*The Development of Southern French
and Catalan Society, 718–1050*

THE DEVELOPMENT OF
Southern French and Catalan Society, 718-1050

BY ARCHIBALD R. LEWIS

UNIVERSITY OF TEXAS PRESS : AUSTIN

Published with the assistance of a grant from the Ford Foundation under its program for the support of publications in the Humanities and Social Sciences.

Library of Congress Catalog Card No. 65-11147
Copyright © 1965 Archibald R. Lewis
All rights reserved

ISBN 978-0-292-72941-4

To my wife, E. C. L.

CONTENTS

Introduction xi
Abbreviations Used in Notes xvii

PART I
Southern France and Carolingian Conquest, 718–778

I. Southern France in the Early Eighth Century 3
II. The Carolingian Conquest, 718–778 20

PART II
Southern France, Catalonia, and the Carolingian Empire, 778–828

III. The Expansion into Gascony and Catalonia 37
IV. The Carolingian System 50
V. Southern French and Catalan Society (778–828) . . . 69

PART III
The Decline of Royal Power, 828–900

VI. Civil War, Invasion, and the Breakdown of
Royal Authority 91
VII. The Governmental System of the Midi and Catalonia . . 114
VIII. The Church (828–900) 136
IX. Southern French and Catalan Society (828–900) . . . 155

PART IV
The Failure of the Territorial State, 900–975

X. The End of Royal Influence 179
XI. The Breakup of Principalities and the Court System . . . 195
XII. The Military System of the Midi and Catalonia 220
XIII. The Church (900–975) 242
XIV. The Society of the Midi and Catalonia 261

PART V
The Age of the Principes, 975–1050

XV. The New Militarism 287
XVI. The Church (975–1050) 315
XVII. The Continued Failure of Principalities 337
XVIII. The *Principes* and Public Order 360
XIX. Southern French and Catalan Society (975–1050) . . . 382
Conclusion 401
Bibliography 405
   I. Primary Materials, 407
   II. Secondary Materials, 415
Index 433

MAPS

Map 1. Southern France (*circa* 700) 5
Map 2. Southern France and Catalonia (*circa* 814) 95
Map 3. Southern France and Catalonia (*circa* 930) 183
Map 4. Southern France and Catalonia (*circa* 980) 291
Map 5. Southern France and Catalonia (*circa* 1050) 363

INTRODUCTION

IN THE LATE twelfth and the thirteenth centuries when the armed might of the nobles and monarchy of Northern France began to expand south into the Midi, the Northern French discovered in Southern France and Catalonia a society very different from their own. The society with which the Northern French barons were familiar was a feudal one in which a great portion of the land was held feudally as fiefs, and in which feudal duties consisted of regular military service, regular court service, and special dues or aids rendered to an overlord by his vassal (who tended to be essentially a fighting man). This was not true of the Midi. Many years later, in the sixteenth and seventeenth centuries, historians who were engaged in examining France's institutional past became aware of this fact. Since that time scholars have often noted various unique aspects of the society of these regions. They have noted the prevalence of allodial land to be found there, the important role played by women in society and in the feudal system, a great emphasis on money, an apparent institutional and class fluidity, the survival of Roman and Visigothic law, and the weak or negative nature of the feudal obligation—all of which are in contrast to the Northern French custom and practice.[1]

Are these features which distinguished Southern French and Catalan society from that north of the Loire merely regional peculiarities—variants of the institutions and customs which are to be found in Northern France? Or do they represent something more than that? This is the first question which needs to be answered. And if they do represent more than regional differentiations, are there sufficient similarities among the various portions

[1] On these peculiarities perhaps the best brief account is to be found in the excellent monograph by F. Ganshof, *Qu'est-ce que la féodalité?* pp. 97, 107–109, 114, 155–156, 169–170, 184–185, 207. See also R. Boutruche, *Une société provinciale en lutte contre le régime féodal: L'alleu en Bordelais et en Bazadais du XIe au XIIIe siècle,* and *Seigneurie et féodalité*; and H. Richardot, "Le fief routurier à Toulouse," in *Revue historique de droit français et étranger,* vol. XIII (1935) and "Francs fiefs: essai sur l'exemption totale ou partielle des services de fief," in *ibid.,* vol. XXVII (1949).

of Southern France and Catalonia, as a whole, so that one can view the society to be found there as a unit which can be studied from an institutional point of view?

While the following pages will attempt to answer this last question in the affirmative, it might be well *in advance* to note that in the late eleventh century there was already a consciousness of such a unity present in Southern France and Catalonia. This explains why those nobles who followed Raymond of Saint-Gilles and Bishop Ademar of LePuy on the First Crusade called themselves Provençals and so distinguished themselves from their Norman and Northern French companions of arms. It also explains why some decades earlier Raoul Glaber, in commenting on the customs and habits of those nobles who followed Constance of Provence north upon her marriage to King Robert of France, should be so struck by the traits which they displayed and which marked them off from the Northern French society of which he approved. By the time of the Albigensian Crusade such differences were to be settled in blood. As early as the eleventh century, then, before the Troubadour society of the Midi had developed, one can distinguish in contemporary accounts and attitudes a certain fundamental difference between Southern French and Catalan society and its feudalism, and that found in Northern France.

In the light of these facts it seems surprising to note that there exists no study of the origins and development of Southern French and Catalan society as a whole, except in Molinier's fragmentary and out-dated article, written many decades ago for the revised *Histoire Générale de Languedoc,* concerning its feudal institutions. Nor does a great deal exist in the way of regional studies from which such a synthesis might be constructed. True we have Brutail's examination of Roussillon, and Breuil's view of eleventh-century Gascony. We possess Poupardin's studies of the Rhone Valley region in his histories of the kingdoms of Provence and Burgundy, as well as Manteyer's and Bousquet's studies of Provence proper. We possess the admirable works of Abadal i de Vinyals on Catalonia, and Higounet's history of the county of Commignes, as well as his important demographic studies. We possess Boutrouche's illuminating views on the Bordelais. We have a series of important articles concerning the role of Roman law in the Midi and Catalonia written by Tisset, Gouron, Hilaire, Didier, Valls-Taberner, and others. We even get some view of Auvergne in certain works by Saigne and Boudet. But only in Tenant de la Tour's history of the Limousin or Fournier's work on Auvergne do we find the kind of regional study which makes Duby's Maconnais and Garaud's article on Poitou so valuable to the institutional historian.

Introduction xiii

On the other hand original sources from which such a study might be constructed are surprisingly full in comparison with their nonexistence for many regions north of the Loire. For the earlier Carolingian period, for instance, we possess a number of reliable chronicles, as well as the charters and capitularies of the monarchs themselves. After the time of Charles the Bald, when such Carolingian materials become scantier and less pertinent, we begin to find hundreds of charters from every region collected in the cartularies of important cathedral churches and abbeys, as well as some contemporary eleventh-century chronicles. For one region, the Spanish March, such materials have only recently been made available to historians through the work of Catalan scholars in publishing their rich documentary collections. For the other regions of the Midi the more significant collections have long been available in published form. Except for Gascony and Provence, as a matter of fact, sufficient published and unpublished materials do exist to allow one to trace the origins and development of Southern French and Catalan society with some hope of success.

What seems to have hindered such a study, then, is not the lack of materials from which it might be constructed—at least as far as the sources are concerned—but something else. This something else has been the particular preoccupations of those able and talented historians who have examined these regions. In general such gentlemen have used one of two approaches in their studies. First, they have insisted on treating Southern France and sometimes Catalonia as parts of a France which was then considered as a unit. Historians using this approach have begun by considering these regions as parts of a centralized Carolingian system which began to disintegrate about the end of the ninth century. Their eyes have been fixed and their attention riveted on the Carolingian element which Southern France and Catalonia had in common with other parts of France. Naturally, under the circumstances, a concern with Charles the Bald or the comital agents of the Carolingian monarchy has seemed more important than an examination of the society of the Midi and the Spanish March in which they had to function. Carolingian machinery of government, even in disintegration, has been the chief interest of such historians until they can pick up the story again in the thirteenth century with an analysis of the Capetian governing system.

A second preoccupation of historians examining Southern France and Catalonia has been equally important in preventing them from dealing with the society of these regions. I refer to what, for want of a better term, might be called their genealogical interests. This, of course, began early with Baluze and DeVic and Vaissette in the seventeenth century, and has continued ever since. Those who have shared it have concentrated their efforts on the discovery of the origins of the various noble houses which arose in the Midi and Catalonia in the tenth and eleventh centuries. They have carried back their interest into the earlier Carolingian period where, with remarkable ingenuity, they have attempted to untangle the family relationships of those nobles who held comital and viscontal charges from the Carolingians in these regions.

Such studies have given us important information, but in their zeal to uncover family relationships, they have tended to ignore the society in which such families functioned and had their being. Individual noble houses, as a result, have emerged from the obscurity of charter and chronicle. The society in which they lived and breathed has remained more unknown to us than is necessary.

While the author of this study would be the first to acknowledge his deep debt to such scholars as Lot, Halphen, Levillain, Auzias, Bloch, Dhondt, and others, too numerous to mention, whose point of view is different from his own, it is his belief that much can be gained by viewing the origins of Southern French and Catalan society in a way somewhat different from theirs. The following pages will attempt to do this, by concentrating attention upon the society of the Midi and Spanish March itself from the eighth to the mid-eleventh centuries. They will, whenever possible, use *local* chronicles, charters, and the like—even those of Carolingian origin—rather than those which may reflect a more distant scene. It is hoped that what may emerge, then, is a history of this whole region which recognizes its relationship to external forces like the Carolingian monarchy or the Papacy, but which is more concerned with local manifestations of even these external influences. It is hoped further that out of this will emerge a clearer picture of the society which had developed in Southern France and Catalonia by the year 1050 than exists at the present time.

Finally the author wishes to express his debt of appreciation to the many scholars, archives, and libraries in Southern France, Catalonia, and the United States that have assisted him in so many ways in his research. In France he is indebted to the archivists and staffs of the archives of Nîmes, Marseille, and Toulouse who made materials available to him, and particularly to M. Marcel Gouron and his assistants, of the archives of Hérault, who gave him every possible assistance for so many months. To M. de Dainville, archivist of Montpellier, go his thanks for special help and encouragement. Above all he is grateful to Professors Pierre Tisset, André Gouron, and Jean Hilaire of the University of Montpellier; Philippe Wolff, of the University of Toulouse; and George Duby, of the

Introduction

University of Aix-en-Provence; all of whom generously gave him of their time and made valuable suggestions.

In Catalonia he is grateful for help given him by Professor F. Undina-Martorell and his staff, of the archives of Aragón; and to the late Professor Jaime Vicens-Vives and his assistants, of the Historical Seminar of the University of Barcelona, as well. Finally he must thank Don Ramón de Abadal i de Vinyals and Sr. José Rubio for generously giving him of their time.

In the United States he is much indebted to the entire staff of the Widener Library at Harvard University and similarly to the Sterling Library of Yale University, the Princeton University Library, and the University of Texas Library for use of their fine collections, and to Professors Robert Lopez, of Yale University; Joseph R. Strayer, of Princeton University; Robert G. Albion, of Harvard University; and Ramón Martínez-López and Raphael Levy, of The University of Texas, for assistance and advice. He also thanks his student Philip Isett, whose research on Visigothic Septimania has proved very helpful. All errors in this study are the author's own; however, without the assistance of these scholars the mistakes would have been more numerous and the lacunae more noticeable.

Finally, he must acknowledge his debt to the Ford Fund for the Advancement of Education, the American Council of Learned Societies, the American Philosophical Society, and the Research Institute of the University of Texas for grants from their organizations which freed him from teaching duties and made possible both the research and the writing of this study. Without their generous assistance neither would have been possible.

Austin, Texas

ABBREVIATIONS USED IN NOTES

Abbreviations	Full Titles
Abadal, *Els Comtats de Pallars i Ribagorça*	R. de Abadal i de Vinyals, *Catalunya Carolingia*, III: *Els Comtats de Pallars i Ribagorça*.
Ademar de Chabannes	Ademar de Chabannes, *Chronique*, ed. A. Chavanon.
Annals of Aniane	*Annales Anianences*, in *Hist. Gen. de Lang.* II.
Astronomus, *Vita Hludovici*	Astronomus, *Vita Hludovici imperatous*, ed. G. Pertz.
Boretius, *Capitularia*	A. Boretius and G. Krause, *Capitularia regum Francorum*, in *Mon. Gen. Hist. Capitularia*.
Cart. de la Réolle	*Cartulaire de prieurie de Saint-Pierre de la Réolle* [Gironde], ed. C. Grellet-Balguerie, in *Archives Historiques de la Gironde*, V (1864).
Cart. de Saint-André-le-bas	*Cartulaire de Saint-André-le-bas de Vienne*, ed. U. Chevalier.
Cart. de Sainte-Croix	*Cartulaire de l'abbaye de Sainte-Croix en Bordeaux*, ed. P. Ducaunnes-Duval, in *Archives Historiques de la Gironde*, XXVII (1892).
Cart. de Saint-Sernin	*Cartulaire de l'abbaye de Saint-Sernin de Toulouse*, ed. C. Douais.
Cart. de Saint-Victor	*Cartulaire de Saint-Victor de Marseille*, ed. B. Guéraud.
Catalunya Carolingia, II	R. de Abadal i de Vinyals, *Catalunya Carolingia*, II: *Els Diplomes Carolingia à Catalunya*.
Chron. of Moissac	*Chronicon Moisacense*, ed. G. Pertz, in *Mon. Ger. Hist. Scriptores*, I.
Chron. of Uzès	*Chronicon Ucenense*, in *Hist. Gén. de Lang.*, II.
Cros-Meyrévielle, *Documents*	*Histoire du Comté et de la Vicomté de Carcossonne* (Piecès justicifatives), by J. Cros-Meyrévielle.

Fredegarii cont.	Fredegariis, *Chronicon quod dicitur Fredegarii continuatio*, ed. R. Krusch.
Gallia Christiana	*Gallia Christiana in Provincias ecclesiasticas distributas*, Vol. V.
Hist. Gén. de Lang.	*Histoire Générale de Languedoc*, ed. Privat.
Liber Feudorum	F. Miguel Rossell (ed.), *Liber Feudorum Maior*.
Marca hispanica	P. de Marca, *Marca hispanica sive limes hispanicus*.
Nithard, *Histoire*	Nithard, *Histoire des fils de Louis le Pieux*, ed. P. Lauer.

I
SOUTHERN FRANCE
AND CAROLINGIAN CONQUEST
718–778

CHAPTER I

Southern France in the Early Eighth Century

IN THE YEAR 718 that part of France south of the Loire and Burgundy lay between two powers which were to affect its destiny for more than a century. To the north we find regions which were dominated by the Carolingian family—a family which Pepin of Heristal had established in power over Austrasia and Neustria and whose authority was being further increased by his able son, Charles Martel. To the south lay Spain, conquered by the Arab and Berber forces of Musa and Tarik—forces which were about to cross the Pyrenees in an advance toward the heartland of Western Europe.

The Midi which faced these two adversaries in the early eighth century was a region without any over-all political cohesion of its own. It consisted of four relatively distinct areas. The largest of these was an Aquitaine which lay south of the Loire and west of the Rhone Valley, with its southern borders reaching the Narbonnaise in the east and a Gascon frontier along the Garonne in the west. Aquitaine had been part of the Merovingian Frankish state since the time of Clovis, but by the eighth century was controlled by a duke or *princeps* called Eudes. He and his heirs, Hunald and Waiffre, were to control its destiny for the next fifty years.

We find a second rather amorphous principality known as Provence, which probably consisted of the Rhone Valley south of Lyon and east of Aquitaine and the Narbonnaise, up to the crests of the French Alps— roughly the area occupied by the old Roman Provincia. Provence was controlled by a series of local magnates who bore the title of patrician. We know little about these patricians beyond their names with one exception, and we do not even know whether or not they belonged to the same family like the *principes* of Aquitaine. Provence, like Aquitaine, had long been nominally a part of the Merovingian Frankish state, though soon after the death of Dagobert it had managed to achieve a large measure of autonomy under native princes.[1]

West of Provence along the shores of the Mediterranean we find the third distinct region of Southern France, the Narbonnaise or Septimania, as it was called. Unlike Aquitaine and Provence, the Narbonnaise had never been conquered by the Merovingians. Instead, for three hundred years it had been under Visigothic rule. Its boundaries seem to have been the Rhone on the east, a series of fortified cities like Uzès, Lodève, and Carcassonne on the north, the Pyrenean high country inhabited by the Basques on the west, and the Pyrenees and Mediterranean to the south.[2] Though it had not shared the political history of Aquitaine and Provence, like them it seems to have had an instinct for autonomy, which in the late seventh century led to a serious revolt by a local Gothic magnate called Paul, a rising which had to be suppressed by Wamba, king of Visigothic Spain.[3]

The fourth region of the Midi was Gascony which occupied the remaining region of Southern France north of the Pyrenees. It is difficult to give Gascony's boundaries in any exact way. A later Carolingian writer summed it up by saying that the Gascons lived across the Garonne and among the Pyrenees. Following his lead we might hazard the opinion that Carcassonne and Roussillon formed the eastern boundary, the Garonne its northern border, the Atlantic its western one, and the Pyrenees its southern one. On the other hand it is uncertain whether Bordeaux and the Bordelais were part of Gascony or part of Aquitaine during this period.[4] It is equally difficult to be sure that the Pyrenees formed Gascony's southern border, since other Basques lived south of them in Northern Spain. These Spanish Basques, who were similar in race and culture to their French Gascon compatriots, occupied an expanse of Spanish soil northwest of Saragossa in Pallars, Ribagorça, Aragón, Navarre, and Asturias and were generally independent of and at times hostile to the Visi-

[1] E. Duprat in *Bouches du Rhône: Encyclopédie départementale*, II, 248–250; G. de Manteyer, *La Provence du Ier au XIIe siècle*, pp. 100–154.

[2] The basic work on the Narbonnaise in the pre-Carolingian period remains A. Dupont, *Les cités de la Narbonnaise première dupuis les invasions germaniques.*

[3] Julian of Toledo, *Historia Excellentissimi Wambae Regis*, ch. 5, in *España sagrada*, vol. VI; *Chronologia et series regum Gothorum*, in *Hist. Gén. de Lang.*, II, col. 19–20; *Divisio terminorum episcopatum provinciae Narbonensis*, in *ibid.*, II, col. 20–21.

[4] On Basques on the French side of the Pyrenees see J. Jaurguin, *La Vasconie*, I, 80 ff. On the fact that these Basques *"trans Garronam et circa Pireneum montem habitant"* see *Annales Regni Francorum*, ed. G. Kurze, anno. 816, p. 141.

Map 1. SOUTHERN FRANCE (*circa* 700).

gothic rulers of Spain. They appear to have maintained close ties with those Gascons who lived north of the Pyrenees. That this represented any formal political unity, however, appears doubtful, for it seems clear that during this period the Basques of France were ruled by a native family of dukes or *principes* who bore the name of Loup or Lupo. They, like the Spanish Basques, were independent of their Narbonnaise and Aquitanian neighbors.[5]

One more region might also be mentioned—Catalonia, which was to be closely associated with the Midi after 778, though not before. In 713-714, however, Catalonia had been overrun by the Moors who occupied all of it with the possible exception of the Urgell region, where there is some evidence of the survival of an independent native Church and monastic tradition. Yet even here one must be careful, for there is some evidence that all of this part of Northern Spain was less conquered outright by the Moslems than handed over to them by dissident Visigothic nobles, one of whom, a certain Cassius, apostatized from the Christian Church and set up an important Islamic dynasty in the region, the Banu Kasi.[6] During the period covered by this chapter Catalonia followed the destiny of the rest of Moslem Spain rather than that of the Midi.

So much for the political geography of Southern France and the Spanish borderlands. But what of its ecclesiastical divisions? Only in Septimania do we find political and ecclesiastical boundaries coinciding. The Narbonnaise consisted of seven bishoprics: Elne, Carcassonne, Béziers, Agde, Maguelonne, Lodève, Nîmes, and Uzès under the archbishop of Narbonne.[7] Provence on the other hand seems to have had a positive plethora of metropolitans: Aix, Embrun, and Arles near the lower Rhone, and Lyon and Vienne further north.[8]

Even more complex seems to have been the situation in Aquitaine and Gascony. By the late seventh century there were three archbishoprics in this part of France. The archbishop of Bourges was over the bishops of Northern and Central Aquitaine, the metropolitan of Bordeaux controlled

[5] On the Basque-inhabited lands in Northern Spain see J. Lacarra, *Vasconia medieval: Historia y Filología*, pp. 14-20.

[6] On this change to Islamic control in Northeastern Spain see R. de Abadal i de Vinyals, "El paso de Septimania del dominio godo al franco a través de la invasión sarracena," in *Cuadernos de Historia de España*, XIII, 9-15.

[7] *Divisio terminorum episcopatum provinciae Narbonensis*, col. 20-21. By the seventh century these bishoprics had been completely integrated into the Visigothic kingdom and their bishops were regularly represented at Church councils held at Toledo (*Hist. Gén. de Lang.*, I, c. 7, no. 16).

[8] On the bishops of Provence see *Bouches du Rhône*, II, 248-249.

Southern Aquitaine and perhaps part of Western Gascony, the archbishop of Couserans the rest of Gascony. Gascony may also have had a special bishop of its own.[9] Like Provence, then, Western France south of the Loire lacked the ecclesiastical precision of Septimania.

When one tries to examine the pre-Carolingian governmental system of the Midi in greater detail than the above generalities, one finds evidence rather scant. We do have evidence that the Narbonnaise was governed by counts,[10] and that the Visigoths kept their mint at Narbonne in operation during the early years of the eighth century.[11] We hear also of counts in Aquitaine, where about 650 St. Didier's brother was count of Albi[12] and where, at the time of Duke Waiffre, similar officials are found in Poitou, Berry, and Auvergne.[13] On the other hand there is less evidence that counts existed during this entire period in Provence, though the patricians certainly exercised comital powers.[14] As for Gascony—it seems clear that it was without counts in the pre-Carolingian period, its only known rulers being its *duces* and *principes* who appear to have presided over tribal chiefs and families.[15] The counts of Aquitaine and the Nar-

[9] *Hist. Gén. de Lang.*, II, no. 3, col. 40–41, and C. Higounet, *Le comté de Commignes de ses origines à son annexation à la Couronne*, I, 12–15. The above charter mentioning the Council of 673 contains among its witnesses a bishop who calls himself the bishop of the Basques. See also mention of bishoprics in Auvergne, and at Bourges, Rodez, Agen, Angoulême, Périgord, and Cahors, in *Vie de Saint Didier*, ed. R. Poupardin, VIII, 27–28.

[10] See the mention of counts in the Narbonnaise in the late seventh century in Julian of Toledo, *Historia Excellentissimi Wambae Regis*, ch. 5. On the Gothic Count Misemundus, who was the ally of Pepin the Short in the Narbonnaise see *Chronicon Ucenense*, in *Hist. Gén. de Lang.*, II, col. 25–27 (hereafter cited as *Chron. of Uzès*). On the Gothic count of Maguelonne who was the father of St. Benedict of Aniane see *Vita Benedicti Anianensis*, ed. E. Waitz, bk. I, in *Mon. Ger. Hist. Scriptores*, XV, 201.

[11] On the money of Narbonne coined as late as the reign of Witiza (701–711) see *Hist. Gén. de Lang.*, VII, 324.

[12] *Vie de Saint Didier*, I–II, 1–9, and V, 21.

[13] Fredegarius, *Chronicon quod dicitur Fredegarii continuatio*, ed. R. Krusch, ch. 125, 129–130, 134, in *Mon. Ger. Hist. Scriptores rerum Merov.*, II, 187, 189–190, 192 (hereafter cited as *Fredegarii cont.*).

[14] See account of testimony given to a later Carolingian court (in 780) by the aged Bishop Maurontius concerning the power exercised by pre-Carolingian patricians of Provence over the abbey of Saint-Victor of Marseille, in *Cartulaire de l'abbaye de Saint-Victor de Marseille*, ed. B. Guéraud, no. 31, pp. 43–46 (hereafter cited as *Cart. de Saint-Victor*).

[15] One of the earliest references to such *duces* or *principes* of Gascony is in 673 when a document refers to a certain *"Lupo duce"* in *Hist. Gén. de Lang.*, II, no. 3.

bonnaise, like their Carolingian successors, led local armed forces into battle and controlled at least some of the fortresses located in the areas they ruled.[16] Slight evidence from Provence suggests that its patricians had similar authority.[17]

On the other hand we know nothing about the judicial role played by such counts in Southern France and even less of the court system in existence—except for some indication that in Provence the patrician could and did act in a legal capacity.[18] What we can say with some assurance is that Visigothic law was in use in the Narbonnaise,[19] and that Roman law survived in both Aquitaine and the Valley of the Rhone.[20] Neither seems to have been in use, as far as we can tell, in Gascony.

See also reference to this same Lupo at about the same period in a document which says that he controlled a number of cities in Aquitaine (*Miracula Sancti Martialis Lemovicensis*, ed. D. Bouquet, bk. II, ch. 3, in *Recueil des Historiens des Gaules et de la France*, III, 580). Later in 769, Lupo *dux* of the Gascons, submitted to Charlemagne (*Annales Laurissense*, in *Mon. Ger. Hist. Scriptores*, I, 148; Einhard, *Vie de Charlemagne*, ed. L. Halphen, ch. 5, p. 445; and Astronomus, *Vita Hludovici imperatoris*, ed. G. Pertz, ch. 2, in *Mon. Ger. Hist. Scriptores*, II, 608 [hereafter cited as Astronomus, *Vita Hludovici*]).

[16] Count Misemundus or Ansemundus in 752 turned over to Pepin fortresses at Nîmes, Maguelonne, Agde, and Béziers (*Chron. of Uzès*, col. 25–26; *Annales Anianenses*, in *Hist. Gén. de Lang.*, II, col. 5–6 [hereafter cited as *Annals of Aniane*]; and *Chronicon Moisiacense*, ed. G. Pertz, in *Mon. Ger. Hist. Scriptores*, I, 293–294 [hereafter cited as *Chron. of Moissac*]). See also the account of the independent authority in Aquitaine exercised in 761 by Umbert, count of Bourges, and Bladino, count of Auvergne, according to *Fredegarii cont.*, ch. 125, p. 187.

[17] Though the *Chron. of Moissac*, p. 291, says that the Moslems seized Arles in 734, another contemporary source says that in 737 the patrician Maurontius turned Avignon over to them (*Fredegarii cont.*, ch. 19, pp. 177–178). This would imply that at this date he still controlled this city and its *castra*. Another local source agrees with the *Chron. of Moissac* (*Annals of Aniane*, cols. 3–5). Duprat in *Bouches du Rhône*, II, 131–132, A. Molinier in "Sur les invasions Arabes dans le Languedoc," in *Hist. Gén. de Lang.*, II, 550–552, and H. Zotenburg in *ibid.*, pp. 557–558, follow the Fredegarius version.

[18] See account of court of 780 already mentioned (*Cart. de Saint-Victor*, no. 31).

[19] The Visigoths of Narbonne only surrendered this city to Pepin in 759 when he assured them they could continue to use their own Visigothic laws (*Chron. of Moissac*, p. 294, and *Annals of Aniane*, col. 6–7).

[20] See Chapter 3, Section II, on the survival of Roman and Visigothic law in Aquitaine and the Valley of the Rhone in later Carolingian times. For a more contemporary example of the use of Roman private law see the will of Abbo, dating from 739, in *Cartulaire de l'église Cathédrale de Grenoble*, ed. J. Marion, pp. 34–49, and the comments on its Roman legal content in G. Chevrier, "L'évolution de l'acte à cause de mort en Dauphiné du VIIe à la fin du Xe siècle," in

Southern France in the Early Eighth Century   9

If our evidence of pre-Carolingian institutions is too slight for our liking, we know more concerning the pre-Carolingian military organization of Southern France. When Charles Martel and Childebrand advanced down the Rhone Valley with their Frankish and Burgundian levies, they found the principal cities of Provence, like Arles and Avignon, protected by walls formidable enough to call for siege operations.[21] The same seems to have been true of *civitates* of Septimania like Uzès, Nîmes, Mauguio, Agde, Bèziers, Carcassonne, and especially Narbonne.[22] This region also contained *castella* located outside fortified cities like the Castellum of Millia which in 678 was mentioned as in existence between Nîmes and Maguelonne.[23]

In Aquitaine we learn that St. Didier, about 650, rebuilt the walls of Cahors and reconstructed the *castella* of the city, as well as the Castrum Mercurio in Cahors itself.[24] At about the same time we hear of a Castrum Garnomo near Bordeaux.[25] A little later in the eighth century there was a *castrum* in Velay, probably at LePuy.[26] In the early eighth century when Toulouse was attacked by the Moslems, it apparently possessed fortifications.[27]

Later on about 735 we hear of the Castrum of Blavia near Bordeaux and other *castra* in the suburbs of the city,[28] and when Pepin conquered Aquitaine between 761 and 768 we hear of similar fortifications everywhere. Our accounts make it clear that the major *civitates* of this region, like Bourges, Limoges, Poitiers, Saintes, Clermont, Périgord, and An-

---

Recueil de la société historique de droit et des institutions des pays du droit écrit, I (1948).

[21] *Chron. of Moissac,* p. 292. *Fredegarii cont.,* ch. 20, p. 178, mentions a siege of Avignon and its *castra* in 737 by Childebrand, the brother of Charles Martel.

[22] On Charles Martel's destruction of the *castra* and walls of the *civitates* of the eastern Narbonnaise after he retreated from before Narbonne in 738 or 739 see *Annals of Aniane,* col. 4–6; *Chron. of Moissac,* p. 292; and *Fredegarii cont.,* ch. 20, pp. 177–178. On Pepin the Short's long siege of Narbonne, which did not fall until 759 see *Chron. of Moissac,* p. 294; *Annals of Aniane,* col. 6–7; and *Chron. of Uzès,* col. 26–27. Obviously the Narbonnaise was heavily fortified during this period, as it had been in Visigothic times.

[23] *Divisio terminorum episcopatum provinciae Narbonensis,* col. 21.

[24] *Vie de Saint Didier,* II–III, 16–19, and VIII, 50.

[25] *Hist. Gén. de Lang.,* II, no. 3.

[26] *Hist. Gén. de Lang.,* II, no. 208, contains references to the castle of Viviers, which date from the seventh century.

[27] *Chron. of Moissac,* p. 290; *Annals of Aniane,* col. 2–3; and *Chron. of Uzès,* col. 25.

[28] *Fredegarii cont.,* ch. 15, p. 176.

goulême were fortified.²⁹ There were also a number of detached fortresses like Thouars in Poitou, Castelluc in Auvergne, Bourbon in Berry, Turenne in the lower Limousin, Scalas in Quercy, Perrucé in Périgord, and a number of other unspecified *castella* and *roccas*.³⁰

There is also ample evidence that the profession of arms was a general one, so much so that in Southern Aquitaine a church council in the late seventh century had to forbid the carrying of arms and the waging of war by priests.³¹ In the Narbonnaise and Aquitaine there was a military class led by counts and *principes* which furnished opposition to invading Moors and Carolingians alike.³² The assassination of St. Didier's brother shows us a society in Quercy and the Albigeois which was tumultuous and quarrelsome,³³ just as Abbo's will mentions land, in 739, which he had acquired by conquest.³⁴

On the other hand there does seem to be some indication that pre-Carolingian Southern France did not possess a military class as well organized as those *vassi* of Frankish origin whom Charles Martel enriched with Church lands³⁵ and who followed him and his successors into battle. When the Carolingians advanced down the Rhone they found that Maurontius, patrician of Provence, had invited Moslem forces to garrison his cities, probably because he could not muster sufficient warriors of his own.³⁶ And in Aquitaine during Pepin's final nine-year campaign, we again and again find mention of Gascons, probably mercenaries, who formed at least a portion of the levies available to Duke Waiffre and his counts.³⁷ On the other hand there is no evidence of the use of such outside auxiliaries in either Septimania or Gascony.

---

²⁹ *Ibid.*, ch. 126, 129, pp. 187–189, *Annales Laurissenses*, pp. 142–144. On walls of Limoges which were destroyed by Pepin see a later account in "Ex historia monasterii usercensis," in *Cartulaire de l'abbaye d'Uzerche*, ed. J. Champéval, pp. 13–14.

³⁰ *Fredegarii cont.*, ch. 25, 125–126, 129, pp. 180, 187–189, and *Annales Laurissenses*, pp. 142, 144, 146.

³¹ *Hist. Gén. de Lang.*, II, no. 3.

³² See Chapter 2, Section I, on the warlike nature of this society.

³³ *Vie de Saint Didier*, II, 15–16.

³⁴ *Cart. de Grenoble*, pp. 34–38. It is interesting to note that Abbo's will mentions no fortresses within or near his domains.

³⁵ A. Boretius and V. Krause, *Capitularia regum Francorum*, in *Mon. Ger. Hist. Capitularia*, I, nos. 10–12, pp. 29–32 (hereafter cited as Boretius, *Capitularia*).

³⁶ See Note 17. Local authorities and sources mention Moslem conquest rather than a collaboration between Maurontius and the Moslems.

³⁷ Ademar de Chabannes, who may be drawing upon an unknown source from Aquitaine, says that as early as 718 Eudes, duke of Aquitaine, used Gascons in his

Southern France in the Early Eighth Century 11

When we turn to the pre-Carolingian Church organization, we find that we can discover little, in no small measure because of the destruction of Church records by both the Moslems and Carolingians in the course of their campaigns in the Midi. For instance we do not know more than the names of any pre-Carolingian abbeys in the Narbonnaise,[38] which makes us suspect that, unlike those in Urgell, none survived Moslem occupation.[39] In Provence we can only be sure that Saint-Victor of Marseille[40] and Lérins[41] continued active of the pre-Carolingian monastic establishments of this region. For Aquitaine we possess more information, but still too little for more than generalizations.

What emerges from what we do know, however, is a picture of a church and a monastic system closely linked to the ruling, landholding classes. This was no innovation of this period, but rather represented a continuation of a state of affairs which had existed since late Roman and early Merovingian times. Thus the example of Aredus and his grandson, who in 572-573 seem to have endowed the abbeys of Saint-Martial and Vigeois in the Limousin with considerable landed property,[42] was copied often in the next two centuries. We know this from the record of seventh-century gifts of land to the church of Viviers[43] and those given to churches and abbeys in Quercy and the Toulousain dating from the same period. New abbeys were also still being established, as we learn from the case of the abbey of Saint-Gerri established by St. Didier at Cahors[44] or that of

---

wars with Charles Martel (Ademar de Chabannes, *Chronique*, ed. A. Chavanon, I, 51, pp. 51-52 [hereafter cited as *Ademar de Chabannes*]). The more contemporary *Fredegarii cont.*, ch. 10, agrees. In 742 Duke Hunald had Gascon allies (*ibid.*, ch. 25). In 761 Count Bladino of Clermont had Gascons in his garrisons (*ibid.*, ch. 125). So did Count Humbert of Bourges in 762 (*ibid.*, ch. 126). During Duke Waiffre's last years of struggle in 764-766, he had Gascon assistance (*ibid.*, ch. 130-131).

[38] They are Saint-Basil of Nîmes, Saint-André of Agde, and Saint-Gilles, probably located in the Rhone delta (*Hist. Gén. de Lang.*, I, ch. 6, no. 70).

[39] On the survival of Visigothic abbeys in Urgell see R. de Abadal i de Vinyals, *Els Primers Comtes Catalans*, pp. 115-120, and "La batalla del adopcionisme en la destintegración de la Iglesia visigoda," in *Real Academia de Buenas Letras de Barcelona*.

[40] See *Cart. de Saint-Victor*, no. 31, and Introduction to this cartulary by B. Guéraud, pp. i-xxii.

[41] See *Cartulaire de l'abbaye de Lérins*, ed. H. Moris and E. Blanc, and *ibid.*, I, 293, no. 290.

[42] *Cartulaire de l'abbaye de Vigeois*, ed. M. de Montegut, no. CLI, pp. 95-97.

[43] *Hist. Gén. de Lang.*, II, no. 208.

[44] *Vie de Saint Didier*, VI, 22-23.

newly founded Moissac which gained in 680 the landed estates belonging to Nizezius.[45] As late as 739 Abbo left his vast estates in the Middle Rhone region to the newly founded abbey of Novalese in Italy.[46]

The biography of St. Didier, which portrays him acting more like the ruler of Quercy than its bishop again illustrates how closely entwined the Church in the Midi was with the governing system of the region.[47] So do gifts by patricians of Provence to the abbey of Saint-Victor of Marseille, as revealed at a later period,[48] and the fact that in 780 the aged bishop of this city bears the same family name as its last patrician.[49] Except in Gascony there seems to have existed a close relationship and collaboration between bishop and monastery on the one hand and count and leading landowners on the other.

This leads us to a consideration of the economic life of Southern France in the first years of the eighth century, on the eve of Moorish and Carolingian intervention. By this time, it is clear, the outside commerce enjoyed by this region was in a definite state of decline. There is no evidence, for instance, to show the presence of Syrian and Greek merchants in the *civitates* of the Midi, as had been the case a century earlier.[50] We do still find a reference to fine silks,[51] however, and, judging from later Carolingian evidence, it is possible that some Jewish merchant colonies still survived.

At the same time one notices an interesting change in the coinage which is in use. During the last years of the seventh century contemporary accounts still mention gold being used in Quercy and the Toulousain,[52] a fact which seems confirmed by gold found in coin hoards at Bordeaux[53]

---

[45] *Ibid.*, VII, 25–26, for mention of abbey of Moissac. On land acquired by Moissac see *Hist. Gén. de Lang.*, II, no. 4, col. 42–45.

[46] *Cart. de Grenoble*, pp. 34–48.

[47] *Vie de Saint Didier*, II–III, 16–19.

[48] *Cart. de Saint-Victor*, no. 31, mentions a series of gifts to this monastery by patricians of Provence.

[49] *Ibid.*

[50] Dupont, *Les cités de la Narbonnaise*, pp. 210–212.

[51] The abbey of Moissac included *pallios* worth 200 *solidi* in the purchase price they paid to Nizezius for certain large tracts of land in 680 in the Toulousain region (*Hist. Gén. de Lang.*, II, no. 4, col. 45).

[52] The same charter mentions 700 *solidi* (*ibid.*).

[53] P. Le Gentilhomme, *Mélanges de Numismatique Merovingienne*, pp. 9–10. See also comments by J. Lafaurie in *Settimane de studio del Centro di studi sull'- alto medioevo*, VIII (1960), 254–257, and in *Revue Numismatique*, XXIII (1959–1960), 153–210.

and along the Loire[54] and the Rhone.[55] By 718, however, this seems no longer to have been true. Silver seems to have replaced gold as a medium of exchange. It was coined at Narbonne[56] and in Aquitaine[57] and is the only metal found in hoards like Plaissac on the Garonne[58] and Cimiez in Provence.[59] Such coin hoards also reveal the growing economic localism of the Midi, particularly in the Rhone Valley,[60] though they do seem to point to a trade route which was still active along the western shores of Aquitaine to Bordeaux and then along the Garonne to Narbonne and Marseille.[61] There is also some evidence that some spices and oriental wares were still reaching Fos in the early eighth century.[62] Compared to the earlier Merovingian period, however, by 718 Southern France seems to have been more isolated from the main trade currents of Northern Europe and the Mediterranean than had been the case earlier.

All of this contributed to making land in the Midi its most important source of wealth. And it seems clear that this landed wealth was still held in the early eighth century in much the same way that it had been owned in late Roman and early Merovingian times. It was still largely in the hands of the same sort of Gallo-Roman aristocrats whom we meet at the time of Sidonius and Avitus.[63] It must not, however, be thought that such families had a monopoly of land ownership. Side by side with them we find a sizable Frankish element—numerous in the Limousin, Rouergue, and the Albigeois, and present as far south as Carcassonne.[64] A Visi-

[54] Le Gentilhomme, *Mélanges de Numismatique Merovingienne*, pp. 120–125, on hoard discovered at Baugisière.
[55] *Ibid.*, pp. 125–130, on hoard discovered at Buis in the Rhone Valley.
[56] *Hist. Gén. de Lang.*, VII, 324.
[57] *Ibid.*, p. 367.
[58] Le Gentilhomme, *Mélanges de Numismatique Merovingienne*, pp. 126–128.
[59] A. Morel-Fatio, *Catalogue raisonné de la collection des deniers merovingiens des VIIe et VIIIe siècles de la trouvaille de Cimiez.*
[60] See A. Lewis, "Le commerce maritime et la navigation sur les côtes de la Gaule atlantique du Ve au VIIIe siècle," in *Le Moyen Age*, LIX (1953), 277.
[61] *Ibid.*, pp. 270–276.
[62] L. Levillain, *Examen des chartes de Corbie*, p. 220.
[63] E. Salin, *La Civilisation Merovingienne*, I, 25–30.
[64] M. Brouens, "Le peuplement germanique de la Gaule entre Méditerranée et l'ocean," in *Annales du Midi*, XLVIII (1956), 17–37. On this large Frankish element in Rouergue, which, in part, may date from Carolingian times, see C. Higounet, "Observations sur la seigneurie rurale et l'habitat en Rouergue du IXe au XIVe siècle," in *ibid.*, LXII (1950), 121–134. On the similar situation in the Limousin see G. Tenant de la Tour, *L'homme et la terre de Charlemagne à Saint Louis*, pp. 87 ff.

14   Southern France and Carolingian Conquest

gothic element is present in the Narbonnaise too in this same period.[65] One finds this Frankish element mentioned in contemporary accounts, for when Duke Eudes of Aquitaine met and defeated the Moslems near Toulouse in 721, his army is said to have been composed of both Franks and Aquitanians.[66] Judging by his name Eudes himself was of Frankish origin. Long before the Carolingians, then, a considerable Frankish element had settled in parts of Aquitaine. It also needs to be emphasized that Franks and Burgundians were settled in the Middle and Lower Rhone Valley before the time of Charles Martel. Abbo, patrician of Provence, bore a Frankish name, and we find similar northern Frankish soubriquets among the servants whom he mentioned in his will.[67]

It seems highly probable, however, that by the early eighth century such Frankish and Burgundian elements had been largely absorbed into the prevailing Gallo-Roman population of Provence[68] and Aquitaine, just as in the Narbonnaise the Visigothic element had become a part of the essentially Gallo-Roman society of Septimania.[69] Only in Gascony does one find what may represent an unmixed stock, and even here there seems to be some evidence that in Couserans and the Bordelais, Gascons were still advancing into what had earlier been Gallo-Roman areas.[70]

Whether its owner was of Gallo-Roman, Frankish, Burgundian, or Visigothic origin, however, the *villa* was still the prevailing unit of landholding, as had been the case since late Roman times. St. Didier, for example, gave *villas* as an endowment to the abbey he founded in Quercy

[65] Dupont, *Les cités de la Narbonnaise*, pp. 200–201. Visigothic elements seem to have settled in some numbers near Béziers, Perpignan, Narbonne, and Carcassonne—that is to say in Western Septimania. Some of this Gothic population, however, may represent later Carolingian *aprisio* holders.

[66] *Annals of Aniane*, col. 2; *Chron. of Uzès*, col. 25; and *Chron. of Moissac*, p. 290.

[67] Abbo's will mentions men who bear such names as Astruald, Siguald, and Merobert, and who hold benefices from him (*Cart. de Grenoble*, pp. 34–48). This seems to show a Frankish and Burgundian element present in Dauphiny in 739. On Clothair II's absorption of Provence into the Merovingian realm in the early seventh century see H. Adelson, "Early Medieval Trade Routes," in *American Historical Review*, LXV (1960), 2–3.

[68] Again it is the will of Abbo mentioned earlier which shows how romanized Abbo and other Franks had become in this part of France in the early eighth century. On this see also Chevrier, "L'evolution de l'acte."

[69] Dupont, *Les cités de la Narbonnaise*, p. 201.

[70] On this Gascon penetration and mixing with a non-Gascon population see Higounet, *Le comté de Commignes*, I, 13–15.

and to the churches which he restored there and in the Albigeois.[71] Our sources make clear that the estates of Nizezius located between the Tarn and the Garonne were organized as *villas* in 680.[72] We find *villas* mentioned in Vivarais as well as *mansi*.[73] In Provence, around Marseille, the *villa*, made up of *colonicas*, seems to have prevailed,[74] while as far north as Dauphiny, Abbo's will shows the same pattern of land used in the Rhone Valley.[75] We have every reason to believe that the same thing was true in the Narbonnaise also, though this belief rests on conjecture alone.

Some landowners in this period controlled only a *villa* or two. More typical, however, seems to have been a class of large estate owners, controlling vast areas—men such as St. Didier and Nizezius in Aquitaine, or others like them in Velay, or magnates like Abbo who possessed so much property in Dauphiny. Nor were men alone in possessing such estates. We find women like Bobila, the *senatrix Romana* of Quercy, who owned property in their own right.[76] We also find a large class of *servi* or *coloni* living on such *villas* as they had in late Roman time, though a group of freedmen also seems to have existed.[77] It is worth noting that the prevailing system of landholding for the upper class was allodial and that land-

---

[71] *Vie de Saint Didier*, IX, 31–38. On the continuation into the ninth century of this *villa* pattern in this region see Higounet, "Observations sur la seigneurie rurale en Rouergue," pp. 17–23. The rare charter of 756–757, issued by Duke Waiffre in Aquitaine only mentions *villas* in Auvergne (*Cartulaire de Brioude*, ed. H. Doniol, no. 26, pp. 47–48). Ademar de Chabannes also mentions that during the course of his war with Duke Waiffre between 761 and 768 Pepin gave two *villas* to the canons of Saint-Martial and Saint-Etienne of Limoges (*Ademar de Chabannes*, I, 58, pp. 60–61).

[72] On the nineteen *villas* of Nizezius acquired by the abbey of Moissac in 680 see *Hist. Gén. de Lang.*, II, no. 4. See also an analysis of these estates in C. Higounet, "L'occupation du sol du pays entre Tarn et Garonne au moyen âge," in *Annales du Midi*, LXIV (1952), 312–314.

[73] *Hist. Gén. de Lang.*, II, no. 208.

[74] See mention of the *villas* of Caladio and Alpheus owned by the abbey of Saint-Victor of Marseille in *Cart. de Saint-Victor*, no. 31, pp. 43–45. On the prevailing *villa* system in Provence see R. Latouche, "Quelques aperçus sur le manse en Provence au Xe et au XIe siècles," in *Recueil des travaux offerts à M. C. Brunel*, II.

[75] *Cart. de Grenoble*, pp. 34–48.

[76] *Vie de Saint Didier*, IX, 33.

[77] See mention of *coloni* of the *villa* of Rusticiago in Rouergue at the time of St. Didier (*Vie de Saint Didier*, VIII, 27). See also the serfs of five *villas* owned by Nizezius in the Toulousain in 680 (*Hist. Gén. de Lang.*, II, no. 4, col. 42–43).

owners could and did freely sell or will their estates or give them to abbeys and churches.

There can be little doubt that in this period the allod was the prevailing type of landholding to be found. But it is important to note that we have evidence of another sort of tenure—the *precarium* or *beneficium*.[78] In the biography of St. Didier we find a reference to *beneficia* which were given out by nobles and magnates of the region and something called *beneficiendo* or *cohemendo* which seems somewhat similar to Carolingian commendation.[79] In a document from Provence from later Carolingian times we hear how Metrannus, patrician of Provence, about 700 A.D. gave a *villa* to the abbey of Saint-Victor *pro beneficio* and that his successor Abbo did the same *in beneficium*.[80] More explicit is information concerning landholding found in Abbo's will, dealing as it does with land over a wider area in the Valley of the Rhone and in Dauphiny. This will mentions land which *"Australdus habet in beneficio"* or which *"Bartona libertus noster in benefitium habet,"* and others as well. There is also a reference to *"fidele meo Protadio."*[81] In a rare document from Auvergne dating from 756–757 we also find Waiffre, *princeps* of Aquitaine, giving a *villa* to a certain Gédéon, as a life *precarium*, in return for another *villa* and two pounds of silver—this some five years before the final Carolingian offensive against Aquitaine.[82] Though we have no surviving charters from pre-Carolingian Septimania, from what we know of Visigothic Spain during this period we can fairly assume that such *precaria* are to be found in the Narbonnaise too.[83]

---

[78] Ganshof has noted the lack of any satisfactory study of the *precarium* of Merovingian times. This seems especially true of pre-Carolingian Southern Gaul (F. Ganshof, "L'origine des rapports féodo-vassiliques," in *I problemi della Civiltà Carolingia*, p. 48 n.).

[79] *Vie de Saint Didier*, IX, 32.

[80] *Cart. de Saint-Victor*, no. 31.

[81] *Cart. de Grenoble*, pp. 34–48. It is worth noting that while humble freedmen like Bartone are given benefices, the mention of a *fidelis* Protadio may show a more honorable relationship between Abbo and some of those who held his land.

[82] *Cart. de Brioude*, no. 26, pp. 47–48.

[83] C. Sánchez-Albórnoz has made it clear that various types of tenure of this sort, both military and nonmilitary in nature, were common in Visigothic Spain, and thus also in Septimania which was part of this realm. See his "España y el feudalismo Carolingia," in *I problemi della Civiltà Carolingia*, pp. 111–124, and *El "stipendium" hispano-godo y los orígines del beneficio pre-feudal*. A canon of the thirteenth council of Toledo seems to imply that much land was held in this fashion by magnates in Septimania, who as vassals of King Wamba had their land confiscated for disloyalty (*Canon I, XIIIth Council of Toledo*, in *España sagrada*,

Unfortunately the examples of *precaria* and *beneficia* dating from this period in the Midi are so few that it is difficult to be certain about their exact nature or the conditions under which they were given. In the case of Gédéon it is clear that the *precarium* granted was for a lifetime only and that he had to make a definite payment in both land and money for it.[84] Concerning the others we know little, except that in certain cases they were not given in return for military service and were not the monopoly of the upper classes. Several of Abbo's *precaria* granted to freedmen make this clear.[85] What seems more important, however, is the evidence which can be drawn from these examples that a *precarium* frequently was a private grant by an allodial landholder who chose this method of disposing of rights to his property. The *precarium*, then, was a right to use an allod under certain conditions prescribed by its owner.[86] As in Visigothic Spain or Lombard Italy,[87] then, there existed in the Midi conditional grants of land called *beneficia* or *precaria* before the period of the Carolingians.

A final word concerning land in Southern France during these years

---

VI, 29). On Wamba's law of 683 which forbade churches giving out their land as *precaria* or *sub stipendium* see *Lex Visigothorum*, IV, 5–6, in *Mon. Ger. Hist. Leges*, I, 202.

[84] *Cart. de Brioude*, no. 26, pp. 46–47. Note that when Pepin in 743 or 744 *in theory* returned to the Church the estates he had given his vassals, he ordered those who held such lands to pay a *cens* to the Church owner and receive from it a charter of *precarium* (Boretius, *Capitularia*, I, nos. 10–12, pp. 29–32). Ganshof notes that in 779 these were called *"precaria verbo regis"* (*Capitulary of Heristal*, anno 779, in Boretius, *Capitularia*, I, no. 20, art. 13, p. 32). Such *precaria* seem similar to that in Auvergne which Duke Waiffre gave to Gédéon. Perhaps Waiffre was copying Charles Martel and Pepin in an attempt to raise forces to protect his realm against Carolingian attacks.

[85] In the eighth century, before Charles Martel attracted important magnates into ties of vassalage by distributing Church lands to them in 743, vassalage in Frankish domains generally was reserved for men of humble condition (Ganshof, "L'origine des rapports féodo-vassiliques," pp. 35–42). This remained true also under Pepin the Short and even under Charlemagne (see Boretius, *Capitularia*, I, nos. 15, 16, 104, pp. 38, 44, 215). This seems generally true also of all Southern France north of Septimania during this period.

[86] Ganshof reports the same thing for *precaria* and benefices in general (Ganshof, *Qu'est-ce que la féodalite?* pp. 22–24, and "L'origine des rapports féodo-vassiliques," p. 49).

[87] On pre-Carolingian Italian feudalistic institutions and customs that parallel those of Visigothic Spain and Merovingian Southern France see P. Leicht, "Il Feudo in Italia nell'età Carolingia," in *I problemi della Civiltà Carolingia*, pp. 71–107.

seems in order. How much vacant or uncultivated land was there? We know that there was a great deal of it in later Carolingian times in the Narbonnaise, in Roussillon, in the Rhone Valley, in Aquitaine, and in Catalonia. Most historians have tended to explain this fact by calling attention to the six decades of disorder in the Midi between 718 and 778. In other words they have given the blame to invading Moslem and Carolingian forces for a devastation to which they ascribe such a condition.

Such views seem exaggerated, to say the least. Except for two razzias, one which reached Autun about 722[88] and another Poitiers in 732,[89] Moslem raids were confined to the Narbonnaise, Rouergue, the Albigeois, Velay, and the Lower Rhone Valley, and even here they seem to have lasted for only a few decades. Carolingian conquest of the Rhone Valley between 736 and 739 was a swift affair and Carolingian activities in Septimania seem to have been confined to the same period and to the years 752–760, when the subjugation of this region and nearby Southern Aquitaine was finally completed. Pepin's conquest of the rest of Aquitaine, though destructive, took place over an eight-year period between 761 and 768. Gascony was not entered by Carolingian forces until 769 and then again in 778 during the campaign against Saragossa. Thus neither the military activities of the Moslems nor of their Carolingian rivals really explain the vast amount of uncultivated land found in the Midi after 778, though they help explain some of it.

Thus we must look for another explanation. Perhaps the most satisfactory one lies in the fact that the society of the Midi—and this includes Catalonia—had not in the period before 718 begun to use land very effectively. The *villa* system, which still seems to have been the dominant method of landowning, simply did not provide a way of settling new land which the *coloni* who dwelt on such *villas* might well have desired to cultivate for themselves. Nor do we have any evidence that the Church in the Midi was any more enterprising in this respect.[90] Not until the Carolingians established a new land policy were the waste places of the

[88] *Annals of Aniane*, col. 2–3.
[89] *Ibid.*, col. 3–4; *Chron. of Moissac*, pp. 291–292; and *Fredegarii cont.*, ch. 13, p. 175.
[90] Here Higounet's study of the cultivation of Moissac's land located between the Tarn and the Garonne in this period and in later Carolingian times is of vital importance. He shows that *only old used land* was cultivated. New lands were not exploited until much later (Higounet, "L'occupation du sol du pays entre Tarn et Garonne au moyen âge").

Midi to be put to the plow or brought into effective use, and this in a new and different era.

Such then was the pattern of Southern French society on the eve of Moslem and Carolingian intervention. It was a region which consisted of large estates (except perhaps in Gascony), which were generally cultivated by serflike *coloni* and which were run by an aristocracy of allodial landholders, who made some use of *precaria* as well. It was a region whose Church, except in Gascony, seems to have been closely linked to the same landholding class and whose government, divided into four great regions, was in the hands of counts and similar officials. Throughout its area, again with the exception of Gascony, Roman and Visigothic law had survived, and the aristocracy, who were frequently fighting men, relied in part on castles and other fortresses to defend themselves. The society was one, however, in which neither government nor military service was well organized and in which the economy was increasingly local. Its two stronger neighbors, Moslem and Carolingian, were soon to intervene in its affairs and bring it to a new and different era.

CHAPTER II

The Carolingian Conquest 718–778

IN 718 MOSLEMS from Spain crossed the Pyrenees into Southern France. In so doing they set in motion a series of events which was to end sixty years later with most of the Midi in Carolingian hands. By 778 Provence, the Narbonnaise, and Aquitaine had been forcibly added to the Carolingian Empire, while Gascony had accepted its nominal overlordship. The Moslems had been driven back across the Pyrenees, and Carolingian armies had begun the task of liberating a band of Spanish territory where Christian Catalonia, Aragón, and Navarre were to arise.

As we examine these years one fact stands out—the slowness of the Carolingian advance to the south. Not until 732 do we find Carolingian armed forces in the Midi. Even after this date their advance seems to have been a spasmodic one. Periods of activity seem to have alternated with periods of quiescence. Thus we find them active between 732 and 739, between 752 and 759, from 760 to 769, and again in 778. During the remaining years of these six decades they did little.

It was Moslems from Spain, as a matter of fact, who began outside intervention in Southern France, not the Carolingians. Charles Martel, who was busy consolidating his authority north of the Loire and in Germany, seems to have had little inclination to follow their lead initially. True, Aquitaine and Provence, which were menaced by this Moslem invasion, were nominally part of the Frankish domains he ruled as mayor of the palace; and true also, Eudes, duke of Aquitaine and a partisan of some of the later Merovingians, was hostile to him and his pretensions. But Charles was in no very strong position at the time, and he seems to have been more concerned with the menace of the Frisians than with events in the Midi.[1] Thus he did not react in any effective way to the news of the Moslem invasion of the Narbonnaise.

[1] On the hostility which existed between Duke Eudes of Aquitaine and Charles Martel, as well as the latter's difficulties with the Frisians prior to 732 see *Frede-*

So it was that when the forces of Islam reached Narbonne in 720 and established themselves there and turned it into a permanent base for future operations, they did so with only local, ineffective opposition.[2] After all, the Narbonnaise had always been Visigothic rather than Frankish, and so the Moslem conquest could easily be considered an extension of their activities in Spain—wiping out the last traces of Gothic opposition to their rule—rather than any immediate threat to Frankish territory.

If such thoughts existed in the minds of the Franks, Aquitanians, and Provençals, however, they were soon rudely dispelled. Almost at once the Moors advanced from Narbonne into Aquitaine where, late in 720 or early in 721, they were defeated before the walls of Toulouse by an Aquitanian-Frankish force led by Duke Eudes.[3] Checked in this direction, the Moslems appear to have contented themselves with a consolidation of their position in the Narbonnaise, occupying Carcassonne in 725 and perhaps some of the other *civitates*[4] and launching razzias into Rouergue and the Albigeois, one of which seems to have reached as far north as Autun.[5] Such raids, it would seem, did not concern Duke Eudes too much, or perhaps his fear of his Carolingian rival, Charles Martel, was greater still, for we learn that some time before 731 he allied himself to the Moslem ruler of Cerdanya, by giving him his daughter in marriage— an alliance which he may have felt would secure his southern frontiers.[6]

---

garii cont., ch. 10, p. 174; *Chron. of Moissac*, pp. 291–292; *Ademar of Chabannes*, I, 51, pp. 51–52; and *Annals of Aniane*, cols. 2–3.

[2] On the Moslem conquest of Spain and advance toward Septimania the best account is still F. Codera y Zaidín, "Límites probables de la dominación árabe en la cordillera pirenaica," in *Collección de Estudios Árabes*, VIII. See the more recent account in R. de Abadal i de Vinyals, "El paso de Septimania del dominio godo al franco a través de la invasión sarracena," in *Cuadernos de Historia de España*, XIII.

[3] All three Southern French sources—the *Chronicles of Uzès* and *Moissac* and the *Annals of Aniane*—mention this victory which Eudes won at Toulouse (*Annals of Aniane*, col. 2–3; *Chron. of Uzès*, col. 25; and *Chron. of Moissac*, p. 290).

[4] Only the *Chronicles of Moissac*, which may reflect special local knowledge of nearby areas, mentions the Moslem conquest of Carcassonne in 725 or 726. Both Zotenburg and Molinier accept the fact that this conquest did take place (H. Zotenburg, "Sur les invasions Arabes dans le Languedoc," in *Hist. Gén. de Lang.*, II, 555–556; and A. Molinier, "Sur les invasions Arabes dans le Languedoc" in *ibid.*, pp. 549–550).

[5] Later sources mention Arab raids into Rouergue near Conques and into Velay, but the contemporary *Annals of Aniane* tells us of this raid as far north as Autun (*Annals of Aniane*, col. 3–4, and Molinier, "Sur les invasions Arabes," p. 550).

[6] This alliance of Eudes with the Moslems of Cerdanya is mentioned in *Frede-*

If Eudes hoped to secure himself from Moslem attack by this alliance with a ruler who controlled the eastern passes from Spain into Septimania, he was doomed to disappointment. For in 731 the new governor of Spain, Abd-ar-Rahman, who was not a party to this alliance, entered the lists against him. In doing so, Abd-ar-Rahman avoided the passes of the Pyrenees controlled by Eudes' Moslem ally and instead, with a large army, crossed into France by way of Pampeluna and the western Basque country. Moving north he met and destroyed an army led by Eudes outside Bordeaux and sacked the city. Eudes fled north to ask Charles, his Carolingian rival, for assistance, while the victorious Moslems followed, spreading destruction in their wake and sacking abbeys like Saint-Hilaire of Poitiers.[7]

News of this Moslem advance north seems to have at last alerted Charles Martel to his danger and so, with an army of heavily armed *vassi* whom he had enriched with Church lands, the Carolingian mayor of the palace moved south to meet the Moors. Outside Poitiers in 732 the Franks won a victory, and the Moslems retreated south leaving Abd-ar-Rahman, their commander, dead on the field of battle.[8]

There is little evidence that Charles Martel moved to follow up this victory, and it seems clear that its chief beneficiary was Duke Eudes, who probably did homage to Charles and then regained control of his duchy of Aquitaine, dying undisturbed a few years later in 735. A contemporary source gives us an explanation of Charles' inactivity in Aquitaine at the time, for it tells us how in 734 he was busy pacifying Burgundy, which he turned over to trusted followers or *fideles* after its conquest.[9] Only upon Eudes' death in 735 do we find him active in Aquitaine, this time leading an expedition as far south as Bordeaux which he captured despite its formidable fortifications. It seems probable, though, that this expedition was less an attempt to conquer Aquitaine than a show of force to make sure that Hunald, son and successor of Eudes, would acknowledge

---

garii cont., ch. 13, p. 175. See also Zotenburg, "Sur les invasions Arabes," pp. 555–556. Perhaps this alliance with a ruler of a region inhabited by Basques was simply a continuation of Eudes' old pro-Basque policy (see Chapter I, Section I, note 37).

[7] *Annals of Aniane*, col. 4–5; *Chron. of Moissac*, p. 291; and *Fredegarii cont.*, ch. 13, p. 175.

[8] The advance north to Poitiers was a raid or razzia, not a Moslem attempt to conquer this part of France. Thus, some historians have tended to overestimate the importance of Charles Martel's victory. On this see Zotenburg, "Sur les invasions Arabes," p. 557.

[9] *Fredegarii cont.*, ch. 14, p. 175.

The Carolingian Conquest

Carolingian overlordship.¹⁰ Whatever its cause, Charles does not appear to have kept possession of Bordeaux and other parts of Aquitaine. Instead he returned north to his domains beyond the Loire.

In 736, however, he was ready to move south. But this time he concerned himself not with Aquitaine but with the Rhone Valley south of newly conquered Burgundy. The reasons for this are obscure. A passage from the *Annals of Aniane* gives us a possible explanation. This tells us that some time prior to 736 Moslems from the Narbonnaise had occupied Arles, perhaps on the invitation of Maurontius, patrician of Provence, and for four years had been raiding widely in the Rhone Valley.¹¹ Perhaps such activities had begun to menace Charles in Burgundy, or perhaps they furnished him with a needed excuse. At any rate in 736, after occupying the Lyonnais and the Middle Rhone region and placing his *judices* or supporters in the principal *civitates*,¹² Charles and his brother Childebrand advanced down the Rhone with a Frankish and Burgundian force. They besieged and captured Arles and Avignon and then moved west into Septimania. The *civitates* of the eastern Narbonnaise surrendered to the Frankish forces, and in 739 these forces defeated a Moslem army at Buerre not far from the Moslem base of Narbonne.¹³

Charles did not follow up this victory with a seizure of Narbonne and an expulsion of the Moors from the Midi. Perhaps, as has been suggested, he did not have sufficient siege equipment to take this stronghold which could be supplied from the sea. More probably, however, he was deterred by other happenings. Hunald, *princeps* of Aquitaine, was hostile and threatened his long line of communications to the north.¹⁴ More impor-

---

¹⁰ *Ibid.*, ch. 15, pp. 175–176.

¹¹ *Chron. of Moissac*, p. 291, and *Annals of Aniane*, col. 4–5. Duprat believes that the Moslems were not invited in by Maurontius until *after* Charles Martel had intervened in Provence about 736 (E. Duprat in *Bouches du Rhône: Encyclopédie départementale*, II, 131–132). This agrees with *Fredegarii cont.*, ch. 20, p. 177.

¹² *Fredegarii cont.*, ch. 18, pp. 176–177, says that in 737 Charles Martel took Lyon with a Burgundian army and subjugated Marseille and Arles and there *"constituit suis judicibus."* No local chronicle, however, mentions the conquest of these last two cities during this campaign. It therefore seems more reasonable to believe that they were conquered later in 737 during Childebrand's expedition against Avignon and the rest of Provence proper.

¹³ *Chron. of Moissac*, p. 291; *Annals of Aniane*, col. 5–6; and *Fredegarii cont.*, ch. 20, pp. 177–178. See also Molinier, "Sur les invasions Arabes," pp. 551–552.

¹⁴ The *Annals of Aniane*, in mentioning Waiffre's later attacks on Frankish troops blockading Narbonne during the period 752–759, says that Waiffre attacked Pepin *"as his father had done Charles Martel."* This seems to imply at

tant, Maurontius, patrician of Provence, from his unconquered city of Marseille, raised a revolt against him from the rear. Charles was forced to withdraw from Septimania to the Lower Rhone, destroying many of the *castella* of the region and the fortifications of such *civitates* as Agde, Béziers, and Mauguio as he retreated. Once in Provence with Lombard assistance he appears to have crushed all opposition. Patrician Maurontius had to flee for refuge to the Alps. Though the Narbonnaise had escaped him, by 739 Provence and the Valley of the Rhone were Carolingian.[15]

Charles Martel returned to the north after this campaign, and a little later in 742 we learn of a revolt by Hunald, duke of Aquitaine. Charles had to invade Auvergne and capture the castle of Castelluc before Hunald would return to his allegiance—a peace, however, which left Aquitaine still effectively in the latter's hands.[16] Hunald was succeeded peacefully in 745 by his son Waiffre, and Charles' heirs who succeeded him in the same year made no attempt to disturb the status quo. We can only guess at the reasons for this peaceful decade in the Midi. One reason may have been the fact that Charles Martel left his domains to his two sons, which meant that until his brother had retired to a monastery, Pepin, Charles' able son, did not have a free hand. A second reason may have been the fact that Pepin was more concerned with events in Germany, his intervention against the Lombards in Italy, and his efforts to replace the Merovingians as kings of the Franks with his own Carolingian family than he was with Aquitaine or Septimania. Not until 752 was Pepin, who now securely held the position as Frankish king, free to concern himself with the Midi.

Once the decision was made in 752 Pepin turned his attention to Septimania, taking up where his father had left off in 739. He led a strong Frankish army south. In the Narbonnaise a local Gothic count, Ansemundus, went over to him and delivered into his hands the cities of

---

the very least a threat to Charles' forces in the Narbonnaise from the duke of Aquitaine in the period 736–739. (*Annals of Aniane*, col. 6–7).

[15] Note 13 contains the references to Charles' withdrawal during which he destroyed the walls of Mauguio and the Arena of Nîmes. The *Annals of Aniane* also says he took hostages with him. The *Fredegarii cont.*, ch. 20, contains the fullest account and mentions the destruction of Nîmes, Agde, and Béziers, and a number of other *castra*. Then (with Lombard help) he expelled Maurontius from Provence in 738 (*Fredegarii cont.*, ch. 21, p. 178). On this see Duprat in *Bouches du Rhône*, II, 132. Charles' alliance with the Lombards against the Moslems and the patrician of Provence explains his reluctance during this period to assist the Papacy in Italy.

[16] *Fredegarii cont.*, ch. 25, p. 180.

Nîmes, Agde, and Béziers, while still another local magnate did the same for Mauguio.[17] All but unopposed, Pepin and his forces advanced to the outskirts of Narbonne, the principal Moslem base.

What followed is somewhat confused in our sources, but they agree that for some seven years Frankish forces invested Narbonne without taking the city. What caused this delay? There seem to have been several reasons for it. In the first place we learn that Count Ansemundus, Pepin's Gothic ally, was killed outside Narbonne, thus limiting local support.[18] This seems to have been followed by a revolt at Nîmes in the Frankish rear, a rising which ended in the placing of this region under a Frankish governor, a certain Count Radulf.[19] Finally we hear of an attack on the Narbonnaise by forces under the control of Duke Waiffre of Aquitaine.[20] All these developments must have made the Frankish position before Narbonne difficult to maintain. So it was not until 759 that Pepin secured the city, and then only after promising the Gothic inhabitants of this region their own laws and probably their own government. Thereupon, we are told, they killed the Moslem garrison and delivered the city over to him.[21]

Pepin's conquest of Narbonne eliminated the last effective stronghold which the Moslems held north of the Pyrenees and was probably followed by an advance south in which he or his Gothic allies secured Roussillon.[22]

[17] *Chron. of Moissac*, p. 293; *Chron. of Uzès*, col. 26; *Annals of Aniane*, col. 6; and *Vita Benedicti Anianensis*, ed. E. Waitz, ch. I, in *Mon. Ger. Hist. Scriptores*, XV, 201.

[18] Only the *Chron. of Uzès*, col. 26, mentions the death of Ansemundus in 753.

[19] *Ibid.* Again it is only this local chronicle which mentions the revolt of Nîmes and Uzès against the Franks and its suppression which resulted in these cities' being placed *"sub Franchorum dominio"* in 754.

[20] While the *Fredegarii cont.*, ch. 35, mentions the hostility of Duke Waiffre to Pepin and the fact that he gave asylum to Pepin's enemies in 753 after Pepin had become king of the Franks, it is only *local* chronicles that mention his attacks on the Frankish forces besieging Narbonne (*Chron. of Moissac*, p. 294; and *Annals of Aniane*, col. 6–7).

[21] The surrender of Narbonne by its Goths in 759, which is mentioned by both the *Annals of Aniane* and the *Chronicle of Moissac*, was an important event. By allowing these Goths their own laws and probably also their own government, Pepin made them his most dependable allies in the Midi. They helped him conquer a hostile Aquitaine. Indeed from this time on an alliance with the Goths of this region remained the cornerstone of Carolingian policy here. It insured Gothic loyalty to the Carolingians, but was probably also the reason for the continued hostility of Gascons and Aquitanians who were old enemies of these Goths.

[22] The advance into Roussillon, which was certainly Carolingian by Charlemagne's time, probably took place immediately after the fall of Narbonne. We

Soon afterwards we are told of a more important conquest, for one local chronicle tells us that after the fall of Narbonne Pepin's forces moved north and west to occupy Toulouse, Rouergue, and the Albigeois.[23] By 760 both Septimania and Southeastern Aquitaine were Carolingian.

It was this last conquest which led to a Carolingian assault on Aquitaine proper, probably the most difficult operation which had been attempted so far. True, Pepin, the Frankish monarch, had certain advantages in this struggle. Thanks to his Gothic allies, he appears to have had a firm hold on Septimania, while the Moslems driven south of the Pyrenees and involved in the civil wars which attended the arrival of Abd-ar-Rahman I in Spain, were no longer a menace. Waiffre's domains lay exposed to Pepin on three sides, the north, the east, and the south. On the other hand the rugged terrain of the Massif Central which Waiffre controlled and the many fortified cities and *castella* of the region favored the defense. In addition to this, Waiffre appears to have countered Pepin's alliance with the Goths of the Narbonnaise by making a similar arrangement with Duke Lupo and the Gascons south of the Garonne, which assured him of Gascon troops and assistance when needed.[24] He also appears to have begun to confiscate Church lands in Aquitaine—probably binding his followers to him by generously distributing such property among them, as Charles Martel had done some decades earlier in Northern France.[25]

In 760 our sources reveal that Pepin, after denouncing Duke Waiffre's spoilation of the Church, sent an army into Berry and Auvergne which ravaged a large part of Aquitaine, or as the chronicler puts it, *"maximam partem Aquitaniae,"* with fire and sword.[26] The next year two of Waif-

---

have no proof of this fact, however. See Molinier, "Sur les invasions Arabes," p. 554.

[23] The *Chronicle of Uzès* says that Rouergue was conquered and a Frankish count installed there in 754 (*Chron. of Uzès*, col. 27). The *Annals of Aniane* and the *Chronicle of Moissac* mention the conquest of Toulouse, Albi, and Rouergue as taking place *after* the fall of Narbonne in 759. The latter two accounts seem more plausible, since Gothic assistance was probably necessary to secure these regions for Pepin (*Annals of Aniane*, col. 7; and *Chron. of Moissac*, p. 294).

[24] On the Gascons who fought with Duke Waiffre see *Fredegarii cont.*, ch. 125–126, 130–131, pp. 186–190.

[25] *Ibid.*, ch. 124, p. 185.

[26] It is interesting to note that Pepin was the aggressor and that Duke Waiffre asked for peace in 760 (*ibid.*). Only when it became apparent that only complete conquest would satisfy Pepin did the war continue to the death.

fre's border counts, those who controlled Bourges and Auvergne, replied in kind by ravaging Burgundy.²⁷ Pepin's answer to this was an expedition into Auvergne which captured the key fortresses of Bourbon and Clermont, killed a number of Gascon auxiliaries who were fighting for the Aquitanians, and forced Count Bladino of Auvergne to submit.²⁸ With Auvergne in his hands, the next year he attacked Berry and Poitiers. Bourges surrendered with its Count Humbert, and so did the fortress of Thouars and the count of Poitou. Gascons fighting for these counts were deported across the Loire into Northern France.²⁹

Then in 763 Pepin advanced further into the heart of Duke Waiffre's domains with a raid which carried his forces through the Limousin as far south as Quercy. For the next three years a seesaw struggle took place. Pepin captured such fortified *civitates* as Poitiers, Limoges, Saintes, Angoulême, and Périgord and a number of *castella* and destroyed their fortifications if he did not feel he could garrison them. At the same time he occupied and rebuilt certain other fortresses with his Frankish levies. Duke Waiffre seems to have followed a policy of destroying such Frankish-held castles if he could capture them and raising revolts in Pepin's rear like that led by Count Bladino in Auvergne. Under the circumstances the war became a bitter affair, and Pepin began to wage it with deliberate frightfulness, for we are told he burnt *villas*, destroyed vineyards, and depopulated monasteries.³⁰

By the end of 765 it seems clear that such brutal tactics had destroyed resistance in central Aquitaine and in 766–767 it was the turn of Périgord, Angoulême, and the Bordelais, close to the Gascon allies of Duke Waiffre. In a series of campaigns the *castella* and *civitates* of these regions were reduced and the countryside so devastated that *"nullus colonus terram ad laborandam"* escaped unscathed. Waiffre's Gascon allies were badly defeated, and in 768 the pro-Frankish peace party of nobles led by Count Humbert of Bourges and other magnates submitted. Most of Waiffre's family were captured, and he was killed in a forest in Périgord

²⁷ *Ibid.*, ch. 125, p. 187.
²⁸ *Ibid.* See also the more general account in *Annales Laurissenses*, anno 761, in *Mon. Ger. Hist. Scriptores*, I, 142.
²⁹ *Fredegarii cont.*, ch. 126, pp. 187–188; *Annales Laurissenses*, anno 762, p. 142.
³⁰ Our sources mention that Franks were placed in fortresses in Berry and that a number of castles were occupied. (*Fredegarii cont.*, ch. 129–130, pp. 189–190; and *Annales Laurissenses*, anno 763, 765, 766, pp. 144–145). Again in 765 Duke Waiffre attempted in vain to make peace.

as his son Hunald escaped south to Gascony.[81] Pepin, who had led this war to a successful conclusion, died soon afterwards.

One last flurry of resistance followed. Pepin's death appears to have raised hopes again among the Aquitanians and their Gascon allies, and Hunald, son of Duke Waiffre, raised the standard of revolt. In vain. Pepin's heirs, Charles and Carloman, immediately moved south to the Garonne where they put down the revolt. Then we are told they built a fortress at Fronsac on the Dordogne to control this sensitive border region and crossed the Garonne into Basque territory. Unable to resist, Lupo, duke of Gascony, surrendered Hunald to them and submitted himself.[82] The ten-year campaign in Aquitaine was over at last and even the Gascons had been forced to accept a nominal Carolingian suzerainty. What had begun with the Moslem invasion of the Narbonnaise in 718 had ended half a century later with the Carolingians supreme in the Midi.

For the next nine years our sources contain no information on events in Southern France. Probably they were peaceful years, as the Carolingians concerned themselves with other problems and other parts of their Empire. During this period Carloman, Charlemagne's brother, retired to a monastery leaving the latter supreme in the Frankish Empire. Charles himself was fully occupied with problems arising in Saxony and Bavaria, and with his first campaigns in Italy. Under the circumstances the Midi could claim little of his attention.

All this changed, however, in 778. In this year dissident Moslem nobles of Saragossa and Northeastern Spain, in revolt against the emir of Cordova, Abd-ar-Rahman I, invited Charlemagne to intervene in Northern Spain, promising him suzerainty of the region north of the Ebro. Charlemagne seems to have been attracted by this prospect and gathered together a large army which included Gascon and Aquitanian contingents and invaded Spain. He appears to have used western Pyrenean passes and to have entered Spain by way of Pampeluna. This campaign was a failure, despite efforts of Carolingian chroniclers to conceal the fact, and Charlemagne had to withdraw across the mountains without having accomplished anything. Emboldened by his failure, Basques in the Pyrenees rose against him and massacred his rear guard. Charles had to return and punish them for their treachery. But he also had to do more. He seems

---

[81] *Fredegarii cont.*, ch. 131–135, pp. 190–192; *Annales Laurissenses*, anno 767, 768, p. 146.

[82] *Annales Laurissenses*, anno 769, p. 148; Einhard, *Vie de Charlemagne*, ed. L. Halphen, ch. 5, p. 445; and Astronomus, *Vita Hludovici imperatoris*, ed. G. Pertz, ch. 2, in *ibid.*, II, 608.

The Carolingian Conquest

to have been forced to a realization that the ties which bound Gascon and Aquitanian to him were very fragile ones indeed.[33] This realization probably explains why he almost immediately reorganized Aquitaine and inaugurated new policies in the Midi—policies which will be examined in later chapters.

With the year 778, then, we reach the end of one era and the beginning of a new one. The conquest of the Midi by the Carolingians had been completed, but it was already apparent that something needed to be done to provide for a better organization of areas south of the Loire which had been added to the Carolingian Empire. Equally important, the events of 778 had shown the nominal and superficial nature of Gascony's submission, and this presented a problem for the future. As for Spain, despite the failure of Charlemagne's intervention, it continued to beckon as an area in which something might be accomplished in the future.

Such then is the story of the Carolingian conquest of the Midi and their first campaign across the Pyrenees on Spanish soil. But it raises some important questions. Of these the one that most needs answering is why the conquest of the Midi proceeded so slowly and was attended by so many difficulties. Why did it take sixty years, and why at the end of the period was Carolingian control so fragile that it demanded a drastic reorganization soon after 778?[34]

One answer certainly lies in the field of geography. To conquer Provence, Gascony, and Aquitaine, the Carolingians had to operate very frequently in a mountainous terrain near the Alps, Cévennes, and Pyrenees quite different from the flat plains of Northern France and Germany to which they were accustomed. This terrain gave every advantage to its native defenders. While such terrain does not appear to have hindered the conquest of Provence, it undoubtedly prolonged the resistance of Aquitaine and kept Gascony from ever being completely Carolingian.

But more than geography lies behind Carolingian difficulties. What of the role of Moslem opposition to them? Can we blame it for the slowness of their advance? This seems unlikely. Moslem forces never proved very worthy opponents to the Carolingians, except in Spain. Down to 778 they lost every battle they fought with Frankish contingents. This was true at Poitiers in 732 where they were badly mauled, in 736–737 when

---

[33] On this expedition see R. de Abadal i de Vinyals, "La expedición de Carlomagno a Zaragoza, el hecho histórico," in *Coloquios de Roncevalles. Augusto 1955.*

[34] See F. Ganshof, "Une Crise dans le règne de Charlemagne, les années 778 et 779," in *Mélanges Charles Gaillard.*

they failed to hold cities like Arles and Avignon, and in 739 when they were crushed at the Battle of Buerre. Outside Narbonne between 752 and 759 they did not dare meet Carolingian troops in the open field. It seems clear then that though Moslem forces represented the principal excuse for Carolingian intervention in the Midi, they were not a real obstacle to a successful Carolingian advance to the Pyrenees.

This leads one to the conclusion that neither geography nor the Moslems furnished the Carolingians with real difficulties but rather something else—the resistance of the local inhabitants and society of the Midi, whether it be in Provence and the Valley of the Rhone, in Septimania, in Aquitaine, or in Gascony. And we can discern a general pattern which this resistance seems to have taken. Upon the arrival of Frankish forces in each region, the inhabitants would almost always submit initially, but such submission was always temporary and nominal. It was almost always followed by a revolt when a Charles Martel, a Pepin, or a Charlemagne was in difficulties or when they tried to transform a nominal suzerainty into something more real and enduring.

Thus in Aquitaine the submission of Eudes to Charles Martel in 732 did not mean a Carolingian Aquitaine, but a tie, fragile in nature, made necessary by Eudes' defeat at the hands of the Moslems.[35] Equally formal were the submissions of Hunald in 735 and 742, each time the result of a Carolingian invasion of his principality.[36] Waiffre's attempted intervention in the Narbonnaise during the years 752–759 shows the inherent opposition of his family to the Carolingians[37]—an opposition which did not end until the brutal campaigns of Pepin and his sons during the years 760 to 769 finally made Aquitaine Carolingian.

In much the same way the inhabitants of Provence and the Lower Rhone Valley submitted in 736–737 only to stage a revolt in Charles Martel's rear when the opportunity arose—a revolt which only ended when Maurontius, patrician of Provence, was driven out and the rebellion crushed by Lombard and Frankish troops.[38] During the same period Charles Martel's campaign in Septimania again proved how little he could rely upon native Gothic counts and the local population for support against the Moslems. And this was repeated during the years 752–759, when, after the death of Count Ansemundus, the inhabitants of Nîmes revolted and native rule had to be done away with and the region put

[35] *Fredegarii cont.*, ch. 13, p. 175; *Chron. of Moissac*, p. 291.
[36] *Fredegarii cont.*, ch. 15, 25, pp. 176, 180.
[37] *Ibid.*, ch. 35, p. 181; *Annals of Aniane*, col. 6; and *Chron. of Moissac*, p. 293.
[38] *Fredegarii cont.*, ch. 20, p. 178.

under a Frankish count.[39] Narbonne, as a matter of fact, only became Carolingian in 759 after Pepin had specifically guaranteed its inhabitants their own laws and perhaps their own native rulers.[40] Charlemagne's experience in Gascony in 778 seems to have shown him the same unreliability as far as the native population and its rulers were concerned.[41]

In the face of this apparently deep-seated unyielding attitude of local populations and their leaders in every part of Southern France, the Carolingians, during this period, seem to have followed two policies. On the one hand, wherever possible, they made alliance with local magnates in the regions they conquered, like Count Ansemundus in Septimania, the Goths of Narbonne, or a Count Humbert of Berry. On the other hand they found it wiser not to put too much trust in such allies to control these regions. So they early began to introduce into Southern France their own Northern Frankish *vassi* to serve as rulers and garrisons of the areas which they had conquered. Thus in 734 we hear how Charles Martel, having conquered Burgundy, turned over authority to his *fideles*.[42] A little later our sources tell us that in the Lower Rhone Valley he placed the *civitates* under the control of his own officials or *judices*.[43] In the Narbonnaise Pepin placed Frankish counts in control of Nîmes, Uzès, and Rouergue after revolts developed in these areas.[44]

In Aquitaine during the fierce campaigns of 760–779 we again and again hear of Franks whom Pepin stationed in the castles and fortresses of the region.[45] Later on, the Astronomus, writing of Aquitaine in 778, correctly explains this basic Carolingian policy by saying that Charlemagne made sure that all abbots and counts of this region were Franks, and that he also introduced into the land large numbers of Frankish

[39] *Chron. of Uzès*, col. 27.
[40] *Chron. of Moissac*, p. 294; *Chron. of Uzès*, col. 27; and *Annals of Aniane*, col. 7.
[41] See Ganshof, "Une Crise dans le règne de Charlemagne."
[42] *Fredegarii cont.*, ch. 14, p. 175.
[43] *Ibid.*, ch. 18, pp. 176–177.
[44] *Chron. of Uzès*, col. 26–27.
[45] On the occupation of Bourges by Pepin's counts see *Fredegarii cont.*, ch. 126, p. 187. On the occupation of *civitates* and *castella* in the rest of Aquitaine between 762 and 765 see *ibid.*, ch. 129, p. 189. On the occupation of Berry in 766 see *Annales Laurissenses*, anno 766, p. 146. On the building of the castle of Fronsac on the Dordogne see *ibid.*, anno 769, p. 148. See also references to castles fortified by Charlemagne in this region in *Annales Regni Francorum*, ed. G. Kurze, and in M. Garaud, "La construction des châteaux et les déstinées de la *vicaria* et du *vicarius* Carolingiens en Poitou," in *Revue historique de droit français et étranger*, XXXI (1953), 54–60.

warriors who were called *vassi*.[46] In fact only in the region about Narbonne and in Gascony was such a policy not followed prior to 778.

To this policy, which has been called Frankish colonization by churchmen, officials, and warrior garrisons, one should add one more feature of Carolingian conquest and control—the ruthless crushing of opposition. Historians have often commented on Charles Martel's confiscation of land in the Rhone Valley and noted how he replaced a native clergy, after 739, with one recruited from the north.[47] Contemporary chronicles have left us a picture of his destruction of *civitates* in Septimania, like Mauguio for instance.[48] In Aquitaine Pepin's campaigns present a picture of deliberate frightfulness in which *villas* were burnt, crops and vineyards laid waste, and monastic establishments depopulated,[49] and the end of such campaigns seems to have been followed by confiscations of land which passed from the hands of native landowners into that of Carolingian *vassi* or swelled the royal *fisc*.

It thus seems fair to say that the Carolingian conquest of Southern France, at least down to 778, was more than a simple taking over of certain regions by a distant monarch. It resulted in conditions which represented, in many areas of Southern France, a deliberate, sustained, and fundamental assault upon the pre-existing society and institutions. Local magnates and the local Church down to 778 suffered serious damage as a result of Carolingian policies, which deliberately introduced alien officials, churchmen, and others into the Narbonnaise, Provence, and Aquitaine, along with a Frankish proto-feudal system quite different from that familiar to these areas. Resistance was general, but ineffective, except in some parts of the Narbonnaise and Gascony. Unlike the Midi's earlier conquerors, the Visigoths and the Merovingians, we must regard the Carolingians as bringing with them into Southern France certain funda-

---

[46] Astronomus, *Vita Hludovici*, ch. 3, p. 608. On benefices given such vassals see *Capitulare Aquitanicum*, anno 768, ch. 5, 9, in *Mon. Ger. Hist. Capitularia*, I, no. 18, p. 43.

[47] A particularly ruthless ecclesiastical policy seems to have been followed in the area of the Upper and Middle Rhone Valley. Yet in Provence in 780 we find a certain Maurontius still bishop of Marseille, obviously of the old family of the patricians of Provence (*Cart. de Saint-Victor*, no. 31, pp. 43–46).

[48] "*Castra illis regionis vastabat*" is the term used in *Fredegarii cont.*, ch. 21, p. 178.

[49] In Aquitaine, where resistance was prolonged, we find in our sources phrases like "*maximam partem Aquitaniae ignibus concremant*," or "*monasteria multa depopulata*," or "*nullus colonus terram ad laborandam.*" See *ibid.*, ch. 124, 130, 133, pp. 186, 189, 191.

mental changes. These triumphed over local opposition, at least initially, and brought a new system and pattern of development to the lands which lay south of Poitou and Burgundy.

One final word concerning these decades of war and change—the economic results which followed. We have already noted that neither Carolingian conquest nor Moslem depredations suffice to explain the extent of vacant and unused land found in the Midi after 778. This state of affairs was the result of longer-range and more fundamental causes. This is true. But nevertheless one cannot escape the fact that these sixty years did see much destruction, particularly of churches and abbeys which were unable to resist, and of *villa* life also. It is significant that so much reconstruction was necessary in the Midi after 780. Nor can we escape feeling that the disappearance of every mint south of Poitou and Burgundy was in part the result of these disorderly patterns of life during these years,[50] as was the almost total disappearance of the Midi's external commerce. Thus it was that the Midi not only faced the future in 778 under the alien and different rule of the Carolingians, it also faced it with its churches in ruins, its *villa* life disorganized, and its economic life at a level lower than had been the case in 718—all this was to provide a challenge which its new overlords had to face in planning its future.

[50] M. Prou, *Catalogue des Monnaies Carolingiennes*, p. cxi–cxx; and A. Lewis, "Le commerce maritime et la navigation sur les côtes de la Gaule Atlantique du Vᵉ au VIIIᵉ siècle," in *Le Moyen Age*, LIX (1953), 297.

II
SOUTHERN FRANCE, CATALONIA,
AND THE CAROLINGIAN EMPIRE,
778–828

CHAPTER III

The Expansion into Gascony and Catalonia

THE FAILURE of Charlemagne's Spanish expedition of 778 had many important consequences for the Midi and the Carolingian Empire. Among them was a realization by this monarch that two regions on the southern boundaries of his empire, Gascony and the borderlands of Moslem Spain just across the Pyrenees, presented problems which demanded new solutions. This, of course, does not mean that Charlemagne felt free to devote much attention to either area. Other more pressing problems seem to have had priority: such as Saxony and the marches of Germany; Italy and the Papacy; the Church; and a necessary reorganization of the structure of his government. After 778, however, it seems clear that Charlemagne had become aware of the fact that new methods were needed to deal with the Gascons, and that there existed in Spain, beyond the Pyrenees, a Christian population, many of whom were ready for liberation from the Moslem yoke.[1]

One might sum up Charlemagne's Gascon problem as follows. Here was a mountainous region too remote and difficult to conquer, over which he lacked any really effective control. True, Lupo, the Gascon duke or *princeps*, had submitted to him in 769, after he had crossed the Garonne in pursuit of Hunald of Aquitaine, and, according to Frankish accounts, had placed Gascony under Carolingian overlordship.[2] But the events of 778 had certainly proved the limited value of such suzerainty. For, as we

---

[1] On the initial basic problems of this era see F. Ganshof, "Une Crise dans le règne de Charlemagne, les années 778 et 779," in *Mélanges Charles Gaillard*, and R. de Abadal i de Vinyals, "La expedición de Carlomagno a Zaragoza, el hecho histórico," in *Coloquios de Roncevalles. Augusto 1955*.

[2] Astronomus, *Vita Hludovici*, ch. 3, p. 608; Einhard, *Vie de Charlemagne*, ed. L. Halphen, ch. 5, p. 445; and *Annales Regni Francorum*, ed. G. Kurze, anno 769, p. 136.

have noted, when Charlemagne was returning from Spain to France, Basques in the Pyrenees, perhaps encouraged by Duke Lupo, had risen against him and ambushed his rear guard in the mountain passes—an action which later gave rise to the celebrated legend of Roncesvalles. Contemporary accounts tell us that Charlemagne returned to avenge this defeat with his main body and restored his authority over the region which lay on the other side of the Pyrenees.[3]

But Charlemagne did more than this. He seems to have taken certain steps which had the effect of diminishing the authority of Duke Lupo and his family over Gascony. This probably explains why in 778 he appointed a certain Séguin as count of Bordeaux, for in so doing he gave Carolingian backing to a western Gascon family who seem to have been rivals of Lupo.[4] More important still, a little later he organized a second county in Gascony on the borders of the Toulousain, the county of Fézensac, which we learn was entrusted to a Count Burgund, who, judging from his name, was certainly not a Gascon. When Burgund died about 801, he was replaced by a certain Liutard, who again was not of Gascon origin.[5] General supervision of this Gascon frontier seems to have been placed in the hands of Chorson, count or duke of Toulouse.[6]

It seems obvious that such policies displeased the Gascons, and in 787 or 789 we learn that Chorson was captured by Odalric, son of Duke Lupo of Gascony, and forced to make an agreement which Charlemagne considered so shameful that he deprived him of his *honorem* of Toulouse and replaced him in 790 with Count William, the famous St. Guillem, who was closely related to the Carolingian royal house.[7] Our sources tell us that Count William restored the Gascons to obedience and that Odalric was banished to perpetual exile.[8]

For the next two decades Gascony appears to have accepted Carolingian authority, though not without some grumbling, and Duke Lupo in 801–802 assisted Louis the Pious and Count William of Toulouse in their expedition against Barcelona by leading a Gascon contingent of troops into battle on the Carolingian side.[9]

---

[3] Astronomus, *Vita Hludovici*, ch. 3, p. 608; Einhard *Vie de Charlemagne*, ch. 9, p. 448; *Chron. of Moissac*, anno 778, p. 296; and *Annals of Aniane*, anno 778, col. 7–8.

[4] Astronomus, *Vita Hludovici*, ch. 3, p. 608.

[5] *Ibid.*, ch. 5, 13, pp. 609, 612.

[6] *Ibid.*, ch. 3, 5, pp. 608–609.

[7] *Ibid.*, ch. 5, p. 609.

[8] *Ibid.* See also L. Auzias, *L'Aquitaine Carolingienne 778–987*, pp. 32–36.

[9] *Chron. of Moissac*, anno 803, p. 307; Astronomus, *Vita Hludovici*, ch. 13, pp.

Charlemagne, however, does not appear to have been willing to rely only on a friendly count of Bordeaux, a Frankish count of Fézensac, and the military and diplomatic skill of his principal viceroy in the Midi, the count of Toulouse, to keep control over Gascony. He enlisted the Church on his side as an ally as well. This policy seems to have begun quite early, for we are told that when he had restored his authority over the high Pyrenees in 778 he divided the land between bishops and abbots and began to baptize the pagan Basques of this region.[10] This encouragement of Church and monastic organizations in Gascony soon bore some fruit, for in 790 we hear of a Gascon bishop, Abraham of Commignes, who attended a Church conclave at Narbonne.[11] A little later we begin to hear, for the first time, of Gascon monasteries, for the Council of Aix-la-Chapelle held in 816 speaks of three Gascon abbeys and one *cella*—all unknown to us from other sources and none of which survived into a later period.[12] Perhaps the Carolingians, with some success, were attempting in Gascony to pursue the same policy of founding abbeys which was going on in Septimania with their blessing under the leadership of St. Benedict of Aniane.

In Septimania and along its borders to the south and east of Gascony Charlemagne's 778 expedition into Spain seems to have had equally important consequences. The failure of his attempt on Saragossa seems to have caused a number of Spanish Christians, who rose in his support, to seek refuge north of the Pyrenees. Charlemagne decided to welcome these *spani* or *hispani*, as they were called, who, judging from their names, were of Gothic, Spanish, or even Gascon origin.[13] He gave them waste lands, or *aprisiones*, as they were called, upon which they could

---

612–613; and Ermold Niger, *Carmina in honorem Hludovici*, ed. E. Dummler, I, vers. 164–167, 273–278, 304–313, 615, in *Mon. Ger. Hist. Scriptores*, I, 472–475.

[10] Only one source, the *Annals of Aniane*, mentions the baptizing of *"Basconorum vel paganorum"* (*Annals of Aniane*, anno 778, col. 7–9). On the limited Christianization of Navarre and other Basque regions nearby during this period see J. Lacarra, *Vasconia medieval: Historia y Filología*, pp. 15–30.

[11] C. Higounet, *Le comté de Commignes de ses origines à son annexation à la Couronne*, I, 18.

[12] "Council of Aix-la-Chapelle," in P. Labbé, *Sacrosancta Concilia*, IX, 603. On the date of this conclave see F. Ganshof, "Note sur la date de deux documents administratives émanant de Louis le Pieux," in *Recueil des travaux offerts à M. C. Brunel*, I, 511–514.

[13] See the list of large *aprisio* holders, one of whom is called Wasco, who petitioned Charlemagne in 812, in R. de Abadal i de Vinyals, *Catalunya Carolingia II. Els Diplomes Carolingis a Catalunya*, pp. 313–314 (hereafter cited as *Catalunya Carolingia*, II).

settle, mainly in Roussillon and about Narbonne.[14] In doing so he accomplished two purposes which were of importance to him. In the first place he provided settlers for some of the wide expanse of deserted and uncultivated land in this part of the Midi. In the second place he assured his empire of warriors who could defend its southern borders in case of an Islamic attack.

The arrival of these *hispani*, however, and the generous Carolingian reception of them seems to have had a secondary effect. It began or at least it speeded up a liberation from Moslem rule of certain territory across the Pyrenees. Perhaps as early as 781 Pallars and Ribagorça, high in the Pyrenees, came under the control of the counts of Toulouse.[15] In 785, we learn that Gerona had accepted Frankish control and nearby Besalu as well.[16] A little later the Urgell-Cerdanya region, where Moslem rule had long been only nominal, accepted Carolingian overlordship.[17] This liberation of a strip of country in Spain which was to become the Spanish March was not only hailed and welcomed by Spanish *aprisio* holders who had found a refuge on Carolingian soil, it was also probably assisted by them and by the Gothic native counts of Septimania and Roussillon.

There seems to be little doubt that these developments alarmed the rulers of Cordova. At any rate in 793 the Moors launched a counterstroke—a full scale invasion of the Midi. William, count of Toulouse, took to the field to oppose these Moslem invaders only to be defeated near Carcassonne. The walled cities of Narbonne and Gerona, however, stood firm and the Islamic army withdrew into Spain without accomplishing anything of a permanent nature.[18]

Despite the Moslem invasion of 793, the general success of the Caro-

---

[14] Abadal dates this original grant in 780. It addresses his *fideles* in Aquitaine, Septimania, and Provence concerning these grants (*Catalunya Carolingia*, II, 399–410, and appendix I, p. 412).

[15] P. Ponsch, "Les origines de l'abbaye d'Arles," in *Études Roussillonnaises*, IV (1954–1955), 69–71.

[16] *Chron. of Moissac*, anno 785, p. 297; *Annales Barcinonenses*, ed. G. Pertz, ch. 23, in *Mon. Ger. Hist. Scriptores*, XXIII, 2.

[17] R. de Abadal i de Vinyals, "La batalla del adopcionisme en la desintegración de la Iglesia visigoda," in *Real Academia de Buenas Letras de Barcelona*, pp. 69–74. See also F. Codera y Zaidín, "Límites probables de la dominación árabe en la cordillera pirenaica," in *Colección de Estudios Árabes*, VIII, which points out the nominal nature of Moslem control of this region.

[18] *Annals of Aniane*, anno 793, col. 8–10; *Chron. of Moissac*, anno 793, p. 300; and *Chron. of Uzès*, col. 27.

Expansion into Gascony and Catalonia 41

lingians in spreading their authority over Gascony and across the Pyrenees seems to have had echoes in Christian Spain. Thus in 794 we hear of an embassy from Christian Asturias visiting Toulouse,[19] and in 797 and 798 we learn of other ambassadors from this part of the Iberian peninsula reaching Charlemagne's capital of Aix-la-Chapelle[20]—all this in spite of the controversy over Adoptionism which from 794 to 799 threatened to divide the Carolingian Church from its Spanish coreligionists.[21]

By 796 the Carolingians again had taken the offensive, and a raiding expedition was sent across the Pyrenees.[22] Two years later Louis the Pious, now of age and, as king of Aquitaine, in official charge of the Spanish-Gascon border, ordered Count Borell of Urgell-Cerdanya to move south into Ausona and Berga and to repair the deserted castles of Ausona, Cardona, and Casserès.[23] In 799 Navarre seems to have accepted Carolingian overlordship under a certain Count Velasco.[24]

By 801 these preliminary probings gave way to a major offensive. A large force of Franks, Burgundians, Aquitanians, and Provençals was assembled, supported by important contingents of Gascons under Duke Lupo and of Goths who were commanded by Bera, probably count of Roussillon.[25] Though Louis the Pious officially headed the expedition, actual field command seems to have belonged to Count William of Toulouse. This force crossed the Pyrenees and advanced south to capture the important city of Barcelona and the nearby castle of Tarrassa.[26]

For the next ten years our sources tell us of regular Carolingian advances into Moslem territory. Though none of the major Islamic-held centers in the Ebro Valley like Tortosa, Lérida, Huesca, and Saragossa

[19] Astronomus, *Vita Hludovici*, ch. 8, p. 611.
[20] *Annales Luricanes*, ed. E. Waitz, anno 797, in *Mon. Ger. Hist. Scriptores*, I, 184; *Annales remanies*, ed. G. Pertz, anno 798, in *Mon. Ger. Hist. Scriptores*, I, 185; Einhard, *Vie de Charlemagne*, ch. 16, p. 451. On these embassies see also M. Défourneaux, "Charlemagne et la monarchie Asturienne," in *Mélanges Louis Halphen*, pp. 177–184.
[21] On Charlemagne's reaction to Adoptionism see *Annals of Aniane*, anno 794, col. 10–11; and Abadal, "La batalla del adopcionisme."
[22] The *Chronicle of Moissac* says that this army penetrated *in fines Sarracenorum*" (*Chron. of Moissac*, anno 796, pp. 302–303).
[23] Astronomus, *Vita Hludovici*, ch. 8, p. 611.
[24] J. Pérez de Urbel, "Lo viejo y lo nuevo sobre el origin del Reino de Pamplona," in *Al-Andalus*, XIX (1954), 1–30.
[25] See note 9 on sources mentioning this expedition. See also R. de Abadal i de Vinyals, *Els Primers Comtes Catalans*, pp. 219–221.
[26] *Ibid*. For the best assessment of the role of Duke William of Toulouse in this campaign see P. Tisset, *L'abbaye de Gellone au diocèse de Lodève*, pp. 31 ff.

were captured, the frontier seems to have been moved south beyond the Llobregat River line in Catalonia and in Urgell as well.[27] In the same period between 809 and 812 Aragón came under the control of a Frankish count called Aureolus,[28] while Navarre under Count Velasco held to its Carolingian allegiance.[29] Carolingian hegemony over a strip of territory stretching from Pampeluna to the Mediterranean became a reality. Nor was activity confined to land frontiers. On the sea a newly built Carolingian navy began activities, and in 813 we hear of a victory won over a Moslem Spanish flotilla by Count Ermengaud of Ampurias—a victory which was followed by Carolingian hegemony being extended to the Balearics.[30] In 812[31] and again in 815[32] Cordova was forced to seek peace from the war which her Frankish adversaries were waging against her with increasing success.

Such Carolingian advances south, however, were not destined to continue. By 812 Duke William of Toulouse had retired to the shelter of the abbey of Gellone to end his days as a monk, and his statesmanship and military ability were lost to the Midi.[33] His successor at Toulouse, Count Begon, does not appear to have had his ability. Charlemagne was nearing the end of his days, and his son and successor Louis the Pious had his eyes fixed on the succession and the imperial problems he would be called upon to handle. So it was that when a certain Enneco, allied to the Moslem border lords of Tudela, the Banu Kasi, succeeded Count Velasco in Pampeluna no really effective counterstroke to this anti-Carolingian action took place.[34] An army was sent out which advanced on Pampeluna, but it appears to have met with little success and barely es-

---

[27] Astronomus, *Vita Hludovici*, ch. 14–17, pp. 613–617.
[28] J. Lacarra, *Orígines del condado de Aragón*, pp. 1–13.
[29] Pérez de Urbel, "Lo viejo y lo nuevo"; and R. de Abadal i de Vinyals, "La Catalogne sous l'empire de Louis le Pieux," in *Études Rousillonnaises*, V (1956), 148–152.
[30] *Annales Regni Francorum*, anno 813, p. 140. On Carolingian naval power in this region see A. Lewis, *Naval Power and Trade in the Mediterranean A.D. 500–1100*, pp. 176–178. Since Louis the Pious' jurisdiction did not extend over this region in 813, these expeditions are not mentioned by his biographer. He mentions only ships constructed along the Atlantic shores of Aquitaine (Astronomus, *Vita Hludovici*, ch. 15, p. 615).
[31] *Chron. of Moissac*, anno 812, pp. 309–310.
[32] Astronomus, *Vita Hludovici*, ch. 25, p. 620.
[33] On Duke William's connection with Abbey of Gellone see Tisset, *L'abbaye de Gellone*, pp. 38–72.
[34] Pérez de Urbel, "Lo viejo y lo nuevo."

Expansion into Gascony and Catalonia   43

caped ambush at the hands of hostile Gascons in the passes of the Pyrenees. Enneco remained ruler of Navarre.[35]

After 814 the situation took a further turn for the worse. The death of Charlemagne brought Louis the Pious to Aix-la-Chapelle, too far away from Gascony to direct things there. His son Pepin, who succeeded him as king of Aquitaine, was too young to rule effectively and lacked experience. So, when the revolt in Navarre spread across the mountains into Gascony in 816, all that seems to have been done was to deprive Count Séguin of Bordeaux, whom the Carolingian chroniclers refer to as *"dux Gasconorum,"* of his county—either because he had collaborated with these rebels or because he had failed to suppress the revolt.[36]

This action of Louis the Pious seems to have had little effect on the situation for we learn that in 817 the revolt had spread to Aragón, where Count Asnar Galindo, successor to Count Aureolus and loyal to the Carolingians, was driven from power by his cousin Count García Malo who had allied himself to Enneco of Navarre.[37] Asnar Galindo fled east to seek refuge in Frankish controlled territory. From Aragón the revolt spread still further north into central and eastern Gascony. Our chroniclers are in disagreement as to the leader of this rising. Most speak of a certain Lupo Centulle, who was probably a member of the old Gascon ducal family.[38] One calls the leader of the rebellious Gascons, García Mucí, who it is said was elected prince in 818.[39] Probably the latter account refers to events in Aragón, the former to a local leader in Gascony. What does seem apparent is that by 818 Navarre, Aragón, and all Gascony had been lost to the Carolingians.

It was the crisis caused by these successful revolts which was probably in part responsible for the Carolingian reorganization of Aquitaine, Septimania, and the Spanish March in 817. By this time the incompetent Begon had been succeeded by the abler Count Berengar at Toulouse, who, as viceroy for the young king Pepin of Aquitaine, had the immediate

[35] Astronomus, *Vita Hludovici,* ch. 18, pp. 615–616; Auzias, *L'Aquitaine Carolingienne,* pp. 66–67.

[36] Astronomus, *Vita Hludovici,* ch. 26, p. 620; *Chron. of Moissac,* anno 816, p. 312; *Annals of Aniane,* anno 816, col. 11–12; and *Annales Regni Francorum,* anno 816, p. 142.

[37] Lacarra, *Orígines del condado de Aragón,* pp. 13–14; and C. Higounet, "Les Aznars, un tentatif de groupement des comtés gascons et pyrénéens au IXe siècle," in *Annales du Midi,* LXI (1949), 5–10.

[38] Astronomus, *Vita Hludovici,* ch. 32, p. 624, mentions that this Gascon leader rebelled in 819. So too does *Annales Regni Francorum,* anno 819, p. 145.

[39] *Annals of Aniane,* anno 818, col. 12.

responsibility of keeping order in Gascony. To fit his command new boundaries were drawn for Aquitaine so that they included the entire Gascon border to the west, Pallars-Ribagorça and the Urgell-Cerdanya-Besalu complex to the south and Carcassonne-Razès to the east. The rest of Septimania and the maritime counties of Roussillon, Ampurias, and Gerona-Besalu-Barcelona were placed under the direct control of Louis the Pious himself. This in effect gave control over these maritime regions to three counts. Count Bera controlled the counties of Barcelona-Besalu-Gerona. Count Gaucelm, son of Duke William of Toulouse, was in charge of Ampurias-Roussillon. And Count Leibulf of Provence ruled Provence and Septimania.[40]

Once this reorganization of comital charges had been completed Count Berengar of Toulouse proceeded to act. He and Count Warin of Auvergne, we are told, led an army into Gascony, overthrew the rebel Lupo Centulle and by 820 had restored Carolingian authority over most of Gascony.[41] Lupo Centulle's successor seems to have been a certain Count Aznar who appears to have been more loyal to the Carolingian house. It is possible, however, that this victory only restored the situation in part, since neither Aragón nor Navarre was recovered, and it is probable that the rebellion in Western Gascony also was not suppressed.

Then in 820 it was Catalonia's turn. In this year Count Bera of Barcelona-Gerona was accused of disloyalty by a certain Goth, Sanila, challenged to a judicial duel as a traitor and, when he lost, deprived of his counties.[42] These counties were then bestowed on a Frank, Count Rampon. At about the same time Count Asnar Galindo, the exiled ruler of Aragón, was given Count Borell's old counties of Urgell-Cerdanya.[43] Most historians have seen in the removal of Count Bera proof of the existence of a ninth-century sense of Catalan nationalism in this part of the empire—a basic hostility to the Franks lying at the bottom of this

---

[40] Boretius, *Capitularia*, I, 227. On the over-all significance of this reorganization see F. Ganshof, "Observations sur l'Ordinatio Imperii de 817," in *Festschrift Guido Kisch*. On its significance for Catalonia and neighboring regions see R. de Abadal i de Vinyals, "La catalogne sous l'empire de Louis le Pieux," pp. 352–354, and *Catalunya Carolingia* III. *Els Comtats de Pallars i Ribagorça*, pp. 95–97 (hereafter cited as Abadal, *Els Comtats de Pallars i Ribagorça*).

[41] *Annales Regni Francorum*, anno 819, p. 150; Astronomus, *Vita Hludovici*, ch. 32, p. 625; and *Chron. of Moissac*, anno 818, p. 314.

[42] *Annales Regni Francorum*, anno 820, p. 152; Ermold Niger, *Carmina in honorem Hludovici*, I, vers. 1794–1873; and Astronomus, *Vita Hludovici*, ch. 33, p. 625.

[43] Abadal, *Els Primers Comtes Catalans*, p. 222.

Expansion into Gascony and Catalonia 45

incident. More plausible, however, seems to be the view of Catalonia's distinguished historian of the Carolingian period, Abadal i de Vinyals. For him this removal of Count Bera was the work of Count Gaucelm of Roussillon, son of Duke William and brother of the ambitious Count Bernard of Septimania. It was not a nascent Catalan nationalism, then, but a family rivalry between the sons of Duke William and the family of Count Bellon of Carcassonne and his relatives which explains this incident—a rivalry incidentally which was to last for many years. And, as he points out, in this rivalry it was the Gothic counts of the region who uniformly were to remain loyal to the Carolingian house, the Frankish ones, disloyal.[44]

Whatever lay behind Count Bera's removal, and we can never be exactly sure, one thing seems clear. It was followed by a more aggressive policy along the Moslem frontier of Catalonia, for we learn of an invasion of Moslem territory in 822, probably led by Rampon, the new count of Gerona-Barcelona, and Asnar Galindo, newly installed as count of Cerdanya-Urgell.[45] We know nothing of the results which were achieved by this campaign, but we are told that two years later an ambitious attempt to regain Navarre led by Count Asnar of Gascony and Count Ebles, controlling one of the regions bordering on Gascony, ended in complete disaster. Both counts were captured by their enemies. Count Ebles was sent as a prisoner to the emir of Cordova. Count Aznar was released, which suggests that his interest in this expedition was at best lukewarm.[46] Navarre was not regained and Carolingian control over Gascony was weakened still further.[47]

It seems probable that the failure of this expedition caused Louis the Pious serious concern. At any rate, in 826 he called to Aix-la-Chapelle his son Pepin, king of Aquitaine, and the counts who controlled the

[44] J. Calmette stresses a Catalan nationalism in "Rampon, Comte de Gerona et Marquis de Gothie," in *Le Moyen Age,* V (1901), and "Le sentiment national dans la Marche de'Espagne au IXe siècle," in *Mélanges Ferdinand Lot.* See the more plausible arguments against this point of view in Abadal, "La Catalogne sous l'empire de Louis le Pieux," pp. 147–152, and *Els Primers Comtes Catalans,* pp. 222–230.

[45] *Annales Regni Francorum,* anno 822, p. 151; and Astronomus, *Vita Hludovici,* ch. 35, p. 626.

[46] *Annales Regni Francorum,* anno 824, p. 154; and Astronomus, *Vita Hludovici,* ch. 37, p. 628. See also F. Codera y Zaidin, "Expedicion a Pamplona de los condes francos Elbo y Aznar," in *Colección de estudios Árabes,* VII, 185–198.

[47] In 828 a further Gascon revolt took place (Astronomus, *Vita Hludovici,* ch. 42, p. 632).

Spanish border—"*custodes limitibus Hispaniae,*" in the words of our source.[48] We do not know what transpired at this conference but soon afterwards we learn that Bernard of Septimania was given both Rampon's counties of Barcelona and Gerona and the Septimanian counties which had been the *honores* of Count Leibulf. Since his brother Gaucelm was already count of Ampurias-Roussillon, these two sons of Duke William of Toulouse were now in charge of the entire coastal region of the Midi from the Llobregat to the Rhone. Well does Count Bernard merit the title of *dux Septimaniae* given him by Nithard.[49] The Carolingian frontier in the Midi was now in the hands of two viceroys, Bernard of Septimania and his rival to the west, Count Berengar of Toulouse.

A large faction in Catalonia, however, opposed Bernard's assumption of power as count of Barcelona. As a result a serious revolt broke out led by a certain Aizo and other relatives and friends of the late Count Bera. This revolt, which appears to have been given help from Cordova, did not succeed in capturing the city of Barcelona which Count Bernard defended successfully. But it did have serious results for Catalonia. Due to it much territory which had been gained from the Moslems between 802 and 815 was lost. This included Ausona with its plain of Vich, which suffered devastation, and other border land in Berga, Urgell, and to the south of Barcelona itself.[50] Many decades were to pass before they were to be regained.

Worse still an attempt to send a relief expedition to Catalonia in 828 ended in failure. Armed forces were gathered together and entrusted to Pepin, king of Aquitaine and his brother Lothaire. But they never reached the Pyrenees. Two counts who were held responsible for this fiasco were degraded by the angry emperor, but the damage had been done. In Catalonia, as in Navarre, Aragón, and Gascony, the Carolingians had been forced to pull back without any effective assistance having been sent to their officials who controlled their southern marches.[51] The peace

[48] *Annales Regni Francorum,* anno 826, pp. 154–155; Astronomus, *Vita Hludovici,* ch. 40, p. 630.

[49] Nithard, *Histoire des fils de Louis le Pieux,* ed. P. Lauer, p. 10 (hereafter cited as Nithard, *Histoire*). Abadal, "La Catalogne sous l'empire de Louis le Pieux," pp. 170–177, and *El Primers Comtes Catalans,* p. 222.

[50] *Annales Laurissenses,* anno 827–829, pp. 216–218. Astronomus, *Vita Hludovici,* ch. 40–41, pp. 630–631. See also Abadal, "La Catalogne sous l'empire de Louis le Pieux," pp. 174–176. On the results of Aizo's revolt see R. de Abadal i de Vinyals, *La Plana de Vich,* pp. 11–21.

[51] Astronomus, *Vita Hludovici,* ch. 41, p. 631; *Annales Regni Francorum,* anno 828, p. 156.

Expansion into Gascony and Catalonia 47

made with Cordova merely ratified this *fait accompli*—a shrunken Carolingian prestige and authority on the borders of the Midi.[52]

There is one other aspect of Carolingian expansion into the Spanish March during these years, however, that needs to be emphasized, for in many ways it was as important as the establishment of secular non-Moslem government and authority. I refer to the reorganization and expansion of the Church in Catalonia and Pallars and Ribagorça, and particularly its monastic establishments. As in Gascony this church was strongly backed by the Carolingian monarchs who saw it as a bulwark and basis of their authority in this part of Spain.

It should be emphasized, however, that the problem of the Church in this region was quite different from that in Gascony. In Gascony the Church was weak because of the paganism of a large number of the Basques, who had never been converted to Christianity and because the simple tribal organization which seems to have prevailed there made any kind of Church organization difficult to establish.[53] The task in Gascony, like that in Saxony, was to create a Church organization almost from scratch.

In the Spanish March, one finds quite a different situation. Here the inhabitants of the land were practicing Christians with a long tradition of church, parish, and monastic organizational experience behind them. On the other hand the years of Moslem occupation had borne heavily on this Church. Of the former Visigothic dioceses of the region only four, Barcelona, Gerona, Urgell, and Elne seem to have survived Moslem rule, though one might add Rhoda in Ribagorça also. And we can only be sure of two abbeys, both in Urgell, which continued their life without interruption during this same period, though a third, San-Cugat, near Barcelona, might well be added to these two.[54]

---

[52] It is worth noting that the year 829 saw the beginning of a crisis in the Carolingian Empire when Louis the Pious attempted to set up a kingdom for his fourth son Charles from territory already allotted other sons (Theganus, *Vita Hludovici imperatoris*, ed. G. Pertz, ch. 35, in *Mon. Ger. Hist. Scriptores*, II, 597; Nithard, *Histoire*, p. 8; *Annales Xantenenses* and *Annales Vedastini*, ed. B. de Simson, anno 829, p. 7). This made any further action along the frontiers impossible except defensive ones.

[53] The episcopal and monastic organization which the Carolingians set up in Gascony did not survive. Those monastic establishments mentioned at the Council of Aix-la-Chapelle in 817 are not found in the tenth century when monasteries revive in Gascony.

[54] Abadal, "La Catalogne sous l'empire de Louis le Pieux," pp. 32–33, and *Els Primers Comtes Catalans*, pp. 115–116.

Liberation by the Carolingians was followed almost immediately by a revival of such churches and abbeys and a re-establishment of religious life on the parish level also. Carolingian rulers assisted this movement almost at once by granting special privileges to cathedral churches. Before 828 the bishopric of Gerona received important immunities by imperial grant[55] and those of Urgell and Elne are mentioned in royal charters dating from 823[56] and 825[57] respectively. Barcelona's privileges were given later.[58]

More important, however, is evidence of encouragement and support given to the monastic movement, particularly during the reign of Louis the Pious. This took the form of the encouraging of the foundation of new abbeys and the granting of special privileges and lands to such establishments, as well as the revival and strengthening of older ones. Two rather distinct areas seem to have been the regions in which initially this monastic movement was most active. One was in the general region Vallespir-Besalu-Roussillon. The second further to the west consisted of Urgell, Pallars, and Ribagorça.

In the former region we find that the oldest abbey established in this period was Sainte-Maria of Arles, which seems to have been founded by Abbot Castellanus, a Spanish refugee, about 779–781.[59] In 820 Louis the Pious gave Arles special privileges and placed it under royal protection.[60] In nearby Roussillon two other new foundations, Saint-Genesius des Fonts and Saint-André de Sureda received similar privileges from the emperor in 819[61] and 823[62] respectively. So did Saint-Stephen of Banyols in Besalu in 822[63] and the nearby abbeys of Albaniya and Les Escoules which seem to date from about the same period.[64] In the more westerly region in Urgell the abbeys of Saint-André de Tresponts and Saint-Sernin de Tabernoles, which appear to have been Visigothic foundations, show new life and vigor in this period.[65] And to them in Charlemagne's last years were added two new establishments, Aláo in Ribagorça

---

[55] *Hist. Gén. de Lang.*, II, no. 46.
[56] *Catalunya Carolingia*, II, 260–262.
[57] *Hist. Gén. de Lang.*, II, no. 189.
[58] *Catalunya Carolingia*, II, 66.
[59] Ponsch, "Les origines de l'abbaye d'Arles," pp. 69–99.
[60] *Catalunya Carolingia*, II, 20–26.
[61] *Ibid.*, pp. 206–207.
[62] *Ibid.*, pp. 268–269.
[63] *Ibid.*, pp. 45–47.
[64] *Ibid.*, pp. 205, 226.
[65] Abadal, *El Comtats de Pallars i Ribagorca*, pp. 20–35.

Expansion into Gascony and Catalonia

and Gerrí in Pallars, while in 823 Senterada in Pallars was founded on land given by the emperor Louis the Pious himself.[66] Often, however, it is clear that local counts furnished the driving force which led to the foundation of such monasteries, as the examples of Count Matfred of Urgell,[67] Count Gaucelm of Roussillon[68] and Count Rampon of Barcelona-Gerona,[69] all of whom helped found abbeys, clearly show. All of these, incidentally, were of Frankish origin. Already then as part of the Carolingian expansion into the Spanish March, we see evidence of a spread of monasticism and a more vigorous and growing Church.

Such then is the story of the Carolingian expansion into Gascony and the Spanish March during the years between 778 and 828. It is a story of a slow but steady advance under Charlemagne down to 812 or 813, and then during the time of Louis the Pious of a steady contraction of the areas under Carolingian control. This contraction began in Navarre, then affected Aragón, then Gascony, and finally Catalonia, until by 828 much of what had been gained earlier had been lost. But not all of it, particularly in Catalonia, Pallars, and Ribagorça where newly founded abbeys and re-established bishoprics gave a promise of continued life, future vigor, and expansion. But when Louis the Pious and his heirs began to quarrel over their inheritance, even such authority as still belonged to these rulers in the Midi and Catalonia began to crumble, leaving the nobility, the bishops, and the abbots of these regions the *de facto* heirs of the Carolingian monarchy.

[66] *Catalunya Carolingia*, II, 260–262.
[67] *Ibid.*
[68] *Ibid.*, pp. 268–269.
[69] *Ibid.*

CHAPTER IV

The Carolingian System

WHEN CHARLEMAGNE became undisputed ruler of the Frankish realm soon after his father Pepin's death, the Carolingians already had forced the greater part of Southern France to accept their rule. Between 778 and 812, as has been noted, Charlemagne expanded his authority still further and added to the empire Gascony and a strip of Spanish territory stretching from Navarre to Barcelona. Though part of these gains was lost between 812 and 828, much remained. What was the method used during this period to control this region which consisted of the Midi and the Spanish March? How did Charlemagne and Louis the Pious govern this vast expanse of territory down to 828, and what changes did they make in the system of government which they found already present in these regions or which they had inherited from their predecessors? In short, what was the nature of the Carolingian governing system here?

We might begin by emphasizing that at the summit of the Carolingian governmental system was the head of the Carolingian family, who bore the title of king up to 800, of emperor afterwards. Backed by the power of the Church, this Carolingian monarch was ruler by the grace of God, and rebellion against him was, in theory at least, disobedience to the Almighty. As ruler of the Franks, Lombards, and the other peoples who made up this vast empire, he was supreme judge and lawgiver, general, and administrator. In practice he was head of the Church. He was not a despot, however, and his authority was absolute rather than arbitrary, since he was limited by both law and custom. He did not have the right, for instance, of taxing his subjects directly, nor could he arbitrarily interfere with their property or rights, except in war, without following the cumbersome legal procedures of the time.

The chief limitation upon the power of the Carolingian monarch, how-

The Carolingian System   51

ever, does not appear to have been the result of the restraining influence of law, custom, and other precedents. It lay in the paucity of his financial resources. He did not have adequate money to pay for a self-perpetuating bureaucracy of officials who could govern in his name, or resources which enabled him to hire soldiers to fight for him. In this respect his government was inferior to that of his Moslem and Byzantine neighbors. In addition the extent of the Carolingian empire made it impossible for a monarch to supervise personally remote regions, as might have been possible had the empire been smaller. Though efforts were made, as we will note, to get around such limitations, no real solution of a governmental sort was ever devised in the Carolingian period.[1]

To deal with such a vast empire with the inadequate governmental machinery at his disposal, Charlemagne adopted some interesting expedients. One of them was to set up his heirs as sub-kings over portions of his domains. Thus in 781 he organized a kingdom of Aquitaine with his eldest son Louis as king. This kingdom of Aquitaine seems to have consisted of all of Southern France south of the Loire and west of the Rhone along with its Gascon and Spanish borderlands.[2] A little later he gave a second sub-kingdom of Italy to his other son Pepin.[3] Most historians have seen this kingdom of Aquitaine as an example of Charlemagne's realistic recognition of proud Aquitanian particularism. No doubt this is so in part. But it might also be wise to note that it was useful to him in other ways. It gave his heir governmental experience, and it also provided a valuable and even necessary intermediate government between Aix-la-Chapelle and local regions in Southern France and Catalonia.[4]

Louis the Pious continued his father's policy after he became emperor himself in 814 and appointed one of his sons, Pepin, king of Aquitaine,[5]

[1] On the structure of the Carolingian empire see A. Kleinclausz, *L'Empire Carolingien*; L. Halphen, *Charlemagne et l'empire Carolingien*; and H. Fichtenau, *Der karolingische Imperium*.

[2] Astronomus, *Vita Hludovici*, ch. 4, p. 609; and *Chron. of Moissac*, anno 781, p. 297.

[3] See the formal division of the empire between Louis the Pious and his brother Pepin which Charlemagne prepared in 806 in anticipation of his death in "Divisio Imperii," in Boretius, *Capitularia*, I, no. 45.

[4] It is worth noting that Charlemagne included in his son Louis' kingdom of Aquitaine areas like Gascony, Septimania, and the Spanish March which had never been included in the earlier independent duchy of Aquitaine of Eudes, Hunald, and Waiffre. Auzias' contention, then, that the setting up of this kingdom was a sop to Aquitaine's particularism seems somewhat exaggerated. See L. Auzias, *L'Aquitaine Carolingienne (778–987)*, pp. 1–63.

[5] Astronomus, *Vita Hludovici*, ch. 24, p. 619. See the arguments against the

though three years later he altered its boundaries by taking away from it the coastal counties of Septimania and Catalonia.[6] But he soon went much further and extended the practice of setting up sub-kingdoms in the empire to the point of dividing all of it among his three sons, Lothaire, Louis, and Pepin.[7] Charlemagne had never done this, but had kept direct authority over most of the empire.[8] Louis' action had evil results for the empire, not only in provoking his nephew Bernard in Italy to revolt,[9] but even more so when Judith, his new queen, presented him with a fourth son Charles, whose inheritance had to be carved out of lands already allotted to his older brothers. This, of course, led directly to the civil wars in Louis' last years and afterwards, which did so much to weaken and destroy the Carolingian empire.

Down to 828, however, what authority was vested in the sub-king of Aquitaine? If one follows the Astronomus or Ermold the Black, one would believe that it was considerable. Other information, however, con-

young Pepin's bearing the royal title this early in L. Levillain, *Recueil des actes de Pépin I et Pépin II, rois d'Aquitaine*, p. cliv. At any rate at this early date Pepin was too young to exercise any effective royal authority.

[6] Boretius, *Capitularia*, I, 227. See the comments of R. de Abadal i de Vinyals on these changes in "La Catalogne sous l'empire de Louis le Pieux" in *Études Roussillonnaises*, V (1956), pp. 351–354.

[7] On Louis the Pious' determination to set up an indivisible empire in 817, in contrast to the divided empire which Charlemagne planned in 806 see F. Ganshof, "Observations sur l'Ordinatio Imperii de 817," in *Festschrift Guido Kisch*, pp. 16–28. Perhaps a more logical comparison, however, would be between the "Ordinatio of 817" and Charlemagne's early investiture of Louis as king of Aquitaine in 781 and Pepin as king of Italy a little later. The "Divisio of 806" was a will which was only effective *for the future*. Louis' division of 817, if it is regarded as a will, was certainly written too early. If it was a system of setting up his sons and nephews as viceroys, it was so all-inclusive that it compromised Louis' own power as emperor. Despite Ganshof's contentions, then, it seems to have been a major blunder, from which much evil arose. Not the least of these evils was the revolt in Italy of Bernard, Louis' nephew, who as viceroy felt slighted by the "Ordinatio of 817."

[8] See note above on the basic differences between the way in which Charlemagne and Louis planned the division of the empire, and Charlemagne's greater wisdom. To mark out the *entire* empire for such a division seems folly so early in his reign despite the obvious safeguards to imperial unity which the "*Ordinatio* of 817" contained.

[9] The *Ordinatio* left Italy as a kingdom in the hands of Bernard ("Ordinatio Imperii," ch. 17, in Boretius, *Capitularia*, I, no. 136, p. 273). This did not satisfy Bernard, however, who revolted almost at once. The revolt was put down and the kingdom of Italy was extinguished. Halphen, *Charlemagne et l'empire*, pp. 242–245.

tradicts them. Down to Charlemagne's last year it seems clear that Louis' role in his kingdom was unimportant, and that he was closely supervised from Aix-la-Chapelle.[10] Only when Count William of Toulouse had retired to his monastery do we find Louis having any real scope or initiative in policy matters. Similarly Pepin, his son, seems to have been given little room for maneuver as king of Aquitaine during his early years. This was to come later.[11] The use of sub-kingdoms which, as applied to our area, refers to the kingdom of Aquitaine, did not, then, down to 828, mean a really separate governmental system. Rather it meant a training ground for heirs and a useful regional adjunct to power exercised by Carolingian monarchs from their capital in the north.

If power was not really exercised in the Midi and the Spanish March down to 828 by the kings of Aquitaine, where does one find it? One finds it in the counts who were appointed by Carolingian rulers to govern various parts of Southern France and Catalonia. As had been true in the pre-Carolingian era, the count was the basic official of the Carolingian

[10] All evidence seems to show that Charlemagne handled foreign affairs which affected the borders of the kingdom of Aquitaine, though Louis was its king after 781. See his removal of Duke Chorson in 789 for making an unsatisfactory agreement with the Gascons (Astronomus, *Vita Hludovici*, ch. 5, p. 609). This incidentally also shows him disposing of *honores* in this subkingdom. Note also that after a preliminary visit of an Asturian embassy to Louis' court at Toulouse in 794 (*ibid.*, ch. 8, p. 611) serious negotiations between the empire and the Spanish kings in 797 and 798 were transferred to Aix-la-Chapelle. See M. Défourneaux, "Charlemagne et la monarchie Asturienne" in *Mélanges Louis Halphen*, pp. 179–184. Most important we have no evidence that Louis, as king of Aquitaine, ever disposed of any *honores* or any of the royal *fisc*. All charters we possess from this period bear the name of Charlemagne *not* Louis.

[11] For limitations on Pepin's power as king of Aquitaine see the "Ordinatio Imperii," ch. 4–5, 708, 10, 12–16, 18, in Boretius, *Capitularia*, I, 270–274; and Ganshof, "Observations sur l'Ordinatio Imperii de 817," p. 24. On the other hand he was also given, in theory, a right to exercise certain powers in disposing of the crown's revenues in his domains (the *fisc*), in allotting *honores*, and in fighting defensive wars, which Louis himself never seems to have had as king ("Ordinatio Imperii," ch. 3, 7, 12, in Boretius, *Capitularia*). Until 827, however, he does not appear to have exercised such authority, for as late as 826 it was Louis who called to Aix-la-Chapelle the *"custodios limitibus Hispaniae"* according to *Annales Regni Francorum*, ed. G. Kurze, anno 826; and Astronomus, *Vita Hludovici*, ch. 40, p. 630. Then in 827 Pepin began to issue royal charters in his own name, which marks the beginning of later troubles. See the grant of Pepin to the abbey of Lagrasse in 827 in Levillain, *Recueil des actes de Pépin I et II*, no. 23, and in 828 a grant to the abbey of Montolieu in *Cartulaire et archives des communes de l'ancien diocese et de l'arrondissement de Carcassonne*, ed. M. Mahul, I, 70.

governmental system. He was a man of proven ability, often related to the royal house, who was given a charge or *honorem* as it was called, as ruler of a district, which he exercised in the name of the monarch. He was a kind of sub-king in this district, exercising all the functions of government. He led into battle the army of his county, consisting of the *ban,* or levy of free-born men, and was responsible for the county's defense and its fortifications. He managed the *fiscus* of the crown, that is to say, the royal estates of his county and such dues and levies as the king had a right to exact. He was responsible for law and order and presided over the royal courts in cases brought before them. He was in charge of the mint, which he operated in the name of the monarch. Except where royal immunities or private seigneurial jurisdiction intervened, he was supreme in his county. A count did not receive a salary for his services, but was rewarded by a share in the fines of the county courts and other revenues which were the perquisite of his office. Often too he was given land owned by the monarch as his own. The eagerness with which men sought the dignity of count seems to show that the office carried with it ample rewards.

At the time of Charlemagne, the general rule seems to have been that a count controlled only a single county in the Midi, with the exception of the count of Toulouse, often called a *dux* or duke in our sources, who always seems to have had a wider field of action, serving as a kind of viceroy in charge in the Southern French frontier.[12] Toward the end of Charlemagne's reign, however, one other extraordinary command may have been created for Count Leibulf of Provence who seems to have controlled a number of counties in Septimania.[13]

Under Louis the Pious this seems to have changed, and we get increasing evidence of several counties being entrusted to one man like Count Gaucelm of Ampurias-Roussillon, Count Bernard of Septimania, or Count Berengar of Toulouse.[14] If a count controlled a border county facing the enemy, he seems to have borne the title of *marchio* as well as

---

[12] "Chorso, *dux Tholosanus"* is the title given this official in 789 in Astronomus, *Vita Hludovici,* ch. 5, p. 609. The same title is given his successor Duke William of Toulouse a little later.

[13] On Count Leibulf's large number of *honores* see Abadal, "La Catalogne sous l'empire de Louis le Pieux," p. 353 and P. Février, "La donation faite à Lérins par le comte Leibulfe," in *Provence Historique,* VI (1956).

[14] Nithard calls Bernard *dux* of Septimania (Nithard, *Histoire,* p. 10). On his other multiple *honores* in the Midi in 829, if not earlier, see Abadal, "La Catalogne sous l'empire de Louis le Pieux," pp. 67–73.

The Carolingian System

count. In one case, Gascony, where hereditary non-Carolingian rulers continued to exist, we find the title of *dux* used—the equivalent of the pre-Carolingian title *princeps*, though even here there was, no doubt, an attempt made to force the Gascons to conform to Carolingian practices in use elsewhere.[15]

Carolingian counts in the Midi made use of officials of their own in this period. They often had a deputy or viscount who assisted them in their court or presided over it in their absence[16] and vicars, who were subordinate officials presiding over districts of their counties known as *vicaria* and who seem to have had a competence to judge cases of minor importance.[17] In areas of the Midi where Roman and Visigothic law was in use, when the counts or their viscounts held court, they were assisted by legal officials known as *judices* or *saiones*, men skilled and versed in the interpretation of the law.[18] Whether Roman, Frankish, or Visigothic law was used, however, and whether count, viscount, or vicar presided over a tribunal, one essential ingredient which made such a court legal was the presence of a group of leading landowners or magnates of the district. These magnates or landowners are called *scabini* or *boni homines* in our documents, but they sometimes seem to have included some given the title of *vassi dominici*.[19] It was their presence which seems to have made public action taken by such courts legal and official.

While the count was the leading official of his county, there were others who, in a sense, shared his authority. These were the archbishops,

[15] Seguin is called *dux Vasconorum* in 816 (*Annales Regni Francorum*, anno 816, p. 14). Earlier in 789 Lupo is called *dux* of the Gascons (Astronomus, *Vita Hludovici*, ch. 5, pp. 609).

[16] Actual reference in local charters to viscounts are rare indeed for this period, though we know the Carolingians had a place for them in their governing system. One is found at Narbonne, however. His court is mentioned in a charter of 791 (*Hist. Gén. de Lang.*, II, no. 10). And a certain Viscount Stephen is mentioned in a charter dealing with a court held there in 834 (*Catalunya Carolingia*, II, 442–444).

[17] Our documents give us no references to vicars in the Midi during this period. The first reference is in a document of 845 from Marseille which mentions Rotbert, vicar of Count Adelbert as presiding over a court (*Cart. de Saint-Victor*, no. 26).

[18] These are mentioned in documents dating from 780 and 845 from Marseille (*Cart. de Saint-Victor*, nos. 26, 31), and at Narbonne in 782 and 791 (*Hist. Gén. de Lang.*, II, nos. 6, 10).

[19] Two *vassi dominici* are reported present at a court in Narbonne in 782 (*Hist. Gén. de Lang.*, II, no. 6). There is also a mention of a certain Bertrand, *vassus dominicus*, in a document from Auvergne dating from 823 (*Cartulaire de l'abbaye de Conques en Rouergue*, ed. A. Desjardins, no. 460).

bishops, and abbots of important monasteries. More often than not appointed by the Carolingian monarchs, possessing important lands in local areas of the Midi, such churchmen eagerly sought and generally received special privileges from the crown. The most important were the royal immunities which placed their churches or abbeys under royal protection and which gave them a right to hold their own courts and manage their properties free of fiscal interference by the counts.[20] Often, as happened in the case of the archbishop of Narbonne[21] and a number of abbeys,[22] such rights led to disputes with counts of the region which could only be settled by court action. Equally frequent, however, is evidence of close co-operation between count and viscount on the one hand and bishop and abbot on the other.[23]

To control their counts the leading weapon available to the Carolingians, besides support for their potential rivals, the abbots and bishops of the local region, was removal from office. Down to 828 such action was not uncommon. More common, however, seems to have been the practice of making certain that sons did not succeed to their father's *honores* so that no family could make itself supreme in a particular region.[24] Still another was the use of *missi* sent out by the central govern-

[20] All important abbeys in the Midi and Catalonia possessed such immunities from the time of Louis the Pious. So did almost all bishoprics and archbishoprics. On the Midi see E. Lesne, *Histoire de la propriété ecclésiastique en France*, I–II. For Catalonia see Abadal, "La Catalogne sous l'empire de Louis le Pieux," pp. 32–53, and *Els Primers Comtes Catalans*, pp. 115–147.

[21] *Hist. Gén. de Lang.*, II, nos. 6, 10.

[22] See, for instance, an argument in 832 over a *cella* belonging to the abbey of Arles (*Hist. Gén. de Lang.*, II, no. 80). Or in 835 similar troubles over the usurpation of land belonging to the church of Urgell (*Catalunya Carolingia*, II, 284–285). For land belonging to the church of Maguelonne during this period see *Cartulaire de Maguelonne*, ed. J. Rouquette and A. Villamagne, I, no. 1. On land of Saint-Victor's near Marseille lost to a count see *Cart. de Saint-Victor*, no. 31, and on other interference with the rights of the bishop of Marseille by comital agents in 845 see *ibid.*, no. 26.

[23] For examples of close cooperation between the Church and the counts of Carcassonne and other regions of the Midi in 793 see J. Cros-Meyrévielle, *Histoire du comté et de la vicomté de Carcassonne*, Document no. 4 (hereafter cited as Cros-Meyrévielle, *Documents*); in 813 see *Hist. Gén. de Lang.*, II, no. 23; in 820 *ibid.*, no. 50; in 821 Cros-Meyrévielle, *Documents*, no. 11; in 822 *Catalunya Carolingia*, II, 45–47; in 823 *ibid.*, pp. 260–262 and *Cartulaire de l'abbaye de Beaulieu*, ed. M. Deloche, no. 185; in 827 *Cart. de Carcassonne*, II, 212.

[24] For an exception to this rule see the county of Carcassonne where control remained in the hands of the same family throughout this period. R. de Abadal,

ment to investigate complaints and hold courts to correct abuses.[25] None of these methods, however, seems to have been really satisfactory in keeping counts from entrenching their families firmly in particular districts of the Midi or the Spanish March.

This being the case, Charlemagne and Louis the Pious made use of another method which had been begun by their predecessors—vassalage or *fidelitas*. All counts, bishops, and abbots[26] who were given *honores* had to do homage to the monarch for them and in a special ceremony swear an oath of personal allegiance. This solemn oath and ceremony established a special tie between him who swore it and the ruler, a tie which, according to the *Manual of Dhuoda*, could not be broken as long as either was alive.[27] Nor were counts and important churchmen the only ones who were bound to the ruler by such ties. In the Midi, as elsewhere in the empire, are to be found a class of important landowners known as *vassi dominici*, who were given land belonging to the royal *fisc* as life benefices in return for an oath of allegiance or *fidelitas*.[28] These men, often Frankish in origin, and known as *fideles*, seem to have had special military responsibilities, which meant they were to present themselves fully equipped for campaigns upon call of king or count.[29] In Septimania and Catalonia the important *aprisio* holders, who appear to have done homage to Carolingian rulers, were in many ways similar to the *vassi*

"Un diplôme inconnu de Louis le Pieux pour le comte Oliba de Carcassonne," in *Annales du Midi*, LXI (1949), 350–357.

[25] For examples of such *missi* see the record of a court held at Marseille in 780 in *Cart. de Saint-Victor*, no. 31, and in 782 in Narbonne in *Hist. Gén. de Lang.*, II, no. 60.

[26] The first proof of such oaths of *fidelitas* and homage by bishops, abbots, counts, and *vassi dominici*, according to Ganshof, dates from 837 (*Annales Bertiniani*, ed. Waitz, anno 837, p. 15). See also for 838 Astronomus, *Vita Hludovici*, ch. 59, p. 644. On the other hand, as early as 802 a ceremony similar to this swearing of *fidelitas* or homage to the ruler took place when such royal vassals as counts, bishops, and abbots swore to be loyal to Charlemagne in a ceremony presided over by *missi dominici*. See "Capitulare missorum," ch. 2 and 4 in Boretius, *Capitularia*, I, no. 25, pp. 66–67. Again in a charter of 842 Pepin II calls an abbot, Radulf, a *fidelis* of his (*Cart. de Beaulieu*, no. 6).

[27] E. Bondurand, *L'éducation Carolingienne: Le Manuel de Dhuoda*, XV, 89–90.

[28] Such *vassi dominici* are mentioned along with bishops, abbots, and counts as doing homage to Charles the Bald in 837 (*Annales Bertiniani*, anno 837, p. 15).

[29] On the duty of royal vassals to present themselves for campaigns when summoned see F. Ganshof, "L'origine des rapports féodo-vassiliques," in *I problemi della Civiltà Carolingia*, pp. 44–45, 57–59, 64.

dominici.[30] Two ties then bound local leaders of Southern France and Catalonia to the Carolingian monarchs—one the tie of office, lay or ecclesiastic, the other the bonds of vassalage or *fidelitas*. And so important did Carolingian rulers believe such ties of vassalage to be, that they encouraged the counts to bind their followers to them in the same manner.

Such a description of the system used by the Carolingian to govern the Midi, however, leaves out certain things of importance. The first is the matter of the Frankish character of their administration. In an earlier chapter we noted how, as they conquered regions in the Midi, Charles Martel and Pepin made a practice of introducing into such areas their own officials. The *fideles* and *judices* to whom Charles Martel gave the governing power and church offices in Burgundy and the Rhone Valley,[31] the Frankish Count Radulf whom Pepin placed over Uzès and Nîmes,[32] and the garrisons he established in *castella* in Aquitaine[33] are cases in point. According to the Astronomus, Charlemagne followed the same policy in Aquitaine about 778, when he appointed as abbots and counts men of Frankish origin exclusively.[34] The county of Fézensac in Gascony, given to a series of non-Gascons, seems to illustrate a similar policy used in this part of the Midi as well.[35]

In examining men who were appointed as counts later on by Charlemagne and Louis the Pious many historians have been impressed by the number of these officials who were of Frankish origin. Specific families like that of the Nibelungen, of Count William of Toulouse, of Count Frédélon of Toulouse, or Rannoux of Poitiers immediately spring to mind. So does the removal of Count Bera and his replacement after 820 by a series of Frankish counts of Barcelona.[36] So important have these facts seemed to some historians that they have pictured the Carolingians as

---

[30] See the charter in which John of Fontjoncouse is called a *fidelis* in *Catalunya Carolingia*, II, appendix XIII, 443, and the general oath of homage given Louis the Pious in 816 by the large *aprisio* holders (*ibid.*, appendix IV, 420).

[31] *Fredegarii cont.*, ch. 14, 18, pp. 175–177.

[32] *Chron. of Uzès*, anno 754, col. 26–27.

[33] *Fredegarii cont.*, ch. 126, p. 186; *Annales Laurissenses*, in *Mon. Ger. Hist. Scriptores*, I, anno 766, p. 146; and "Capitulare Aquitanicum," anno 768, in Boretius, *Capitularia*, I, no. 18, p. 43.

[34] Astronomus, *Vita Hludovici*, ch. 3, p. 608.

[35] *Ibid.*, ch. 13, p. 612.

[36] See comments on this general policy of colonization in Ganshof, "L'origine des rapports féodo-vassiliques," pp. 58–59. See the objections to such a thesis as it concerns the removal of Count Bera in 820 in Abadal, "La Catalogne sous l'empire de Louis le Pieux," pp. 147–170, and *Els Primers Comtes Catalans*, pp. 222–224.

The Carolingian System

leaders of a group of Austrasian noble families, tied to them by blood and vassalage, through whom they conquered and governed their empire and kept control over the Church. Such a view regards Carolingian government in the Midi as one run by a Frankish minority who used it and the Church to dominate a large and inarticulate Southern French and Catalan majority.

Did the Carolingians go further than this, however, and establish throughout Southern France colonies of Franks as military garrisons to hold down the local population? The Astronomus certainly implies as much when he tells us of Franks, who were called *vassi*, whom Charlemagne established throughout Aquitaine.[37] But what evidence can we find to back up his assertion? Here Septimania seems of particular importance since it had never been Frankish prior to the eighth century and any evidence of Frankish colonies there must date from the Carolingian period. It seems important then to note that we do find much evidence of a Frankish element in the population of these regions which, a century or more later, still considered itself somewhat distinct. At Nîmes the presence of a Frankish element seems to be clearly indicated by the use of Frankish or Salic law as late as 898.[38] A century later about Maguelonne the local counts specifically state they still are following it too.[39] Nearby in the vicinity of Agde and Béziers we hear of a certain *"villa Franconica,"*[40] while a charter of a century or more later contains the name of a witness who still calls himself Salic.[41] Two *vassi dominici*, who, judging by their names, seem to be Franks, are mentioned as attending a court held at Narbonne in 782,[42] while the use of Salic as well as Visigothic and Roman law in the law courts as late as the tenth century[43] seems to point to Frankish settlers in this part of the Midi.

For Provence our information is scantier but here too the use of Salic law in courts which were held near Marseille in the late eighth and early

---

[37] Astronomus, *Vita Hludovici*, ch. 3, p. 608.

[38] *Cartulaire de l'église cathédrale de Notre Dame de Nîmes*, ed. E. Germer-Durand, no. 8.

[39] *Liber Instrumentorum Memorialium: Cartulaire des Guillems* [Montpellier], ed. A. Germain, no. 376.

[40] *Cartulaire d'Aniane*, ed. A. Cassan and E. Meynial, no. 306, which dates from the period 814–840. See also the charter of 802 which mentions a number of Frankish names, as well as a *villa franconica* (*ibid.*, no. 12).

[41] See charter of 955 in "Catulaire de l'Évêché d'Agde" (unprinted), no. 7, p. 36.

[42] *Hist. Gén. de Lang.*, II, no. 6.

[43] At Alzonne in 918 (*Hist. Gén. de Lang.*, II, nos. 137–140) and at Narbonne in 955 (*ibid.*, V, nos. 160–161).

ninth centuries,[44] seems to indicate the presence of a Frankish element. Further north in Aquitaine we find more evidence of a Frankish population. As late as the tenth century a landholder giving land to the abbey of Saint-Chaffre speaks of himself as being of Frankish origin.[45] In the Rouergue, near Conques, we hear of a *vassus dominicus* who, judging from his name, was Frankish.[46] In the Limousin an examination of the names of those who cultivated the *villa* of Cavalicus, once part of the royal *fisc*, shows clearly that they were Franks.[47] In fact an analysis of family names in the Limousin found in charters dating from this and later periods by Tenant de la Tour seems to show that a surprising proportion of this province's population came from north of the Loire originally.[48] In all of the Midi north of Narbonne, Carcassonne, and the Garonne, then, we can establish the presence of sufficient Franks to indicate that a certain colonization took place here in Carolingian times and perhaps even later.

But there is still another way in which the problem might be approached—through an examination of castles and fortifications. We know that when the Carolingians were conquering Southern France their task was made difficult by the presence of large numbers of fortified *civitates* and *castella*. If we have evidence that they maintained such fortresses after conquest, this could be considered to represent a continuing need for the use of military force during the reigns of Charlemagne and Louis the Pious—a possible index of basic resistance to their rule. Now there seems to be some indication that many of the fortified *civitates* of the Midi, whose walls were destroyed by the Carolingians in the course of conquest, were not refortified. Cases in point are Mauguio, Limoges, Périgord, Bordeaux, Marseille,[49] and others which fell easy

[44] See reference in a charter of 845 to *scabini* called *"tam romanes quam salices"* (*Cart. de Saint-Victor*, no. 26).

[45] *Cartulaire de l'abbaye de Saint-Chaffre du Monastier*, ed. U. Chevalier, no. 268.

[46] *Hist. Gén. de Lang.*, II, no. 81, and *Cart. de Conques*, no. 460. See comments on the large Frankish population in the Rouergue in C. Higounet, "Observations sur la seigneurie rurale et l'habitat en Rouergue du IX⁰ au XIV⁰ siècle," in *Annales du Midi*, LXII (1950), 121–132.

[47] F. Delage and G. Brussel, "Un domaine carolingien au Limousin, Cavalicus" in *Bulletin de la société archéologique et historique de Limousin*, LXXXIV (1952–1954), 43–52.

[48] G. Tenant de la Tour, *L'homme et la terre de Charlemagne à Saint Louis*, pp. 100 ff.

[49] The walls of Mauguio were destroyed by Charles Martel in 739 (*Chron. of Moissac*, anno 739, p. 291; *Annals of Aniane*, col. 5–6; and *Fredegarii cont.*, ch.

prey to Viking and Moslem raiders later in the century. Some like Barcelona, Gerona, Toulouse, Vienne, and perhaps Avignon[50] remained fortified.

When we consider castles, however, the situation seems to be a little different. Though our information is scant, there is indication of the continued use of *castella* and the building of new ones in parts of the Midi and the Spanish March between 778 and 828. Some of these fortresses were near the frontiers, like Tarrassa[51] close to Barcelona and Ausona, or like Casserès and Cardona which Louis the Pious ordered Count Borell to rebuild in 798,[52] or Fronsac, constructed by Charlemagne near the Gascon border in 769.[53]

Others, located in the interior, cannot have been the result of the needs of frontier defense. This seems true of the *castellum* owned by the church of Gerona in the *vellula nova* of Vellosa in Ampurias in 834.[54] It also

---

20, pp. 177–178). They were not rebuilt until late in the tenth century ("Chronicon Vetus Magalonense," in *Cart. de Maguelonne*, I). On Pepin's destruction of the walls of Limoges in the eighth century and Bishop Turpin's refortification of the city in 905–914 see "Historia monasterii Uzercensis," in *Cart. d'Uzerche*, pp. 13–14. On the destruction of the fortifications of Périgord and of other *civitates* in the Limousin and Angoulême see *Fredegarii cont.*, ch. 129–130, pp. 189–190, and *Annales Laurissenses*, anno 765, 766, pp. 144–145. There is no mention of Bordeaux's walls in records from the ninth century, which leads one to assume that they did not exist. Marseille presents the same situation as Bordeaux in this century. Note that the canons of Marseille in 923 had to take refuge in the castle of Fos to escape Moslem attack (*Cart. de Saint-Victor*, no. 1).

[50] On the walls of Barcelona, which were able to resist a Moslem siege in 828 see Astronomus, *Vita Hludovici*, ch. 43, pp. 636–637. Both Gerona and Narbonne had fortifications which allowed them to resist Moslem attack in 793 (see P. Ponsch, "Les origines de l'abbaye d'Arles," in *Études Roussillonnaises*, IV, 70–72; and also *Chron. of Moissac*, anno 793, p. 290; *Chron. of Uzès*, col. 27; and *Annals of Aniane*, col. 9–10). In 844 Toulouse possessed city walls (*Cartulaire de l'abbaye de Saint-Sernin de Toulouse*, ed. C. Douais, no. 3). About Vienne see G. Letonnelier, "Essai sur l'origine des châtelains et des mandements en Dauphiné," in *Annales de l'Université de Grenoble*, I (1889), 7; *Cartulaire de Vienne*, no. 4, in *Cartulaire de l'abbaye de Saint-André-le-bas de Vienne*, ed. U. Chevalier, pp. 214–215. About Avignon see *Cart. de Vienne*, no. 4, pp. 214–215; also see R. Poupardin, *Recueil des actes des rois de Provence (855–928)*, p. 38.

[51] On mention of this castle in 801 see *Catalunya Carolingia*, II, appendix II, 415. In 844 *ibid.*, II, 423–425.

[52] Astronomus, *Vita Hludovici*, ch. 8, p. 611.

[53] *Annales Laurissenses*, anno 769, p. 148; Astronomus, *Vita Hludovici*, ch. 2, p. 608; and *Ademar of Chabannes*, II, 70–71.

[54] *Catalunya Carolingia*, II, 121–124.

applies to the fortress called Turres in Agde which a certain Rainald owned in 824[55] or the nearby castles of Mesoa and Turres granted by Charles the Bald as benefices to certain landowners of the Béziers region in 844.[56] Further east in Lodève, we learn that the abbey of Aniane owned a castle called Montecalmense, which is mentioned in 787 and 829[57] and seems to have been near the monastery. To the south we hear of a *castrum* of Substantion in 801, and one at Novumvillaco in 813,[58] both in the county of Maguelonne or Melgueil, as well as that of Anduze near Nîmes mentioned in 821.[59]

We have less information concerning Provence. But we do know that in 798 there was a *castrum* near the abbey of Lérins[60] and in 781 one at Nantes[61] outside Marseille. Further north along the Rhone it seems probable that the castles of Pilep and Saint-Just at Vienne mentioned between 865 and 870[62] date from this earlier period, as does the Alpine fortress of Maurienne which guarded *clusae* leading to Italy.[63]

For Aquitaine too there are indications of the existence of castles dating from this period. There is the castle of Vitry built in Velay by Count Berengar about 830[64] and the *rocca* in Rouergue which Liutard gave to the abbey of Conques.[65] In Auvergne the abbey of Saint-Julien de Brioude seems to have been located in or near the Castrum Victoriacum,[66] while in the Limousin the castle of Turenne is mentioned in the mid-eighth century as well as later on.[67] There may also have been other *castra* in the Limousin-Quercy region which Count Roger gave to the abbey of Char-

---

[55] *Cartulaire de Gellone,* ed. A. Cassan and E. Meynial, no. 278.

[56] *Hist. Gén. de Lang.,* II, no. 105. See also mention of the castle of Popian in 804 (*Cart. de Gellone,* no. 143).

[57] *Cart. d'Aniane,* nos. 1, 55. See also mention of a *castellanus* in "Cart. de l'Évêché d'Agde" (unprinted), no. 15.

[58] *Cart. d'Aniane,* no. 254.

[59] *Ibid.,* no. 147.

[60] *Cart. de Lérins,* no. 290.

[61] *Cart. de Saint-Victor,* no. 83.

[62] Poupardin, *Recueil des actes des rois de Provence,* p. ii.

[63] *Chartes du diocèse de Maurienne,* ed. A. Billiot and F. Abrieux, no. 1, in *Académie Impériale de Savoie: Documents,* II, 5–7.

[64] *Hist. Gén. de Lang.,* II, no. 68.

[65] *Cart. de Conques,* no. 1.

[66] *Cart. de Brioude,* no. 252.

[67] K. Zeumer, *Formulae, Merovingici et Karoli Aevi,* in *Mon. Ger. Hist. Leges,* V, p. 325.

The Carolingian System 63

roux between 769 and 799.⁶⁸ South of Poitou and Burgundy, then, castles continued to be built and occupied, and they remained of some importance. All this would seem to show that in some respects Carolingian government in the Midi remained an alien one, which was imposed on the local population by means of Frankish officials and churchmen and buttressed by the establishment of *vassi dominici* and other colonists from the north who kept control of local areas for the Carolingian monarchs by maintaining older castles and fortresses and building new ones. But before we accept this as a final conclusion, we should consider other evidence which points to quite different conclusions for the period after 778—especially as far as Septimania and Catalonia are concerned.

Let us first consider those counts whom the Carolingians appointed to office in regions south of the Loire and in the Valley of the Rhone. Even as early as the reign of Pepin many were not Frankish. There is that Gothic count of Mauguio or Maguelonne, the father of St. Benedict of Aniane, who delivered this city to Pepin and was maintained in office afterwards even under Charlemagne.⁶⁹ Then there were those Goths to whom Pepin in 759 guaranteed the use of their own laws and who, in return, delivered over to him the city of Narbonne. From this time on there is every indication that most of the counts south of Carcassonne and Narbonne were Gothic rather than Frankish, like Borell of Ausona, Bellon of Carcassonne, and Bera of Barcelona.⁷⁰ Even the removal of Bera in 820 does not appear to have been based on his nationality but, as has been noted, was the result of other factors. And the almost simultaneous appointment of Asnar Galindo, a Spaniard from Aragón as count of Urgell-Cerdanya is further indication of a willingness to use a non-Frank in a sensitive border area of the empire.⁷¹ Can we be sure also that Dhuoda of Uzès was not, as her name certainly implies, of Southern French origin, like Count Leibulf of Provence, who, if he was not Provençal, certainly owned private allodial property in Arles?⁷²

---

⁶⁸ *Chartes et documents pour servir à l'histoire de l'abbaye de Charroux*, ed. P. Monsabert in *Archives Historiques de Poitou*, XXXIX, 10–11.

⁶⁹ *Vita Benedicti Anianensis*, ed. E. Waitz, I, in *Mon. Ger. Hist. Scriptores*, XV, 201; and *Hist. Gén. de Lang.*, II, no. 314.

⁷⁰ Abadal, "Un diplôme inconnu de Louis le Pieux," pp. 352–357.

⁷¹ *Catalunya Carolingia*, II, 325–326.

⁷² See Leibulf's property in Arles called *"ex rebus proprietas"* in *Cart. de Lérins*, nos. 247, 248; and Février, "La donation faite à Lérins par le comte Leibulfe," pp. 23–37.

In Aquitaine one finds a similar situation. It was a group of Aquitanian counts led by Count Humbert of Bourges who made the final surrender of this region to Pepin in 768.[73] And while historians have paid close attention to the Astronomus' statement that Charlemagne gave to Franks the *honores* of counts and abbots throughout Aquitaine, they have failed to notice the contradiction to be found in his next statement. For he lists among the nine counts actually appointed at least two who were non-Frankish, Humbert of Bourges, who is obviously the same Aquitanian count mentioned in 768, and Séguin of Bordeaux, who was a Gascon.[74]

Gascony, Aragón, and Navarre were certainly areas of Southern France and its borderlands which were least responsive to Carolingian authority. Yet even here the same policy seems to have been followed. In Navarre Charlemagne backed Count Velasco, a Basque of Spanish descent,[75] and in Aragón accepted as successor to Aureolus, who was probably a Frank, Asnar Galindo, a native of the region.[76] This latter's loyalty was such, as a matter of fact, that when he was overthrown, he sought refuge in Carolingian territory. Even in Gascony use was made of the native Basque ducal family, though attempts seem to have been made to diminish their over-all authority.[77]

More striking, however, than this use of non-Franks as counts is another policy which was inaugurated about 780—that of welcoming Spanish refugees into the Midi. These *hispani*, who were frequently given large tracts of vacant land to settle as *aprisiones*, were probably few in number. Abadal estimates them as numbering some fifty in all, and we know of some forty-two by name who went to Aix-la-Chapelle in 812 to present their grievances to the emperor.[78] But what is significant is not their numbers, but the fact that from 780 on these refugee *milites* were given special treatment by the Carolingians—not only in Catalan counties like Barcelona, Gerona, Ampurias, and Roussillon, but in Septimania in the counties of Carcassonne, Narbonne, Béziers, and also in Provence. Their quasi-proprietorship was protected from the encroachment of the local counts by a special capitulary, and, like the *vassi dominici*, they even

---

[73] *Fredegarii cont.*, ch. 131–135, pp. 190–192; and *Annales Laurissenses*, anno 767, 768, p. 146.

[74] Astronomus, *Vita Hludovici*, ch. 3, p. 608.

[75] J. Pérez de Urbel, "Lo viejo y lo nuevo sobre el origin del Reino de Pamplona," in *Al-Andalus*, XIX (1954), 1–30.

[76] J. Lacarra, *Orígines del condado de Aragón*, pp. 1–14.

[77] L. Auzias, *L'Aquitaine Carolingienne (778–987)*, pp. 40–67.

[78] *Catalunya Carolingia*, II, 313–314.

appear to have done homage in person to Carolingian rulers for their lands.[79] Can one still consider that the Carolingians followed a policy of Frankish domination of the Midi in the light of their use and treatment of such large *aprisio* holders—not to mention the more numerous proprietors of small *aprisiones* who were given land by the emperors of Aix-la-Chapelle and their subordinates?

As a matter of fact we cannot even be sure that all *vassi dominici* and other similar landholders in the Midi were Franks. The case of Dodila is instructive in this respect. In 813 Dodila, an important landholder, left property to Psalmodi and two other abbeys. This land, the charter reveals to us, was located in Rouergue, Uzès, and Maguelonne and was allodial and had been inherited from his father Gregory. Yet in the same charter we learn that Dodila, whose name does not seem Frankish, served Charlemagne as a warrior, just as the better known John of Fontjoncouse had done.[80]

This reliance on non-Frankish *milites* and warriors, as a matter of fact, seems to have been a regular feature of Carolingian policy—particularly after 778. The most important military effort of the Carolingians during this period was the expedition sent into Catalonia in 801–802 which ended in the conquest of Barcelona. What troops were used on this expedition? Our sources are explicit in explaining that they were Franks, a contingent of Provençals under Count Leibulf, some Aquitanians, Gascons commanded by Duke Lupo, and an important Gothic element under Count Bera.[81] As late as 820 we find a Frankish Count Rampon fighting side by side with a Spaniard, Count Asnar Galindo, in an invasion of Moslem territory,[82] while a Frankish Count Ebles joins a Gascon Count Aznar in attacking Navarre.[83]

A closer look at those holding interior castles proves equally revealing, for it shows how few seem to have been in the possession of the Frankish lay officials of the region concerned. Thus it is the church of Gerona which

---

[79] See Abadal's excellent account of these *aprisio* holders in "La Catalogne sous l'empire de Louis le Pieux," pp. 257–274.

[80] *Hist. Gén. de Lang.*, II, no. 24.

[81] Ermold Niger, *Carmina in honorem Hludvici*, ed. E. Dummler, I, vers. 273–278, in *Mon. Ger. Hist. Scriptores*, I, 472; Astronomus, *Vita Hludovici*, ch. 13, pp. 612–613; and *Chron. of Moissac*, anno 803, p. 307.

[82] *Annales Regni Francorum*, anno 822, p. 152; Astronomus, *Vita Hludovici*, ch. 34, p. 626.

[83] *Annales Regni Francorum*, anno 824, p. 153; Astronomus, *Vita Hludovici*, ch. 37, p. 628. See also F. Codera y Zaidín, "Expedición a Pamplona de los condes francos Elbo y Aznar," in *Colección de Estudios Árabes*, VII, 185–199.

owned the castle of Vellosa in Ampurias,[84] the abbey of Aniane that of Montecalmense.[85] Conques was proprietor, after 801, of the *rocca* given it by Liutard,[86] just as Charroux gained possession of certain fortresses given this abbey by Count Roger of Limoges.[87] It also seems probable that Brioude was the immediate proprietor of that castle located nearby in Auvergne.[88] Other *castra* were under private control, like that Turres near Agde,[89] those nearby *castella* granted *jure beneficario* by Charles the Bald in 844[90] or the castle of Nantes in Provence which was a privately owned allod.[91] Thus, at the time of Charlemagne and Louis the Pious many fortresses seem to have been used more for the protection of abbeys, churches, and private individuals than as an integral part of the governmental system.

When one examines the Church during the same period, its non-Frankish character seems just as obvious. The most important churchman in the Midi was St. Benedict of Aniane, who served as an important advisor to the emperor Louis the Pious. His abbey of Aniane and its *cellas* were in large measure responsible for the monastic revival which took place in the Midi from Psalmodi to Carcassonne. Yet he was a Goth, the son of a count of Maguelonne.[92] Maurontius, who was a bishop of Marseille about 780, seems to have been a member of the old family of Gallo-Roman patricians of Provence.[93] St. Benedict's principal collaborators in the Midi consisted of Gothic and refugee Spanish churchmen like Nimfridius of Narbonne, Abbot Castellanus of Arles, and Archbishop Agobard of Lyon.[94] Without exception those churchmen and abbots who were responsible for the somewhat later revival of monasticism in Catalonia and Pallars and Ribagorça were non-Frankish.[95] Even in Aquitaine the

[84] *Catalunya Carolingia*, II, 121–124.
[85] *Cart. d'Aniane*, nos. 1, 55.
[86] *Cart. de Conques*, no. 1.
[87] *Chartes de l'abbaye de Charroux*, pp. 10–11.
[88] *Cart. de Brioude*, no. 252.
[89] *Cart. de Gellone*, no. 278.
[90] *Hist. Gén. de Lang.*, II, no. 105.
[91] *Cart. de Saint-Victor*, no. 83.
[92] See *Vita Benedicti Anianensis*, and *Annals of Aniane*, anno 782, col. 9–10 on Benedict's role in founding abbeys *"in Gociam"* and Aquitaine.
[93] *Annals of Aniane*, anno 782, col. 9–10.
[94] Abadal, "La Catalogne sous l'empire de Louis le Pieux," p. 269.
[95] R. de Abadal i de Vinyals, "La batalla del adopcionisme en la desintegración de la Iglesia visigoda" in *Real Academia de Buenas Letras de Barcelona*, and *Els Primers Comtes Catalans*, pp. 115–147.

The Carolingian System   67

names of men like Aguarnius, bishop of Cahors in 783,[96] or Ferreolus, abbot of Brioude (817–834),[97] or Anastasius, abbot of Conques about 823,[98] reveal that they sprang from Gallo-Roman stock. The Church south of Poitou and Burgundy was even less Frankish than lay officialdom.

Finally it is worth emphasizing that the Carolingians allowed the inhabitants of Southern France and Catalonia to use their own law— which would have been unlikely if they had been intent on dominating these regions in the interests of a Frankish minority. Thus not only were the Goths of Narbonne promised their own laws in 759,[99] but afterwards records reveal a use of Visigothic law and procedure in every court south of Narbonne and Carcassonne.[100] *Aprisio* holders were similarly allowed to continue the use of a non-Frankish legal system.[101] Roman law also continued to be important over much of the Midi both in courts and in a more private capacity. We find it used in courts in Provence between 780 and 845,[102] in tribunals a little later held at Nîmes,[103] and it seems to have been the basis of the property law used in Rouergue.[104] The personality of the law, which was maintained, whether it be Salic, Roman, or Visigothic is a rather clear indication of the equal treatment which the Carolingians accorded all the inhabitants of the Midi—whatever their origins.

What emerges when one examines the Carolingian governmental system of Southern France and Catalonia, then, is a very different picture from that given us by Auzias, Calmette, and Dhondt. There was a use made of Frankish officials as counts throughout these regions, which is not surprising considering that they helped win the Midi for the Carolingians

[96] *Hist. Gén. de Lang.*, II, no. 7.
[97] *Le Grand Cartulaire de Saint-Julien de Brioude, essai de reconstruction*, ed. Anne Marie and Marcel Boudet, no. CCXCVI, p. 83.
[98] *Cart. de Conques*, no. 460.
[99] *Chron. of Uzès*, anno 759, col. 26–27, and *Chron. of Moissac*, anno 759, p. 294.
[100] See record of courts held in Narbonne in 855 (*Cart. de Carcassonne*, IV, 192–193), and in 862 (*ibid.*, I, 71–72); or record of courts held in Roussillon in 832 (*Hist. Gén. de Lang.*, II, no. 80), and in 865 (*Cartulaire roussillonnais*, ed. B. Alart, no. 1); or in Nîmes in 898 (*Cart. de Nîmes*, no. 8).
[101] *Catalunya Carolingia*, II, 417–419.
[102] *Cart. de Saint-Victor*, nos. 31, 36.
[103] See record of court held in Nîmes in 876 in *Cart. de Nîmes*, no. 1, and in 902 (*ibid.*, no. 9).
[104] In a grant of land to Conques in 801 Liutard states he is acting *"secundum quod* lex romana *docet de post mortem causa donatis"* (*Cart. de Conques*, no. 1). And see the very similar statement of Rudolf, count of Turenne in a charter of 823 from the Limousin (*Cart. de Beaulieu*, no. 185).

and were their relatives and familiars. There is evidence of some Frankish settlement or even colonization of these same regions. But except for the extreme southwest beyond the Garonne in Gascony, Aragón, and Navarre, the Carolingian system of government after 778 stands revealed as a multinational or multi-racial one. Once conquest had been completed, this became even truer than it had been earlier under Pepin and Charles Martel.[105] One change, the use of *aprisiones* in Septimania and Catalonia is a specially good example of privileges given the non-Frankish population. Even more important, as we approach 828 we become more and more aware of the fact that there was a steady infiltration of non-Franks into both the Carolingian secular administration and the Church, which was resulting in a slow but inexorable modification of both toward a very different system than that envisaged by the distant emperors of Aix-la-Chapelle. Two forces, then, were at work in the Midi and Catalonia during this period and interacting upon one another. The first was that system of government imposed by the Carolingians. The second was the society of the Midi, which, surviving Carolingian conquest, continued as an element of importance.

[105] It is not surprising that this should be so, for those scholars whom Charlemagne drew to Aix-la-Chapelle during this same period were also multinational as far as their origin was concerned. If the Carolingian renaissance was more than a Frankish affair, why not the Carolingian administrative system too?

CHAPTER V

Southern French and Catalan Society (778–828)

DURING THE reigns of Charlemagne and Louis the Pious a number of changes took place in the society of Southern France and Catalonia, which were more significant than the purely governmental ones discussed in the last chapter. These changes helped to modify the nature of this society and to lay the bases for its development. The most important were the emergence of a new method of landholding, especially in Septimania and Catalonia, the development of a set of personal relationships which might be called proto-feudal, and the revitalization of the Church, particularly in respect to its monastic institutions. To these should be added two more: the beginnings of an agricultural revolution which put vacant and unused land in cultivation, and a limited but no less real revival of trade.

Several points, however, need to be stressed before we proceed to examine such developments in detail. The first is the fact that the changes of these decades took place within the context of the existing society and institutions of these regions, which had the effect of limiting them and modifying them in a number of ways. The second point, equally important, is that such changes as took place did so unevenly. Not every part of Southern France and the Spanish March was affected by them in the same way. Thus, for various reasons, Septimania and Catalonia seem to have been the areas most affected by such developments, Gascony and Provence the least, with Aquitaine and the Rhone Valley area lying somewhere in between.

Remembering such qualifications let us first consider that innovation in landholding which must be ascribed to the Carolingians. It may be recalled that in our first chapter, dealing with pre-Carolingian society, we noted two systems of landholding which were to be found in the Midi. One, much the more common, was the system of holding land allodially in full outright ownership. The other was a use of *precaria* or benefices in which land was held conditionally. To these two systems the Carolingian monarchs added a third, the *aprisio*.

The *aprisio* did not appear until 780, when, as has been noted, Charlemagne had to face the problem of providing for Spanish refugees who had fled to the Midi after the failure of his Saragossa expedition of 778. He solved this problem by allotting to these *hispani* tracts of uncultivated land in Septimania belonging to the royal *fisc*, which they were to hold under special conditions.[1] The first such specific grant that we know of was one at Fontjoncouse near Narbonne given to John, the hero of Pont, in 795.[2] Two different types of refugees were given such allotments, the important ones or *majores*, who arrived in the Midi with servants and many followers, and the less important ones known as *minores*.

As territory south of the Pyrenees was gradually liberated from the Moslem yoke, the *aprisio* system was extended into Catalonia,[3] until by 812 such holdings were to be found over a wide area in the maritime Catalan counties of Barcelona, Gerona, Ampurias, and Roussillon, as well as around Narbonne, Carcassonne, and Béziers, and in Provence.[4] Judging from Charlemagne's original edict which set up the *aprisio* system, such holdings may have spread into parts of Aquitaine also.[5]

In 812 disputes between *aprisio* holders and the local counts and inhabitants of the regions in which they were located caused some forty-two important *spani* settled in Carolingian domains under this system to carry their complaints to Aix-la-Chapelle to the emperor Charlemagne himself. They may have been accompanied by some *minores* or smaller *aprisio* holders.[6] As a result of their complaints Charles' successor Louis the Pious in 815 and 816 regulated the status of *aprisiones* in edicts which embodied

---

[1] *Catalunya Carolingia*, II, 412.
[2] *Ibid.*, pp. 309–311.
[3] *Ibid.*, p. 415. This extended the *aprisio* system to the inhabitants of newly liberated Barcelona and Tarrassa. In this connection see Charles the Bald's specific extension of *aprisiones* to *Goti* and *Ispani* in Barcelona and the castle of Tarrassa in 844 (*ibid.*, pp. 423–425).
[4] Both *aprisio* owners and the counts of Barcelona, Gerona, Ampurias, Roussillon, Narbonne, Béziers, Carcassonne, and Provence were summoned to Aix-la-Chapelle in 812 (*ibid.*, appendix XII, p. 412).
[5] In 780 Charlemagne addressed his original statute setting up *aprisiones* to his *fideles* in Aquitaine, as well as Septimania and Provence (*ibid.*, appendix I, p. 412). Louis the Pious added that *aprisio* holders were settled "in that portion of Spain liberated by our marcher lords." See R. de Abadal i de Vinyals, "La Catalogne sous l'empire de Louis le Pieux," in *Études Roussillonnaises*, V (1956), 259–260.
[6] *Catalunya Carolingia*, II, 313–314.

principles found in his father's original grant of 780 and his extension of *aprisio* rights to the inhabitants of Barcelona and Tarrassa about 802.[7] In 844 Charles the Bald made some minor changes and issued another capitulary concerning *aprisiones*.[8]

From these Carolingian enactments we learn the exact nature of an *aprisio*, particularly one held by one of the *majores* like John of Fontjoncouse or Asnar Galindo. In the first place important *aprisio* holders did homage for their holdings to the Carolingian emperor. In 812 such seems to have been the case as regards the forty-two *majores* who journeyed to Aix-la-Chapelle.[9] A little later on, in 814, Louis the Pious calls Wimar a *vassalus* in renewing the grant of Charlemagne to him and his brother —a grant of land *"ab herema"* in which they had organized the *villa* of Ceret.[10] In 815 John of Fontjoncouse is called a *fidelis* by Louis when he has his land reconfirmed by the emperor.[11] So is Sunifred in a charter in 829 which concerns his *villa* or *aprisio* of Fons Cooperta.[12] The statutes reveal another fact—they were all free men. They paid, therefore, no special dues or *cens* to the counts or their agents, and they had the right to settle disputes among themselves and those whom they brought in to cultivate their holdings in accordance with their own Visigothic law, without recourse to the official tribunals of the counts. The one exception concerned criminal cases or *majores causas* in which the counts were still to have jurisdiction, just as they did in cases involving disputes between *aprisio* holders and the native inhabitants of their districts.[13]

Such privileges enjoyed by the large *aprisio* holders also carried with them certain responsibilities. The most important one was the duty of military service. These *milites*, as they were sometimes called, were required, upon call, to join the count's army and take part in frontier campaigns. They also had to furnish horses and purveyance to royal *missi* and envoys traveling to and from Spain. They were also permitted to receive benefices from counts and to enter into a dependent relationship with them in return for such grants of lands.[14]

---

[7] *Ibid.*, pp. 415–419.   [8] *Ibid.*, p. 336.   [9] *Ibid.*, p. 420.
[10] *Ibid.*, pp. 318–319. In this charter this *aprisio* is called a benefice, although it is said to have been given by Charlemagne and put into cultivation *"ab herema."*
[11] *Ibid.*, pp. 320–321.   [12] *Ibid.*, p. 324.
[13] *Ibid.*, p. 336. See also A. Dupont, "Considérations sur la colonisation et la vie rurale dans le Roussillon et la Marche d'Espagne," in *Annales du Midi*, LXVII (1955), 223–238.
[14] Dupont "Considérations sur la colonisation," pp. 223–238. See also Abadal, "La Catalogne sous l'empire de Louis le Pieux," pp. 260–274.

72   *Southern France, Catalonia, and the Carolingian Empire*

All the above seems to make a large *aprisio* holder all but identical with one of the *vassi dominici* who had very similar privileges and very similar responsibilities.[15] Wherein lies the difference? It lies in their rights of proprietorship over their lands. A large *aprisio* holder held his land in what Charles the Bald in 844 called quasi proprietorship.[16] He could, like an allodial landholder, sell or exchange it or leave it to his sons, nephews, or other relatives. Indeed, Carolingian monarchs themselves, in individual cases, began to transform some *aprisiones* into allods early in the ninth century. Thus in 814, in renewing the *aprisio* of Wimar and his brother, Louis the Pious expressly regranted it to them as *"jure proprietario,"* or full allodial ownership.[17] In the case of the charter referring to Sunifred's *aprisio* in 829 we find the same wording, *"jure proprietario."*[18] Later on in Catalonia custom seems to have prescribed full allodial ownership after thirty years. Perhaps this already was the case at the time of Louis the Pious.

Large *aprisio* holders, then, occupied a position between *vassi dominici* on the one hand and allodial landholders on the other. But what of small holders who were given *aprisiones*: the *minores*? What about these and their rights? We know less about them than the *majores*, other than that they were dissatisfied with their situation in 815 and complained about how they were being oppressed by the *majores*.[19] They were certainly numerous, particularly a little later where they formed a considerable element in the population of Catalonia.[20] Like the *milites* who help *aprisiones*, the

---

[15] See F. Ganshof's remarks on the similarity between these *aprisio* holders and *vassi dominici* in *Qu'est-ce que la féodalité?* pp. 59–60, and "L'origine des rapports féodo-vassiliques," in *I problemi della Civiltà Carolingia*, pp. 50–52. Note for example the interchangeability of terms by the time Louis the Pious in the case of Wimar or Guimar who is called a *vassulus* but holds what is obviously an *aprisio* (*Catalunya Carolingia*, II, 318).

[16] *Catalunya Carolingia*, II, 336.

[17] *Ibid.*, pp. 318–319.

[18] *Ibid.*, p. 324. Note that at about this time a capitulary of Louis the Pious speaks of royal vassals *"qui ad marcam nostram constituti sunt custodiendam aut in longinquis regionibus sua habent beneficia vel* res proprias" "Capitulare missorum," ch. 4, in Boretius, *Capitularia*, I, no. 148, pp. 300–301. The *"res proprias"* referred to above were obviously land owned outright (*"jure proprietario"*) given to *fideles, aprisio* holders, and vassals, similar to those mentioned in this note and in note 17.

[19] *Catalunya Carolingia*, II, 420.

[20] See mention of small *aprisio* holders in Roussillon in 861 in *Hist. Gén. de Lang.*, II, no. 156; in the Barcelona region in 862 in *Catalunya Carolingia*, II, 357–358; in Besalu in 866 in *Hist. Gén. de Lang.*, II, no. 167, and *Catalunya Carolingia*,

minores seem to have been free men, who were given their grants of *aprisiones* by larger landholders: counts, churches, or abbeys. In return they appear to have put it into cultivation and to have paid the original proprietor a *cens*, sometimes one third of the crop. They were certainly also subject to call for military service and responsible for the same *corvées* and purveyance as the more important *aprisio* holders.[21] Later on it was they who were the actual cultivators who repopulated the county of Ausona which Count Guifred changed from a deserted region into an important part of Christian Catalonia.[22]

What seems to have made *aprisiones* important, however, was not such grants to Spanish refugees, who were few in number, but the extension of the system to others—particularly in Catalonia. This seems to have begun as early as 802 when the grant of *aprisio* rights to the inhabitants of Barcelona and Tarrassa expressly included in its provisions extension of the system to Goths as well as *hispani*.[23] Such Goths, and Gascons as well, are specifically mentioned as holding *aprisiones* in Besalu some years later in a grant by Charles the Bald to the abbey of Santa-Julia del Mont[24] and also in a charter from Roussillon dating from the same period.[25] Equally interesting is evidence of the extension of this system of landholding to the Urgell-Cerdanya region. The *aprisio* granted Count Asnar Galindo here is a case in point.[26] By the end of the century in this part of Catalonia, and in Pallars and Ribagorça as well, the *aprisio* had become one of the principal methods used to extend the area of settlement along the frontiers of the Spanish March.

Which leads us to a final question. Was the *aprisio* system used elsewhere in the Midi, as well as in Septimania and Catalonia where it took firm root? There is some indication that it was. A little later we find

---

II, 219–221; in Vallespir in 878 in *ibid.*, pp. 70–71; in Besalu in 889 in *ibid.*, pp. 363–364; in Gerona in 891 in *ibid.*, pp. 365–366; in the Narbonnaise and Confluent in 891 in *ibid.*, pp. 109–111.

[21] A later charter, from 891, mentions *"homines hostalienses vel Ispani,"* and speaks of the dues which these men owe the *fisc* (*Catalunya Carolingia*, II, 110–111). See also Abadal, "La Catalogne sous l'empire de Louis le Pieux," pp. 265–266.

[22] See R. de Abadal i de Vinyals, *Els Primers Comtes Catalans*, pp. 73–110, and *La Plana de Vich*.

[23] *Catalunya Carolingia*, II, 415.

[24] *Ibid.*, pp. 219–221.

[25] *Hist. Gén. de Lang.*, II, no. 167.

[26] *Catalunya Carolingia*, II, 325–326.

aprisiones mentioned in charters from both Razès and the Toulousain.[27] More interesting is evidence that there existed a similar system during this period in Rouergue where it appears to have been called *attracto* as early as 801.[28] As for Gascony, lack of charters preclude anything except a conjecture that the system was not unknown in this part of the Midi. Nowhere, though, does it appear to have become as important as it did in Catalonia and the rest of the Spanish March.

To understand landholding systems found in the rest of the Midi, however, we must look for something other than *aprisiones,* interesting and unique though this system may be. North of the Pyrenees a system of *honores, precaria,* and *beneficia* seems to have been much more important. The *honores,* as they were called, present the easiest problem. An *honor* was a position, office, or charge, a county or series of counties, an archbishopric, a bishopric, or an abbey given to an individual by a Carolingian monarch; for it the individual did homage personally in a regular ceremony, and it therefore established between him and this ruler the special bond or tie of *fidelitas.*[29] *Honores* of a secular nature could be revoked and often were at the pleasure of the ruler, either because of disloyalty or incompetence or both.[30] When revocation seemed in order the monarch generally carried it out before an assembly attended by the important magnates and churchmen of the empire. The same is true of the bestowing of such *honores.*

Somewhat different were the benefices which Charlemagne and Louis the Pious gave to important supporters. Like *honores* such benefices were grants of land which established, through the personal ceremony of homage the bond of *fidelitas,* and those who received them were called

---

[27] In Carcassonne-Razès in 908 (*Cart. de Carcassonne,* I, 253), and in the Toulousain in 965 and 966 (*Hist. Gén. de Lang.,* V, no. 116 and *Cart. de Saint-Sernin,* no. 396).

[28] In the charter in which a certain Liutard gives land to Conques, he says this land is *"tam de alode quam de adtracto"* (*Cart. de Conques,* no. 1).

[29] See the excellent summary of this system in Ganshof, *Qu'est-ce que la féodalité?* pp. 28 ff.

[30] The Midi and Catalonia provide two excellent examples of this. One is the removal of Duke Chorson of Toulouse by Charlemagne in 789 (Astronomus, *Vita Hludovici,* ch. 5, p. 608). The other is the removal of Count Bera in 820 by Louis the Pious (*ibid.,* ch. 33, p. 625). Still another case is the removal of Count Séguin by Louis the Pious in 816 (*ibid.,* ch. 26, p. 620). Both Chorson and Bera were called to Aix-la-Chapelle and degraded there, Bera after losing a judicial duel to his accuser, the Goth Sanila.

Southern French and Catalan Society (778–828)   75

fideles and sometimes *vassi*.³¹ But, in the Midi during this period, a benefice seems to have consisted essentially of a grant of *land* rather than an *office*. The royal *fisc*, consisting as it did of confiscated, conquered, and vacant land, seems to have been the source from which benefices were given, as it was for *aprisiones* which much resemble them. Unlike the *honor*, however, the *beneficia* seem to have been lifetime grants, unless disloyalty forced their withdrawal from the recipient. Sometimes, however, they were even given for longer periods of time.³²

Counts in addition to their *honores* often received from the Carolingian monarchs grants of *beneficia*, a fact which shows that an individual could hold an *honor* as an official and a benefice as a *fidelis* at the same time. The *villa* which Count Robert had held *"in beneficium"* from Louis the Pious and which this emperor gave to the bishop of Maguelonne in 819 is a case in point.³³ Equally instructive is the dispute between Count Milon and the archbishop of Narbonne in 782 in which the former claimed he held certain *villas "in beneficio"* from Charlemagne.³⁴ The *aprisio* granted Asnar Galindo in Cerdanya which became the subject of a dispute between the later counts of this region and Galindo's heirs similarly reveals the difference between benefices and *aprisiones* given to individuals in a private capacity and *honores* which were public charges even though both established the personal bond of *fidelitas*.³⁵ Probably those lands given by Count Roger of Limoges to the abbey of Charroux between 769 and 799 were also benefices granted to him by Charlemagne since a general confirmation of this gift by a special charter signed by the monarch is to be found also.³⁶

Royal benefices, however, were also given to a class of landowners or *milites* known as *vassi dominici*. Perhaps it was to this group that the

³¹ In the Midi and Catalonia during this period the terms *vassi, vassali*, and *fideles* seem to be used interchangeably in our documents, so that it seems impossible to distinguish among them in any juridical sense. On a possible difference between them see C. Odegaard, *Vassi and Fideles in the Carolingian Empire*.

³² For an example of such a benefice which, a little later, could be inherited see Charles the Bald's grant of the castles of Mesoa and Turres near Béziers in 844 (*Hist. Gén. de Lang.*, II, no. 105).

³³ *Cart. de Maguelonne*, I, no. 2.

³⁴ *Hist. Gén. de Lang.*, II, no. 6.

³⁵ *Catalunya Carolingia*, II, 325–326.

³⁶ *Chartes de l'abbaye de Charroux*, pp. 10–11, 55–62. The charter purporting to be that issued by Count Roger, however, seems to be either a forgery or a later interpolation (*ibid.*, pp. 55–62).

Astronomus refers when he says that Louis the Pious, as king of Aquitaine, gave land to *"viros militares."*[37] A clearer example of this class, however, was Bertrand, a *vassus dominicus* who, with the permission of the emperor in 823, exchanged lands which he held belonging to the royal *fisc* for others in Rouergue which were the property of the abbey of Conques.[38] Another was a certain Ebolatus, called a nobleman, who in 817, with the permission of the emperor, gave lands and *villas* he held to the monastery of Maz d'Azil in the Toulousain.[39] Sometimes even grants of lands to the Church are similarly called *beneficia*, like the property and privileges given Saint-Victor of Marseille by Charlemagne in 790.[40] It is clear then that Carolingian rulers in distributing land from their *fisc* to officials and important supporters, made use of benefices which in turn seem to have carried with them the obligation on the part of the recipient to appear as part of the armed forces when summoned by proper authority.[41]

Carolingian capitularies make it clear that these rulers also expected their *fideles* and *vassi*, particularly their counts, to similarly give their own followers benefices and so bind these latter to them by the same ties of *fidelitas*. Indeed the capitulary of 815 specifically allowed large *aprisio* holders to enter into such ties with counts, despite the *fidelitas* they owed the emperor.[42] But there may have been some reluctance in parts of the Midi to follow such practices. The long struggle, in the end successful, of the heirs of John of Fontjoncouse to escape this sort of control by the local counts is an interesting case in point.[43] Even more significant is a little noted statement of the Astronomus who tell us that Louis, while king of Aquitaine, forbade individuals to give out *"annona militaris quas vulgo foderum vocant."* This, incidentally, may well be the first appear-

[37] Astronomus, *Vita Hludovici*, ch. 7, p. 611.
[38] *Cart. de Conques*, no. 460.
[39] *Hist. Gén. de Lang.*, II, no. 46.
[40] *Cart. de Saint-Victor*, no. 8.
[41] On this see Ganshof, *Qu'est-ce que la féodalité?* pp. 44–45, and especially note 47 which lists the sources in the capitularies of Charlemagne and Louis the Pious.
[42] *Catalunya Carolingia*, II, 417–419. This is also found in Boretius, *Capitularia*, I, no. 132, p. 262. See the same permission in the charter of 844 which Charles the Bald gave to the inhabitants of Barcelona and Tarrassa (*Catalunya Carolingia*, II, 425).
[43] *Catalunya Carolingia*, II, 442–444. This is a record of a court held in 834, before which John's heirs testified of their difficulties with the counts of the Narbonne region.

ance of word "fief" in the Midi, or anywhere else.[44] It also seems to forbid the very practice of private commendation which later Carolingian enactments encouraged counts and other officials to practice. The very prohibition against such practices, though, is proof that they were not uncommon.

To discuss benefices, however, and confine one's attention to those given out by Carolingian monarchs and their officers and *fideles*, is to ignore the wider use of this system of landholding and the very similar *precaria* by other elements in the population of the Midi and Catalonia during this period. The *precaria* granted by churches and abbeys are of particular interest in this respect. In the Lyonnais, for instance, we find a record of a grant of a *villa* in 825 by the abbot of Savigny to a certain Marfinus, a landowner of the region, as a life *precarium*, in return for an annual payment of six *denarii* as a *cens*.[45] Similarly in a list of property owned by the abbey of Saint-Victor of Marseille, compiled sometime between 802 and 813, we find several *colonicas* and one *villa* which had been given to individuals as benefices. These benefices are mentioned as owing a *cens* in kind to the abbey.[46] Similar benefices were given to individuals of very humble circumstances, like the land which a certain Pinaud and his family had held in 803 for six years *"pro beneficio"* from the abbey of Caunes in the Narbonnaise. The charter describing this benefice reveals that they are to pay a *cens* or *tasca* for the property and hold it *"per precaria"* from now on.[47] A little later in 826 the inhabitants of two other *villas* testify before a court of *boni homines* that they hold land *"per beneficium"* from the same monastery.[48] In 820 in the nearby county of Carcassonne we hear that the abbey of Lagrasse has given two *villas* as *precaria* or a *beneficium* to Count Oliba and his wife in return

---

[44] Astronomus, *Vita Hludovici*, ch. 7, pp. 610–611. Marc Bloch in his *La Société Féodale*, I, 254–256, felt that the word "fief" had a different derivation, and found it first used in the late ninth century in Burgundy. It would seem more logical to me, however, to derive it from the term *foderum* found here. In this connection one of the earliest uses of the term is in a Southern French charter of 899 (see *Cart. de Maguelonne*, no. 3).

[45] *Cartulaire de l'abbaye de Savigny, suivi du petit cartulaire de l'abbaye d'Ainay*, ed. A. Bernard, no. 16.

[46] "Descriptio Mancipiorum Ecclesiae Massiliensis," Nos. F, H, in *Cart. de Saint-Victor*, Bk. II, 638, 642, 644.

[47] *Hist. Gén. de Lang.*, II, no. 15.

[48] *Ibid.*, col. 72–73.

for an annual payment of twenty *solidi* as a *cens*. This grant is clearly stated to be for a lifetime only.[49]

That the practice of churches granting benefices to prominent individuals had spread into Catalonia is revealed by a charter which in 835 Louis the Pious gave to the church of Urgell. In this charter he forbids this church's giving *"in beneficium"* any of its property located in the counties of Urgell, Berga, Cardona, Cerdanya, Pallars, and Ribagorça.[50] The same prohibition is to be found in another charter which concerns the Limousin given by the same emperor in 817 to the church of Saint-Etienne of Limoges. In it, in granting a *cella* to this church, the emperor forbids it be given away *"in beneficio."*[51] Two charters from nearby Auvergne show the same practice there. One dating from the period 817 to 834 tells of a *villa* given by the abbot of Brioude as a life *precarium* to two landowners, Aigobert and Gouraud.[52] The second, dating from 834, mentions a *mansus* and some vines which a certain priest has *"in beneficio"* and which a certain Witard has given to the same abbey.[53]

Perhaps we should add still another kind of benefice or *precarium* which concerned abbeys and churches of this period—those which resulted from gifts of land in which the owner keeps a life usufruct for himself and his family, often for more than one generation—generally with the payment of a regular *cens* to the religious establishment concerned. Charters illustrating such practices in this period are to be found from Auvergne and Rouergue in Aquitaine and from Béziers and the Maguelonne region of Septimania.[54]

Finally, we have a few examples of still another type of benefice or *precarium*—that used in the settlement of new land. An example of this, and the earliest which is to be found in the Midi, is an agreement between Bishop Wadald of Marseille and two individuals and their families in 817. By this agreement the latter were given some vacant land in the Arles region which they agreed to put into cultivation. After five years the

[49] *Ibid.*, no. 56.
[50] *Catalunya Carolingia*, II, 284–285.
[51] *Cartulaire de l'église de Saint-Etienne de Limoges*, ed. J. de Font-Réaulx, in *Bulletin de la société archéologique et historique du Limousin*, LXIX (1922), no. 86.
[52] *Grand Cart. de Brioude*, no. CCXCVI.
[53] *Cart. de Brioude*, no. 17.
[54] For examples in Auvergne see *Grand Cart. de Brioude*, no. CCCXXXVI, and *Cart. de Brioude*, nos. 252, 127, 231. For Rouergue see *Cart. de Conques.*, no. 1. For Septimania see *Hist. Gén. de Lang.*, II, no. 24, and *Cart. d'Aniane*, nos. 306 and 123.

land, now cultivated, was to be evenly divided between the church of Marseille and the cultivators. The cultivators' half, however, was clearly a *precarium* since they were to hold it for a lifetime only and could not dispose of it except with the consent of the bishop.[55] It seems probable that the grant of land by Caunes to Pinaud and his family, first as a benefice for six years and then as a *precarium*, was a similar *precarium* or agreement to put land into cultivation.[56] So too was that benefice in Auvergne which Witard mentions that he gave to a priest to set out *"vineale unum ad plantadum."*[57] All three seem similar to a system found later on all over the Midi, which is known as *medium plantum*.

Examination of *honores, beneficia*, and *precaria* during this period then, seems to lead to the following conclusions. They can be divided into three categories. The first consists of those *honores* and benefices given officials and *milites* and the like by Carolingian rulers and their counts. Those who receive them do so as *fideles* and *vassi* and in return are expected to render service of a military and governmental nature to those who grant them. But the second category of benefices or *precaria* seem quite different and much more similar to those found in the Midi in the pre-Carolingian period. These grants are in the form of land also, but they appear to carry with them no obligation of a military or governmental sort. They may carry with them some sense of clientage, that is all. And in almost every case they call for a payment in kind or in money, sometimes merely symbolical, which is referred to as a *cens*. They are also almost always limited to one lifetime. Equally interesting is the fact that such grants can be large ones of a *villa* or more, like those given to a Marfinus in the Lyonnais, or an Aigobert in Auvergne, or an Ebroin in Provence, or a Count Oliba in Carcassonne. Or they can consist of much smaller and less important pieces of property. Finally there is a third type of *precarium*, still rare in the Midi, but perhaps growing in importance. This consists of a grant of uncultivated land by a lay or ecclesiastical landowner which is given under a special agreement which has as its object the bringing of this property into cultivation and its division between landowner and cultivator after this end has been accomplished.

In the light of all this, the *aprisio*, examined earlier, assumes an interesting place in this society. The large *aprisio* holding seems to very much resemble a benefice given a supporter by a ruler or important official. Its

[55] *Cart. de Saint-Victor*, no. 163.
[56] *Hist. Gén. de Lang.*, II, no. 15.
[57] *Cart. de Brioude*, no. 17.

purpose was essentially military or governmental. On the other hand the small *aprisio* holding seems very much like the *medium plantum* both in its purpose and in its final result.

The foregoing pages, however, dealing as they do with the development and uses of the *aprisio* system and *honores, beneficia,* and *precaria* in the Midi and Catalonia may give the reader quite an erroneous impression—an impression that such systems of landholding were the most prevalent or important ones to be found in these regions during the reign of Louis the Pious and Charlemagne. Actually nothing could be further from the truth. The prevailing system remained allodial, just as had been the case in pre-Carolingian times. In the Rhone Valley, in Provence, in Septimania, the Toulousain, Rouergue, Auvergne, and the Limousin this is true, without exception. Frequently such allods were large estates like those belonging to Lempteus and his wife in the Vienne, Valence, and Grenoble regions about 830,[58] or those *villas* in the Limousin and Quercy which were the allodial property of Count Roger of Turenne in 823,[59] or those in Uzès, Maguelonne, and Rouergue which Dodila owned in 813.[60] They might include a castle like that owned by Sigebert and his wife in Provence in 790,[61] or a piece of property as small as the *mansus* which the priest Ardebert gave to Brioude in 817.[62] It seems also clear that allodial landowners understood the difference between such allods, owned outright, and lands held conditionally as benefices and *precaria*. We know this because two charters from Aquitaine show us landowners who specifically invoke the provisions of Roman law as giving them the right to dispose of their allods as they please[63]—the first of many such references to be found later in the Midi which use Roman law as a general protection of allodial rights.

It is equally interesting to note that the women of the Midi in this period, as earlier, could own allodial land in their own right. The case of Karissima in Auvergne, who, between 817 and 834, gave a *mansus* to her son Deacon Franausius, while keeping a life usufruct of it for herself, is a

[58] *Cart. de Grenoble,* no. 7.
[59] *Cart. de Beaulieu,* no. 185.
[60] *Hist. Gén. de Lang.,* II, no. 24.
[61] *Cart. de Saint-Victor,* no. 83.
[62] *Cart. de Brioude,* no. 252.
[63] That of 801 which shows Liutard giving his allods to Conques (*Cart. de Conques,* no. 1), and that of 823 which tells of the gifts of Count Roger of Turenne to a son, a daughter, and a church (*Cart. de Beaulieu,* no. 185).

case in point.⁶⁴ So is that of a certain Bestila, who, in 829, gave property which she had inherited to the abbey of Aniane.⁶⁵

Though small property owners like the above, owning only a *mansus* or so, are to be found, it was the *villa* which still seems to have been the prevailing unit of landholding in the Midi during this period. And most of these *villas*, judging from our sources, still seem to have been cultivated by a class of serfs or *coloni*, as had been the case before the Carolingians arrived. We find such serfs in the Lyonnais and Dauphiny, in Provence, in Septimania, in the Narbonnaise, and the Toulousain, and in Rouergue, Auvergne, and the Limousin.⁶⁶ Despite *aprisiones* and a wider use of *precaria* and benefices, then, the old landholding system of the Midi still continued relatively unchanged throughout the reigns of Charlemagne and Louis the Pious.

All of which brings us to the Church, the biggest landowner of all. What happened to it during this period? Here we find that, after the destruction caused by the conquest of Pepin and Charles Martel, the Church began to revive almost everywhere in the Midi and Catalonia. This seems particularly true of Septimania. Here, sparked by St. Benedict and his abbey of Aniane, we find established from the Rhone to Canegou in the Narbonnaise a whole series of new monasteries and *cellas*.⁶⁷ These establishments were soon joined by others newly established in Western Languedoc like Saint-Polycarpe in Razès, Arles in Vallespir, and Lagrasse, Saint-Hilaire, Caunes, and Montolieu⁶⁸ near Narbonne and Carcassonne.

⁶⁴ *Grand Cart. de Brioude*, no. CCCXXXVI.
⁶⁵ *Cart. d'Aniane*, no. 313.
⁶⁶ See mention of *colonicas* at Lyon in 805 in *Cartulaire Lyonnais*, ed. M. Guigue, I, no. 2. Serfs in Provence, Septimania, and the Narbonnaise are mentioned in *Cart. de Saint-Victor*, no. 291, and in "Descriptio Manciporum," in *ibid.*, pp. 633–656; in *Hist. Gén. de Lang.*, II, nos. 24, 30, 49, 71. *Ibid.*, no. 7, mentions the freeing of a serf in the Toulousain. Others are mentioned in Rouergue, Auvergne, and the Limousin in *Cart. de Conques*, no. 1; in *Hist. Gén. de Lang.*, II, nos. 47, 48; in *Grand Cart. de Brioude*, no. CVII; and in *Cart. de Beaulieu*, no. 185.
⁶⁷ See *Annals of Aniane*, anno 782, col. 9–10. On work of St. Benedict of Aniane in encouraging the building of abbeys in Aquitaine and "Gocia" (that is to say Septimania and the Spanish March) see also *Vita Benedicti Anianensis*, in *Mon. Ger. Hist. Scriptores*, XV. On Septimanian monasteries and *cellas* associated with Aniane see *Cart. d'Aniane*, nos. 1, 8, 9, 13.
⁶⁸ On Saint-Polycarpe in Razès founded by Atala see Abadal, "La Catalogne sous l'empire de Louis le Pieux," p. 269. See also the charter of Carloman which mentions that this abbey was founded by Charlemagne, in *Cart. de Carcassonne*, II, 598. About Arles see *Catalunya Carolingia*, II, 20–26, and P. Ponsch, "Les

A large proportion of these abbeys were founded on uncultivated land belonging to the royal *fisc*, land which was provided by the Carolingian rulers who also extended to them royal protection and other privileges.

A little later this movement spread into Catalonia where we find, as we have already noted, similar foundations in Roussillon, Ampurias, and Besalu dating from the reign of Louis the Pious[69] matching a somewhat earlier monastic revival which took place in Urgell, Pallars, and Ribagorça.[70] Even Gascony, where three monasteries and one *cella* existed by 817, shared in part in this founding and spread of monastic institutions.[71] Nor were cathedral churches ignored by Carolingian monarchs. Charlemagne granted immunities and other privileges to the church of Narbonne[72] and Louis the Pious extended them to Nîmes in 814, to Maguelonne in 819, and to Elne a little later.[73] Somewhat similar rights were given to the cathedral churches of Gerona and Urgell[74] as well.

Carolingian monarchs began to give special privileges and lands to the church in Aquitaine even earlier than was the case in Septimania or the Spanish March. The earliest indications of their interest seem to be Pepin's gifts of *villas* to Saint-Martial and Saint-Etienne of Limoges between 765 and 768[75] and Charlemagne's grant of lands and *villas* to Saint-Cybard of Angoulême in 770.[76] A little later, Louis the Pious, as king of Aquitaine, perhaps influenced by the example of St. Benedict of Aniane, made it a regular practice to restore the churches and abbeys of Poitou, the Limou-

origines de l'abbaye d'Arles," in *Études Roussillonnaises*, IV (1954–1955), 69–99; about Lagrasse see *Cart. de Carcassonne*, II, 208–209; about Saint-Hilaire see Cros-Meyrévielle, *Documents*, no. 4; about Caunes see *Cart. de Carcassonne*, IV, 67; and about Montolieu see Cros-Meyrévielle, *Documents*, no. 8.

[69] In addition to those abbeys mentioned in Chapter I, which were founded by Louis the Pious, there were others dating from these years such as Alet, founded by Count Bera in 813 (*Hist. Gén. de Lang.*, II, no. 23), and Saint-Clinian given privileges by Louis the Pious in 820 (*ibid.*, no. 71).

[70] On older foundations, like Taverna and Aláo, and new ones, like Santa-Grata, Gerrí, and Oveix, in Pallars and Ribagorça see Abadal, *Els Comtats de Pallars i Ribagorça*. On Senterada in Urgell, which was founded in 823 by Louis the Pious, see *Catalunya Carolingia*, II, 260–262.

[71] P. Labbé, *Sacrosancta Concilia*, IX, 603.

[72] See references to the property and privileges of the archbishop of Narbonne which were protected by a court in Narbonne, in *Hist. Gén. de Lang.*, II, no. 6.

[73] *Hist. Gén. de Lang.*, II, no. 30; *Cart. de Maguelonne*, no. 1; *Catalunya Carolingia*, II, 102–103.

[74] *Catalunya Carolingia*, II, 121–124, 284–285.

[75] *Ademar de Chabannes*, I, 50, pp. 60–61.

[76] *Ibid.*, II, 1, pp. 70–71.

Southern French and Catalan Society (778–828) 83

sin, Quercy, Auvergne, Velay, Rouergue, and the Toulousain.[77] To such restored monasteries like Moissac and Conques[78] should be added new foundations and *cellas* like Charroux in the Limousin,[79] and Mas d'Azil near Toulouse,[80] or the *cella* which Louis granted Saint-Etienne of Limoges in 817.[81] By this year the Council of Aix-la-Chapelle mentions thirteen abbeys in Aquitaine, four in the Toulousain and fourteen in Septimania.[82]

West of Aquitaine in the Valley of the Rhone as in Provence, however, our records show less evidence of rebuilding or of new foundations which date from this period. Lérins seems to have been given privileges by these Carolingian monarchs[83] and so was Saint-Victor of Marseille,[84] but there are few other indications of a vigorous monasticism. In fact that inventory in 802 of property belonging to Saint-Victor of Marseille seems to show a significant decay of the patrimony of this abbey, with only about half the *villas* belonging to it still in cultivation.[85] That this was not merely local can be seen when one examines the church of Lyon which, according to Bishop Ledrad in 807, needed a complete rebuilding of its churches and monastic establishments and which had many *villas* belonging to its patrimony vacant and uncultivated like those of Saint-Victor of Marseille.[86] In this part of Southern France a reformed and revitalized Church was still a distant prospect rather than a present reality.

Now there has been a general tendency on the part of historians to give to Carolingian rulers the credit for most of this church revival and monastic vigor which we find in Southern France and Catalonia during this period. There is much truth in this, for without their support it could

[77] Astronomus, *Vita Hludovici*, ch. 19, pp. 616–617. The Astronomus mentions twelve older monasteries which were rebuilt (*"reparata"*) and nine new ones founded, mostly in Septimania and the Toulousain.
[78] *Hist. Gén. de Lang.*, II, no. 7; *Cart. de Conques*, no. 580. See also mention of the Abbey of Saint-Antonin to which Louis the Pious gave privileges in 818 (*ibid.*, no. 48).
[79] *Chartes de l'abbaye de Charroux*, no. 3.
[80] *Hist. Gén. de Lang.*, II, no. 46.
[81] *Cart. de Saint-Etienne de Limoges*, no. 86. On the immunity given this cathedral church by Charlemagne and Louis the Pious see *ibid.*, no. 85.
[82] Labbé, *Sacrosancta Concilia*, IX, 603.
[83] This rests on a charter which may be spurious but purports to be one given the abbey in 798 by Pepin, king of Italy and brother of Louis the Pious (*Cart. de Lérins*, no. 290).
[84] *Cart. de Saint-Victor*, no. 8.
[85] *Ibid.*, no. 291, and "Descriptio mancipiorum" in *ibid.*, II, 633–656.
[86] *Cart. Lyonnais*, nos. 2, 7.

not have succeeded, just as there would have been no Carolingian Renaissance without their support. But one must also not lose sight of the fact that there was also strong *local* support for the Church, and without such support the revival could not have taken place either. The Astronomus, as a matter of fact, mentions the laity of Aquitaine who assisted Louis the Pious in his work of rebuilding the abbeys and churches of this region.[87] One should add churchmen too. Individual cases bear this out whether it be a bishop, like Aguarnius of Cahors who in 783 gave a number of *villas* to Moissac,[88] a count, like Roger of Turenne who in 823 endowed establishments in the Limousin[89] or a simple landowner, like Liutard who in 801 gave property to Conques.[90] In Septimania and Provence landowners like Dodila, the benefactor of Psalmodi[91] and Sigefred who gave generously to Saint-Victor of Marseille[92] reveal the same local support given the church.

Around Narbonne and in Catalonia we find the same thing happening. It was upon the request of Count Rampon that Louis the Pious gave privileges to Saint-Stephen of Banyols in 822,[93] just as it was on the plea of Count Gaucelm of Roussillon and Count Matfred of Urgell that a year later he granted immunities to the abbeys of Saint-André de Sureda and Senterada.[94] In 827 when King Pepin of Aquitaine gave a *villa* to Lagrasse[95] and in 835 when he added property to the patrimony of Montolieu[96] he did so at the request of Count Oliba of Carcassone. The founding of new abbeys and *cellas* in the Midi and Catalonia, then, like the revitalization of older establishments and churches, owed much to local initiative. It was a joint effort of Carolingian monarchs, of Carolingian officials, and of churchmen and landholders who represented the society of Southern France and Catalonia.

There remains one final aspect of this church revival that needs to be examined—its economic results. We have already noted how most of the newly founded abbeys and *cellas* in Septimania, Aquitaine, and the Spanish March were located on uncultivated and vacant land which the

[87] Astronomus, *Vita Hludovici*, ch. 19, p. 617.
[88] *Hist. Gén. de Lang.*, II, no. 7.
[89] *Cart. de Beaulieu*, no. 185.
[90] *Cart. de Conques*, no. 1.
[91] *Hist. Gén. de Lang.*, II, no. 24.
[92] *Cart. de Saint-Victor*, no. 83.
[93] *Catalunya Carolingia*, II, 45–47.
[94] *Ibid.*, pp. 260–262, 268–269.
[95] *Cart. de Carcassonne*, I, 70.
[96] *Ibid.*, pp. 70–71.

Southern French and Catalan Society (778-828)

monks had to put into cultivation, either through their own efforts or by calling in cultivators to do this for them.[97] This new land which was broken for cultivation was sometimes called an *aprisio* since it much resembled those grants of vacant land given *hispani* and others in the same regions.[98] How extensive were such lands which were put into cultivation by the abbeys of the region? It is difficult to say. But it would be unwise to overestimate the extent of such land during the reigns of Charlemagne and Louis the Pious. The same is true of similar results of clearing and cultivation by the laity. In Catalonia only a beginning was made and the same seems to be true of Auvergne and central Aquitaine.[99] As for Provence and the Valley of the Rhone, the vacant *colonicas* of the abbey of Saint-Victor and the church of Lyon show that much remained to be done in this respect.[100] And here it seems to have been the *medium plantum* system rather than the *aprisio* which was the method used in putting new land into cultivation. But despite such limitations there can be little doubt that in many parts of Southern France and Catalonia enough was accomplished to result in some increased agricultural production, which in turn made possible an increase in the population of the countryside. A beginning had at least been made, for the first time since

[97] A charter issued by Louis the Pious in 819 says that Conques was founded where Moslem *"illam terram pene totam devasterunt,"* and an *oratorio* was constructed *"in heremum"* (*Cart. de Conques*, no. 580). In 807 a charter of Charlemagne's gave to the abbey of Lagrasse, from the royal *fisc*, a whole valley and land that was obviously uncultivated (*Cart. de Carcassonne*, II, 209–210). In 819 Louis the Pious gave to the abbey of Saint-Genesius de Fonts land *"ex heremo traxerunt ex apprisione"* (*Catalunya Carolingia*, II, 206–207). In 822 the abbey of Saint-Stephen of Banyols was founded in what our charter calls a "desert" (*ibid.*, pp. 45–47), while in 823 Senterada was founded on land called *"herema,"* (*ibid.*, pp. 260–262).

[98] The term *ex apprisione* is used in a charter of 819 which mentions land belonging to Saint-Genesius des Fonts (*Catalunya Carolingia*, II, 206–207), while in Roussillon according to a charter of 834 the church of Elne is given land which *"sui homines ex heremo traxerunt"* (*ibid.*). Ten years later Possidonius of this church is said to possess a *villa* which *"de heremo vastate ad culturam frugem perduxisset"* (*ibid.*, pp. 263–265). See also mention of the *apprisiones* of an abbey in Pallars and Ribagorça in F. Valls-Taberner, *Els origines dels comtats de Pallars i Ribagorça*, p. 5.

[99] See later chapters on the great amount of clearing done in these regions in the late ninth and tenth centuries.

[100] See earlier references to those *"colonicas absas"* found in the Lyonnais and in Provence. See also the comments of R. Latouche, "Quelques aperçus sur le manse en Provence au Xe et au XIe siècles," in *Recueil de travaux offerts à M. C. Brunel*, II, 101–103.

the Roman Empire, in reversing the tendency toward rural depopulation. A foundation had been laid for further agrarian progress in parts of Southern France and Catalonia.

Peace and order and this limited agrarian advance all help explain another feature of this period—a certain commercial revival. One aspect of this can be seen in the revival of mints. In 750 there was not a single mint in operation in Carolingian territory south of Poitou and Burgundy.[101] They were rare elsewhere in Carolingian territory, but they did exist. After 770 this situation began to change. As a result, during the reign of Charlemagne we find mints reviving at Vienne, Arles, Avignon, Uzès, and Marseille in the Valley of the Rhone, and at Béziers, Carcassonne, and Narbonne in Septimania, and Barcelona in Catalonia.[102] In Aquitaine existing mints at Clermont and Poitiers were joined by others which were located at Saint-Maixent, Melle, Limoges, Augoulême, Saintes, Agen, and Toulouse.[103] During the reign of Louis the Pious others were established at Ampurias, and at Bordeaux and Dax in Gascony.[104] Coin hoards dating from the early years of Louis the Pious' reign discovered at Veuillen in Poitou[105] and at Belvezet near Uzès[106] show a wide circulation of money in the Midi during this period in contrast to the localism found during the immediately pre-Carolingian period.

This increased economic activity was reflected in commerce which reached the Atlantic coasts of Aquitaine from Northwestern Spain[107] and in commerce carried on by Arab and Jewish traders who reached Arles and other ports in Septimania and Provence.[108] Though overland trade with Northwestern Italy via the *clusae* was more important than that which arrived by sea,[109] the latter was important enough so that Louis the Pious felt it worth while to grant the bishop of Marseille in 822 the *teloneum* on salt and on ships which arrived in this region from Italy.[110] Agricultural growth and internal commerce had thus stimulated sufficient trade by 828 so that the Midi was now linked with Italy, Spain, and the wider Mediterranean world of commerce.

[101] M. Prou, *Catalogue des Monnaies Carolingiennes*, pp. xci–cix.
[102] A. Lewis, *The Northern Seas A.D. 300–1100*, p. 187.
[103] *Ibid.*, p. 190.   [104] *Ibid.*   [105] *Ibid.*, p. 188.
[106] *Ibid.*, pp. 188–189.
[107] *Ibid.*, pp. 191–192.
[108] Theodulphus, bishop of Orleans, *Pavrensis ad Judices*, ed. E. Dummler, in *Mon. Ger. Hist. Poet. Lat. Aevi*, I, 499; and Ibn Khodâdbeh, *Book of Routes*, ed. R. de Groje, in *Biblioteca Geographiae Arabiae*, IX, 114–116.
[109] Lewis, *The Northern Seas*, pp. 184–185, 189.
[110] *Cart. de Saint-Victor*, no. 11.

Such then was the society of the Midi and the Spanish March at the time of Charlemagne and Louis the Pious. It was a society which still remained essentially what it had been before the Carolingian conquest, but one to which the new *aprisio* system, more use of *precaria* and benefices, and a revived Church were bringing some significant changes. It was one in which a reviving agriculture, a new series of mints, and new commerce were, for a period, modifying its parochialism and bringing it into the main stream of development of the Carolingian Empire. Such economic growth, however, was to prove in some ways abortive, as the sons of Louis the Pious in their quarrels over their heritage broke asunder the Carolingian Empire and helped bring a new and less hopeful era to lands which lay south of the Loire.

III
THE DECLINE OF ROYAL POWER, 828–900

CHAPTER VI

Civil War, Invasion, and the Breakdown of Royal Authority

THE LAST YEARS of the reign of Louis the Pious saw the beginning of a period of disorder which was to affect most regions of Southern France and the Spanish March for some seven decades. By the end of this period royal authority had all but vanished over the lands which lay south of Poitou and Burgundy. A new order of things had emerged in which real, *de facto* power had passed into the hands of a series of noble families who, by hereditary right, ruled local areas and were powerful enough to ignore the royal government.

The story of the emergence of such independent local ruling families is a complex one, and historians are still very much in disagreement over the details which attended the process and even, in some respects, over basic causes. It does, however, seem to be agreed that this change was due to a series or combination of factors. Perhaps the most important one was the civil strife which continued intermittently among various members of the Carolingian royal house and then between them and the rising Capetian family. Almost equally important as a basic factor were invasions by Vikings and Moslems which proved the inability of the royal government to protect its realm. Finally there was the policy of elevating certain officials to great authority by giving them command over two or more counties of the empire which, more often than not, resulted in their disloyalty to the central authorities as they attempted to make themselves completely independent.

All three of these factors were, as a matter of fact, interrelated. Dissension within the empire and civil war encouraged outside attack. Danger along the frontiers and actual invasions made it necessary to give broad powers over wide areas to certain counts. Such officials increased their authority still further by playing one side against the other in the disputes which the various heirs of Louis the Pious had with one another. They could even negotiate or ally themselves with foreign invaders. Finally they could become powerful enough to revolt openly, which encouraged invaders and started the whole cycle going again.

Faced by this dangerous cycle Carolingian rulers strove to maintain their authority by maintaining peace, whenever possible, along their frontiers and by delicately balancing the power of their dangerous subordinates, the counts, by removing some from office and playing the rest one against the other as the occasion demanded. The remarkable thing is that they succeeded in maintaining their authority as long as they did, from the time of Bernard of Septimania to that of Boson of Provence. Yet in each crisis they were forced to give up a little more royal authority to gain support, until by the time of Charles the Fat they had little power left. When Eudes, of the new Capetian family, became king late in the century, he found himself a monarch who possessed only shadowy rights south of Poitou and Burgundy. An old era had ended and a new one was at hand.

Within this pattern of development let us examine in some detail the events of this period. By 829 Louis the Pious' premature division of his empire among his heirs was already affecting Southern France and Catalonia. One son, Pepin, as we have noted, ruled the sub-kingdom of Aquitaine, now smaller in extent than had been the case earlier, since in 817 Septimania and the maritime counties of Catalonia had been taken from it and placed under direct imperial control. Provence, the Lyonnais, and Viennois formed part of a middle kingdom which was marked out as the portion of Lothaire, Louis' oldest son.[1] In actual control of the frontiers of each of these regions were subordinate officials who exercised authority over wide areas. Berengar, count of Toulouse, who bore the title of *dux* and *marchio*, seems to have been in charge of the Gascon border and the interior counties of the Spanish March. Bernard, son of Duke William of Toulouse, controlled Septimania and Barcelona as *dux* and *marchio*, while his brother Gaucelm was count of Ampurias and Roussillon.[2] Provence at this time was probably also controlled by a *dux* and

---

[1] "Ordinatio Imperii," in Boretius, *Capitularia*, I, no. 136, pp. 270–271. In 829, however, Louis changed his division of the empire, by attempting to set up a special kingdom for his fourth son, Charles, the issue of his second marriage (Theganus, *Vita Hludovici imperatoris*, ed. G. Pertz, ch. 35, in *Mon. Ger. Hist. Scriptores*, II, 597; and Nithard, *Histoire*, I, ch. 3, p. 8). This set in motion revolts among his older three sons which from 830 on helped to destroy the unity of the empire.

[2] On Berengar see J. Calmette, "Comtes de Toulouse inconnus," in *Mélanges*

Civil War, Invasion, and Breakdown of Royal Authority 93

marchio, as it was after 835, but we do not know the name of the count who controlled it as heir to Count Leibulf's authority.³

Difficulties along the frontiers, which we have discussed earlier, seem to have been the reason for the establishment of such extraordinary commands—difficulties marked by the failure to recover Aragón and Navarre after the disastrous expedition of Count Ebles and Count Aznar in 824 (which left a restive Gascony), and the revolt of Aizo in Catalonia in 826, which resulted in the loss of Ausona and other border marches that had been gained between 802 and 814. In the face of such a crisis Count Bernard had held firm in Barcelona⁴ and Count Berengar seems to have restored the situation along the borders of the Toulousain, but they could do little more without additional military assistance.⁵ This assistance they did not receive, since the army raised in Northern France by Pepin and Lothaire never reached them. The peace which had to be made with Cordova in 828 left the custodians of the empire's southern frontiers still very much on the defensive.⁶

Such was the situation in the Midi when, in 830, while leading an expedition into Britanny, Louis the Pious' three older sons revolted against him, most probably because of resentment over his plans to carve a kingdom for Charles, his fourth son, out of land already allotted to them.⁷ This revolt seems to have had important repercussions in the Midi and Catalonia. Count Berengar of Toulouse stayed loyal to the emperor Louis. Count Bernard of Septimania favored his rebellious sons. There-

---

Antoine Thomas, pp. 83–88, and R. de Abadal i de Vinyals, "Un diplôme inconnu de Louis le Pieux pour le comte Oliba de Carcassonne," in *Annales du Midi*, LXI (1949), 345–350. On Bernard and Gaucelm see J. Calmette, *De Bernardo, Sancti Willelmi filio*. For sources see *Annales Regni Francorum*, ed. G. Kurze, anno 829, p. 154; Astronomus, *Vita Hludovici*, ch. 43, pp. 636–637; and Nithard, *Histoire*, I, ch. 4, p. 10. For an over-all view see R. de Abadal i de Vinyals, "La Catalogne sous l'empire de Louis le Pieux," in *Études Roussillonnaises*, V (1956), 67–80.

³ It was perhaps Warin, brother of Bernard of Auvergne, who was duke and *marchio* under Lothaire in 843. See E. Duprat in *Bouches du Rhône: Encyclopédie départementale*, II, 132–134.

⁴ Astronomus, *Vita Hludovici*, ch. 43, pp. 636–637.

⁵ *Ibid.*, ch. 42, p. 632.

⁶ *Ibid.*, ch. 41, p. 631, and *Annales Regni Francorum*, anno 828, p. 152. See a summary of situation in R. de Abadal i de Vinyals, *Els Primers Comtes Catalans*, pp. 222–223.

⁷ On the background of this revolt see Theganus, *Vita Hludovici*, ch. 36, p. 598, and Nithard, *Histoire*, I, ch. 4–5, pp. 8–10. See also F. Ganshof, "Observations sur l'Ordinatio Imperii de 817," in *Festschrift Guido Kisch*, pp. 30–31.

Map 2. SOUTHERN FRANCE AND CATALONIA (*circa* 814).

key to symbols

Counties

Al—Albigeois	Me—Melgueil
Am—Ampurias	Na—Narbonne
An—Angoulême	Ne—Navarre
Ar—Aragón	Nm—Nîmes
Au—Ausona	Pa—Pallars
Av—Auvergne	Pe—Périgord
Ba—Barcelona	Po—Poitou
Be—Berga	Pr—Provence
Br—Berry	Qu—Quercy
Bs—Besalu	Ra—Ribagorça
Bx—Bordeaux	Ro—Rouergue
Bz—Béziers	Rs—Roussillon
Ca—Carcassonne	Sa—Saintonge
Ce—Cerdanya	Su—Suse
Fe—Fézensac	To—Toulouse
Ga—Gascony	Ur—Urgell
Ge—Gerona	Uz—Uzès
Gv—Gevaudun	Ve—Velay
Lm—Limousin	Vn—Viennois
Ly—Lyonnais	Vv—Vivarais

fore, when Louis won out, Bernard fled to Catalonia where he and his partisans held out against both Louis and his loyal Count Berengar of Toulouse until the latter's death in 835. With Berengar's death Count Bernard returned to imperial favor, and as his reward received Toulouse and other counties of Septimania.[8] It was probably due to Bernard that Count Asnar Galindo, a partisan of Berengar, was then removed as count of Urgell-Cerdanya and this charge given to Sunifred, a relative of Count Oliba I of Carcassonne.[9] Not until 838, however, was Sunifred able to drive Asnar Galindo from Pallars and Ribagorça which he had usurped in these troubled times.[10] It is also probably the shift of power to Bernard from Berengar which was responsible for troubles with Aznar, count of Hither Gascony, who in 836 is reported to have been killed in a revolt and who was succeeded by his brother Sánchez over the strong objections of Pepin, king of Aquitaine.[11]

By 838 peace had come to the Midi and Spanish March in regions along

---

[8] Abadal, "Un diplôme inconnu de Louis le Pieux," pp. 50–53, and "La Catalogne sous l'empire de Louis le Pieux," pp. 70–95. See also M. Chaume, "Bérenger, Comte de Toulouse," in *Annales du Midi*, LII (1940), 65–67.

[9] It seems probable that this Sunifred is the same Sunifred who in 829 is called a *fidelis* by Louis the Pious and who was a son of Count Borell of Urgell-Cerdanya-Ausona (*Catalunya Carolingia*, II, 324). According to a charter of 873 he was the father of Counts Guifred and Miró of Cerdanya (P. de Marca, *Marca hispanica sive limes hispanicus*, I, appendix 27 [hereafter cited as *Marca hispanica*]). Abadal in his "Un diplôme inconnu de Louis le Pieux," pp. 53–57, advances the connection between Counts Guifred and Miró and the earlier Count Bellon of Carcassonne was through the distaff side, since Count Sunifred married Ermissende, a daughter of Count Bellon. This would make Guifred and Miró of Cerdanya and Oliba II and Acfred of Carcassonne first cousins. In later writings he has preferred to regard Count Sunifred as descended only from Count Bellon, and do away with any identification of him as that *fidelis* of Louis the Pious who is called the son of Count Borell (see Abadal "La Catalogne sous l'empire de Louis le Pieux," pp. 83–91, and *Els Primers Comtes Catalans,* pp. 222–225). On the whole Abadal's first solution of the problem seems the more reasonable one, and it is probably wiser to accept his original identification of this Sunifred with Sunifred the *fidelis* of 829 and so make him grandson of *both* Count Borell and Count Bellon.

[10] See Abadal, *Els Comtats de Pallars i Ribagorça*, pp. 107–108, on Asnar Galindo's usurpation of these counties. See also the comments of C. Higounet, "Les Aznars, un tentatif groupement des comtés gascons et pyrénéens au IXe siècle," in *Annales du Midi*, LXI (1949).

[11] *Annales Bertiniani*, ed. E. Waitz, anno 836, p. 12. See also Higounet, "Les Aznars," and L. Auzias, *L'Aquitaine Carolingienne (778–987)*, pp. 89–90.

Civil War, Invasion, and Breakdown of Royal Authority 97

the frontiers. But it did not last for long. For in that year King Pepin died and a group of Aquitanian nobles led by Ermenon, count of Poitou, defied the emperor Louis and proclaimed Pepin's young son Pepin II, king of Aquitaine. Louis was forced to lead an army in Aquitaine to put down this rebellion and, according to Ademar of Chabannes, replaced a number of the disloyal counts. He gave Rannoux the county of Poitou, Turpio that of Angoulême, and made Landry count of Saintes.[12] Count Bernard of Septimania, who appears to have stayed neutral during this rebellion, was not removed from office. Perhaps this was because Louis did not feel strong enough to do this. More probably, however, he died in 840 before he had an opportunity to act.

This first period of civil wars, though, had other results for the Midi besides those already discussed. It encouraged outside attacks. These began in 838 when Pepin II was rebelling in Aquitaine and when Count Asnar Galindo was being expelled from Pallars and Ribagorça by partisans of Count Bernard. The first was an attack by Moslem pirates on Marseille, interesting because for twenty-five years the coasts of Provence had been free of such assaults.[13] The second was a Viking attack directed against Aquitaine which since 820, also, had been free of such raids.[14] It was probably in response to this Viking raid that Louis, in reorganizing Aquitaine following Pepin II's revolt, gave to Séguin the county of Bordeaux and bestowed on him the title of *dux* of Bordeaux.[15] Probably he hoped, in doing so, to set up an important command which would guard the Garonne River entrance into Aquitaine. Perhaps with the same idea in mind in the same year he made Count Warin *dux* and *marchio* of Provence, a position he certainly held in 843, if not earlier.[16]

These attempts by the emperor Louis in his last years to reorganize and bring peace to the empire, however, were to prove unsuccessful, for when

[12] *Ademar de Chabannes*, III, 16, p. 132. On the other hand Loup of Ferrières in 840 writes that Rainald, not Turpio, was count of Angoulême, and he mentions that Gerald, who favored Pepin, was count of Saintonge rather than Auvergne. Loup de Ferrières, *Correspondence*, ed. L. Levillain, 17, 1, in *Mon. Ger. Hist. Epistolae*, I, 98.

[13] Duprat, in *Bouches du Rhône*, p. 134.

[14] H. Shetelig, *An Introduction to the Viking History of Western Europe*, pp. 109–110; A. Lewis, *The Northern Seas A. D. 300–1100*, p. 251; and T. Kendrick, *History of the Vikings*, pp. 227–228.

[15] *Ademar de Chabannes*, III, 16, p. 132.

[16] See Duprat in *Bouches du Rhône*, pp. 133–140, on the changes which took place in Provence during this period.

he died in 840 civil wars broke out at once. These civil wars were complex in character, particularly as far as Charles the Bald, Louis' son and heir for France, was concerned. On the one hand, in alliance with his brother, Louis of Germany, he directed his efforts against his other brother, Lothaire, and his middle kingdom of Lorraine. On the other hand, within his domains he had to deal with his nephew Pepin II, who was attempting to set up an independent kingdom of Aquitaine. Down to 843, it was his struggle with Lothaire which claimed most of his energies, a struggle that need not concern us here.[17] After that time, for a decade he devoted his attention primarily to Pepin II.

The war in Aquitaine between Charles and Pepin II was a long and bitter one, primarily because Pepin had been given time to entrench himself solidly in the southern portion of this province along the borders of Gascony, and because Bernard of Septimania was again playing an equivocal role. Charles was fortunate to be freed of Bernard by his death in 844 but his son, William, an open ally of Pepin, made trouble for him despite the loyalty displayed by the Gothic counts of Carcassonne and Catalonia.[18] Charles even suffered a serious defeat in 845 that forced him to make a temporary peace with Pepin, his rival.[19] Gradually, however, the tide turned. In 849, Count Frédélon deserted Pepin and surrendered to Charles the important city of Toulouse.[20] In 850, Sánchez, duke of Gascony, submitted.[21] William, rebel son of Bernard of Septimania, who in 848 and 849 appears to have invaded Catalonia and allied himself with the Moslems, was beaten in battle and then slain when he tried to take refuge in Barcelona in 850.[22] When Pepin was delivered to Charles in 852 as a prisoner by the duke of Gascony,[23] Aquitaine seemed to be firmly in

[17] Charles the Bald, however, was on the Gascon frontier in 842 which shows his interest in rallying doubtful Aquitaine lords to his side during this period (F. Lot and G. Tessier *et alii, Recueil des actes de Charles II le Chauve*, I, 25). See note 12 on the pro-Pepin sentiment among some of these lords.

[18] Abadal, *Els Primers Comtes Catalans*, p. 223.

[19] *Ibid.*, pp. 180–181.

[20] *Chronici Fontanellensis fragmentum*, ed. G. Pertz, anno 849, in *Mon. Ger. Hist. Scriptores*, II, 42.

[21] *Ibid.*, anno 850, p. 43.

[22] On William's attempts to seize Catalonia after occupying Barcelona and Ampurias see *Annales Bertiniani*, anno 848, and *Chron. Fontanellensis*, anno 849, p. 43. See also Abadal, *Els Primers Comtes Catalans*, pp. 181–182.

[23] *Annales Bertiniani*, anno 852, and *Chronicum Aquitanicum*, ed. G. Pertz, anno 852, in *Mon. Ger. Hist. Scriptores*, II, 252.

Charles' hands. Pepin, however, made one last effort to secure his inheritance. In 862 or 863 Marquis Humfrid revolted against Charles along with Charles' son whom he had made sub-king of Aquitaine.[24] Pepin, released from custody during the disorders that ensued, raised the standard of revolt again. This time he did not hesitate to ally himself with Viking invaders of the Midi.[25] Thwarted in this last effort, he died soon afterwards leaving no heirs who could dispute control over the Midi with Charles the Bald.

This long struggle over Aquitaine between Carolingian rivals lasting from 840 to 852 and then again from 862 to 865 only partly explains the disorders which affected the Midi and Spanish March during this period. Equally disturbing were invasions by Moslems and by Viking pirates which bore particularly heavily on certain regions. Let us first consider those attacks which originated in Moslem Spain. The first such attack was launched by Cordova in 842, some fourteen years after peace had been made in 828. It was timed to coincide with that period of intense disorder in the Carolingian Empire which followed the death of Louis the Pious. Directed against Cerdanya, the invasion had little success, since it seems to have been contained by Count Sunifred of Urgell-Cerdanya before it reached the other side of the Pyrenees.[26] It was perhaps as a reward for this success that in 844 Sunifred was given the counties of Barcelona and Gerona upon the death of Bernard of Septimania. He apparently handled the defense of Catalonia and its marches skilfully, for in 847 envoys from Cordova went to Rheims to make peace with Charles the Bald.[27]

This peace did not last long. By 848 Count Sunifred was dead and William, rebel son of Bernard, had invaded Catalonia. Taking advantage of the inevitable disorders which ensued, the Moslems, probably in alliance with William, attacked and took the city of Gerona.[28] They continued hostilities after William's death in 850, and we learn that in 851—

[24] On this revolt see J. Calmette, "Onfroy, Marquis de Gothie," in *Études Médiévales*.

[25] See J. Calmette, "Le siège de Toulouse par les Normands," in *Annales du Midi*, XXIX (1917), 171–183.

[26] J. Millás-Vallicrosa, "Els textos d'historiadors musalmans referents a la Catalunya carolingia," in *Cuaderns d'Estudi*, XIV, nos. 103–104. See also C. Sánchez-Albornoz, "La auténtica batalla de Clavejo," in *Cuadernos de Historia de España*, IX, 105–109.

[27] *Annales Bertiniani*, anno 847.

[28] *Annales Bertiniani*, anno 852; *Chron. Fontanellensis*, anno 849, p. 42 and Millás-Vallicrosa, "El textos," nos. 107–108.

852 a Moslem army captured Barcelona itself and sacked it.[29] They also appear to have extended their attacks toward the Northwest into Navarre and Gascony where at about this time they seem to have captured Duke Sánchez and his brother-in-law Count Ermenon of Périgord in battle.[30] It may have been this Moslem threat which caused Duke Sánchez to desert Pepin and come to terms with Charles the Bald both in 850 and in 852. This new solidarity on the Carolingian side, however, did not stop the Moslems from making one more important raid on Catalonia, one in which in 856 they captured the castle of Tarrassa near the city of Barcelona.[31] Then they negotiated peace with Marquis Humfrid, Charles the Bald's new viceroy in the Midi, a peace which was to last some thirty years down to the time of Count Guifred later in the century.[32]

No doubt such Moslem incursions between 842 and 856 caused serious damage in parts of the Spanish March, but they did not directly affect the rest of the Midi. Quite different, however, was the case of another set of invasions, those which took place in Aquitaine and Gascony during the same period and were the result of the activities of Viking pirates. Serious Viking attacks seem to have begun in 843, five years after their first probing raid of 838. In this year, while all eyes were fixed on the civil war between Pepin II and Charles the Bald, the Vikings invaded the Loire region.[33] Next year, after wintering on the island of Noirmoutier, they began an assault on the Garonne region. Meeting little opposition from local counts, who, as the chronicler puts it, were busy fighting each other, they penetrated far into the interior and for some five years plundered the land without serious opposition. Séguin, count of Bordeaux and Saintes, who seems to have been charged with the defense of the Garonne,

[29] Millás-Vallicrosa, "El textos," no. 109; *Annales Bertiniani*, anno 852; and Sánchez-Albornoz, "La auténtica batalla."
[30] *Miracles de Sainte Foy* in *Recueil des Historiens de Gaules et de la France*, ed. D. Bouquet *et alii*, VII, 656, and *Translatio Sanctae Faustae e Vasconia*, in *ibid.*, pp. 344–345. See also *Chronicon de Sebastian de Soulanges*, in *España sagrada*, ed. E. Flórez, XIII, 691.
[31] Both the *Annales Bertiniani*, anno 852, and the *Chron. Aquitanicum*, anno 852, mention that Sánchez, count of Gascony, surrendered Pepin II to Charles the Bald. On the Moslem conquest of the castle of Tarrassa see Millás-Vallicrosa, *"El textos,"* no. 109.
[32] See Abadal, *Els Primers Comtes Catalans*, pp. 178–187, on these decades of peace along the Moslem-Catalan frontier.
[33] Lewis, *The Northern Seas*, p. 251. See also *Chronique de Nantes*, ed. R. Merlet, pp. 14–18, and *Annales Engolensis*, ed. G. Pertz, in *Mon. Ger. Hist. Scriptores*, XVI, 484.

was slain by the invaders in 845, and they ranged widely, sacking Bordeaux, Saintes, Angoulême, Périgord, Poitiers, and other centers here and in Gascony, as well as a number of monasteries and *castella*.[34] The end of the civil war between Pepin and Charles the Bald may have reduced their freedom of action to a certain extent, but they could still launch periodic raids into the interior from their fortified island bases along the coast. Such raids were only interrupted by their great Mediterranean expedition under Hastings and Bjorn between 859 and 862, which seems to have stripped the coast of Aquitaine of pirates temporarily.[35] After their return in 862, however, they again began to raid the interior, killing Count Turpio of Angoulême in 863[36] and with the help of Pepin II launching an unsuccessful attack on Toulouse.[37] By 870 Archbishop Frotaire had been forced by their activities to abandon Bordeaux[38] and in 875 the abbey of Saint-Cybard of Angoulême felt their fury.[39] Gradually, however, their attacks slackened off, as local counts like Vulgrin raised castles against them which effectively limited their freedom of action. Down to 930, however, they continued to vex Western Aquitaine with their raids, and indeed the Viking menace remained endemic along western Gallic shores right into the first years of the eleventh century.

While portions of Aquitaine, Gascony, and the Spanish March were feeling the effect of such invasions, the Mediterranean shores of the Midi did not escape unscathed. This is particularly true of Provence. Information concerning Provence during this period is limited, but we do know that in 842 the Moslems followed up their raid on Marseille with another on Arles.[40] Six years later, in 848, Marseille was attacked again, this time by Greek pirates.[41] These attacks may have been the result of disturbed conditions in this region following the revolt of Duke Fulcrad, successor

---

[34] *Ademar de Chabannes*, III, 17, p. 134, and *Chron. Aquitanicum*, anno 845, p. 252.

[35] See A. Vasiliev, *The Russian Attack on Constantinople in 860*, for the best account of this expedition.

[36] *Ademar de Chabannes*, III, 19, p. 136, and *Chron. Aquitanicum*, anno 863, p. 252.

[37] See Calmette, "Le siège de Toulouse par les Normands."

[38] Johannis VIII, *Papae Epistolae*, in Migne, *Patrologia latina*, CXXVI, no. 36, and *Annales Bertiniani*, anno 877, p. 149. See also Archbishop Frotaire's interest in the abbey of Brioude where he served as abbot from 874 to 879, after his flight from Bordeaux (*Cart. de Brioude*, nos. 132, 334, 236, 197, 268).

[39] *Ademar de Chabannes*, III, 19, p. 137.

[40] Duprat in *Bouches du Rhône*, pp. 134–135.

[41] *Ibid*.

to Warin in 845, a revolt which the emperor Lothaire does not appear to have completely suppressed.[42] Whatever the causes, the Moslem pirate menace continued. In 859 Arles was fortified against such attacks[43] and at about this time the monks of Psalmodi were forced to abandon their abbey in the Camargue.[44]

For a brief period the Moslem menace was even replaced by another, that of the Vikings. In 859–860, the Mediterranean expedition of Hastings and Bjorn, after plundering abbeys in Roussillon, wintered in the Camargue. During their stay they seem to have raided over a wide area, as far north as Valence where they were checked by Count Gerald of Vienne.[45] When the Vikings sailed away the Moslems returned and seem to have set up a pirate base at Maguelonne. Efforts made by the archbishop of Arles in 869 to defeat them failed[46] until the building of castles and other fortifications in the region so limited their effectiveness that between 884 and 889 they shifted their center of activity to the east. At Fraxinetum during this period they established a base from which they were for many years to vex the coasts and the interior of Provence.[47]

During these years of Moslem depredations in Provence, this region, like the rest of the Valley of the Rhone, was disturbed by Carolingian rivalries. This part of the Midi in 840 had been allotted to the emperor Lothaire and in 843 was still part of his middle kingdom. When he died about 855 his domains were divided among his sons, Lothaire II inheriting Lorraine, Louis II Italy, and Charles Provence.[48] Charles' kingdom of Provence, stretching along the Rhone from the Lyonnais to the Mediterranean, seems to have been only loosely controlled by this ineffectual prince. Real authority lay in the hands of Count Gerald of Vienne who was in direct charge of the Lyonnais and Viennois.[49] When Charles died about 865 his domains excited the cupidity of his uncle, Charles the

---

[42] *Ibid.*, pp. 132–133. Note, however, that in 845, according to a charter of this date, Marseille was ruled by a Count Adalbert (*Cart. de Saint-Victor*, no. 26).
[43] Duprat, in *Bouches du Rhône*, pp. 151–152.
[44] *Ibid.* Note that monks fled from Psalmodi to a new home near Substantion during this period.
[45] Vasiliev, *The Russian Attack on Constantinople*, pp. 301–318. See also L. Levillain, "Giraut, Comte de Vienne," in *Le Moyen Age*, LV (1949).
[46] Duprat, in *Bouches du Rhône*, p. 136.
[47] On the castle built in the Camargue about this period see *ibid.*, p. 280. On Moslems in this region and nearby see A. Lewis, *Naval Power and Trade in the Mediterranean A.D. 500–1100*, pp. 135–170.
[48] See R. Poupardin, *Le Royaume de Provence sous les Carolingiens*, pp. 1–106.
[49] See Levillain, "Giraut, Comte de Vienne," and E. Fournial, "Recherches sur

Civil War, Invasion, and Breakdown of Royal Authority 103

Bald, who, victorious over Pepin of Aquitaine, felt free to make an attempt to add Provence to his kingdom. Other claimants included Charles' brothers, Lothaire of Lorraine, and Louis of Italy. Charles, however, proved the stronger and after one earlier unsuccessful attempt in 870 led an army into the Valley of the Rhone, defeated Count Gerald and took control of the region, which he turned over to his *fidelis* and kinsman, Boson, who ruled it as duke.[50]

Charles' ambitions, however, included more than Provence, and when Louis II of Italy, who held the title of Emperor, died, he hastened to gather together an army which he led to Rome and where he received the imperial title from the Pope in 876.[51] Then, after his death in 877 while returning to France, Boson usurped Provence and in 879 assumed the title of king.[52] Such presumption seems to have annoyed his royal neighbors, and armies led by Charles the Fat of Germany and Carloman and Louis III of France invaded Boson's new kingdom and drove him from Vienne. By 887 he was dead, a fugitive in the Alps, and his kingdom seemed destined to disappear into the domains of the French Carolingian family.[53]

This, however, did not happen. Louis II and Carloman died without heirs who were of age, and Charles the Fat proved totally incompetent. As a result, in 887 the French nobility north of the Loire conferred the royal title on Eudes of the Capetian family. The Midi in general was reluctant to accept Eudes as king, and so, during this period, it was not difficult for Louis, the son of Boson, to reconstitute his father's kingdom of Provence from Lyon to the Mediterranean with himself as king. From this time on, for many years, this kingdom was to enjoy a political existence separate from the rest of the Midi.[54]

---

les comtes de Lyon au IXe et Xe siècles," in *Le Moyen Age,* LVIII (1952), 221–225.

[50] See the mention of Duke Boson in a charter which Charles the Bald gave to the church of Vivarais in 877 (*Hist. Gén. de Lang.,* II, no. 187).

[51] See F. Lot and L. Halphen, *Le règne de Charles le Chauve (842–877),* pp. 200 ff, on the circumstances surrounding this expedition. On a coin of Charles' minted in Rome and found in a hoard unearthed at Avignon see Lewis, *The Northern Seas,* p. 388 n.

[52] *Cart. de Grenoble,* no. 70.

[53] See Boson's last charter given to the bishop of Maurienne, high in the Alps (Chartes de Maurienne, no. 1). On his loss of Lyon to his Carolingian enemies in 880 see *Annales Bertiniani,* anno 880, p. 151.

[54] See charter given by King Louis to the church of Saint-Etienne of Lyon in 892 in *Cart. de Grenoble,* no. 81.

It is against this background of revolts, of civil wars, and of invasions that various noble families assumed independent power in various parts of Southern France and Catalonia. Just how they did so and in exactly what period they achieved independence from royal authority is the matter which now claims our attention; for only when we have examined each region can we come to any final conclusions as to how power moved from the hands of Carolingian monarchs to the now hereditary counts and dukes who replaced them as the governors and rulers of the lands which lay south of Poitou and Burgundy.

In the examination of this problem, Gascony presents the fewest difficulties, though our information concerning this region is quite limited. Here throughout the entire period of Carolingian dominance, we have evidence of the existence of a family of native dukes or *principes* who held authority over Gascony by hereditary right. The Carolingians had made periodic attempts to reduce the power of this Aznar family, by setting up a Frankish county of Fézensac within their domains[55] or by backing, at times, a rival family, the Séguins, as dukes of Gascony.[56] But they were never able to destroy the Aznars. Thus, in 850 and 852, when Sánchez came to terms with Charles the Bald, our sources speak of him as *dux* of Gascony.[57] This, incidentally, marks the last real evidence of Carolingian control of this region. From this time on, into the next century, the Aznars seem to have ruled their Gascon domains in full *de facto* independence, without sharing even nominal authority with the kings of France.

The story of the development of a similar *de facto* independence for other families in various parts of the Midi and Catalonia, however, presents more complex problems. In the first place, we must emphasize that the greater number of officials appointed as counts by Carolingian monarchs between 828 and 900 for various reasons never did lay the basis for hereditary family authority over the regions which they governed. Many examples of this spring to mind, like Counts Aléran and Odalric

---

[55] See Astronomus, *Vita Hludovici*, ch. 13, p. 612, on the setting up of the county of Fézensac.

[56] The first reference we have to the Séguin family comes from 778 when Charlemagne makes a Séguin count of Bordeaux (*ibid.*, ch. 3, p. 608). They are last mentioned holding office in 845 when Duke Séguin is killed by the Vikings (*Chron. Aquitanicum*, anno 845, p. 252, and *Ademar de Chabannes*, III, 7, p. 134). Early in the eleventh century however a Séguin is still mentioned as holding the office of archbishop of Bordeaux.

[57] See note 30 on references to Sánchez of the Aznar family.

and Marquis Humfrid in Septimania and Catalonia,[58] Count Landry in Saintonge, Count Appolonius in Agde and Béziers,[59] Count Gerald in the Vienne region[60] or even the powerful Bernard, marquis of Gothia from 865 to 879.[61] Other families, from all appearances firmly entrenched in their local regions, disappeared in the course of the century or shortly thereafter like the Séguins of Bordeaux[62] or the family of the counts of Turenne in the lower Limousin.[63]

There were a number of other important families, however, who were amazingly successful both in establishing themselves in certain regions and in surviving until they could achieve *de facto* independence in the regions they governed. Let us examine what evidence we can find concerning eleven such families, three in Western Aquitaine, two in Central Aquitaine, four in Catalonia and the Narbonnaise, one in Septimania, and one in the Valley of the Rhone. This may allow us to discern some pattern in their success.

Let us begin with Western Aquitaine. The first family that concerns us is one that goes back at least to 838 when two brothers, Ermenon, count of Poitou, and his brother Turpio, count of Angoulême, had established themselves in this part of the Carolingian Empire. Ermenon, who supported Pepin II in 838, was deprived of his *honorem* of Poitou by Louis the Pious,[64] but a little later he seems to have acquired the county of

---

[58] See Abadal, *Els Primers Comtes Catalans*, p. 53; Calmette, "Onfroy, Marquis de Gothie"; and M. Chaume, "Onfroi, Marquis de Gothie, ses origines et ses attaches familiales," in *Annales du Midi*, LII (1940).

[59] Appolonius is first mentioned as count in 848 (*Hist. Gén. de Lang.*, II, no. 138). He is last mentioned in a charter of 872 (*ibid.*, no. 182). Probably, as a partisan of Bernard of Gothia he lost out in the changes that took place from 872 to 879.

[60] See Levillain, "Giraut, Comte de Vienne," on this powerful count who controlled the Middle Rhone region for many decades.

[61] See J. Calmette, "Les comtes Bernard sous Charles le Chauve," in *Mélanges Louis Halphen*; J. Dhondt, *Etude sur la naissance des principalités territoriales en France*, pp. 190–206; and Abadal, *Els Primers Comtes Catalans*, pp. 3–9, 40–49.

[62] See note 56.

[63] We possess a charter issued by Rudolf, count of Turenne in 823, *Cart. de Beaulieu*, no. 185. The family supported Pepin II in 848 (*ibid.*, no. 7). In 866 Gotfred, of this family, was still count (*ibid.*, no. 3). Yet by 870 Count Bernard of Toulouse controlled this region (*ibid.*, no. 27). In 887 a certain Gotfred, who seems to bear no title, gave land to Beaulieu (*ibid.*, no 169). Again in 898 another, or the same, Gotfred is a donor to Beaulieu (*ibid.*, no. 29). Then the family disappears from the history of Quercy and the Limousin.

[64] *Ademar de Chabannes*, II, 16, p. 132.

Périgord, where he married a sister of Sánchez, duke of Gascony. A son by this union, Arnaud, was Count of Fézensac with some claim to Gascon overlordship in 864.[65] Both Count Turpio and Count Ermenon died in the 860's, the former in 863 fighting the Vikings,[66] the latter in 866 fighting Landry, count of Saintes.[67] But the family seems to have continued to have importance, for a son of Count Ermenon, Ademar, was count of Poitou and may have had some power in the Limousin from 890 to 902,[68] finally dying without issue in 926.[69]

A second family of importance is one which became established in Angoulême and Périgord in 869, when Charles the Bald appointed a certain Vulgrin as count of these regions and perhaps of Saintonge as well.[70] Vulgrin died in 886 and left two sons: William who became count of Périgord and gained Agen from the count of Toulouse, and Aldouin who became count of Angoulême.[71] This family was allied to the earlier lords of the region, for a sister of Count William of Périgord, Santia, married Ademar, count of Poitou, mentioned earlier.[72] The descendants of these counts continued in possession of their counties into the tenth century.

A third family is one descended from a certain Rannoux, himself a son of Count Gerald of Auvergne, to whom in 838 Louis the Pious gave the county of Poitou.[73] He was succeeded by his son Rannoux II who held Poitou as count until 890, when he was replaced by Ademar.[74] His son Ebles Manzur, however, in 902 managed to drive out Ademar and to recover the county.[75] He transmitted it to his descendants, the famous counts of Poitou and dukes of Aquitaine of later history.

[65] *Ibid.*, III, 21, pp. 141–142; "Aquitaniae Historiae Fragmentum," in *Ademar de Chabannes*, p. 199; and *Translatio Sanctae Faustae*, ch. 2, p. 727. See also L. Levillain, "Ademar de Chabannes, généalogiste," in *Bulletin de la société des antiquaires de l'ouest*, XXIX (1934), 246–248.

[66] *Chron. Aquitanicum*, anno 863, p. 252, and *Ademar de Chabannes*, II, 19, p. 136.

[67] *Ademar de Chabannes*, III, 19, p. 136.

[68] *Ibid.*, III, 21, pp. 140–141.

[69] *Chron. Aquitanicum*, anno 930, p. 253. *Ademar de Chabannes*, III, 23, p. 143, gives the date as 923.

[70] *Ademar de Chabannes*, III, 19, pp. 136–137.

[71] *Ibid.*, III, 20 and 23, pp. 137–138 and 143–144, and *Chron. Aquitanicum*, anno 886, p. 253.

[72] *Ademar de Chabannes*, III, 23, p. 145.

[73] *Ibid.*, III, 16, p. 132.

[74] *Annales Vedastes*, ed. B. de Simson, anno 881, p. 335; *Ademar de Chabannes*, III, 21, pp. 140–141. See also F. Lot, *Fidèles ou vassaux?* pp. 55–56.

[75] Lot, *Fidèles ou vassaux?* p. 55.

Turning from Western Aquitaine, let us examine Auvergne where we find a particularly important family descended from Count William of Gellone who was count of Toulouse under Charlemagne. Certain early members of this family, like Count Gaucelm of Roussillon, Count Bernard of Septimania and the latter's rebellious son, William, have already been mentioned during the period of their importance under Louis the Pious and Charles the Bald, when the center of their power was located in Septimania and Catalonia. Though the victory of Charles the Bald over Pepin seems to have dimmed their prospects in his part of the Midi, a son of Count Bernard, who bore his father's name, was able to salvage from the wreck of the family fortunes a position as count of Auvergne in 846.[76] He had a brother, Count Warin, who held a number of important posts.[77] More important, his son, who succeeded him, was the famous Count Bernard Plantevelue, who rose to great authority during the last years of the reign of Charles the Bald. He added to his *honores* the counties of Autun, the Lyonnais, Gevaudun, the Toulousain, and others in the Midi.[78] He died about 886 and his son, Duke William the Pious, was not able to keep all his father's *honores*. Enough remained, however, in Auvergne, the Lyonnais, Autun, and Gevaudun[79] to make him and his heirs important lords of Southern France until well into the tenth century.

The principal rival of the Bernards of Auvergne was a family more recently established in the Midi, descended from Frédélon, whom Charles the Bald had made count of Toulouse in 849.[80] With various intervals

[76] See J. Calmette, "Les comtes d'Auvergne et les comtes de Velay sous Charles le Chauve," in *Annales du Midi*, XVI (1904), and "La Famille de Saint Guillem," in *ibid.*, XVIII (1906). See also the charter of 846 which marks his assumption of power in Auvergne (*Cart. de Brioude*, no. 172).

[77] See mention of Count Warin in a charter of 859 in *Cart. de Brioude*, no. 56, and also that of 868 in *ibid.*, nos. 266–267. See also F. Lot, "Etudes Carolingiennes: Les comtes d'Auvergne entre 846 et 877; Les Comtes d'Autun entre 864 et 878" in *Bibliothèque de l'Ecole des Chartes*, CII (1941).

[78] L. Auzias, "Recherches d'histoire carolingienne, II: Le personnel comtal et l'authorité comtale en Septimanie méridionale (872–878)," in *Annales du Midi*, XLV (1933), and "Les relations de Bernard Plantevelue avec les princes carolingiens de 880 à 885," in *Le Moyen Age*, XXXI (1935). See also Abadal, *Els Primers Comtes Catalans*, pp. 53–70.

[79] Duke William the Pious controlled Brioude in 893 (*Cart. de Brioude*, nos. 98, 165, 182). On his power in the Lyonnais see Fournial, "Recherches sur les comtes de Lyon," p. 225–243. On his authority in Velay see *Hist. Gén. de Lang.*, V, 146, and E. Delcambre, "Géographie historique de Velay, du pagus, au comté et au baillage," in *Bibliothèque de l'Ecole des Chartes*, XCVIII (1937).

[80] *Chron. Fontanellensis*, anno 849, p. 43.

during which rivals were appointed to this position, Frédélon was succeeded by his brother Count Raymond in 862, and then Raymond's son, Bernard, in 865.[81] From Toulouse the family of Frédélon extended their authority over Rouergue, the Albigeois, Quercy, and the Limousin during these years.[82] For a moment in 872 when Bernard, count of Toulouse, was murdered by partisans of Bernard Plantevelue and his *honores* were taken over by the latter,[83] it seemed that the family of Frédélon was doomed to obscurity. They rallied, however, and recovered their former *honores* and, even more important, turned out to be the principal beneficiaries of the fall of Bernard of Gothia in 879. His *honores* in Septimania east of Carcassonne and Narbonne fell to them. After the death of Bernard Plantevelue in 886, Eudes, son of Bernard of Toulouse, and his sons, Raymond and Ermengaud, became the most important lords in Southern France, possessing counties which stretched from the borders of Gascony and of Périgord to the Rhone.[84]

South of the *honores* accumulated by the House of Toulouse during these years three other closely related families of Gothic origin came to control domains below Carcassonne and Narbonne which included all of what was to become Catalonia. The oldest of these families was that of Carcassonne, going back to Bellon, who was appointed count of this region by Charlemagne. The descendants of Count Bellon seem to have

---

[81] See Dhondt, *Etude sur la naissance des principalités*, pp. 185–206, on the circumstances and the activities of the House of Toulouse during these years.

[82] Note that in 860 Count Raymond I of Toulouse signed the will of Archbishop Rodulf of the House of Turenne (*Cart. de Beaulieu*, no. 1). In 870 a charter reveals to us Count Bernard of Toulouse presiding over a court which returned to the abbey of Beaulieu land which had been usurped (*ibid.*, no. 27). And in the same year a charter which Charles the Bald gave to the abbey of Vabres calls him *"Tolosanus Marchio et dilectissimus nobis fidelis"* Lot and Tessier, *Recueil des actes de Charles II le Chauve*, I, no. 339.

[83] On the murder of Bernard in 872 see *Annales Bertiniani*, anno 872, and Abadal, *Els Primers Comtes Catalans*, pp. 43–45.

[84] It is hard to escape the feeling that the survival of the Toulousain House in this period following the murder of Bernard was primarily due to the effective action taken by their kinsman, Archbishop Frotaire. Frotaire kept control of the abbeys of Beaulieu and Brioude and as archbishop of Bourges (he had previously been archbishop of Bordeaux) maintained his family's authority until the death of their rival, Bernard Plantevelue. On Frotaire's authority and its effectiveness throughout the Midi see Chapter III, Section III. See also *Cart. de Saint-Etienne de Limoges*, no. 8; *Cart. de Brioude*, nos. 197, 234; and *Grand Cart. de Brioude*, nos. *CCLXXV, CCLLLI*. On his role in the distribution of the *honores* of Bernard of Gothia see Lot and Tessier, *Recueil des actes de Charles II le Chauve*, I, no. 428.

controlled Carcassonne almost without a break for a century. Bellon was succeeded by his sons, Gisclafred and then Oliba I, and then the latter was followed by his sons Oliba II of Carcassonne and Acfred I of Razès, who continued in authority down into the first years of the next century.[85]

The second important family of this region was that of Ampurias-Roussillon. Its founder seems to have been a certain Count Sunyer I, who Abadal convincingly argues was a son of Count Bellon and a brother of Count Oliba I of Carcassonne.[86] Some time after his death in the 840's, after a succession of Frankish counts, Ampurias and Roussillon came under the control of his son, Sunyer II, who was to rule it in conjunction with his brother Dela from the 870's on.[87]

Even more important was a third such family, that of the celebrated Count Guifred the Hairy of Barcelona. The founder of this family's fortunes was a Count Sunifred of Urgell-Cerdanya-Confluent, who ruled these counties from 844 to 848 and in addition was count of Barcelona and Gerona. Abadal believes that Count Sunifred was a fourth son of Count Bellon of Carcassonne to whom he most certainly was related, but it seems more probable that he was descended from Count Borell of Ausona, the original Gothic count of this region.[88] After his death his *honores* of Barcelona and Gerona went to a series of Frankish counts. Urgell-Cerdanya-Confluent, however, was given to a certain Count Saloman. The *Gesta of Barcelona* and most historians have advanced the view that Saloman was a Frank, but Abadal rather convincingly argues that he was a Goth and a relative of Sunifred's.[89] Sometime after Count Saloman's death about 870, Guifred, son of Sunifred, was invested with these counties which he probably governed with his brother, Count Miró.[90] By

[85] Abadal, *Els Primers Comtes Catalans*, pp. 7-9, 41-50, gives the background of the establishment of the House of Carcassonne-Razès. See also his "Un diplôme inconnu de Louis le Pieux," pp. 52-57.

[86] On Count Sunyer's establishing himself in Ampurias see Abadal, *Els Primers Comtes Catalans*, pp. 8-9, 13-24. Though Abadal's surmises as to the close relationship between the counts of Ampurias-Roussillon and those of Carcassonne-Razès seem reasonable, they are, of course, impossible to prove.

[87] Abadal, *Els Primers Comtes Catalans*, pp. 49-50.

[88] See note 9.

[89] Abadal, *Els Primers Comtes Catalans*, pp. 30-39. See the opposing view that Saloman was a Frankish count in P. Ponsch, "Le role de Saint-Michel de Cuxa dans la formation de l'historiographie de Catalogne et l'historiographie de la legénde de Wilfred le Velu," in *Études Roussillonnaises*, IV (1954), 157-159, and "Le Confluent et ses comtes du IXe au XIIe siècle," in *Études Roussillonnaises*, I (1951), 10-106.

[90] Abadal, *Els Primers Comtes Catalans*, pp. 46-49.

878, Count Guifred and his brothers had added to their domains the counties of Gerona and Barcelona. From this time on this group of counties stretching from Barcelona to Pallars and Ribagorça were to be governed by Count Guifred, Count Miró, and Count Radulf and their descendants.[91] Thus, starting with Count Bellon of Carcassonne in Charlemagne's time, there developed a group of related counts who by 878 ruled this whole region by hereditary right and in full *de facto* independence.

One other area, close to Catalonia, remains to be considered. I refer to the counties of Pallars and Ribagorça. From the time of its reconquest this remote trans-Pyrenean region had been ruled as a district of the Toulousain by the counts of Toulouse—except for the brief period when Count Asnar Galindo had taken over authority there as a usurper. About 872, however, during the disorders which attended the murder of Count Bernard of Toulouse by the followers of Bernard Plantevelue, a certain Ramón made himself count of both Pallars and Ribagorça by usurpation.[92] From this time on, he and his descendants were to govern these counties without even nominal ties with the rulers of the Frankish monarchy.

This leaves two more families to be considered. One of them is by far the most insignificant which we have considered so far, since it confined its authority to a single county—that of Melgueil or Maguelonne. Furthermore, we know little concerning it except that its founder seems to have been a certain Count Robert of Frankish origin who governed this county at the time of Louis the Pious.[93] In the last years of the century his probable descendants, Countess Guillaumette and her son Count Bernard, were still in possession of it and were able to pass it on to their descendants.[94]

The last family is one we have already examined in some detail, the royal family of Provence. They were, as we have noted, the last to become established in the region they were to rule, going back to the time when Boson, the founder of the family's fortunes, was made duke of Provence and the Valley of the Rhone about 875 by Charles the Bald.[95] We have explained how in 879 he made himself king of Provence[96] and how after

[91] *Ibid.*, pp. 53–70.
[92] *Ibid.*, p. 45. See also Abadal, *Els Comtats de Pallars i Ribagorça*, pp. 116–127, and his "Els precepts comtals carolingis per al Pallars," in *Boletín de la Real Academia de Buenas Letras de Barcelona*, XXVI (1954–1958).
[93] Count Robert is mentioned in a charter of 819 (*Hist. Gén. de Lang.*, II, no. 51).
[94] *Cart. de Maguelonne*, no. 1.
[95] Duke Boson is mentioned in 877 in a charter in *Hist. Gén. de Lang.*, II, no. 197.
[96] *Cart. de Grenoble*, no. 70.

Civil War, Invasion, and Breakdown of Royal Authority 111

his death in 887 his son Louis, taking advantage of the accession of King Eudes, reconstituted his father's kingdom. From this time on into the tenth century Louis and his kinsman, Count Hugh of Arles, were to control this region in the Rhone Valley as a separate and distinct kingdom.[97]

Now when we come to analyze these twelve families who by the year 900 had come to exercise ruling authority over Southern France and the Spanish March by hereditary right a number of things seem apparent to us. First of all we are struck by the fact that all of them, with the exception of the dukes of Gascony, gained a real and *de facto* independence between the years 870 and 890, a period which comprised the last years of Charles the Bald, the three short reigns of his Carolingian successors, and the first years of King Eudes of the Capetian line. It was during these two decades that Northern French monarchs lost effective control over the Midi and Catalonia.[98]

Furthermore, we can mark the steps in this process. The murder of Count Bernard of Toulouse and the taking over of his *honores* by Bernard Plantevelue in 872, followed as it was by the loss of Pallars and Ribagorça, seems to be the first step.[99] The famous Assembly of Quiersy in 877 where the magnates protected their rights of succession to their *honores* seems a second.[100] The deprivation of the *honores* of Bernard of Gothia in 879 by the magnates and their redistribution seems a third step.[101] Finally, after the disastrous reign of Charles the Fat, the accession of Eudes represented the final step, since the lords of the Midi could, by claiming a Carolingian loyalty, in effect make themselves independent.[102]

[97] *Ibid.*, no. 81.

[98] The *Annales Bertiniani,* anno 877, pp. 137-138, mentions a revolt of the magnates which forced Louis the Stammerer, heir to Charles the Bald, to confirm rights given them by his predecessor. This helped to make *honores* and benefices hereditary. On this change see F. Ganshof, "L'origine des rapports féodovassiliques" in *I problemi della Civiltà Carolingia*, pp. 53-56.

[99] *Annales Bertiniani,* anno 872, p. 134, and Abadal, *Els Primers Comtes Catalans,* pp. 41-50.

[100] The Assembly of Quiersy did not make all *honores* hereditary, only those assigned to the magnates who were accompanying Charles the Bald on his Italian campaign (see "Capitulare Carisiacense," ch. 9, and "Capitula excerpta in conventu Carisiacense," ch. 3, in Boretius,*Capitularia,* I, nos. 281, 282, pp. 358, 362). On the other hand it did help to serve as a precedent for making all other *honores* hereditary too.

[101] Abadal, *Els Primers Comtes Catalans,* pp. 62-66.

[102] Most of the magnates in the Midi and Catalonia were reluctant to accept Eudes as king, as seen by their refusal to date their charters by his reign. The exception seems to have been the House of Toulouse judging by a charter of 892 from Nîmes (*Cart. de Nîmes,* no. 5).

This is just what they did. Out of civil wars, rebellions, invasions, and royal weakness, then, there developed a group of noble families who now ruled south of Burgundy and Poitou by hereditary *de facto* right.

Examination of these families, however, shows us more than this fact, well known to historians. For though all of them, except the Gascon dukes, owed their *final* independence to the events of the years 870–890, the circumstances which led each family to establish itself firmly in the local district varied immensely. One family, the Gascon dukes, goes back to the pre-Carolingian period. All the other eleven were initially appointed to power over the region or regions they came to rule by Carolingian monarchs—with the exception of Ramón of Pallars-Ribagorça who probably was in charge of the region as a subordinate of the counts of Toulouse prior to 872.[103] But the dates when they began to establish themselves in their regions vary immensely. Four began to establish themselves during the reigns of Charlemagne, and the first years of Louis the Pious—the family of Melgueil, that of Carcassonne, that of the Bernards of Auvergne, that of Ademar of Poitou. Four others seem to date from the very last years of Louis the Pious and the early years of the reign of Charles the Bald—the family of Toulouse, that of Rannoux of Poitou, and those of Ampurias-Roussillon and Urgell-Cerdanya-Besalu. Three became firmly established in their regions very late—that of Vulgrin of Angoulême-Périgord, that of Ramón of Pallars-Ribagorça, and that of Boson of Provence. Viewed in this way then, the development of independent ruling families in these regions was a slow, evolutionary process in some cases, a rapid affair in others—dependent on the special and varied circumstances which affected every family quite differently. Such facts seem to preclude any sudden revolutionary forces at work in the process, such as some historians have seemed to emphasize.

Even more interesting is an analysis of the nationalities represented by these families. As far as we can tell, one was Gascon, one Hispano-Gascon, three Gothic, six Frankish, and one either Frankish or Gallo-Roman.[104] In the case of the Gascon dukes, their support may have been due to a dislike of alien Frankish rule. In the case of the others we have no reason or facts upon which we can base such an opinion. In fact, the

---

[103] See note 92.

[104] The dukes of Gascony were of Gascon origin, the counts of Carcassonne, Ampurias, and Barcelona were Gothic, the counts of Melgueil, Toulouse, Auvergne, Angoulême, and Poitou, and the kings of Provence-Burgundy were Frankish, the counts of Pallars and Ribagorça were Hispano-Basque, and the counts of Périgord were either Frankish or Gallo-Roman.

Civil War, Invasion, and Breakdown of Royal Authority 113

last two families who managed to establish themselves in our regions, those of Vulgrin and Boson, were Frankish ones who established their authority in areas which were overwhelmingly Gallo-Roman in character. Even a nascent nationalism, except in Gascony, is hard to discern as a cause of the failure of the Carolingians to maintain their authority over Southern France and Catalonia.

To sum up then, civil wars and invasions weakened the imperfect system of centralized control which the Carolingians had established in Southern France and the Spanish March. Special circumstances, the most important being the short reigns of Charles the Bald's successors and the accession of King Eudes allowed the leading ruling counts of the Midi and Catalonia to establish their families as hereditary and independent *in fact* of royal authority. This, however, more often than not, was the result of no sudden, revolutionary situation, but the culmination of a slow, gradual evolution of authority which, for most of these families, took many decades. This process, inevitable under the circumstances, rather than any supposed national consciousness of portions of the Midi and the Spanish March explains in large measure the new situation which by 900 had arisen out of the failures and weaknesses of the Carolingians.[105]

---

[105] Both Calmette and Dhondt have emphasized nationalities as a cause of the disintegration of Carolingian rule in the Midi and Catalonia. So does Auzias in his *L'Aquitaine Carolingienne*. See the wise words of Abadal on this subject, which, while they refer to Catalonia, can also be applied to the entire Midi, as well. He says that the major problem of the period was not an incipient nationalism but a split between the powerful landowners and the less powerful mass of the population. Abadal, *Els Primers Comtes Catalans*, pp. 226–227. If we add a split between crown and magnates, we have a real explanation of what happened to the Carolingian Empire in this part of France and Catalonia.

CHAPTER VII

The Governmental System of the Midi and Catalonia

IN THE LAST chapter we have been primarily concerned with the decline of the royal government south of Poitou and Burgundy as we traced the civil wars and invasions of this period and the rise of certain noble families to positions of hereditary, *de facto* independence in regions they had originally controlled as subordinate officials appointed by Carolingian monarchs. This, however, leaves unanswered the important question of how these developments changed the governmental system as established in the reigns of Charlemagne and Louis the Pious. What has become of government in Southern France and Catalonia by the year 900?

At this point it might be well to reiterate that in the early ninth century the Carolingians entrusted their government to counts who could be assisted in performing their duties by certain subordinates—viscounts and vicars—and who were often supervised by special officials or *missi* sent out by the monarchs. Such a system was in theory the one established everywhere in the Carolingian Empire and implemented by capitularies and other decrees issued by the monarchs. How did this system actually work out in practice, though, in our regions? What use was actually made of viscounts and vicars in Southern France and Catalonia during this period?

Here we note an interesting fact. We have little evidence of the use of such subordinate officials by counts during the reign of Louis the Pious. In fact, clear evidence exists for two only—one of Thouars in Poitou, who is mentioned in 833,[1] and a Viscount Stephen who presided over a court

[1] *Chartes poitivines (833–1160) de l'abbaye de Saint-Florent de Samaur*, ed. P. Marchegay, no. 33, in *Archives historiques du Poitou*, II (1873), 46. On the lack of viscounts in Poitou until late in the ninth or early in the tenth century see M. Garaud, "Les circonscriptions administratives du comté de Poitou et les auxiliaires du comté au Xe siècle," in *Le Moyen Age*, LIX (1953), 11–13.

in Narbonne in 834 which considered a case involving the *aprisio* of John of Fontjoncouse.[2] We hear more of them, however, during the early years of the reign of Charles the Bald. In a charter given a church in the Pallars-Ribagorça region by Count Frédélon about 850, we find a reference to viscounts and other officials of the court.[3] In 855 there is a mention of a certain Viscount Lambert in Angoulême.[4] In 859 another charter from Roussillon mentions a Viscount Richelme.[5] Four years later, after being called a *fidelis* by Charles the Bald, a certain Isembert is called a viscount and *missus* in the Narbonne area.[6] We also find several references to *missi* during these years. Count Bernard of Auvergne refers to himself as a *missus* in presiding over a court in a case involving a serf of the royal *fisc* in 851,[7] and Count Saloman is called a *missus* in a case involving the archbishop of Narbonne in 862.[8]

After 870, judging by our sources, royal *missi* disappear, but we find viscounts appearing throughout the Midi and Catalonia. In Provence and the Valley of the Rhone, for instance, where we find counts mentioned at Vienne in 842[9] and at Marseille in 845,[10] but no viscounts, by 870 such subordinate officials begin to appear. The first reference to them dates from this year when we find two viscounts assisting Count Gerald in a court held at Vienne.[11] In 902 we find another assisting Count Hugh of Arles in a similar capacity in the same city.[12]

[2] *Catalunya Carolingia*, II, 442–444. See also the mention of a viscount's court in 791 in *Hist. Gén. de Lang.*, II, no. 10. In both these years Narbonne formed part of a large *honor* or a group of *honores* ruled by a single count. In 791, for instance, it was probably ruled by Duke William of Toulouse. In 834 it was one of the *honores* of Bernard of Septimania. Hence a viscount in this important city.

[3] See the charter in F. Valls-Taberner, *Els origines dels comtats de Pallars i Ribagorça*, p. 5. On the possible spuriousness of this charter see G. Tessier, "A propos de quelques actes toulousains du IXᵉ siècle," in *Recueil de travaux offerts à M. C. Brunel*, II, 566–580.

[4] *Cartulaire de l'église d'Angoulême*, ed. I. Nanglard, I, no. 52.

[5] *Hist. Gén. de Lang.*, II, no. 150.

[6] *Cart. de Carcassonne*, II, 598, mentions an Isembert as a *fidelis* of Charles the Bald in 859. A little later he is called a viscount and *missus* (*Cart. de Carcassonne*, I, 71–72).

[7] *Grand Cart. de Brioude*, no. CXIV.

[8] *Catalunya Carolingia*, II, 325–326.

[9] *Cartulaire de l'abbaye de Saint-André-le-bas de Vienne*, ed. U. Chevalier, appendix no. 2, pp. 211–213 (hereafter cited as *Cart. de Saint-André-le-bas*).

[10] *Cart. de Saint-Victor*, no. 26.

[11] *Recueil des chartes de l'abbaye de Cluny*, ed. A. Bernard and A. Bruell, I, no. 15, pp. 18–20.

[12] *Cart. de Vienne*, no. 1, appendix 1, pp. 219–221.

In Septimania at Nîmes we find a viscount who is presiding over a court in 876, another acting in the same capacity in 892 and still a third present at a court headed by Count Raymond of Toulouse in 898.[13] In Béziers too, where Appolonius was count as late as 872, viscounts appear also. A certain Rainald, called a *fidelis* in 881 by King Carloman by 897 seems to be serving as viscount and in the same year is succeeded by his son-in-law, Boson, who bears the same title.[14] In 875 in the Narbonne-Carcassonne region we find a certain viscount, Berold, who is presiding over a court[15] and a little later in 883 a viscount, Sunifred, present at a tribunal headed by Count Oliba II.[16] In 898 in the same region Viscount Aton of Albi presides over another court as a special *missus* or representative of Count Eudes of Toulouse—a court in which Count Oliba II this time is referred to as a *missus*. At about this same time we also find a viscount at Toulouse.[17]

In Roussillon and the rest of Catalonia we again find such officials. In the former region in 875 there is record of a court held with a *missus* of Count Bernard of Gothia presiding.[18] Some four years later we find a reference to a Viscount Franco, called a *fidelis* of Count Guifred of Barcelona-Cerdanya.[19] In 898 we learn of a Viscount Ermenico who is assisting at a court presided over by Count Sunyer II of Ampurias-Roussillon.[20]

We have no proof that viscounts existed in Auvergne during these years. But in 876 we first hear of a viscount of Limoges, a certain Hildebert, who is called a *fidelis* in a charter given him by Charles the Bald.[21] In the same year we again learn of a viscount at Thouars in Poitou.[22] A little later in 898 we find two viscounts in the Limousin, Ademar and Gausfred, who presided over a court held near Limoges.[23] In the same

[13] *Cart. de Nîmes*, nos. 1, 5, 8.
[14] *Hist. Gén. de Lang.*, V, nos. 4, 17, 18.
[15] *Cart. de Carcassonne*, IV, 70–71.
[16] *Hist. Gén. de Lang.*, V, no. 5.
[17] *Cart. de Carcassonne*, I, 73–74, and Odo, *Vita Sancti Geraldi Aureliacensis*, II, 28, in Migne, *Patrologia latina*, CXXXIII, cols. 685–686.
[18] *Hist. Gén. de Lang.*, II, no. 180.
[19] R. de Abadal i de Vinyals, *Els Primers Comtes Catalans*, pp. 78–79.
[20] *El Archivo Condal de Barcelona en los Siglos IX–X*, ed. F. Udina-Martorell, no. 9.
[21] *Cart. de Saint-Etienne de Limoges*, no. 84.
[22] Garaud, "Les circonscriptions administratives du comté de Poitou," pp. 13–15.
[23] *Cartulaires des abbayes de Tulle et de Roc-Amador*, ed. J. Champéval, in *Bulletin de la société scientifique, historique et archéologique de la Corrèze*, VI (1893), no. 276.

The Governmental System of the Midi and Catalonia 117

year we hear for the first time of a viscount at LePuy, the first of the celebrated Polignac family.[24] To the west in the Angoulême region we learn that Count Vulgrin, sometime between 869 and 878, has appointed a certain Viscount Ramnulf as castellan of the fortress he has built to protect this region from Viking attacks.[25] A charter of 879 shows him still holding this position in Angoulême.[26] Without in any way denying the possibility that a number of other viscounts were placed in office in the Midi and Catalonia during this period, what seems clear is that we do have proof of their existence by 900 at Vienne, Nîmes, Béziers, Narbonne, Carcassonne, Toulouse, Roussillon, Ampurias, Ausona, Angoulême, the Limousin, Poitou, the Albigeois, and Velay.

Why do we find such viscounts in so many regions of the Midi and of Catalonia at a time when they seem to be rare in the rest of the Carolingian Empire? No final response to this question can be given, but a plausible answer seems to be that during this period single individuals came to control many counties or *honores*. Under the circumstances counts and marquises like Bernard of Septimania, Bernard of Gothia, or Frédélon and Raymond of Toulouse needed help in governing the regions entrusted to them. True, they could use counts for the task and subordinate such counts to themselves by special ties of vassalage or *fidelitas*. Such a system seems to have been used in the Quercy-Limousin region by Raymond of Toulouse about 860 where he appears to have subordinated the counts of Turenne to his authority.[27] It was certainly attempted in Carcassonne where in 872 Count Oliba II did homage for his county to Count Bernard of Toulouse.[28] Such subordination may have continued down to 898 and even afterwards.[29]

But the difficulties arising from such subordination of one count to another were very real, as the murder of Count Bernard in 872[30] and the revolt of Count Asnar Galindo in Urgell in 838[31] clearly showed. It therefore seems probable that counts who controlled a large number of

[24] A. Jacotin, *Preuves de la maison de Polignac*, I, 21.
[25] *Ademar de Chabannes*, III, 20, p. 138, and "Aquitaniae Historiae Fragmentum," in *ibid.*, pp. 197–198.
[26] *Cart. d'Angoulême*, no. 40.
[27] According to a charter of 860 Raymond I controlled the abbeys of Solignac and Beaulieu (*Cart. de Beaulieu*, no. 1). Yet in 854 Gotfred was still count of Turenne (*ibid.*, no. 186).
[28] *Cart. de Carcassonne*, V, 228.
[29] *Ibid.*, I, 73–74.
[30] *Annales Bertiniani*, ed. E. Waitz, anno 872.
[31] Abadal, *Els Comtats de Pallars i Ribagorça*, pp. 107–108.

honores generally preferred, when possible, to entrust power to subordinates who, bearing the title of viscounts, were far enough down the ladder not to attempt to usurp the authority entrusted to them.

Therefore, it was to a viscount that Bernard seemed to have entrusted Narbonne in 834 and viscounts whom the counts of Toulouse used in governing the trans-Pyrenean lands of Pallars and Ribagorça down to 872[32] and a Viscount Richelme whom Marquis Humfrid appointed as a *missus* in Roussillon in 862.[33] After 870 similar magnates, controlling a large number of counties, seem to have used viscounts more extensively. At a time when Count Gerald of Vienne and Count Hugh of Arles controlled large areas in the Valley of the Rhone we find viscounts appearing there,[34] just as the family of the counts of Toulouse seem to have established them in Nîmes, Béziers, Narbonne, Toulouse, Albi, and the Limousin.[35] The counts of Carcassonne, who controlled both Carcassonne and Razès, seem to have established such officials in Carcassonne,[36] while Marquis Bernard established them in Razès[37] and Count Guifred seems to have been responsible for their appointment in Ausona and other portions of his domains.[38] It was probably Duke William the Pious of Aquitaine, who controlled many counties, who established a viscount of LePuy in 898,[39] just as it was Count Vulgrin, controlling several counties, who seems to have established the first viscounts in Angoulême.[40] Even the viscounts of Thouars may have been made necessary by the special authority exercised over a border region of Aquitaine by Rannoux II during

---

[32] *Catalunya Carolingia*, II, 442–444.

[33] Valls-Taberner, *Els origines des comtats*, p. 5.

[34] *Cart. de Saint-André-le-bas*, appendix no. 2, pp. 211–213.

[35] On a viscount at Nîmes see *Cart. de Nîmes*, no. 1. On one at Béziers see *Hist. Gén. de Lang.*, V, no. 17. On one at Narbonne see *ibid.*, no. 5. On one at Albi see mention of Aton, viscount of Albi, who served as *missus* of Count Eudes at Carcassonne in 898 (*Cart. de Carcassonne*, I, 73–74). On one in the Limousin see *Cart. de Saint-Etienne de Limoges*, no. 84.

[36] See mention of Viscount Berald in 875 in *Cart. de Carcassonne*, IV, 70–71, and in 883 in *Hist. Gén. de Lang.*, V, no. 5.

[37] *Catalunya Carolingia*, II, 442–444.

[38] See Abadal, *Els Primers Comtes Catalans*, pp. 76–81, on the organization of Ausona and the establishment of viscounts by Guifred.

[39] See E. Delcambre, "Géographie historique du Velay du pagus, au comté et au baillage," in *Bibliothèque de l'Ecole des Chartes*, XCVIII (1937), 37–41.

[40] *Ademar de Chabannes*, III, 20, p. 138. The "Aquitaniae Historiae Fragmentum," in *ibid.*, pp. 197–198, says that Gislebert was given the castle of Marillac at the same time that Ramnulf was given Matas and made viscount. It also calls Ramnulf the *"fidelissimus amicus"* of the count.

this period.⁴¹ Viscounts in the Midi and Catalonia, then, were not created by usurpation, but were initially a response to a governmental need of the period.

While there seems to be little doubt that the initiative in appointing viscounts came from the counts, the dukes, and the marquises, it also seems clear that Carolingian rulers, down to the time of Eudes, were not content to allow them to be responsible only to their immediate superiors. They, therefore, seem often to have established close ties with such viscounts. That is the meaning of the fact that Isembert is called a *fidelis* by Charles the Bald in 859 five years before he appears as a viscount at Narbonne.⁴² It explains why the same monarch in granting land to Hildebert, viscount of Limoges in 876, refers to him also as his *fidelis*.⁴³ Five years later in 881. Carloman refers in like terms to a certain Rainald, who we learn is serving as viscount of Béziers a little later.⁴⁴ While Carolingian rulers were willing to let their counts make use of such subordinates, they seem to have wished to tie them directly to the monarchy also by ties of vassalage or *fidelitas*, at least down to 887. After this date, such a relationship seems largely to have disappeared.

This leads to the final and difficult question as to whether or not the charge of viscount had, like that of count, become an hereditary one by the end of this period. It certainly rapidly became so in the next century, as viscounts followed the example set for them by their superiors, the counts. Down to 900, however, we can be sure that viscounts passed their position or *honor* on to their heirs in two cases only. One is in Béziers where Viscount Boson succeeded his father-in-law in 897.⁴⁵ The other is in Angoulême where Viscount Ramnulf was succeeded by his sons soon after the death of Count Vulgrin in 886.⁴⁶

When we turn from consideration of viscounts to the less important subordinates of the counts, the vicars, we find ourselves facing greater difficulties. Our documents make it clear that in some portions of the Midi like Auvergne, Velay, the Limousin, and neighboring Poitou—that is to

---

⁴¹ Note that when Rannoux II established a viscount at Thouars he had claims to a wider region than Poitou proper and is called *"dux maximae partis Aquitaniae"* in 889 according to *Annales Vedastes*, ed. B. de Simson, anno 889, p. 335.
⁴² *Cart. de Carcassonne*, II, 598.
⁴³ *Cart. de Saint-Etienne de Limoges*, no. 84.
⁴⁴ *Hist. Gén. de Lang.*, V, no. 4.
⁴⁵ *Ibid.*, no. 18.
⁴⁶ See *Ademar de Chabannes*, III, 23, pp. 144–145, on the restoration of Viscount Ramnulf's *honores* to his heir by Count Bernard, son of Count Vulgrin.

say in Aquitaine—counties were divided into districts known as *vicaria*.[47] South of these areas of Southern France, however, we do not at first find such *vicaria* mentioned, and we find that almost everywhere south of Poitou and Burgundy evidence of actual vicars exercising their charges is rare. In 845, we find one presiding over a court at Marseille.[48] Two are mentioned in a charter from Angoulême dating from 855.[49] At about the same time they may have been used under the title of *centenarii* by the counts of Toulouse in Pallars and Ribagorça.[50] After 870 references to them are slightly more numerous in our sources. We find them at Vienne in this year attending a court presided over by Count Gerald.[51] They are found at Nîmes in 876,[52] and one is mentioned in the *civitas* of Limoges in 884.[53] About 881 a Vicar Fredanci seems to have served as a castellan of a frontier fortress in Ausonia as a *fidelis* of Count Guifred.[54] This is all. Useful minor officials they seem to have remained, but not too widely distributed until well into the next century.

Even rarer than the vicars are the *vassi dominici*, judging by our sources. We find them mentioned only twice after 828, once in 852 attending a court in Narbonne presided over by Count Oldaric[55] and again in 870 in the Toulousain at a court held by Count Bernard of Toulouse.[56] Then they seem to have disappeared. Did they actually cease to exist, or did they become vassals of the counts instead of vassals of the Carolingian rulers and continue to attend the courts of the counts in this capacity after 887? It is difficult to say. All we can be sure of is that there is only one indication of such a survival of *vassi dominici* in this new role. In a court held

[47] On such *vicaria* in Auvergne see H. Doniol's introductions to the *Cart. de Brioude* and the *Cartulaire de Sauxillanges*. For Velay see Delcambre "Géographie historique du Velay." For the Limousin see Deloche's introduction to the *Cart. de Beaulieu*. For Poitou see M. Garaud, "Les origines des Pagi poitevins du moyen-âge," in *Revue historique du droit français et étranger*, XXVI (1948); "La construction des châteaux et les déstinées de la *vicaria* et du *vicarius* Carolingiens en Poitou, in *ibid.*, XXXI (1953); and "Les circonscriptions administratives du comté de Poitiers et les auxiliaires du comté au Xe siècle," in *Le Moyen Age*, LIX (1953).
[48] *Cart. de Saint-Victor*, no. 26.
[49] *Cart. d'Angoulême*, no. 52.
[50] Valls-Taberner, *Els origines des comtats*, p. 5.
[51] *Chartes de Cluny*, I, no. 15.
[52] *Cart. de Nîmes*, no. 1.
[53] *Cart. de Saint-Etienne de Limoges*, no. 3.
[54] Abadal, *Els Primers Comtes Catalans*, pp. 88, 98.
[55] *Hist. Gén. de Lang.*, II, no. 139.
[56] *Ibid.*, no. 174.

at Nîmes in 898 presided over by Count Raymond I of Rouergue we do find two men, called *vassi*, in attendance.[57] Elsewhere, all is silence for the Midi and Catalonia.

To sum up, then, the governmental system of the Midi did change during the years from 828 to 900 from what it had been under Charlemagne and Louis the Pious. Not only did noble families establish themselves as *de facto* hereditary rulers of important regions, but in the process the use of viscounts became more widespread, along with some use of vicars in a minor but important subordinate capacity. As this happened *vassi dominici* disappeared though some of their functions may have been taken over or transformed into those of *vassi* beholden to local counts instead of to Carolingian and Capetian monarchs who lived north of the Loire.

A discussion of officials and governmental administration found in Midi and Catalonia after 828, however, and of the changes which took place in their character, is still incomplete without an examination of two other important governmental phenomena. The first is the institution of a system of co-comital authority in certain regions south of Poitou and Burgundy. The second is the new power exercised in government by women. Both are a feature of the next century. Both already seem to have appeared by the year 900.

It is difficult to see how either of these developments owes anything to previous, prevailing Carolingian governmental practices. Carolingian monarchs always gave an *honor* or a group of *honores* to a single official whom they bound to them by the oath and ceremony of homage and *fidelitas*. They do not appear to have allowed women to exercise local governmental functions, since such charges always included the responsibility of military service at the pleasure of the monarch. Yet soon after 870 we find both developments in the Midi.

These two phenomena seem to have appeared at the moment when public office in our regions was transformed into hereditary familial right. As this happened, counts, who held their authority still in *theory* from late Carolingian monarchs, began *privately* to associate with themselves brothers or sons who bear the title of counts and who take a share in governing their domains. It is in Catalonia and the Carcassonne region that we first find this system in effect. Here certain counts like Oliba

[57] *Cart. de Nîmes*, no. 8. On the possibility that these *vassi* were royal *vassi dominici* see F. Ganshof, "L'origine des rapports féodo-vassiliques," in *I problemi della Civiltà Carolingia*, p. 43 n.

II of Carcassonne, Sunyer II of Ampurias-Roussillon, and Guifred of Barcelona-Gerona-Cerdanya-Urgell legally owed their office to Carolingian monarchs. Yet we find, associated with them as counts after 870, other members of their families who seem to share authority with them. Thus, along with Oliba II we find his brother Acfred I and then, at the turn of the century his sons, Bencio and Acfred II.[58] In Ampurias-Roussillon Count Dela, a brother of Sunyer II, is mentioned in our documents.[59] In the *honores* he controls Count Guifred seems to have associated with him his brothers Count Miró the Old and Count Radulf.[60] Nearby in Pallars and Ribagorça after the death of Count Ramón, late in the century, two of his sons, Isarn and Llop, serve as co-counts of Pallars and two others, Bernard and Miró, as co-counts of Ribagorça.[61]

This system cannot be considered a purely Spanish one confined to regions under the influence of the Christian kingdoms of the Iberian peninsula, since it is also found in the rest of the Midi. When the counts of Toulouse recovered their authority from the slipping grasp of Bernard Plantevelue and his family, they instituted a similar system in their domains, where Count Eudes associated with himself his son Raymond of Rouergue as count over a portion of his *honores* and a little later another son, Ermengaud, as well. In Western Aquitaine after Count Vulgrin died in 886, his sons, William and Aldouin, ruled his counties of Angoulême and Périgord in common and transmitted this tradition to their heirs.[62] By 898, in the Limousin we find the same practice with two viscounts, Ademar and Gausfred ruling a part of this region in common.[63] By 900, then, in the Limousin, in Angoulême, in Languedoc, and in Catalonia and the Spanish March a new governing system had made its appearance.

One reason for this development may well have been a purely practical

[58] See the mention of co-counts Oliba II and Acfred of Carcassonne-Razès in *Marca hispanica*, I, appendix 39, and *Hist. Gén. de Lang.*, II, no. 184. See also Abadal, *Els Primers Comtes Catalans*, pp. 13–24, 244–246.

[59] See Abadal, *Els Primers Comtes Catalans*, pp. 18–24, 199–201, on the co-counts of Ampurias-Roussillon.

[60] See *Hist. Gén. de Lang.*, II, no. 184, and Abadal, *Els Primers Comtes Catalans*, pp. 13–24, 234–246, 249–250.

[61] On documents dating from as early as the late ninth century showing such co-counts see Abadal, *Els Comtats de Pallars i Ribagorça*.

[62] See Chapters I and II, Section IV on the power of the counts of Toulouse and their method of governing their *honores*. Ademar of Chabannes says that the heirs of Count Vulgrin *"communem haberunt totum honorem"* (*Ademar de Chabannes*, III, 23, pp. 144–145).

[63] About those viscounts (who were perhaps brothers) who jointly presided over a court see *Cart. de Tulle*, no. 276.

The Governmental System of the Midi and Catalonia 123

one—the need of governing large areas or multiple counties with inadequate governmental machinery or personnel. One possible answer to this problem was the use of viscounts, as we have mentioned. But an even better method was to designate a brother or a son, or both, as co-rulers and so assure one's family of direct control of regions which might otherwise slip away. In Catalonia and Carcassonne-Razès such a co-ruler's rights were often limited to his own lifetime and do not seem to have been inherited by his issue.[64] In the rest of the Midi this does not appear to have been so.

Another consideration, however, seems more important—a subtle but real change in the nature of power exercised by counts after 870. As they made their authority private and hereditary, they came to think of it as a private family possession and so subject to traditions of the equal division of family property among all heirs—as Roman and Visigothic law provided. Naturally, therefore, all heirs shared in a county or counties as they shared in other family property. Such a change emphatically did *not* make authority feudal in the commonly accepted sense of the word, but it did make it familial and caused it to be shared among a count's family and heirs in a new way.

It was this change which also seems to explain the new and different role played by women in the governing system of the Midi and of Catalonia. Earlier in the century women in these regions were almost always associated with their husbands in private charters and even possessed considerable property in their own name. In a public capacity, however, they appear to have been unimportant and subordinate to their husbands or sons who, as counts and viscounts, exercised the real authority. As public office became a private family matter, however, women's position changed. Since in the ninth century, like the twentieth, women tended to outlive their husbands, women, as wives and particularly as widows, often became the heads of these families who exercised rights as rulers over the counties and *honores* of their regions. As such, they began to share authority in a new way with their husbands and their sons. A Countess Ermissende of Carcassonne or a Countess Guinelda, wife of Count Guifred of Barcelona-Cerdanya, now appear in contemporary documents as equal to their spouses and begin to exercise a certain political authority in their own right.[65] Thus in 883 Countess Berteiz of Toulouse in her

[64] See Abadal, *Els Primers Comtes Catalans*, pp. 199–201, on the way this system worked in Catalan counties.
[65] See *ibid.*, pp. 241–246. For mention of Countess Guinelda after 885 see especially *Marca Hispanica*, I, appendices 53, 404.

own right signed a charter which left to the abbey of Vabres considerable property.[66] In 899 Countess Guillaumette of Melgueil acted with a similar authority in dividing her lands between the Church and her heirs.[67] The way was opened toward an era in which women like Countess Garsinde and Viscountess Arsinde and others were to dominate so much of the Midi in the next century. More important, then, than the *de facto* hereditary independence of noble families or the appearance of viscounts or the disappearance of *vassi dominici* was this important change from public authority to family control which not only led to the use of co-counts, but to a special and real authority exercised by women—an authority all but unknown north of the Loire.

These important changes in the way in which *honores* or counties were held and in the administrative officials who ruled them south of Poitou and Burgundy, were not, curiously enough, reflected in the legal system. Down to 900, at least, the system of law and of courts continued in a form like that established by the earlier Carolingian rulers. Courts, judging from our documents, continued to be held in most regions and were presided over by counts, or their legal representatives, the viscounts, the vicars, and the *missi*. Everywhere we find in attendance at these tribunals the same *judices, scabini,* and *boni homines* whom we have met with earlier, obviously representing the principal local landowners or magnates of the region. In areas south of Carcassonne, in addition, we find present those special *saiones* or wise men versed in the law which Visigothic procedures required.[68]

Courts of such Carolingian-type are found meeting at Marseille in 845, at Vienne in 870, at Nîmes in 876, 892, and 898 and at Béziers in 897.[69] Our records concerning them are even more numerous for western Languedoc where we find them held at Narbonne in 855[70] and at Carcassonne in 862, 873, 875, 883, and 898.[71] In nearby Roussillon we find them

---

[66] *Hist. Gén. de Lang.*, II, nos. 164, 203.

[67] *Cart. de Maguelonne*, I, no. 3.

[68] See the excellent article on the survival of Visigothic law into this period by A. Gouron, "Les étapes de la pénétration du droit romain au XIIe siècle dans l'ancienne Septimanie," in *Annales du Midi*, LXIX (1957), 104–111.

[69] *Cart. de Saint-Victor*, no. 26; *Chartes de Cluny*, I, no. 15; *Cart. de Nîmes*, nos. 1, 5, 8; and *Hist. Gén. de Lang.*, V, no. 18.

[70] *Cart. de Carcassonne*, IV, 192–193.

[71] *Ibid.*, I, 71–72 (862), 73–74 (898); IV, 70–71 (875); Cros-Meyrévielle, *Documents*, no. 17 (873); and *Hist. Gén. de Lang.*, V, no. 5 (883).

The Governmental System of the Midi and Catalonia 125

meeting in 832, 858, 865, and 868,[72] and in Confluent in 874.[73] Though our records for Aquitaine concerning them are less extensive, we do find one held in the Toulousain in 870,[74] another in Rouergue in 878,[75] a third in Auvergne in 851,[76] and a series of others in the Limousin in 870, 887, and 898.[77] One which may vary slightly from the accepted pattern is to be found meeting in Angoulême in 868,[78] as well.

In addition to such secular tribunals we find evidence of other courts in these regions. These are ecclesiastical ones presided over by bishops and abbots. They were in line with Carolingian practice which, in granting immunities to abbeys and churches, gave them the right to establish courts for those subject to their authority. The earliest example of such a court in our sources is one held in the Limousin over which Bishop Stodile of Limoges presided and in which a dispute between a nearby abbey and a *vassus* of the bishop was handled.[79] The next is a tribunal presided over by Archbishop Frédol of Narbonne in 865 to consider a dispute over land between a priest and the abbey of Caunes.[80] Finally we hear of a third, a court of the abbot of Arles in Vallespir held in 875 and concerned with a similar property dispute.[81] Several points concerning these courts should be of interest to us. In the first place, all three seem to concern themselves with cases involving disputes and individuals subject to their legal authority. They are not, then, courts which conflict with the jurisdiction of secular tribunals. Secondly, they seem remarkably like the secular courts of the period. In each case the presiding officer seems to be assisted by the same type of *boni homines* or *judices* we meet in secular courts, and the procedure seems the same except that many of those present are clerics instead of laymen. Except for this, however, one might be dealing with any typical Carolingian court.

[72] *Hist. Gén. de Lang.*, II, no. 80 (832), 150 (858), 169 (868); *Cart. roussillonnais*, no. 1 (865).
[73] *Hist. Gén. de Lang.*, II, no. 173.
[74] *Ibid.*, no. 174.
[75] *Ibid.*, no. 201.
[76] *Grand Cart. de Brioude*, no. CXIV.
[77] *Cart. de Beaulieu*, no. 27 (870), 164 (887); *Cart. de Tulle*, no. 276 (898).
[78] *Cart. d'Angoulême*, no. 37. This court, which seems to have had no presiding officer, appears more like the informal assemblies found in the next century than a Carolingian tribunal.
[79] *Cart. de Saint-Etienne de Limoges*, no. 3.
[80] *Hist. Gén. de Lang.*, II, no. 165.
[81] *Ibid.*, no. 175.

In fact there is only one case in the Midi in which we seem to find evidence of a different sort of legal procedure. This is in the record of the settlement of a dispute between the abbot of Aniane and a nearby landowner some time between 829 and 840. This settlement was not apparently the result of the meeting of a court, but rather the result of an informal gathering which took place between the parties concerned in the castle of the abbey. The resulting agreement is called a *conventia* and seems to be the first example of this sort found in the Midi[82]—a precedent perhaps for the common use of this type of settlement of disputes in later centuries.

Not only did courts remain much what they had been in the earlier Carolingian period, but so did the law which was used in them, though there is some evidence that the legal concepts of this law were not always clearly understood by the parties concerned—particularly in the case of Roman and Visigothic law. Nevertheless, personality of the law continued in use. South of Narbonne and Carcassonne it was Visigothic law which seems to have been used almost exclusively and indeed our sources show it specifically invoked by name at tribunals held in Narbonne in 855,[83] in Carcassonne in 862,[84] and in Roussillon in 865 and 868.[85] It is also mentioned in a court in Nîmes held in 898.[86] Salic law, however, did not die out and continued to be used by certain individuals. Documents dating from 845 mention it at Marseille,[87] and in Auvergne in 859[88] and at Nîmes in 898.[89] Roman law is also referred to at Marseille in 845[90] and in the Limousin in 841, 851, 865, and 871.[91] It is difficult, however, to be sure that we should attach too much legal significance to such references to various types of law, except in those areas where Visigothic procedures were omnipresent. Elsewhere whatever law is said to be used, the courts seem very similar one to another. Procedures differ little and findings seem still to be rendered in the same way by lay officials and churchmen who were assisted by *judices* and *boni homines* in

[82] *Cart. d'Aniane*, no. 55.
[83] *Cart. de Carcassonne*, IV, 192–193.
[84] *Ibid.*, I, 71–72.
[85] *Cart. roussillonnais*, no. 1; *Hist. Gén. de Lang.*, II, no. 169.
[86] *Cart. de Nîmes*, no. 8.
[87] *Cart. de Saint-Victor*, no. 26.
[88] *Cart. de Brioude*, no. 43.
[89] *Cart. de Nîmes*, no. 8.
[90] *Cart. de Saint-Victor*, no. 26.
[91] *Cart. de Beaulieu*, no. 20 (841), 186 (865); *Cart. de Saint-Etienne de Limoges*, no. 3 (851), 8 (871).

attendance. From the standpoint of law the world of the Carolingians still lingered on relatively unchanged during this period south of Poitou and Burgundy.

While we can come to some definite conclusions as to changes which took place in the administrative and judicial side of government in our regions, the military aspects of it are more difficult to analyze with any precision. Yet it is clear that in these turbulent years in the Midi and Spanish March the military side of its governmental system must have been its most important responsibility. Moslem invasions of Provence, Catalonia, and other parts of the Spanish March, and Viking raiding activities in Gascony, Aquitaine, and even, for a brief period, in the Mediterranean, account for this fact. So do the civil wars which took place between Charles the Bald and Pepin II from 840 to 865 and the struggle over Provence and the Valley of the Rhone which lasted down to 887 or 890. Nor was this all. There is ample evidence that these turbulent decades abounded in private quarrels between magnates which tended to be settled by forceful means.

Ademar of Chabannes, for instance, comments on the fact that the nobles of Aquitaine, or the *duces* as he calls them, were so busy fighting each other during the period 845-852 that they had no time to deal with Viking invaders.[92] Later on, in 866, we hear of a battle to the death between Count Ermenon of Périgord and Count Landry of Saintes in a castle in Angoulême.[93] The men of Bernard Plantevelue in 872 kill Bernard of Toulouse.[94] In fact, the election of Boson as king of Provence in 879 seems to have been due to the desire of churchmen of the Rhone Valley to restrain disorders.[95]

Even where neither civil war nor invasions had any direct impact we find evidence in our documents of continual struggle. In 859 and 860 we find Archbishop Rodulf of Bourges complaining of the presence of evil men in the Limousin—*"infestorum malorum hominum."*[96] A little later in the Rouergue the same phrase is used about 894, when Viking invasions had ceased to be a problem.[97] In charters from the Auvergne region

[92] *Ademar de Chabannes*, III, 17, p. 134.
[93] *Ibid.*, III, 19, pp. 136-137, and *Chronicum Aquitanicum*, ed. G. Pertz, anno 866, in *Mon. Ger. Hist. Scriptores*, II, 252-253.
[94] *Annales Bertiniani*, anno 872.
[95] *Cart. de Grenoble*, no. 70, pp. 265-267. No nobles seem to be listed in this charter.
[96] *Cart. de Beaulieu*, nos. 1, 24.
[97] *Ibid.*, no. 76.

which give land to the abbey of Brioude during this period we also find that a surprising amount of this property was acquired by *conquest*.[98] Charters mentioning this fact are to be found dating from the years 858, 859, and 860, then again in 870 and 873 and finally in an unbroken sequence in 881, 882, 883, 888, 890, 891, 892, 893, 895, 898, 899, and 900.[99] The same thing is revealed for the Lyonnais in 857,[100] for the Vienne region in 870 and 875,[101] and for the Valence area in 889.[102]

Unfortunately when we try to discover specific evidence of the military system in use during this period we find little really pertinent information. The *Manual of Dhuoda* with its general references to *fidelitas* helps little.[103] Nor do the generalities of Carolingian capitularies. It seems probable that Carolingian monarchs like Pepin II, Charles the Bald, and Carloman, regularly summoned into battle their *fideles,* the counts, the *vassi dominici* and the important *aprisio* holders, and that counts did the same for their *vassi.* We hear of the *men* of Bernard Plantevelue who killed Bernard of Toulouse in 872.[104] We learn of Bernard of Septimania invading Catalonia and being killed by the *Goti* of Barcelona in 850.[105] We find a reference to the *fideles* who followed Count Guifred and Count Miró between 878 and 898 and helped repopulate the plain of Vich and

[98] The phrase *ex conquestu* in charters does not necessarily mean conquest, but land acquired by means other than gift or inheritance. Such land, however, if found in large amounts, as in this region, shows an instability in the pattern of landholding, *some* of which was certainly due to actual loss of land by the weak and seizure of it by the powerful. On the meaning of *conquestu* see *Cart. de Brioude,* no. 126, which mentions land *"per parentes vel per conquestem."*

[99] *Cart. de Brioude,* nos. 13, 19, 43, 56, 60, 85, 102, 119, 126, 208, 225, 227, 271, 277, 282, 311, and *Grand Cart. de Brioude,* nos. CCCVIII, CCCLXXII. Fortunately we have some corroborative evidence of disorders in the very region where the abbey of Brioude was located. In a rare narrative, written at about this time concerning Gerald, the self-appointed count by Aurillac, St. Odo of Cluny mentions brigands in the forests, the disturbed state of the countryside, and private wars being waged. Odo, *Vita Sancti Geraldi Aureliacensis,* in Migne *Patrologia latina,* CXXXIII.

[100] *Cart. de Savigny,* no. 19.

[101] *Cart. de Vienne,* no. 106, 109.

[102] *Cartulaire de Saint-Barnard de Romans,* ed. U. Chevalier, no. 4.

[103] This document, dating from the early part of the ninth century, may still be true of its later years. See E. Bondurand, *L'education Carolingienne: Le Manuel de Dhuoda,* XV, 89–91.

[104] *Annales Bertiniani,* anno 872.

[105] *Ibid.,* anno 848, and *Chronici Fontanellensis fragmentum,* ed. G. Pertz, anno 849, in *Mon. Ger. Hist. Scriptores,* II, 43. See also Abadal, *Els Primers Comtes Catalans,* pp. 181–182.

The Governmental System of the Midi and Catalonia

garrison its castles.¹⁰⁶ But we can tell little of how they were mustered into service and how they fought.

This is particularly true of those who battled invaders. We learn that Count Séguin of Bordeaux was captured and killed while fighting the Vikings in 845,¹⁰⁷ that Count Rannoux of Poitou fled from them in 852,¹⁰⁸ that Count Turpio in 863 was slain while opposing them,¹⁰⁹ and that Toulouse was able to beat them off a little later.¹¹⁰ That is all. Just so we learn of the failure of the archbishop of Arles in a campaign against Moslem pirates in the 850's¹¹¹ and of the success of Count Gerald of Vienne in 869¹¹² without having any details which might help us in getting a true picture of the military organization of the areas involved.

What such information, slight though it may be, seems to emphasize is the fact that the military organization which existed during this period was rather ineffective. The failure to destroy Moslems established in Provence or to expel Vikings from Aquitaine, like the difficulties experienced by Carolingian rulers in overcoming the resistance of Count Gerald and King Boson in Vienne, seems to reflect a failure in military organization. So does Count Guifred's defeat and death in battle against the Moslem lords of Lérida in 897 or 898.¹¹³ In contrast to the disciplined warriors whom Charles Martel and Pepin led south between 718 and 768 or those whom William, count of Toulouse, led against Barcelona in the campaign of 801–803,¹¹⁴ the fighting men of the Midi seem disorganized and poorly led during this period. Except for some early successes in Ausona and Berga by Counts Miró and Guifred,¹¹⁵ as a matter of fact, we do not know of a single military operation of any consequence involving warriors of Southern France and Catalonia during these years which was a success.

¹⁰⁶ *El Archivo Condal de Barcelona*, no. 38.
¹⁰⁷ *Ademar de Chabannes*, III, 17, p. 134.
¹⁰⁸ *Ibid.*, III, 18, pp. 136–137.
¹⁰⁹ *Ibid.*, III, 19, p. 138.
¹¹⁰ See J. Calmette, "Le siège de Toulouse par les Normands," in *Annales du Midi*, XXIX (1917).
¹¹¹ See L. Levillain, "Giraut, Comte de Vienne," in *Le Moyen Age*, LV (1949).
¹¹² E. Duprat, in *Bouches du Rhône*, II, 136.
¹¹³ P. Ponsch, "A propos de la date du décès de Wilfred le Velu," in *Études Roussillonnaises*, II (1952), 132–134.
¹¹⁴ See Chapter II, Section I, and Chapter I, Section II, on Carolingian successes in these campaigns.
¹¹⁵ Abadal, *Els Primers Comtes Catalans*, pp. 191–198. Particularly melancholy is the record of the failure to stop Moslem invasions of Catalonia in 852 and 856.

There is still one more way, however, in which we may gain some knowledge of the military aspects of the government of this period. That is by an analysis of information concerning castles and other fortifications. By examining the occupation of old castles and the building of new ones and by studying their distribution we can get some indication of military organization. We can also learn something by examining what we can discover of castle ownership and the power of castellans over the surrounding countryside.

Our first problem concerns evidence of the existence of castles and other fortifications in various parts of the Midi and Catalonia between 828 and 900. By the end of the century it is clear that there were a number of such fortified centers in the Rhone Valley and in Provence. We find mention of a castle at Tournon in 855[116] and two *castella* at Vienne between 855 and 860.[117] In 887 we hear of the fortress of Châtel in Maurienne which guarded the *clusae* leading to Italy.[118] Seven years later there is a reference to a Castle of Inchas near Vienne.[119] In addition to such castles, Lyon is mentioned as having walls in 892 and Vienne in 849 and 899.[120] In Provence we learn of a *castrum* located at Venasque in 862 and one built in the Camargue in 869.[121] Others are referred to at Tournon in 879 and Incia at about the same time.[122] After Moslem attacks in 859 Arles seems to have been fortified, while in 898 Avignon possessed walls.[123]

To the east in Septimania the castle of the Arena of Nîmes was again being used in 876.[124] So was the nearby castle of Anduze mentioned between 876 and 897.[125] Aniane still possessed its castle in Lodève about 840[126] and we have every reason to believe that the nearby castles of Mel-

---

[116] R. Poupardin, *Recueil des actes des rois de Provence (855-928)*, p. 20.
[117] *Ibid.*, p. 11.
[118] *Chartes de Maurienne*, no. 1.
[119] *Cart. de Grenoble*, no. 27.
[120] On the walls of Lyon see *ibid.*, no. 81. On the walls of Vienne and the castle of Castellione beyond the walls mentioned in 849 see *Cart. de Vienne*, no. 4. On the walls of the city mentioned in 899 see *Cart. de Grenoble*, no. 20.
[121] Poupardin, *Recueil des actes des rois de Provence*, p. 27; Duprat, in *Bouches du Rhône*, p. 275.
[122] Poupardin, *Recueil des actes des rois de Provence*, pp. 38, 57.
[123] Duprat, in *Bouches du Rhône*, pp. 132-134; Poupardin, *Recueil des actes des rois de Provence*, p. 38.
[124] *Cart. de Nîmes*, no. 1.
[125] *Ibid.*, no. 2.
[126] *Cart. d'Aniane*, no. 55.

The Governmental System of the Midi and Catalonia 131

gueil and Substantion were still occupied.[127] Near Béziers we hear of the *castra* of Mesoa and Turres,[128] while Narbonne possessed city walls half of whose *turres* Charles the Bald gave to the archbishop of the city in 844.[129] Near Carcassonne we find a castle of Minerbe in 873, one at Alzonne in 888, and evidence of fortifications at the abbey of Montolieu by 898 if not before, since it is now called the Castrum Mallesti.[130] In Razès in 900 there was a *castrum* of Por near the abbey of Saint-Jacques de Joucan.[131]

To the south in Roussillon our documents speak of a castle of Corbi in 832, a *rocca* at Fruesendi in 854 and several other *roccas*, which Marquis Humfrid had *"in beneficio"* and which were given to Count Sunyer in 862.[132] Perhaps one of these was the castle of Saint-Stephen of the *rocca* of Ponus whose castellan is referred to in a charter dating from 865.[133] In Catalonia proper there is a mention of the castle of Vellosa in Gerona in 834 and 844 with the nearby *castellum fractum* and in the same *pagus* one at Monte Aspero which dates from at least 889.[134] Barcelona was protected by walls throughout the period and so was the important fortification of Tarrassa referred to in documents dating from 844 and 874.[135] Ampurias had at least one castle, that given to a certain Stephen by Charles the Simple in 899.[136]

Further to the west the activity of Count Guifred and his brothers in advancing their frontiers to include Ausona and the marches of Berga resulted in the building of a large number of castles. One in Besalu called Castellaris is mentioned in 871, one at Montgrony in 887 and a third at Tarabaldi in 892[137]—all in Ausona. Others at Manressa, Cardona, Besaura, Kastellionem, Casserès, and many other places date from this

---

[127] At least the castle of Substantion is mentioned in 1005 ("Cartulaire de Psalmodi" [unpublished], fol., p. 16).
[128] *Hist. Gén. de Lang.*, II, no. 105.
[129] *Ibid.*, no. 115.
[130] Cros-Meyrévielle, *Documents*, no. 17; *Cart. de Carcassonne*, II, 217; I, 73–74.
[131] *Cart. roussillonnais*, no. 3.
[132] *Hist. Gén. de Lang.*, II, no. 80; *Catalunya Carolingia*, II, 348; *Cart. roussillonnais*, no. 1.
[133] *Catalunya Carolingia*, II, 121–124, 127–130.
[134] *Ibid.*, pp. 13–15, 423–425.
[135] *Ibid.*, pp. 423–425, 431–433.
[136] *Hist. Gén. de Lang.*, V, no. 25.
[137] *Catalunya Carolingia*, II, 176–178; *El Archivo Condal de Barcelona*, nos. 4, 8. See also the castle of Torello mentioned first in 881 in Abadal, *Els Primers Comtes Catalans*, p. 88.

period also.[138] So do the many small *turres* or castles which we find scattered throughout Pallars and Ribagorça.[139]

To the north in Aquitaine we find Toulouse possessing walls in 844[140] and capable still of resisting Norse attacks two decades later, while on the Gascon borders there is a record of at least one castle, that of Cerrucium which before 847 was given to Astronove by Pepin II.[141] Other regions of Aquitaine contained a number of *castella* which the Vikings sacked between 844 and 848.[142] Among them perhaps was the castle of Rancogne in Angoulême mentioned in 866.[143] We also know that some time between 869 and 877 Count Vulgrin raised two castles in the same region and in the Saintonge to thwart Viking raiders, the fortresses of Marillac and Matas.[144] A little later, soon after 886, Count Aldouin rebuilt the walls of Angoulême.[145]

To the east in Quercy we find a reference to a castle of Cosilacum near Cahors which seems to have been in existence in 844 and one in Castellione overlooking the Dordogne.[146] In 859 the castle of Turenne in the Limousin was occupied.[147] So was one at Castellacus mentioned in 885 and one at Ségur in 888.[148] In the same year in nearby Poitou we find reference to a tower at Château Larchier.[149] In our documents concerning Auvergne we find a reference to a *castrum* of Mozérat in 864[150] and ten years later in 874 to the fortifications of the abbey of Brioude and to a *castrum* at Aurillac as well.[151] As early as 825 LePuy had a *castrum* built by Count Berengar.[152]

---

[138] *El Archivo Condal de Barcelona*, no. 9, and Abadal, *Els Primers Comtes Catalans*, pp. 87–90.
[139] On the large number of *turres* scattered through these regions see Abadal, *Els Comtats de Pallars i Ribagorça*.
[140] *Cart. de Saint-Sernin*, no. 3.
[141] *Hist. Gén. de Lang.*, II, no. 131.
[142] *Ademar de Chabannes*, III, 17, p. 134.
[143] *Ibid.*, III, 19, p. 136.
[144] *Ibid.*, III, 20, and "Aquitoniae Historiae Fragmentum, in *ibid.*, pp. 197–198.
[145] *Ademar de Chabannes*, III, 23, pp. 143–144.
[146] *Cart. de Beaulieu*, no. 34; *Hist. Gén. de Lang.*, II, no. 121.
[147] *Cart. de Beaulieu*, no. 33.
[148] *Ibid.*, nos. 55, 166; G. Tenant de la Tour, *L'homme et la terre de Charlemagne à Saint Louis*, pp. 300–301.
[149] *Cartulaire de l'abbaye de Saint-Cyprien de Poitiers*, ed. Redet, in *Archives historiques du Poitou*, III (1874), no. 400, p. 271.
[150] *Cart. de Brioude*, no. 176.
[151] *Ibid.*, no. 132.
[152] *Hist. Gén. de Lang.*, II, no. 67.

This incomplete list of castles and fortified *civitates* dating from this period—incomplete because of a lack of documentary materials—does seem to show certain things. It makes clear that there was a certain concentration of castles in three regions, in Provence and Eastern Languedoc near the mouth of the Rhone, in Western Aquitaine, and in Catalonia. It suggests that this concentration was the result of reactions to invasion, or in the case of Catalonia a response to armed advance into frontier areas. A Count Vulgrin in Angoulême or local magnates in Provence and the Nîmes area, or a Count Guifred in Catalonia seem to have been responsible for the fortifications of such regions, often in response to outside pressure. For other parts of the Midi, like the Carcassonne region, the Middle Rhone Valley, or Auvergne and the Limousin, no such explanation is possible. Here the occupation of old castles and the building of new ones must be regarded rather as a response to the insecurity which prevailed during these years. This seems particularly true of fortifications which protected abbeys like Aniane, Brioude, and Montolieu.

Furthermore, some indication of defense matters can also be gained from an analysis of castle holding. In most cases we are ignorant as to who actually controlled a particular castle or fortified city. In other cases we can be more precise. A large number of them, perhaps even a majority of them, were under the direct control of the authorities, such as the counts and other representatives of secular government. The castles of Inchas and Châtel[153] in the Upper Rhone Valley region, those of Turenne and Ségur[154] in the Limousin, the castles of the Arenas and Anduze[155] in the Nîmois, and those built by Vulgrin in Angoulême[156] and Count Guifred in Ausona[157] are cases in point. Others built on land which belonged to the royal *fisc* seem to have been controlled, at least initially, by castellans

---

[153] *Cart. de Grenoble*, no. 27 (originally the castle of Inchas belonged to King Louis of Provence-Burgundy); *Chartes de Maurienne*, no. 1 (originally Châtel belonged to King Boson).

[154] During this period the castle of Turenne probably belonged to the counts of Turenne (See *Cart. de Beaulieu*, no. 33). On Ségur, the central castle of the viscounts of Limoges, see Tenant de la Tour, *L'homme et la terre*, pp. 300–305.

[155] In 876 the castle of the Arenas seems to be in the possession of the viscounts of Nîmes (*Cart. de Nîmes*, no. 1). By the late ninth century the fortress of Anduze belonged to Viscount Frédélon of Anduze (*ibid.*, no. 2).

[156] See *Ademar de Chabannes*, III, 20, p. 138, and "Aquitaniae Historiae Fragmentum," in *ibid.*, pp. 197–198, on the circumstances of the building of these castles by Count Vulgrin.

[157] On the castles in Ausona and elsewhere in Catalonia built by Count Guifred see Abadal, *Els Primers Comtes Catalans*, pp. 80–110.

tied to Carolingian rulers by ties of vassalage or *fidelitas*. Such seems to have been the case of Mesoa and Turres near Béziers held *"jure beneficiario"* from Charles the Bald, Cerrucium on the Gascon border which Charles the Bald gave to Astronove, the *rocca* of Fruesendi in Roussillon which Sunald and Riculf held as a benefice in 854 and other *roccas* in Ampurias held *"ad beneficium"* from Charles the Bald down to 862.[158]

A surprising number of fortresses, however, either were originally or during the course of the century became the possessions of archbishops, bishops, and abbeys. The archbishops of Narbonne were given one half of the *turres* of Narbonne, the bishop of Maurienne the castle of Châtel, the bishop of Gerona the castle of Vellosa.[159] The abbots of Aniane controlled the *castrum* of Montecalmense about 840; the abbey of Moissac, that of Cerrucium after 847; Lagrasse, Alzonne after 888; Saint-Paul de Fontclara, one-third of Monte Aspero in 889.[160] Brioude's fortifications after 874 seem to have belonged to the abbey, as did Montolieu's in 898.[161] Both church and private individuals then seem in this period to share in a military defense system which one would tend to think of as one belonging to the secular authorities alone—just as had been true earlier—a proof, perhaps, of the ineffectiveness of the governmental system established in these regions.

What, however, did control or ownership of such a castle imply? Did castellans of the period tend to have authority over territory which surrounded their fortresses and to levy special dues upon it, as they were to do later on? Did *mandamenta* already exist? In at least two cases there is definite indication that they did. In 881 we hear of the *appendici* or *terms* of the castle of Torello[162] in Ausona and in 887 the fortress of Châtel in the Alps is mentioned along with *"villis villaribusque subjectis eodem castro."*[163] Did this mean that dues of a special nature were levied on the surrounding countryside? Perhaps so. In 848, on the plea of Count Appolonius of Agde, Charles the Bald forbade the levying by the laity of certain dues called *"mansionaticum, portaticum, salinaticum et hospitalicum"*—this in a region close to the fortresses of Mesoa and

---

[158] *Hist. Gén. de Lang.*, II, no. 105, 131; *Catalunya Carolingia*, II, 348, 357–358.

[159] *Hist. Gén. de Lang.*, II, no. 115; *Chartes de Maurienne*, no. 1; *Catalunya Carolingia*, II, 121–124.

[160] *Cart. d'Aniane*, no. 55; *Hist. Gén. de Lang.*, II, no. 131; *Cart. de Carcassonne*, II, 217; *Catalunya Carolingia*, II, 13–15.

[161] *Cart. de Brioude*, no. 132; *Cart. de Carcassonne*, I, 73–74.

[162] See Abadal, *Els Primers Comtes Catalans*, pp. 78–79, 88.

[163] *Chartes de Maurienne*, no. 1.

The Governmental System of the Midi and Catalonia 135

Turres.[164] In 874 the bishop of Barcelona asked the help of the same ruler against what he called the insolence of the castle of Tàrrassa and two *Goti* who were usurping lands belonging to his church.[165] Near Carcassonne in 883 a certain Ermenard, in returning land he had taken unjustly from the abbey of Saint-Hilaire retained a *receptum* over this property belonging to the monastery.[166] Already then, though opposed, it would seem, by important elements in the population, *mandamenta* were being formed around the castles to be found in these regions.

Examination of castles then, of their occupation, their building, their control, and their distribution—as well as evidence of exactions which were levied beyond their walls—seems to show the same changes revealed in other aspects of military organization or in the administration of *honores*. It shows us a Midi and a Catalonia in transition from a Carolingian governmental system to something quite different in which local nobles, churchmen, and private individuals more and more tend to exercise power which was once the prerogative of the Carolingian government. Much of the old Carolingian system still remained, particularly the courts and the legal system, but much had already begun to be profoundly altered in spirit and in substance towards a new and unusual system of government which we will be examining in later chapters.

[164] *Hist. Gén. de Lang.*, II, no. 133.
[165] *Catalunya Carolingia*, II, 431–433.
[166] Cros-Meyrévielle, *Documents*, no. 19, pp. 24–25.

CHAPTER VIII

The Church (828–900)

No CONSIDERATION of the decay of the Carolingian system in the Midi and Catalonia would be complete without special attention being paid to the Church, which was, as we have noted, an integral part of this system. Charlemagne and Louis the Pious had helped to make the Church of these regions a powerful force by placing most archbishoprics, bishoprics, and abbeys under special royal protection, endowing them with tracts of land belonging to the royal *fisc,* and giving them special privileges. The most important of such privileges were the immunities which freed important churchmen and their domains from interference from counts and their agents, which allowed them to maintain a court system separate from that of the secular authorities in many ways, and which in effect gave them authority over many laymen who were dependent upon them. As a result, archbishops, bishops, and abbots south of Poitou and Burgundy were, during this period, men possessing great power, in practice—if not in theory—often sharing authority over local regions with those counts and viscounts who nominally controlled them in the name of the monarch.

Recognizing the importance of such churchmen in the empire Louis the Pious like Charlemagne had followed the policy of tying them to him personally by having them take the special oath of *fidelitas* required of counts and *vassi dominici,* which in certain respects made the domains of important church officials *honores* and the churchmen themselves *vassi* or *fideles* of the monarch.[1] In addition to their responsibilities and loyalty to a church organization, then, such churchmen had a special and personal

---

[1] *Annales Bertiniani,* ed. E. Waitz, anno 837, p. 15. On earlier oaths of churchmen to Charlemagne's *missi* see "Capitulare Missorum," ch. 2, 4, in Boretius, *Capitularia,* I, no. 25, pp. 66–67.

The Church (828-900)

tie which bound them to Carolingian rulers—in some ways more important than that which linked them to a distant Pope in Rome.

From 828 on Carolingian rulers of the Midi and Catalonia continued to maintain, in effect, this same system and, as a matter of fact, seem to have found the Church a much more dependable basis of support than their secular officials and organization. Pepin II or Charles the Bald, Carloman, or even Eudes was always ready to give protection and support to the Church and could generally count upon its support in turn. Despite this fact, however, changes had taken place in the Southern French and Catalan Church by the year 900—changes not only in regard to the Church's organization and authority, but also in its relationship to the monarchs who lived north of the Loire. Civil wars, invasions, and the rise to authority of independent noble families affected the Church as they did the secular system of courts, administration, and military organization. The Church which emerged by the first years of the tenth century in many ways was not the same Church which we find in 828.

Until well into the reign of Charles the Bald, however, changes which took place in the Church seem less apparent than those in other parts of the Carolingian governing system or even in the society of the Midi and Catalonia. St. Benedict of Aniane and his successors among the important churchmen of the century continued to support the Carolingian rulers of the empire, and in return the Church's privileges and power were maintained by such monarchs to the best of their ability.[2] In fact, down to the time of Hincmar of Rheims the Church was the strongest bulwark of support for the monarchy, and the monarchy was fully cognizant of this fact.[3]

Nowhere do we see this more clearly revealed than in an examination of the monastic establishments of the period. As we have noted, the years between 778 and 828 saw a monastic revival in the Midi and Spanish March. With the full backing of Charlemagne and Louis the Pious, older abbeys were reformed and reconstituted and new ones established south of the Loire and of Burgundy, especially in Aquitaine, Septimania, the Spanish March, and even in Gascony. In most parts of the Midi and Catalonia this continued to be true after 828 also. In Aquitaine, for in-

[2] See Agobard's letter to Louis the Pious in 833 in support of imperial Carolingian unity (*Agobardi Lugdunensis archepiscopi*, no. 15, in *Mon. Ger. Hist. Epistolae*, ed. E. Dummler, V, 223-226). See also L. Halphen, *Charlemagne et l'empire Carolingien*, pp. 240-280.

[3] On Church support for the Carolingians in this period see especially F. Lot and L. Halphen, *Le règne de Charles le Chauve (842-877)*.

stance, not only were the privileges of older establishments renewed by Carolingian rulers, but new or reconstituted abbeys were set up with royal approval and privileges, like Saint-Chaffre du Monastier in Velay, Saint-Jean d'Angély in Saintonge or Saint-Cybard of Poitiers.[4]

Even more interesting is the continued founding of new abbeys in Catalonia. It was early in this period that Saint-Clement of Regulla in Roussillon, Saint-Medir in Gerona, Eixalada in Confluent, Saint-Martin des Escoules in Besalu, and Saint-Salvador in Urgell[5] were founded. A few years later, about 866, another, Santa-Julia del Mont was added.[6] Charles the Bald bestowed on each of these new monasteries generous grants of land from the royal *fisc* and many other privileges. He was equally generous to the cathedral churches of this region and to other abbeys, old and new, further west in Pallars and Ribagorça.[7]

Soon after 840, however, in Gascony, in parts of Western Aquitaine and in Provence this monastic revival came to a halt and a decline set in. It seems clear that in the former two regions this was due to Viking invasions which bore particularly heavily upon monastic establishments which seem to have represented rich prizes and sources of booty for Norse raiders. Those monasteries which were destroyed during the years 844–852, or a Saint-Cybard of Angoulême sacked in 875,[8] illustrate the damage done during the course of Viking raids. No wonder the monks of Saint-Hilaire of Poitiers moved to the interior to escape the Vikings who ravaged their cloister.[9] Nor were abbeys alone disorganized by such attacks. Even Archbishop Frotaire thought it wiser to abandon his see of Bordeaux and, about 870, to seek refuge in the interior also.[10] As a result a number of abbeys like Saint-Jean d'Angély disappear from our records not to reappear until the next century.

It seems clear that the weak Gascon monastic movement was also adversely affected by Viking attacks and the disorders of the period. Not one Gascon abbey founded in Carolingian times appears to have survived

---

[4] *Hist. Gén. de Lang.*, II, no. 128; *Ademar de Chabannes*, III, 16, p. 132.
[5] *Catalunya Carolingia*, II, 10–13, 80–90, 154–156, 180–182, 246–248.
[6] *Ibid.*, pp. 219–221.
[7] On privileges given to the church of Gerona see *ibid.*, pp. 127–130. On those given churches of Pallars and Ribagorça see Abadal, *Els Comtats de Pallars i Ribagorça* and "Els precepts comtals carolingis per al Pallars," in *Boletin de la Real Academia de Buenas Letras de Barcelona*, XXVI (1954–1958).
[8] *Ademar de Chabannes*, III, 17, 19, p. 134, 137.
[9] *Ibid.*, III, 19, p. 137.
[10] Johannis VIII, *Papae Epistolae*, in Migne, *Patrologia latina*, CXXVI, no. 36.

The Church (828-900) 139

into the tenth century. They simply disappeared.[11] The secular church organization seems to have been disorganized by this period of disorders as well. Not only did the archbishopric of Bordeaux cease to function, but so did that of Auch, further in the interior, whose cathedral church was still in ruins early in the tenth century.[12] Whether other bishoprics continued in existence is uncertain. No wonder the relics of Sainte-Foi were brought to Conques about 878 for safekeeping.[13] There was no security for them in Gascony.

It seems probable that in Provence and the lower Rhone Valley Moslem pirate attacks had a similar bad effect on monasteries and upon the Church in general. Soon after 850 such attacks seem to have caused the monks of Psalmodi to leave their abbey and take refuge farther west in Septimania.[14] Lérins ceased for a period after 830 to keep charters,[15] and Saint-Victor of Marseille entered a period which can only be described as one of decadence.[16] Whether all of the above, however, was due to Moslem pirate activities is very questionable. As some historians have pointed out, some of it was the result of a general insecurity found in these regions after 828, particularly in the countryside far from the protective walls of the *castra* and *civitates* of the region. Monastic establishments in rural areas were adversely affected by such disorders, whatever their origin.[17] Any monastic revival which had occurred stopped in Provence and in many cases abbeys which were in existence simply disappeared.

[11] See references to abbeys in Gascony by the Council of Aix in 815 or 816, in P. Labbé, *Sacrosancta Concilia*, IX, 603. None of these seem to have survived into the tenth century.

[12] *Cartulaires du chapitre de l'église métropolitaine Sainte Marie d'Auch*, ed. C. Lacaye La Playne-Barris, in *Archives Historiques de la Gascoyne*, fasc. III, no. 77.

[13] See *Miracles de Sainte Foy*, in *Recueil des Historiens de Gaules et de la France*, ed. D. Bouquet *et alii*, VII, 650–661; and *Translatio Sanctae Faustae e Vasconia*, in *ibid.*, pp. 344–351.

[14] E. Duprat, in *Bouches du Rhône*, p. 138.

[15] The last charters in this period from the *Cartulaire de Lérins* date from 824 (see *Cart. de Lérins*, nos. 247, 248). Then all is silence for more than a century and a half.

[16] For Saint-Victor's cartulary we find only one charter (dating from 884) after 845. Then all is silence for decades. We know that in 923 the canons of Marseille settled in the abbey of Saint-Gervais near Fos (L. Albanes-Chevalier, *Gallia Christiana Novissima*, nos. 62, 76). This may account for this silence. See *Cart. de Saint-Victor*, no. 9, on the charter of 884.

[17] Duprat, in *Bouches du Rhône*, pp. 149–153.

140   *The Decline of Royal Power*

It would be wise, however, not to generalize from such areas about the Midi as a whole. For in regions not affected by such conditions there is ample evidence that older monasteries continued to grow after 840 and that new ones were founded. This seems true of Aniane, Gellone, Conques, Lagrasse, Saint-Hilaire, Montolieu, Arles, Brioude, Saint-Chaffre, Savigny, Moissac, and Saint-Sernin of Toulouse[18]—to name only

[18] On the land which Aniane possessed and its *cellas* which stretched through Septimania see the privileges of the abbey confirmed by Louis the Pious in 837 (*Cart. d'Aniane*, nos. 7, 13), and a charter of Charles the Bald (*ibid.*, no. 41); for additional private gifts of land see *ibid.*, nos. 55, 59, 61, 113, 123, 150, 306, 311, 313, 319, 412. Most of Gellone's charters which date from this period are of doubtful validity. On the problem of that abbey's lost charters see P. Tisset, *L'abbaye de Gellone au diocèse de Lodève*, pp. 61 ff. See *Cart. de Gellone*, no. 113, on land given the abbey. The growth of Conques was slow until, in 838, Pepin I gave the abbey land which belonged to the royal *fisc* (*Cart. de Conques*, no. 581). Its next important gifts came from Bernard Plantevelue in 882 and 883 (*ibid.*, nos. 4, 153); for other gifts see *ibid.*, nos. 108, 212, 409. For Lagrasse see privileges and grants of land given it by Pepin I of Aquitaine in 838 in Cros-Meyrévielle, *Documents*, no. 12, and other royal bounty from Charles the Bald in 854 (*Hist. Gén. de Lang.*, II, no. 140); in 855 and 876 (*Cart. de Carcassonne*, II, 264–266). For private gifts see *ibid.*, pp. 214, 216, 217. Lagrasse in this period seems to be the most important abbey in Septimania, except perhaps for Aniane. Concerning property owned by Saint-Hilaire see privileges and land given this abbey in 844 (*Hist. Gén. de Lang.*, II, no. 124) and in 855 (*Cart. de Carcassonne*, V, 59–60). See Pepin I's gifts of land to Montolieu in 828 (*Cart. de Carcassonne*, I, 70–71) and those of Eudes in 888 (*ibid.*, p. 75). On the growth of Arles see P. Ponsch, "Les origines de l'abbaye d'Arles," in *Études Roussillonnaises*, IV (1954–1955), 69–99. Brioude grew to become the most important abbey of Central France during this period, judging from its cartulary, which shows an accumulation of many small pieces of property as gifts (see *Cart. de Brioude*, nos. 13, 17, 19, 24, 26, 29, 43, 56, 60, 62, 77, 82, 85, 86, 95, 98, 102, 110, 116, 119, 126, 131, 144, 165, 168, 173, 182, 197, 199, 200, 207, 208, 210, 212, 215, 219, 225, 226, 227, 231, 240, 245, 254, 263, 269, 277, 278, 282, 283, 289, 297, 304, 309, 311; and *Grand Cart. de Brioude*, nos. CCLXXV, CCLXXXIV, CCCXXII, CCCXLVII, CCCLIX, CCCLXXII, CCCXXXVII, CCCC). For the privileges given Saint-Chaffre by Pepin II in 845 see *Hist. Gén. de Lang.*, II, no. 128; for those given by Charles the Bald in 876 and 877 see *Cartulaire de l'abbaye de Saint-Chaffre du Monastier*, ed. U. Chevalier, nos. 33, 196, 430; for extensive private gifts of land to the abbey, some large, some small, see *ibid.*, nos. 58, 59, 60, 61, 62, 65, 66, 67, 68, 69, 70, 72, 339, 386. Savigny's records for this period are incomplete due to their destruction early in the tenth century. See a partial record of property accumulation in *Cart. de Savigny* nos. 18, 19, 24, 26, 27. We know little about gifts of land to Moissac after the bishop of Cahors' extensive gift in 783 (*Hist. Gén. de Lang.*, II, no. 7), except for a second large addition to the abbey's lands in 847 (*ibid.*, II, no. 13). On the privileges which Charles the Bald gave to Saint-Sernin in 844 see *Cart. de Saint-Sernin*, no. 3.

The Church (828-900)

a few of the established ones which have left records for us. As for new ones, the best examples of this development are Tulle and Beaulieu in the Limousin, Aurillac in Auvergne and Vabres in the Albigeois,[19] which were all the result of pious foundations by the leading magnates and churchmen of Aquitaine during this period. A reconstituted Saint-Barnard de Romans in Dauphiny and Saint-André-le-Bas outside Vienne[20] represent the same tendency in the Middle Rhone Valley region. Toward the end of the century in Catalonia when Counts Miró and Guifred had reestablished control over this region, we find new abbeys being founded, like Cuxa to which the abbey of Eixalada was transferred in 879, and nearby Ripoll and Saint-Joan de les Abadesses, as well as Saint-Paul de Fontclara in Gerona and Santa-Cecilia de Elins in Urgell.[21] The decline of Carolingian authority which took place, then, did not result in an end of the monastic revival in many parts of the Midi and of Catalonia. Rather the movement seems to have kept an amazing vitality and ability to spread into certain regions.

[19] We have only a few late ninth-century charters showing gifts of land to Tulle (*Cart. de Tulle*, nos. 45, 53, 457, 658). Beaulieu, which seems to have been the most important abbey in Central Aquitaine, has extremely full records. For royal charters giving privileges and land to the abbey see those of Charles the Bald in 859 (*Cart. de Beaulieu*, no. 5), in 864 (*ibid.*, no. 4), in 876 (*ibid.*, no. 19). See also charters of Carloman in 882 (*ibid.*, no. 8); and Eudes in 889 (*ibid.*, no. 12). For the record of extensive private gifts to Beaulieu between 859 and 900 see *ibid.*, nos. 1, 3, 4, 13, 17, 18, 19, 22, 25, 29, 33, 43, 45, 51, 52, 54, 55, 63, 68, 79, 81, 87, 112, 115, 127, 130, 131, 133, 140, 142, 152, 153, 155, 156, 157, 158, 161, 162, 165, 168, 169, 171, 172, 173, 175, 176, 177, 179, 183, 186. No charters survive from Aurillac, but we have an account of the founding of this abbey late in the century in Odo, *Vita Sancti Geraldi Auriliacensis*, in Migne, *Patrologia latina*, CXXXIII. Charters given Vabres in 863 and 870 by Charles the Bald are found in *Hist. Gén. de Lang.*, II, nos. 159, 175. For other gifts of land to this abbey see *ibid.*, nos. 160, 164, 186, 203.

[20] Though Saint-Barnard de Romans was founded in 817 (*Cart. de Saint-Barnard de Romans*, no. 1), it is not until late in the century that we see any evidence of growth (*ibid.*, nos. 3, 4). For Saint-André-le-Bas and its slow growth during this period see *Cart. de Saint-André-le-bas*, nos. 86, 137.

[21] On the early history of Saint-Michael of Cuxa and its accumulation of property see P. Ponsch, "Le domaine foncier de Saint-Michel de Cuxa au IXe, X^e et XIe siècles," in *Études Roussillonnaises*, II (1952), 68–80, and "Les origines de Saint-Michel de Cuxa," in *ibid.*, pp. 7–19. On the foundation of Ripoll and Saint-Joan de les Abadesses see R. de Abadal i de Vinyals, *Els Primers Comtes Catalans*, pp. 130–147. For the charter which tells how Ripoll was founded by Count Guifred and his wife see *Marca hispanica*, appendix 45. For Saint-Joan de les Abadesses see *Catalunya Carolingia*, II, 216. About Saint-Paul de Fontclara and Santa-Cecilia des Elins see *Catalunya Carolingia*, II, 13–15, 250–252.

Newly founded abbeys, like old ones, continued to seek and to receive charters assuring them of royal privileges and royal protection even when the actual authority of the Carolingians had become rather nominal in many parts of the Midi and Catalonia. Witness Charles the Bald's charters given to Vabres in 863, to Brioude in 874, to Caunes (Aude) in 875, Lagrasse and Saint-Chaffre in 876, and Dovera in 877;[22] or Louis le Bègue's to Arles-sur-Teche in Vallespir in 878;[23] or Carloman's charters given Arles (Auch), Santa-Cecilia de Elins, and Saint-Polycarpe in Razès in 881 and to Beaulieu in 882.[24] Nor did this end with a new Capetian line, for we have Eudes' diploma for Montolieu dating from 888 and ones for Saint-Polycarpe in Razès, Saint-Paul de Fontclara, and Beaulieu[25] in 889 as well as Charles the Simple's charters given Saint-Joan de les Abadesses in 899 and Saint-Jacques-de-Joucan in 900.[26]

Royal charters, those given late in the period and earlier ones too, did more than assure the recipients of immunities and royal privileges. They represent a continuing policy of distributing land belonging to the royal *fisc* to such establishments and to the churches of these regions—especially vacant and uncultivated land which needed settlement. This policy, of course, antedates the reign of Charles the Bald. In 828, for instance, we find Pepin I of Aquitaine giving two *villas* to the abbey of Montolieu and in 835 adding another on the plea of Count Oliba I of Carcassonne.[27] Three years later he gave to Conques a *villa* called Fiscellum, a significant name, as well as an important tract of forest land and four other *villas*.[28] Meanwhile in 834 the Emperor Lothaire also bestowed property on the church of Elne in Roussillon, consisting of certain *"villas ex heremo."*[29] At the same time his father Louis the Pious was giving the same type of land to the abbey of San-Salvador in Urgell.[30]

These earlier gifts of royal *fiscal* land to abbeys, however, seem rather insignificant in comparison with the bounty which began to be distributed by Charles the Bald soon after his accession. Probably Charles' gifts of

[22] *Hist. Gén. de Lang.*, II, no. 159 (Vabres), 197 (Dovera); *Cart. de Brioude*, no. 334 (Brioude); *Cart. de Carcassonne*, II, 216 (Lagrasse); IV, 72 (Caunes); *Cart. de Saint-Chaffre*, nos. 33, 196, 430, (Saint-Chaffre).
[23] *Catalunya Carolingia*, II, 33–36.
[24] *Cart. Roussillonnais*, no. 2; *Catalunya Carolingia*, II, 250–252; *Hist. Gén. de Lang.*, V, no. 2; *Cart. de Beaulieu*, no. 8.
[25] *Cart. de Carcassonne*, I, 73; *Hist. Gén. de Lang.*, V, no. 9; *Catalunya Carolingia*, II, 13–15; *Cart. de Beaulieu*, no. 12.
[26] *Catalunya Carolingia*, II, 216–217; *Cart. roussillonnais*, no. 3.
[27] *Cart. de Carcassonne*, I, 70–71.   [28] *Cart. de Conques*, no. 581.
[29] *Catalunya Carolingia*, II, 102–103.   [30] *Ibid.*, pp. 246–248.

The Church (828-900)   143

land from the royal *fisc* were due to the fact that he was competing for Church support in the Midi and Catalonia with his rival, Pepin II of Aquitaine. Whatever the causes, however, it was in the year 844 that his activities in this respect were most noticeable. In this year he gave royal property to the abbey of Psalmodi in the Camargue, to the church of Narbonne, to Caunes, Saint-Hilaire, and Saint-Polycarpe in the Carcassonne region and to Saint-Clinian on the borders of the Toulousain.[31] Nor were church establishments in Catalonia neglected. Saint-Clement of Regulla in Besalu and San-Senterada in Urgell received similar royal gifts, as did Saint-André de Sureda, Saint-Peter of Albaniya and the church of Gerona.[32] In answer to Charles' generosity, in 845 Pepin II gave land from the royal *fisc* to Saint-Chaffre du Monastier (Haute-Loire)[33] and gave to Bishop Stodile and the canons of the church of Saint-Etienne of Limoges two *villas* belonging to the royal *fisc*.[34]

Judging from extant charters a slackening of royal distribution of property then ensued, for down to 864 we learn of only two gifts of royal lands to abbeys, one to Saint-Clement of Regulla in 850,[35] and a large number of *villas* in the Narbonne region and in Confluent, Gerona, Ampurias, and Besalu added to the patrimony of the abbey of Lagrasse in 855.[36] Later in Charles' reign, however, he continued to endow abbeys with land belonging to the royal *fisc*. In 864 he gave a *villa* to Beaulieu in the Limousin[37] and two years later the Catalan abbey of Santa-Julia del Mont was the recipient of similar generosity.[38] In 876 Beaulieu again received royal land[39] as did Saint-Velesius of Albi;[40] and in this year and 877 so did Lagrasse[41] and the abbey of Dovera in the Vivarais.[42]

---

[31] *Hist. Gén. de Lang.*, II, nos. 122 (Psalmodi), 114 and 115 (Narbonne), 125 (Caunes), 124 (Saint-Hilaire), 172 (Saint-Polycarpe, 113 (Saint-Clinian).

[32] *Catalunya Carolingia*, II, 180–182 (Saint-Clement), 263–265 (San-Senterada), 271–272 (Saint-André de Sureda), 5–8 (Saint-Peter), 127–130 (Gerona).

[33] *Hist. Gén. de Lang.*, II, no. 128.

[34] *Cart. de Saint-Etienne de Limoges*, no. 80.

[35] *Hist. Gén. de Lang.*, II, no. 137.

[36] *Cart. de Carcassonne*, II, 214–215.

[37] *Cart. de Beaulieu*, no. 4.

[38] *Hist. Gén. de Lang.*, II, nos. 219–221. See in this same year a charter referring to a gift of a *villa* to the *cella* of Saint-Vincent (*ibid.*, no. 167).

[39] *Cart. de Beaulieu*, no. 9.

[40] This grant of land *ex fiscos* to Saint-Velesius probably took place earlier than 870. In this year, however, it is mentioned in a case before a court presided over by Bernard, count and marquis (*Hist. Gén. de Lang.*, II, no. 174).

[41] *Cart. de Carcassonne*, II, 216.   [42] *Hist. Gén. de Lang.*, II, no. 197.

144   The Decline of Royal Power

Charles' death in 877 did not halt this policy, for his immediate successors continued to follow it. In 878 King Louis le Bègue gave *fiscal* land to the abbey of Arles in Vallespir and to the churches of Gerona and Barcelona,[43] while in 881 Carloman did the same for the church of Narbonne, and the abbeys of Arles (Auch), Saint-Polycarpe in Razès and Santa-Cecilia in Urgell.[44] The next year in 882 he conferred a grant of royal *villas* on the abbey of Beaulieu.[45] The accession of Eudes did not change matters either. Though Eudes had little authority over the Midi and Catalonia, he did not hesitate to give royal property to Montolieu in 888 or to add new gifts to the patrimony of Saint-Polycarpe in Razès and to newly founded Saint-Paul de Fontclara in 889.[46] In the Valley of the Rhone his rivals and contemporaries adopted a similar policy, for we find King Boson in 887 giving the bishop of Maurienne a castle and surrounding territory,[47] and his son, King Louis, endowing the church of Saint-Etienne of Lyon in 892 with a number of *villas*.[48] When Charles the Simple's accession to power brought the Carolingians back into authority, he, too, continued such distribution of property to ecclesiastical establishments. In 898, he gave three *villas* and a piece of woodland to the church of Roussillon and a year later gave other royal rights and *fiscal* land to the churches of Gerona and Narbonne.[49] If the royal *fisc* south of Poitou and Burgundy was exhausted by 900, it was in no small measure due to the lavish endowments given the Church by monarchs between the year 828 and the end of the century.

In the light of the above it seems almost paradoxical to insist that the last years of the ninth century saw actual royal authority over many of the monasteries and churches of the Midi and Catalonia in a state of eclipse. By this time it was the important families of their regions rather than the monarchs who had become the principal patrons and proprietors of such monasteries and churches. Not that either refused to accept royal bounty. They did not. But the situation had definitely changed. It seems

---

[43] *Catalunya Carolingia*, II, 33–36; 131–134.
[44] *Hist. Gén. de Lang.*, V, nos. 3 (Narbonne), 2 (Saint-Polycarpe); *Cart. roussillonnais*, no. 2 (Arles); *Catalunya Carolingia*, II, 250–252 (Santa-Cecilia).
[45] *Cart. de Beaulieu*, no. 8.
[46] *Cart. de Carcassonne*, I, 73 (Montolieu); *Hist. Gén. de Lang.*, V, no. 9 (Saint-Polycarpe); *Catalunya Carolingia*, II, 13–15 (Saint-Paul de Fontclara).
[47] *Chartes de Maurienne*, no. 1.
[48] *Cart. de Grenoble*, no. 31.
[49] *Catalunya Carolingia*, II, 107–108, 145–147, 373–374.

clear, for instance, that Vabres, despite its royal charter, was controlled and protected by the house of Toulouse-Rouergue,[50] and that Brioude, except for a brief period, was under the control of that of Auvergne,[51] just as the counts of Turenne at first occupied a similar position in regard to Beaulieu.[52] In Catalonia San-Cugat, Saint-Joan de les Abadesses, Cuxa, and Ripoll were all under the protection of the family of Count Guifred.[53] Like the *honores*, which they came to control as hereditary counts, the abbeys, too, came under the control of the leading families of the Midi and the Spanish March who by 900 had replaced the monarchs in their role as protectors and patrons of such establishments. What is important to emphasize, however, is that this change did *not* stop monastic growth in most parts of these regions. Rather, it continued.

Despite the continued existence and growth of a number of older monastic establishments and the founding of new ones after 828, though, it would not be exact to assume that all was well with abbeys and churches which were located in regions not subject to Viking attack or raids by Moslem pirates. Nothing could be further from the truth. Growth did exist and so did new foundations which were the result of the piety of prominent laymen. But at the same time, our records reveal that during these years Church lands presented a temptation to avaricious rulers, officials, and magnates who often encroached upon them and usurped such land for their own use and that of their supporters.

We have many examples of this. For instance, in Provence we hear of the usurpation of a *teloneum* belonging to the abbey of Saint-Victor of

[50] In a charter of 862 referring to a gift he is giving to the abbey of Vabres, Count Raymond of Toulouse forbids a *king* or any other man to exchange this property he is giving to the abbey or grant it out as a benefice. This implies a certain control over this abbey by the Toulousain house. Indeed in this same charter Raymond says he and his son are the *defensores* of the abbey (*Hist. Gén. de Lang.*, II, no. 160). By 883 a charter refers to Count Bernard of Toulouse as its *custos* (*ibid.*, no. 203).

[51] Between 846 and 869 charters of Brioude refer to Counts Bernard and Warin as lay abbots. In 893 lay control over the abbey by this same family of counts seems to have been re-established with Duke William as lay abbot (see *Cart. de Brioude*, nos. 98, 165, 208).

[52] The case of Beaulieu is less clear than Brioude or Vabres, yet charters dating from 859, 860, 866, and 878 seem to show control over this abbey by the counts of Turenne and their family (see *Cart. de Beaulieu*, nos. 1, 3, 4, 19, 21, 33).

[53] Abadal, *Els Primers Comtes Catalans*, pp. 131–147. On the foundation of Saint-Joan de les Abadesses see particularly *El Archivo Condal de Barcelona*, no. 38. On Ripoll *Marca hispanica*, appendix 45.

Marseille by Count Adalbert about 845 and of the loss of lands near Fréjus by the same abbey several decades later.[54] We hear of a *villa* taken unjustly from Psalmodi by Count Bernard of Septimania in 844[55] and of another at Bizago belonging to the church of Nîmes twice taken by avaricious magnates, once in 876 and again in 892.[56] This same church was victimized by a certain Rostagnus in 898, who seems to have seized one of its churches.[57] Further north in the Valley of the Rhone in the 860's Count Gerald of Vienne seems to have seized domains belonging to the church of Viviers,[58] and at about the same period Lothaire II of Lorraine usurped four *villas* belonging to the church of Saint-Etienne of Lyon.[59]

About 840 our documents reveal to us the loss of land belonging to Aniane as the result of its seizure by a neighboring landowner[60] and the usurpation by a count of property near Béziers belonging to the archbishop of Narbonne.[61] Such usurpations seem to have been so extensive that about 881 the archbishopric of Narbonne is reported reduced to penury.[62] Other nearby church property at Béziers was taken by Viscount Rainald a little before 897.[63] To the east around Carcassonne the abbey of Caunes was forced to institute lawsuits in 855 and 875[64] before it was able to regain land taken from it by local landowners, as was Montolieu in 862 and 898[65] and Saint-Hilaire in 883.[66] In the case of Montolieu's suit in 898 the guilty party seems to have been Count Oliba II of Carcassonne. To the south we learn that Lagrasse was victimized in a similar fashion by a landowner of Confluent in 865, Eixalada in Roussillon in 868, and the abbey of Arles (Auch) about 875[67] when its land was usurped in Vallespir. In the latter year the church of Elne seems to have

[54] *Cart. de Saint-Victor*, nos. 9, 26.
[55] *Hist. Gén. de Lang.*, II, no. 122.
[56] *Cart. de Nîmes*, no. 1, 5.
[57] *Ibid.*, no. 8.
[58] *Hist. Gén. de Lang.*, II, no. 162.
[59] *Cart. de Grenoble*, no. 30.
[60] *Cart. d'Aniane*, no. 55.
[61] *Hist. Gén. de Lang.*, V, no. 3.
[62] *Ibid.*
[63] *Hist. Gén. de Lang.*, V, no. 18.
[64] *Cart. de Carcassonne*, IV, 70–71, 192–193.
[65] *Ibid.*, I, 71–72, 73–74.
[66] *Hist. Gén. de Lang.*, V, no. 5.
[67] *Ibid.*, II, no. 63, 165, 169.

The Church (828-900)

lost some of its property in the same way.⁶⁸ So did the church of Barcelona according to a complaint made to Charles the Bald in 874.⁶⁹

There are records which show similar incidents taking place in Aquitaine. In the Albigeois we hear of a certain Leopardo, a *vassus dominicus* who attempted to take over the domains of the abbey of Velesius about 870⁷⁰ and of a certain Teutbert who usurped a *villa* belonging to the church of Angoulême in 868⁷¹ and of a similar loss suffered by Karissima, abbess of Saint-Sernin of Albi in 878.⁷² In the Limousin it was a *vassus* of the bishop of Limoges, Stodile, who in 851 appears to have been illegally in possession of land belonging to the *opus* of Saint-Etienne of Limoges,⁷³ just as in 870 it seems that the newly founded Beaulieu has lost a church by usurpation to a certain Adon or Aton.⁷⁴ Between 882 and 886 it was the family of the counts of Toulouse who seem to have taken from this abbey the important *villa* of Orbaciaco,⁷⁵ which was given to the monastery by Charles the Bald in 876⁷⁶ and confirmed as its possession by Carloman in 882.⁷⁷ Such examples tell the story clearly. Everywhere in Southern France and Catalonia during these years usurpation of church lands continued and represented a constant threat to religious establishments.

Important as it is to note such usurpations, it is equally important to emphasize something else—the fact that few succeeded permanently. Again and again we find churches and abbeys in our regions able to recover land they had lost to rapacious magnates, officials, and rulers. This, for instance, seems to have been true in almost every case mentioned above. How was this managed? Often it was the result of action taken by the monarchs of the period, a Charles the Bald, a Charles of Provence, a Carloman, a Louis of Provence or a Charles the Simple,⁷⁸ who intervened

⁶⁸ *Ibid.*, no. 189.
⁶⁹ *Catalunya Carolingia*, II, 431–433.
⁷⁰ *Hist. Gén. de Lang.*, II, no. 174.
⁷¹ *Cart. d'Angoulême*, no. 37.
⁷² *Hist. Gén. de Lang.*, II, no. 201.
⁷³ *Cart. de Saint-Etienne de Limoges*, no. 3.
⁷⁴ *Cart. de Beaulieu*, no. 27.
⁷⁵ On the *villa* of Orbiac now in the possession of the counts of Toulouse see *ibid.*, nos. 2, 10.
⁷⁶ *Ibid.*, no. 9.
⁷⁷ *Ibid.*, no. 8.
⁷⁸ For the example of a *villa* returned by Charles the Bald to Psalmodi in 844 see *Hist. Gén. de Lang.*, II, no. 122. For those returned to the church of Viviers see

and by specific charter forced the return of lands which had been usurped. Sometimes we find an important nobleman, like the count of Toulouse or count of Rouergue helping to institute legal proceedings which resulted in the return of such property.[79] Such seems to have been the case with property belonging to Montolieu in 898[80] or Notre Dame of Nîmes in 892.[81] Sometimes property was returned as the result of the activities and influence of an important churchman like Archbishop Frotaire of Bourges or Archbishop Arnulf of Narbonne.

At this point it might be worthwhile to examine in some detail the activities of certain of these churchmen in attempting to protect the patrimony of the churches and abbeys of the Midi and Catalonia. These may reveal something of the forces at work in our regions and reactions to such forces on the part of the Church. In 874 we suddenly learn from our documents that the abbey of Brioude, which had long been under the control of the counts of Auvergne and which had been exploited by them, is now controlled by Archbishop Frotaire of Bourges.[82] Almost immediately we find the abbey given a most interesting charter by Charles the Bald in which he takes this monastery under his royal protection and specifically allows it to elect its own abbot.[83] Frotaire must have been the choice of the monks of Brioude, for charters down to 893 speak of him as abbot, until in that year Duke William the Pious of Aquitaine regained control as lay abbot.[84] For two decades, then, Archbishop Frotaire and his successors were able to protect Brioude from one of the most powerful noble families of the Midi. Nor was Archbishop Frotaire active only in protecting Brioude. We find him doing the same for the abbey of Beaulieu in the Limousin. We have already noted how some time between 882 and 886 the family of Toulouse usurped a royal *villa* given Beaulieu by Charles the Bald. Yet in 886 we find Frotaire intervening in the

---

ibid., no. 162. For others near Fréjus which in 884 were restored to the abbey of Saint-Victor see *Cart. de Saint-Victor*, no. 9. For still others returned by Charles of Provence see *Cart. de Grenoble*, no. 31. For a charter showing Charles the Simple's efforts to protect the domains of the archbishop of Narbonne see *Catalunya Carolingia*, II, 438–439.

[79] For a charter showing the intervention of Count Bernard of Toulouse in the Limousin in 870 to help Beaulieu recover land which had been usurped see *Cart. de Beaulieu*, no. 27.

[80] *Cart. de Carcassonne*, I, 73–74.
[81] *Cart. de Nîmes*, no. 5.
[82] *Cart. de Brioude*, no. 132.
[83] *Ibid.*, no. 334.
[84] *Ibid.*, no. 98.

matter. He does so by purchasing this *villa* for some thirty pounds of silver from those who had taken it,[85] and then makes certain that both Bernard and Raymond of Toulouse attest to a charter of 887 in which he returns it to Beaulieu.[86] In 884 he is even active in protecting church establishments in distant Provence. For in this year a charter given by King Carloman, in which he orders the return of lands in Fréjus taken from Saint-Victor of Marseille, mentions that he does so on the plea of Archbishop Frotaire.[87]

Equally instructive is evidence of similar activities by Arnulf, archbishop of Narbonne a little later in the century. It would probably not be in error to consider that Archbishop Arnulf's influence was responsible for the return of land usurped from his *opus* in Béziers and for the efforts which resulted in the recovery of lands which Viscount Rainald gave back to the church of Béziers in 897.[88] We might well consider him also as in no small measure responsible for Montolieu's successful suit against Count Oliba II of Carcassonne in 898.[89] Whatever the facts concerning the above, however, we do know he made a serious effort to protect not only his own church's possessions but also those of his province. He did so by procuring from Charles the Simple, a charter in 899 which not only forbade laymen, counts, and others to interfere with the church of Narbonne but which also put all bishops and abbots of the region under this monarch's direct protection. And, interesting to note, Charles states that he does so on the plea of Archbishop Arnulf.[90] Like Archbishop Frotaire, Archbishop Arnulf was enlisting the aid of the monarch and others to protect his Church from lay usurpation.

Still a third interesting example from this later period concerns the church and bishop of Nîmes. In 876 our records inform us that a certain local magnate had usurped a *villa*, called Bizago, belonging to the church of Nîmes. Bishop Gislebert regained it, after a lawsuit.[91] Yet in 892 it seems that another magnate, a certain Genesius, had taken it illegally, claiming that King Eudes had given it to him. According to our sources,

[85] *Cart. de Beaulieu*, no. 10.
[86] *Ibid.*, no. 11.
[87] *Cart. de Saint-Victor*, no. 9.
[88] See reference to *fiscos* usurped by a count in 881 in *Hist. Gén. de Lang.*, V, no. 3, and to the return of land to the church of Béziers by the viscount in *ibid.*, no. 18.
[89] *Cart. de Carcassonne*, I, 73–74.
[90] *Catalunya Carolingia*, II, 438–439. On other privileges given the archbishop by this monarch see *ibid.*, pp. 109–111, 373–374.
[91] *Cart. de Nîmes*, no. 1.

Bishop Gislebert went to see King Eudes, found him hunting and poured out his complaints against Genesius' usurpation. He ascertained that Eudes had made no such gift to Genesius and got Eudes to send a letter to Count Raymond of Rouergue, the overlord of Nîmes, who in turn sent letters to this effect to his viscount, Allidaf. Allidaf held a court which considered the case, and the testimony of Bishop Gislebert and the letters of King Eudes and Count Raymond proved conclusive. Genesius was forced to return Bizago to the church of Nîmes.[92]

These examples show how important churchmen used their influence and that of rulers and courts to prevent a spoilation of the Church. But they do not mean that other methods were not also used to protect Church lands. Whenever possible this sort of assistance was solicited by hard-pressed bishops and abbots, particularly late in this period. More normal, however, was another procedure. This was to get land which had been usurped given back by a local tribunal, presided over by a count or his representative. Most of the restitutions of Church lands came in this fashion. There were certain reasons for this fact. In the first place, a local tribunal would be more cognizant of the pertinent facts in a case and have a greater interest in the outcome than some more distant authority far from the scene. Even more important, such a court containing, as it always did during these years, the important landowners of the region as *judices* or *boni homines*, provided a forum which represented local public opinion. Such public opinion, in a period when government was breaking down, was probably the most important weapon which a church or abbey could enlist to force avaricious laymen to disgorge the Church property which they were occupying. Already, especially in a case we find in Angoulême in 868,[93] the Church in the Midi and Catalonia was making use of procedures which were to lead to the *guirpitios* that in the next century were a major protection of their property and their rights.

We might sum up the question of usurpation of Church lands in this period, then, as follows. As government broke down we have ample evidence that usurpation of Church property took place in every part of the Midi and Catalonia with counts, viscounts, rulers, and simple landowners as the guilty parties. At the same time, except in Gascony, Western Aquitaine, and Provence, there is evidence that the Church in general was able to protect itself against such loss of property with some degree of success. Using local tribunals, influential churchmen, sympathetic officials,

[92] *Ibid.*, no. 5.
[93] *Cart. d'Angoulême*, no. 37.

and Carolingian and other rulers in various ways, down to 900 at least, the Church was able more often than not to secure the return of such property and to grow and expand its patrimony and influence in most of the regions which lay south of Poitou and Burgundy.

Yet when all this has been said it still remains true that it was a very different Church which emerged into the tenth century from that which we find several decades earlier. That of 900, in contrast to the Church of 828, was already well on the way to being an institution taken over and becoming a part of the family system which controlled the machinery of secular government also. This, rather than outright usurpation, was the fate of abbey and bishopric in every part of the Midi and Catalonia.

Why was this so? Why did the Church avoid loss of its land by outright usurpation only to succumb to a different and more subtle sort of pressure by the end of this period? We must begin by reiterating the fact which was noted earlier, that the initial revival of Church power and monastic institutions in our regions was not solely the result of Carolingian interest. Local officials and important families played an important role in Church revival even before 828, witness St. Benedict of Aniane,[94] Duke William of Toulouse,[95] and the Gothic counts of Carcassonne and Catalonia and their relations.[96] After 828, as real Carolingian authority over Southern France and the Spanish March declined, local participation in and control of the Church increased in importance. By the second half of the reign of Charles the Bald we can see a good deal of evidence of this. As we have noted, the counts of Toulouse not only founded Vabres. They became the *custodes* and *defensores* of this abbey,[97] just as the Bernards of Auvergne did in the case of Brioude.[98] Aurillac was identified with the counts of this region by its founder, St. Gerald.[99] Not only did the counts of Turenne in the person of Rodulf, archbishop of Bourges assist Bishop Stodile of Limoges in founding Beaulieu. It remained almost a family affair for this line of counts throughout the century, even after they lost their exalted

---

[94] *Vita Benedicti Anianensis*, ed. E. Waitz, in *Mon. Ger. Hist. Scriptores*, XV, and *Annals of Aniane*, anno 782, col. 9–10.

[95] See *Vita Sancti Guilelmi ducis ac monarchi*, in *Acta Sanctorum*, May VI, cols. 811–820, and this work, Chapter III, Sec. II.

[96] See R. de Abadal i de Vinyals, "La Catalogne sous l'empire de Louis le Pieux," in *Études Roussillonnaises*, IV–VI (1955–1957), and Ponsch, "Les origines de l'abbaye d'Arles," pp. 83–99.

[97] *Hist. Gén. de Lang.*, II, nos. 110, 203.

[98] See note 51.

[99] See Odo, *Vita S. Geraldi*.

position.[100] They also built a convent at Cahors whose first abbess was Irmena of their family.[101] In 873 we find a church being consecrated in Capçir by the counts of Carcassonne and Cerdanya and by the archbishop of Narbonne—all of whom seem to be members of the same family group.[102] We have noted the independent course of Archbishop Frotaire, but we need also to emphasize that he was a kinsman of Counts Bernard and Raymond of the House of Toulouse.[103]

By the last years of the century abbeys and churches had become completely entwined in the families of importance who dominated these regions. Sunifred, brother of Acfred I of Razès and Oliba II, was abbot of Lagrasse[104] and another Sunifred, the brother of Counts Guifred and Miró, was abbot of Arles in Vallespir.[105] When Count Guifred and his wife founded the nunnery of Saint-Joan de les Abadesses, they gave it to their daughter Emma who became the first abbess.[106] By 899 we find that the bishopric of Maguelonne is held by one relative of Countess Guillaumette of Melgueil, while the other succeeds her as count.[107] We hear of a Centulle as abbot of Saint-Polycarpe of Razès in 844 who seems obviously a member of a local Gascon noble family,[108] and of a Rostagnus somewhat later, who served as abbot of Saint-Chaffre and who obviously comes from a family of importance in this part of the Rhone Valley.[109] Gombard, bishop of Angoulême from 897 to 941, was a member of the comital family who controlled Angoulême and Périgord.[110] The important lay *prepositi* of abbeys similarly tend more and more to represent important families in the regions where such monasteries are located. Witness the role of the viscounts of Limoges and Turenne as *prepositi* of

---

[100] *Cart. de Beaulieu,* nos. 17, 29, 46, 169, refers to later gifts of this family to this abbey.
[101] *Ibid.,* no. 184.
[102] *Hist. Gén. de Lang.,* II, no. 184.
[103] *Cart. de Beaulieu,* no. 11.
[104] *Cart. de Carcassonne,* II, 216, and *Hist. Gén. de Lang.,* II, no. 200.
[105] See Abadal, *Els Primers Comtes Catalans,* pp. 13–24, for the ramifications of this family.
[106] *El Archivo Condal de Barcelona,* no. 38. On Emma's relationship with Count Sunifred see *ibid.,* no. 10.
[107] *Cart. de Maguelonne,* I, no. 3.
[108] *Hist. Gén. de Lang.,* II, no. 154.
[109] *Cart. de Saint-Chaffre,* nos. 33, 72.
[110] *Ademar de Chabannes,* III, 23, p. 144.

Tulle, Solignac, and other abbeys[111] and of similar families who seem to be connected with the abbey of Brioude in Auvergne.[112]

In addition to examples of the direct participation and interest of such families in the abbeys and churches of these regions we have still another type of evidence. This is provided by grants of land given by such establishments as *precaria* and benefices to important neighboring landowners. These also go back to earlier Carolingian times, but seem much more numerous after 828. Such grants were generally for a lifetime only and required only a nominal payment of a *cens* to the abbey or church in question. They do not seem to have represented the establishment of any military relationship or obligation between the recipient and the ecclesiastical grantor, but only a certain more general dependence on a client-patron basis. Perhaps, it is true, some *precaria* masked usurpation of church land. This seems particularly true of certain land given out in this manner by the abbey of Brioude in 846 and 864.[113] Perhaps the *precarium* or benefice which the abbey of Lagrasse gave Countess Richelde for a twenty-year period in 837 represents the same thing.[114]

But most other *precaria* of which we have a record seem quite different in character. Those granted by Savigny in 857, 858, 888, and 889,[115] or those which Brioude gave out in 874, 888, and about 890[116] are examples. So also are those in which individuals gave land to abbeys and churches but reserved the usufruct for the donor and his family upon the payment

---

[111] G. Tenant de la Tour, *L'homme et la terre de Charlemagne à Saint Louis*, pp. 236–280, 516–536.

[112] According to the *Cartulaire de Brioude* Adalgisius was *prepositus* in 846, in 859, and in 868, thus holding office for more than twenty years (*Cart. de Brioude*, nos. 56, 161, 172. In 874 we find a certain Ictor called *custos* and *castellanus* (*ibid.*, nos. 132, 263). Then from 892 to 896 when control of Brioude was again in the hands of the counts of Auvergne we find a certain Eldefredus as *prepositus* (*ibid.*, nos. 82, 144, 181, 207).

[113] See the gift of a large piece of the abbey's land by Count Bernard and the *prepositus* Adalgisius to a certain Eldefredus (who was probably the same man who had served as *prepositus* from 892–896) in return for *one* mansus (*Cart. de Brioude*, no. 172), and a similar exchange of property between Count Bernard and the abbot of Mozat in (*ibid.*, no. 176).

[114] *Hist. Gén. de Lang.*, II, no. 91.

[115] *Cart. de Savigny*, nos. 23 (857), 20 and 28 (858), 21 (888), 1 and 3 (889). See one also referred to in a charter of 883 in *ibid.*, no. 2.

[116] *Cart. de Brioude*, nos. 132 (874) and 38 (888). For land given a certain Aton in 890 which transformed this vassal into a man occupying a *precarium* which paid a *cens* to this abbey see *ibid.*, no. 60.

of an annual *cens,* which, in effect, established the same kind of client-patron relationship between the possessor of this property and the church establishment concerned.[117] All mark the growth of abbeys and churches which protected or even controlled segments of the lay population and which in turn were protected by them. A beginning was being made toward the development of the powerful lord abbots and lord bishops of the next century who, through their family relationships and use of Church lands, were to dominate important portions of the Midi and Catalonia.

By 900, then, the Church in Southern France and the Spanish March had escaped from the danger of a crude usurpation of the land which belonged to it, only to succumb to what was to prove a more subtle form of control. Its abbeys and churches, like secular *honores,* had been absorbed in various ways into the system of family control of these regions, either through the institution of lay abbots, *defensores,* or *custodes* or because the bishops, archbishops, abbots, and *prepositi* were chosen from members of the dominant families in each region. The *precaria* given to representatives of the same families reinforced such bonds of interest and control. An independent Church in *one* sense of the word still existed, opposed to crude use of its lands by the laity and depending upon monarchs, important churchmen, and nobles friendly to it to protect it from such a fate.

But the battle, for all practical purposes, was actually already lost. For as local bishoprics and *abbatia* became filled with members of the local ruling families or their supporters, these families began to consider such positions as family property. Church *honores,* like secular ones, became a matter of family possession and family control. The Church in the Midi and Catalonia might and did continue to grow in the late ninth century, but it grew in a society which was subject to and part of the family control of regions in which its establishments were located. After 900, despite its struggles, the Church, like the governmental machinery of the Carolingian monarchy, had changed from an independent power exercised under the direction of a distant ruler, to one exercised by important families of these regions. It is this kind of Church which we will be examining in later chapters.

[117] These are particularly numerous, as shown by charters, at Aniane, Beaulieu, and Brioude.

CHAPTER IX

Southern French and Catalan Society (828–900)

As ROYAL authority disappeared in Southern France and Catalonia and both the governmental system and the Church passed into the control of important noble families, certain changes took place in the society which was forced to adjust itself to new conditions. For certain portions of this area, however, we are ignorant of the nature of such changes. This is simply because in Gascony, much of Western Aquitaine, and Alpine regions east of the Rhone, the disorganization caused by outside invasions and troubled internal conditions was so complete that we have almost no record whatsoever of these years. For the rest of the Midi and Catalonia, however, we possess sufficient documentation so that we can get a rather clear idea of the changes through which society passed during this period.

Let us first consider the matter of landholding, a key point in understanding Southern France and the Spanish March. Here we might begin by reiterating that up to 828 there were several ways in which land was held. The first was the allod, or full allodial ownership. The second was the *aprisio*, large or small. The third was the *beneficium* granted by Carolingian rulers to counts, viscounts, bishops, abbots, *vassi dominici*, or other *fideles*, or by counts and viscounts to their own *vassi* or *fideles*. The fourth was the benefice or *precarium* of a different sort given out by a church establishment or a private individual.

Let us begin by considering the allod during the period from 828 to 900. In a preceding chapter we noted that the prevailing system of landholding was allodial, even during the reigns of Charlemagne and Louis the Pious. After 828 this continued to be true. Perhaps the best proof of this fact comes from an analysis of charters dating from this period by which private individuals gave property to churches and abbeys south of Poitou and Burgundy. What do they reveal? They show, after we eliminate all grants by the monarchs, which must be examined under a separate category, that we have a record of some 258 pieces of property given by private individuals to the Church in various parts of Southern France and Catalonia. Of these 82 are from Auvergne, 64 from the Limousin and Quercy, 12 from Rouergue and the Albigeois, 6 from Angoulême-Périgord, and 1 from the Toulousain[1]—which covers Aquitaine. The Rhone Valley is covered by 7 from the Lyonnais, 15 from the Vienne-Dauphiny area, 14 from Velay, Valence, Vivarais, and 1 from Provence.[2] From Septimania we have 25, covering the region from Nîmes to Béziers and some 11 from the area of Narbonne-Carcassonne.[3] From Roussillon and the rest of Catalonia we have some 25 such charters.[4] We thus have a representative sample from a wide area of Catalonia and the Spanish March.

Property concerned in such gifts to abbeys and churches seems to have varied a great deal in size. Of those listed above some 86 represent property which can be called small holdings of a *mansus*, a field, a vineyard, or less. Some 70 represent medium-sized property of more than a *mansus* but less than a *villa*. The remaining 102 are holdings of at least a *villa* and frequently even more extensive tracts of land.

It is not the size of such holdings which interests us here, however, but how such property was owned. And here we note an important fact. Only

[1] Most of these Auvergne charters are from the *Cart. de Brioude* and *Le Grand Cart. de Brioude*. A few are from the *Hist. Gén de Lang.* and the *Cart. de Saint-Chaffre*. The majority of the Limousin and Quercy charters are from the *Cart. de Beaulieu*. Others are from the *Cart. de Saint-Etienne de Limoges*, the *Chartes de Charroux*, the *Hist. Gén. de Lang.*, and the *Cart. de Tulle*. Those for Rouergue and the Albigeois are from the *Cart. de Conques* and the *Hist. Gén. de Lang.* Included also are charters from the *Cart. d'Angoulême*, the *Fragments du cartulaire du Monastère de Paunat*, ed. R. Poupardin and A. Thomas for Angoulême-Périgord, and one from the *Hist. Gén. de Lang.* for the Toulousain.

[2] See the *Cart. Lyonnais*, the *Cart. de Savigny*, the *Cart. de Grenoble*, the *Cart. de Vienne*, the *Cart. de Saint-André-le-bas*, the *Cart. de Saint-Barnard de Romans*, the *Chartes de Maurienne*, the *Chartes de Cluny*, the *Cart. de Saint-Chaffre*, the *Hist. Gén. de Lang.*, and the *Cart. de Saint-Victor*.

[3] From the "Cartulaire de Psalmodi" (unprinted), the *Cart. d'Aniane*, the *Cart. de Gellone*, the *Cart. de Maguelonne*, the *Cart. de Nîmes*, the "Cartulaire de l'Evêché d'Agde" (unprinted); the *Livre Noir ou Cartulaire du chapitre cathédral de Béziers*, ed. J. Rouquette, the *Hist. Gén. de Lang.*, the *Cart. de Carcassonne*, the *Catalunya Carolingia*, II, *Marca hispanica*, the *Cart. roussillonnais*, and Cros-Meyrévielle, *Documents*.

[4] From *Catalunya Carolingia*, II; *Marca hispanica; Hist. Gén. de Lang.*; the *Cartulario de San Cugat des Valles*, ed. J. Ruis Serra; the *Archivo Catederal de Barcelona*, ed. S. Puig y Puig; and *El Archivo Condal de Barcelona*.

Southern French and Catalan Society (828-900) 157

5 out of these 258 gifts of land to churches and abbeys during these years consist of anything but allodial land. These 5 came from a relatively small region of the Midi, 2 from Auvergne, 2 from the Limousin and 1 from Angoulême. Using this land then as a fair sample of the rest, we find privately held land in the Midi was 98 per cent allodial, or if we consider only Aquitaine where all our non-allodial land seems to be concentrated, it was 90 per cent allodial. These proportions are probably high, since allodial land was easiest to give to ecclesiastical establishments. Nevertheless, it is clear, in the light of this evidence, that we must regard allodial land as the prevailing system in the Midi and Catalonia.

The five cases of non-allodial land are also worth careful analysis. Two of them represent land given to the abbey of Brioude in Auvergne in 896 and 898[5] in which the consent of another individual is mentioned in the charter—thus probably reflecting land held as *precaria* or benefices. Those from the Limousin concern gifts of land to the church of Saint-Etienne of Limoges in 884[6] and to the abbey of Beaulieu in 887.[7] The first speaks of the consent of a certain Ermenicus whom the charter calls the lord of the giver. The second mentions the consent of a certain Matfred and his sons—probably members of a landowning family prominent in this region in the next century. That from Angoulême is a gift of a number of *villas* and other property given in 852 to the abbey of Saint-Cybard in which the charter states that Charles the Bald gives his consent —thus identifying this land as a benefice from the monarch.[8] Only in this last case do we seem to be involved with any important piece of property, for each of the others represents only a medium-sized holding.

These documents tell us something else also about allodial landholding. For in the same general region of Aquitaine in which we find some cases of nonallodial land, we find evidence of a resistance to any control over the right of an owner to dispose of his holdings as he sees fit—the major feature of the allod. Thus in 859 in giving a gift of some property of medium size to Brioude, a certain Ancelmus says that he is following Salic law which gives him this right.[9] In the Limousin, on the other hand, we find Roman law invoked in a general way as giving a man the right to dispose of his property as he wishes—a far more accurate statement from the legal point of view. We find Roman law referred to in this way

[5] *Cart. de Brioude*, nos. 64, 254.
[6] *Cart. de Saint-Etienne de Limoges*, no. 3.
[7] *Cart. de Beaulieu*, no. 43.
[8] *Cart. d'Angoulême*, no. 136.
[9] *Cart. de Brioude*, no. 43.

in 841 by a certain Boson who is selling large tracts of land to Bishop Rodulf, of the family of the counts of Turenne, for 1,500 *solidi*.[10] We find it mentioned again in 865 in a charter by which Count Gotfred and his wife are giving a number of *villas* and other property to their son.[11] We find it invoked and the Theodosian Code referred to specifically by name by a certain Frotaire in 871 in a gift to the canons of Saint-Etienne of Limoges.[12] The allodial right of disposing freely of one's property, then, seems to have been a jealously guarded one in the only region of the Midi in which we find traces of nonallodial land.

A few other important things emerge from an examination of these grants of property to churches and abbeys. They show us, as noted earlier, that in the Midi there were large, medium, and small landholders who possessed allods during this period and that each type was relatively numerous. They also help us to understand something of how such land was acquired. Judging from our examples, allodial land was acquired in various ways by those who owned it. Most of it seems to have been inherited. Some came as a gift or grant from a ruler or someone else in authority, some by purchase or exchange. Other allods were acquired by *aprisio* or by *attracto*—that is by settlement on wasteland. Some was acquired by other means including force or conquest. All these methods seem to have been in use and, provided they were legal, would make such land an allod, owned outright by the possessor and freely disposable if he so desired.

Along with this privately held allodial land, however, we find another sort: that which was the property of Carolingian monarchs themselves. This land—consisting of estates and *villas* and churches and much unused and unoccupied land which had been conquered by the Carolingians— made up the royal *fisc*. In the last chapter we have already shown how much of this royal *fisc* was distributed by these monarchs in the course of the century to churches and abbeys, mainly in Septimania and Catalonia where such land, much of it unoccupied, seems to have been extensive. Such royal property given to the Church need not concern us here.

What we do need to consider, however, is that land which Carolingian rulers gave out in the form of large and small *aprisiones* or in benefices conferred on their *fideles* and *vassi dominici*. What had happened to this property by the year 900 and what methods were used in holding it?

[10] *Cart. de Beaulieu*, no. 86.
[11] *Ibid.*, no. 186.
[12] *Cart. de Saint-Etienne de Limoges*, no. 8. Perhaps the Frotaire who is mentioned in this charter is Archbishop Frotaire.

Let us first consider *aprisiones*. This form of quasi proprietorship had been begun by Charlemagne, who used it to make large grants of land belonging to the royal *fisc* in Septimania and Catalonia, and was continued by his son, Louis the Pious. By 828, however, large *aprisiones* seem to have begun to change their character. They began to become allodial and indistinguishable from private property held as allods elsewhere in Southern France and the Spanish March. This process was not the result of usurpation of such a status by *aprisio* holders themselves. It was a result of a deliberate royal policy which, by specific grants, transformed property held as *aprisiones* into allods. A number of specific cases illustrate this change. One of the earliest goes back to the year 832 when a certain Wimar and his brother, both of whom are called *fideles* by Lothaire, were given a charter which expressly changed into an allod the *aprisio* which they had received from Charlemagne. The charter states they are now to hold it *"jure proprietario."*[13] A year later they are given another charter by Louis the Pious, in which Wimar is called a *vassalus*, which confirms this change in their land.[14] Still another interesting case is the well-known *aprisio* of John of Fontjoncouse in the Narbonnaise which was the subject of specific royal charters in 834, 844, and 849. John's heirs, his son and brother, are also called *fideles* in these charters, and by 849 it is clear that their *aprisio* has been transformed into an allod which they hold *"jure proprietario."*[15] In 847 we have another case, this time an *aprisio* held by a certain Alphonse and his nephews near Narbonne, which they inherited from the former's brother and which is now theirs *"jure proprietario."*[16] In 854 two *Goti*, Sunald and Riculf, called *fideles*, are given in full ownership the *aprisio* in Roussillon which their father and grandfather held from the Carolingian rulers.[17] In 889 a certain Ansemundus and his wife, in giving an allod to Bishop Agilbert of Béziers, state that they got this land *"ex aprisione parentum suorum"* and *"per praeceptum regum,"* probably from Charles the Bald.[18] Finally for an example of a nonroyal *aprisio* which became an allod we have the land given to the nunnery of Saint-Joan de les Abadesses in 898 by Gotmar, bishop of Ausona. In giving the allod to Saint-Joan, Gotmar expressly states he had received this land as an *aprisio* from his uncle, Count Sunifred.[19]

[13] *Catalunya Carolingia*, II, 328.
[14] *Hist. Gén. de Lang.*, II, no. 84.
[15] *Catalunya Carolingia*, II, 338–339, 343–344, 442–444.
[16] *Ibid.*, pp. 341–342, and *Hist. Gén. de Lang.*, II, no. 132.
[17] *Catalunya Carolingia*, II, 348.
[18] *Hist. Gén. de Lang.*, II, no. 163.
[19] *El Archivo Condal de Barcelona*, no. 10.

Not every *aprisio*, though, became an allod at once. There is some indication that Carolingian monarchs were reluctant to alienate them completely if they contained fortresses. Thus in the Béziers region those two *hispani* who held *aprisiones* in which the *castra* of Mesoa and Turres were located, were given this property *"jure beneficiario"* in 848 instead of *"jure proprietario."* Since this charter, however, gave them the right to sell, bequeath, or exchange this land, there is little doubt that their rights of quasi proprietorship, stated in this grant, were quite similar to those pertaining to an allod.[20] Again in 854 the fortress or *rocca*, in the *aprisio* given Sunald and Riculf as an allod, is expressly excluded from such status and is called a *beneficium*.[21] With these exceptions it seems clear that we are face to face with an inevitable trend which was transforming *aprisiones* into allods—even when, as in the case of Asnar Galindo's *aprisio*, it had changed hands. By 862 this property had become an allod and was in that capacity protected from usurpation by the public authority of the region.[22]

While there can be little doubt that these large *aprisiones* became allods in the course of the century, what about small ones? Such less important ones, initially, had a less independent status than larger *aprisiones* and were subject to certain dues and duties—perhaps even a *cens*. Did they, too, become allods? It is hard to say. We find many references to such *aprisiones* in Roussillon, in the rest of Catalonia, and in Pallars and Ribagorça in documents dating from these years. But they are vague as to their exact status. We do find a reference to two such *aprisiones* in Roussillon though, which had become allods by the end of the century, two pieces of small property acquired as allodial land by the Bishop of Elne in 861 and 869.[23] If our information from these southerly regions is slight concerning smaller *aprisiones*, we have more from Auvergne where this method of landholding seems to have been known as *attracto*. Such property, so-called, is given to Brioude in a number of charters dating from 861, 876, 877, and 891[24] (five cases in all). Every one of them is allodial land. In general then we can probably fairly say that the tendency was for small *aprisiones* to become allods just like the larger ones.

This leads us to a consideration of those benefices which Carolingian monarchs also gave to their *fideles* and which tend so much to resemble

[20] *Catalunya Carolingia*, II, 335–337, and *Hist. Gén. de Lang.*, II, no. 132.
[21] *Catalunya Carolingia*, II, 348.
[22] *Ibid.*, pp. 325–326.
[23] *Hist. Gén. de Lang.*, II, nos. 156, 172.
[24] The phrase is *"tam de alode quam de atracto"* in *Cart. de Brioude*, no. 110 (866). See also *ibid.*, nos. 263 (876), 197 and 260 (877), 212 (891).

aprisiones. During these years did they too become allods? Our evidence again clearly indicates that they did, again with the full concurrence of the monarchs.[25] Let us examine some examples of such changes in land given to lay and church *fideles*. The first two cases we know of go back to the time of Louis the Pious. In 829 this monarch gave to his *fidelis* Sunifred a *villa* near Narbonne, which the charter states had been held earlier by his father, Count Borell. Now it is to be his *"jure proprietario."*[26] Four years later another *fidelis* of the emperor, called his *vassallo*, is given a *villa* in the Toulousain on the same terms.[27]

After 840 when Charles the Bald and Pepin II were competing for support, such gifts of royal land seem more numerous. In 842 Charles gave to his *fidelis* Miró six *villas* in the Carcassonne region in full allodial ownership.[28] In the same year we hear of a gift made by Pepin II to Bishop Rodulf of Limoges whom he calls *"fidelis nostri,"* of two *villas "jure proprietario."*[29] In 843 a similar gift of lands belonging to the royal *fisc* was made by Charles to his *fidelis*, Sunifred, one which included *villas* in Roussillon, Confluent, Cerdanya, and Urgell (Andorra).[30] In 844 he gave a *mansus* and church outright to his *fidelis* Hilduco,[31] and in the same year bestowed on his *fidelis*, the archbishop of Narbonne, one half of the city of Narbonne and its *turres* as an allodial possession.[32] It was probably at about this time that Pepin II gave to Astronove the castle of Cerrucium on the Gascon border as an allod, which in 847 the latter gave to the abbey of Moissac.[33] In the next year, in 848, this same ruler gave to Bishop Rodulf of Limoges two more *villas* in the Limousin *"jure proprietario,"*[34] while Charles matched this gift with one of a *villa* in the Agde region and a *mansus* near Substantion to his *fidelis* Deodatus (Deusdat), the latter on the plea of Count Appolonius of Agde.[35]

---

[25] During his bitter struggle with Pepin II of Aquitaine in 845 Charles the Bald stated in a charter that he was giving away land from his *fisc* to gain supporters by necessity *"in beneficiario jure aut in allode."* See "Capitularia de Beauvais," anno 845, ch. 20, in Boretius, *Capitularia*, II, 403.
[26] *Catalunya Carolingia*, II, 324.
[27] *Hist. Gén. de Lang.*, II, no. 81.
[28] *Cart. de Carcassonne*, III, 418.
[29] *Cart. de Beaulieu*, no. 6.
[30] *Catalunya Carolingia*, II, 333–334.
[31] *Hist. Gén. de Lang.*, II, no. 131.
[32] *Ibid.*, no. 115.
[33] *Ibid.*, no. 131.
[34] *Cart. de Beaulieu*, no. 7.
[35] *Hist. Gén. de Lang.*, II, no. 134.

The defeat of Pepin II in 852 did not end Charles' gifts of royal lands as allods to his supporters. Rather, they continued. In 853 we find him giving a certain *fidelis* Teutmund seven *mansi* in Confluent *"jure proprietario."*[36] Six years later in 859, on the plea of Marquis Humfrid, he gave to his *fidelis* Isembert two *villas* and a church in the Narbonne region.[37] In the charter this gift is called *"in proprium aeternaliter."* In the same year, again on the petition of Humfrid, he gave to his *fidelis* Aureol two *villas "jure proprietario."*[38] Ten years later he gave to his *fidelis* Dido, *vassus* of Otger, two *villulas* in Roussillon as allodial property.[39] An even more generous gift followed in 870. In this year he gave to Count Oliba II of Carcassonne *fiscal* lands and a number of churches in Ausona and Carcassonne. In his charter he says he concedes these lands to Oliba *"aeternaliter ad jus proprium."*[40] In 876 Hildebert, viscount of Limoges, was given the *villa* of Cavalicus in the Limousin *"jure beneficiario."* At first glance this seems to be a gift of land on more limited terms than the preceding ones, but careful examination of the charter shows it is actually the gift of a benefice for two lifetimes, since it specifies not only Hildebert as the recipient but his son also.[41] Whatever Charles' intent concerning this land, it became allodial, since it is so specified in 916 when Hildebert gave it to a nearby church establishment.[42] Finally in 877, just before his death, Charles made another gift of land to Count Oliba II of Carcassonne. This consisted of property taken from the *"infideliter Etilius Berani* [Bero]," which was now given to Oliba as *"rebus suae proprietatis."*[43]

Carloman continued this practice. In 881, on the plea of Count Appolonius he gave to his *fidelis* Rainald several *villas* and a church *"in proprietatem."*[44] In 885 we find an allod in the possession of Ermenicus, a leading magnate of the Limousin, which he says he acquired from this monarch.[45] In the next year two *villas* given to the abbey of Beaulieu by

[36] *Catalunya Carolingia*, II, 313–314.
[37] *Cart. de Carcassonne*, II, 598.
[38] *Catalunya Carolingia*, II, 353–354.
[39] *Ibid.*, pp. 359–360.
[40] Cros-Meyrévielle, *Documents*, no. 16.
[41] *Cart. de Saint-Etienne de Limoges*, no. 84.
[42] *Cart. de Beaulieu*, no. 71. On the change of this land to allodial status see F. Delage and G. Brussel, "Un domaine carolingien au Limousin, Cavalicus," in *Bulletin de la société archéologique et historique du Limousin*, LXXXIV (1952–1954).
[43] Cros-Meyrévielle, *Documents*, no. 18.
[44] *Hist. Gén. de Lang.*, V, no. 4.
[45] *Cart. de Beaulieu*, no. 55. This even included a castle.

Charles and Carloman are called *"res proprietatis"* by Count Raymond of Toulouse.[46] Two years later in Cerdanya Count Guifred and his wife own an allod which they say they got from a certain Sesenardo who received it *"per praeceptum regis."*[47]

Eudes, Charles' Capetian successor, acted in similar fashion. In 889 this monarch granted to Count Guifred vast tracts of land *"de fisco"* as his allodial property[48]—a grant which was probably as generous as that given to Count Oliba II by Charles the Bald in 870. In the same year, on the plea of the bishop of Gerona, he gave a certain Peter a *villa* as an allod located in this region of Catalonia.[49] Nor did the return of the Carolingian family to power with Charles the Simple change matters. For in 898 we find him, on the plea of his *fidelis* Robert, giving another *fidelis*, a certain Theodosius, land belonging to the royal *fisc* in Narbonne and Roussillon, as well as property in Besalu and Gerona, as his full allodial possession.[50] A year later, in 899, on the instance of Arnulf, archbishop of Narbonne, he gave his *fidelis* Stephen a number of *villas "in jus proprietatis et in allodem perpetualiter."*[51] Nor was Charles the Simple alone in making such grants. In 902 his contemporary, King Louis of Provence, acted similarly in the Valley of the Rhone, where he gave to his *fidelis* Viscount Berilon *fiscal* property belonging to the crown *"jure proprietario."*[52]

These numerous examples show what happened to land which belonged to the royal *fisc* south of Poitou and Burgundy. As Dhondt and others have pointed out, by 900 the *fisc* had been exhausted by the extensive gifts to the Church, to counts and viscounts, and to other *fideles*—a fact which helps to explain the end of royal authority in these regions. But what they have *not* emphasized is a point of equal importance to us. That is that such land was given by the monarchs to individuals in such a way that it *expressly* became the full allodial possession of those who had earlier held it as royal benefices or *aprisiones*. By 900 the royal *fisc* had disappeared in such a way that it swelled the allodial possessions of leading families in these regions and of the Church. From this time on, except in Catalonia and Pallars and Ribagorça, where *aprisiones* continued to be granted by the counts from land belonging now to the *fisc*, we find no more land granted in the fashion of Charlemagne and Louis the Pious to their *fideles*.

[46] *Ibid.*, no. 10.
[47] *Marca hispanica*, appendix 45.
[48] *Catalunya Carolingia*, II, 363–364.
[49] *Ibid.*, pp. 365–366.
[50] *Ibid.*, pp. 369–370.
[51] *Hist. Gén. de Lang.*, V, no. 25.
[52] *Cart. de Vienne*, no. 11.

We have no evidence of royal property still existing, only allodial family possessions which followed the general rules which governed allodial land south of Poitou and Burgundy.[53]

Which brings us to a final question. Did counts and viscounts who were gaining full *de facto* independence and control over their *honores* as hereditary family possessions and who transformed benefices and *aprisiones* given them by the monarchs into allods, succeed in transforming the large *aprisio* holders or *fideles* of the Carolingian monarchs into *vassi* or *fideles* who held such property from them? Were Carolingian vassals changed into comital ones and their land made dependent on the new rulers of these regions? It is frequently asserted that this is what took place, and a case in Auvergne in which the nephew of a royal vassal did homage to the duke of Aquitaine for his uncle's land is cited as the proof of the fact. This particular case, however, seems a poor proof for such a development, since it shows not a willingness to transfer such an allegiance, but an unwillingness to do so on the part of the royal vassal concerned. Furthermore, the source reporting it dates from the next century.[54]

As far as our regions are concerned down to 900, the evidence seems clear and unequivocal. We have no *single* case in which we can either directly or indirectly prove that such a transfer to a count or viscount of *fidelitas* or of land belonging to a royal vassal or *aprisio* holder took place. What we do find is some *attempts* on the part of counts to achieve this. The *aprisiones* of John of Fontjoncouse near Narbonne[55] and that of Asnar Galindo in Cerdanya[56] are cases in point. So are certain lands belonging to the Church which usurpers claimed were given to them by counts, or even bishops as benefices.[57] But in every case, as far as we can tell, such claims were denied and the land in question returned to full allodial ownership of the individual or church or abbey concerned. South of Poitou and Burgundy the allodial principle triumphed, and no such

---

[53] One finds this same development elsewhere in France. The benefices of the Nibelungen in Autun in Central France also became hereditary allods in the late ninth century. See L. Levillain, "Les Nibelungen historiques et leurs alliances de famille," in *Annales du Midi, L* (1937), 346–353.

[54] Odo, *Vita Sancti Geraldi Auriliacensis,* I, ch. 32 in Migne, *Patrologia Latina,* CXXXIII, col. 660–661.

[55] See the charter of 834, a record of a court case, explaining how the counts tried to take over this *aprisio,* in *Catalunya Carolingia,* II, 442–444.

[56] *Ibid.,* pp. 325–326.

[57] For examples see *Hist. Gén. de Lang.,* II, nos. 150, 169, 189, and *Cart. de Saint-Etienne de Limoges,* no. 3.

Southern French and Catalan Society (828-900)

transfer of land or loyalty seems to have taken place during this period. The results of this fact will be examined in later chapters.

Nevertheless, in the Midi and Catalonia we do have some evidence that vassals and *fideles* existed, though they were not royal ones transformed into men with a new dependence upon the counts of these regions. In 844 in giving *aprisio* privileges to the inhabitants of the city of Barcelona and the castle of Tarrassa, Charles the Bald in his charter gave to these *Goti* the right to commend themselves to counts as *vassi*, as the Franks were accustomed to do.[58] By 858 such *vassi* existed in Roussillon, for in the year we find Viscount Richelme declaring that he gave four churches to *"homine suo Tructerio."*[59] A decade later before a court presided over by Count Saloman a certain Recosind, a Goth, states that he was given certain church lands as a *benefice* by his lord.[60] In 875 before another court held in this part of Catalonia a certain Arnold claims that he holds land belonging to the church of Elne *"per beneficium"* of the count.[61] A posterior document of 913 mentions the *fideles* of Count Guifred who assisted him in occupying Ausona after 878.[62]

In Aquitaine a *vassus* of Bishop Stodile of Limoges is mentioned in 851[63] and certain grants of lands a little later in this same region imply the same sort of dependent relationship, particularly one already noted, in 884, in which in giving land to Beaulieu a certain Daniel mentions his *lords* Deusdet and Ermenicus.[64] We also find two *vassi*, obviously dependent on the count of Rouergue-Toulouse, who are mentioned at Nîmes in 898.[65] These cases, however, are few in number. In contrast to the widespread, full allodial ownership of land without dependence and other ties, evidence of this sort seems unimportant. By 900 Carolingian-type feudal relationships and control over land seem to have largely disappeared in

[58] *Catalunya Carolingia*, II, 423–425. This is a right similar to that which Louis the Pious gave to *aprisio* holders in 815. The fact, however, that Charles the Bald felt it necessary to include it in this charter reflects on the whole the *rarity* of such types of commendation among the non-Frankish population of this region, rather than its prevalence.

[59] *Hist. Gén. de Lang.*, II, no. 150.
[60] *Ibid.*, no. 169.
[61] *Ibid.*, no. 189.
[62] *El Archivo Condal de Barcelona*, no. 38.
[63] *Cart. de Saint-Etienne de Limoges*, no. 3.
[64] *Ibid.*, no. 5.
[65] *Cart. de Nîmes*, no. 8. On the possibility that these *vassi* may be royal *vassi dominici* rather than comital ones see F. Ganshof, "L'origine des rapports féodo-vassiliques," in *I problemi della Civiltà Carolingia*, p. 19 n.

the Midi. The whole method whereby such monarchs had used *honores* and royal *fiscal* land to tie individuals to them through homage and *fidelitas* was in full decay. A few vestiges of the system remained which counts and others attempted to keep alive. But these were only vestiges. What we find is a society in which, with the possible exception of Catalonia, these have disappeared, leaving private allodial land under control of important families as the normal pattern found everywhere south of Poitou and Burgundy.

If our information concerning these years shows a disappearance of land given out in the Carolingian fashion to *vassi* and *fideles* in return for military and other services, and its transformation into allodial land everywhere in the Midi and Catalonia, what of those very different *precaria* and benefices which had long been a feature of this society? I refer to grants of land by individual landowners or church establishments, long known south of Burgundy and Poitou, which did not resemble Carolingian grants. These were grants of allodial land, generally for a lifetime, in return for a definite payment of a *cens* and what is more important, grants which seem to have involved, as far as we can tell, no oath of homage or *fidelitas* on the part of the recipient. The grantor remained owner or had the *dominio* over the land involved. But he did *not* become lord of the individual who received it in the Carolingian sense, though no doubt he who received such land at a nominal yearly *cens* was in some ways the client or dependent of him who gave it.

This sort of *precaria* or benefice did not disappear along with those of the Carolingian variety. Instead, we find a good deal of evidence of its continued use, particularly by church establishments in Central France, in the Lyonnais, the Viennois, Velay, Auvergne, the Limousin, and Rouergue. Thus we find seven such *precaria* granted by the abbey of Savigny to important nearby magnates between the years 857 and 889, all calling for a yearly payment in kind or in money of a nominal sort.[66] Four were *precaria* of more than one lifetime.[67] Three were limited to a lifetime only.[68] This giving out of such *precaria* was not confined to Savigny. The nearby church of Saint-Etienne of Lyon followed suit, as we learn from the fact that King Lothaire II of Lorraine held two of its *villas* in such a manner between 863 and 868,[69] and its benefices are referred to in a

---

[66] *Cart. de Savigny*, nos. 1, 2, 3, 20, 21, 23, 25.
[67] *Ibid.*, nos. 1, 2, 3, 21.
[68] *Ibid.*, nos. 20, 23, 25.
[69] *Cart. de Grenoble*, no. 30.

charter of King Louis of Provence in 892.[70] Similar benefices seem to have been included in the domains of the church of Viviers in 877,[71] and it was probably such practices that caused two donors of land to the church of Saint-Maurice of Vienne in 871 and 889[72] to state that their property given to this church could not be alienated or given out as benefices.

In Auvergne similar practices seem not uncommon either. In 857 we find evidence that a church *"cum ipso beneficio"* was given to the abbey of Brioude[73] and that a villa *"ad beneficium"* was granted in 869 to a *"vir nobilis"* Hildegare,[74] a grant which Archbishop Frotaire reconfirmed in 874 when he became abbot of this monastery.[75] In the charter which tells us of this reconfirmation we find a mention of the fact that Hildegare in return for this grant gave to the abbey a *mansus* and some land planted in vines and promised a yearly *cens* of five *solidi*. In 888 we hear of a church and other property in the Cantal given by the same monastery to a certain Cunibert as a *precarium* for which he is to pay eight *solidi* a year in *cens*.[76]

In the Limousin where large *prestaria* and *precaria* were to become such a feature of the use of church lands in the next century, we find them in this period, too. In 859 Archbishop Rodulf and Abbot Garnulf of Beaulieu seem to have been given a church as a *precarium* by the bishop of Limoges, for which they were to pay seven *solidi* annually.[77] That gift of two *mansi* by Daniel in 884 to Saint-Etienne of Limoges seems to have represented not only land which Deusdet held as a benefice, but also additional property for which he must annually pay seven *solidi* to the canons of the church.[78] Such practices may help explain why donors forbade grants of *precaria* or benefices from lands they were giving Beaulieu in 866, 878, 887, 893, and 899.[79] We possess similar prohibitions in charters which mention land given to the abbeys of Vabres and Conques in Rouergue dating from 862 and 892,[80] as well as evidence of *precaria* which the latter

[70] *Ibid.*, no. 31.
[71] *Hist. Gén. de Lang.*, II, no. 197.
[72] *Cart. de Vienne,* nos. 108, 110.
[73] *Cart. de Brioude,* no. 77.
[74] *Grand Cart. de Brioude,* no. CXCI.
[75] *Cart. de Brioude,* no. 132. This charter clearly states that this *villa* is a precarium which owes a *cens* to the abbey.
[76] *Ibid.*, no. 38.
[77] *Cart. de Beaulieu,* no. 33.
[78] *Cart. de Saint-Etienne de Limoges,* no. 5.
[79] *Cart. de Beaulieu,* nos. 3, 22, 46, 156, 162.
[80] *Hist. Gén. de Lang.*, II, no. 160; *Cart. de Conques,* no. 153.

monastery gave to a certain Askipito and his son, in 900, in return for an annual *cens* of wine *"in vestitura."*[81]

Judging from our documents fewer such *precaria* were in use in more southern regions of the Midi or in Catalonia. Yet we do find proof of just such a *precarium* which in 837 the abbey of Lagrasse gave to Countess Richelde of Carcassonne in return for an annual *cens* of forty *solidi*—a large sum.[82] Some years later in 898 a *precarium* granted by the abbey of Montolieu in the same general region is mentioned.[83] We also find a reference to lands in Roussillon which in 861 were held *"de beneficio"* from the church of Elne,[84] and in nearby Urgell as early as 840 a charter of Count Sunifred's speaks of land belonging to the church of Urgell held *"sub beneficio."*[85] Perhaps it was such practices which caused Louis the Pious in 835 to forbid the holding *"in beneficium"* of any lands belonging to the Church which were located in Urgell, Berga, Cerdanya, Cardona, Pallars, and Ribagorça.[86]

Though the origin was different, the practice whereby owners gave land to a church or abbey and reserved the usufruct of such property for more than one generation or for more than one person, generally with payment of a *cens*, in effect set up *precaria* or benefices similar to those mentioned above. A charter from Périgord dating from 856, which calls this a *"beneficium usufructarium,"*[87] and one from Auvergne dating from 880[88] makes this clear. Such a practice seems to have been an increasingly popular one in the Midi. We find many examples of it in our documents: in Auvergne in charters of Brioude dating from 834 to 898,[89] in Lodève in one from Aniane dating from 840,[90] and one from Saint-Barnard de Romans which bears the date 889.[91]

In this same period we also find our first clear references to a fief or *feudum*, where it seems to be a synonym for *beneficium*. The first reference is in a charter from the abbey of Brioude which dates from 895–896.

[81] *Cart. de Conques*, no. 56.
[82] *Hist. Gén. de Lang.*, II, no. 91.
[83] *Cart. de Carcassonne*, I, 73–74.
[84] *Hist. Gén. de Lang.*, II, no. 156.
[85] *Ibid.*, no. 98.
[86] *Catalunya Carolingia*, II, 284–285.
[87] *Cart. de Paunat*, no. 7.
[88] *Cart. de Brioude*, no. 219.
[89] *Ibid.*, nos. 17, 26, 38, 60, 85, 102, 131, 165, 197, 212, 225, 240, 268, 279, 289, and many others.
[90] *Cart. d'Aniane*, no. 123.
[91] *Cart. de Saint-Barnard de Romans*, no. 4.

Southern French and Catalan Society (828–900)

This charter uses the term *"cum feudo"* in reference to some property exchanged by this monastery.[92] The second is from the Melgueil region where it is used in describing a gift of lands to the church of Maguelonne in 899.[93]

Last of all we have several references to that system later called *medium plantum* in which vacant land is given by an allodial owner to an individual who then puts it into cultivation, with the property being divided equally after five years between the cultivator and the original owner. An actual contract of this nature is found in a charter from Auvergne dating from the period 887 to 889[94] and we have what seems to be a reference to land of this nature in a charter dating from 879.[95] In the next century, this system of *medium plantum* was to become one of the most important ways in which new land was put into cultivation in the Midi and in Catalonia.

Such then is a description of the various types of landholding found south of Poitou and Burgundy during this period and of the various changes in such systems which are apparent. But no discussion of landholding by this society would be complete without at least some examination of serfs and serfdom. In early chapters we noted the existence of serfs in the Midi down to 828. After 828 we continue to find them relatively numerous, judging from our sources of information. This seems particularly true of parts of Aquitaine, particularly the Limousin, Rouergue, Quercy, Angoulême, and Périgord, those centers of the old Roman *villa* system. Charters dating from 841, 859, 860, 863, 865, 866, 878, 879–884, 885, 893, and 899[96] testify to the presence of serfs in the Limousin and Quercy, while they are also found in Rouergue and the Albigeois, according to charters dating from 838, 862, and 865.[97] In Angoulême and Périgord they are mentioned in 855 and 888.[98] They seem to be rarer in Auvergne where only one serf appears in our documents, one who in 851 was living on land belonging to the royal *fisc.*[99]

Judging from our sources, serfs seem to be rarer in the rest of the Midi. We find a reference to four serfs near Avignon in 897[100] and no mention

[92] *Cart. de Brioude,* no. 7.
[93] *Cart. de Maguelonne,* I, no. 3.
[94] *Grand Cart. de Brioude,* no. CCXXXI.
[95] *Cart. de Brioude,* no. 268.
[96] *Cart. de Beaulieu,* nos. 20 (841), 18 (859), 19 (860), 112 (863), 186 (865), 3 (866), 46 (878), 17 (879–884), 55 (885), 155 (893), 22 (899).
[97] *Cart. de Conques,* no. 581; *Hist. Gén. de Lang.,* II, nos. 160, 164.
[98] *Cart. d'Angoulême,* no. 52; *Cart. de Paunat,* no. 11.
[99] *Grand Cart. de Brioude,* no. CXIV.
[100] *Hist. Gén. de Lang.,* V, no. 17.

of others in the rest of the Valley of the Rhone or Septimania. On the other hand, it seems clear that there still existed a certain number of serfs in a region generally thought of as free from such bondage, the region of Roussillon, Confluent, Cerdanya, and Ausona. Here charters dating from 874, 876, 887, 898, and 898–917[101] attest to their presence. This would tend to make one believe that the settlement of such regions at the time of Count Miró and Count Guifred was, at least initially, a more aristocratic affair than has sometimes been assumed with the *fideles* of these counts who staked out *aprisiones* bringing into these regions a number of serfs who assisted them in the initial task of clearing the soil for cultivation. Whatever the explanation of this fact, it is clear that here and in Aquitaine serfdom still remained, as late as the year 900, an institution which had not yet begun to disappear.

Finally we need to consider the role of women in the ownership of property. In this period, as in earlier ones, we find them everywhere the proprietors of large and small estates and able to dispose of them as freely as men. Our documents, for instance, reveal such women owning and disposing of property in 857, 860, and 876[102] in Velay; in 882 in Dauphiny;[103] in 829, 840, and 899[104] in the Melgueil region; and in 889 near Béziers.[105] We find a woman who owns a *villa* in the Narbonnaise in 850[106] and others who possessed *villas* and other property in Roussillon in 876[107] and in Ausona in 900.[108] In Aquitaine charters show them in the same role; such as some from Auvergne which date from 891 and 898[109] and others from the Limousin dating from 844, 847, and 860.[110] Some of these women, like Countesses Aiga and Rotrudis and Abbess Irmenna of the Turenne family, or Karissima, abbess of Saint Sernin of

---

[101] *Ibid.*, II, nos. 162 (874), 190 (876); *El Archivo Condal de Barcelona*, no. 4 (887), 10 (898), 9 (898–917).

[102] *Cart. de Saint-Chaffre*, nos. 59 (857), 60 (860), 72 (876).

[103] *Cart. de Vienne*, no. 99.

[104] *Cart. d'Aniane*, nos. 313 (829), 55 (840); *Cart. de Maguelonne*, I, no. 3 (899).

[105] *Cart. de Béziers*, no. 6.

[106] *Cart. de Carcassonne*, II, 214.

[107] *Hist. Gén. de Lang.*, II, no. 190.

[108] *El Archivo Condal de Barcelona*, no. 12.

[109] *Cart. de Brioude*, nos. 85, 102.

[110] In the charter of 844 Countess Aiga's relatives sign as witnesses to signify, it would seem, their consent (*Cart. de Beaulieu*, no. 34). According to the 847 charter Abbess Immena seems to be acting without her family's consent (*ibid.*, no. 184). For the 860 charter see *ibid.*, no. 19.

Albi, or Berteiz, countess of Toulouse, or Guillaumette, countess of Melgueil, were not only important landowners, they were important personages in their own right. Perhaps the best symbol of such women, however, was Emma, to whom Count Guifred, her father, gave land to found the nunnery of Saint-Joan de les Abadesses about 885[111] and to whom Gotmar, bishop of Ausona, gave his *aprisiones* in 898.[112] A somewhat posterior document sums up her role and position as follows, "the late Count Guifred gave to his daughter, Abbess Emma, the *honor* of the nunnery of Saint-Joan, so that all *men* who inhabited it should be under her control."[113] Emma, the powerful and able abbess of Ausona, then, is a symbol of those other women who in later centuries were to wield so much power and influence in every segment of the life of Southern France and Catalonia.

Such was the landholding system found in the Midi and the Spanish March between the years 828 and 900. It was one which was essentially based upon allodial ownership of land both large and small and one where in some regions there were still a considerable number of serfs. It was a system in which by 900 large *aprisio* holdings and benefices, established by the Carolingians, had changed until they were indistinguishable from allodial property. It was one which still seemed to preserve some vestiges of Carolingian vassalage, but now only as a tie maintained by local counts, viscounts, and bishops in an unimportant role: the more important and more numerous *precaria* and benefices which existed were those given out by churches and individuals in return for a *cens* instead of in return for *fidelitas* and military service or even court service. It was a system in which women, who were in many respects the equal of men, were playing an increasingly important role. By 900, in fact, it was a system which in many ways seems to have resembled that of pre-Carolingian times more than it did that to be found at the time of Charlemagne and Louis the Pious. The Carolingians had come and then they had declined, but the society of the Midi remained relatively intact, remaking the landholding system of Carolingian times into one which was different from that of Northern France and more nearly suited to their own traditions and their own needs.

As a final view of this society, let us examine its economic development

[111] *El Archivo Condal de Barcelona*, nos. 3, 4; *Catalunya Carolingia*, II, 216–217; and *Marca hispanica*, appendix 45.
[112] *El Archivo Condal de Barcelona*, no. 10.
[113] *Ibid.*, no. 38.

during this period. During these decades land remained the most important basis of the economic life of these regions. In some parts of the Midi and Catalonia, therefore, the clearing of the soil and the colonization of vacant land, a feature of the earlier Carolingian period, continued. This seems to be particularly true in Auvergne, which was far enough away from the regions which the Vikings and Moslems devastated not to be affected by their raids. Evidence of land held by *attracto* or *medium plantum* seems to point to activity of a colonizing nature by peasant cultivators in this region.[114] Perhaps during these years there also continued to be a similar movement in nearby areas like those near the Tarn, in the Toulousain, where we hear of land belonging to Raymond of Toulouse which in 862 was being put into vineyards.[115] If so, it was a very limited movement, for we find nothing of a similar nature in any other part of Septimania, Gascony, or Aquitaine north of Narbonne and Carcassonne. In the Valley of the Rhone we have one reference in Velay to a *villa "ad heremum"* in 857,[116] which seems to imply clearing; that is all. Elsewhere all is either silence or as in the case of the Lyonnais in 892 we hear of deserted land and *villas* called *"absas et vastitas."*[117] Obviously Auvergne and parts of Velay and the Toulousain were islands of agricultural progress in a sea of agricultural stagnation and decay.

To the south in Roussillon, Confluent, and parts of Catalonia, however, we sense a different mood. Here, throughout these years, the new settlement of land started by Charlemagne and Louis the Pious continued. We hear of new abbeys being founded in waste places and of land being cleared by the monks. We find many references to *aprisiones*. Even more important between 878 and 898 we have that advance of Count Guifred, Count Miró and their *fideles* into Ausona, Berga, and Barcelona beyond the Llobregat and a beginning made of colonizing land deserted since the revolt of Aizo in 826–828.[118] This advance was the only one which we find in our regions during this period, and it was to have very important consequences for Catalonia. Nevertheless, one must not overestimate the actual extent of the repopulation which was accomplished in Guifred's

---

[114] For examples of *attracto* land see *Cart. de Brioude,* nos. 110, 197, 212, 260, 263. For *medium plantum* see *ibid.,* no. 268, and *Grand Cart. de Brioude,* no. CCXXXI.
[115] *Hist. Gén. de Lang.,* II, no. 160.
[116] *Cart. de Saint-Chaffre,* no. 69.
[117] *Cart. Lyonnais,* I, no. 2.
[118] See Abadal, *Els Primers Comtes Catalans,* pp. 73–110, and *La Plana de Vich* for excellent accounts of this colonization.

Southern French and Catalan Society (828–900)   173

time. This able count did regain such regions and organize them politically, and he began a restoration of the Church, particularly in Ausona. But the actual resettlement of much of this region came later. A beginning was made on the fringes of his reconquest only, by abbeys like Saint-Joan and Ripoll and by his *fideles* to whom he allotted land.[119] But not until well into the next century was sufficient colonization achieved so that this region had a full population.

If our evidence seems to show some continuing agricultural advance in two portions of the Midi, the Massif Central and the general region of Catalonia which are in contrast to a general agrarian stagnation and decay elsewhere, what of trade and commerce? Did limited advances noticeable at the time of Charlemagne and Louis the Pious continue, or did such progress show the effect of the same troubled times which set back agricultural progress in so much of the Midi? Here our evidence is scant, but on the whole significant.

In the first place, examination of our charters shows that a use of money continued in those regions for which we have evidence, that is to say in most of Aquitaine, in the Valley of the Rhone, in Septimania, and in Catalonia. Only in remote areas like Pallars and Ribagorça do phrases like *"in rem valentem,"* that sign of a barter economy, appear very often in charters.[120] One should not, however, attach too much significance to this continued use of money. For we also find that in certain regions mints, active during the early years of Charles the Bald and of his father, Louis, had begun to disappear. First to disappear were those in Gascony and along the Garonne at Dax, Bordeaux, Agen, and Saintes—all of which were in areas which were much exposed to Viking attacks.[121] At about the same time Marseille ceased to coin money, and a little later the mints at Uzès, Nîmes, Béziers, and Maguelonne had disappeared also.[122] By 900 the only mints left in the Midi seem to have been those located at Vienne, Avignon, and Arles in the Rhone Valley; Narbonne, and Carcassonne in Septimania; Barcelona, Gerona, and Ampurias in Catalonia; and Toulouse, Limoges, Melle, Clermont, and LePuy in Aquitaine.[123] It seems worth

[119] *El Archivo Condal de Barcelona*, no. 38.
[120] See the large number of examples of payments in kind found in the charters contained in Abadal, *Els Comtats de Pallars i Ribagorça*. For examples from Auvergne see *Cart. de Brioude*, nos. 219 (880), 131 (881), 289 (881), 223 (882), 225 (888), 18 (893), 277 (895), 26 (898), 85 (898).
[121] See A. Lewis, *The Northern Seas A.D. 300–1100*, pp. 286–287.
[122] *Ibid.*
[123] *Ibid.*, pp. 290–291.

noting that in general it is in regions in which agricultural progress continued in Central Aquitaine and in Catalonia that mints continued their activities.

At the same time the external commerce of most of the Midi also declined. Judging from the lack of Southern French coins in Northern French coin hoards which date from this period, there was less contact between these northern parts of France and the Midi than had been true earlier.[124] The most important trade was that in the hands of Jews of Verdun who were still carrying slaves south through the Midi on their way to Moslem Spain.[125] Some contacts were still maintained with Italy via Alpine *clusae*,[126] but less by sea from the mouths of the Rhone. Only from Catalonia by sea and overland, especially from Ampurias, was much contact maintained with Mediterranean Moslem and Christian lands nearby.[127]

This growing economic localism is best illustrated, perhaps, by certain coin hoards which date from this period and which show the circulation of money in portions of the Midi. The first we should consider is one from Brioux, near Melle in Poitou, which dates from about 870. All of the coins found in this hoard were either minted at Melle or other places in Aquitaine with one exception, a silver denier from Pavia in Italy.[128] A somewhat later coin hoard dating from the first years of the tenth century and found nearby at Bonnevaux is even more revealing. It contains money minted during the reigns of Charles the Bald, Carloman, Eudes, and Charles the Simple. Those dating from the reign of Charles the Bald come from mints all over Northern and Western France. Those struck in Carloman's reign come from Toulouse, Limoges, and Melle. Those of Eudes' came from Limoges alone, and those of Charles the Simple are only from Melle.[129] In these two hoards one can see the increasing localism of this part of the Midi.

Lest this be thought unusual, a coin hoard from Avignon of about the same date throws light on similar conditions along the lower Rhone during this period. This hoard contains coins minted during the reigns of

---

[124] *Ibid.*, pp. 291–293.
[125] *Ibid.*, p. 287.
[126] *Ibid.*, pp. 295–296.
[127] A. Lewis, *Naval Power and Trade in the Mediterranean A.D. 500–1100*, pp. 137–153.
[128] E. Gariel, *Les monnaies royales de France sous la race carolingienne*, pp. 75–81.
[129] *Ibid.*, pp. 124–137.

Charles the Bald, Carloman, and Charles the Fat, as well as some coined by the archbishop of Arles early in the tenth century. Those minted by Charles the Bald came from Clermont, Toulouse, and one from Italy. Those of Carloman's reign came from Arles and Substantion. Those from the reign of Charles the Fat came from Béziers, Uzès, and Nîmes. Those minted later came only from Arles. Here again we see localism triumphing as we reach the year 900.[130]

To sum up then, the economic conditions of regions south of Poitou and Burgundy show a steady deterioration from 828 to 900 and especially after 875. As royal authority declined and the governmental system, the Church, and society changed, the agrarian growth and economic advance which characterized the period of Charlemagne and Louis the Pious stopped, except in parts of Catalonia and Central Aquitaine. As this happened, mints disappeared and commerce declined, too, leaving localism triumphant almost everywhere—a localism which was to increase in the decades ahead. It was this local agrarian economy which in no small measure was to determine the conditions under which the Midi and the Spanish March were to operate in the next century.

[130] *Ibid.*, pp. 147–153.

IV
THE FAILURE OF THE TERRITORIAL STATE,
900–975

CHAPTER X

The End of Royal Influence

BY THE FIRST years of the tenth century Frankish monarchs who lived north of the Loire had lost all effective control over Southern France and Catalonia. Real authority over the Spanish March, Gascony, Septimania, Aquitaine and the Valley of the Rhone was now in the hands of noble families, who, by hereditary right, seem to have exercised such functions of government as remained and who tended to dominate the Church as well. This end of the power of the royal government, however, did not destroy all vestiges of influence which French monarchs still exercised over these regions. Some remained down to the middle of the tenth century and even afterwards, until it disappeared, not to be found again until the middle of the twelfth century.

Let us examine this ending of royal influence over the Midi and Catalonia and the reasons for it. We might perhaps best begin by considering the matter of royal presence in these regions. From 900 on our evidence seems to show that kings of France rarely traveled south of Poitou and Burgundy. When they did, they seem to have confined their visits to regions like Auvergne and Western Aquitaine which were close to their northern centers of authority. Of all these kings, Raoul seems to have shown the most interest in the Midi, traveling to LePuy and Auvergne[1] and acting for a period in a military capacity in the Limousin, Quercy, and adjoining regions.[2] Louis IV probably made several visits to Western

[1] A charter dating from 924 probably was given during this visit to Velay (*Hist. Gén. de Lang.*, V, no. 49). See also a charter granted at the request of Raoul's *fidelissimus miles* Dalmatius, who was probably a viscount of Velay or Auvergne in *Cart. de Carcassonne*, I, 76.

[2] For example see the charters which Raoul gave to Tulle in 933 and 935 during his visit to this region (*Cart. de Tulle*, nos. 15, 598).

Aquitaine and Auvergne.[3] Lothaire certainly visited LePuy.[4] In contrast to a Charles the Bald or a Carloman, however, northern French rulers seem to have showed little direct interest in their southern domains, if by interest one means actual visits.

We have, however, other indices of interest, besides actual visits, which need to be examined. That is evidence of charters issued by these rulers which concern the Midi and Catalonia and are proof of continuing ties of homage or *fidelitas*, which linked important noble families of these regions to a distant crown. Before examining these two points, however, we must emphasize that there were at least two regions of Southern France and the Spanish March in which neither of these two forms of continued royal influences are to be found in this period. I refer to the Valley of the Rhone and to Pallars and Ribagorça. The Valley of the Rhone, after 890, had kings of its own and so did not recognize, even in theory, northern French monarchs,[5] while Pallars and Ribagorça from the late ninth century on had counts who both in theory and in fact possessed power independent of the kings who lived north of the Loire.[6]

Elsewhere, however, charters and evidence of homage seem to point out that some royal influence remained in most regions south of Poitou and Burgundy down into the reign of Lothaire. Lest we overestimate the importance of this influence, however, we need to understand its true basis and nature in the light of the political realities of the period. The first of these political realities was the rivalry which existed between the older Carolingian family and the new rising power of the Capetians. This rivalry led to a practice of choosing monarchs alternately from these rival houses between the years 887 and 938. First Eudes was made king.[7] Then

---

[3] See Louis IV's confirmation of the privileges of Saint-Pons de Thomières in 939 in *Hist. Gén. de Lang.*, V, no. 73. This does not necessarily mean he was present in person in this part of the Midi. On the other hand two charters issued by him in 942 seem to prove that he visited Aquitaine. One was the charter he gave to Saint-Jean d'Angély (*Cartulaire de Saint-Jean d'Angély*, ed. G. Musset, no. 1). The other was one he gave to Saint-Hilaire of Poitiers (*Cart. de Saint-Sernin*, no. 289). For the charter he issued in 941 during his visit to Auvergne see *Cart. de Brioude*, no. 338. See the record of another visit to Auvergne in 944 (Flodoard, *Annales*, ed. P. Lauer, anno 944).

[4] See a charter dating from 955 given to the church of LePuy during his visit to Velay (*Hist. Gén. de Lang.*, V, no. 97).

[5] On the situation which existed in this region during the early tenth century see R. Poupardin, *Le Royaume de Bourgogne (888-1038)*, pp. 1-109.

[6] See Abadal, *Els Comtats de Pollars i Ribogorça*.

[7] On the results of the assumption of royal office by Eudes see J. Dhondt, *Etude*

The End of Royal Influence 181

his Carolingian rival Charles the Simple succeeded him in 898.[8] Then there was a return to the Capetians with Raoul.[9] And finally in 938 Louis IV re-established his family in control of the monarchy for most of the rest of the century until the Capetians finally won out permanently at the time of Hugh Capet.[10]

This rivalry was one in which the noble families of the Midi and Catalonia could take very little part, even if they had wished to do so. Election of monarchs seems to have been a prerogative of Northern French magnates and churchmen, who encouraged Capetian-Carolingian rivalry since this forced each monarch to bid for their support with important concessions. But it did have serious political effects upon the magnates who controlled political power south of Poitou and Burgundy.

Much more important for the Midi and Catalonia during this period, though was another rivalry—one which involved the House of Toulouse and neighboring noble families, and one of which historians have been much less aware. This rivalry, like that between Carolingians and Capetians, also went back into the last years of the ninth century. It seems to have been the result of the ambitions of the Toulousain family to dominate the Limousin and Auvergne to the north and the Carcassonne-Narbonne region to the south of their broad domains which stretched from Angoulême and Périgord to the Rhone. Their claims and ambitions in the Limousin brought them into conflict with Ebles of Poitou and his heirs, who, having recovered their ancestral county from Count Ademar in 902, had hopes of extending their authority to the south.[11] Their claims to Auvergne resulted in an enmity between their house and the heirs of Bernard Plantevelue, who controlled this region during the first years of the tenth century. Then, after the death of Count Acfred, the last direct heir of this house, it led to additional friction with the House of Poitou which also had a claim to Auvergne.[12] It was probably a common

---

sur la naissance des principalités territoriales en France, pp. 160–250; L. Auzias, *L'Aquitaine Carolingienne (778–987)*, pp. 180 ff, and E. Favre, *Eudes, comte de Paris et roi de France (882–898)*.

[8] For this reign see A. Eichel, *Charles le Simple*.

[9] See P. Lauer, *Louis IV, d'Outremer*, pp. 1–65, on the rivalry between Capetians and Carolingians during this period.

[10] See Lauer, *ibid.*, and F. Lot, *Les Derniers Carolingiens: Lothaire, Louis V, Charles de Lorraine*.

[11] *Ademar de Chabannes*, III, 21, pp. 140–141, and "Aquitaniae Historiae Fragmentum," *ibid.*, p. 199.

[12] *Ademar de Chabannes*, III, 23, p. 143. Ademar says Ebles Manzur was count

Map 3. SOUTHERN FRANCE AND CATALONIA (*circa* 930).

key to symbols

Noble Families Dominating the Regions (all boundaries are approximate)

Ar—Aragón
Au—Auvergne
AP—Angoulême-Périgord
AR—Ampurias-Roussillon
BC—Barcelona-Cerdanya
CR—Carcassonne-Razès
Ga—Gascony

Me—Melgueil
Na—Navarre
Po—Poitou
Pr—Kingdom of Provence-Burgundy
PR—Pallars-Ribagorça
TR—Toulouse-Rouergue

opposition to the House of Toulouse which caused these two families to be linked by marriage alliance early in this period.

To the south, Toulousain claims to a special overlordship over Narbonne, Carcassonne, and Razès seem to have been the basic cause of an enmity which existed between the heirs of Oliba of Carcassonne and the family of Toulouse—a conflict which also had its roots in the last years of the ninth century.[13] In this conflict it would seem that the House of Carcassonne could generally count on the support of its relatives, the Gothic counts who controlled Catalonia.[14] But they probably sought other allies also, and this was the cause of that marriage alliance with the family of the Bernards of Auvergne, which finally resulted in Acfred II of Carcassonne-Razès succeeding William II as count of Auvergne in the 920's.[15] During most of our period, then, we find the House of Toulouse in basic conflict with the noble families who controlled Poitou, Auvergne, and Carcassonne—families who were linked by close ties and marriage alliances.

If the House of Toulouse had its enemies in the Midi, it had its allies too. Its counts seem to have maintained a close alliance with the Western Aquitanian noble house of Angoulême-Périgord, whom they tied to their house by a marriage alliance and the concession of the county of Agen, which also linked them to that associated noble house descended from Ermenon.[16] They also seem to have maintained close and friendly ties with the hereditary dukes of Gascony.[17] To the east they did the same with the counts who controlled the Lower Rhone Valley and Provence.[18]

---

of both Poitou and Auvergne. That he was count of the latter seems very doubtful, since we find no reference to him in either the *Cart. de Brioude* or the *Cart. de Sauxillanges* during this period. All he had was a *claim* to Auvergne.

[13] On the investiture of Count Bernard of Toulouse with the counties of Carcassonne and Razès in 872 by Charles the Bald see *Cart. de Carcassonne*, V, 221.

[14] See R. de Abadal i de Vinyals, *Els Primers Comtes Catalans*, pp. 3–60, 120–160, on the ties which linked the counts of Carcassonne with those of Catalonia.

[15] See Abadal, *ibid.*, pp. 48–49, on Acfred II (of Carcassonne) and his inheritance of the county of Auvergne through his mother who was a sister of Duke William the Pious.

[16] *Ademar de Chabannes*, III, 20, p. 139, mentions the marriage of William, count of Périgord, with the sister of Count William of Toulouse, a union which brought to the former the county of Agen.

[17] Flodoard mentions that Lupus Aznar Vasco accompanied Counts Raymond and Ermengaud of Toulouse when they did homage to King Raoul for their lands (Flodoard, *Annales*, anno 932).

[18] Bertha, countess of Rouergue, seems to have been a daughter of the count of

The End of Royal Influence 185

Thus the House of Toulouse and its allies controlled a wide belt of territory, during this period, which effectively separated their northern enemies in Poitou and Auvergne from their southern adversaries in Carcassonne-Razès and Catalonia. In the continuing struggle both sides found royal influence a useful weapon, just as both the Carolingians and Capetians sought the support of these same powerful magnates in the course of their own rivalry.

With this in mind let us consider what can be learned from an examination of charters which were issued by northern French monarchs and from acts of homage by the magnates of the Midi and Catalonia to these same rulers. We must begin by noting again that the accession of Eudes marked the opening of a new era for French monarchs and their power in the lands which lay south of Poitou and Burgundy. The nobles of most of these regions only accepted Eudes as king with extreme reluctance,[19] and those of the Rhone Valley used his accession as an excuse to rally to the new king of Provence, Louis, son of Boson.[20] As far as can be ascertained most of the magnates of Aquitaine, Septimania, and Catalonia refused to do homage for their *honores* to a king whom they considered to be little more than a usurper.[21] The exceptions seem to have been Ademar, count of Poitou,[22] and the House of Toulouse, who became Eudes' only dependable supporters in the Midi.[23]

As a result the return of the Carolingian line to power in 898, with Charles the Simple, could not help but be hailed as a victory by the anti-Toulousain party. They used it as an occasion to drive Count Ademar from Poitou in 902,[24] and the Gothic counts of Carcassonne and Catalonia did homage to Charles for their lands and *honores*, something they had refused to Eudes.[25] It seems probable that it was in recognition of this support that Charles the Simple gave to the magnates of this faction

---

Provence. See the charter of 960 which mentions the lands she possessed in Provence (*Hist. Gén. de Lang.*, V, no. 107).

[19] Concerning Catalonia see comments of Abadal in *Els Primers Comtes Catalans*, pp. 235–239.

[20] See the charter of 892 which Louis signs as king of Provence in *Cart. de Grenoble*, no. 31. This does not mention Eudes.

[21] See Abadal, *Els Primers Comtes Catalans*, and Dhondt, *Étude sur la naissance de principalités*.

[22] *Ademar de Chabannes*, III, 21, p. 140.

[23] See account of the letter which Eudes wrote to Count Raymond of Toulouse in 892 on behalf of the church of Nîmes in *Cart. de Nîmes*, no. 5.

[24] *Ademar de Chabannes*, III, 21, p. 140.

[25] Abadal, *Els Primers Comtes Catalans*, p. 257.

charters which contained many privileges. He confirmed to the heirs of Count Guifred control over lands which had belonged to the royal *fisc* in Catalonia[26] and generously endowed abbeys like Saint-Jacques de Joucan in 900[27] and Lagrasse in 908[28] which were controlled by his Gothic supporters. He seems to have done the same for the archbishop of Narbonne, who was menaced by Toulousain encroachment also.[29]

About 909, however, we begin to notice a certain change in the policies which Charles the Simple pursued in Southern France. In this year Charles gave to the abbey of Psalmodi a charter in which he refers to Raymond of Toulouse as *marchio* and as a *fidelis,* which implies that he had done homage to him for his *honores* in the Midi.[30] Whether such an act actually took place or not, there can be little doubt that Charles' relations with his Gothic supporters grew cooler after this period. He issued no more royal charters which were in their interest and in 914, when Archbishop Arnulf of Narbonne was murdered, he attempted to name as his successor a bishop of Béziers who appears to have been the candidate of the House of Toulouse. In the face of the united opposition of the counts of Catalonia and Carcassonne this attempt ended in failure and with it most of Charles' influence in the Midi.[31] Only one more charter, given in 924 to the abbey of Solignac in the Limousin, probably at the behest of the Toulousain house, testifies to his influence south of Poitou.[32]

Toward the end of Charles' reign it became apparent that Raoul of the Capetian family would succeed him as king. The enemies of the Toulousain family, who had been checked by Charles' defection to this house, again appear to have taken heart. At any rate in 924 we find Raoul, with the consent of Count William II of Auvergne, giving a charter to Adelard, bishop of LePuy, in which he granted to him the *burg* of this city and the right to coin money.[33] Two years later the same Count Wil-

---

[26] See the record of land which the king gave to Count Guifred II in 911 in *El Archivo Condal de Barcelona,* no. 33, and the charter recording another royal grant to Guido, bishop of Gerona, in 922 (*Catalunya Carolingia,* II, 379–380).
[27] *Cart. roussillonnais,* no. 3.
[28] *Hist. Gén. de Lang.,* V, no. 34.
[29] *Ibid.,* V, no. 25, and *Catalunya Carolingia,* II, 373–374, 438–439.
[30] *Hist. Gén. de Lang.,* no. 37.
[31] *Ibid.,* nos. 114, 116, 126. On the resistance to this see Abadal, *Els Primers Comtes Catalans,* pp. 262–264. He dates the end of royal influence of an effective sort in Catalonia from 922, except in the case of a few abbeys which kept royal connections.
[32] *Cart. d'Uzerche,* no. 1306.
[33] *Hist. Gén. de Lang.,* V, no. 49.

The End of Royal Influence   187

liam did homage to Raoul for his *honores* of Auvergne, Velay, Gevaudun, and the Lyonnais.[34] Soon afterwards about 929 this same monarch rewarded a certain Oliba with wide royal lands and rights in Besalu.[35] And in 931 on the petition of his *"fidelissimus miles Dalmatius"*—probably Viscount Dalmace of LePuy—he granted certain privileges to the abbey of Montolieu, which was located in a region controlled by the counts of Carcassonne.[36]

It was probably the results of such royal favor to their enemies which caused Count Ermengaud and his nephew Count Raymond Pons, whom our source calls *"principes Gothorum,"* to hasten north in 932 to do homage to Raoul for their lands, bringing with them their ally Sánchez, the hereditary duke or *princeps* of Gascony.[37] If they hoped by this act of homage to disarm Raoul and checkmate their rivals, however, they were doomed to disappointment. For it was at about this period that this monarch in the company of Count Ebles Manzur of Poitou entered the Limousin and Western Aquitaine at the head of a force of Northern French warriors.[38] Raoul and his allies succeeded in their immediate objective, which was to destroy the last Viking bands which appear to have still been operating freely in this region of France. But their expedition had still another result. This was to deliver the Limousin and perhaps a part of Quercy into the hands of the Poitevin house, as we learn from a charter that Raoul gave to the abbey of Tulle in 933, which mentions that this monastery is being reformed by Count Ebles of Poitou and Viscount Ademar of Scalas.[39]

Faced by this danger to his authority in the Limousin and the northern portion of his domains, Raymond Pons of Toulouse seems to have made peace with his enemies in the Carcassonne region. He must have then taken the offensive in the Limousin. At least he and his allies regained the southern portion of this province, for in 935, in another charter which Raoul gave to Tulle there is no mention of Count Ebles, but only of Ademar, who is now called count *"in partibus Cahors"*[40]—which seems to imply if not a break with his Poitevin ally at least an accommodation with Raymond Pons and the Toulousain House and their allies.

[34] Flodoard, *Annales*, anno. 926.
[35] *Catalunya Carolingia*, II, 386.
[36] *Cart. de Carcassonne*, I, 76.
[37] Flodoard, *Annales*, anno 932.
[38] See *Cart. de Tulle*, nos. 15, 598.
[39] *Ibid.*, no. 15.
[40] *Ibid.*, no. 598.

Such an accommodation, however, was of short duration. By 938 Raoul was dead and had been succeeded by Louis IV of the Carolingian family. It seems probable that initially Louis tried not to take sides in the dispute of the Midi. True, soon after his accession he gave a generous charter to the abbey of San-Cugat near Barcelona, the foundation most favored by the counts of Barcelona.[41] But he balanced this grant by giving a similar charter in 939 to the newly founded abbey of Saint-Pons of Thomières which Raymond Pons had established as a repository for his family's interests in the Narbonnaise.[42] By 941 Louis IV seems to have leaned closer to Raymond Pons, who became his principal ally in the Midi. A contemporary source tells of a meeting between Raymond and the king at which he probably did homage to him for his *honores* and brought his supporters with him to do likewise. The chronicler in this instance mentions him in the following terms: *"Regimundo Gothorum principe ceterisque proceribus Aquitanorum."*[43] That he controlled at least a part of Auvergne and the Limousin in this period seems clear from another charter dating from this same year which Louis IV issued to the Auvergnat abbey of Chanteuges. In this charter the king speaks of Raymond Pons as *princeps* of Aquitaine.[44]

By 942, however, it seems that Louis had changed allies and that the House of Poitou was back in favor. In that year we find him in Western Aquitaine where he reformed the abbey of Saint-Jean d'Angély in the Saintonge.[45] He appears to have done so in close alliance with the count of Poitou, for in the same year we find him giving two churches to the abbey of Saint-Hilaire of Poitiers. In this charter we find among the witnesses William Caput Stupe of Poitou signing as count and *marchio* along with his brother Ebles, who was later to be bishop of Limoges and abbot of Saint-Hilaire.[46] In the same year he gave a charter to Tulle as well.[47] Two years later in 944 we find him giving privileges to ecclesiastical establishments in the Barcelona region on the petition of Count Geoffrey of Ampurias-Roussillon and Bishop Gotmar of Barcelona.[48]

Certainly this friendship and alliance between the king and the Poitevin

---

[41] *Catalunya Carolingia*, II, 183–186. See also grant to Ripoll in *ibid.*, p. 162.
[42] *Hist. Gén. de Lang.*, V, no. 73.
[43] Flodoard, *Annales*, anno 944.
[44] *Cart. de Brioude*, no. 338, and *Hist. Gén. de Lang.*, V, no. 75.
[45] *Cart. de Saint-Jean d'Angély*, no. 1.
[46] *Cart. de Saint-Sernin*, no. 389.
[47] *Cart. de Tulle*, no. 15.
[48] *Catalunya Carolingia*, II, 226–228, 389–390.

The End of Royal Influence 189

house represented a danger to the family of Toulouse and their interests in Aquitaine, but it did not last for long. For in 944 Ebles Manzur died leaving his domains to his son Count William Caput Stupe. In the confusion that followed the claims which the House of Poitou had to Auvergne had to be abandoned temporarily. Perhaps the Limousin also had to be abandoned, at least the southern portion of it, though Ebles, William's brother, was able to assume the office of bishop of Limoges.[49] Louis apparently took no action during this period in either the Limousin or Auvergne, but he did continue to maintain close and friendly relations with the counts of Catalonia. At any rate in 948 and 953 we find him granting charters containing a number of privileges to the monastery of Saint-Peter of Rhodes.[50] In 951 we find him granting additional privileges and confirming the land of the newly established abbey of Monserrat, near Barcelona,[51] and in 952, on the pleas of Counts Guifred and Sunyer doing the same for Cuxa and Saint-Peter of Camprodon.[52]

By 954, however, Louis was dead and his son Lothaire had succeeded him without a struggle. Lothaire's accession seems to mark the end of most royal influence in areas south of Poitou. When Count William Caput Stupe of Poitou, for instance, in 955 took control of much of Auvergne,[53] Lothaire did little except to renew in 955 the privileges of the church of LePuy which may have been threatened by this conquest.[54] We have no record, for instance, of any homages to him by any magnates who lived south of Poitou.[55] Nor does he appear to have been consulted or even considered when, for a brief period in the 960's, the House of Toulouse-Rouergue re-established a measure of control over the Limousin and parts of Auvergne.[56] Then for several decades there is little evidence of royal

[49] See mention of Bishop Ebles in a Limousin charter which dates from 951 (*Cart. d'Uzerche*, no. 120). On his building of castles at Limoges in 944 see *Ademar de Chabannes*, III, 27, p. 147.

[50] *Catalunya Carolingia*, II, 229–231, 231–234.

[51] *Ibid.*, pp. 256–257.

[52] *Ibid.*, pp. 77–78, 92–93.

[53] *Chartes de Cluny*, I, no. 825. It seems questionable, however, that William exercised much real authority over Auvergne in this period. For instance none of the charters found in the *Cartulary of Brioude* mention him.

[54] *Hist. Gén. de Lang.*, V, no. 97.

[55] On the failure of the lords of the Midi and Catalonia to do homage for their lands to French kings from this time on see J. Lemarignier, "Les Fidèles du roi de France," in *Recueil de travaux offerts à M. C. Brunel*, II.

[56] See the record of a court held in the Limousin in 960 by Count Raymond I of Rouergue (*Cart. de Beaulieu*, no. 47). See the record of land which Raymond owned in this same region according to his will which dates from 961 (*Hist. Gén.*

influence, except a charter which Lothaire gave to Cuxa in 958 reaffirming the privileges of this abbey,[57] and one ten years later which was given to San-Felix de Guixolds near Barcelona.[58] The only other sign of royal interest in the Midi was this monarch's apparent acquiescence in the assumption of the title of duke of Aquitaine by William Fierebras of Poitou in 973.[59] By 975, even by 954, the French monarchs, who had lost their *power* in the Midi and Spanish March in the late ninth century, had also lost their *influence* over such regions in their kingdom.

We might sum up our conclusions concerning royal influence in lands which lay south of Poitou and Burgundy, then, as follows. Despite outward appearances based on the issuing of charters and specific evidence of homages, from the time of Eudes on, French monarchs had no actual power over any part of Southern France and Catalonia. During these years of Capetian-Carolingian rivalry, however, they were able to maintain a certain illusion of authority or rather of influence. This seems to have been largely the result of the acute rivalry which existed between the House of Toulouse and its neighbors to the north and to the south. Thanks to this rivalry for some decades French monarchs were able to play one faction against another and thus force each side to seek their support and periodically to renew their homages to the crown. By the reign of Lothaire, however, even these outward signs of royal authority ended. The *principes* and churchmen of the Midi and Catalonia moved toward a new destiny in which they ceased to concern themselves, except spasmodically, with these monarchs who lived north of the Loire.

Yet some residue of royal tradition remained, if not of real royal influence. Except in the Valley of the Rhone and Pallars and Ribagorça, charters continued to be dated from the reigns of those monarchs who lived north of the Loire. True the phrase *"regnanti Jesu Christe"* seems to appear frequently enough to indicate a certain indecision and frustration, particularly toward the end of the tenth century,[60] and a somewhat puzzled count of Bigorre, just to be safe, in a charter dating from 945 refers to both the reigns of Louis IV of France and García of Aragón.[61]

---

de Lang., V, no. 111). Note that in this will he left land which he owned in Auvergne to Brioude.

[57] *Catalunya Carolingia,* II, 96–98.

[58] *Ibid.,* pp. 202–204.

[59] F. Lot, *Fidèles ou vassaux?* p. 67.

[60] When Eudes became king much of the Midi had difficulty in deciding to recognize him. This was even more noticeable in the late tenth century as the Carolingian line came to an end.

[61] *Hist. Gén. de Lang.,* V, no. 84.

The End of Royal Influence

But even granting such facts, a tradition that the kings of France were the overlords of Southern France remained, although it had little political substance. It was this tradition which was to flower again some two centuries later, when in the twelfth century French kings again advanced south of the Loire and began to re-establish their authority over areas which had not known their power or their presence for many, many decades. Royal influence ceased in the Midi and Catalonia by 975, if not earlier, but the memory of it remained for the future.

As royal influence faded, something began to replace it on a level more important than the local one. In Catalonia, curiously enough, it seems that one such influence was that of the caliphate of Cordova, which, in a sense, was a reaffirmation, after more than a century, of the fact that Catalonia formed a part of the Iberian peninsula. We begin to find Cordovan influence in Catalonia about 950, at the very moment when the influence of the French monarchy had all but disappeared. At about this time an embassy representing Count Borell of Barcelona visited Abd-ar-Rahman III's capital of Cordova.[62] A little later in 966 after a border conflict with the Moslems, peace was made which strengthened such ties.[63] In 971 and 974 two other embassies were sent to Cordova.[64] These embassies seem to have resulted in a new relationship being established in which the counts of Barcelona became, for all practical purposes, vassals of the powerful Moslem rulers to the south of them—a status which was to continue until the great Moslem attack which Almansor launched against Barcelona in 985. This attack opened a new and difficult period for Catalonia and its Islamic neighbors. Fading Carolingian influence then resulted for a time at least in a certain Moslem predominance as far as Catalonia was concerned.

This new status, however important it may have been temporarily, was less important than still another outside influence which we now begin to find, not only in the Spanish March but in the rest of the Midi. I refer to the power and influence of the Papacy. The growth of Papal influence during this period of the tenth century and its importance to Catalonia has long been known to historians, ever since the appearance of the important studies of Kehr, a German scholar, several decades ago. Kehr showed how, as royal ties to the north loosened, Catalan counts, nobles, and churchmen, starting about 950, began to look to Rome for a protection and interest they could no longer expect from distant French mon-

[62] Abadal, *Els Primers Comtes Catalans*, pp. 316–318.
[63] *Ibid.*, pp. 318–320.
[64] *Ibid.*, pp. 320–321.

archs. They thus multiplied such Papal connections,[65] which were to end in the twelfth and thirteenth centuries with these portions of the Iberian peninsula firmly tied to the see of St. Peter.

Though this Catalan story is well known and documented, it has been less appreciated that this was not merely a Catalan affair. For during these years we find exactly the same thing happening in the rest of the Midi also, even in the Valley of the Rhone with its separate local royal house. Our first documentary proof of this new Papal influence, as a matter of fact, comes from Dauphiny where in 932 a charter was issued by Pope John to the Abbey of Saint-Barnard de Romans which had special ties linking it to the Papacy.[66] This Papal bull represented an attempt to protect this monastery from depredations which it suffered at the hands of Sylvius, a nearby local magnate, and it ordered the latter to make amends for damage he had caused this establishment. These amends were to include a payment of one hundred pounds of silver and the freeing of some six hundred serfs—a stiff penalty indeed.

Such Papal intervention may have been effective, for it continued in later years. In addition to favors bestowed on Catalan religious establishments, in 950 Pope Agepitus II began extending Papal protection into other parts of the Midi. In 950 this pontiff gave the abbey of Montolieu a charter which confirmed this abbey's rights over its domains and gave it special authority over a number of churches.[67] In 951 Lagrasse secured a similar charter affirming Papal protection of its patrimony,[68] and so did Saint-Chaffre du Monastier in Velay.[69] This was followed by still another Papal charter given the new abbey of Lézat on the borders of Gascony.[70] Papal intervention in the affairs of the Church of the Midi had begun, and so had Papal protection for its abbeys—an intervention which was to have momentous consequences in the future.

Important as Pope John's intervention in the affairs of Saint-Barnard de Romans was to prove in the future, and that of Pope Agepitus in

[65] See P. Kehr, "Papsturkunden in Spanien: Vorarbeiten zur Hispania Pontifica I. Katalanien," in *Abhandlungen der Gesellschaft der Wissenschaften*, XVIII (1926).

[66] *Cart. de Saint-Barnard de Romans*, no. 13. Much earlier, however, is evidence of such ties set up by Gerald of Aurillac for his new monastery (see Odo, *Vita Sancti Geraldi Aureliacensis*, II, 4, and III, 4, in Migne *Patrologia latina*, CXXXIII, cols. 672–673, 691).

[67] *Cart. de Carcassonne*, I, 78.

[68] *Ibid.*, II, 224–225.

[69] *Cart. de Saint-Chaffre*, no. 375.

[70] *Hist. Gén. de Lang.*, V, no. 97.

The End of Royal Influence 193

Catalonia, Gascony, Velay, and Septimania, it was another outside ecclesiastical power which, in the immediate future, was to affect these regions more profoundly. I refer to the abbey of Cluny. Cluny, which had been established early in the tenth century by Duke William the Pious of Aquitaine, was a foundation which was soon to enjoy complete ecclesiastical independence. It very early began to exercise authority and influence over neighboring regions which lay south of Poitou and Burgundy. As one would expect the first evidence of such influence is to be found in regions like the Lyonnais, Auvergne, and Forez which were very close to Cluny itself. Thus as early as 927[71] we have evidence that Cluny had begun to accumulate property in Auvergne as the result of gifts by individuals impressed by Cluny's piety and reforming zeal. Other gifts followed in 929, 936–937, 954, 959, 963, 964–965, 966, and 975.[72] Perhaps the most important acquisition of all was the important abbey of Sauxillanges which between the years 950 and 952 became one of Cluny's daughter houses[73]—one of the first great abbeys to acknowledge Cluny's authority in this way.

In Forez we find similar gifts to Cluny in 927–942, in 965, and in 969,[74] while in 943 the abbey had sufficient property in this region to grant to a local nobleman, Aicard, a *villa* as a *precarium*.[75] Nearby in the Vienne region donors gave land to Cluny in 937 and 975,[76] and even more important in 943 King Conrad of Provence-Burgundy gave to her an important charter which placed all her property in his kingdom under his royal protection.[77] An examination of Cluny's charters of this period reveals this abbey's need of royal protection in the Valley of the Rhone, for they show that extensive gifts were being made to her. These gifts, which consisted of *villas,* churches, and other property seem to have been made in Valence in 928 and 975, in Uzès in 946 and 948, in Digne in 956–967, in Provence proper in 958, and in Apt in 959–960.[78] One of them

---

[71] *Chartes de Cluny,* I, no. 333.
[72] *Ibid.,* I, nos. 378 (929); 458, 459, 460 (936–937); 872, 873, 876 (954); II, nos. 1060, 1068 (959); 1149, 1156, 1164, 1167 (963); 1183 (964–965); 1206, 1208 (966); 1209 (975).
[73] *Ibid.,* I, no. 792, and *Cartulaire de Sauxillanges,* ed. H. Doniol, no. 16.
[74] *Chartes de Cluny,* I, no. 342 (927–942); II, no. 1189 (965); 921 (969).
[75] *Ibid.,* I, no. 642.
[76] *Ibid.,* I, no. 476 (937); II, no. 1311 (975).
[77] *Ibid.,* I, no. 622.
[78] *Ibid.,* I, no. 367, and II, no. 1390 (Valence); I, nos. 693, 724 (Uzès); II, nos. 1013 (Digne); 1052, 1066 (Provence); 1071 (Apt).

was the abbey of Saint-Armand bestowed on Cluny by Boson, count of Provence in 958.[79]

Though Cluny seems to have accumulated property and to have increased her influence primarily in Auvergne and the Valley of the Rhone, during these decades, we also find her extending her influence into other parts of the Midi. For instance sometime between 932 and 942, probably in 937, Bernard, count of Périgord, gave to her the abbey of Sarlat,[80] and she accumulated other property in the Limousin and Quercy during the same period. No wonder when Mayeuil, the venerable abbot of Cluny, was captured and held for ransom in 972 by Moslem brigands in the Alps while on a journey to Rome,[81] such an outcry arose in the Midi, an outcry which probably had a great deal to do with the final expulsion of these Moslem brigands from their pirate base of Fraxinetum in Provence. For by this time Cluny, from a simple abbey free of local, secular, and ecclesiastical control, had grown into a power in its own right. It had become a potent force capable of protecting abbeys, churches, and even individuals throughout the Midi in a lawless age in which such protection was a practical necessity. Already Cluny was on the way to becoming the powerful house which it became under St. Odilon's leadership later on in the next century.

The disappearance of royal influence over Southern France and the Spanish March then, created, about 950, a vacuum which needed to be filled in some way. Immediately the caliphate of Cordova assumed a certain suzerainty over Catalonia. More important, however, were two other outside powers, the Papacy and Cluny, which by 975 had spread their influence into most of the regions lying south of Poitou and Burgundy, bringing with them at least some assurance of a protection which Northern French monarchs could no longer provide.

[79] *Ibid.*, II, no. 1052.
[80] *Gallia Christiana*, II, anno 937, col. 595.
[81] Raoul Glaber, *Historiarum libri V*, ed. R. Prou, I, IV, 9, pp. 10–12.

CHAPTER XI

The Breakup of Principalities and the Court System

THE STORY of the decline and disappearance of royal authority and influence in Southern France and Catalonia brings up a most important question. What took its place beyond such influence as could be exerted by the Papacy, Cluny, and the caliphs of Cordova? Were the important noble families who emerged as masters of local regions and the local Church able, as a result, to create principalities on the bones of a decayed Carolingian system? Such seems to be the contention of a recent historian who has examined this question and who appears to postulate such a development as all but automatic.[1] Yet there is little evidence that he is correct. The fact seems to be instead that when Carolingian royal control of the Midi and the Spanish March ended in the last years of the ninth century, the leading magnates were unable to create territorial states in its place, despite all efforts to do so.

What then did happen? The story of the first three quarters of the tenth century is one not of the success but of the failure of the territorial state in these regions, and of a continuing decay of such machinery of government as survived—except perhaps in Catalonia which in many ways presents a unique situation. By 975 what had emerged in Southern France was not principalities, but a system which was so disorganized in a political sense that it approached anarchy—an anarchy that only slowly began to develop into a more orderly pattern of government.

Perhaps the best way to make clear this continuing decay of governmental organization and the failure of organized principalities to emerge

[1] See J. Dhondt, *Étude sur la naissance des principalités territoriales en France*, for an expression of this point of view. In this work Dhondt makes the assumption, without proof, that the decline of royal power *automatically* made for principalities.

is to examine our regions in 900 and contrast them with the situation to be found in 975. At the earlier date, as we have already emphasized, political authority had moved from the Northern French monarchs into the hands of a group of noble families. One of these had assumed a royal title and controlled the general region of the Rhone Valley. The other eleven dominated the rest of Southern France and the Spanish March as counts —two in Septimania, three in Catalonia, one in Gascony, and four in Aquitaine. Assisting them and sharing a measure of authority with them were a number of viscounts who had already made their appearance at Vienne, Nîmes, Béziers, Narbonne, Carcassonne, Toulouse, Roussillon, Catalonia, Albi, the Limousin, Angoulême, and Velay—at least thirteen in all, if not more.[2]

What do we find by 975? We find that the number of independent comital and viscontal families has multiplied, until we can list some hundred and fifty who hold their authority by hereditary right. In some regions like Provence, the Limousin, Auvergne, and Languedoc these families are so numerous that it is all but impossible to disentangle them or to discover with any accuracy their origins. Nor does a catalogue of such families exhaust the list of those in control of these regions, for by 975 in certain areas like Languedoc, Auvergne, and Catalonia, for instance, we find minor officials, vicars and *comtors,* whose independent authority over local regions seems almost as great as that exercised by counts and viscounts. The number of families in positions of authority had so multiplied in most of the Midi that the age of the *princeps* had become the period of the *principes.* Nor does the above suffice in explaining the extent of the diffusion of political power. For we must add to such secular ruling families ecclesiastical magnates as well; bishops like those of Limoges, Angoulême, LePuy, and Grenoble, or archbishops like those of Lyon, Vienne, and Narbonne. Such churchmen during this period were often the almost unchallenged masters of large parts of the Midi.

How did this decay and fragmentation of principalities come about? Why were families who controlled important portions of the Midi and Catalonia in 900 unable to create any form of principality—feudal or nonfeudal, which was capable of resisting progressive disintegration? And what happened to the governmental system of the Midi and the Spanish March as a result of such failures? These are the questions which demand answers. One might approach the answers in various ways, but

[2] See Chapter II, Section III, for a description of how viscounts came to develop in the Midi and Catalonia.

perhaps a good method is to concentrate on a certain number of the ruling families who appear to have controlled the Midi and Catalonia in 900, and to trace their history and that of the regions where they were powerful down to 975. We need not consider all twelve of the families who appear to have been dominant in 900, but only the more important ones. What should emerge is a general pattern which may allow us to make important generalizations.

Interestingly enough, it is not difficult for us to ascertain the relative importance of leading families in the Midi and Catalonia during these years. A number of terms or titles used to describe them in our sources make clear to us what individuals were endowed with more than ordinary authority or prestige. These terms are "king," "*dux*," "*marchio*," and "*princeps*," which, while they are not always precise, distinguish those who bore them from the less important counts and viscounts. Using such titles as a guide we discover that we can with profit focus our attention on the House of Poitou, the family of the Bernards of Auvergne and their successors, the kings of Provence and their principal supporters, the family of Hugh of Arles and those who succeeded them in authority, the House of Toulouse, the counts of Ampurias-Roussillon, the heirs of Counts Guifred and Miró in Catalonia, the counts of Pallars and Ribagorça, and the dukes of Aquitaine. We might also pay some attention to the House of Angoulême-Périgord and the family of Carcassonne-Razès, though they are not exactly similar to the examples cited above.

The eight families listed above, and their successors, all had representatives between 900 and 975 who were called "king," "*dux*," "*marchio*," or "*princeps*." For instance William the Pious is called duke of Aquitaine and the successor to his authority in Auvergne, Count Guy of Clermont, bears the title "*princeps Arvenorum*."[3] Ebles Manzur and his heirs of the

---

[3] William is called "count" and "marquis" in a charter which dates from 898 to 911 (*Cart. de Brioude*, no. 64). Another charter dating from 907 refers to him as "duke" (*ibid.*, no. 228). Again a charter of 917 which established the abbey of Sauxillanges calls him "count" and "marquis" (*Cart. de Sauxillanges*, no. 146). His heir, Count William II, seems to bear no title other than "count," however (see *Cart. de Brioude*, nos. 66, 318, 324). The next ruler of this line, Acfred, is only called "duke" once in a charter dating from 928 (*Cart. de Sauxillanges*, no. 13). In other charters of 922, 923, 926, and 927 he is simply called "count" (*Cart. de Brioude*, nos. 15, 30, 167, 315, and *Grand Cart. de Brioude*, no. CCCCXXXIII). Charters from Auvergne from late in this period dating from 954 to 986 mention Guido or Guy (of the Clermont family) as "count" (*Cart. de Sauxillanges*, no. 363). Note this latter is during that period when some historians claim Duke William Caput Stupe of Aquitaine controlled Auvergne.

House of Poitou are variously referred to as "count" and *"marchio"* or *"dux"* until after 973 they bear the title of dukes of Aquitaine by hereditary right.[4] In the Valley of the Rhone not only is Louis the Blind called "king,"[5] but his chief supporter Hugh of Arles, is called "count," *"marchio,"* and *"dux"*[6] in contemporary documents, before he too assumed a royal Italian title. Their successors in authority over these regions bear similar titles. Conrad is called "king,"[7] Geilin of Valence-Velay is referred to as *"marchio"* and *"princeps,"*[8] and William of Provence is variously styled "count" and *"marchio"* and *"dux."*[9]

Ermengaud and Raymond Pons of the House of Toulouse-Rouergue in 932 are called *"principes Gothiae,"*[10] and a little later, in documents dating from these years, the latter is referred to as *"Gothorum princeps,"*[11] *"princeps Aquitanorum,"*[12] and *"dux Aquitanorum."*[13] Just after 975 Count Geoffrey of Ampurias-Roussillon is called *"dux,"*[14] while Count Guifred and his heirs in Barcelona-Gerona-Ausona are variously styled

---

[4] A charter of 930 from the Limousin calls Ebles Manzur "count" (*Cart. de Tulle*, no. 14), while in 942 another refers to his son William as "count" and *"marchio"* (*Cart. de Saint-Sernin*, no. 289). In still another given to Saint-Jean d'Angély in 945 he is called "duke" (*Cart. de Saint-Jean d'Angély*, no. 242). A later charter dating from 971 from this same region also refers to his son William Iron Arm as "duke" (*ibid.*, no. 192). On members of this house continuing to bear the title of "duke" after 973 see F. Lot, *Fidèles ou vassaux?*, p. 67.

[5] See the use of this title in charters dating from 902 and 903 in *Cart. de Vienne*, nos. 11, 12, 13, and in 923 in *Chartes de Cluny*, I, no. 237.

[6] See charters of 910 (*Cart. de Vienne*, no. 14); of 917 (*Cart. de Saint-Barnard de Romans*, no. 9); of 920 (*Cart. de Saint-André-le-bas*, no. 124); and of 928 (*Cart. de Saint-Barnard de Romans*, no. 11).

[7] *Cart. de Saint-Barnard de Romans*, no. 11.

[8] See references to Count Geilin as *"nobilissimus vir et potens"* and *"princeps noster"* in *Hist. Gén. de Lang.*, V, no. 110 and as "marquis" in a charter of 937 (*ibid.*, no. 20).

[9] He is called *"dux"* in Raoul Glaber, *Historiarum libri V*, ed. R. Prou, I, IV, 9, p. 12.

[10] Flodoard, *Annales*, ed. P. Lauer, anno 932.

[11] In 933 a charter calls him "count" and *"marchio"* (*Hist. Gén. de Lang.*, V, no. 57). A charter issued by King Louis IV in 939 again refers to him as *"marchio"* (*ibid.*, no. 59). Still another local charter dating from 924 calls him *"Narbonensium principem"* and "marquis" (*ibid.*, no. 50).

[12] *Cart. de Brioude*, no. 338, dated 941. This charter was issued by King Louis IV.

[13] See charters dating from 937 and 939 which Raymond himself issued (*Hist. Gén. de Lang.*, V, nos. 67, 69, 74).

[14] *Catalunya Carolingia*, II, 210, 394.

"count" and *"marchio," "princeps,"* and *"dux."*[15] Those who succeeded Count Miró in Cerdanya-Besalu seem to have frequently been called *"marchio,"*[16] as were the counts of Pallars and Ribagorça in this period.[17] Late in the ninth century the hereditary rulers of Gascony are called *"dux"*[18] and probably continued to bear this title into the tenth century. The majority of these titles which show a special importance or authority seem to be survivals from Carolingian times when the terms "king," *"dux,"* and *"marchio"* were used to designate certain officials who possessed a special authority—particularly in regions close to the frontiers.[19] There is one exception to this—*"princeps."* This does not seem to have been found in the ninth century,[20] but is a return to pre-Carolingian eighth-century practices—a significant fact in many ways, since it seems to reflect the different characteristics which this period had from those found at the time of Charlemagne, Louis the Pious, or Charles the Bald.

Leaving aside this matter of titles, however, let us examine in some detail the families whose representatives bore them. We might well begin with the House of Poitou and the lands ruled by this family down to 975. In doing so we will not consider the county of Poitou itself. Poitou proper was always directly involved in Northern French affairs and had a governmental system which resembles that of Maine and Anjou to the north

[15] A charter dating from 906 calls the count of Barcelona "count and *marchio"* (J. Villanueva, *Viaje literario a las Iglesias de España*, XI, appendix 11). Another of 908 calls him *"princeps et marchio"* (*Hist. Gén. de Lang.*, V, no. 35). Still a third dating from 904 calls him "count" and *"marchio"* (*Cart. de San Cugat*, no. 2). See the use of the term *"princeps"* for Count Borell in charters dating from 947 and 974 in *Marca hispanica*, appendix 84, 118. See same in a letter of Gerbert dated 985 in J. Havet, *Lettres de Gerbert*, no. 45, p. 296. He is also called *"dux Gothiae"* in 972 (*Marca hispanica*, ap. 112, 113).

[16] On use of the title *"marchio"* by the counts of Cerdanya-Besalu see R. de Abadal i de Vinyals, *Els Primers Comtes Catalans*, pp. 294–296.

[17] See a number of charters in Abadal, *Els Comtats de Pallars i Ribagorça*, for use of this term in this region by members of the comital house.

[18] See C. Samarin, "Les institutions en Gascogne," in R. Fawtier and F. Lot, *Histoire des institutions français au Moyen Age*, I, 186–190.

[19] Judging from these examples, there seems little doubt that the title *"marchio"* no longer meant a count holding a frontier region, as had been the case earlier. Now it meant a very important nobleman.

[20] The first use of *"princeps"* in late Carolingian times seems to come from a charter dating from 878 which refers to Bernard, *"princeps Gothorum"* (undoubtedly Bernard of Gothia), and a *"princeps Urso"* (perhaps the count of Provence) (*Hist. Gén. de. Lang.*, V, no. 1). This charter is of local not royal provenance, however.

rather than that common to the rest of the Midi.[21] It will therefore be eliminated from consideration here. What we will consider, however, is the role of this family in their advances south and southwest into the Limousin, Saintonge, Quercy, and Auvergne which are part of our Southern French complex.

Now perhaps the most important thing for us to note in this regard is that for the greater part of this period the counts of Poitou, despite their assumption, at times, of rather grandiose titles and their wide claims, had little authority beyond their own county of Poitou. For a brief period, about 930, Count Ebles Manzur may have conquered the Limousin and entered Saintonge and Quercy,[22] but by the time of his death, the control exercised by his family had shrunk to authority over Limoges, where his son was bishop, and over the nearby abbey of Saint-Martial.[23] If we may believe Ademar of Chabannes, even this power at Limoges had to be exercised through an auxiliary bishop, and the nobles of the Limousin, after the death of Bishop Ebles, recovered control of this see for members of their own families.[24] After 950 or 960 castles constructed in the new march or county of La Marche by Count Boson and his successors seem to have effectively barred the count of Poitou's entrance into the Limousin.[25] As for Auvergne, until 955 a combination of local opposition and Toulousain influence kept the counts of Poitou from achieving control over this region. At least the western portion of it became theirs in 955,[26] but there is a serious question whether such control as they could establish here was very effective until the time of Duke William Iron Arm.[27]

[21] On the survival of Carolingian elements in Poitou which remained strong in contrast to the weakness of these elements in the rest of the Midi see M. Garaud, "Les circonscriptions administratives du comté de Poitiers et les auxiliaires du comté au Xᵉ siècle," in *Le Moyen Age*, LIX (1953), 11–61.

[22] See *Cart. de Tulle*, no. 15.

[23] See *Ademar de Chabannes*, III, 24, pp. 146–147, on the building of castles at Limoges by Bishop Ebles.

[24] On the control of the bishopric of Limoges by its viscontal family see G. Tenant de la Tour, *L'homme et la terre de Charlemagne à Saint Louis*, pp. 260–280.

[25] On the appearance of these counts in the tenth century see G. Thomas, *Les comtes de la Marche de la maison de Charroux (Xᵉ siècle–1177)*.

[26] See *Chartes de Cluny*, I, no. 825, on the nobility of Auvergne doing homage to William, count of Poitou, in 955. On Ebles' earlier supposed control of Auvergne see *Ademar de Chabannes*, III, 23, p. 143.

[27] Since a few years later a charter, which does not mention the Poitevin house, calls Guy of Clermont "*princeps Arvenorum*," it seems that their control over this region was minimal (*Cart. de Sauxillanges*, no. 363). Since there is also no men-

The Breakup of Principalities and the Court System   201

The counts of Toulouse-Rouergue continued to exert a powerful influence in Auvergne for some decades more²⁸ and so did the bishop of Auvergne, Etienne, and his family at Clermont.²⁹ Down to 975, then, it seems fair to say that the counts of Poitou had made some progress in Saintonge,³⁰ had controlled for brief periods parts of the Limousin, and had assumed after 955 a shadowy suzerainty over parts of Auvergne. That is all. The rise of this house to real authority as dukes of Aquitaine must be considered a later phenomenon, for beyond Poitou proper they were still unable, in this period, to create any effective principality—only claims for the future.

Even more interesting is the case of the family of Bernard Plantevelue and its power over Auvergne and adjoining regions. Bernard's son William the Pious, duke of Aquitaine, was able to retain control over much of the land which his father ruled, Auvergne, Velay, Gevaudun, the Lyonnais, and Autun.³¹ Upon his death about 914 his nephew William II seems to have succeeded to all of his *honores* except Autun.³² William's successor, Count Acfred, however, was less powerful than his predecessors. He is not mentioned in charters from the Lyonnais or Velay.³³ Even more important his will of 927 left his property not to his relatives, but to his *fideles* and *amicos*, the viscounts and important landowners of Auvergne, particularly those who controlled Clermont and LePuy. And when we analyze his estate we are amazed to discover what a limited one it is,

---

tion of this house in charters of Brioude or Sauxillanges during these years, this would seem to indicate that they had little effective control over Auvergne.

²⁸ See will of Raymond I of Rouergue which mentions land in Auvergne belonging to the Toulousain House (*Hist. Gén. de Lang.*, V, no. 111).

²⁹ See the charters of the *Cart. de Brioude* and the *Cart. de Sauxillanges* which reveal the power of this family in Auvergne throughout this period.

³⁰ See the charter of Saint-Jean d'Angély of 945 in which the count of Poitu is called a duke (*Cart. de Saint-Jean d'Angély*, no. 242).

³¹ On the power of Duke William the Pious in the Lyonnais see E. Fournial, "Recherches sur les comtes de Lyon aux IXᵉ et Xᵉ siècles," in *Le Moyen Age*, LVIII (1952). See references to his power in Auvergne in *Cart. de Brioude*, nos. 64, 228, and *Cart. de Sauxillanges*, no. 146.

³² On William II's power in Auvergne see *Cart. de Brioude*, nos. 66, 318, 324. On his control of the Lyonnais see Fournial, "Recherches sur les comtes de Lyon," and reference to him as count of Lyon in 921 in *Cart. de Savigny*, no. 12. For Velay see *Hist. Gén. de Lang.*, V, no. 49.

³³ See reference to Acfred's land which was located in Auvergne, Velay, and Gevaudun according to his will of 927 (*Grand Cart. de Brioude*, no. CCCCXXXIII). In a charter dating from 928 he is referred to as "duke" (*Cart. de Sauxillanges*, no. 13).

consisting of a few *villas* and other property scattered through Auvergne, Velay, and Gevaudun.[34] What must have represented formidable power and huge estates in Duke William the Pious' time was reduced to limited authority and small property holdings at the time of Count Acfred.

Furthermore following the death of Count Acfred, no true successor to even this authority appeared. Certainly Raymond Pons of Toulouse tried to take Auvergne about 940–941,[35] and Count William Caput Stupe of Poitou achieved a partial control of the region about 955.[36] But neither of these nor native houses like the viscounts of Clermont or those of LePuy succeeded in building up a true principality during this period. Auvergne and Velay remained regions controlled by viscounts and *comtors* and the prey to the ambitions of neighboring lords in Poitou, Rouergue, and Gevaudun.[37] As for the Lyonnais, by 975 it had passed to the control of a completely new dynasty which was descended from important landowners of this region, who seem to have had no connection with the previous or present rulers of Auvergne.[38]

If Auvergne and those surrounding regions, controlled by the heirs and successors of Bernard Plantevelue, disintegrated into political disunity, what of the nearby kingdom of Provence-Burgundy? Here we find a very similar story. In 900 control over the Valley of the Rhone south of Lyon was officially in the hands of its king, Louis of Provence. Actual authority, however, seems to have been exercised by Hugh of Arles and his brother Boson, who, as far as we can tell, distributed *honores* and acted in the name of this blind monarch, particularly after his return from Italy.[39]

[34] *Grand Cart. de Brioude*, no. CCCCXXXIII.
[35] Note that Raymond was called *"princeps Aquitanorum"* when he was present with the lay and secular *"procures"* of the province when Louis IV gave a charter to the abbey of Chanteuges in 941 (*Cart. de Brioude*, no. 338).
[36] *Chartes de Cluny*, I, no. 825. Yet a few years later Aldegardis of the Clermont family is called "countess" (*Cart. de Sauxillanges*, no. 188).
[37] See the excellent descriptions of Auvergne during this period in "Etude historique sur la vicomté de Carlat" in *Documents historiques relatifs à la vicomté de Carlat*, ed. G. Saigne, II, lix–lxxvii, and Introduction to the *Cartulaire du Peuré de Saint-Flour*, ed. M. Boudet, pp. lvii–clxvi.
[38] See Fournial, "Recherches sur les comtes de Lyon," on the appearance of this new family of counts in the Lyonnais.
[39] See R. Poupardin, *Le Royaume de Bourgogne (888–1038)*, pp. 1–138, on the career of Louis of Provence, and *ibid.*, pp. 138–160 on Count or Duke Hugh. See also charters dating from 908, 912, 917, and 928 in *Cart. de Saint-Barnard de Romans*, nos. 6, 9, 11, and *Cart. de Grenoble*, no. 24. There is an additional reference to Hugh in a charter dating from 920 in *Cart. de Saint-André-le-bas*, no. 124.

The Breakup of Principalities and the Court System 203

With Louis' death, however, they were unable to keep their authority, despite efforts to give their lands to relatives and to carve out careers for themselves in Italy.⁴⁰ In 938, Conrad became king of a new kingdom of Burgundy which included in it all Louis' holdings.⁴¹ The Middle Rhone region south of Vienne fell into the hands of Count Geilin, who also dominated the Vivarais and Velay for a time,⁴² while Provence went to a certain Boson, the father of Count William of Provence, who was to make his authority effective over this region and drive the Moslems from Fraxinetum in 972.⁴³

As these changes took place, however, it seems clear that King Conrad's actual authority did not extend much beyond his capital of Vienne and its immediate vicinity. Nor is there much evidence that any of the kings or magnates of the Rhone Valley, like Count Hugh, Count Boson, or Count Geilin ever exercised much authority over Alpine regions east of the Rhone. These areas remained, as far as we can tell, disorganized and lawless, the prey of brigands and Moslem freebooters down to the end of our period. Only then do we find a group of new families in Savoy, Dauphiny, and Provence, aided by churchmen like Bishop Isarn of Grenoble, begin the task of restoring order on a local basis by the building of castles, the cultivation of abandoned soil, and a restoration of churches and abbeys.⁴⁴ But this colonization seems to have proceeded with little assistance given to such nobles by either the kings of Provence or their principal vassals.⁴⁵ As principalities, the kingdom of Provence and its successor the kingdom of Burgundy must be rated as failures.

⁴⁰ In 937 Hugh attempted to give land belonging to the royal *fisc* and consisting of 700 *mansi* to a nephew (*Cart. de Vienne*, no. 22, pp. 232-233). This did not prevent Conrad from becoming king of Provence-Burgundy the next year.

⁴¹ On the circumstances surrounding Conrad's assumption of authority in this region see Poupardin, *Le Royaume de Bourgogne*.

⁴² A charter of 937 from LePuy calls Geilin a "marquis" (*Hist. Gén. de Lang.*, V, no. 70), and another dating from 961 calls him "princeps" and *"nobilissimus vir et potens"* (*Cart. de Saint-Chaffre*, no. 345).

⁴³ See reference to Count Boson in 958 in *Chartes de Cluny*, II, no. 1052, and again in 965 in *Cart. de Saint-Victor*, no. 29. On Count William's expulsion of the Moslems see Raoul Glaber, *Historiarum libri V*, I, IV, 9, p. 12.

⁴⁴ A posterior charter of 1100 refers to the work of Bishop Isarn (950-974) in colonizing Alpine regions (*Cart. de Grenoble*, no. 16). In a more contemporary document of 938 there is a reference to land which has been devastated by the pagans (perhaps the Hungarians), which is given to Canon Ubold by Archbishop Sobbo of Vienne *"in prestaria"* (*Cart. de Vienne*, no. 23).

⁴⁵ Neither King Conrad nor the principal lay nobles of the Middle Rhone region seem to have played any role in the colonizing activities mentioned in note 44. In

In some ways an examination of that vast extent of territory which the House of Toulouse controlled in 900 is even more interesting. This territory stretched from the Rhone to Périgord and Angoulême, and from the shores of the Mediterranean, the borders of Carcassonne, and the Pyrenees to Auvergne and the northern borders of the Limousin. It had few frontiers in any formal sense of the word, which was one reason for the friction between the Toulousain house and its neighbors in Carcassonne-Razès, Auvergne, Poitou, and to some extent in Gascony. As far as we can tell, early in the tenth century this whole region formed a rather complex family co-dominion which was controlled by two sons of Count Eudes, Raymond and Ermengaud.[46] Upon Raymond's death his son Raymond Pons represented the Toulousain branch of the family and Ermengaud the Rouergue branch.[47] Of the two, Raymond Pons, down to his death about 950, seems to have been the more powerful,[48] though a certain Count Hugh, a nephew, perhaps had some authority also.[49] After his death his widow Countess Garsinde seems to have been more powerful than Raymond Pons' heir, Count William Taillefer, judging from her will which dates from 972.[50] But these years saw an even greater family authority exercised by the Rouergue branch consisting of Count Raymond I of Rouergue,[51] his son Raymond II,[52] and the latter's brother Bishop

---

contrast to the churchmen who were active here, in Provence it was Count William and the secular nobility who took the lead.

[46] See reference to Count Raymond in 919 in *Cart. de Conques*, no. 322, and to *"Ermengaudo principe"* in 934 in *Hist. Gén. de Lang.*, V, no. 54.

[47] In 932 Raymond Pons and Ermengaud, called *"principes Gothiae,"* did homage to King Raoul (Flodoard, *Annales*, anno 932). A charter of 922 refers also to *"comites nostri Ermengaudi et Raymundo"* *Hist. Gén. de Lang.*, V, no. 47.

[48] *Hist. Gén. de Lang.*, V, nos. 50, 55, 59, 69, 74, and *Cart. de Brioude*, no. 338, all refer to Raymond as "marquis," "duke," or *"princeps."*

[49] See mention of Hugh in 934 in *Hist. Gén. de Lang.*, V, no. 54. In 940 he is referred to as a witness to a charter from the Narbonne region (*ibid.*, no. 74), and again in 949 (*ibid.*, no. 89). It is probably he who is referred to in Countess Garsinde's will of 972 (*ibid.*, no. 126).

[50] *Ibid.*, no. 126.

[51] Raymond I's will which dates from 961 shows he exercised considerable authority over the whole Midi (*ibid.*, no. 111). See evidence of his influence in the Limousin in 960 as evidenced in his presiding over a court in 960 according to a local charter (*Cart. de Beaulieu*, no. 47).

[52] For references to Raymond II of Rouergue in 961 and 965 see *Cart. de Nîmes*, nos. 61, 66. For another reference in 972 see *Hist. Gén. de Lang.*, V, no. 125.

Hugh of Toulouse.⁵³ This Rouergue predominance seems to have continued down to the early years of the eleventh century.

What concerns us here, however, is not the complexities of authority and influence exercised within the House of Toulouse-Rouergue, but rather something else—evidence of their steadily shrinking authority over Languedoc. We first see this clearly when we examine the Narbonne-Carcassonne region. Here in 918, 922, and 924⁵⁴ charters seem to show that the counts of Toulouse exercised a large measure of control over these regions. Yet in 933 Count Raymond Pons was forced by a court of leading lay and ecclesiastical magnates of the region to give up his efforts to enforce his rights over lands belonging to the abbey of Montolieu.⁵⁵ Thereafter direct control by the Toulousain family seems to have been largely confined to the abbey of Saint-Pons of Thomières⁵⁶ and after 949 even this authority seems to have been a limited one. In nearby Béziers we find the same story repeated. In the year 937, when Raymond Pons gave land to Saint-Nazaire of Béziers, he seems to have acted with considerable authority over this region.⁵⁷ After this date this ceases to be true, and down to 975 his house is not even mentioned in the local charters of this part of Septimania.⁵⁸

Lest this be thought unusual, an examination of the Nîmes region reveals the same pattern of development. Early in the century both Count Raymond and his son Raymond Pons were the powerful overlords of Nîmes and were mentioned as such in certain lawsuits which took place in

---

⁵³ For an early reference to Bishop Hugh of Toulouse, whose will we possess from later in the century, see a charter of 949 in *Hist. Gén. de Lang.*, V, no. 89.

⁵⁴ In 918 Viscount Bernard, *missus* of Count Raymond, settled a dispute between the abbey of Montolieu and the vicar of the castle of Alzonne (*Cart. de Carcassonne*, I, 188–189). A letter of 922 from the archbishop of Narbonne speaks of *"comites nostri"* Ermengaud and Raymond (*Hist. Gén. de Lang.*, V, no. 47). In 924 Eudes, viscount of Narbonne gave to the abbey of Montolieu an allod which his father received from Charles the Bald. He does so only with the consent of Raymond, count of Toulouse who is called Pons, *"Narbonensium principem"* (*ibid.*, no. 50).

⁵⁵ *Ibid.*, no. 57.

⁵⁶ See *ibid.*, no. 74, on Pons' founding of Saint-Pons de Thomières. For his widow's continued control of this abbey as late as 969 see *ibid.*, no. 117.

⁵⁷ *Ibid.*, no. 68.

⁵⁸ See charters of 967 and 969 which mention only the viscounts of Béziers and not the Toulousain House in *Cart. de Béziers*, no. 30, and *Hist. Gén. de Lang.*, V, no. 118. The second charter is the will of Viscount Reginald.

this area in 902, 915, and 928.[59] Then all is silence down to 961 and 965, when we find a record of certain gifts to the cathedral church of Notre-Dame of Nîmes by Countess Bertha, widow of Count Raymond I of Rouergue. In the charters referring to this gift of *villas,* Countess Bertha in 961, following what was the common practice of the period, forbade their alienation from church control, saying that if this was done they would revert to her son, Count Raymond II of Rouergue or *"ipsam potestatem de Nemauso publice."*[60] In 965 this curious phrase is explained by a repetition of the preceding phrase except that *"ipsam potestatem publice"* is identified. It is the viscount of Nîmes.[61] By 965, then, even the Toulouse-Rouergue family had to publicly recognize those who really controlled Nîmes—not they but the hereditary viscounts of the city.

When we examine what happened to the power of the Toulousain family in the northern and western portions of their domains we find the same thing happening. We do find a reference to their authority in Rouergue in 910 and 919[62] and in the Albigeois in 926, 934, 935, and 943.[63] Then all is silence, and from local records it seems clear that these regions were controlled by viscontal families, like those of Albi, Rodez, and Carlat, just as similar families controlled Auvergne. Similarly in Quercy and the Limousin we have references to Toulousain overlordship in 930 and 932, as well as one in 972 which refers to an earlier period about 930 or 940.[64] Yet after this period, except for a court held by Raymond I of Rouergue in the Limousin in 960,[65] we find no other proof of effective overlordship. The viscounts of Cahors and the Limousin obviously now control these regions in their own right.

The same story seems to have been repeated toward the south and southwest of these domains. We are told that about 950 the count of Toulouse gave the county of Agen to the House of Angoulême-Périgord.[66] And at about this same time we learn of a certain Arnaud, who was probably related to the family of Carcassonne, who became the ruler of that

---

[59] *Cart. de Nîmes,* nos. 9 (902), 16 (915), 32 (928).
[60] *Ibid.,* no. 61.
[61] *Ibid.,* no. 66.
[62] *Cart. de Conques,* no. 322.
[63] *Hist. Gén. de Lang.,* II, no. 207 (926); V, nos. 59 (934), 63 (935), 78 (943).
[64] *Cart. de Tulle,* no. 14 (930); *Cart. de Beaulieu,* no. 48 (932); *Hist. Gén. de Lang.,* V, no. 122 (972).
[65] *Cart. de Beaulieu,* no. 47.
[66] *Ademar de Chabannes.* III. 20. p. 138.

The Breakup of Principalities and the Court System 207

region which late in the century we know as the county of Commignes.[67] None of the few charters which we possess for this region between 950 and 975 even mention the Toulousain house.

The best proof, however, of the declining fortunes of the family of Toulouse-Rouergue and of their failure to establish a territorial state comes from a series of wills which date from late in the period—one of Raymond I of Rouergue's dating from 961,[68] one of Countess Garsinde's from 972,[69] and a little later one left by Hugh, bishop of Toulouse.[70] Naturally, these wills put forward the best case possible for family and personal possessions, and they do prove to us that down to 975 this family was still a powerful one, controlling a number of castles, churches, and allods through all of Languedoc. But when we examine these wills in detail we find that actual *possession* of most of this property, as opposed to its *ownership*, is generally in the hands of magnates and churchmen of these regions, not the House of Toulouse.[71] By 975, then, not only had this family failed to create a principality in the Midi, but they had been forced to watch both their authority and much of their property slip away into the hands of others. After 975 for many decades it was the counts of Commignes, of Carcassonne-Razès, and of Périgord, and the viscounts of the Limousin, of Cahors, Rodez, Albi, Nîmes, Béziers, Lautrec, and Narbonne, who really controlled Languedoc. All that was retained by the House of Toulouse was control over some scattered abbeys, castles, and allods, and a tradition of overlordship, which in the next century could be used by Raymond of Saint-Gilles to create a new and different principality.

When we turn from Languedoc to Gascony again disintegration seems to have been the order of the day, though we lack detailed information concerning how it happened. In the ninth century Gascony seems to have been a vast rather politically amorphous region, consisting of a county of Fézensac, some areas under the control of the counts of Toulouse and a large area ruled by the hereditary dukes of Gascony.[72] By 975 this had

---

[67] See C. Higounet, *Le Comté de Commignes de ses origines à son annexation à la Couronne*, I, 22–27, and P. Ourliac, "L'origine des comtes de Commignes," in *Recueil de travaux offerts à M. C. Brunel*, II.
[68] *Hist. Gén. de Lang.*, V, no. 111.
[69] *Ibid.*, no. 126.
[70] *Ibid.*, no. 183.
[71] See references to wills in notes 69 and 70 above.
[72] Amalvinus is called *"dux Bordelensis"* in 906 (F. Lot, *Études sur le règne de*

ceased to be the pattern. Instead, in eastern Gascony we find a whole series of independent counties and viscounties: Commignes, Bigorre, Astarac, and Fézensac, and in the western part Béarn, Lomargue, Tartas, Tursan, Marsan, and several others.[73] Probably the dukes of Gascony still exercised some control over western Gascony,[74] but eastern counties and viscounties had become independent of ducal authority. So they were to continue down into the eleventh century.

In some ways, however, the Spanish March, consisting of Pallars, Ribagorça, and Catalonia, provides us with the most interesting case study of all, for here in the late ninth century Count Guifred had established the most workable and successful large principality of all as an heir to Carolingian authority. What happened then to his work during the first three quarters of the tenth century? As far as Pallars and Ribagorça are concerned the answer is a simple one—a progressive and almost complete disintegration followed the death of its first Count Ramón. First Pallars and Ribagorça were divided into separate counties, and then subdivided as three and four co-counts divided authority still further and left it to their heirs.[75] Ampurias-Roussillon stayed relatively stable and unchanged throughout this period.[76]

When we consider the rest of Catalonia, though—that part ruled by the heirs of Count Guifred and Count Miró—we begin to notice some interesting things happening. In a certain sense throughout this period a large amount of Catalan unity was maintained by this family, and Guifred's direct heirs, who controlled the Barcelona-Gerona-Ausona region, could claim some primacy over the rest by bearing the title of *princeps*, even after 975.[77] They could intervene in some cases in the affairs of abbeys which were located beyond regions which they ruled directly.[78] About 950,

---

Hugh Capet, p. 378 n), and in 904 a certain García Sánchez is called *"comtes et marchio in limitibus oceani" Gallia Christiana,* I, inst., col. 170. These attest to the vagueness of any over-all ducal control of Gascony in the early years of the tenth century. See also Samarin, "Les institutions en Gascogne," I, 186–189.

[73] Samarin, "Les institutions en Gascogne," I, 187–190, and Higounet, *Le Comte de Commignes,* I, 21–36.

[74] Samarin, "Les institutions en Gascogne," I, 186–187.

[75] See Abadal, Introduction to *Els Comtats de Pallars i Ribagorça* on this fragmentation of authority.

[76] R. de Abadal i de Vinyals, *Els Primers Comtes Catalans,* pp. 297–298.

[77] Count Borell of Barcelona is called *"Hispanica duce, marchisco, comtes"* in 988 in *Cart. de San Cugat,* no. 217, and in 992 in *Catalunya Carolingia,* II, 72.

[78] See account of the election of the bishop of Gerona in 908 in the presence of *"princeps marchio"* Guifred II (*Hist. Gén. de Lang.,* V, no. 38). On the court in

The Breakup of Principalities and the Court System 209

however, despite the tradition of Barcelona's supremacy, we begin to notice a certain separation taking place between the counties of Cerdanya-Besalu-Confluent-Berga under Miró's descendants and Barcelona-Gerona-Ausona-Urgell controlled by Count Borell and his brother Count Ermengol.[79] This situation, a little later, seems to have led to an outright hostility between Count Oliba Cabreta who controlled the former and Count Borell who controlled the latter, with Urgell, under Count Ermengol, following still a third path of its own.[80] By 975 the forces of disintegration were beginning to affect a Catalonia which had not known them earlier.

This disintegration which was affecting the ruling family's unity was made worse, it would seem, by a growing independence which more and more began to be assumed by viscounts, vicars, and other important landowners who controlled castles and broad lands along Catalonia's frontiers. In 928, for instance, we find Viscount Leopardo selling to his son for some 1,000 *solidi* a castle and its surrounding territory without bothering to secure the permission of one of the counts.[81] In 940 another important lord, Sendredo, freely exchanged the castle of Tarrassa for some other property which belonged to the bishop of Barcelona.[82] In 954 the viscounts of Cerdanya and Urgell, neither bothering to secure a count's permission, made an agreement covering their frontier castles of Queralt and Miralès.[83] Two years later another marcher lord, Hennego, freely bought from a certain Aigo a *turre* and much property nearby for 800 *solidi*,[84] and in 957 left to the abbey of San-Cugat land and the rights to justice he had over the territory of the castle of Arampuña.[85] Two years later Daniel, another frontier lord, also left a *turre* and land near the castle of Olerdula to San-Cugat without securing Count Borell's permission.[86]

Ausona jointly presided over by Counts Miró of Cerdanya and Sunyer of Barcelona in 913 see *El Archivo Condal de Barcelona*, no. 38. Or note Count Borell's role in 949 in choosing the abbess of Saint-Joan in *ibid.*, no. 128, or the intervention of Counts Borell and Miró of Barcelona in the affairs of the cathedral of Vich in 957, in *ibid.*, no. 138.

[79] On the growth of the authority of the Cerdanya-Besalu branch of the Catalan comital house see P. Ponsch, "Le Confluent et ses comtes du IXe au XIIe siècle," in *Études Roussillonnaises*, I (1951), 190–309.

[80] *Ibid.*, pp. 270–282.
[81] *El Archivo Condal de Barcelona*, no. 91.
[82] *El Archivo Catedral de Barcelona*, no. 20.
[83] *Hist. Gén. de Lang.*, II, no. 209.
[84] *Cart. de San Cugat*, no. 45.
[85] *Ibid.*, no. 49.
[86] *Ibid.*, no. 56.

In 963 Hennego bought from Count Miró the castle of Masquefa, near Barcelona's frontier, for some 1,000 *solidi*.[87] All this makes it clear that along the frontiers of Catalonia there existed a good deal of independence —an independence that definitely limited the authority of the counts of Catalonia. So Catalonia, too, began to be affected by the same forces of disintegration which we find in the rest of the Midi, though down to 975 such forces were weaker here than elsewhere.

This examination of the leading families of the Midi and the Spanish March makes it clear that no principalities arose to take the place of Carolingian government. But it leaves unanswered the basic question as to why this was so. The first and most important reason we can give has to do with the operation of the family system in Southern France and Catalonia. As we noted earlier in all our regions, by 900, families had become the controlling element in government, as they took over what in Carolingian times had been *honores*. During the first generation or so family solidarity tended to preserve a certain unity in regions which a particular family controlled, witness Catalonia immediately following Count Guifred's demise;[88] or Languedoc down to the death of Raymond Pons and Ermengaud;[89] the Valley of the Rhone under the control of Count Hugh of Arles and his brother Boson;[90] or Angoulême-Périgord where, according to Ademar of Chabannes, Count Bernard and his brother, Count William Taillefer, *"communem habuerunt totum honorem eorum ipse."*[91] In some ways this family system continued to work effec-

---

[87] *Ibid.*, no. 65.

[88] Note the cooperation in 904 between Count Miró of Cerdanya-Besalu and his niece, Abbess Emma, the daughter of Count Guifred, in a matter concerning land which belonged to the nunnery of Saint-Joan (*El Archivo Condal de Barcelona*, no. 16). Note similar close cooperation between Count Miró and Count Sunyer of Barcelona in a court case in 913, previously mentioned (*ibid.*, no. 38). In the next generation this remains the pattern also as seen in the cooperation between Count Borell of Barcelona and Count Sunifred of Urgell in 949 (*ibid.*, no. 128).

[89] A charter of 922, which speaks of *"comites nostri Ermengaudius et Raymundus,"* shows this close relationship (*Hist. Gén. de Lang.*, V, no. 47). So does Flodoard's account of how Raymond Pons and Ermengaud as *"principes Gothiae"* came *together* to do homage to King Raoul for their lands in 932 (Flodoard, *Annales*, anno 932).

[90] For an example of such family cooperation see the gift of a *villa* and many *mansi* which Hugh of Arles made to his nephew and heirs in 937 (*Cart. de Vienne*, no. 22).

[91] *Ademar de Chabannes*, III, 23, p. 145.

The Breakup of Principalities and the Court System 211

tively even after 975, as in Cerdanya-Besalu, Carcassonne-Razès,[92] and Provence under the immediate heirs of Count Boson of Arles.[93]

But eventually the principle of *divisio* and the habit of allowing widows to continue to control their husbands' estates triumphed over family unity. Countess Garsinde, for instance, in 972 appears to have given to her own family in Narbonne, and to special friends and relatives, land that belonged to the House of Toulouse, and even threatened her nephew Hugh with disinheritance if he disputed her distribution. In this will she also seems to have disinherited Count William Taillefer of Toulouse, her son or stepson. The division of land in Gascony among the Aznar heirs and their relatives effectively dismembered this region into a whole series of counties and viscounties.[94] On a minor scale a similar *divisio* resulted in the county of Béziers being divided between two viscounts, one at Agde and one at Béziers,[95] and began to spawn a series of miniscule viscounties in the Limousin out of what originally was a viscounty of Limoges,[96] a county of La Marche,[97] and a county of Turenne.[98] It was later to break up

[92] For the Cerdanya-Besalu comital family see the charter of 964 in which Sunifred, count of Cerdanya, Oliba Cabreta, count of Besalu and Miró—all brothers—join in giving land to the nunnery of Saint-Joan (*El Archivo Condal de Barcelona*, no. 162). See also action in concert taken by Countess Arsinde of Carcassonne and her sons in 957 and 959. *Hist. Gén. de Lang.*, V, nos. 106, 109.

[93] See how Count Boson and his sons Counts Roubaud and William jointly presided over a court at Arles in 965 (*Cart. de Saint-Victor*, no. 29), and the close cooperation between Counts William and Roubaud revealed by another charter of 970 (*ibid.*, no. 598).

[94] For a typical *divisio* see a charter which shows how two sons divide family land in Uzès in 946 (*Chartes de Cluny*, I, no. 693). Or the *divisio* set up by the viscount and viscountess of Narbonne in 966 for their sons (*Hist. Gén. de Lang.*, V, no. 115). Or another shown in a charter from the Limousin dating from 913 (*Cart. de Beaulieu*, no. 89).

[95] See reference to Viscounts Eudes and Teudo of Béziers and Agde, who were brothers and heirs of Bishop Reginald of Béziers in 933 (*Hist. Gén. de Lang.*, V, no. 58).

[96] See also a charter of 930 mentioning Viscounts Gausbert and Ademar, who were perhaps brothers (*Cart. de Tulle*, no. 346). They are mentioned in a charter of the same year as well from Beaulieu (*Cart. de Beaulieu*, no. 49).

[97] See reference to Viscounts Ademar, Boson (of la Marche?), Odolrico, Gausbert, Boson, and John, all of this region, in a charter of 931 (*Cart. de Tulle*, no. 641).

[98] The family of Count Robert of Turenne or Cahors is mentioned in a charter of 932 (*Cart. de Beaulieu*, no. 108). Viscounts who may be of the same family are referred to in another charter which dates from 946 (*Cart. de Tulle*, no. 487).

the county of Provence and that of Carcassonne-Razès. Familial control in which wives, sons, and daughters shared in a principality and in which no primogeniture existed, ended any possibility of organized states emerging in the Midi and the Spanish March during these years.

There was, however, still another force at work in this process of political fragmentation. I refer to the tendency to transform into allods land which was given to *fideles* by their lords. Some of this land, no doubt, was from the start given in this manner, but the rest was transformed in the course of this period. Such a tendency, of course, was nothing new. We have commented on it earlier in the distribution of land from the royal *fisc* by Carolingian rulers. It continued under their successors, the independent nobles of the Midi and Catalonia. Only this can explain why Count Acfred possessed so little property in Auvergne and neighboring regions when he made his will in 927, a will incidentally which left even this property to *fideles* instead of to his own family. By 930 there was no comital *fisc* left in Auvergne.[99]

Exactly the same thing happened in the Valley of the Rhone. In 902, for instance, we find King Louis of Provence giving land belonging to his royal *fisc* to his *fidelis*, Viscount Berilon, *"jure proprietario"*[100] and doing the same with other family property in Rodez which he distributed to two other *fideles*, Teutbert and Bernard.[101] In 903 he went further and gave to all his nobles the right to freely dispose of, sell, or will their own property as they pleased.[102] Just before 910 he gave considerable property to Count Hugh of Arles [103] and followed it up with distribution of land from the *fisc* to his *fidelis* Gerard in 915,[104] to Inglebert in 923[105] and to the church of Vienne in 927.[106] Probably it was land which originally was part of the royal *fisc* which Hugh, now king of Italy, gave to his nephew in 937—some 700 *mansi* according to the charter[107]—and from this same source came those five *villas* with which he endowed the abbey of Saint-Barnard de Romans in 928.[108] It seems probable that even before King

[99] See the distribution of the comital *fisc* of Auvergne and Gevaudun in 927 in *Grand Cart. de Brioude*, no. CCCCXXXIII.
[100] *Cart. de Vienne*, no. 11.
[101] *Hist. Gén. de Lang.*, V, no. 29.
[102] *Cart. de Vienne*, no. 12.
[103] *Ibid.*, no. 14.
[104] *Ibid.*, no. 16.
[105] *Chartes de Cluny*, I, no. 237.
[106] *Cart. de Vienne*, no. 21.
[107] *Ibid.*, no. 22.
[108] *Cart. de Saint-Barnard de Romans*, no. 11.

Conrad of Burgundy succeeded to Louis' position in the valley the greater part of the royal *fisc* had been dissipated, and with it royal control over this region. Yet King Conrad continued to act in a similar fashion with what little was left. In 943 we find him giving the abbey of Saint-Genesius to a certain Hermarus,[109] a *turre* to Saint-Victor of Marseille[110] and as late as 975 giving to a nobleman, Artald, two *villas* as a benefice, which, since it was a grant for two lifetimes, probably soon became the latter's allodial property.[111]

In regions controlled by the House of Toulouse we find the same tendency at work, though there can be little doubt that this family was more reluctant to alienate its property than the kings who controlled the Valley of the Rhone. Nevertheless our sources tell us of a certain Repertus in 923 who controlled an allod at Nîmes which had at one time been *fiscal* land.[112] A charter of 930 from the Limousin contains a statement by Viscount Ademar of Scalas that the land which it refers to, an allod, originally belonged to Count Raymond who gave it to the viscount's father.[113] Our sources also mention another allod, a *villa*, owned by Arnold of Commignes which the latter received from Count Hugh of the Toulousain house,[114] and a fief or *feus* in Quercy which a certain Raimulf in 972 says Count Hugh gave to his grandfather.[115] Still another charter dating from 942 concerns an *honorem* given to the abbey of Saint-Pons of Thomières by Viscount Aton of Albi which the latter states was a gift to him from Raymond Pons,[116] while the will of Raymond I of Rouergue in 961 mentions a fief given to Sánchez in Gascony by this count which is to be changed into the latter's allod.[117] Such dissipation of property, which ended in becoming allodial land in the hands of important local magnates, then, was a real feature of the failure of the House of Toulouse to create a strong principality in Languedoc during this period.

There is little need to burden these pages with the even more numerous examples of this tendency which could be cited from Catalonia and Pallars and Ribagorça, where a continuing policy of granting *aprisiones* meant the exhaustion of vacant land belonging to the comital *fisc* and its transfor-

---

[109] *Cart. de Vienne*, no. 24.
[110] *Cart. de Saint-Victor*, no. 1041.
[111] *Cart. de Vienne*, no. 239.
[112] *Hist. Gén. de Lang.*, V, no. 89.
[113] *Cart. de Nîmes*, no. 22.
[114] *Cart. de Tulle*, no. 14.
[115] *Hist. Gén. de Lang.*, V, no. 122.
[116] *Ibid.*, no. 77.   [117] *Ibid.*, no. 111.

mation into allods which were owned by both large and small landowners. Suffice it to say that dozens of examples could be cited, particularly from regions close to the frontiers of the Spanish March.[118] Enough has already been said, though, to show how the tendency of land granted to *fideles* to become allodial was a feature of this period, and one which must bear a large share of the responsibility, along with the workings of the family system, for the failure to develop territorial states south of Poitou and Burgundy.

As attempts to create principalities failed and those which existed disintegrated into small, amorphous and often unstable counties and viscounties, what happened to the machinery of government which had survived the end of Carolingian authority? Here an examination of law and the court system is particularly pertinent, since it seems to have survived more intact than any other aspect of Carolingian government down to the first part of the tenth century. What happened to it now during this period of further governmental disintegration?

Our first impression seems to convince us that very little change took place during the tenth century in the surviving legal system of most of Southern France and Catalonia. Personality of the law continued in the Valley of the Rhone, in Aquitaine and in Septimania where we find references in a number of our documents to Roman, Gothic and Salic law and precedents.[119] Even more important, certain courts continued to be held in the Carolingian fashion and are presided over by the official representatives of secular authority, that is to say by kings, counts, viscounts, *missi*, and vicars. We find two such tribunals which were held in the Valley of the Rhone in 912 and 926[120] over which King Louis of Provence and Hugh of Arles respectively presided, and two others at Arles in 965 and 967–968[121] which met under the aegis of Count Boson of Provence and his son Marquis William. At Nîmes we find a record of similar tribunals which met in 902, 909, 915, and 928[122] under the legally

[118] See *Cart. de San Cugat*, nos. 5 and 206 (912), 7 (914), 9 (917), 20 (941), 47 (956), 69 (964), 79 (965), 86 (966), 98 and 102 (972); *El Archivo Condal de Barcelona*, nos. 58 (918), 60 (919), 81 (975), 84 (927), 110 (937, 942), 124 (948), 151 (961), 157 and 159 (962), 160 (963); *Catalunya Carolingia*, II, 379–380 (922); F. Miguel Rossell, *Liber Feudorum Maior*, no. 395 (939) (Hereafter cited as *Liber Feodorum*).

[119] For example see the court held in 918 at Alzonne (*Cart. de Carcassonne*, I, 188–189), or that held at Arles in 967–968 (*Cart. de Saint-Victor*, no. 290).

[120] *Cart. de Grenoble*, no. 24 (912); *Chartes de Cluny*, I, 256 (926).

[121] *Cart. de Saint-Victor*, nos. 29 (965), 290, (967–968).

[122] *Cart. de Nîmes*, no. 9 (902), 12 (909), 16 (915), 32 (928).

The Breakup of Principalities and the Court System 215

constituted authority of the count of Toulouse and his viscounts and *missi* Abbo and Frédélon. Church and lay officials jointly presided over similar courts which met in the Narbonne-Carcassonne region in 918, 933, and 955,[123] and there is also a record of a vicar's court which was held in Razès in 958.[124] To the south in Catalonia we find the same sort of tribunals which were held by the counts of this region in 904 and 912.[125] Though our record in this respect is not as complete for the turbulent lands which made up Aquitaine, we do find in our documents a reference to a vicar's court which met in Rouergue in 934,[126] and one which in 960 was held in the Limousin and which was presided over by Raymond I of Rouergue.[127]

As far as we can tell, too, all these courts seem to follow the same general pattern as those found in the earlier Carolingian period. In each one the official or officials presiding over the court were assisted by minor officers, such as viscounts and vicars, and by *judices* and that group of leading landowners of the region where the court was held, who still went by the name of *boni homines, rachimburgs, scabini,* or in one case *principes.*[128] Despite the presence of some men called *fideles*[129] at some of these tribunals and even the mention of *vassi dominici* at a Provençal court,[130] it is clear that these courts were not feudal ones. They still represent the regional organization of earlier Carolingian times based upon a district, and the *boni homines* who attend do so because of their residence in a region and not because of a personal tie linking them to the count or viscount who was presiding. Formal courts, then, in this period still seem regional in essence rather than personal.[131]

There were other tribunals too which seem to have survived from the Carolingian period, ecclesiastical ones. Some of them seem to follow the usual pattern of such courts in the ninth century, which means that their jurisdiction lay in the privileges granted them in immunities from the

[123] *Cart. de Carcassonne,* I, 188–189 (918); *Hist. Gén. de Lang.,* V, no. 57 (933), 98 (955).
[124] *Ibid.,* no. 104.
[125] *El Archivo Condal de Barcelona,* nos. 16 (904), 35 (912).
[126] *Cart. de Conques,* no. 155.
[127] *Cart. de Beaulieu,* no. 47.
[128] The term *"principes"* is used for some of those who attended the court held at Arles in 965 (*Cart. de Saint-Victor,* no. 29).
[129] See record of court held in Dauphiny in 912 in *Cart. de Grenoble,* no. 24.
[130] This is in that court held at Arles in 967–968 (*Cart. de Saint-Victor,* no. 29).
[131] See comments on a similar situation in Burgundy during this same period in F. Estey, "The Fideles in the County of Mâcon" in *Speculum,* XXV (1955).

crown, one of the more important being a church or an abbey's right to maintain its own tribunal. For instance the important church council that met at Azillan in 902 acted in just such a fashion in forcing a certain cleric called Tetbald to give up land he was holding unjustly which belonged to the church of Sainte-Eulalia.[132] So did a tribunal of the abbey of Saint-Joan de les Abbadesses which in 912 forced a certain Tudesco to acknowledge Abbess Emma's ownership of land that he claimed.[133] Even that curious court presided over by Bishop Hucbert of Nîmes in 921, in which the churchmen present as *boni homines* are called *vassi* in our documents, seems essentially like a court of Carolingian times since it dealt with tithes unjustly appropriated by landowners who seem to have been dependent on the church of Nîmes—and thus within the competence of this court.[134]

In this age of decaying governmental forms, however, certain other church tribunals seem somewhat more unusual, particularly in parts of Central France. An example of such a court is one held by Bishop Etienne II of Auvergne, who certainly had a court of his own as early as 945,[135] and also in 958.[136] This court, according to our sources, was one attended by churchmen and important laymen or *principes* of Auvergne, and forced a certain Calistus to give back land which he had usurped from Amblard, a canon of Clermont. Three years later this same prelate held still another court, with his *fideles* in attendance, at the church of Saint-Martin and forced his vassal Gerard to return a *mansus* which he had unjustly taken from the abbey of Sauxillanges.[137] What makes these tribunals unusual is the fact that Bishop Etienne, who presided, seems to be acting not as a churchman who could hold such courts by virtue of a royal immunity, but as the embodiment of *public* authority in Auvergne replacing the secular government of the period. Furthermore if the court of 961 seems an unusually feudal one for this period, that of 958 does not fit such a category, since its presiding officer, in this case the bishop, is still assisted by neighboring *boni homines*, called *principes* here, who, as in Carolingian times, represent the force of local public opinion in giving their backing to the verdict reached by the court.

As governmental authority and forms decayed still further in most of

---

[132] *Hist. Gén. de Lang.*, V, no. 28.
[133] *El Archivo Condal de Barcelona*, no. 35.
[134] *Cart. de Nîmes*, no. 21.
[135] *Grand Cart. de Brioude*, no. CCCXXXV.
[136] "Archives du Puy du Dome" (unprinted), XVIII, soc. A, cat. 4.
[137] *Cart. de Sauxillanges*, no. 86.

our regions, except perhaps Catalonia and Provence, the destiny of the Midi was to see more such unusual tribunals like that held by Bishop Etienne in 958. Such courts were not feudal, but rather seem to have been informal gatherings of leading landowners and churchmen of a particular region, who met together to decide matters which earlier in Carolingian times had come before a *mallus publicus*. Sometimes such assemblies or gatherings are called courts, sometimes they are not. But irrespective of their title, they performed one of the major functions of public tribunals, that of forcing an individual landowner to justify his ownership or occupancy of a certain piece of property, and, if he could not furnish satisfactory proof, to formally return it to its rightful claimant in an action or ceremony known as *guirpitio* or *werpio*, which frequently included a written *carta evacuonis*.[138] One might well think of such tribunals as courts without presiding officers or a public authority in the Carolingian sense of the word.

No study of this informal *guirpitio* system, which we begin to find in the Midi during this period,[139] has ever been made, so a few observations concerning it seem very much in order. It seems clear that in part it was derived from the Carolingian court system, which also provided a very similar method of giving up land illegally held before a *mallus publicus* which was attended by *boni homines* and presided over by an official, and the formal writing of a *carta evacuonis* at the conclusion of the case.[140] One might then simply consider the *guirpitio* system a Carolingian court meeting informally without a presiding officer; a system made necessary by the breakdown of government.

Nevertheless it seems wise also to note another possible origin of *guirpitios* which we find in the Midi in increasing numbers; a private origin. All through the ninth and tenth centuries in the Midi landowners made it a practice to gather together groups of important witnesses to attest the validity of their private charters and wills, particularly those in which important property was at stake. This was particularly true of charters giving land to church establishments. The formula seems clear: an individual and members of his or her immediate family swear to

---

[138] We find a series of such *cartae evacuonis* in the documents referred to in most of the notes found here from no. 145 to no. 150.

[139] Ganshof defines a *guirpitio* as a ceremony whereby a vassal gives land back through a judicial act (F. Ganshof, *Qu'est-ce que la féodalité?* p. 167). Such a definition seems out of place for the Midi in this period, where anyone, *vassal or not*, can act in this fashion before a formal or informal tribunal.

[140] See record of court cases found in Section III dating from the late ninth century for examples of this procedure.

their gift and they ask others present to affirm or to witness their oath. The number and importance of these witnesses seem to be in direct proportion to the importance of the land in question. They are referred to in such charters as friends, neighbors, or noblemen or *boni homines* and their names are almost always given.[141] The validity of a private legal act involving transfer of property rights in this period seems more and more to be dependent *in practice* upon a public opinion represented by the presence and affirmation of members of one's family, one's friends, and one's important neighbors.

What could be more natural, then, as the family system superseded government in the Midi and public courts broke down, than to gather together the same sort of *boni homines, nobiles viri,* and neighbors to decide matters concerning disputed land, since such assemblies were already being used in a private capacity to attest the grants of such lands by individuals or their wills in the charters of the period. Certain remnants of the public court system in the Midi and these private procedures then coalesced in the tenth century to create the *guirpitio* system. Groups of *boni homines* deriving their authority from their habit of attending the public courts and their use as witnesses to private agreements and family charters began to informally assume the right to judge disputes concerning land, where no other clear jurisdiction existed. Since the authority of these *boni homines* and others who met informally in such assemblies rested essentially upon public opinion, they strove to arbitrate disputes rather than use force, but this does not mean they were without power. They had a great deal, and continued to use it in this period and later on.

We find in the Midi, as public tribunals disappear, an increasing number of such *guirpitios* used to settle disputes over land. Perhaps those witnesses who attested the return of land to the abbey of Tulle in 922 by Ademar, count of Scalas, formed such an informal tribunal,[142] as did those who, a charter shows us, were present sometime between 923 and 935 when Gotfred returned the church of Stanquillières to the abbey of

---

[141] For some examples of this see the charter of 930 from the Limousin which tells how Gausbert, viscount of Tulle, and his fellow viscount, Ademar, gave the abbey of Tulle a *villa*. The charter says that they do so in the presence of *"boni homines"* (*Cart. de Tulle,* no. 396). Or see the charter recording a gift of land to Saint-Augustin of Limoges by Bishop Turpin between 936 and 942 which says he does so *"consentientibus nostris consanguineis seu optimatibus Limovicensi pago degredientibus"* (*Cart. de Saint-Etienne de Limoges,* no. 15). Or see the charter which reports a gift to Cluny by Archbishop Gerard of Aix in 948, which says this is an *"actum apud Sanctum Saturninum publice"* (*Chartes de Cluny,* I, 724).

[142] *Cart. de Tulle,* no. 12.

Beaulieu in this same part of the Limousin.[143] It seems probable too that such an informal group handled the trial by combat in 946 which decided a dispute over a church between Tulle and Viscount Odalric of Saint-Cyrico.[144] Whatever we may decide concerning these earlier *guirpitios,* real or potential, judging from our charters there can be little doubt concerning later ones. Thus we can be sure that such an informal court procedure was used in the Limousin in examples which date from 951, 959, and 969–970.[145] We find it in use in the Périgord area in 970,[146] in Rouergue in 958 and 964[147] and in Auvergne about 950 and in 961 and 962.[148] In Septimania we find examples of it in charters dating from 939, 972,[149] and shortly after 975, though only later does it appear to have taken firm root in the Narbonnaise or Catalonia. It is found in the Valley of the Rhone in 926, 932, 968, and 970.[150] After 975 it became the normal system of handling disputes over property in most regions north of Catalonia.

Thus as government disappeared in the Midi and Catalonia the older court system decayed also. As it did more and more disputes which had been carried before public tribunals had to be handled in a new way. This new way was the use of gatherings of an informal nature attended by *boni homines, nobiles viri,* or *principes.* Such gatherings were not feudal, though feudal elements sometimes attended them. They were regional or local reflections of public opinion as represented by the leaders or powerful men of a particular district. And their verdicts had the force of law through their very importance. The fate of the Carolingian legal system in the Midi, then, was not to disappear into feudalized courts, but to disappear and to be replaced by assemblies of important landholders and church magnates who rendered such rough justice as was possible under the circumstances and who kept disorders to a minimum at a time when there was little judicial authority upon which society could depend.

[143] *Cart. de Beaulieu,* no. 56.
[144] *Cart. de Tulle,* no. 599.
[145] *Cart. d'Uzerche,* no. 120 (951); *Cart. de Saint-Etienne de Limoges,* no. 157 (959); *Cart. de Tulle,* no. 345 (969–970).
[146] *Cartulaire du prieuré conventual de Saint-Pierre de la Réolle [Gironde],* ed. C. Grellet-Balguerie, no. 171, in *Archives Historiques de la Gironde,* V (1864), 171–172.
[147] *Cart. de Conques,* nos. 293 (958), 193 (964).
[148] *Cart. de Sauxillanges,* nos. 58 (950), 86 (961); *Cart de Brioude,* no. 336 (962).
[149] *Cart. de Gellone,* no. 420 (939); *Hist. Gén. de Lang.,* V, no. 121 (972).
[150] *Chartes de Cluny,* I, no. 272 (926); *Cart. de Saint-Barnard de Romans,* no. 13 (932); *Cart. de Savigny,* nos. 116 (968), 158 (970).

CHAPTER XII

The Military System of the Midi and Catalonia

IN THE LAST two chapters we have seen how, during the first three quarters of the tenth century, principalities based on family rule tended to disintegrate in regions south of Poitou and Burgundy and how, when this happened, the public court system of the Carolingians tended to disappear almost everywhere and to be replaced by an informal *boni homines* system of justice. But what of the military aspects of government? What happened to the military system and in what form did it emerge by the year 975?

Obviously we must examine this military system in terms of the demands placed upon it by a need for defense against outside attack and against internal disorders. Let us first consider defense against outside attack. Earlier, in the ninth century, as we have noted, there were three regions which were particularly subject to invasion. They were Western Gascony and Aquitaine where Viking pirates concentrated their activities, the Spanish March close to the hostile Moors of Spain, and Provence and Alpine regions east of the Rhone where Moslem freebooters and other brigands seem to have operated with relative freedom. By the first years of the tenth century the problem presented by the Vikings ceased to be a serious one in Gascony and Western Aquitaine. As far as we can tell, after 900 these raiders left Gascony alone[1] and by 906 Bordeaux had recovered sufficiently to be able to send trading ships to Christian Asturias.[2] As for Aquitaine, about 930 King Raoul and Count Ebles

---

[1] The brief chronicle found in the cartulary of Auch says that in the early tenth century, at the time of Count Bernard Lupo, Auch was a *"civitas de ruina murorum"* and that *"cetera civitates Vasconie destructae erant"* (*Cart. d'Auch,* no. 77, pp. 77–79). Then rebuilding began.

[2] See the mention of the fleet of Bordeaux and of Amalvinus, *dux* of Bordeaux in 906 in *Bibliothèque Nationale, Mélanges Colbert,* XLVI, 97.

Manzur of Poitou defeated the last Viking bands who were operating in this part of France.³ Hereafter, except for occasional coastal raids which continued down into the eleventh century, Aquitaine ceased to be disturbed by Viking activity.⁴

The story of Moslem Spanish aggression is a somewhat similar one. Early in the tenth century, still reacting to Count Guifred's activity in advancing his frontiers to the south, Moslem lords of the Ebro Valley continued to carry on warfare with the Christian Spanish March. Llop ibn Mohammed, who had slain Count Guifred in battle about 897 or 898,⁵ continued hostilities after the latter's death. In 904, according to our sources, he attacked Pallars in force, capturing some seven hundred prisoners, among them Isarn, grandson and heir of Count Ramón of Pallars-Ribagorça.⁶ Four years later his contemporary, Al-Tamil, lord of Huesca, invaded Ribagorça and occupied Rhoda.⁷ He followed this up, the next year, with a raid on Catalonia in which the frontier castles of Alguaire, Gualter, and Oliola were captured and in which some three hundred prisoners and much booty were taken.⁸ In 912, after assaults on Navarre and Aragón, he turned again to Catalonia and launched another campaign against this region, in the course of which Count Sunyer of Barcelona was routed near Tarragona.⁹ Two years later he was less fortunate and met his death during a similar razzia into Catalan territory.¹⁰

After some two decades of constant war, the death of Al-Tamil in 914 brought relative peace to the Spanish March. This was due, however, less to Catalan strength than to a new political situation which had developed in Moslem Spain, one caused by the rise to power of Abd-ar-Rahman III. Abd-ar-Rahman III about 918 began an effort, eventually successful, to unite all Moslem Spain under his rule, which meant, among other things, ending the *de facto* independence of Moslem marcher lords in the Ebro

---

³ A charter from the cartulary of Tulle mentions damage done by the Vikings in this region (*Cart. de Tulle*, no. 289). See the charter of 935 which mentions the restoration of order in the Limousin too (*ibid.*, no. 598).
⁴ See A. Lewis, *The Northern Seas A.D. 300–1100*, pp. 405–406, on late Viking raids along the coasts of Aquitaine.
⁵ P. Ponsch, "A propos de la date du décès de Wilfred le Velu," in *Études Roussillonnaises*, II, 132–134.
⁶ Abadal, *Els Comtats de Pallars i Ribagorça*, p. 123.
⁷ R. de Abadal i de Vinyals, *Els Primers Comtes Catalans*, pp. 313–314.
⁸ *Ibid.*   ⁹ *Ibid.*, p. 314.
¹⁰ See the accounts of Moslem historians in J. Millás-Vallicrosa, *Els textos d'historiadors musalmans referents a la Catalunya carolingia*, in *Cuaderns d'Estudi*, XIV, 151–155.

Valley. Facing such a Cordovan threat, which they viewed with as much concern as the Christian kings of Léon, Castile, and Navarre did, the rulers of Saragossa, Huesca, and Lérida felt it wiser to keep peace along the frontiers of Pallars, Ribagorça, and Catalonia.[11] And when, about 940, these Moslem marcher lords had been absorbed into Abd-ar-Rahman's centralized caliphate, by hastening to accept Cordova's suzerainty, the counts of Barcelona were able to continue this peaceful co-existence until almost the end of the century.[12] After 914, then, peace rather than war generally prevailed along the frontiers of the Spanish March.

Our third region, Provence and Alpine areas east of the Rhone, presents a somewhat different picture. In this part of the Midi the great Hungarian raid of 938 did some damage, particularly in the Lyonnais.[13] The principal problem, however, and a continuing one, was caused by the activities of those Moslem freebooters who had established themselves at Fraxinetum and were raiding the interior. Though it is difficult to estimate the extent of the damage they caused, we do know that their raids forced the canons of Saint-Victor of Marseille to abandon this city about 923 and to transfer this establishment to land protected by the walls of the castle of Fos.[14] We also learn from later records of certain damage which the raiders did in the region of Aix.[15]

Finally as the rule of Louis the Blind and his viceroy, Hugh of Arles, proved to be increasingly ineffective, they moved north into␣Alpine regions, where, aided by local brigands and perhaps even some local nobles, they became a menace to traffic crossing the *clusae* into Italy. In 972 they were bold enough to capture the celebrated St. Mayeuil, abbot of Cluny, on his way back to his abbey after a visit to Rome.[16] It was this action which probably at last forced action against them. Though King Conrad the Peaceful appears to have done nothing, his principal vassals were spurred into action. Bishop Isarn of Grenoble began to build castles and

---

[11] Abadal, *Els Primers Comtes Catalans*, pp. 316–318.

[12] The best account of the reign of Abd-ar-Rahman III is to be found in E. Lévi-Provençale, *L'Espagne Musulmane au Xe siècle*. See also Abadal, *Els Primers Comtes Catalans*, pp. 318–321.

[13] Several charters mention Hungarian devastation of this region. For the Vienne region see a charter of 938 (*Cart. de Vienne*, no. 23). For the Lyonnais a charter of 949 (*Cart. de Savigny*, no. 38).

[14] *Cart. de Saint-Victor*, no. 1.

[15] See later charters in the *Cart. de Saint-Victor* and the *Cart. de Lérins*, for mention of the damage done by Moslems in Provence.

[16] Raoul Glaber, *Historiarum libri V*, I, IV, 9, p. 10.

to restore order to Dauphiny.[17] Even more important, William, count of Arles, rallied the local nobility of Provence and in 972 led them to a victory over the Moslems of Fraxinetum. He not only expelled the raiders from this pirate base, but also, by encouraging the building of castles in remote regions of Provence, began to bring order at last to Alpine regions which had not known it since the time of Louis the Pious.[18] After more than a century in a disorganized state, Alpine regions east of the Rhone at last got something like effective government.

Let us turn from this examination of external enemies to the problem of internal disorder. Our sources contain less information than we would like to have concerning this aspect of the Midi's development. For many regions we have no information at all. For others, however, charters of the tenth century, like those of the ninth, by telling us of land acquired by "conquests," that is by means other than inheritance, give us some indication of local conditions. For the Limousin and Quercy, for instance, such charters date from the period 923 to 945, with mention of land which was called *"ex conquestu"* or *"per conquestem"* in documents which date from the years 923, 926, 927, 930, 932, 937, and 945.[19] Ademar of Chabannes gives us some additional information. He tells us how Bernard, count of Périgord, killed Viscount Lambert of Marillac and his brother Bernard soon after 920, and how his uncle Count William Taillefer of Angoulême restored this *honorem* a little later to their brother, Viscount Odalric.[20] He also informs us of how, late in this period, about 973–974, Boson the Old, count of La Marche, tore down the castle of Brosse, which Duke William of Poitou had erected in the former's domains.[21]

When we examine charters from Auvergne and Rouergue we get much more evidence of instability than we find in the Limousin and Western Aquitaine. Some thirty charters from Conques dating from the period 901–974 mention land whose owners acquired it *"ex conquestu."* Five of these date from the period before 925, twelve from the period 925–950, and fifteen from the years 951–974.[22] Evidence from Auvergne

---

[17] *Cart. de Grenoble*, no. 16.
[18] Raoul Glaber, *Historiarum libri V*, I, IV, 9, p. 12. See also E. Duprat, in *Bouches du Rhône*, pp. 255–258.
[19] *Cart. de Beaulieu*, nos. 38, 56, 132, 174, and *Cart. de Tulle*, nos. 229, 596.
[20] *Ademar de Chabannes*, III, 23, p. 145.
[21] *Ibid.*, III, 29, p. 150.
[22] *Cart. de Conques*, nos. 6, 25, 89, 91, 109, 110, 113, 114, 124, 132, 151, 157, 189, 200, 208, 227, 230, 235, 250, 288, 324, 340, 357, 391, 413, 424, 434, 436.

seems to be even more complete. Some seventy-six charters from this region mention *"ex conquestu"* land—most in the central and southern portions of this province. Thirty-one date from the period down to 925, twenty-eight from the years 926 to 950, and eighteen from the years 951 to 975.[23] In contrast to this our sources from the nearby regions of the Albigeois and Velay give us little information about such instability of land ownership.

The basic political situation which helped create this instability of landholding in the Limousin and Quercy for some two decades and which caused what seems to have been a state of endemic disorder in Rouergue and Auvergne is known to us. It was the conflict which took place over these regions between the House of Toulouse and the Houses of Bernard of Auvergne and of Ebles Manzur of Poitou. This long conflict helped to create factions and what might be termed chronic civil war in these parts of the Midi. By 950 such disorders appear to have ceased in the Limousin, but they continued unchecked in Auvergne and Rouergue because no political authority strong enough to stop them existed.[24] Nor was any to appear here until the twelfth century.

When we consider the Valley of the Rhone proper our charters also give us some evidence of similar disorders. We find certain references to *"ex conquestu"* land in charters dating from 908 and 923[25] which concern Dauphiny; in ones from 937, 947–948, and 956–957[26] which deal with the Vienne region; and in ones from 968 and 970[27] from the Lyonnais. Such land ownership changes in the Vienne region may well have

[23] Both the *Cart. de Brioude*, and the *Cart. de Sauxillanges* contain numerous examples in charters dating from this period.

[24] Contemporary charters reflect this political instability by ceasing in many cases to use the term county, which earlier was normal. See for instance the charter issued by King Raoul which calls Ademar a count *"in partibus Cahors"* in 935 (*Cart. de Tulle*, no. 598); or that dating from 936–942 which mentions the *"optimates Limovicensi pago"* (*Cart. de Saint-Etienne de Limoges*, no. 15); or that from Quercy dating from 969–974 which mentions the *"urbem Cahors,"* though it refers to property in the countryside (*Cart. de Beaulieu*, no. 148). For Auvergne we have a charter of 901 which speaks of *"in orbe Arvernio"* (*Cart. de Brioude*, no. 32). Another of 930 mentions *"in orbe Arvernico"* (*ibid.*, no. 4). Then two of 935 speak of the *"patria Arvernica"* (*ibid.*, nos. 153, 186). The same expression is found in charters of 939, 940, 945, and 946 in *ibid.*, nos. 40, 158, 246, and 3.

[25] *Cart. de Saint-Barnard de Romans*, nos. 7 (908), 10 (923).

[26] *Chartes de Cluny*, I, no. 476 (937); *Cart. de Saint-André-le-bas*, nos. 99 (947–948), 145 (956–957).

[27] *Cart. de Savigny*, nos. 59 (968), 123 (970).

The Military System of the Midi and Catalonia 225

been associated with a change in dynasties after the death of Louis the Blind.[28] Those found in Dauphiny in part seem related to the rise of a local family, that of Sylvius, to a position of authority.[29] Those in the Lyonnais were probably the result of Artald's assumption of the power and authority of count about the year 970.[30] In contrast to Auvergne and Rouergue, though, our sources seem to show that the Valley of the Rhone suffered only occasional disorders in specific areas for short periods of time—except in Alpine areas and Provence, of course.

Such then is an analysis of what we can discover concerning internal and external disorders in Southern France and the Spanish March during the period 900 to 975, in the light of which we must consider military aspects of government. But though such an analysis helps to explain why some form of military organization was necessary in most of the Midi and Catalonia, it tells us nothing more. To get some answers to the question of what form this military organization took we must turn to what we can discover about castles and their use during the period. Before we do so, however, we must remember that our sources are incomplete. All we can hope for, as in previous periods, is some indications of military organization. We must also, generally, take it for granted that most of the fortresses and fortifications which were to be found in these regions in late Carolingian times continued to be used during this period, unless we have specific evidence to the contrary.

With this in mind let us first consider Auvergne and Rouergue where, as has been pointed out, disorders were almost constant during these decades. Curiously enough, though, our sources reveal fewer fortresses in this part of Central France than we might expect. We do nevertheless find some. One is a *castellum* near Sauxillanges mentioned in a charter which dates from about 928.[31] Still another is the important fortress of Castelluc, referred to several times in our sources.[32] Others are a place called Casterole, found in a document of 945[33] and 958, and that *rocca*

[28] On this change see R. Poupardin, *Le Royaume de Bourgogne*, pp. 163–197, and R. Busquet, "Rois de Bourgogne et comtes de Provence," in *Provence Historique*, III (1950–1951), 147–150.

[29] Charters dating from 922, 932, 969, 970, and 971 show the power which Sylvius exercised in Dauphiny (*Cart. de Saint-Barnard de Romans*, nos. 10, 13, 38, 40, and *Cart. de Saint-Chaffre*, no. 322.

[30] See E. Fournial, "Recherches sur les comtes de Lyon au IXᵉ et Xᵉ siècles," in *Le Moyen Age*, LVIII (1952), 233–249.

[31] *Cart. de Sauxillanges*, no. 13.

[32] *Cart. de Brioude*, nos. 75, 81, 170, and *Cart. de Sauxillanges*, nos. 376, 182.

[33] *Grand Cart. de Brioude*, nos. CCCXXXV, CCCCVII.

which, we are told, was held in 961 by two Auvergnat nobles, Genesius and Aimery.[34] Late in our period we also find references to a *castrum* called Yconensium near Monte Asenario[35] and another called Brézac or Bresantium located near the abbey of Aurillac.[36] For Rouergue, charters of the region speak of a castle of Salmegro in 937[37] and another called a *turre* or *castrum* not far away in 957.[38]

We have more evidence of castles and other fortifications in use during this period in Quercy, the Limousin, and other regions of Western Aquitaine. Ademar of Chabannes tells us that the walls of Angoulême which we know were in existence in 918[39] were rebuilt by Count Aldouin sometime before 916,[40] and the *Cartulary of Uzerche* mentions the work of refortifying Limoges by Bishop Turpio in the same period.[41] In 922 and 930[42] our sources mention the *castrum* of Fouilloux as well as one called Bellum located near Cahors.[43] We learn of three more located near the abbey of Tulle during this period, Echelles or Scalas,[44] one at Stanquillières[45] and one called Moncieux,[46] as well as that of Uxelladuno which King Raoul gave to this monastery in 935.[47] In 941, 944, 947, and 975 we learn of a *rocca* owned by a certain Guitard and his family.[48] And we hear of a place called Castres given to the abbey of Beaulieu in 943.[49] From the pen of Ademar of Chabannes we learn how Bishop Ebles of Limoges, about 944, built the castle of Saint-Hilaire near this city and surrounded the abbey of Saint-Martial with fortifications.[50] West of the

---

[34] *Hist. Gén. de Lang.*, V, no. 111.
[35] *Cart. de Sauxillanges*, no. 145.
[36] *Cart. de Saint-Flour*, no. 1.
[37] *Hist. Gén. de Lang.*, V, no. 71.
[38] *Ibid.*, no. 102.
[39] *Cart. d'Angoulême*, no. 2.
[40] *Ademar de Chabannes*, III, 23, p. 144.
[41] "Ex historia monasteri Usercensis," in *Cart. d'Uzerche*, ed. Champéval, pp. 13–14.
[42] *Cart. de Tulle*, no. 12 (922), 14 (930).
[43] *Ibid.*, no. 14.
[44] *Ibid.*, no. 290.
[45] *Cart. de Beaulieu*, no. 56.
[46] *Cart. de Tulle*, no. 14.
[47] *Ibid.*, no. 598.
[48] *Ibid.*, nos. 537, 472, 556.
[49] *Cart. de Beaulieu*, no. 159.
[50] *Ademar de Chabannes*, III, 25, p. 147.

The Military System of the Midi and Catalonia 227

Limousin in Saintonge we learn of the castle of Ostend in 956,[51] south of the newly erected *castrum* of Melle.[52]

When we look further south toward an area in Rouergue, Quercy, and the Toulousain which was definitely controlled directly by the House of Toulouse, we find references to a large number of such fortifications in the will of Raymond I of Rouergue, and a little later in the period in those of Countess Garsinde and Hugh, bishop of Toulouse. Raymond's will mentions a *rocheta* near Albi, five castles near Moissac, and some twelve others scattered through his domains which he is leaving to his son, Raymond II, and his other heirs.[53] Garsinde's will of 972 refers to a castle near Saint-Pons of Thomières and one near Castres, as well as one in Lodève owned by Bishop Frotaire.[54] Bishop Hugh of Toulouse in his will mentions the castle of Durimane belonging to Bishop Frotaire and that of Sexago in Razès held by the count and countess of Carcassonne.[55]

Charters from Septimania give us still more information concerning such fortresses and fortifications. We have mention of the walls of Nîmes in 925[56] and of castles at Anduze and Roquador[57] nearby at about this same time, as well as one called Salaves mentioned in a charter of 959.[58] Our records show that the castle of Substantion was still in use in 923 and 926.[59] So was a *castrum* called Lunet near Béziers, which is mentioned in a charter of 909,[60] one near Agde referred to in a document of 929,[61] and a *turre* near the church of Saint-Martin to which we find other references in a charter dating from late in the period.[62] Further to the west near Narbonne and Carcassonne we learn of a castle located in 902 and

---

[51] *Cart. de Saint-Jean d'Angély*, no. 62.
[52] *Chartes et documentes pour servir à l'histoire de l'abbaye de Saint-Maixent* [Poitou], ed. A. Richard, no. 67, in *Archives Historiques de Poitou*, XVI (1886), 85.
[53] *Hist. Gén. de Lang.*, V, no. 111.
[54] *Ibid.*, nos. 125, 126.
[55] *Cart. de Saint-Sernin*, no. 280.
[56] *Cart. de Nîmes*, no. 25.
[57] *Ibid.*, no. 2, and *Cart. de Gellone*, no. 117 (Anduze); *Cart. de Nîmes*, nos. 32, 33 (Roquador).
[58] *Cart. de Nîmes*, no. 57.
[59] *Cart. de Gellone*, no. 72.
[60] *Hist. Gén. de Lang.*, V, no. 37.
[61] *Cart. de Gellone*, no. 73.
[62] *Ibid.*, no. 281.

904 near the abbey of Lagrasse,[63] a nearby one called Leorte found in 950,[64] one at Montolieu in 925,[65] and a *castrum* called Alzonne referred to in a charter dating from 918.[66] Somewhat later about 959 we find a source which mentions a *turre* sold to the archbishop of Narbonne by Viscount Matfred as well as the *castrum* of Boxia which he left to his son Raymond in 966.[67]

When we turn to the Valley of the Rhone again we find evidence of a number of these fortifications. Our sources reveal that Lyon and Vienne during this period were still fortified,[68] as was LePuy whose *burg* belonged to the bishop of the city.[69] We learn of a castle at Mont Burton near Vienne in 965,[70] of one at Crussal in 943[71] and of another one called Mezengo in Velay at about this same period.[72] In 950 there seems to have been at least one in Vivarais.[73] A little earlier, in 947, the bishop of Valence gave to a certain Gibernus the right to build a castle in this region,[74] and a little later, between 950 and 976, Bishop Isarn of Grenoble, according to a posterior source, began constructing such castles in Dauphiny.[75] Further in the interior we find *castra* mentioned in 928 near Gap, and nearby in 950 at Barret and in 967 at Lurs.[76] In addition to pre-existing fortifications we hear of a castle at Fos in 923,[77] of a *turre* near Marseille in 950,[78] and in 970 of four *castra* in various parts of this province, one near Marseille, two near Aix, and one near Fréjus.[79]

---

[63] *Cart. de Carcassonne*, II, 218, and *Hist. Gén. de Lang.*, V, no. 30.
[64] *Cart. de Carcassonne*, II, 223–224.
[65] Cros-Meyrévielle, *Documents*, no. 21.
[66] *Cart. de Carcassonne*, I, 188–189.
[67] *Hist. Gén. de Lang.*, V, nos. 104, 115.
[68] For Vienne see charter of 924 in *Chartes de Cluny*, I, no. 241. Somewhat later see mention of walls of the city in *ibid.*, II, no. 900. For walls of Lyon see "Cart. d'Ainay," no. 192, in *Cart. de Savigny*, pp. 697–698.
[69] *Hist. Gén. de Lang.*, V, no. 49.
[70] *Cart. de Vienne*, no. 28.
[71] G. Letonnelier, "Essai sur les origine des châtelains et des mandaments en Dauphiné" in *Annales de l'Université de Grenoble*, I (1889), 10.
[72] *Cart. de Saint-Chaffre*, no. 106.
[73] *Hist. Gén. de Lang.*, II, no. 208.
[74] G. Columbi, *Episcopi Valentiniani*, VII, 61.
[75] *Cart. de Grenoble*, no. 16.
[76] *Cart. de Conques*, no. 431 (Gap); *Gallia Christiana*, Nov. I, Inst. 73 (Barret), Inst. 443 (Lurs).
[77] *Cart. de Saint-Victor*, no. 1.
[78] *Ibid.*, no. 1041.
[79] *Ibid.*, no. 23.

The Military System of the Midi and Catalonia 229

When we turn from the Midi to the Spanish March we find even more evidence of such fortresses, as we would expect upon approaching the Moslem frontier. Leaving aside for a moment the border marches of Catalonia and Pallars and Ribagorça let us consider information from counties which were fairly far removed from the frontier. When we do so our sources mention a *turre* which was located in Roussillon not far from Elne[80] and other fortifications nearby in 947,[81] two *castra* called Castellano and Turres Betses referred to in documents from Confluent in 952 and 958,[82] a Castrum Falconis in Vallespir in 936,[83] and two called Bertin and Castellaris in Perelada in 948.[84]

When we approach the frontier such castles multiply. Our sources give us information of some twenty-two located near the Moslem border in the counties of Barcelona, Ausona, and Manressa during these years. In the order of their appearance by date in our documents they are Kastellionem, Cervallo, Cleriana, Cervilione, Subirats, Besaura, Rosidors, Marro, Miralès, Queralt, Palumbi, Vidde, Manressa, Arampuña, Olerdula, Castelito, Gellito, Masquefa, Turre Hostalde, Mulier, Castelfels, and Montmell.[85] For the interior regions of Berga-Cerdanya-Besalu we have a record of some thirteen of them: Gratos, Llaiers, Casserès, Lucano, Usalito, Ravinas, Nuret, Olone, Montgrony, Nebule, Spugnole, Saint-Martin, and Agremundo.[86] For Pallars and Ribagorça, in addition to the numerous *turres* which dotted the mountainsides,[87] we find mention of

[80] *Hist. Gén. de Lang.,* V, no. 83.
[81] *Cart. roussillonnais,* no. 7.
[82] *Catalunya Carolingia,* II, 92–93 (952), 96–98 (958).
[83] *Hist. Gén. de Lang.,* V, no. 65.
[84] *Catalunya Carolingia,* II, 229–231.
[85] *El Archivo Condal de Barcelona,* nos. 9 (Kastellione), 17 (Marro), 47 (Cervallo), 67 (Besaura), 93 and 100 (Rosidors), 130 (Manressa), 132 (Palumbi, Queralt); *Cart. de San Cugat,* nos. 2 (Cervallo), 5 (Cervilione), 7 (Cervallo), 9 (Subirats), 45 (Vidde), 51 (Cleriana), 56 (Olerdula), 65 (Castelito, Gellito, Masquefer), 67 (Subirats), 87 (Mulier), 88 (Castelito), 95 (Gellito), 96 (Arampuña), 97 (Arampuña, Castelfels), 98, 99, and 105 (Castelfels), 107 (Arampuña); *Liber Feudorum,* nos. 445 and 447 (Cleriana); *Hist. Gén. de Lang.,* II, no. 209 (Miralès, Queralt); *Archivo Catedral de Barcelona,* nos. 23 (Turre Hostalde), 24 (Montmell).
[86] *El Archivo Condal de Barcelona,* nos. 16 (Gratos), 72 (Llaiers), 73 (Casserès), 78 (Llaiers), 80 (Usalito), 81 (Agremundo), 91 (Ravinas), 113 (Nuret), 121 (Llaiers), 123 (Montgrony), 129 (Nuret), 130 (Nebule, Spugnole), 167 and 168 (Usalito), and appendix B., p. 444 (Lucano); *Cart. roussillonnais,* no. 7 (Olone); *Hist. Gén. de Lang.,* II, no. 209 (Saint Martin).
[87] See Abadal, *Els Comtats de Pallars i Ribagorça,* for the large number of *turres* in this region.

castles at Leovalles, Castellous, and Lemignano,[88] to name only a few. Obviously the Spanish March was a land of castles.

We might sum up our evidence of the existence of castles, then, as follows. Except for Gascony, for which we have no evidence of the existence of such fortress, our documents show that a great many more castles existed by the year 975 than were to be found in 900. How many more it is difficult to say. The preceding pages, though, give proof of the existence of some one hundred castles and other fortifications north of the Pyrenees and between forty and fifty in the Spanish March. Though in our sources only a few castles are definitely stated to be ones which were newly built during these decades, it seems fair to say that this was an important period for the construction of such fortresses, particularly in Aquitaine, Septimania, Provence, and the Spanish March.

This brings us to an even more important question. Who owned and controlled these castles that were the basis of military power south of Poitou and Burgundy during this period? Often we cannot be sure. In other cases our information is more precise. Many of the castles north of the Pyrenees seem to have been the outright allodial possessions of the principal counts, viscounts, and *principes* of these regions. Some, no doubt, became so in the course of these years. This seems to have been the case for those seventeen castles and one *rocheta* scattered through Languedoc which are mentioned in 961 in the will of Raymond I of Rouergue[89] or the three fortresses mentioned by Countess Garsinde in 972.[90] Ademar, count of Scalas, seems to have owned at least some of the castles found in Quercy and the Limousin about 930,[91] as did Count Acfred in Auvergne at about the same time.[92] During this period our sources show us that Viscount Bernard of Albi acquired at least two castles, one at Solenegra in 937 and another *castrum* or *turre* in 957.[93] By 928, Frédélon, progenitor of the later marquises of Anduze, seems to have been in full control of his castle.[94] In Narbonne the viscontal family disposed of at least three castles which were their allodial possessions, in 950, 959, and 966.[95] In the Valley of the Rhone, for which our informa-

[88] *Hist. Gén. de Lang.*, V, nos. 82 (Leovalles); 95 (Castellous, Lemignano).
[89] *Ibid.*, no. 111.
[90] *Ibid.*, nos. 125, 126.
[91] *Cart. de Tulle*, no. 14.
[92] *Cart. de Sauxillanges*, no. 13.
[93] *Hist. Gén. de Lang.*, V, no. 102.
[94] *Cart. de Nîmes*, nos. 32, 33.
[95] *Cart. de Carcassonne*, II, 223–224 (950); *Hist. Gén. de Lang.*, V, nos. 105 (959), 115 (966).

The Military System of the Midi and Catalonia 231

tion concerning castles is less precise, at least one such fortress, that of Treslia, was owned by King Conrad of Burgundy-Provence about 950.[96]

In Catalonia where the counts tended to control most castles, we still find other individuals who owned such fortresses. Examples of this are the castle of Ravinas, which Viscount Leopardo sold in 928,[97] or that of Spugnole given away by Countess Adelaise in 950,[98] or Masquefa which Hennego, a border marcher lord, acquired as an allod in 963.[99] Sometimes such an individual owned only a small fortress, or *turre*, like those mentioned in 956 and 959[100] which were given to the abbey of San-Cugat. In Catalonia, as in the rest of the Midi then, a number of powerful nobles controlled castles which were their allodial property.

If members of the secular nobility owned a number of these castles, so did the Church, which, as a matter of fact, seems to have steadily increased the number of such fortresses in its possession. In the Limousin and Quercy, for example, we know of some five castles belonging to the abbey of Tulle, as well as one owned by the abbey of Beaulieu,[101] and several which were built at Limoges about 944 by Bishop Ebles.[102] Further to the south the will of Raymond I of Rouergue, dating from 961, makes it clear that this important noble contemplated that a number of his castles would ultimately go to the churches of Albi and Cahors or to abbeys like Figeac, Moissac, Marcillac, and Brioude.[103] Eleven years later Countess Garsinde's will left similar fortresses to Saint-Vincent of Castres and Saint-Pons of Thomières,[104] as well as consenting to a gift of one to Saint-Michael of Gaillac.[105] About 975 a similar castle became the allodial possession of the abbey of Gellone.[106]

In the Carcassonne-Razès region in 900 we find that the *castrum* of Por is the allodial possession of the abbey of Saint-Jacques de Joucan,[107] while Lagrasse owned two castles, one near the monastery itself,[108] and another

---

[96] *Cart. de Saint-Victor*, no. 1041.
[97] *El Archivo Condal de Barcelona*, no. 91.
[98] *Ibid.*, no. 130.
[99] *Cart. de San Cugat*, no. 65.
[100] *Ibid.*, nos. 45 (956), 56 (959).
[101] *Cart. de Tulle*, nos. 12, 14, 290, 598; *Cart. de Beaulieu*, no. 56.
[102] *Ademar de Chabannes*, III, 25, p. 147.
[103] *Hist. Gén. de Lang.*, V, no. 111.
[104] *Ibid.*, no. 126.
[105] *Ibid.*, no. 123.
[106] *Cart. de Gellone*, no. 281.
[107] *Cart. roussillonnais*, no. 3.
[108] *Hist. Gén. de Lang.*, V, no. 38.

it acquired about 950.[109] Montolieu, as has been noted, remained fortified throughout this period.[110] The archbishop of Narbonne in 959 acquired a *turre* as part of his possessions.[111] To the south we learn of another *turre* belonging to the abbey of Cuxa,[112] of a *castrum* owned by Saint-Joan de les Abadesses,[113] and several *turres* which belonged to the abbey of San-Cugat near Barcelona.[114]

A similar situation seems to have existed in the Valley of the Rhone. From 924 on in Velay the *burg* of LePuy belonged to the bishops of this city,[115] while, as we have noted, Bishop Isarn of Grenoble was responsible for the construction of castles throughout his domains sometime between 950 and 974.[116] Even in Provence by 950 the abbey of Saint-Victor of Marseille had acquired a *turre* or fortress, that of Treslia.[117] In this period as in Carolingian times, the Church, like other landowners owned a large number of the fortresses which are to be found in the Midi and Catalonia.

In addition to the ownership of such fortresses, however, there is another question which we need to consider—that which concerns the occupation of them. Many of those who owned such fortresses as allods were in no position to actually occupy them personally, particularly if they were nobles or churchmen who owned more than one. What then did they do with them? Various solutions of this problem are to be found during this period. One of the more interesting appears to have been the use of a system of joint ownership, a sort of *divisio* which continued into later periods. Under this system the ownership of a castle, or its allod, to use a contemporary phrase, was divided. One half belonged to the occupant: one half to an owner who did not live in it. An example of such castle ownership is to be found in a charter, dating from 957 which tells us of a castle acquired by Bernard, viscount of Albi. When Bernard took this over, one-half of this fortress was owned by a certain Senegunde and her four sons "*ad proprium allodum*," the other half by Bligardis and her two sons in the same manner.[118] The castle of Cenceno which Countess Garsinde gave to Saint-Pons of Thomières in 972 was similarly divided

[109] *Cart. de Carcassonne*, II, 223–224.
[110] *Ibid.*, p. 218, and Cros-Meyrévielle, *Documents*, no. 21.
[111] *Hist. Gén. de Lang.*, V, no. 105.
[112] *Catalunya Carolingia*, II, 96–98.
[113] *El Archivo Condal de Barcelona*, no. 9.
[114] For example see a charter of 959 in *Cart. de San Cugat*, no. 56.
[115] *Hist. Gén. de Lang.*, V, no. 49.
[116] *Cart. de Grenoble*, no. 16.
[117] *Cart. de Saint-Victor*, no. 1041.
[118] *Hist. Gén. de Lang.*, V, no. 102.

as an allod between this countess and her relative Adelaise of Narbonne and the latter's two sons.[119] In 961, in his will, Raymond of Rouergue mentions one-half of certain castles that he was giving to the abbey of Moissac and *his part* of the castle of Gordo, which suggests the same kind of joint ownership.[120] So does his mention of a *rocca* in Auvergne which he says Genesius and Aimery hold *in common*.[121] Joint ownership, particularly by members of the same family, then, was one way in which the problem of controlling castles was solved.

Still another was a system similar to that used by the Carolingians in the Midi and Catalonia, that of giving out castles as benefices or fiefs. The abbey of Tulle and some of the secular lords of the Limousin seem to have used this system for some of the castles they owned.[122] And in Valence it was the method contemplated by Bishop Aurilbert in about 943, when he allowed Gibernus to build a castle which he would then hold as a *precarium* from this pontiff.[123] The castle of Ulmo, which Bishop Frotaire held and which he gave to Gaillac in 972, seems to have been a similar benefice given to the bishop by the House of Toulouse.[124] So was the castle of Sexago, which, we learn the count and countess of Carcassonne held as

[119] *Ibid.*, no. 125. See also a charter of 950 in which a certain Ermengardis gives *her part* of the castle of Leorte to the abbey of Lagrasse (*Cart. de Carcassonne*, II, 223–224).

[120] *Hist. Gén. de Lang.*, V, no. 111.

[121] *Ibid.*

[122] A charter of Tulle gives the history of such a castle during the tenth and eleventh centuries, in this case the castle of Moncieux, which was given out as a benefice. The castle originally was given to Tulle by Ademar, viscount of Scalas, who, along with his wife, kept possession of it as a lifetime benefice or usufruct. Then, about 935 the monks gave the castle as a benefice to a certain Donarel, son of Viscount Ademar. A little later Bernard, viscount of Turenne received the castle as a benefice with the surrounding area (*"cum caslania"*). He held it only as a lifetime usufruct and paid the monks a *cens* for it. Then Viscount Archimbaud of Comborn and his son were given the castle as a benefice and paid the abbey a *cens*. This carries the castle down to the end of this period (*Cart. de Tulle*, no. 290). It is worth noting that Tulle granted this castle as a benefice on a lifetime basis *only* during these years. A *cens*, proof of the abbey's allodial ownership of the castle, regularly was paid by its possessors. And thirdly the abbey shifted possession of the castle pretty much to suit itself, or as prudence, in terms of a strong *defensor* in the neighborhood, dictated.

[123] G. Columbi, *Episcopi Valentiniani*, XVII, 21.

[124] *Hist. Gén. de Lang.*, V, no. 123. This charter shows that the castle of Ulmo and other *honores* were only given to Gaillac with the *permission* of Count Raymond II of Rouergue, his lord.

a fief from Bishop Hugh of Toulouse,[125] the castle of Parisio which a certain Malbert had *"a feo,"* or the fortress held by Isarn and Arnold in the same way in 961 from Raymond of Rouergue.[126] It seems probable also that at least some of the castles which were the subject of an agreement between the viscounts of Urgell and Cerdanya in 954 were held as fiefs too, since Count Ermengol of Urgell is mentioned specifically in the agreement, in what seems to be his capacity as overlord.[127]

Sometimes such arrangements could be very complex, judging from our sources. The allodial owner of the castle of Sexago was the bishop of Toulouse, Hugh of the Toulouse-Rouergue family. The House of Carcassonne held this castle as a fief from the bishop.[128] Yet the actual occupant was neither of these, but a certain Gilbert, called a vicar, who in 958 presided over a court held in the castle, which met to decide a case involving a dispute over land in the nearby region.[129] Did Gilbert hold this castle in sub-infeudation as castellan from the count and countess of Carcassonne? We cannot say for sure, though it seems probable that he did. One thing though does seem clear. Castles given as benefices, like other land given out in this fashion, had a way of being lost to their owners and tended to become the allodial possession of those who held them. Thus we see attempts to put a time limit of one or two lifetimes on such grants.

Perhaps it was this fact—that castles so easily tended to slip away into the full possession of their occupants—that explains still a third method of giving out grants, that is called the *guarda* or *baillem* system, which we begin to find in this period. Under this system, judging from certain specific examples found a little later, a castle was given out to an individual castellan, but the grant was revokable and limited to a certain period of time, probably less than a lifetime. Such a *guarda* or castle ward is mentioned in the will of Bishop Hugh of Toulouse which speaks of a castle "in *the hands*" of a certain Frotaire but *"in guarda"* of Bernard and Gausbert.[130] Again in a document from the Spanish March we learn that the two castles of Miralès and Queralt were held *"in baillem"* by a certain Berengar de Araquel.[131]

---

[125] *Cart. de Saint-Sernin*, no. 280.
[126] *Hist. Gén. de Lang.*, V, no. 111.
[127] *Hist. Gén. de Lang.*, II, no. 209.
[128] *Cart. de Saint-Sernin*, no. 280.
[129] *Hist. Gén. de Lang.*, V, no. 104.
[130] *Cart. de Saint-Sernin*, no. 280.
[131] *Hist. Gén. de Lang.*, II, no. 209. See also the mention of a *"garda"* in a charter given to the abbey of San Cugat in 938 by King Louis IV (*Catalunya Carolinga*, II, 183–193).

The Military System of the Midi and Catalonia

Such then is the picture of the ownership, control, and occupation of castles in the Midi and Catalonia during this period. From it we can see that a variety of methods were used. Castles were owned allodially by important secular nobles, by counts, viscounts, and even minor vicars and other landowners. They belonged to various church establishments also. Sometimes these owners actually lived in the fortresses they owned as allods. Sometimes they kept a measure of control over them by joint ownership with others. Sometimes they granted them out as benefices. Sometimes they used a more flexible and less dangerous system of *guarda, baillem*, or castle ward. What is striking is how many types of castle ownership and control were in use during this period, which seems to be a reflection of the disorganized state of the military and governmental systems of the period. Yet it is worth noting too that we seldom hear during these years of a castle which was the subject of dispute or declared to be illegally built of occupied. The two exceptions are the destruction by Queen Matilda of Provence-Burgundy in 965 of a castle built near Vienne,[132] and the action of Count Boson of La Marche in destroying a castle which Duke William of Poitou built in his domains in 973–974.[133] Castles may have been held or owned in a variety of ways, but down to 975, at least, the direct problems represented by them had not yet become very serious ones for the security of the Midi.

When we probe beneath the surface, however, we begin to see by 975 that the increase in the number of such castles and the methods used in their ownership and control had already begun to bring certain changes to this society. Dimly we can see the outline of a new system of militarism which was arising in Southern France and the Spanish March. For as castles spread everywhere we begin to find along with them a special class of warriors or *milites* spreading too. These *milites* seem to differ from their predecessors in the period of Charlemagne or Charles the Bald in one important respect. The warriors of the previous period in the Midi and Catalonia were *first* important landowners and officials and *then* warriors. They seem to have been essentially a militia, or part-time warriors, to use a modern term. The *milites* whom we find appearing in this tenth century are first of all professional fighters and *then* landowners, judges, and officials. The emphasis had changed, hence their title of *milites*. Their homes were not the unfortified manor houses or the *villas* in the countryside, but the castles and fortifications which steadily increased in number

[132] *Cart. de Vienne*, no. 28.
[133] *Ademar de Chabannes*, III, 29, p. 150.

throughout this period.[134] Such fighting men were not a completely new phenomenon. They had been found earlier. But now they were found everywhere in the Midi and Catalonia in regions where they had been unknown before.

Perhaps our earliest documentary reference to this new class, interestingly enough, comes from Quercy and the Limousin early in the tenth century where a charter of about 925 speaks of a certain man as a *miles*.[135] A little later, about 935, in a charter giving to Tulle the castle of Uxelladuno, King Raoul speaks of the *milites* inhabiting such castles who were going outside of the walls and were oppressing *"loca monarchia."*[136] By 971 the number of such *milites* must have grown, since in that year the abbot of Beaulieu forbade his *judices servum*, who administered the domains belonging to the abbey, to make themselves into *milites* and to carry the lance and the spear. If they did, he threatened, they would be returned to the serfdom from which they had emerged.[137] This interesting document not only shows us the new *milites* in the Limousin, but also

---

[134] With the *possible* exception of three cases—one a *miles* mentioned in a charter dating from 925 from the Limousin (see note 135), one a royal charter of 931 which calls Dalmatius, viscount of LePuy, a *miles* (see note 138), and one dating from 925 which calls Landry of Roussillon a *miles* (see note 141)—the term *miles* or *milites* found in charters of this period are not substitutes for the words *vassus* or *vassi*. They do not denote *social rank* and cannot be translated by the term *knight* or *knights*. They clearly are occupational terms which denote *fighting men* and those garrisoning castles. See, for example, reference in a charter of 935 from the Limousin to the *milites* of the castle of Uxelladuno or, according to a charter of 972, the *milites* living in the castle of Ulmo (*Hist. Gén. de Lang.*, V, no. 123), or those mentioned in the charter of 954 who are called *milites* of the *castra* of Miralès and Queralt located near the Moslem border of Catalonia (*ibid.*, II, 209). Their duties seem to be essentially military rather than feudal, during this period, or at least these two duties have not yet coalesced to form the feudal fighting man. If one doubts this, the abbey of Beaulieu's refusal to allow its lay officials (*judices*) to become *milites* would be conclusive. What the abbey refused to allow them to do in 971 was to *arm themselves* as *milites* (*Cart. de Beaulieu*, no. 50). Down to 975 then in the Midi and Catalonia, those called *milites* were mounted, armed men living in fortresses with others of their kind. They were not yet a fighting and governing feudal class in the society of these regions.

[135] This *miles* is a certain Analgorius who received a *villa* and a church *"ad fevum"* from Viscount Ademar of Scalas (*Cart. de Tulle*, no. 289). See however earlier references to such *milites* in this same region in Odo, *Vita Sancti Geraldi, Auriligiensis*, I, 8, 18, 31, 37–39, cols. 647, 654, 660–665.

[136] *Cart. de Tulle*, no. 598.

[137] *Cart. de Beaulieu*, no. 50.

The Military System of the Midi and Catalonia 237

gives us some idea of how they were recruited from the ranks of the minor officialdom and even serfs of the period. It also shows us the opposition to this class which already existed in this part of France.

Such *milites* were not confined to the Limousin. We find them elsewhere. In 931 a charter of King Raoul speaks of Dalmatius, viscount of Lepuy, as a *miles*,[138] and in 975 another charter from nearby Auvergne mentions land belonging to *"belli homini."*[139] A document dating from 968, from the Lyonnais, mentions *milites* near the city of Lyon.[140] We find them in Roussillon according to charters which date from 925 and 953.[141] They are mentioned in the Toulousain in 972.[142] A charter of 954 from Urgell gives us still more information and is the earliest which we possess embodying an agreement between those who own a castle and those who occupy it—agreements which were to be common later on in the Midi and Catalonia. In this agreement between the viscounts of Urgell and Cerdanya we find mention of the *milites* of the castle of Saint-Martin and those of the *castra* of Miralès and Queralt. There is also a reference to the military service which was expected of these *milites*, the *hostes et cavalcades*.[143] Here we see clearly a reference to such professional warriors and their military duties as they existed along the frontiers of Catalonia.

Even where we do not have a direct reference to such *milites* we do have indirect evidence of their presence in the castles of the period and of their effect upon the surrounding countrysides. Such garrisons of professional warriors required special provision for support in dues levied on lands located near their fortresses, in contrast to Carolingian warriors who appear to have been scattered about the countryside on land from which they could support themselves. Hence we begin to find in our documents references to such special dues which were levied in addition to the or-

---

[138] *Cart. de Carcassonne*, I, 76.

[139] *Cart. de Conques*, no. 228. These were probably *milites*, so called, who lived on land near a tract given to Conques during this period. See also charters of 913 and 916 which mention a certain *cavalarius* who lived near the abbey of Brioude (*Cart. de Brioude*, nos. 5, 151, 100).

[140] "Cart. d'Ainay," no. 3, in *Cart. de Savigny*.

[141] "Landry, *miles*" is the expression used in a charter of 925 (*Cart. de Carcassonne*, II, 221). See also a charter of 953 which mentions in a general way *"boni homines, clericos, et milites"* who were present at the dedication of a church in Vallespir (*Cart. roussillonnais*, no 8). The use of a term such as *milites* in this region seems to be a Carolingian survival, since such terms are also used in documents of the late ninth century originating in this part of the Midi.

[142] *Hist. Gén. de Lang.*, V, no. 123.

[143] *Ibid.*, II, no. 209.

dinary *cens*. The most common appear to have been what were called the *receptum* or *albergum*, but north of the Pyrenees they are called by other names too, such as *usaticos, questas, tallias,* or *firmancias,* this last apparently representing service in labor which was exacted as well as service in kind. In 918, for instance, at a court held in the castle of Alzonne near Carcassonne there is a mention of such services, which, it is said, were owed by an allod belonging to the abbey of Montolieu.[144] In 933 in the same region we find Count Raymond Pons giving up exactions which his men, probably those from nearby castles, were levying on an allod of the same abbey—dues in the form of levies in wine, bread, and pigs, which were probably such *albergos* or *receptas*.[145]

In the Lodève region near the abbey of Gellone, where castles were also common, we hear of a place in 930 which is called *"Malos Albergos,"*[146] surely a suggestive reference to such dues and the popular reaction to them. In the Albigeois whose many castles made it one of the more militarized parts of the Midi during this period, a charter issued by Raymond Pons in 936 mentions a variety of such exactions.[147] So does one of 942 in which Viscount Aton of Albi gives certain lands to Saint-Pons of Thomières—which, incidentally lumps such dues under the general term *potestatum*.[148] In 972 Countess Garsinde of Toulouse mentions similar rights of *"usaticos, tallias, et albergos"* which she has over land in this same region.[149] As we have already noted, we know of similar exactions levied from castles in the Limousin in 935[150] and of *receptas* owed the abbey of Beaulieu in 971.[151]

As might be expected, however, Catalonia, a land covered with castles, provides us with a good deal of evidence of such dues, many of which, no doubt, developed directly from those which were owed to Carolingian officials by *aprisio* holders and which were now taken over by those who controlled the fortresses of this region. In Ausona, whose government Count Guifred organized around its castles, as early as 899 we find a

---

[144] These services, *"circa, quarta et cavalcata,"* are said to be those which the *spani* (that is *aprisio* holders) are expected to render to constituted authorities.
[145] *Hist. Gén. de Lang.,* V, no. 57.
[146] *Cart. de Gellone,* no. 36.
[147] *Hist. Gén. de Lang.,* V, no. 67.
[148] *Ibid.,* no. 77.
[149] *Ibid.,* no. 125.
[150] *Cart. de Tulle,* no. 598.
[151] *Cart. de Beaulieu,* no. 50. Beaulieu, however, forbids laymen to be given *receptas* belonging to the abbey in this charter.

The Military System of the Midi and Catalonia 239

mention of such dues, which a charter calls *"obsequia et servicia."*[152] In a later document dating from the period 898–917 they were simply called *servicia*. In 913 a vicar of Count Miró's, who no doubt controlled one of the castles of the region, in attempting to levy them upon land belonging to Saint-Joan de les Abadesses, called them *"hostem et alium regale servicium."*[153] A charter from nearby Urgell dated 927 mentions a *receptum*,[154] and one of 942 speaks of *"tasca et servicium"* which were levied in the vicinity of the castle of Laiers.[155] By 957 similar dues are to be found in the frontier marches of Barcelona where castles had multiplied, for in this year Hennego, an important marcher lord, mentions the *rights* and *justice* he possesses in the territory of the castle of Arampuña.[156] Our best description of such dues though comes from a charter which Bishop Vivas of Barcelona gave to the inhabitants of his castle of Montmell in 974. In this charter, which is called a *pactum*, he gave special privileges to those who lived under the jurisdiction of this castle. They included not only a right to freely sell or exchange their land, but also exemption from any dues which might be levied on their houses, their pigs, their horses, their cattle, and their sheep.[157] By 975, then, throughout Catalonia and nearby Pallars and Ribagorça, it had become the custom for the *milites* of a castle to levy dues on the inhabitants of the surrounding countryside—dues, which, while originally Carolingian regalian ones, now pertained to a particular castle and those who owned and occupied it.

This leads us to our final question. Did this building of castles and the appearance of a class of professional *milites* who lived in them, and the dues and services levied in the counties of such fortresses, result in a spread of *mandamenta* throughout the Midi and Catalonia during this period? Did the castle and its surrounding territory begin to be a governing unit? We have already noted several cases for the late ninth century: one from Savoy and several from Ausona, in which this seems to have been the case. Now there can be little doubt that such *mandamenta* were beginning to appear in many more parts of Southern France and the Spanish March. In 928, for instance, we learn of land held in the "territory" of the castle of

---

[152] See Abadal, *Els Primers Comtes Catalans*, p. 88, on the duties which new inhabitants of Ausona were expected to render to constituted authorities. See also *Catalunya Carolingia*, II, 289–299.
[153] *El Archivo Condal de Barcelona*, nos. 8, 38, and appendix A.
[154] *Ibid.*, no. 92.
[155] *Ibid.*, no. 121.
[156] *Cart. de San Cugat*, no. 49.
[157] *Archivo Cathedral de Barcelona*, no. 24.

Garza, located in the county of Gap,[158] and about 970 a charter from Provence mentions land *"in termino de Castro Marigno," "in termino Castro Lambisco,"* and *"in termino Castro Petro Castellano."*[159] Even before Moslems had been expelled from Fraxinetum, Provence and neighboring regions were being divided into *mandamenta*.

We find a similar system in Aquitaine where a charter dated 930 from Quercy mentions *"Scalas castrum cum omni caslania."*[160] Another from Auvergne dating from 975 refers to land *"in territorio Castelluc."*[161] At about this same period we hear of land at Nîmes located *"in vicario Ariensi sub Castro Exunatis."*[162] Those rights of justice over neighboring regions possessed by the vicar who was castellan of the *castrum* of Sexago in Razès in 958 suggest the same kind of territory under the control of a castle.[163]

But again it is the Spanish March which makes clear how widespread this system had become by the year 975. Here along the entire frontier from Tarragona to Ribagorça, where castles were numerous, the castle had become the unit of government controlling its vicinity which was known as its *territorium*, its *appendicium*, or its *termino*. One could cite dozens of charters showing such an organization of land along these frontiers.[164] They make clear that here *mandamenta* already existed, in which vicars and others who served as castellans were exercising rights of government and exacting dues from the *homines* of their *castra* and the territory nearby.

We might sum up our conclusions concerning the military system of the Midi and Catalonia, then, as follows: between 900 and 975, as principalities disintegrated and the legal system of the Carolingians disappeared, almost everywhere a growing militarization took place. This was marked by a building of castles in every part of the Midi and Catalonia, the ap-

[158] *Cart. de Conques*, no. 431.
[159] *Cart. de Saint-Victor*, no. 23.
[160] *Cart. de Tulle*, nos. 14 and 290.
[161] *Cart. de Sauxillanges*, no. 376.
[162] *Cart. de Gellone*, no. 111.
[163] *Hist. Gén. de Lang.*, V, no. 104.
[164] See Abadal, *Els Primers Comtes Catalans*, pp. 87–88, on this system in Ausona after it was repopulated by Count Guifred. Among others see references in 921 to the *appendicii* of the castle of Besaura (*El Archivo Condal de Barcelona*, no. 67); or land which in 941 was located in the *appendicii* of the castle of Castelloi (*ibid.*, no. 129); or land said to be located in 955 *"in termino"* of the *castrum* of Cervello (*Cart. de San Cugat*, no. 40); or that which in 974 is located *"in termino"* of the *castrum* of Arampuña (*ibid.*, no. 103).

The Military System of the Midi and Catalonia

pearance in many regions of a special class of *milites*, and the levying of special dues near these castles to support the garrisons of *milites*. Finally in various regions this resulted in such castles and the territory becoming what one might already call *mandamenta* in which the castellan who controlled such a fortress began to exercise a certain independent jurisdiction or government of his own. The process was by no means complete by the year 975, except perhaps along the frontiers of the Spanish March and in Alpine regions of Provence. But it had begun, despite opposition to such *mandamenta* and the exactions they encouraged, in such regions as the Limousin, the Carcassonne area, and the Viennois. Nor had any uniform system yet been developed to own and to control such fortresses. But already in 975 the outlines of this new military system in the Midi and Catalonia are discernable, a military system which was to increase in importance in the decades which were to follow.

CHAPTER XIII

The Church (900–975)

FEW ASPECTS of society and government in the Midi have been dealt with by historians more cursorily and with less understanding than the Church during the first three quarters of the tenth century. Yet few have more importance. The picture which has generally been presented to us is one of a moribund, secularized, feudalized Church, preyed on by a rapacious aristocracy, and one which steadily deteriorated until it was rescued by the Cluny Reform movement and the Peace of God. Only one important study which deals with our region—Tenant de la Tour's examination of the Limousin—has registered a strong dissent from the prevailing opinion in showing a Church much healthier and more vital than most historians have been willing to believe existed.[1]

Curiously enough the prevailing picture of this Church which historians have given us seems to have been derived from an insufficient study of it. It has been arrived at by mixing together facts concerning this Church, which cover a period of more than two centuries, from late Carolingian times to the period of the Investiture struggle, and even more important by abstracting from this period a few examples of simony and lay control of the most glaring sort and considering them as typical. For the period from 900 to 975 such views seem to be in particular need of correction, and a more serious effort needs to be made to understand the organization, role, and importance of the Church, before they can be accepted as valid.

Let us begin by considering whether the Church in the Midi and Catalonia was moribund or vital and expanding during these years. Here we note at once a crucial factor. One of the more important facts concerning

[1] See G. Tenant de la Tour, *L'homme et la terre de Charlemagne à Saint Louis*, pp. 175–183, for an excellent account of the general growth and well-being of the Church in the Limousin during this century.

The Church (900–975)

the Church in these regions after 900, as before, is that it continued to grow and expand. One of the best indices of this growth is to be found in the number of new monasteries which were established and the number of old ones which were reformed and given new life. In Auvergne we find at least two such monasteries, Sauxillanges which was founded about 917 by Count William II of Auvergne[2] and Chanteuges to which Louis IV gave privileges about 941.[3] In nearby Velay we have Chamalières which seems to have been established or re-established about 933–937[4] at about the same time that Bishop Godeschalc of LePuy was reforming Saint-Chaffre.[5] In the Limousin there is Tulle which Ademar, viscount of Scalas, reconstituted about 930,[6] and which received privileges from King Raoul about 935.[7] In nearby Angoulême Count William of Angoulême and Count Bernard of Périgord appear to have restored the Abbey of Saint-Cybard[8] soon after Saint-Jean d'Angély was reformed and received a new charter from King Louis IV.[9] To the south of Aquitaine among the other new abbeys which were established the most important were Saint-Pons of Thomières founded near Narbonne by Count Raymond Pons of Toulouse, which received royal privileges in 939,[10] and Sainte-Marie de Canon given to Lagrasse in 943.[11]

Gascony, where Carolingian efforts to establish a vital Church had ended in failure, presents a particularly important example of Church growth during this period. New abbeys and rebuilt churches became the order of the day, particularly in eastern Gascony near the borders of Périgord, the Toulousain, and Carcassonne-Razès. At the turn of the century, according to a somewhat later source, Gascony was a land in which the *civitates* and churches like Auch had been reduced to ruins.[12] Yet by 920 a beginning was made of reconstituting the archbishopric of Auch with the assistance of Count William García of Fézensac.[13] Some two decades

[2] *Cart. de Sauxillanges*, no. 146.
[3] *Cart. de Brioude*, no. 338, and *Hist. Gén. de Lang.*, V, no. 75.
[4] The first charters of the *Camalarium de St. Egidius* date from the 930's. They record gifts of very small pieces of land to this establishment (*Cartularium conventus St. Egidii Camaleriarum* [LePuy], ed. H. Fraisse, nos. 113, 115, 168, 259, 290 [hereafter cited as *Cart. de Saint-Egidius*]). Perhaps this house was a revitalized one during this period rather than a completely new foundation.
[5] *Hist. Gén. de Lang.*, V, no. 70. See the charter of the Pope confirming its privileges in *Cart. de Saint-Chaffre*, no. 375.
[6] *Cart. de Tulle*, nos. 14, 290.
[7] *Ibid.*, no. 598.
[8] *Ademar de Chabannes*, III, 24, p. 145.
[9] *Cart. de Saint-Jean d'Angély*, no. 1.
[10] *Hist. Gén. de Lang.*, V, nos. 73, 74.
[11] *Cart. de Carcassonne*, II, 222–223.
[12] *Cart. d'Auch*, no. 77.
[13] *Ibid.*, no. 55.

later, about 940, the abbey of Lézat was founded by a viscount of Lautrec[14] and in 945 a certain Raymond, who was probably count of Bigorre, gave land and privileges to the new abbey of Saint-Savin.[15] In 954 the nearby abbey of Saint-Martin de Lez was important enough to receive a charter from the Pope,[16] while a little later, perhaps about 970, Count Bernard of Périgord restored the abbey of Saint-Sour de Geniac by returning it to its abbot.[17] In a region in which the Church had been in a decline since the time of Louis the Pious, we suddenly find it growing and expanding —though not in Western Gascony, which still was not much affected by this revival.

In the Valley of the Rhone the same tendencies seem to have been at work. The monastery of Ainay in the Lyonnais begins to show new life.[18] So does Saint-Barnard de Romans which in 908 was reformed and rebuilt by Archbishop Alexander of Vienne.[19] We hear of a new church or abbey of Saint-Vincent near Grenoble,[20] and of the priory of Saint-Michael de la Cluse in Maurienne about 950.[21] In Provence and neighboring regions Cluny's influence in revitalizing monastic establishments can be seen in the gift of the priory of Saint-Sernin de Port of Arles to this establishment by Archbishop Gerald in 945,[22] as well as a very similar gift of the abbey of Saint-Armand in 958.[23]

The Spanish March presents an equally revealing picture of the foundation of new monasteries, particularly in regions close to the Moslem frontiers where there had been few such establishments in the previous century. In 922 the new abbey of Amer received a royal charter from Charles the Simple,[24] and in 944 the *cella* of Saint-Peter of Rhodes in Perelada was raised to the status of an independent monastery and given royal privileges too.[25] A year later in 945 two new nunneries were estab-

[14] *Hist. Gén. de Lang.*, IV, 126–128, 488–489.
[15] *Ibid.*, V, no. 84.
[16] *Ibid.*, V, no. 97.
[17] *Cart. de la Réolle*, no. 171.
[18] For gifts of land to Ainay during this period see "Cart. d'Ainay," nos. 2, 138, 169, 192, in *Cartulaire de l'abbaye de Savigny, suivi du petit cartulaire de l'abbaye d'Ainay*, ed. A. Bernard.
[19] *Cart. de Saint-Barnard de Romans*, no. 6.
[20] *Cart. de Grenoble*, no. 11.
[21] *Chartes de Maurienne*, no. 5.
[22] *Hist. Gén. de Lang.*, V, no. 81.
[23] *Chartes de Cluny*, II, no. 1052.
[24] *Catalunya Carolingia*, II, 379–380.
[25] *Ibid.*, pp. 226–228.

lished in the Spanish March to join their sister house of Saint-Joan de les Abadesses. One of them, San-Pedro de les Puellas, was founded near Barcelona by the bishop and the count and countess of Barcelona,[26] while the other, the nunnery of Burghals, was established in Pallars by Count Isarn.[27] At about this same period Counts Borell and Miró of Barcelona also established the abbey of Montserrat in a castle very close to the frontier,[28] and a decade or so later we hear of two other new abbeys in this part of Barcelona: Santa Maria de Castelfels[29] and San Felix de Guixolds.[30]

What does this all mean? It shows clearly that the Church in the Midi and Catalonia during this period was anything but moribund. New, restored, and reformed abbeys and nunneries which were the result of the joint efforts of churchmen and prominent lay nobles are the symbol everywhere of a revived and more vital Church life and Church organization. In some regions like Gascony and the Valley of the Rhone they even represent a movement in regions which had not known such interest in the Church for more than a century. In others the trend was but a continuation of progress in this respect which had not appreciably slackened since the ninth century. Everywhere what stands out is the fact that the Cluny Reform movement was not an isolated development, but part of a larger Church reform which affected every part of Southern France and the Spanish March. Cluny merely represents the most spectacular example of renewed interest in a reformed, revitalized monasticism.

Still a second indication of vitality is to be found in the expansion of the holdings of abbeys and cathedral churches during these years in every part of Southern France and Catalonia. Such an increase in Church endowments is another index of an interest in the Church by lay society which, of course, provided the abbeys and churches with the gifts of land, both large and small, that made up their holdings. One cannot examine the record of the hundreds of gifts of land to abbeys like Sauxillanges and Brioude[31] in Auvergne; Conques in Rouergue;[32] Tulle and Beaulieu in

[26] *Archivo Catedral de Barcelona*, no. 22.
[27] *Hist. Gén. de Lang.*, V, no. 82.
[28] *Catalunya Carolingia*, II, 256–257.
[29] *Cart. de San Cugat*, no. 89.
[30] *Catalunya Carolingia*, II, 202–204.
[31] *Cart. de Sauxillanges* contains more than a hundred charters showing gifts of lands to the abbey in this period. Some six score charters show the growth of Brioude's landed endowment during this period (See the *Cart. de Brioude* and the *Grand Cart. de Brioude*).
[32] For Conques for the period 900–938 see some forty charters (*Cart. de Conques*, nos. 5, 6, 7, 22, 24, 91, 92, 107, 112, 115, 116, 121, 124, 128, 143, 144, 157,

the Limousin;[33] Saint-Chaffre in Velay,[34] Saint-André-le-Bas in Viennois;[35] Aniane and Gellone[36] near Melgueil; or Montolieu, Lagrasse, and Saint-Hilaire[37] in Western Septimania without being impressed by this regard for monasteries. Ripoll, Saint-Joan de les Abadesses, Cuxa, and San-Cugat[38] are equally impressive when we consider Catalonia. We find a similar expansion of Church domains when we examine the holdings of cathedral churches in Vienne, Nîmes, Béziers, Narbonne, Elne, Angoulême, and Limoges.[39]

161, 177, 182, 185, 200, 208, 220, 230, 231, 251, 262, 291, 306, 321, 322, 343, 352, 357, 391, 406, 432). Charters from the period 939–975 show an even greater growth of the abbey's domains.

[33] For Tulle see *Cart. de Tulle*, nos. 12, 14, 15, 16, 59, 60, 62, 90, 108, 109, 124, 125, 126, 183, 184, 185, 208, 226, 228, 229, 249, 262, 283, 285–286, 289, 301, 304, 305, 317, 345, 387, 396, 397, 417–419, 428, 458, 469, 472, 473, 480, 487, 520, 529, 530, 532, 536, 537, 556, 561, 565–568, 587, 591, 592, 597, 598, 599, 641, 781. For the record of more than a hundred gifts of land to Beaulieu in this period see the *Cart. de Beaulieu*.

[34] For the growth of Saint-Chaffre's landed endowment see *Cart. de Saint-Chaffre*, nos. 54, 75, 76–78, 80–81, 84–85, 87–88, 92, 94, 103, 106, 109, 112, 114, 115, 117, 119–121, 125–126, 129, 168, 243, 276, 277, 288, 294, 299, 305, 312, 316–317, 322, 323–325, 328, 331, 332, 334, 336, 340, 343, 345, 346, 375.

[35] See *Cart. de Saint-André-le-bas*, nos. 5, 15, 18, 39, 43, 49, 63, 64, 84, 90, 97–98, 99–100, 102–103, 104, 105, 111, 112, 116, 119, 122–123, 128, 130, 131–132, 133–135, 139, 141, 145, 245.

[36] For Aniane's growth see *Cart. d'Aniane*, nos. 42, 218, 245, 253, 281, 285, 316. For the increase in Gellone's domain see *Cart. de Gellone*, nos. 9, 12, 26, 30, 36, 41, 72–73, 74, 111, 117, 280–281, 420.

[37] For property accumulated by Montolieu see *Cart. de Carcassonne*, I, 74–77, 195, 253–254 and especially the charter of Pope Agepitus dating from 950 which lists all the abbey's holdings (*Cart. de Carcassonne*, I, 78). A complete list of Lagrasse's extensive domain in this period is to be found also in a charter of Pope Agepitus dating from 951 (*Cart. de Carcassonne*, II, 224–225). For Saint-Hilaire's holdings see *Cart. de Carcassonne*, V, 61; *Hist. Gén. de Lang.*, V, no. 53; and Cros-Meyrévielle, *Documents*, nos. 28, 29.

[38] See R. de Abadal i de Vinyals, *Els Primers Comtes Catalans*, pp. 271–278 for the growth of Ripoll during this period; also the charter of Louis IV, dating from 938, in *Catalunya Carolingia*, II, 159–165. *El Archivo Condal de Barcelona* records more than eight score gifts and additions of land to the nunnery of Saint-Joan during this period. See an exact and revealing analysis of Cuxa's growth in P. Ponsch, "Le domaine foncier de Saint-Michel de Cuxa au IXe, X[e] et XIe siècles," in *Études Roussillonnaises*, II (1952). Some two hundred charters record additions to San-Cugat's domains during these years (see the *Cart. de San Cugat*).

[39] See *Cart. de Vienne*, nos. 14, 19–21, 23, 26, 28, 30, 111, 113, 114, 115, 239, for the growth of Vienne. Charters of this period show extensive additions to the domains of the church of Nîmes (*Cart. de Nîmes*, nos. 10, 13–15, 18–19, 22–30,

Unfortunately few special studies of the property accumulated by individual churches and abbeys have been made which concern this period with one exception, that of Cuxa in Confluent.[40] A cursory and incomplete examination of these charters, however, is enough to show one that most of their land was located in regions fairly close to the abbey or church in question. This seems to be particularly true of the church establishments of Auvergne, the Limousin, the Albigeois, Velay, Dauphiny, the Lyonnais, and Provence,[41] most of whose property could probably be included in a circle drawn forty or fifty miles or less about the establishment in question. If property was acquired which was more distant, it was generally exchanged with another religious establishment or even a lay landowner.[42] In a few cases in this period, however, we begin to find important abbeys following the example of Cluny and not only acquiring but also keeping possession of property which was relatively far away, like that in the Gap region of Provence given to Conques in 928.[43] In this

---

34–41, 43–44, 46, 48–49, 53–58, 60–63, 65, 67–69, 71). For Béziers see *Cart. de Béziers*, nos. 12–13, 17–18, 25–28, 31, 34–36; and for Narbonne see *Hist. Gén. de Lang.*, V, nos. 38, 46, 51, 104–105, *Cart. de Carcassonne*, II, 226, and *Cartulaire de la seigneurie de Fontjoncouse*, ed. G. Mouynes, in *Bulletin de la commission archéologique et littéraire de Narbonne*, I (1877), no. 6. For Elne see *Hist. Gén. de Lang.*, V, nos. 60, 62, 72, 76, 83, 105, and *Cart. roussillonnais*, no. 8; and for the church of Barcelona see *Archivo Cathedral de Barcelona*, nos. 20–24. *Cart. d'Angoulême*, nos. 3, 27, 29, 33, 41, 43, 52, 57, give information about Angoulême. See the extensive growth of Limoges church's lands as recorded in *Cart. de Saint-Etienne de Limoges*, nos. 6, 9, 10, 14, 16, 17, 19, 26, 31, 32, 39, 41, 42–43, 44, 45, 104, 108, 144–145, 146, 148, 150–152, 153, 157, 163.

[40] Ponsch, "Le domaine foncier de Saint-Michel de Cuxa."

[41] Examination of the *Cart. of Brioude* and the *Grand Cart. de Brioude* shows that most of this abbey's property is located in the general area of Auvergne. See *Cart. de Tulle*, *Cart. de Beaulieu*, *Cart. de Saint-Etienne de Limoges*, *Cart. d'Uzerche*, and *Cart. de Vigeois* for the local nature of most of the holdings of the Limousin abbeys and churches. In the Albigeois the *Cart. de Conques* and *Cartulaire de Vabres*, ed. A. Molinier, in *Hist. Gén. de Lang.*, II, emphasize that most of these abbeys' domains are nearby; and the *Cart. de Saint-Chaffre* and *Cart. de Saint-Egidius* make the local pattern of holdings in Velay obvious. In addition to the localism revealed in Dauphiny by an examination of the *Cart. de Grenoble*, see that shown when one examines the *Cart. de Saint-Barnard de Romans*, *Cart. de Saint-André-le-bas*, and *Cart. de Vienne*. See also the same pattern in the *Cart. de Savigny and Ainay* in the Lyonnais, and of the *Cart. de Saint-Victor* (nos. 1, 23, 107, 1041) in Provence.

[42] For examples of such exchanges during this period see *Cart. de Saint-Chaffre*, no. 85; *Chartes de Maurienne*, no. 5; and *Cart. de Béziers*, nos. 32, 34, 38. For exchanges of land on an even more local level see *Cart. de Nîmes*, nos. 45, 59.

[43] *Cart. de Conques*, no. 431.

respect the holdings of the great abbey of Lagrasse, as revealed in charters given this monastery by Charles the Simple in 908[44] and Pope Agepitus in 951[45] are of particular interest. They show that the domains of this abbey were located near Carcassonne, in Razès, in the Toulousain, in the Narbonne area, in the Albigeois, in Rouergue, in Besalu, in Urgell, in Roussillon, in Ausona, in Gerona, and in Barcelona, thus covering a tremendous area of the Midi and Catalonia. Montolieu's holdings, as shown in charters of the period, were almost as extensive.[46] Even Gellone, which was still a monastery with a relatively small domain, possessed considerable property in Rouergue at some distance from its central abbey.[47] Though we are far from the situation we find in the next century when monasteries like Conques and Saint-Victor of Marseille, to mention only two prominent ones, owned land all over Southern France, abbeys were beginning to expand their holdings beyond their local regions and to assume an importance which Cluny had already achieved.

In previous chapters we have pointed out how this growing Church continued, down to 950, to rely upon royal charters and privileges to protect its rights, and it is clear that new abbeys in particular sought such privileges whether it be in Catalonia, the Narbonnaise, Septimania, or Aquitaine.[48] We have also pointed out how after 950 more and more reliance began to be placed on Papal protection in most regions of the Midi and Catalonia, and how the influence of Cluny, another outside power, steadily increased, particularly in Auvergne and the Valley of the Rhone. As royal protection became less helpful then, the Church now often turned to the distant Papacy and nearby Cluny to gain the protection

[44] *Hist. Gén. de Lang.*, V, no. 34.
[45] *Cart. de Carcassonne*, II, 224–225.
[46] See the list of Montolieu's holdings in Raoul's charter of 932 (*Hist. Gén. de Lang.*, V, no. 56) and that of Pope Agepitus in 951 (*Cart. de Carcassonne*, I, 78).
[47] *Cart. de Gellone*, no. 134.
[48] For examples in Catalonia see royal charters given to Catalonian abbeys like Amer in 922 (*Catalunya Carolingia*, II, 18–19), or San Cugat in 938 (*ibid.*, pp. 183–193), or Saint-Peter of Rhodes in 944 (*ibid.*, pp. 226–228), or Montserrat in 951 (*ibid.*, pp. 256–257), or Cuxa in 958 (*ibid.*, pp. 96–98). In the Narbonnaise note the royal charter given Saint-Jacques de Joucan in 900 (*Cart. roussillonnais*, no. 3), or Lagrasse in 908 (*Cart. de Carcassonne*, II, 219–220), or Montolieu in 932 (*Hist. Gén. de Lang.*, V, no. 56), or Saint-Pons de Thomières in 939 (*ibid.*, no. 73). See royal charter given to Psalmodi in Septimania in 909 (*Hist. Gén. de Lang.*, V, no. 37), and those given in Aquitaine to Tulle in 935 (*Cart. de Tulle*, no. 598), to Chanteuges in 941 (*Cart. de Brioude*, no. 338), or to Saint-Jean d'Angély in 942 (*Cart. de Saint-Jean d'Angély*, no. 1).

which Northern French monarchs were no longer able to provide.⁴⁹ Down to 975, however, neither of these two outside influences, Cluny or Rome, could really play a very important role in the Midi and Catalonia. We must therefore look elsewhere for the methods whereby the Church was able to survive in the turbulent world of the tenth century. We must look to the more local scene.

When we do so, we must again emphasize, that, with certain exceptions, the possessions of abbeys, their *abbatia*, to use a contemporary term, and the domains of cathedral churches tended to grow in regions close to their establishments. Such growth, of course, made these establishments, whether they willed it or not, important and powerful, and it made the bishops, abbots, and others, who controlled or shared in the control of them, important figures in the life of their local regions. What was the result of this? The most important result had already begun before the tenth century, the tendency of important church officials to be chosen from the ranks of the family which held secular authority over the region in which the archbishopric, bishopric, or abbey was located. In other words the tendency was for the Church to become part of the family system which controlled Southern France and Catalonia during these years.

We can see this tendency at work everywhere. In Provence by 950 the family of the viscounts of Marseille controlled the bishopric of this city in the person of Honoratius, brother of Pons and Guillaume, who were its viscounts.⁵⁰ In the Béziers region the bishopric of Béziers was under the control of the viscounts of the city, as revealed by the fact that Reginald, bishop of Béziers, was a brother of Viscount Boson and that in his will of 969 he emphasized such family connections.⁵¹ By the last years of the period a similar situation prevailed at Narbonne, judging from a charter of 966, which mentions the archbishopric as if it were almost the family possession of the viscounts who ruled this city.⁵² In the Toulousain Hugh, who was bishop of Toulouse and a member of the House of Toulouse-Rouergue, reveals in his will the same kind of close family ties,⁵³ while the choice of Frédélon as abbot of Vabres emphasizes the same kind of

---

⁴⁹ See Chapter I, Section IV, on the way the protectors of these abbeys changed during the tenth century.
⁵⁰ Bishop Honoratius is mentioned as the brother of Viscount William of Marseille in *Cart. de Saint-Victor*, no. 23.
⁵¹ *Hist. Gén. de Lang.*, V, no. 118.
⁵² *Ibid.*, no. 115.
⁵³ *Cart. de Saint-Sernin*, no. 280.

family connections.⁵⁴ By the middle of the century the viscounts of Albi appear to have controlled the bishopric of this city too, where Bernard was viscount and his brother Frotaire its bishop. ⁵⁵

In Aquitaine proper we find the same system in effect. In the Limousin, except for a brief interval, the family and relatives of the viscount of Limoges provided its bishopric with incumbents,⁵⁶ and several of the lay abbots of Beaulieu and Tulle were also chosen from important viscontal families of the region.⁵⁷ Gombard, bishop of Angoulême, seems to have been a member of the ruling family of Angoulême-Périgord,⁵⁸ just as Ebles, who was bishop of Limoges and abbot of Saint-Hilaire of Poitiers at mid-century, was a brother of the count of Poitou.⁵⁹ Bishop Etienne II of Auvergne was a scion of the viscontal House of Clermont,⁶⁰ and at least one abbot of Saint-Chaffre du Monastier in Velay, Dalmace, was of the viscontal family of LePuy.⁶¹ Already in the person of Bishop Isarn the secular counts of Gravaisdun were beginning to show a measure of control over the church of Grenoble.⁶²

We find a similar situation throughout Catalonia. The first abbesses of Saint-Joan de les Abadesses, Emma and Adelaise, were chosen from the comital family of Barcelona-Ausona,⁶³ just as Ermengardis, the first abbess

⁵⁴ *Hist. Gén. de Lang.*, V, no. 59.
⁵⁵ *Ibid.*, no. 102.
⁵⁶ Tenant de la Tour, *L'homme et la terre*, p. 254.
⁵⁷ See the charters of 945 which mention that Boson, a brother of the viscount of Aubusson, is serving as lay abbot of Tulle (*Cart. de Tulle*, nos. 285, 286). Or note that Dida, abbess of Saint-Marie de Limoges is a sister of Viscount Ademar of Limoges (*ibid.*, no. 428). Or see the mention of the fact that Viscount Ademar of Comborn is serving as an *avoué* of three churches (*Cart. de Saint-Etienne de Limoges*, no. 5). On the lay abbots of Beaulieu see the Introduction to the *Cart. de Beaulieu*, pp. cclii–cclxv.
⁵⁸ *Ademar de Chabannes*, III, 23, p. 144.
⁵⁹ *Ibid.*, III, 25, pp. 147–148.
⁶⁰ Bishop Stephen of Clermont is revealed as the son of Viscount Robert in a charter of 945 (*Grand Cart. de Brioude*, no. CCCXXXV). A little later we note a similar close relationship between Bishop Stephen II and Viscounts Robert and Amblard (*Cart. de Sauxillanges*, no. 179).
⁶¹ *Cart. de Saint-Chaffre*, no. 328.
⁶² On the kinship existing between Bishop Isarn of Grenoble (950–976) and the counts of Gravaisdun see *Cart. de Saint-Barnard de Romans*, no. 27; *Cart. de Saint-Chaffre*, no. 322; and *Cart. de Grenoble*, no. 16. See a similar kinship a little later as regards Bishop Humbert of Grenoble according to *Chartes de Cluny*, III, 2307, and *Cart. de Grenoble*, no. 118.
⁶³ Abbess Emma was the daughter of Count Guifred (*El Archivo Condal de*

The Church (900-975)   251

of Burghals was a daughter of Count Isarn of Pallars.⁶⁴ As the power of
the family of Cerdanya-Besalu increased toward mid-century we begin to
find them dominating the abbey of Cuxa and adding Ripoll to their family
interests by seeing that its abbots were chosen from members of their
house,⁶⁵ and even bringing Saint-Joan under their influence with the selection of Ranlo as abbess of this nunnery.⁶⁶ By 950 not only had this
family come to possess the important monasteries located in their counties
but even the powerful abbey of Lagrasse further to the north.⁶⁷ We are
well on our way toward the period when Bishop Oliba was to be a major
power in Catalonia and much of the Midi.

It must not be thought, however, that it was only through the selection
of members of a particular clan as bishops or abbots that family control
and interests in an abbey or bishopric were maintained during this period,
or that such influence was the monopoly of a single family in each region.
The larger monasteries and the cathedral churches of the Midi and Catalonia possessed other prizes available to neighboring families. These included such offices as that of deacon and *prepositus* which also carried with
them considerable authority. The *prepositi* of the great abbeys of the
Limousin, for instance, seem to have been the monopoly of the leading
noble families of this region.⁶⁸ They seem to have been important posts in
Auvergne also, where again and again our documents show us leading
landholding families represented in the administration of abbeys like
Brioude and Sauxillanges⁶⁹ through representatives who hold such offices.

Barcelona, no. 38). Adelaise who became the next abbess in 949 was a sister of
Count Borell of Barcelona.

⁶⁴ *Hist. Gén. de Lang.*, V, nos. 82, 84. See the kinship between Count Isarn
of Pallars and Bishop Otto who was his brother (*ibid.*, no. 95).

⁶⁵ Abadal, *Catalunya Carolingia*, II, 92–93, and *El Archivo Condal de Barcelona*,
no. 139.

⁶⁶ *El Archivo Condal de Barcelona*, nos. 132, 162.

⁶⁷ *Hist. Gén. de Lang.*, V, no. 94, and Cros-Meyréville, *Documents*, no. 22.

⁶⁸ Tenant de la Tour, *L'homme et la terre*, pp. 520–531.

⁶⁹ At Brioude, Eldefred, already *prepositus* before 900, still holds this position
in 907 (*Cart. de Brioude*, no. 228). In 909 he is called a *fidelis* of Duke William
and is still *prepositus* (*ibid.*, no. 51). Then in 912 our documents mention a new
prepositus called Arlebad. Charters of 916, 922, 923, and 926 show him still
occupying this office (*ibid.*, nos. 100, 76, 169, 112). In 926 he is called a bishop
(*ibid.*, no. 327) and is mentioned by Duke Acfred in his will of 927 as a *fidelis*
(*Grand Cart. de Brioude*, no. CCCCXXXIII). Meanwhile a certain Cunibert is
mentioned in a charter of 927 as *prepositus*. He seems to have held this office to
941 (*Cart. de Brioude*, nos. 86, 261, 338). He is called lay abbot in 930 (*ibid.*,
no. 213). Then in 942 and 950 our documents call him a deacon (*ibid.*, nos. 226,

252   *Failure of the Territorial State*

At Vienne the *prepositi* of the church seem to have been drawn from the members of the family of Ingelbert who assumed this position by almost hereditary right.[70] The church of Nîmes had similar officials drawn from the leading neighboring landholding families.[71] So did the abbeys and cathedral churches of Catalonia.[72] Given a share of church property as *precaria,* such *prepositi* formed an important element in family control of the Church in this period.

All of this seems to show that, as the Church continued to grow and to expand its holdings, it tended to become a power in its own right. It began to develop a bureaucracy of officials of its own, which involved not only the ruling noble families of various regions who controlled the offices of archbishop, bishop, and abbot, but also others who were drawn into it through positions which, though less important, still carried with them considerable authority and control over the domains belonging to church establishments. By 950, if not earlier, each important church establishment was controlled not by a *single* family, but by a group of families of neigh-

---

61). Then between 943 and 956 a certain Joseph serves as *prepositus* (*ibid.,* nos. 113, 124, 293, and *Grand Cart. de Brioude,* no. CCLXXXIII). He is succeeded in this year by a certain Robert who is still in office in 969 (*ibid.,* nos. 69, 83, 177, 189, 246). All of these men seem to have connections with important neighboring landholding families, as seen in these charters. And all seem able to survive the political changes which affected Brioude and Auvergne during this period (except Cunibert, who may have been a partisan of the House of Toulouse).

At Sauxillanges, quite late in this period, we find Eustorgus of the viscontal family of Clermont serving as *prepositus* (*Cart. de Sauxillanges,* nos. 340, 358, 363). See the mention of the gift that he and his brother gave to this abbey in 970 (*ibid.,* no. 441).

[70] A charter of 923 mentions at Vienne a certain Ingelbert who is called a *fidelis* of King Louis of Provence (*Chartes de Cluny,* I, no. 237). After the dynasties had changed in this region in 956 a charter mentions an Ingelbert (perhaps the same one) who is *prepositus* of the church of Vienne (*ibid.,* II, no. 1005).

[71] In 926 a certain Ansemir, of an unknown family, is mentioned as *prepositus* of Nîmes (*Cart. de Nîmes,* no. 29). In 929 another charter says that Frédélon, lord of Anduze is serving as *defensator* of the church (*ibid.,* no. 32). Meanwhile at about the same time a certain Almeradus is mentioned as *prepositus.* He is called deacon in 932 and is mentioned again in a charter of 960 (*ibid.,* nos. 35, 57, 58). Judging from his name Almeradus was a member of the Anduze family.

[72] See references to Deacon Miró of the family of Cerdanya-Besalu between 959 and 964 in *El Archivo Condal de Barcelona,* nos. 131, 144, 162. Abbot Gilmundo of San Cugat, also called deacon, was a member of the viscontal family of Barcelona (*Cart. de San Cugat,* no. 157). See also the interesting will of Deacon Sunifred in Roussillon dating from 967 (*Cart. roussillonnais,* no. 12). All these show that a number of noble families of Catalonia held important church offices.

The Church (900-975) 253

boring regions who shared in various degrees in the privileges and power which came from such churches and abbeys—either through church office or through *precaria* given them in return for their support.[73] It was not a feudal system which triumphed over the Church in this period, but a family system—one which involved more than a single family in the life of each church and abbey of the Midi and Catalonia.

As the Church grew and its organization and its property began to become entwined in the destinies of the leading ruling families of each region we begin to see some interesting results. The Church and its organization often began to take the place of secular political institutions in a rather curious way. As important noble families, like the Houses of Auvergne and Toulouse-Rouergue, found, for instance, that their subordinates or supporters tended to transform property which they gave them into allods, and as their machinery of courts disappeared, and as their control over castles became more precarious, they began more and more to give such property to abbeys and churches, which could not alienate it as easily as secular supporters could and which they could control more easily. This practice seems clearly indicated by the wills of Raymond of Rouergue[74] and Garsinde of Toulouse,[75] who appear to be using the abbey in their region of the Midi as repositories for their property which could then be drawn on at a later time to provide *precaria* for their supporters without the danger of usurpation or alienation that would result if land were given them directly. Others seem to have followed suit. Like the Ottos of

[73] Note that in 948 the abbey of Saint-Barnard de Romans gave a *precarium* to Count Geilin (*Cart. de Saint-Barnard de Romans*, no. 21). Note also that in 950 the church of Vienne gave a *prestaria* to a certain Berilo (probably a viscount of Vienne) which his uncle had held before him (*Cart. de Vienne*, no. 20). In Auvergne, Arlebad, *prepositus* of Brioude, was given a *precarium* by this abbey in 926 (*Cart. de Brioude*, no. 327). A little later in 929 Cunibert, now *prepositus*, is also given a *precarium* by the abbey (*ibid.*, no. 261). In the Limousin Tulle gave the castle of Moncieux as a *prestaria* (*Cart. de Tulle*, no. 290), and gave lands to Viscount Foucher of Tulle in 947 (*ibid.*, no. 317) and gave a *prestaria* to Hugh and Iter in 949 (*ibid.*, no. 184). Note also the lands which Beaulieu granted to its *prepositus* Ranier between 954 and 967 (*Cart. de Beaulieu*, no. 70).

[74] Count Raymond I of Rouergue left property to Conques, Figeac, Aurillac, Beaulieu, Saint-Sernin, Vabres, Brioude, Aniane, Gellone, Saint-Salvador of Albi, and Moissac, and to the churches of Nîmes, Rouergue, Cahors, Agen, and Maguelonne, and a number of others (*Hist. Gén. de Lang.*, V, no. 111).

[75] Countess Garsinde gave property to a number of church establishments in Rouergue: to Saint-Pons of Thomières, Saint-Vincent of Castres, Aurillac, Gaillac, Conques, Vallmagne, Aniane, Vabres, Saint-Just and Saint-Paul of Narbonne, to the churches of Lodève, Béziers, Albi, and a number of others (*ibid.*, no. 126).

Germany in this same period, then, the nobles of the Midi made gifts to the Church as a method of keeping actual control of their property and power which would have been lost under any other method available to them.

We must regard the growth of property and influence among the abbeys and churches of the Midi, then, as in no small measure the result of a definite policy followed by ruling families in entrusting such religious establishments, which they dominated, with control over property that they expected to use in their own interest and that of their supporters. This may have resulted in a feudalized Church, but if so, it was a feudalism quite different from that generally ascribed to it by historians.

As the Church under this system more and more became the key to real power and authority in Southern France and Catalonia we begin to note another interesting development—the bishop who also serves as abbot of a monastery or series of monasteries, and so is able to command authority over a rather wide area. This phenomenon was not an entirely new one. In the late ninth century it was used, for instance, by Archbishop Frotaire.[76] But in the tenth century it became more widespread. Thus we find Bishop Ebles of Limoges not only serving as abbot of Saint-Hilaire of Poitiers but reaching out to control Saint-Martial of Limoges and a number of other abbeys in the Limousin.[77] We discover that Bishop Etienne II was not only abbot of Brioude and Conques but for a considerable period controlled Sauxillanges too.[78] Bishop Godeschalc of LePuy also served as abbot of Saint-Chaffre du Monastier.[79] The archbishops of Vienne controlled the *abbatia* of Saint-Barnard de Romans,[80] and the bishops of Grenoble the monastic establishments of their part of Dauphiny.[81] A Bishop Honoratius of Marseille, we learn, is also abbot of Saint-Victor of Marseille,[82] just as Bishop Bernard served as abbot of

---

[76] See Chapter III, Section III, on Frotaire's role throughout the Midi.

[77] *Ademar de Chabannes*, III, 25, pp. 147–148.

[78] Frontinus is mentioned as a bishop and as abbot of Brioude in 920 (*Cart. de Brioude*, no. 129). In 941 Bishop Etienne of Auvergne was also abbot of the same monastery (*ibid.*, no. 178). See references to his control over Sauxillanges in charters of 970, 971, and 974 in *Cart. de Sauxillanges*, nos. 356, 368, 639. For evidence of his control of Conques in 959 and 962 see *Cart. de Conques*, nos. 405 and 302.

[79] *Hist. Gén. de Lang.*, V, nos. 70 and 99.

[80] See *Cart. de Saint-Barnard de Romans*, no. 55, for a later example of this archepiscopal control of this abbey.

[81] *Cart. de Grenoble*, no. 11.

[82] *Cart. de Saint-Victor*, nos. 23, 29, 290.

The Church (900–975) 255

Aniane.[83] Even in Catalonia we find that Arnulf, bishop of Gerona was also abbot of Ripoll.[84] An age in which a Bishop Oliba could simultaneously serve as abbot of both Ripoll and Cuxa,[85] and an Archbishop Burchard could use such authority to dominate the Lyonnais was already dawning. The ecclesiastical principality had become a reality in Southern France and to some extent in Catalonia.

So far in this chapter we have considered the growth of the Church and its organization almost completely in terms of important noble families of Southern France and Catalonia, who gave their land to religious establishments, and who came to dominate such churches and abbeys as archbishops, bishops, and abbots, or to become part of a church officialdom as *prepositi,* deacons, vicars, and the like. But what of the humbler members of society—those less important families who were not able to share, as the *principes* and *majores* could do, in a governing system which used the Church as an organization instead of the dying secular institutions of the period? Here again we notice an interesting fact. Our sources show that these humble folk too gave their land in large amounts to religious establishments. What they seem to be seeking is not political power or advantage in doing so, but rather protection in a society which offered them little security. The property which they gave, judging from our records, was often received expressly as a usufruct for members of their family for one or more lifetimes, upon payment of a *cens* of generally modest proportions. Perhaps it was even understood that this would continue to be so even after the time specified by the donor in making the gift. But whatever method was used, religious establishments like San-Cugat, or Saint-Joan de les Abadesses, Gellone, or Beaulieu, or Brioude, or Savigny, or Saint-André-le-Bas,[86] as a result of such gifts, began to

[83] *Cart. d'Aniane,* no. 316.
[84] *El Archivo Condal de Barcelona,* no. 139.
[85] See an excellent example of the control of a number of abbeys and a bishopric by one man in the career of Oliba in R. de Abadal i de Vinyals, *L'abat Oliva, bisbe de Vic, i la seva època.*
[86] For examples of such small holdings given to the abbey of San-Cugat in this period see *Cart. de San Cugat,* nos. 7, 11–14, 16–19, 21–22, 24, 26–27, 31–33, 35–37, 39–44, 46, 48, 50, 53–55, 61–64, 74–75, 78, 80–86, 91–93, 95–97, 101–103, 110–111. All seem to represent *allods* whose owners often received them back from the abbey as benefices for which they and their posterity paid a regular *cens* or *tasca.*
For some examples of similar small holdings given to the nunnery of Saint-Joan in the year 908–918, all of them *aprisiones* located in the valley of Vallfogena, see *El Archivo Condal de Barcelona,* nos. 22–29, 31–32, 34, 36–37, 40–46, 48,

build up an acreage of land occupied by humble landowners who had exchanged the dangerous position of independent allodial ownership for the protection which a light fiscal yoke of a *cens* or *tasca* to a church or abbey made available to them. In doing so they not only swelled the property of such establishments in Southern France and Catalonia but they increased Church authority too, just as gifts by more important land owning families had done. The ecclesiastical principality in Southern France and the Spanish March was becoming a reality at the very moment when the secular principality had become an impossibility.

How were such large ecclesiastical principalities administered? It seems clear that the principal officials who were used, whether they be called *prepositi* or vicars or *judices*[87] or even the humble *portarii* were rewarded by being given lands in the form of *precaria*[88] or by being given rights over church property in the form of a share of the court fines or other dues owed to the particular church establishment. Often such lands or rights were held "*in obedientia*"[89] to an abbey or a cathedral church and

---

50–52, 54, and 57. Similar small holdings were given Gellone usually with the proviso that the donor and his heirs have the usufruct of this land (*Cart. de Gellone*, nos. 36, 41, 73, 74, 117).

Cart. de Beaulieu, nos. 67, 70, 73, 74, 96, 106, 126, 129, 139, 143, 148, 149, show other examples of small gifts. In general, however, most property which was given to Beaulieu and other abbeys in the Limousin was larger in extent than the holdings mentioned above. The *Cart. de Brioude* shows that more than 90 per cent of the property this abbey acquired in this period was in the form of small holdings. For similar gifts to Savigny see *Cart. de Savigny*, nos. 28, 33–37, 44, 46, 55, 57, 59, 70, 76, 100, 118–119, 158, 201, 320; and to Saint-André-le-Bas see *Cart. de Saint-André-le-bas*, nos. 39, 43, 84, 102, 116, 123, 129, 130, 131, 136, 138, 139, 141.

[87] See notes 68–70 and references to a *prepositus* at Gellone in a charter of 939 (*Cart. de Gellone*, no. 420), and at Angoulême in 918 according to *Cart. d'Angoulême*, no. 2. There is a mention of the *vicaria* of Saint-André at Gellone, according to the charter of 939 (*Cart. de Gellone*, no. 420). A charter of 934 mentions a vicar at Vabres in 934 (*Hist. Gén. de Lang.*, V, no. 59), and at Conques in the same year (*Cart. de Conques*, no. 155). Still another mentions two vicars at Périgord in 964 (*Cart. de Paunat*, no. 15). *Judices* are mentioned at Nîmes in 928, as serving at a session of a court (*Cart. de Nîmes*, no. 32). A similar mention of them is to be found at Carcassonne in 908 (*Hist. Gén. de Lang.*, V, no. 33). Quite different however are those *judices* which a charter of 971 mentions at Beaulieu. They seem to be administrative officials of the abbey (*Cart. de Beaulieu*, no. 50).

[88] See note 73.

[89] A charter of 913 from Beaulieu mentions land which a certain Ratbad holds "*ad obedientiam*" (*Cart. de Beaulieu*, no. 89). One of 939 from San Cugat men-

The Church (900–975)

even minor officials took an oath of *fidelitas* to an abbey like that required of the *judices* whom we find mentioned at Beaulieu in 971.[90] Their *precaria* and offices were still restricted in most cases to one lifetime during this period,[91] but there was certainly a tendency for them to become hereditary, particularly those which were given to magnates, such as the control of castles either as outright fiefs or as *guardas*[92] for a more limited period of time. Thus we find a promise given to the *"judices servum"* of Beaulieu that if they stayed loyal their sons would inherit their offices,[93] and we see *precaria* renewed by a church like that of Saint-Maurice of Vienne for a certain Berilo, perhaps of the old viscontal family, which his uncle had held before him.[94] What evidence we possess, however, seems to indicate that those who received *precaria* from church establishments, whether they held office or not in this period, were expected to pay a *cens* in return for them, like that owed the abbey of Tulle by Viscount Bernard of Turenne, its *defensor*, for the castle of Scalas and its *caslania*,[95] or the *"dominatio et servitia"* which Bishop Isarn of Grenoble kept over the castles that he allowed nobles to build in Dauphiny soon after 950.[96] Down to 975 the *precaria* which were used by ecclesiastical establishments to pay their officials or to bind leading landowners to them still seem to be *fiscal* in essence rather than military in nature. They established a mild seignorial yoke—that is all; which is probably the reason why their holdings continued to grow during this period.

There remains the important question of how well such an ecclesiastical system worked. Down to 975, as far as we can tell, its seems to have proved a rather effective substitute in most regions for a decaying system

---

tions land held *"in tua subdicione ac senioraticone"* (*Cart. de San Cugat*, no. 17). Brioude, however, furnishes the most numerous examples. A charter of 922 mentions land held *"in servaticione"* and *"per obedientiam"* (*Cart. de Brioude*, no. 30). One of 929 mentions land held *"in ministerio et in fidelitate"* (*ibid.*, no. 261). Others in 939 and 947 mention land held *"in ministerio"* (*ibid.*, nos. 46, 140); or in 964, 967, and 970 land held *"in obedientia"* (*ibid.*, nos. 177, 205, 147).

[90] *Cart. de Beaulieu*, no. 50.
[91] Sometimes rather emphatically, as is revealed by a charter in which the abbot of Tulle gives land in 947 to the viscount of Limoges. He says he does so *"sed in vita sua solummodo"* (*Cart. de Tulle*, no. 317).
[92] For the history of the castle of Moncieux, given out as a *precarium*, see *ibid.*, no. 290.
[93] *Cart. de Beaulieu*, no. 50.
[94] *Cart. de Vienne*, no. 26.
[95] *Cart. de Tulle*, no. 290.
[96] *Cart. de Grenoble*, no. 16.

of secular, family-controlled principalities. True there were abuses, particularly in regions where castles were numerous and a fighting aristocracy was becoming a powerful element in the population. Here the rather sinister figure of the lay abbot—whether it be a Count William II controlling Brioude,[97] a Begon ruling Conques,[98] or a Bernard of Turenne dominating Tulle,[99] or an Aimery in charge of Saint-Martial of Limoges[100] presented a problem for which there was no easy solution. No doubt also there were serious abuses which were the result of family control over abbeys and churches at Marseille, Béziers, Narbonne, and in regions controlled by the House of Toulouse-Rouergue.[101] Yet it is possible to overestimate the seriousness of such abuses. The continued growth of the domains of church establishments throughout the period and the evidence of continuing efforts to reform monasteries bid us take care before we assume that secularization of a brutal sort was the lot of the Church in the Midi and Catalonia. In general familial control of the Church was a mild yoke which was by no means unenlightened and which was not incompatible with either real religious life or intellectual vigor. The career of Gerbert, who got his early training at Aurillac, and evidence of the abbey of Cuxa's intellectual interests in this period, bid us be careful before we assume that a brutal secularization resulted from the rather unusual way in which the abbeys and cathedral churches of the Midi and Catalonia functioned during this period.[102] Cluny's influence spread, for example, not because of the poor state of Church discipline, but because thoughtful churchmen and laymen like Etienne, bishop of Auvergne,[103] or Gerald,

---

[97] A charter of 917 mentions Count William II for the first time as rector of Brioude (*Cart. de Brioude*, no. 318). In the next year he is said to have it under his protection (*ibid.*, no. 66).

[98] See how Begon exploited the abbey of Conques according to a charter of 962 (*Cart. de Conques*, no. 302).

[99] On how Bernard of Turenne acted as *defensor* of Tulle and particularly on how his successor Viscount Archimbaud of Comborn refused to pay the abbey a *cens* for his *precaria* see *Cart. de Tulle*, no. 290. After this period Tulle seems to have given out most of its land as *precaria* to the nobles of the surrounding region.

[100] *Ademar de Chabannes*, III, 29, p. 150.

[101] *Hist. Gén. de Lang.*, V, nos. 111, 126.

[102] On this see L. Nicolau d'Oliver, "Gerbert y la cultura catalana del siglo X," in *Estudis Universitaris Catalans*, IV (1910).

[103] Bishop Etienne is called the *defensor* of lands given to abbeys in Auvergne (*Cart. de Sauxillanges*, nos. 368, 639). See also his efforts to keep peace in this region in 972 with the help of the bishops of Périgord and Cahors and the nobles of Central France (*Cart. Saint-Flour*, no. 1).

archbishop of Aix,[104] or King Conrad of Burgundy-Provence[105] were interested in making a vital, growing Church a more disciplined one. Without that widespread feeling, which in itself was a reflection of the strength and the health of the Church, the example of Cluny would have been meaningless.

Nevertheless one fundamental problem remained by the year 975 which was to clamor for attention in the next decades. This was the problem of how the abbeys and bishoprics of the Midi and Catalonia were to cope with the new class of professional *milites* in the castles which were everywhere being built—even by the Church itself. It was one thing for the Church to accommodate itself to a family control through the choosing of archbishops, bishops, abbots, and *prepositi* from the ranks of the leading families of a region, and to reward such families and officials by grants of *precaria* or fiefs, or castle guard, which were in theory for a lifetime only, even if they were often in practice hereditary and renewable. It was something else for it to accommodate itself to the warriors of a castle who levied tribute on the surrounding territory, whatever their rights over it were, and who were rapidly transforming such *caslania* or *territoria* into *mandamenta*. Here lay the challenge to Church establishments which could not reconcile their older system of milder *fidelitas* or *obedientia* accompanied by *fiscal* lordship with the harsher militarism which emanated from such castles and the *milites* who now occupied them. No wonder Beaulieu forbade its *judices* to become *milites*[106] or that the castle of Brézac in the Limousin which was oppressing local monks was torn down.[107] No wonder too that the monkish scribe of the church of Vienne noted in a charter that 965 was the year when Queen Matilda destroyed the castle of Mont Burton.[108] The new age dawning for the Church and society in Southern France and the Spanish March was one of castle and *milites* in which the Church in particular was to suffer until Peace and Truce of God were established to hold in check the new class of *milites*,

---

[104] See his gift of the priory of Saint-Sernin de Port to Cluny in 945 (*Hist. Gén. de Lang.*, V, no. 81).

[105] See King Conrad's confirming of the privileges and lands of Saint-Chaffre, *circa* 950 (*Cart. de Saint-Chaffre*, no. 322); and his confirmation of Cluny's privileges in 943 before an assembly of all the *"vassi majores et minores"* of his realm (*Chartes de Cluny*, I, no. 622).

[106] *Cart. de Beaulieu*, no. 50.

[107] *Ademar de Chabannes*, III, 29, p. 150.

[108] *Cart. de Vienne*, no. 28.

and the Investiture controversy and First Crusade brought a new and different era to the Church.

We might sum up our conclusions regarding the Church in the Midi and Catalonia as follows. From 900 to 975 the Church as an institution was anything but moribund. It showed a power to expand, and a vitality so great that in many regions it became an institutional substitute for secular organization and government. In addition to its outside protectors, Cluny and the Papacy, it procured its support from important noble families who used it as a repository for their family influence and much of their family property. In turn it rewarded such families with important Church offices, a share of Church lands, and a share of Church revenues. It also gave protection on mild terms to smaller landholders. It kept a form of order in regions like Auvergne, Dauphiny, and the Limousin, where no order of any other sort could exist and, as a result, began to develop something which we might call Church principalities. Such principalities were secular, in part, in their interests and used mild and limited *precaria* of a *fiscal* sort as part of their system of administration and government, but they were not feudal in the classic sense of the word.

Toward the end of this period, however, abuses seem to have become more numerous. Family control, mutually advantageous to church establishments and ruling families, began to become simony and unscrupulous domination in some cases. Even more important the newer military system of castle and professional *milites* began to represent a problem with which the Church, as an institution, was not prepared to cope. This, however, was more a problem of the years after 975 than it was of the earlier period. For down to 975, as principalities disintegrated, royal influence disappeared, and castles grew more numerous throughout Southern France and Catalonia, it was the Church, as an institution, which provided what stability and order existed and which through its power and its organization bridged the gap between a dying Carolingian order and the new era which was being born.

CHAPTER XIV

The Society of the Midi and Catalonia

THE FIRST three quarters of the tenth century—when family-controlled principalities and political institutions were disintegrating, the Church was growing in power and influence, and a new military system based on castles and *milites* was making its appearance—was a difficult period of transition for the society of Southern France and Catalonia. This society found itself caught between a dying Carolingian world and a new, harsher age in the process of being born. How did it react to these changes, and in what form did it emerge by the year 975?

We might begin by reiterating that during this period land was still the basic form of wealth and power for every element on the scene, whether it was the old ruling families of this region, the Church, or the *milites* in the newly arising castles, or even the humbler peasant who dwelt on the soil and tilled it for himself and his betters. It was still a rural world of villages and farms covering a landscape which possessed only an occasional abbey, walled *civitas*, or newly built castle to break the monotony of the agrarian scene. In a few regions like the Spanish March or the Limousin castles were more numerous than elsewhere, but they were not yet the dominant feature of the landscape which they were to be later on.

Life was local and the economy had to be self-sufficient, even more so than in the late ninth century, for the slow growth of trade and commerce, which was beginning to affect Italy and other parts of Western Europe, had not yet reached this region. It remained an economic backwater with little close connection with the outside world, even though by 950 some such contacts were beginning.

In these rural, relatively isolated regions the prevailing system of landholding was still the allod, as far as secular society was concerned. Due to a larger volume of evidence, this can be said with even more assurance in this period than earlier. For in analyzing over 1,600 charters from every part of the Midi and Catalonia, representing transfer of land from individual landowners to Church establishments and other individuals, we discover an interesting fact. Only 4 per cent of such transfers represent land which was other than that owned outright as allods, a figure not appreciably greater than the 2 or 3 per cent which we found for the late ninth century. Let us examine our evidence as to how land was owned and held, however, in a little more detail to show exactly what emerges from a study of each part of Southern France and Catalonia.

We might begin by considering Aquitaine, the Toulousain, and Septimania. From Auvergne we have some 560 charters, which represent 287 transfers of property of small size (a field, a *mansus,* or the equivalent), some 94 transfers of medium-sized property, and some 62 representing large estates (a *villa,* a church, or the equivalent), with the rest indeterminable. Of these, 543 show us property which is allodial and only 17 land which is held in whole or in part conditionally or feudally—a ratio of nonallod to allod of 4 per cent.[1] For the Limousin-Quercy region we have a record of some 126 such transfers of land of which 37 seem to be small holdings, 26 property of medium size, 55 large holdings, and the rest indeterminate. All but 8, or some 6 per cent, are clearly allods.[2] For Angoulême-Périgord our information is less extensive, but we do have evidence of some 14 land transfers; 6 of which are small holdings, 2 medium-sized, and 6 large. All seem to be allods.[3] So are some 16 from Saintonge, Aunis, and lower Poitou which represent gifts of land made during this period to the abbey of Saint-Jean d'Angély.[4]

When we turn to the Rouergue-Albigeois region we find charters which refer to some 91 transfers of property, of which 42 represent large estates or holdings, 22 medium-sized, 24 smaller ones, and the rest indeterminate. Of these only 3 can be considered to be anything but allodial, or 3 per cent of the land in question.[5] For the Toulousain proper we have only

[1] These are from the *Cart. de Brioude,* the *Grand Cart. de Brioude, Hist. Gén. de Lang., Cart. de Sauxillanges, Cart. de Saint-Egidius, Cart. de Beaulieu, Cart. de Saint-Flour, Chartes de Cluny,* and *Cart. de Conques.*

[2] Represented are charters from the *Cart. de Tulle,* the *Cart. de Beaulieu, Cart. de Vigeois, Cart. d'Uzerche, Hist. Gén. de Lang., Cart. de Saint-Etienne de Limoges,* and *Ademar de Chabannes.*

[3] These come from the *Cart. d'Angoulême, Gallia Christiana, Cart. de Vigeois,* and *Cart. de Paunat.*

[4] All from the *Cart. de Saint-Jean d'Angély.*

[5] Represented are charters from the *Cart. de Conques,* the *Cart. de Vabres,* and *Hist. Gén. de Lang.*

The Society of the Midi and Catalonia 263

8 examples of such gifts of land, and only one of them is anything but an allod.[6] For eastern Septimania, from the Rhone to Béziers, we have more information. In examining charters which refer to some 95 transfers of land we find that 34 small, 32 medium-sized, and 24 large pieces of property are described, and the rest are indeterminate. Some 5 of these, or about 5 per cent, may represent nonallodial holdings. The rest are allods.[7] For the Narbonne-Carcassonne region the figures are 38 property transfers of which 18 are large estates, 12 medium-sized, and 5 smaller pieces of land with only 3, or 8 per cent, nonallodial.[8]

One of our best checks on the proportion of allodial to nonallodial land, however, comes from examination of property owned by members of the House of Toulouse, as shown in the wills of Count Raymond of Rouergue, Countess Garsinde of Toulouse, and Bishop Hugh of Toulouse. One would expect that in these wills a large proportion of the land referred to was feudal and was granted out as fiefs or *precaria* to their supporters. But what do we find? Of the 125 pieces of property which can be distinguished by an examination of these wills only 15, or 12 per cent, seem to be feudally held, and one of these is a fief or *feus* which, it is stated, is soon to become an allod.[9] The House of Toulouse, then, like other landowners of the Midi, is shown to have based its power and authority in this period on its allods and not on fiefs.

When we turn to the Valley of the Rhone and contiguous areas under the influence of the kingdom of Provence and its successor, the kingdom of Burgundy, we discover the same pattern of landholding. Examination of the record of some 44 transfers of land from the Lyonnais and Forez, of which 11 are of large-sized property, 16 medium-sized, and 13 small holdings, shows us only 4, or 9 per cent, are nonallodial.[10] For the region near Vienne we have charters describing the transfers of 41 small-sized, 9 medium-sized, and 15 large-sized pieces of land, and the rest indeter-

---

[6] From the *Hist. Gén. de Lang.*, the *Cart. de Saint-Sernin*, the "Cartulaire de Lézat" (unprinted), and the *Cart. de Carcassonne.*

[7] These charters are from the *Cart. de Nîmes, Cart. de Gellone,* "Cart. de Psalmodi" (unprinted), *Cart d'Aniane, Cart. de Maguelonne, Cart. de Béziers,* "Cart. de l'Évêché d'Agde" (unprinted), *Cart. d'Agde,* and *Hist. Gén. de Lang.*

[8] Included are charters from the *Cart roussillonnais; Hist. Gén. de Lang; Marca hispanica; Cart. de Carcassonne;* Cros-Meyrévielle, *Documents;* G. Catel, *Histoire des comtes de Toulouse;* and *Cart. de Fontjoncouse.*

[9] *Hist. Gén. de Lang.*, V, nos. 111, 126 and *Cart. de Saint-Sernin,* no. 280.

[10] From the *Cart. de Savigny,* "Cart. d'Ainay," in *Cart. de Savigny, Cart. de Saint-Chaffre, Chartes de Cluny,* and *Cart. Lyonnais.*

minate. Of these some 8, or 11 per cent, seem nonallodial.[11] For Dauphiny and Valence, out of some 45 properties which our records show were transferred—of which 16 seem to be small holdings, 12 medium-sized, and 14 large-sized—only 3, or 6 per cent, appear to be allodial.[12] The figure for nearby Velay and Vivarais is 77 transfers of land, 17 large, 24 medium-sized, and 35 small in size, with only one case which seems to be other than allodial.[13] For Provence during this period our information is scantier, but an examination of some 18 Provençal charters, most of them referring to transfers of large estates, reveals only allods.[14] For the Valley of the Rhone as a whole then, our figure is 6 per cent of the land nonallodial and 94 per cent allodial, which seems very close to the 5 per cent figure for the rest of the Midi.

Two other regions, Gascony and the Spanish March, still need to be examined. It is during this period that we get detailed information for the first time from charters on Gascony and its landholding system. These show us some 10 transfers of property taking place—all of property in Eastern Gascony near the Toulousain and Carcassonne-Razès. All concern allods only.[15] We have much more information concerning Pallars and Ribagorça and Catalonia proper. The exact figures for the former areas are not included here, but charters show us that 95 per cent of the land in these two counties was allodial.[16] For Catalonia an analysis of some 274 such transfers shows us 156 represent small holdings, 59 medium-sized ones, and 50 larger estates. Of these only 9, or some 3 per cent, can be considered other than allods[17]—a figure even less than that for the Midi as a whole.

Down to 975, then, despite the building of castles and the attempts of

[11] From the *Cart. de Saint-André-le-bas, Cart. de Vienne, Chartes de Cluny,* and *Cart. de Saint-Chaffre.*

[12] From the *Cart. de Saint-André-le-bas, Cart. de Saint-Barnard de Romans, Cart. de Grenoble, Chartes de Cluny,* and *Chartes de Maurienne.*

[13] From the *Cart. de Saint-Chaffre, Cart. de Saint-Egidius, Chartes de Cluny, Hist. Gén. de Lang., Cart. de Saint-Barnard de Romans,* and L. Albanes-Chevalier, *Gallia Christiana Novissima.*

[14] From the *Hist. Gén. de Lang., Chartes de Cluny, Cart. de Saint-Victor,* and Albanes-Chevalier, *Gallia Christiana Novissima.*

[15] From the *Cart. d'Auch,* "Cart. de Lézat" (unprinted), *Cart. de la Réolle,* and *Hist. Gén. de Lang.*

[16] See charters in Abadal, *Els Comtats de Pallars i Ribagorça.*

[17] These charters are from the *Hist. Gén. de Lang.*; *El Archivo Condal de Barcelona; Cart. de San Cugat; Marca hispanica;* J. Villanueva, *Viaje literario a las iglesias de España; Liber Feudorum; Cart. roussillonnais;* and *Archivo Catedral de Barcelona.*

some leading noble families to transform Carolingian benefices and allodial property into land carrying a feudal obligation, it seems clear from this analysis of privately held land that the allod still held its own and that the society of the Midi resisted all efforts to substitute for it other systems of landholding.

But the information about these land transfers is not the only evidence available to us about how the lay population held land. We have still another source of information which emphasizes the predominance of allodial ownership—contemporary reiteration in these same land-transfer charters that a man has a right *by law* to dispose of his property as he wishes. This strong statement seems to be found in charters coming from those regions where we have the most evidence of efforts to curb or modify allodial holdings. Thus in 931, at the height of the period when Raymond Pons was intervening in the Narbonnaise, a landowner in giving property to Saint-Hilaire states that the law allows a man to do with his property— *"de res suas proprias"*—what he wishes.[18] In 949 Arnald, who founded the House of Commignes, in a charter appeals to Roman and Salic law in the same fashion as giving him a right to turn over to the abbey of Montolieu land which he says he acquired from Count Hugh of the Toulousain house.[19] In 970, in giving away property which they owned in the Toulousain, Count Roger of Carcassonne and his wife reiterate this statement.[20] Nearby at Nîmes a certain Bligare in 956 similarly invokes his right by law to sell or exchange his property as he wishes—land which seems to have been originally a fief belonging to Viscount Bernard of Nîmes and his wife.[21] In 909 it is Roman law which is referred to by another landowner, Foucher, in giving to his wife a number of *villas* in Provence and elsewhere.[22]

We find the same resistence to nonallodial land in the very region of the Toulousain, Rouergue, and the Albigeois in which we find the House of Toulouse making use of fiefs. In 910, for instance, Senegunde and her son, Abbot Rudolf of Conques, state in a charter in which they give some land and some churches to the abbey of Conques that Roman law allows one to freely give away one's own property.[23] In 942 another charter from the Albigeois tells us how Raymond and Aimery make a grant to the

[18] *Hist. Gén. de Lang.*, V, no. 53.
[19] *Ibid.*, no. 89.
[20] Cros-Meyrévielle, *Documents*, no. 29.
[21] *Hist. Gén. de Lang.*, V, no. 100.
[22] *Chartes de Cluny*, I, no. 105.
[23] *Cart. de Conques*, no. 7.

bishopric of Albi and give as their right to do so the authority of Roman, Gothic, and Salic law.[24] In 943 a charter from Vabres dealing with another such gift is prefaced with the statement that the law of the emperors and the Church allows a man *"ex nobilis ortus"* to dispose of his property freely.[25] Still another charter dating from 970, in which land is given to the church of Saint-Sernin of Toulouse, mentions rights derived from Roman and Salic law.[26]

Documents originating from Auvergne contain similar declarations. One of them, dating from 944, at about the period of Toulousain intervention in this region, shows us a certain Arlulf giving an allod to his brother and stating that law gives him a right to dispose of his property as he wishes.[27] Another from about 970 contains a similar statement as regards a grant made to the abbey of Sauxillanges.[28] In the Limousin, where *precaria* and fiefs were relatively numerous, three charters which mention land given to Saint-Etienne of Limoges in 950, 968, and 970[29] invoke Roman law in exactly the same way. Though it is clear that by this period any accurate knowledge of the provisions of Roman law and Visigothic law had disappeared in most of the Midi, their memory was still effective and, along with Salic law, they were still being invoked as a protection of allodial rights in regions in which the fief, the benefice, and the *precarium* were gaining a foothold.

Sometimes we find this opposition to a use of the fief even more clearly expressed, however, in charters of this period which contain a proviso that land given a particular Church establishment cannot be alienated or given out as a fief. Such statements are found in charters of 920 and 926[30] from the Limousin; of 908 and 948–950[31] from Dauphiny; of 927 and 970[32] from the Viennois; of 916 and 961[33] from Rouergue; of 943 from Nîmes;[34] and 922 from Melgueil;[35] most of these are regions where we

[24] *Hist. Gén. de Lang.*, V, no. 78.
[25] *Ibid.*, no. 79.
[26] *Cart. de Saint-Sernin*, no. 236.
[27] *Cart. de Sauxillanges*, no. 68.
[28] *Ibid.*, no. 376.
[29] *Cart. de Saint-Etienne de Limoges*, nos. 17 (950), 14 (968), 26 (970).
[30] *Ibid.*, no. 16 (920); *Cart. de Beaulieu*, no. 38 (926).
[31] *Cart. de Saint-Barnard de Romans*, nos. 6 (908), 23 (948–950).
[32] *Cart. de Vienne*, nos. 20 (927), 30 (970).
[33] *Cart. de Conques*, nos. 262 (916), 340 (961).
[34] *Cart. de Nîmes*, no. 44. See somewhat similar prohibitions in charters dating from 936 and 939 in *ibid.*, nos. 39, 41.
[35] *Cart. de Maguelonne*, I, no. 2, and *Hist. Gén. de Lang.*, V, no. 48.

have evidence of disorders, and change, and of some elements of feudalism being introduced. Thus directly and specifically as well as indirectly, by invoking law which protected allodial rights, the society of Southern France seems to have resisted feudalization of its land and to have maintained its traditions of property controlled without limitations by its landowners.

If we come to the conclusion that fiefs and benefices were rare in Southern France and Catalonia, and that where they are found we have evidence of resistance to them on the part of a society which believes land should be allodially owned, there still remains a question to be answered. That is the nature of the fiefs and benefices which existed by grant of the secular landowners of these regions. We do not have too much specific information on this point. But enough evidence is available to show that the grant of a fief could involve any type of property or even any sort of right which an allodial landowner wished to give to an individual in this manner. Often such a fief seems to have been a large tract of land, a castle, or a *villa*, as seems to have been the case frequently in the Limousin, or with much of the property distributed *a feo* by the members of the House of Toulouse-Rouergue.[36] Or it could be a small bit of land, a field, or a *mansus*, such as we find in Auvergne or the Valley of the Rhone.[37] It could even be a large tract of frontier land, which seems frequently to have been the case in Catalonia.[38] Or it could be the simple right to a *cens*, which we find about 936 in regard to the land and eight *"denarii ad fevum"* which Bernard Calvinus and his brother had from the church of Sainte-Marie of Nîmes.[39] It was often, perhaps generally, a grant restricted to one lifetime, which thus reverted to the donor upon the death of the recipient, at least in theory.[40] A fief, then, in this period, was the possession or use of land or of a right over land held for a lifetime or lifetimes as specified by the allodial owner of this property.

Did the receiving of such a fief carry with it duties on the part of the recipient to him who granted it? It certainly implied dependence, a dependence which in some cases probably meant military service owed. This is certainly true for those fiefs connected with the castles of Saint-

[36] *Hist. Gén. de Lang.*, V, nos. 111, 126, and *Cart. de Saint-Sernin*, no. 280.
[37] See for examples charters of 913, 922, and 929 in *Cart. de Brioude*, nos. 84, 76, 261, or one of 927–928 in *Cart. de Saint-André-le-bas*, no. 128.
[38] On such feudally held land see *Cart. de San Cugat*, no. 17.
[39] *Cart. de Nîmes*, no. 51.
[40] For an example of a grant for two lifetimes see a charter of 975 which describes a grant given by King Conrad to a nobleman, Artald, perhaps later on the count of Lyon (*Cart. de Vienne*, no. 229).

Martin, Mirabels, and Queralt on the Catalan frontier in 954 where we find such service of *"hostem et cavalcadem"* definitely specified.[41] Where formal courts still existed a fief may have required attendance at the court of the grantor of such a benefice,—this seems to have been the case in Auvergne in 961, where some *fideles* of Bishop Etienne II definitely attended his court.[42] But there does not yet seem to have been any rule in these matters. One could be a *fidelis* without holding a fief,[43] and one could hold a fief without this automatically establishing a tie of *fidelitas*.[44] Land granted as a fief or benefice and *fidelitas* were not in this period linked together as they tended to be in Northern France.[45] The fief was still tentative, often unpopular, and limited in its application and scope. So it was to remain in these regions into the next century and even later.

[41] *Hist. Gén. de Lang.*, II, no. 209.

[42] *Cart. de Sauxillanges*, no. 86.

[43] In Auvergne note that Duke Acfred, before 926, gave land as an outright gift, not a fief, to his *fidelis* Bertrand (*Cart. de Brioude*, no. 315). Again in 927 in giving his lands to a group of noblemen whom he calls *"fidelos et amicos meos,"* Duke Acfred gives lands as allodial gifts *not* fiefs (*Grand Cart. de Brioude*, no. CCCCXXXIII). In the Valley of the Rhone we find similar gifts of allodial land to individuals called *fideles*. See for instance a gift in 902 to Berilon, a *fidelis* of King Louis of Provence (*Cart. de Vienne*, no. 11); or to Gerald, called a *fidelis*, in 915 (*ibid.*, no. 16); or to Ingelbert, called a *fidelis*, in 923 (*Chartes de Cluny*, I, no. 237). In Aquitaine, writing a little later on in the eleventh century, Ademar de Chabannes tells of a gift of a church made by Count William Taillefer of Angoulême to *"Iterio fidelio suo" Ademar de Chabannes*, III, 24, p. 146. This seems an outright gift, not a fief. In Catalonia in 961 we find Count Borell II of Barcelona selling a large tract of land as an allod to his *fidelis* Ansulfo (*El Archivo Condal de Barcelona*, no. 159). In this period then it seems that it was the *oath of fidelitas* which made one a *fidelis*, *not* the land which was bestowed by an overlord.

[44] Note how a charter in Auvergne dating from 913 mentions land, which is obviously a fief, given to a man who is called not a *fidelis*, but a friend (*Cart. de Brioude*, no. 84). We find charters of 922 and 926 that repeat this situation (*ibid.*, nos. 76, 291). In the Limousin a charter of the same period mentions land given as a benefice or *precarium* by the abbot of Tulle to Viscount Foucher, but speaks of the latter only as *"familiari nostro"* (*Cart. de Tulle*, no. 317). In this period then such grants did *not* automatically establish a tie of *fidelitas* or vassalage. Sometimes they did, however, it must be admitted, as when Joseph, *prepositus* of Brioude, in 945 gives a gift of a *villa* to a certain Salicus *"propter amorem et servicium"* (*Grand Cart. de Brioude*, no. CCLXXXIII).

[45] Note the differences between the situation described in notes no. 43 and 44 and that found elsewhere by Ganshof (F. Ganshof, "Notes sur les origines de l'union du bénéfice avec la vassalité," in *Études d'histoire dédiées à la mémoire de Henri Pirenne*).

The Society of the Midi and Catalonia 269

In examining benefices and fiefs in the above paragraphs we have concentrated most of our attention on those which originated with secular landowners and officials. But there remains still another category of such grants which needs to be considered—those *precaria, beneficia,* and fiefs given from Church lands to laymen or members of the Church. These grants were, in this period, probably more extensive than those which were the result of the action of secular landowners, and are found in every section of the Midi during this period. Our documents, for instance, mention fourteen such grants of *precaria* in the region of the Limousin and Quercy, fourteen from Auvergne, six from Rouergue-Albigeois, and ten from Septimania.[46] In the Lyonnais-Forez region we find mention of some twenty-two of them[47] and they seem relatively common in the rest of the Valley of the Rhone where we find three from Vienne, four from Dauphiny, two from Provence, and two from Velay.[48] We do not find them in Catalonia, however, unless we consider that certain gifts of land to the abbey of San-Cugat near Barcelona between 953 and 973, in which a number of landowners specify that these lands are to be held as permanent *precaria* by their posterity, established them here too.[49]

Careful examination of such *precaria* granted by abbeys, churches, and churchmen shows us some interesting things. In the first place in this period, as in earlier ones, these *precaria* almost always consist of land or rights over land, a castle, a *villa,* a *mansus,* or even a smaller bit of property which belonged to the *opus* or domain of an abbey or church. Secondly, few *precaria* were granted for an unlimited period of time. The general rule during this period remained what it had been earlier, to grant

[46] For the Limousin and Quercy regions see *Cart. de Tulle,* nos. 12, 126, 184, 226, 262, 283, 290, 304, 317, 565–568; *Cart. de Beaulieu,* nos. 49, 75; *Hist. Gén. de Lang.,* V, no. 122. For Auvergne see *Cart. de Brioude,* nos. 37, 46, 51, 58, 86, 140, 141, 177, 228, 261, 327; and *Grand. Cart. de Brioude,* nos. CCCXLIX, CCLXXXIII. See *Cart. de Conques,* nos. 29, 161, 177, 302, 306, 321, for Rouergue-Albigeois. And *Cart. de Béziers,* nos. 18, 24, 27, 28, 36; *Cart. d'Aniane,* no. 316; Cros-Meyrévielle, *Documents,* no. 22; *Cart. de Fontjoncouse,* no. 6; *Hist. Gén. de Lang.,* V, no. 117; *Cart. de Carcassonne,* II, 222–223, for Septimania.
[47] *Cart. de Savigny,* nos. 6, 7, 11, 12, 15, 17, 22, 29, 31, 41, 42, 43, 44, 46, 49, 51, 55, 59, 63, 73; *Chartes de Cluny,* I, no. 642; *Cart. Lyonnais,* no. 6.
[48] *Cart. de Vienne,* nos. 18, 23, 26 (Vienne); *Cart. de Saint-Barnard de Romans,* nos. 6, 20, 21, and *Cart. de Grenoble,* no. 11 (Dauphiny); *Cart. de Saint-Victor,* no. 1040, and *Chartes de Cluny,* II, no. 1071 (Provence); *Cart. de Saint-Chaffre,* no. 299, and *Hist. Gén. de Lang.,* V, no. 70 (Velay).
[49] *Cart. de San Cugat,* nos. 34, 35, 38, 41, 43, 48, 50, 54, 55, 61, 63, 64, 75, 76, 82, 86, 88, 92, 99, 100, 109.

them for one lifetime only, though occasionally two, or even three, lifetimes seem to have been allowed.[50] Third and most important, a payment of a *cens* seems almost always demanded by the donor from the recipient, a *cens* which was always on a yearly basis. True this *cens* in money or kind was often so small that its value was strictly symbolical, but it was seldom omitted. Thus we see that *in theory* a grant *ad fevum* or as a *precarium* from a church establishment in these regions did not differ much from an ordinary *censive* except in the nominal nature of *cens* required.[51] The recipient seems to have clearly understood that while he had the use of this property or right, he was to pay a *cens* as a recognition of the fact that the *dominio* or allod of it still remained in the hands of the religious establishment which gave it to him. In *precaria* granted by churches and abbeys in the Midi, then, again we find an ingrained respect for *allodial property* and the limited rights, at least in theory, of him who possessed such *precaria, beneficia,* or *feva*.

Is there any evidence that in the case of such grants by religious establishments any responsibilities were expected of the recipient more extensive than the payment of the specified *cens?* Was a *precaria* holder expected to render court service or military service upon call of the bishop or abbot who granted him his holding? It is difficult to be sure. If such a holding represented a payment to an individual who held office from a church or abbey, a *prepositus,* a *portarius,* or a *judex servus,* we know he was expected to swear *fidelitas* in a special ceremony.[52] He then held such land *"in obedientia"* to use a current term in use.[53] In some cases this probably meant that he was expected to assist at the court, formal or informal, of the bishop or abbot in question. His duties, however, in this case, did not include military service unless they were specifically mentioned, as might be the case if the holding given him as a fief or *precarium* was a castle belonging to the church or abbey.[54] Sometimes indeed, as in

[50] There is even one *precarium* mentioned in a charter from the Lyonnais which seems to be a permanent one (*Cart. de Savigny,* no. 22).

[51] In most cases the *cens* paid in return for a *precarium* seems to have been in natural products. Sometimes, however, money was used, but then in amounts so small as to be strictly nominal. What the *cens* seems to represent is a recognition by the possessor that allodial ownership was in another's hands.

[52] See for instance the oath required of the *judices servum* at Beaulieu in 971 (*Cart. de Beaulieu,* no. 50).

[53] In addition to those examples of *obedientia* mentioned in the previous chapter note land given out by Lagrasse in 943 and held *"ad obedientiam"* (*Cart. de Carcassonne,* II, 222–223).

[54] This seems probable as far as the castle of Moncieux was concerned, a castle

The Society of the Midi and Catalonia 271

the case of the *judices servum* of the abbey of Beaulieu in the Limousin, the profession of arms by such *fideles* was specifically forbidden.[55]

Many *precaria* given by church establishments in this period, though, did not go to laymen who held offices from the Church at all. They went to important neighboring landowning families. This seems particularly true of the Limousin and Lyonnais[56] and may be true of Septimania also. On what basis were they given? The best answer which we can give to this question is to say that such *precaria* represented the establishment of no reciprocal duties and responsibilities on the part of grantor and grantee, but rather of a vague but no less real bond of clientage without formal contract. The families who received such grants were no doubt expected in a general way to protect the churches or religious houses in question, but their duties down to 975 were still unspecified and amorphous in nature. Probably in some regions, especially in the Limousin, such vague responsibilities of protection were being transformed into rights of domination.[57] But in most of the Midi this trend was still not too far advanced. It was to become a problem in the next century.

We might sum up our conclusions as follows. Until about 975 the Midi and Catalonia were regions in which allodial land predominated and represented a right that was jealously guarded by lay and church proprietors. Despite this fact, use was made of conditional grants of land and rights over land by both lay and ecclesiastical proprietors in the form of *precaria, beneficia,* and *feva.* Such grants were generally limited in their duration and almost always specified the payment of a definite *cens* by the recipient as a recognition of the owner's real ownership of such property and of the temporary nature of the recipient's rights. In a few cases we have evidence of military service or attendance at court in return for such grants—particularly in Catalonia and other parts of the Midi where castles are to be found in large numbers. Elsewhere, however, such grants merely set up a patron-client relationship not unlike that found in the late Roman Empire or pre-Carolingian times. Instinctively the Midi and Catalonia between 900 and 975 seem to have rejected the Northern Frankish

---

which the abbey of Tulle gave to a number of lords during the period (*Cart. de Tulle,* no. 290). In this charter only a *cens* is mentioned, even though some of these lords are called the abbey's *defensores.*

[55] *Cart. de Beaulieu,* no. 50.

[56] See note 47 on a number of *precaria* or *prestaria* which the abbey of Savigny gave to neighboring landholders. Most seem to be simply powerful neighbors of this monastery.

[57] See note 46 on similar *precaria* given out by the abbey of Tulle.

system of the Carolingians, and returned to earlier principles which made conditional grants of land to supporters, neighbors, and friends a way to increase Church and family influence, but which did not disturb or change the basic allodial landholding system that still prevailed.

Having considered use of *precaria, feos,* and benefices, as well as the prevailing allod, we now need to consider that other landholding system which was introduced by the Carolingians, the *aprisio*. The *aprisio*, judging from our sources, seems to have been relatively rare in the Midi during this period. We do find a few references to its use, though. We find such *aprisio* land, called *attracto,* in a charter from Rouergue dating from 916[58] and in two others from the Albigeois and Auvergne from 920.[59] It is mentioned in 908 in the Carcassonne region.[60] Much later a document of 965 mentions it near the abbey of Lézat[61] and not far from the city of Toulouse a year later it is found as well.[62] All these *aprisiones* seem to have been allodial in character and to have gradually merged into the prevailing system of allods in the Midi.

In Catalonia and Pallars and Ribagorça, however, the *aprisio* system did not disappear at all as it did elsewhere in Southern France. Rather it continued important. In Pallars and Ribagorça charters which date from these years reveal that both large and small landholders owned a surprising amount of land which they got *"ex aprisione"* or *"de ruptura"* — land which probably represented a steady expansion of the line of settlement along the Moslem frontiers.[63] The same thing seems to be true of Catalonia, especially in Ausona and Berga, and south of Barcelona where colonization of frontier regions was active. In some thirty-nine charters dating from 904 to 975 we find, therefore, references to *aprisiones*.[64] These documents make clear that land acquired by *aprisio* tended to be allodial, though perhaps the smaller landholders owed some dues to those who had originally granted them their land and were also expected to

---

[58] *Cart. de Conques,* no. 262.
[59] *Hist. Gén. de Lang.,* V, no. 45, and *Cart. de Brioude,* no. 129.
[60] *Hist. Gén. de Lang.,* V, no. 33.
[61] *Ibid.,* no. 116.
[62] *Cart. de Saint-Sernin,* no. 336.
[63] Over a hundred charters which mention such land are to be found in Abadal, *Els Comtats de Pallars i Ribagorça.*
[64] *El Archivo Condal de Barcelona,* nos. 14, 16, 17, 19, 21–52, 55, 58, 60, 67, 70–71, 75, 78, 81, 84–86, 88, 96, 107, 110, 114, 116, 119, 124, 151, 154, 160; *Cart. de San Cugat,* nos. 4, 5, 7, 9, 14, 41, 47, 69; *Liber Feudorum,* no. 395; and *Archivo Catedral de Barcelona,* no. 24.

The Society of the Midi and Catalonia   273

answer the call to military service if the need arose.[65] Even after 975 along the frontiers of Moslem Spain the *aprisio* remained important to Catalan society.

Finally we have everywhere in Southern France and Catalonia proof of an expanded use of that system we have called the *medium plantum*, whereby an allodial owner gave land, which was uncultivated, to an individual or individuals who held it as a *precarium* until it was put into cultivation. Then this property was divided between cultivator and original allodial owner, with the provisio that the cultivator could not sell or dispose of his one half, after division, without the permission of the proprietor who granted it. We will be examining this system in more detail a little later in this chapter, but here we must note it as another system of *precaria*, though a very specialized one indeed.

So far our attention has been fixed on the various methods of landholding which are to be found in the Midi and Catalonia during these years—the allod, the *precarium*, benefice or fief, the *aprisio*, and the *medium plantum*—and their relative incidence and popularity, judging from our documents. But let us now consider another aspect of the landholding system of the period: the size of holdings. Our records show that large estates, smaller ones, and those of medium size continued to exist side by side in every part of our regions. In Auvergne, the Rouergue, and the Spanish March the small holding seems to have been the more usual one in contrast to the Limousin, Western Aquitaine, Gascony, and the Valley of the Rhone where larger estates seem relatively numerous. But this is only true to a limited extent. Everywhere *villas* continue to exist— even in Provence—and everywhere we also find small and medium-sized landowners, too, who jealously guard their right to their allodial property from rapacious neighbors. The beginnings of *mandamenta*, which already were to be found around the castles of the Midi and Catalonia, had not yet managed to engulf the small holder or to change the prevailing landholding system which had been inherited from Carolingian times.

One fact indeed even makes one feel that this period saw a certain increase in the number of independent allodial owners of small-sized property. I refer to the evidence of a decline of serfdom in many parts of the Midi and Catalonia. Not that we do not find evidence of serfs in many

[65] See mention of allods *"cum beneficios et tascas"* which were part of the canonica of Vich in 957 (*El Archivo Condal de Barcelona*, no. 131). And also the agreement made by the bishop of Barcelona with the *"homines"* or inhabitants of the castle of Montmell in 974 which freed them of certain dues and services (*El Archivo Catedral de Barcelona*, no. 24).

regions. We do. Charters dating from 904, 916, 920, 923, 941, 943–948, and 971 show them in the Limousin and Quercy.[66] Another dating from 930 mentions them in Rouergue,[67] and two from 940 and 952 in Angoulême.[68] Nearby Saintonge-Aunis had them too according to documents dating from 914 and 975.[69] So did Auvergne, judging from charters mentioning them found in 917, 926, 927, 928, and 949.[70] We find serfs referred to also in a Toulousain charter of 972,[71] and two from Roussillon of 927 and 967.[72] In the Valley of the Rhone they are found in many regions: near Substantion in 960,[73] and in Provence in 903, 909, 950, and 960,[74] as well as in Dauphiny in 928, 932, and 956,[75] in the Viennois in 904 and 927–948,[76] in the Lyonnais in 945,[77] and in Forez in 927–942 and 960.[78] But we find none at all in certain regions like Septimania, Velay, and the Spanish March, and even where we do find them they seem more numerous in documents dating from the early part of the tenth century than they are in those from the later part.

Why was the old serfdom becoming less important during this period? One notes first of all that it seems to have survived in greatest strength in just those regions where the *villa* remained an important element in the landholding system; in the Limousin and Western Aquitaine and in the Valley of the Rhone, while it was weakest or non-existent where *villas* were less important, as in Auvergne and Septimania and the Spanish March. Even more important, serfs seem to be disappearing in the same areas where our documents show that *aprisiones* and *medium plantum* were making new land available for cultivation by the peasant population. All of which suggests that the gradual disappearance of *villas* and the availability of free land for colonization lies behind the gradual disap-

[66] *Cart. de Beaulieu*, nos. 28, 50, 60, 72, 94; *Cart. de Saint-Etienne de Limoges*, no. 10; *Cart. de Tulle*, nos. 529, 537.

[67] *Cart. de Conques*, no. 6.

[68] *Cart. d'Angoulême*, nos. 29, 3.

[69] *Cart. de Saint-Jean d'Angély*, nos. 203, 250.

[70] *Cart. de Brioude*, nos. 318, 315; *Grand Cart. de Brioude*, no. CCCCXXXIII; and *Cart. de Sauxillanges*, nos. 13, 428.

[71] These are the serfs whom Countess Garsinde freed in her will of 972 (*Hist. Gén. de Lang.*, V, no. 126).

[72] *El Archivo Condal de Barcelona*, no. 92, and *Cart. roussillonnais*, no. 12.

[73] *Hist. Gén. de Lang.*, V, no. 107.

[74] *Ibid.*, nos. 9, 107, and *Chartes de Cluny*, I, no. 105.

[75] *Cart. de Saint-Barnard de Romans*, nos. 11, 13, 30.

[76] *Cart. de Vienne*, nos. 111, 114.

[77] *Cart. de Savigny*, no. 45.

[78] *Chartes de Cluny*, I, no. 342; II, no. 1005.

The Society of the Midi and Catalonia 275

pearance of serfdom, which by 975 had ceased to be an important factor in the Midi or the Spanish March. After this date it was not the older system of serfdom, but the new burdens laid on the peasant population by the castellans and *milites* of the fortresses of the Midi which concern us and which have real importance.

In this Midi and Spanish March of allodial propriety, some fiefs, and *medium plantum,* and of declining serfdom, the status of women remained very important indeed. All that has been said of their power and authority as landholders in their own right and as heads of families in the late ninth century can be reiterated with even greater force in this period too. A Countess Garsinde of Toulouse[79] or a Countess Bertha of Rouergue,[80] who freely disposed of their property and gave fiefs to leading noble families of the Midi, were certainly equal to other magnates whom we find during this period. So were the great ladies of Carcassonne and Catalonia—a Countess Arsinde,[81] a Countess Adelaise,[82] or an Abbess Ranlo.[83] A charter tells us that it was Queen Matilda, rather than her ineffective husband King Conrad, who destroyed the castle of Mont Burton near Vienne.[84] We can find reference in our documents too to women of humbler status who seem to be able to dispose freely of their property: like Emeldis or Widberga who lived near the abbey of Aniane;[85] or the wife of Foucher, whose husband gave to her in 909 *villas* scattered over the Midi from Provence to Rodez;[86] or Dida, who in 920 gave a large estate to Saint-Etienne of Limoges.[87] Of the same stripe was Lady Ava of Auvergne who in 941 gave a number of villas she got *by conquest* to Cluny, while reserving the life usufruct of them for her husband Abbo.[88] In such a society we seem already to be setting the stage for remarkable women like Countess Ermissende and Countess Almodis in the next cen-

---

[79] See gifts of Countess Garsinde referred to in charters in *Hist. Gén. de Lang.,* V, nos. 125, 126. See her power also as reflected in a charter of 969 (*ibid.,* no. 117).

[80] *Cart. de Nîmes,* nos. 61, 66, and *Hist. Gén. de Lang.,* V, no. 107, mention large gifts of land by Countess Bertha of Rouergue.

[81] See *Hist. Gén. de Lang.,* V, no. 106.

[82] On her control of a castle held as an allod see *El Archivo Condal de Barcelona,* no. 130. See also the mention of Countess Elo in 955 and her ownership of much property along the borders of Ausona and Roussillon (*ibid.,* no. 132).

[83] On Abbess Ranlo see *ibid.,* nos. 132, 150.

[84] *Cart. de Vienne,* no. 28.

[85] *Cart. d'Aniane,* nos. 42, 218.

[86] *Chartes de Cluny,* I, no. 105.

[87] *Cart. de Saint-Etienne de Limoges,* no. 10.

[88] *Chartes de Cluny,* I, no. 532.

tury, and, a little later, such a figure as Eleanor of Aquitaine. Troubadours had not yet appeared to sing the praises of the ladies of our regions, but women already occupied positions powerful enough to make such praise natural and even advisable.

This leads us to a final consideration—the economic basis of this society in the Midi and Catalonia. Here we notice a paradox. In many respects the lands which lay south of Poitou and Burgundy were even more agrarian in character and more isolated from the main currents of commerce and trade of the Mediterranean and Atlantic in this period, than they were earlier. Many of the mints which had existed down to 900, for instance, did not re-open during the first three quarters of the tenth century. In fact we can list the existing mints of the Midi during these decades very easily. They were Melle in Poitou, Limoges in the Limousin,[89] Clermont in Auvergne,[90] LePuy in Velay,[91] Toulouse in the Toulousain,[92] Carcassonne and Narbonne in Western Septimania,[93] and Vienne and perhaps Arles in the Valley of the Rhone.[94] Though Barcelona, Gerona, and perhaps Ampurias had the right to coin money in their mints,[95] they rarely did so in this period. In many regions of Southern France and the Spanish March—such as Gascony, Eastern Languedoc, Western Aquitaine, and Alpine regions east of the Rhone—no mints at all seem to have existed.

Examination of coin hoards dating from this period in Northern France seems to point up this same economic isolation for the Midi, since even those found closest to our regions contain almost no coins from existing Southern French and Catalan mints.[96] Our records show an equally limited amount of outside trade and commerce, except perhaps

[89] A. Blanchet and A. Dieudonné, *Manuel de Numismatique*, IV, 336–372.
[90] *Ibid.*
[91] See the right to coin money given to the bishop of LePuy by King Raoul in 924 and King Louis V in 955 (*Hist. Gén. de Lang.*, V, nos. 49, 70).
[92] Blanchet and Dieudonné, *Manuel de Numismatique*, IV, 234–235.
[93] *Ibid.*, pp. 239–243.
[94] L. Rambault, "La Numismatique Provençale," in *Bouches du Rhône: Encyclopédia départmentale*, II, 944–952.
[95] J. Botet y Siso, *Les monedes catalanes*, I, 17–30, 90–110, 136–145. See also a charter of 967 which mentions *solidi* of Guitard (Barcelona), of Sunifred (Ampurias), or Oliba (Vich) (*Cart. roussillonnais*, no. 12). Or the charter of 911 which gave the counts of Barcelona and the bishops of Gerona a right to coin money (*El Archivo Condal de Barcelona*, no. 33).
[96] See references to such coin hoards in A. Lewis, *The Northern Seas A.D. 300–1100*, pp. 82–88.

The Society of the Midi and Catalonia 277

that which proceeded from Catalonia into Moslem Spain.[97] An occasional ship seems to have reached Arles from Italy.[98] Some Jewish merchants from Verdun carried slaves down the Valley of the Rhone to the Iberian peninsula.[99] And ships from Bordeaux and Western Aquitaine still reached Asturias, Ireland, and Western Britain.[100] That is all. Economic localism seems to have become the order of the day, despite the presence of the colonies of Jews at Vienne, Narbonne, and elsewhere.[101]

On the other hand, despite this localism, a money economy remained in force in most parts of the Midi and the Spanish March. True we do find the phrase *"in rem valentem"* in many charters, especially in remoter regions like Pallars and Ribagorça.[102] But a surprising amount of coin and even of gold was available for use, like that given the abbey of Conques by Countess Garsinde of Toulouse[103] or that which was probably minted into gold *solidi* in Uzès during this period.[104] *Mancusi* were in use in Catalonia,[105] and in 920 a bishop could afford to pay Count Hugh of Arles thirty pounds of silver for a *villa*.[106] Many *cens* payments were

[97] Especially after peaceful relations were established about 950 with the caliphate of Cordova. R. de Abadal i de Vinyals, *Els Primers Comtes Catalans*, pp. 317–321.

[98] Lewis, *The Northern Seas*, p. 345.

[99] See F. Ganshof, "Notes sur les ports de Provence du VIIIe au Xe siècle," in *Revue Historique*, CLXXXIII (1938).

[100] On trade which reached England and Ireland from Southwestern France see Lewis, *The Northern Seas*, pp. 333–334, 338. On trade with Northwestern Spain see *ibid.*, pp. 388–389, and "Bibliothèque Nationale: Mélanges Colbert" (unprinted), XLVI, 97.

[101] A charter of 959 mentions Jews at Narbonne and money which Countess Arsinde borrowed from them (*Hist. Gén. de Lang.*, V, no. 106). On them see also J. Régné, *Étude sur la condition des Juifs de Narbonne du Ve au XIVe siècle*, pp. 12–106. See also mention in charters of Jews of Vienne who also served as money lenders (*Cart. de Saint-André-le-bas*, nos. 5, 100, 105, 111).

[102] At times in this period even important lords like the counts of Barcelona had little ready cash. See for instance how Count Borell II in 957 purchased a large tract from the abbey of Ripoll for 2,000 *"solidi in rem valentem"* (*Liber Feudorum*, no. 447). Or note how this same noble in 961 sold land to his *fidelis* Ansulfo for 100 *"solidi in rem valentem"* (*El Archivo Condal de Barcelona*, no. 159).

[103] This was in the form of actual gold objects, however, rather than gold coin. See R. Latouche, "Saint-Foy-de-Conques et le problème d'or aux temps Carolingiens," in *Annales du Midi*, XLVII (1956).

[104] P. Grierson, "Le sou d'or d'Uzès," in *Le Moyen Age*, LX (1954).

[105] Botet y Siso, *Les monedes catalanes*, I, 70–89.

[106] *Cart. de Saint André-le-bas*, no. 124. Note also the charter of 932 which mentions a fine of 100 pounds of silver levied on the nobleman Sylvius for his destruction of the abbey of Saint-Barnard de Romans (*Cart. de Saint-Barnard de*

required to be rendered in coin rather than in kind, and Jews at Vienne seem to have carried on a rather active moneylending business.[107] In Narbonne Countess Arsinde could borrow 1,000 *solidi* from two such Jewish moneylenders and another 300 *solidi* from a certain Gero, giving family allods as security.[108] Southern France and Catalonia were still agrarian and remote in many ways from more advanced economic regions, but a basis already existed for the economic growth and expansion which was to take place soon after 975.

Even more important to note is a fact made clear by our documents, that this was a period of agrarian growth and of expansion of the land which was under cultivation. This was not a completely new development. We have already noted how in the late ninth century in Auvergne, in Rouergue, in the Albigeois and the Toulousain a good deal of new land was cleared for cultivation in regions which were little affected by Moslem and Viking raids. What we find now is an expansion of the areas in which this development took place and an intensification of this movement.

Let us first consider regions north of the Pyrenees. In some cases the purpose seems to have been one of putting back into cultivation land which, for various reasons, was deserted by those who had cultivated it. Such seems to have been the case of that *"mansus apsitus"* in the Cantal mentioned in a charter of Brioude of 903,[109] or the *villa* with a *"vinea deserta"* which the abbot of Saint-Chaffre gave as a *precarium* to a certain Richard in 909,[110] or a similar deserted vineyard near Clermont given out as a *precarium* by Sauxillanges in 972.[111] More important than such tracts which were temporarily without cultivators, however, was new land, not cultivated at all, which needed to be broken to the plough, whether it be a *villa* called *"illos ermos"* mentioned in Rouergue in a charter of 916,[112] or land called *"culturos ermos"* given to a priest near Auch in 950,[113] vacant lands which a landowner acquired from Saint-Marie of Nîmes in 973,[114] or that property lying between two villages, which Bishop

---

Romans, no. 13). Or see land which Archbishop Amblard of Lyon purchased in 961 for 400 *solidi* (*Chartes de Cluny*, II, 1115).

[107] See note 101.
[108] *Hist. Gén. de Lang.*, V, no. 106.
[109] *Cart. de Brioude*, no. 275.
[110] *Cart. de Saint-Chaffre*, no. 299.
[111] *Cart. de Sauxillanges*, nos. 22, 112.
[112] *Cart. de Conques*, no. 262.
[113] *Cart. d'Auch*, no. 47.
[114] *Cart. de Nîmes*, no. 76.

The Society of the Midi and Catalonia

Etienne II of Auvergne in this period gave to Sauxillanges to make fields and vineyards.[115] Once such new or vacant land had been put into cultivation it seems to have been called a *plantada* or a *plantario*, terms found especially in charters from the Limousin dating from 922 to 948,[116] as well as in Auvergne in 925 and 926–929[117] and in Rouergue in 959.[118] The individuals who put them into cultivation are frequently called *plantadores*.[119]

Equally interesting is an analysis of the ways in which this system of developing land operated. In every example which we find referred to in our sources the allodial owner of the vacant land in question seems to have made a definite agreement or contract with the cultivator who did the work, that is the *plantador* or *plantadores*. A document from Angoulême shows that such contracts could be relatively simple affairs. About 918 the bishop and canons of this city, with the consent of the leading lay magnates, issued a charter which provided that anyone who wished to take up lands within two miles of the city and plant vineyards could do so providing they paid an annual modest *cens* to its owners.[120] In Rouergue some three examples show us the abbey of Conques granting out such lands as *precaria* on the basis of a *cens* which was one quarter of the crop—a contract similar to the common *métayage* ones of later periods.[121] In one case the contract was more specific and provided that the cultivator was to pay a definite amount in grain for use of the abbey's land. Such seems to have been the case too in regard to that *precarium* contract which Saint-Chaffre gave to a landowner in Velay in 909.[122]

More usual, however, seems to have been that system we have called the *medium plantum*, which is mentioned by name in a number of charters of this period from Auvergne, Rouergue, Velay, Carcassonne, Vivarais, the Lyonnais, Dauphiny, and Provence. We find a number of

[115] *Cart. de Sauxillanges*, no. 145.
[116] *Cart. de Beaulieu*, nos. 28, 49, 56, 144, 174; *Cart. de Tulle*, nos. 12, 14, 537, 285–286.
[117] *Cart. de Brioude*, nos. 112, 115.
[118] *Cart. de Conques*, no. 405. See mention in a charter of 933 of such *plantadas* at Conques (*ibid.*, no. 9).
[119] See for instance a charter dating from 944 (*Cart. de Sauxillanges*, no. 218), and of a later one of about 975 (*ibid.*, no. 90).
[120] *Cart. d'Angoulême*, no. 2.
[121] *Cart. de Conques*, nos. 100, 177, 405. See also a charter of 910 which mentions a wood *"in medio planto,"* and another mentioning a forest *"in medio planto"* in 932 (*ibid.*, nos. 7, 208). On land newly put into cultivation according to charters of 924 and 929 see *ibid.*, nos. 92, 306.
[122] *Cart. de Saint-Chaffre*, no. 299.

charters from Auvergne which describe this system in some detail. They show that in this region the allodial owner gave vacant land to a *plantador* as a benefice for a period of five years, during which time the cultivator paid nothing to the owner. During this period he was to put the property into cultivation. Then the land, which was now producing as a vineyard or as fields, was divided equally between the original owner and the *plantador* or *plantadores*, with a panel of *boni homines* of the region supervising the division to make sure it was a fair one. Henceforth the *plantador* was the possessor of his half. He could will it to his heirs and hold it as a permanent *precarium*, but he could not sell it or dispose of it without the permission of the original owner. He had what amounted to a sort of quasi-proprietorship over it.[123] Charters reveal that an exactly similar system was used for getting vacant land into cultivation in Provence in 970[124] and in Dauphiny in 976,[125] showing us that this system had a rather wide distribution in the Midi.

In certain cases from the Lyonnais, the Avergnat type of contract for *medium plantum* was modified in one respect. Here charters show us that the time before division of newly cultivated land between allodial owner and *plantador* was often three instead of five years.[126] Otherwise things proceeded in the same manner. In the nearby Limousin, however, we notice a certain variation in the method used. Some eleven charters dating from the period 926–948 show us land being put into cultivation in various locations—one called Vetus Silvia, an apt phrase. But when the land is divided between the original owner and the cultivator we find that it is not on a 50–50 basis. Instead the *plantador* gets only one-third of it, the allodial owner two-thirds.[127]

It seems probable that the success of this system of putting into cultivation new land was such that it established a certain pattern which was

[123] Three charters, dating from 922, 944, and 955, give a clear picture of how this system worked—especially that of 944 (*Cart. de Brioude*, no. 233 [922]; *Cart. de Sauxillanges*, nos. 218 [944], 372 [955]). For other references to *medium plantum* see *Grand Cart. de Brioude*, no. CCXXXVI; *Cart. de Brioude*, no. 234; *Chartes de Cluny*, I, no. 501; and *Cart. de Sauxillanges*, nos. 31, 67, 70, 73, 90, 175, 190, 225, 242, 373, 639.

[124] *Cart. de Saint-Victor*, no. 598.

[125] *Cart. de Grenoble*, no. 10.

[126] "Cart. d'Ainay," in *Cart. de Savigny*, no. 129. This charter dates from 970. See another charter of 932 which refers to land *"ex medio planto"* (*ibid.*, no. 2). For information on a large field divided into such *medium plantum* about 950 in Velay see *Cart. de Saint-Chaffre*, no. 294.

[127] *Cart de Saint-Etienne de Limoges*, nos. 41–45, 104, 144, 148, 150–153.

The Society of the Midi and Catalonia

used for more than purely agricultural purposes. Thus a charter of 970 from the abbey of Sauxillanges tells us how a certain Gausbert, called a *plantario,* made an agreement to rebuild the houses of the village of Brioude which had been destroyed by a fire. He was to have a *precarium* for life or the usufruct of one half of these houses in return for rebuilding all of them.[128] This agreement helps to explain, it seems, how Bishop Isarn and Count William proceeded to resettle Dauphiny and parts of Provence. We are told that Bishop Isarn gave castles and land to various types of colonists—*"nobiles, mediores et pauperes,"* says the charter.[129] But we have a record of only one such agreement between the bishop and such a settler which, dating from 976, seems to refer to a plot of land given on a *medium plantum* basis.[130] It seems probable that a similar method was used in granting the right to build castles or to settle larger tracts of land. Indeed, later charters of this region, showing us castles which were half owned by the bishop and half by those who occupied them, seem to make clear that this was the method used.[131] Similarly from Provence we have a charter of 970 which tells us of land near Fréjus which Count William of Provence gave to a certain Ugo Blavia to put under cultivation and to build edifices on. Once this was done this property was to be divided on a *medium plantum* basis between the count and Ugo.[132] By 975 then the *medium plantum* system seems to have developed into a method which could be used to settle important tracts of land and to establish castles in regions like Dauphiny and Provence which were being newly organized by their rulers.

Which brings us to Catalonia. Here too we find several references to *plantarias* also in 930[133] and 961,[134] and at least one charter, dating from 966, which seems to be the record of a *medium plantum* contract between a certain Lobela and the church of Santa Maria de Arampuña.[135] Despite

[128] *Cart. de Sauxillanges,* no. 90.
[129] *Cart. de Grenoble,* no. 16.
[130] *Ibid.,* no. 10.
[131] See reference in a later charter of 996 to one-half of the castle of Visalia owned by Bishop Humbert of Grenoble (*Chartes de Cluny,* III, no. 2307). And also note one-half of a castle near Vienne given to the same bishop and others by King Rudolf in 1009 (*Cart. de Vienne,* no. 38).
[132] *Cart. de Saint-Victor,* no. 598.
[133] *El Archivo Condal de Barcelona,* no. 98.
[134] *Ibid.,* no. 152.
[135] See reference to a *medium plantum* near Carcassonne in 920 (*Cart. de Carcassonne,* I, 253–254), and what appears to be a *medium plantum* contract in a 966 charter from Catalonia (*Cart. de San Cugat,* no. 85).

all this, however, as we have noted, it was the *aprisio* rather than the *medium plantum* which seems to have been the usual method of colonization and settlement of land in this region during this period. When one begins to examine examples of such large and small *aprisiones* in the charters of the period, however, one begins to realize that there was not a great deal of difference in practice between the average *aprisio* as found in Catalonia and the average *medium plantum* as found elsewhere in the Midi. Some such charters, dating from the period 965–966, mention specifically *aprisiones* which seem to be one-half of certain property which is described.[136] In one case we even have a mention of *boni homines* who set a price of 2,000 *solidi* for a large tract of *aprisio* land which is sold to Bishop Arnulf of Gerona.[137] One must, of course, be careful not to draw too many conclusions from these facts. But at least it seems fair to point out that, judging from these examples, Catalan *aprisiones* were, like *medium plantum,* agreements to put into cultivation new land, which then was divided between the *plantador* or *aprisio* holder and the original proprietor on a 50–50 basis. The difference seems to have been that in Catalonia the original allodial owner had to buy his half from the cultivator, and that which remained was the outright allodial possession of the cultivator or colonist. By the tenth century, then, it seems probable that in Catalonia the *aprisio* had become a sort of *medium plantum,* but one which gave more benefits and rights to the cultivator or colonist who put it into production than was true of the parts of the Midi north of the Pyrenees.

Our evidence, then, which concerns agrarian developments south of Poitou and Burgundy seems to show the following. In most parts of the Midi and Catalonia, with the possible exception of Gascony, this period saw new land put into cultivation and a colonization movement, particularly in regions where this movement had continued through the late ninth century, as in the Massif Central region and the Spanish March. It took the form of grants, by lay and ecclesiastical allodial landholders, of vacant land as *precaria* or *aprisiones* to those who wished to cultivate or settle them. Much of this land became the all but allodial possession of those who received it on a *medium plantum* or *aprisio* basis.

---

[136] *El Archivo Condal de Barcelona,* nos. 17, 58, 63, 75, 76, 79, 86, 93, 94, 104, 110, 118; *Cart. de San Cugat,* nos. 5, 6, 8, 85; *Liber Feudorum,* no. 191; *Hist. Gén. de Lang.,* V, no. 76.

[137] *El Archivo Condal de Barcelona,* no. 139.

Even more important, this proved to be such a successful method that it was extended, until it became a system which assured settlement and colonization by nobles and other of frontier regions like the Spanish March, or of areas which needed to be organized anew, like Dauphiny and Provence. In addition to all of this, by providing a method whereby a simple cultivator could take up vacant land of his own, it probably helped to destroy the older serfdom and to allow serfs to rise to at least the status of tenants. It provided free land which made for free men, and by increasing agricultural productivity helped to lay the basis for a revival of the Midi's economic life which became noticeable about the year 1000.

Our examination of various aspects of the society of Southern France and Catalonia during this period, then, helps us to form some conclusions of importance. We can see that this society was a remarkably healthy and vigorous one, despite the failure of attempts to form principalities, and despite the growth of castles and a new military class which dominated them. It supported an active Church and an expanding monasticism. Even more important its family system, dominated in many cases by able women, protected and even expanded the tradition of allodial ownership of most of its property. Abbeys and churches, as well as individual allodial proprietors, made use of *precaria,* benefices, and fiefs in handling some of their property, but grants of this nature, when found, generally seem to call for a money payment or *cens* instead of special military service or attendance at courts by the recipients. Or such *precaria* and the related *aprisiones* were used to put new land into cultivation in older settled regions or to expand the Midi's frontiers through colonization. The feudal system of the Midi and Catalonia, such as it was, except near newly built castles, was still a limited one which resembled that of pre-Carolingian times much more than it did that which Charlemagne and his house had tried to establish south of Poitou and Burgundy. The allodial landowner, large or small, was still the master of his fate.

Things, however, were beginning to change. Abbeys and churches had begun to accumulate large domains, often made up of the land of small proprietors who had placed themselves under the mild seigneurial control and protection of these establishments. Castellans were beginning a new and harsher domination of regions within reach of the *milites* who lived in their fortresses. And secular lords were beginning to impose a more ruthless and unsympathetic type of control over churches and abbeys which they found nearby. A new and dangerous trend had appeared which was to lead to a certain crisis for this society about the year 1000—a crisis which neither agrarian progress nor general peace could affect or disguise. By 975 the Midi and Catalonia, though they had made remarkable progress in the face of their governmental failure, were forced to face a difficult period in which the new *milites* and their allies were to threaten Church and lay society alike and lay the basis of a new and different society.

V
THE AGE OF THE *PRINCIPES*, 975–1050

CHAPTER XV

The New Militarism

BETWEEN THE years 975 and 1050 the new military system of Southern France and Catalonia, which had grown slowly but steadily throughout the tenth century, became powerful enough to affect almost every aspect of its government, its Church, and its society. To some extent this had been true of regions like the Spanish March, the Albigeois, the Limousin, and parts of Provence before 975. Now, unchecked by any really effective governmental authority, this military system spread until by 1050 every region south of Poitou and Burgundy was affected by the activities of the nobles and *milites* who dominated local areas near the old or newly built castles which they occupied. These nobles and *milites* were not, in many cases, new men, adventurers without background, who had usurped authority. They were often the descendants of the same old ruling families who had for generations dominated their local regions. What was new about them was their method of domination and control. They exercised authority from their castles as knights or *milites*, fighting men who could command respect and fear, not as rich allodial proprietors of broad acres with rights of patronage over their neighbors and nearby church establishments. Thus this period saw the appearance of a harsher, more brutal age than that which had preceded it—one which was to lead directly to a reaction against this new militarism in movements which we know as the Peace of God, the Truce of God, and the struggle against Lay Investiture.

Was this new military system a response to external or internal needs for defense? On the whole our answer must be in the negative, for internal and external pressures on the Midi and Spanish March were relatively inconsequential during these years, particularly when we contrast them with those which we have found in previous periods. Thus north of the

Pyrenees we hear only of occasional Viking raids along the coasts of Aquitaine[1] and a brief flurry of activity by Moslem fleets of Denia along the coasts of Roussillon.[2] That is all. Even in the Spanish March we know of only two important Moslem offensives, one the expedition which Almansor sent into Catalonia in 985, which captured Barcelona,[3] and the other an assault along Catalan frontiers in 1002 which did some damage.[4] From this time on, as a matter of fact, it was the Christian rulers of the Spanish March who were the aggressors, penetrating into Moslem Spain as far as Cordova and beginning that steady advance to the south which we know as the Reconquista[5]—an advance in which the Basque nobles of Gascony to the west participated as allies of Sancho the Great of Navarre.[6] Indeed it is hard not to ascribe the very success of this advance to the new military system which had developed in the Spanish March and its Southern French back country during this period.

When we examine the internal situation we can find some evidence of conflicts which may have stimulated the growth of the new military system. Largely from the pen of Ademar of Chabannes we learn of the efforts of the counts of Poitou, now dukes of Aquitaine, to advance their domains south into Saintonge, Angoulême, the Limousin, and finally Gascony, first in alliance with the Capetians and then with the assistance of the House of Anjou.[7] At first their efforts to the west in Saintonge and Angoulême were more successful than those directed against the Limousin, where the counts of La Marche barred their path.[8] But even in the Limousin by 1027 they had begun to establish a measure of control,[9] as

[1] A. Lewis, *The Northern Seas A.D. 300–1100*, p. 406.
[2] On the activities of the Moslem fleet of Denia see A. Lewis, *Naval Power and Trade in the Mediterranean A.D. 500–1100*, pp. 191–196.
[3] See references to this capture of Barcelona in *Catalunya Carolingia*, II, 72–73 and *Cart. de San Cugat*, nos. 170–171.
[4] The Moslem attack of 1002 is mentioned in *Cart. de San Cugat*, no. 381.
[5] *Ademar de Chabannes*, III, 38, p. 161.
[6] *Ibid.*, III, 70, pp. 194–195.
[7] For references to the dukes of Aquitaine's power in Saintonge in 980, 990, and 1012 see *Cart. de Saint-Jean d'Angély*, nos. 338, 6, 30. For assistance given them by the kings of France see "Aquitaniae Historiae Fragmenta," in *Ademar de Chabannes*, p. 205. For their expansion into Gascony see *Ademar de Chabannes*, III, 69, p. 194.
[8] On the resistance to the advance of these dukes of Aquitaine to the south see *Ademar de Chabannes*, III, 34, 45, pp. 156–157, 167–168, and "Aquitaniae Historiae Fragmenta," in *ibid.*, pp. 205, 208.
[9] Duke William of Aquitaine is mentioned as being at Limoges in a charter of

they did in Western Auvergne.¹⁰ And then a little later by means of marriage alliances and conquest they managed, shortly after 1050, to add western Gascony to their realm.¹¹ A great duchy of Aquitaine had at last been created. But even in the course of this Poitevin advance south there is ample evidence that warfare was by no means constant. There were long intervals of peace, and we have no way of being sure that the military system which we find developing in these years in this part of the Midi was a response to such military activity on the part of the dukes of Aquitaine.

Elsewhere what evidence we have seems to point to disorders which were more sporadic in nature. Thus from Southern Auvergne and Rouergue we find charters dating from between 984 and 1050 which mention land *"ex conquestu."*¹² In one case there is even a reference to a war in which the castle of Castelars near Conques was destroyed¹³—probably the result of an attempt by the lords of High Auvergne, like the viscounts of Carlat and the comtors of Nonette, to seize land belonging to the house of Toulouse-Rouergue. But, judging from our documents, these disorders were less frequent than those which we find in these same regions in earlier periods. To the east in the Vienne region we also know of some disorders attendant upon the attempt of Archbishop Burchard's nephew to succeed him as archbishop of Lyon in 1031—an attempt thwarted by German intervention.¹⁴ We hear of certain conquests which were made by Count Humbert of Savoy as he began to build up a principality in Savoy and other Alpine regions east of Vienne.¹⁵ We find one charter from Provence which mentions damage done by Count Bertrand near Toulon in 1031,¹⁶ which was probably the result of antagonism between his house and that of the viscontal family of Marseille.

1027 (*Cart. de Saint-Etienne de Limoges*, no. 69). Other later references to their power there are found in *ibid.*, nos. 24, 28.

¹⁰ For evidence of the authority of the dukes of Aquitaine in Western Auvergne which seems to have been rather intermittent see *Cart. de Brioude*, no. 323; *Chartes de Cluny*, III, no. 2682; and *Chartes de Charroux*, no. 4.

¹¹ A. Richard, *Histoire des Comtes de Poitou (778-1126)*, I, 270-271.

¹² *Cart. de Conques*, nos. 28, 30, 122, 127, 149, 178, 184, 273, 300, 333, 355, 385.

¹³ *Ibid.*, no. 247.

¹⁴ Raoul Glaber, *Historiarum libri V*, V, IV, 21-22, pp. 130-132.

¹⁵ *Ibid.*, IV, III, 6-7, pp. 96-97; *Cart. de Saint-Chaffre*, no. 434; and *Cart. de Grenoble*, nos. 19, 20. See also G. de Manteyer, "Les origines de la maison de Savoie en Bourgogne (910-1060)," in *Mélanges d'archéologie et d'historie de l'École française à Rome*, XIX (1899).

¹⁶ *Cart. de Saint-Victor*, no. 455.

Map 4. SOUTHERN FRANCE AND CATALONIA (*circa* 980).

key to symbols

Noble Families Dominating the Regions (all boundaries are approximate)

Ad—Anduze
An—Angoulême
Ar—Aragón
As—Astarac
AR—Ampurias-Roussillon
Ba—Barcelona
Ca—Carcassonne
Cl—Clermont
Co—Commignes
CB—Cerdanya-Besalu
Fo—Foix
Ga—Gascony
  (many families)
Ge—Gevaudun
Gr—Gravaisdun
  (Grenoble)

Li—Limousin
  (many families)
LF—Lyonnais-Forez
LM—La Marche
Na—Narbonne
Nv—Navarre
Po—Poitou
Pr—Provence
PR—Pallars-Ribagorça
  (disorganized)
TR—Toulouse-Rouergue
Sa—Savoy
Ur—Urgell
Va—Valence
VR—Viennois—Royal House
  of Burgundy

We find formal war taking place in only one other region—that which stretched from Carcassonne south into Catalonia. Here the ambitions of Count Oliba Cabreta of Cerdanya-Besalu clashed with those of the houses of Carcassonne-Razès to the north[17] and of Barcelona-Urgell to the south.[18] This led for a period to some conflicts in the Berga-Urgell region and warfare to the southwest of Carcassonne in the Pyrenean foothills. Judging from our sources, however, both these conflicts were spasmodic and did not last long.

In other words examination of the Midi and Catalonia gives us little evidence of continual conflict and disorder anywhere in these regions, and in some areas like Eastern Languedoc we have no evidence of any conflicts whatsoever. It therefore is impossible to view the new military system of the period as an automatic response to internal aggression anymore than we can view it as a response to a need for defense against external conflict. If castle building became the order of the day and the class of *milites* steadily grew in number and in influence, we must consider that this happened in response to circumstances other than those which were necessitated by defense against internal or external enemies.

With this in mind, let us examine the new military system of the Midi and Catalonia. Its chief characteristic seems to have been the multiplication of the number of castles everywhere, many more of them than we found earlier. Let us first examine evidence of this which can be found for the region of the Massif Central; that is to say for Auvergne, Rouergue, and the Albigeois. Here documents show the following castles were in use between 957 and 1050: one, whose name we do not know in Rouergue in 984, Lautrec, Castelluz, Mons Pantiaro, Vertasionem, Gergora, Salern, Budrono, Roca Savona, Rochaneuil, Pallerios, Nonette, a castle near Mauhon, Ebaino, Montagut, Bornaz, Balciago, Persc, Conques, Aurose, Castrum Novum, Elnone, Castelaro, Bello [Bellum], Causago, Berencs, Vintronem, Castelnou, Dunine, Geccago, Villamare, Vauro,

---

[17] A charter of 981 mentions attacks by Count Oliba Cabreta (Cros-Meyrévielle, *Documents*, no. 31). Concerning Oliba's expansion at the expense of the counts of Carcassonne-Razès see P. Ponsch, "Le Confluent et ses comtes du IXe au XIIe siècles," in *Études Roussillonnaises*, I (1951), 280–285.

[18] On the hostility which existed between the counts of Barcelona and the counts of Cerdanya-Besalu in this period see Ponsch, "Le Confluent et ses comtes." See also a charter of 1039–1040 which records an agreement between Count Raymond of Barcelona and Count Ermengol of Urgell directed against Count Raymond of Cerdanya (*Liber Feudorum*, no. 146). See another such agreement dating from 1050 also (*ibid.*, no. 147).

The New Militarism 293

Sainte-Felice, Leocono, Capulso, Albi, Yvonis, Vetus Brivate, Brezons, Brosadolz, Cussac, Castro Vetulo, Muret, Mermens, Castro Novo (de Moet), Saint-Ucruze, Turlande, Cayles, Carlat, and Mandillac.[19] Though it seems obvious that most of these castles were new foundations, three of them, judging by the name of *"castrum novuum"* or new castles, were *certainly* newly built. So was another at Albi according to a document which dates from the year 1040.[20]

When we examine evidence of castles existing in the nearby region of Velay and Vivarais we find a similar concentration of fortresses. Those mentioned in our sources of the period are Mercurio, LaFara, Cherssac, Espolede, Saint-Alban, Ussarie, Lardariola, Mont Rochefort, Rochos, Capdeneco, Capitoliensi, Camberliaco, Bisatico, Castellar, Bellomonte, Saint-Desiderio, Chalencon, Bellommen, and Barholmes.[21] Nearby in the Middle Rhone region which comprises Forez, the Lyonnais, the Viennois, Dauphiny, Savoy, and Valence we find reference to such castles as Ionis, Savigny, Saint-Julian, Mons Meruli, Ay, Novum Castellum, Pupet, Beatti Cassiani, Geneva, Grenoble, Visalia, Chanoux, Sentiae, Saint-Barnard, Tehes, Laurico, Turre of Ebrard, Pailhares,[22] as well as new walls which

---

[19] *Cart. de Conques,* nos. 26 (Bello [Bellum]), 34 and 167 (Castelaro), 173 (Balciago), 245 (Conques), 247 (Castelaro), 259 (Rouergue), 355 (Castelaro), 394 (Aurose); *Hist. Gén. de Lang.,* V, nos. 148 (Lautrec), 203 (Causago, Berenco), 204 (Vintronem, Castelnou, Dunine, Geccago, Villamare, Vauro, Sainte-Felice), 225 (Albi); *Chartes de Cluny,* III, nos. 2006 (Mons Pantiaro), 2103 (Castelluz); *Cart. de Sauxillanges,* nos. 290 (Castrum Novum), 302 (Castelluz), 378 (Mauhon), 410 (Gergora), 435 (Vertasionem), 572 (Vetus Brivate), 618 (Nonette), 623 (Pallerios), 635 (Rochaneuil), 660 (Salern), 701 (Budrono, Roca Savona), 757 (Ebaino); *Cart. de Saint-Flour,* pp. cvii–clxvi (Cayles, Carlat, Mandellac), no. 6 (Nonette, Brezons, Brosadolz, Cussac, Castro Vetulo, Muret, Mermens, Castro Novo, Saint-Ucruze, Turlande); *Cart. de Gellone,* nos. 94 (Elnone), 98 (Montagut, Bornaz); *Liber Miraculi Sanctae Fides,* ed. Bouillet, I, 79 (Persc); II, 3–7 (Castrum Novum); *Cart. d'Aniane,* no. 214 (Leocono, Capulso); *Chartes de Charroux,* no. 4 (Yvonix). Castles listed in this and the following sections appear just as they are named in the documents.

[20] *Hist. Gén. de Lang.,* V, no. 216.

[21] *Ibid.,* V, col. 14–23 (Mercurio); V, no. 216 (LaFara, Cherssac, Espolede); *Cart. de Saint-Barnard de Romans,* nos. 46 (Saint-Alban), 66 (Mont Rochefort); *Cart. de Saint-Egidius,* nos. 96 (Saint-Desiderio), 97 (Geneva), 98 (Grenoble), 189 (Lardariola), 204 (Chalencon), 205 (Bellomonte, Bellomnen), 227 (Barholmes), 248 (Bellomonte); *Cart. de Saint-Chaffre,* nos. 182 (Camberliaco), 184 (Capdeneco), 205 (Bisatico), 207 (Castellar), 228 (Capitoliensi).

[22] *Cart. Lyonnais,* I, no. 9 (*Ionis*); *Cart. de Savigny,* nos. 430 (Savigny), 654 (Saint-Julien); *Chartes de Cluny,* III, no. 2307 (Grenoble, Visalia); IV, no. 2925 (Mons Meruli); *Cart. de Saint-André-le-bas,* nos. 179 (Ay), 241 (Geneva); *Cart.*

were built to protect Vienne.[23] Again at least two of these are definitely mentioned as being built during these years: one near Savigny constructed about the year 1000[24] and the new castle near the river Isarn which is mentioned about 1016.[25] So are the new walls and towers mentioned at Vienne in 1019.[26]

When we turn our attention to Provence we find abundant evidence of castles in existence in this period, which is not surprising since this was a region in the Midi organized around newly built castles. Our sources mention Almis, Malaracua, Gap, Arlerc, Avignon, Sparro, Podium Odolinum, Artiga, Vitrola, Colongellos, Revella, Lurs, Petro Foco, Morera, Auriole, Nantes, Geminas, Auribello, Castro de Petro Castellanus, Salerna, Toramenus, Porales, Oleras, Sinna, Cagueli, Buchodenes, Inter Castello, Vite Albano, Vennena, Favat, Condorcet, Forcalquier, Lunis, Altonum, Bar, Charenguges, Guanin, Pictanis, Sarraix, Flaisoe, Turrivis, Castellnova (of Nice), Castellovum, Calars, Agoldi, Gordon, Archinose, Castromuris, Canneto, Castrum of Boson, Boric, Rocheta, Rocca (of Nice), Boxetum, Rochabuna, Saint-Vincent, Auriac, Coruis, Acut, Cagnes, Gontard, Orion, Bruso, Palacionem, Guardec, Caudo Longo, Fos, Gordiano, Podietum de Malanate, Trigantis, Rhodencs, Diylo, Marsens, Sex Forno, Solario, Rodancs, Drome, Ducelea, Tarascon, Senez, Mota, Mugins, and Grasse.[27] Obviously many of these were newly built, but we

---

de Vienne, nos. 39 (Novum Castellum), 40 (Pupet), 44 (Beatti Cassiani); *Chartes de Maurienne*, no. 4 (Chanoux); Raoul Glaber, *Historiarum libri V*, IV, 3, 6–7, p. 97 (Sentiae); *Cart. de Saint-Barnard de Romans*, nos. 80 (Saint-Barnard), 90 (Saint-Barnard); *Cart. de Grenoble*, no. 46 (Tehes); *Cartulaire de Saint-Sulpice en Bugey*, ed. M. Guigue, no. 3 (Laurico, Ebrard); *Cart. de Saint-Chaffre*, no. 73 (Pailhares). See also references to a castle of Iconium in *Cart. de Savigny*, no. 627; to a castle of Maros in *Cart. de Vienne*, no. 38; and to an unnamed castle which the bishop of Maurienne destroyed just prior to 1040, in *Chartes de Maurienne*, no. 6.

[23] *Cart. de Vienne*, no. 46.
[24] *Cart. de Savigny*, no. 430.
[25] *Cart. de Vienne*, no. 46.
[26] *Ibid.*, no. 40.
[27] *Cart. de Saint-Victor*, nos. 64 (Auriole, Nantes, Geminas), 68 (Castellovum), 69 (Auriole, Nantes, Geminas), 70 (Almis), 101 (Orion), 135 (Porales, Oleras, Sinna, Cagueli, Buchodenes), 207 (Vitrola), 237 (Acut), 240 (Gontard), 243 (Gontard), 250 (Boric), 253 (Boric), 255 (Guardec, Caudo Longo, Fos), 261–263 (Vennena), 269 (Artiga), 293 (Rodancs), 295 (Rhodencs, Diylo), 309 (Auriac), 330 (Turrivis), 419 (Castromuris), 425 (Agoldi, Gordon), 446 (Boxetum), 447 (Sex Forno, Salario), 453 (Acut), 475 (Petro Foco), 486 (Salerno), 488 (Inter Castello), 490 (Salerno), 526 (Inter Castello), 534 (Calars), 552

The New Militarism 295

only have definite proof that the new castle of Nice was constructed during this period.[28]

In nearby Eastern Languedoc we find the same pattern of numerous castles built and occupied everywhere. Nîmes which had new walls in 1015[29] had at least four such fortresses in the city whose names we know; Moriocipium, Turre Magna, Juncariot and the *castrum* of Sainte-Marie,[30] as well as nearby Salvense and Anduze.[31] Further to the west our sources mention the castles of Lignano, Turre of Adfaix (Béziers), Substantion, Béziers, Mercariolo, Adellano, Portiars, Pedinates, Mesoa, Varrigo, Florensiaco, Pavalleno, Nibian, Paulianus, Melgueil, Maguelonne, Duas Virginas, Charos, Porcano, Omelas, Rochabuno, Saint-Tiberio, Mellando, Rochafullo, Lunel, Frontiniaco, and Pouget.[32] We have definite proof that

---

(Mota), 558 (Palacionem), 570 (Marsens), 585 (Vite Albano), 621 (Trigantis), 625 (Archinose), 629 (Archinose), 655 (Boson), 666 (Forcalquier), 678 (Forcalquier), 684 (Saint-Vincent), 685 (Saint-Vincent), 721 (Drôme), 772 (Toramenus), 773 (Ducela, Senez), 774 (Petro Castellanus); *Chartes de Cluny*, III, nos. 1784 (Malaracua, Gap), 1987 (Podium, Odolinum), 2466 (Avignon, Colongellos); IV, nos. 2771 (Lunis), 2779 (Altonum, Bar, Charenguges, Guanin, Pictanis, Sarraix; *Cart. de Lérins*, nos. 3 (Avignon), 46 (Flaisoe), 49 (Canneto), 72 (Arlerc), 120 (Mugins, Grasse), 139 (Podietum de Malanate), 149 (Cagnes), 181 (Nice), 201 (Bruso), 222 (Sparro), 234 (Morera), 240 (Rochabuna); *Cartulaire de l'abbaye de Saint-Pons-hors-les-murs de Nice*, ed. E. Cais de Pierlas and G. Saige, nos. 1 (Revella, Lurs), 4 (Rocheta), 6 (Castellnova); *Cart. de Conques*, no. 395 (Auribello); *Hist. Gén. de Lang.*, V, nos. 172 (Favat, Condorcet), 216 (Tarascon); *Cart. de Saint-Chaffre*, no. 390 (Gordiano). See also references to a castle of Cariovolo in *Cart. de Saint-Chaffre*, no. 321; and to a castle of Bellumjocum in *Chartes de Cluny*, IV, no. 2771.

[28] *Cart. de Saint-Pons de Nice*, no. 6.
[29] *Cart. de Nîmes*, no. 92.
[30] *Ibid.*, nos. 77, 88; and *Hist. Gén. de Lang.*, V, no. 188.
[31] *Cart. de Nîmes*, no. 120.
[32] *Hist. Gén. de Lang.*, V, col. 55–56 (Maguelonne); V, nos. 128 (Lignano), 146 (Béziers, Mercariolo, Adellano, Portiars, Pedinates, Mesoa, Varrigo, Florensiaco, Pavalleno), 149 (Paulianus), 206 (Lunel), 209 (Charos, Porcano, Omelas, Rochabuno, Saint-Tiberio, Rochafullo); *Cart. d'Aniane*, nos. 80 (Frontiniaco), 241 (Nibian, Paulianus), 314 (Adfaix); *Liber Instrumentorum Memorialium* [Montpelliers], nos. 370 (Substantion), 376 (Substantion), 480–484 (Pouget); *Cart. de Béziers*, nos. 46 (Nibian), 49 (Béziers, Mercariolo, Adellano, Portiars, Pedinates, Meso, Varrigo, Florensiaco, Pavalleno); *Cart. de Maguelonne*, I, no. 4 (Melgueil, Maguelonne); *Cart. de Gellone*, nos. 37 (Duas Virginas), 59 (Melgueil), 105 (Mellando). See also mention of a castle of Morecuro in *Cart. d'Aniane*, no. 241; of a castle of Popian in *Cart. de Gellone*, no. 141; of a castle of Florentiac in *Hist. Gén. de Lang.*, V, no. 206; and of unnamed castles in *Cart. de Gellone*, nos. 6, 397.

at least one of these, that of Maguelonne, was constructed in this period between 1000 and 1010.[33]

In Western Languedoc and along the borders of Eastern Gascony we find just as many castles mentioned in the documents dating from these years. Among the more important ones are Saint-Pons, Saint-Martin, Choriano, Burg of Villanova, Collio, Colliensi, Sexago, Minerbe, Foix, Razès, Savartione, Castellopendente, Pierrapertusa, Queribus, Durbin, Dourgne, Palejano, Cula, Dunes, Roccamare, Lodet, Durimane, Saint-Hilaire, Lézat, Miravels [Mirabels], Auriac, Saint-Marcello, Porta Spina, Confolencs, and Castro Novo [Castelnau],[34] as well as the new walls and towers of Narbonne[35] and Carcassonne.[36]

When we turn to Gascony, though our sources are not very voluminous for this period, we again find a number of castles mentioned in our documents. One was near the abbey of Blasement[37] and a second, Castello Mousqué,[38] seems to have been not far from the monastery of Lucq. The old castle of Blavia near Bordeaux was still being used[39] as well as a new one built by Count Geoffrey of Angoulême.[40] Not far away were the *castellum* of Fronciac and other *castella* which Count Aldouin of Angoulême acquired as a result of his marriage about 1028 to the daughter of the duke of Gascony.[41]

In Western Aquitaine, that is to say in the Limousin, Quercy, Angoulême, Périgord, Saintonge, and the borders of Poitou documents again show many new castles as well as older ones which have been mentioned

---

[33] *Hist. Gén. de Lang.*, V, col. 55–56.

[34] *Ibid.*, V, nos. 130 (Saint-Pons, Saint-Martin), 151 (Choriano, Villanova), 155 (Miravels), 162 (Minerbe, Foix, Razès, Savartione, Castellopendente), 179 (Saint-Martin, Durbin), 184 (Miravels [Mirabels]), 185 (Dourgne), 199 (Razès), 206 (Auriac, Saint-Marcello, Porta Spina, Confolencs), 226 (Saint-Pons); XIII, 64 (Pierrapertusa); Cros-Meyrévielle, *Documents*, no. 35 (Collio, Colliensi, Sexago), 37 (Cula, Dunes, Roccamare, Lodet), 42 (Palejano); *Marca hispanica*, I, appendix 191 (Queribus); *Cart. de Saint-Sernin*, nos. 138 (Castro Nova), 280 (Durimane); *Chartes de Cluny*, III, no. 1950 (Saint-Hilaire, Lézat). See also references to a castle of Gaillac in *Hist. Gén. de Lang.*, V, no. 162; and to a castle of Caselas in *ibid.*, no. 207.

[35] *Hist. Gén. de Lang.*, V, no. 179.

[36] *Cart. de Carcassonne*, VI, 324.

[37] *Cart. de la Réolle*, no. 14.

[38] *Cartulaire de Saint-Vincent de Lucq*, ed. L. Barrau-Dihigo, in *Revue de Béarn et des Pays Basques*, I (1904), no. 2.

[39] *Ademar de Chabannes*, III, 67, p. 193.

[40] *Ibid.*

[41] *Ibid.*, III, 68, p. 194.

The New Militarism 297

in earlier chapters. Our sources speak of Angély, Belea, Traliburcense, Fracta Bute, Surgiaco, Marestay, Tulle, Tornense, Bré, Montchâtfer, Rochechouart, Turres, Consolente, Solignac, Castello Novo (Limoges), Niolo, Nobiliaco, Botvilla, Marfines, Cohec, Manslé, Castellar, Bellacum, Procea, Concay, Brossac, Roccamolten, Turre (Limoges), Massai, Argaton, Marillac, Roffrac, Martignac, and Saint-Angelus.[42] Many of these, according to the testimony of Ademar of Chabannes and other sources, were newly built during this period.[43]

From references in the relatively abundant sources which we possess for this period, then, we know of the names of some 275 castles and other fortresses which were in use in Southern France north of the Pyrenees during this period. Some 46 were in the Massif Central region of Auvergne-Rouergue-Albigeois, 37 in the vicinity of the Middle Rhone Valley, 86 in Provence, 5 in Gascony, and 34 in Western Aquitaine. By 1050 the castle had spread everywhere and became a symbol of the new militarization of the Midi. What had started slowly in the ninth century had become, by the mid-eleventh, a reality for the society of Southern France in every region south of Poitou and Burgundy.

There remains a consideration of castles in the Spanish March which, as we have already noted, was already covered with fortresses by the year 975. Nevertheless, documents from this region dating from this period give us information about many more of them. They mention Plana de Courts, Saint-Stephen, Livorte, Cabrera, Vultrairo, Pareds, Granario,

[42] *Cart. de Saint-Jean d'Angély*, nos. 5 (Angély), 78 (Traliburcense), 158 (Marestay), 184 (Surgiaco), 247 (Belea), 275 (Fracta Bute); *Cart. de Tulle*, nos. 343 (Montchâtfer), 481 (Tulle); *Cart. d'Uzerche*, nos. 46 (Tornense), 53 (Rochechouart), 54 (Rochechouart), 172 (Bré); *Cartulaire de l'aumônerie de Saint-Martial de Limoges*, ed. A. Laroux, in *Documents historiques de la Marche et du Limousin*, II, nos. 14 (Consolente), 30 (Turres); *Cart. de Saint-Etienne de Limoges*, nos. 28 (Castello Novo), 96 (Solignac); *Cart. de Beaulieu*, nos. 122 (Castello Novo), 175–177 (Niolo, Nobiliaco); *Cart. de Savigny*, nos. 633 (Botvilla), 635 (Marfines); *Cart. d'Angoulême*, I, no. 87 (Castellar), 158 (Cohec, Manslé); *Ademar de Chabannes*, III, 25, p. 148 (Martignac); 34, pp. 136–137 (Bellacum, Concay, Brossac); 36, p. 160 (Turre); 51, p. 174 (Massai, Argaton); 66, p. 186 (Marillac, Roffrac); "Aquitaniae Historiae Fragmenta," in *ibid.*, p. 205 (Bellacum, Procea), p. 208 (Roccamolten); *Chartes de Charroux*, nos. 72–75 (Saint-Angelus). The Turres mentioned in *Cart. de Saint-Martial de Limoges* may be the same place as the castle of Ségur mentioned in *Cart. d'Uzerche*, nos. 18–19. See also reference to the *turre* of Boson in *Cart. d'Uzerche*, no. 48; to the castle of Montemart in *Cart. de Saint-Etienne de Limoges*, no. 46; and to the castle of the abbey or church of Saint-Stephen in *Cart. de Beaulieu*, nos. 175–177.
[43] Some ten castles in all.

Monte Juliaco, Puigreig, Odene, Pinna Nigra, Santa-Crucis, Moralias, Viridaria, Miralles, Montbui, Villademaier, Montegut, Rocheta, Tous, Vivario, Leone, Mallato, Castro Comitale (Barcelona), Audelino, Olivella, Selma, Albinaño, Cedemilla, Aquitaro, Ervilla, Gariago, Aqualonga, Primaliano, Lauro, Calaf, Fonte Rubio, Malerdula, Turres Becces, Castelloi, La Granada, Orpino, Fontaneto, Castellet, Valle Fornes, Mogio, Saint-Vincent de Calders, Nure, Mediam, Santa-Oliva, Berano, Saint-Martin, Besalu, Lucca, Berga, Balcoreigne, Dua Castella, Oris, Curul, Merlen, Voltniger, Sousa, Fallat, Vacherias, Ardaval, Areng, Oriat, Monteclaro, Pontilans, Sandila, Santa-Perpetua, Lordanis, Fores, Fornells, Paladl, Far, Pax, Cubelles, Tarati, Taganarit, Gavan, Banvure, Tamarrit, Villo, Ales, Todela, Medolio, So, Folet, Agudo, Rochamauro, and Castellnou.[44] In addition to these fortresses we find a number of references to *turres* or smaller fortresses, one near San-Cugat,[45] one belonging to Daniel,[46] one belonging to Hennego,[47] another to Igiga,[48] and one to Sunio-

[44] *Cart. roussillonnais*, nos. 14 (Plana des Courts), 43 (Castellnou); *Cart. de San Cugat*, nos. 126 (Saint-Stephen), 139 (Pareds), 151 (Granario), 159 (Mt. Juliaco), 184 (Odene), 217 (Comitale), 253 (Audelino), 277 (Olivella), 287 (Gariago, Aqualonga), 343 (Calaf), 381 (Castelloi), 382 (Fonte Rubio, Malerdula, Turres Becces), 400 (Orpino), 421 (Fontaneto, Castellet), 431 (Modio, Saint-Vincent de Calders), 432 (Mogio, Saint-Vincent de Calders, Nure), 435 (Mediam), 449 (St. Oliva), 451 (Berano), 452 (Saint-Martin), 458 (Turres Becces), 505 (Ardaval), 544 (Saint-Vincent de Calders), 561 (Gavan); *Cart. de Carcassonne*, II, 228 (Livorte); *El Archivo Condal de Barcelona*, nos. 186 (Cabrera), 204 (Miralles, Montbui, Villademaier, Montegut, Rocheta, Tous), 210 (Puigreig), 223 (Comitale), 232 (Ervilla); *Catalunya Carolingia*, II, 211–213 (Vultrairo), 241–244 (Pinna Nigra, Santa Crucis, Moralias, Viridaria); *Hist. Gén. de Lang.*, V, nos. 144 (Vivario), 146 (Leone), 175 (Besalu); *El "Libre Blanch" de Santas Creus* [Barcelona], ed. F. Udina-Matorell, nos. 2 (Selma, Albinaño), 7 (Cademilla, Aquitaro), 9 (Fores); *Archivo Catedral de Barcelona*, nos. 26 (Primaliano, Lauro), 27 (La Granada); *Liber Feudorum*, nos. 113 (Villo, Ales), 121 (Lordanis), 141 (Areng, Oriat), 202 (Taganarit), 205 (Tarati), 207 Valle Fornis), 212 (Tamarrit), 272 (Lucca, Berga, Balcoreigne, Montecalro, Pontilans, Sandila, St. Perpetua), 273 (Dua Castella, Oris, Curul, Merlen, Voltniger, Sousa, Fallat, Vacherias), 353 (Banvure), 431 (Fornells), 437 (Tudela), 440 (Medolio), 441 (Medolio); *Cart. de Saint-Victor*, no. 1048 (Paladl, Far, Pax, Cubelles); Dom Luc D'Achery, *Spicelegium*, III, 392 (So, Folet); Ponsch, "Le Confluent et ses comtes," pp. 302 (Agudo), 303 (Rochamauro); *Marca hispanica*, I, appendix 143 (Castellnou); C. Brousse, "La vicomté de Castellnou," in *Études Roussillonnaises*, IV, 115–132 (Castellnou).
[45] *Cart. de San Cugat*, no. 125.
[46] *Ibid.*, no. 136.
[47] *Ibid.*, no. 527.
[48] *Ibid.*, no. 259.

The New Militarism

fredo,[49] as well as to the new walls of Barcelona which were built about 1030.[50] Of these almost a hundred castles which we find referred to in our sources, a number were definitely built during this period, like the fortress of Castellnou in Vallespir,[51] or those at Berga, Fores, Albinaño, and Castellet,[52] especially along the frontiers where the marcher lords who built them were advancing slowly, but surely, toward Tarragona and Lérida and other Moslem holdings in the Ebro Valley.

Our sources for this period, however, reveal to us more than just evidence of how castles increased in number during these years. They also contain frequent references to *milites*, or, as they are called in some parts of the Midi, *caballarios*. Some seven charters from Auvergne contain references to *milites*, generally speaking of them as *milites* of a certain castle.[53] For Rouergue and the Albigeois we find them mentioned in some five documents of the period, all of which use the term *caballarios*.[54] They are referred to in documents from the Velay region which date from 980, 1022, and 1030,[55] as well as in some ten charters from the Middle Rhone region, the earliest of which dates from the last years of the tenth century.[56]

---

[49] *Ibid.*, nos. 271, 312.

[50] *Archivo Catedral de Barcelona*, no. 40.

[51] *Marca hispanica*, I, appendix 143.

[52] *Liber Feudorum*, no. 372 (Berga); *El "Libre Blanch" de Santas Creus* [Barcelona], nos. 2 (Albinaño), 9 (Fores); *Cart. de San Cugat*, no. 421 (Castellet).

[53] Note in charters of this period such phrases as, Stephen *"miles"* and the *"milites de Salern"* (*Cart. de Sauxillanges*, no. 660); *"ceteri milites de Nonentensis* [Nonette]" (*ibid.*, no. 618); "*Amblard, comtor de oppida Noneda* [Nonette] *et milites suos"* (*Cart. de Saint-Flour*, no. 5); *"Militum de Castelli Novi"* (*Cart. de Sauxillanges*, no. 290); *"consentibus militibus"* (*Cart. de Brioude*, no. 105); and *"milites de Brosadolz"* and *"homines de Crussac"* (*Cart. de Saint-Flour*, no. 6). Obviously in Auvergne the terms *miles* and *milites* still refer to those who bear arms and should be translated as "fighting men" or "military garrison," not "knight" in the later feudal sense of the word.

[54] In Rouergue we find a series of charters which mention dues levied as *recepta* for so many *caballarios* (*Cart. de Gellone*, nos. 93, 98, and *Cart. de Conques*, nos. 23, 254). See also the mention of *"Belli homines"* in *ibid.*, no. 215. Here it would seem that during this period that the term *caballarios* means "horsemen," "fighting men," or "mounted men" rather than a social feudal class as such.

[55] See mention of *"omnes milites"* of Velay in a charter of about 980 and *"milites et feminas de Cherssac"* about 1040 (*Hist. Gén. de Lang.*, V, cols. 14, 23). See also reference to Gerald, the old *"miles de Rochos"* and a *"boschaticum"* or wooden fortress held by "Erato *de* Acarius, Wilhelmo *et* Petro Negro, *militibus*" (*Cart. de Saint-Egidius*, no. 95). We also have a mention of Stephen *"miles de Castro Bisatico"* in *Cart. de Saint-Chaffre*, no. 205. Here it would seem the term sometimes means "fighting men," as in Auvergne, and sometimes "knight."

[56] For the Lyonnais see mention in a charter of about 1000 of *"Alemanni Cabal-*

In the Provence region, where the terms *miles* and *caballarius* seem to be used almost interchangeably, we find thirteen references to this class also, one as early as 979.[57] In Languedoc we find this class referred to less frequently in specific terms, but we still find it mentioned four times starting as early as about 980.[58] On the other hand, in Gascony where, judging from our sources, castles were still relatively rare, there are six documents which mention *milites*, one of which dates from as early as 985, which makes us suspect that there existed here a fairly large class of such warriors.[59] The same seems to be true of Western Aquitaine where eleventh century charters mention them some nine times.[60] Nor was the Spanish

---

arii" or German mounted men or knights in *Cart. de Savigny*, no. 366; about 1020 a charter mentions a *receptum* for one *caballario* (*ibid.*, no. 654); and about 1031 *"milites"* of the German emperor (Raoul Glaber, *Historiarum libri V*, V, 4, 21–22, pp. 130–131). Starting in 1032, we find a series of other documents from the Lyonnais and Dauphiny which mention the terms *"miles"* or *"milites"*: *"Cart. d'Ainay,"* no. 95 in *Cart. de Savigny*; *Chartes de Cluny*, IV, no. 2960; *Cart. de Vienne*, nos. 52, 94; *Cart. de Saint-Barnard de Romans*, nos. 74, 96; and *Cart. de Saint-André-le-bas*, no. 206. Here *miles* already seems to mean "knight."

[57] Somewhat mixed is the situation in Provence. For example see references in charters of 979 to a *"caballarius"* and a *"cavallerius"* in *Cart. de Saint-Victor*, no. 1042, and *Hist. Gén. de Lang.*, V, no. 133. We find charters of 993 mentioning *"milites"* and "Pandulf *miles"* (*Cart. de Saint-Victor*, no. 77, and *Chartes de Cluny*, III, no. 2268). A charter dating from 1010–1046 from Apt mentions *"duobis militibus"* (*Cart. de Saint-Victor*, no. 437). One from Sisteron of 1026 lists among its witnesses *"cetêri circum adstantes milites"* (*ibid.*, no. 655). A charter of 1026–1048 mentions a *"miles"* who is one of the *principes* of Antibes (*Cart. de Lérins*, no. 113), while in 1029 we find a mention of *"cabalarii"* at Arles (*Cart. de Saint-Victor*, no. 209). In 1030 we find that a charter speaks of the brothers of the archbishop of Arles and *"ceteri conmilites"* (*ibid.*, no. 405). A charter of 1033 mentions land owing dues *"pro uno caballo"* near Marseille (*ibid.*, no. 101); while one of 1035 uses the term *miles* (*Cart. de Lérins*, no. 74); and one from Fréjus in 1038 speaks of a *"caballario"* (*ibid.*, no. 29). One of 1050 speaks of fourteen men called *milites* of Lord Arbert of Digne (*Cart. de Saint-Victor*, no. 739).

[58] The same situation seems to prevail in Languedoc as in Provence. A charter of 1020 mentions "Bernard *miles* Pelitus" (lord of Anduze) (*Cart. de Nîmes*, no. 120). There is also a charter from nearby which mentions an *"albergum"* for "IIII *caballarios"* in 1039 (*Cart. d'Aniane*, no. 236). Near Carcassonne according to a charter of 1036 there was a *"miles"* Bernard Odalricus, (Cros-Meyrévielle, *Documents*, no. 41); while a charter of 980 from Toulouse mentions an *"alberc"* (*albergum*) with six *"milites"* (*Cart. de Saint-Sernin*, no. 158).

[59] Charters of 985, 986, 988, 1010–1032, and 1030 mention the term *"miles"* in Gascony. See *Cart. de Lucq*, nos. 1, 3, 8; *Cart. de la Réolle*, no. 2; *Cartulaire de Saint-Jean de Sorde*, ed. P. Raymond, no. 9; *Hist. Gén. de Lang.*, V, no. 195.

[60] In Saintonge we find charters using the terms *"militibus"* referring to Rainald

March without its class of *milites*, though they are specifically called so infrequently; one reference to them was found which dates from 987,[61] another in 1040.[62] In every section of Southern France and Catalonia, then, by 1050 a special class of *milites* had appeared which was recognized as distinct by the society of the period, and which occupied the old and new fortresses of every region south of Poitou and Burgundy.

How were the castles and other fortresses which these *milites* garrisoned owned and held during these years? That is our next question. In this period, as in earlier ones we have examined, many of them were either owned outright by Church establishments or were the allodial possession of important magnates and their families. Our documents from Auvergne and Velay, which mention Ictor of Castro Rochareuil,[63] or Maurice of Castro Pallerios[64] or Amblard, *comtor* of Oppida Noneda[65] or even Gerald, old *miles* of Rochas,[66] certainly imply that each of the above owned the fortress in question as allods. We know, for instance, that in 1020 the castle of Saint-Julian in the Lyonnais was a family allod of the Guerin clan, each member owning a portion of it.[67] Just so the castles of Pupet and Novum Castellum, which King Rudolf gave to his

---

and Robert in 1000 (*Cart. de Saint-Jean d'Angély*, no. 49); referring to Rainald *"miles"* in 1031 (*ibid.*, no. 197); and to "Contantius *miles"* in 1035 (*ibid.*, no. 221); as well as to the *milites* Francho and Mascelinus in 1034 (*Cartulaire de l'abbaye royale de Notre Dame de Saintes*, ed. T. Graslier, in *Cartulaires inédits de la Saintonge*, II, no. 75). In the Limousin a charter of 1030 mentions three *"milites"* of the brother of the *prepositus* of Saint-Etienne of Limoges (obviously vassals) (*Cart. de Saint-Etienne de Limoges*, no. 1056). A charter of 1036 and one of 1044 mention *"miles"* (*Cart. d'Uzerche*, nos. 58, 132–133); while another of 1045 refers to certain *"milites"* (*ibid.*, no. 109). Here, as in Gascony, *miles* seems to mean "knight."

[61] See reference to the viscount of Cardona and his *"conmilites"* in a charter of 987 (*Hist. Gén. de Lang.*, V, no. 141).

[62] The *"milites"* and *"homines"* of the castle of Albiñana are mentioned in a charter of 1040 (*Cart. de San Cugat*, no. 553).

[63] *Cart. de Sauxillanges*, no. 635.

[64] *Ibid.*, no. 623.

[65] *Cart. de Saint-Flour*, no. 6.

[66] *Cart. de Saint-Egidius*, no. 98. See also a charter, dating from 1036–1048, from Eastern Languedoc which mentions Ermengaud of Duas Virginas, Gerald of Popian, Raymond of Giniac, and others. (*Cart. de Gellone*, no. 18). Or one from the Limousin of 1031–1060 which speaks of Stephen of Terrazo, Robert of Vallada, and others (*Cart. de Vigeois*, no. 11). Or see the mention of the *miles* Elias de Malamont in a charter of 1045 (*Cart. d'Uzerche*, no. 109).

[67] *Cart. de Savigny*, nos. 652, 654–658.

wife Queen Ermengaude about 1011, were his allods.[68] At about the same period in Provence we find Bellielis, daughter of Viscount William of Provence, owning one castle outright and one-third of another which was probably part of the family possessions of the house of Marseille.[69] In 1034 a similar one-third ownership of castles is revealed by the gift of certain rights over fortresses to the abbey of Saint-Victor of Marseille by another member of this same family.[70]

When we consider Languedoc and Aquitaine we find the same situation. The castle of Anduze and others nearby seem to have been the outright allodial possessions of the marquises of Anduze.[71] So were a number of castles which Viscount William of Béziers in 990 left to his wife and his daughters in his will.[72] Similarly, examination of the legacies left by Count Roger the Old of Carcassonne reveals that many of the castles in his domains were allods—allods which were often divided in a rather complex way among various members of the family.[73] Just so a charter of 1037 shows us that at least some of the castles which Count Pons of Toulouse gave to his wife Majore as a bridal gift were outright allodial possessions of this important nobleman.[74] In the nearby Limousin the counts of La Marche owned castles like Bellacum and Roccamolten as allods.[75] So did Count Geoffrey, brother of Count Aldouin of Angoulême, who built a new castle near Blavia about 1028,[76] and Aldouin himself, who, we learn, owned the fortress of Fronsac *"in dominio proprietatis."*[77]

Such castles owned as allods by important magnates were particularly common as well in the Spanish March. Many seem to have small fortresses or *turres* like those which our sources show us were owned by lords like Deacon Suniofredo, Hennego, or Igiga.[78] Others were important castles like Montegut which a charter dating from 992 mentions as an allod belonging to Lord Belleron,[79] or Ervilla which Count Raymond Borell of Barcelona and Count Ermengol of Urgell sold to Lord Hennego in this

[68] *Cart. de Vienne*, nos. 39, 40.
[69] *Cart. de Saint-Victor*, no. 135.
[70] *Ibid.*, no. 255.
[71] *Cart. de Nîmes*, no. 120.
[72] *Cart. de Béziers*, no. 49.
[73] *Hist. Gén. de Lang.*, V, no. 162.
[74] *Ibid.*, no. 206.
[75] *Ademar de Chabannes*, III, 34, p. 157, and "Aquitaniae Historiae Fragmenta," in *ibid.*, p. 208.
[76] *Ademar de Chabannes*, III, 67, p. 193.
[77] *Ibid.*, III, 68, p. 194.
[78] *Cart. de San Cugat*, nos. 271, 259, 312, 327.
[79] *El "Libre Blanch" de Santas Creus* [Barcelona], no. 3.

The New Militarism

same year.⁸⁰ The exchange of still another castle, Masquefa, which Hennego made with the abbey of San-Cugat in 998 in return for the castle of Gellito reveals the same kind of allodial ownership.⁸¹ So does the gift of two castles, Mogio and Albiñano, to this abbey by two members of the viscontal family of Barcelona in 1010⁸²—a gift, incidentally, which was unsuccessfully challenged by other members of this family before a court presided over by Count Raymond Borell in 1011.⁸³ A little later, about 1023, we find Count Raymond Berengar I of Barcelona selling as an allod still another castle, for the price of sixty ounces of gold, the buyer being a marcher lord called Guillelm.⁸⁴ And as late as 1048 still another fortress, given to Count Raymond Berengar by Bernard, son of Ermengaud, shows that allodial castle ownership continued in Catalonia, particularly along the frontiers.⁸⁵ In the Spanish March, as elsewhere in the Midi, the castle which was owned outright as an allod by an individual magnate or by important families was still to be found down to 1050.

Along with this allodial ownership of castles, which was a common feature of this period, as it had been earlier, we find still another method of castle control. This was also not new, but perhaps became a more elaborated and highly organized system during these years. I refer to a division of a castle between him who owned it and had *"dominio proprietates"* over it, and him who was in actual possession of it or *held* it. By this time in most examples of this system which we find in Southern France and the Spanish March, this latter individual was said to hold one-half of such a castle *"in feudo"* or *"in beneficio."* A castle held as a fief or benefice, then, generally is thought of as a sort of division in which the possessor divides it with the allodial owner. A somewhat later document seems to be describing the use of this system in Dauphiny during this period when it tells us that the bishops of Grenoble held the allod of the castles built in Dauphiny and the noblemen the *feudum*.⁸⁶ That such an interpretation is the correct one seems to be confirmed by a charter of 996 which shows Bishop Humbert giving to Cluny *his half* of the castle of Visalia.⁸⁷

---

⁸⁰ *El Archivo Condal de Barcelona*, no. 232.
⁸¹ *Cart. de San Cugat*, no. 331.
⁸² *Ibid.*, nos. 431, 432.
⁸³ *Ibid.*, nos. 437–439.
⁸⁴ *El "Libre Blanch" de Santas Creus* [Barcelona], no. 8.
⁸⁵ *Liber Feudorum*, no. 353.
⁸⁶ *Cart. de Grenoble*, no. 16.
⁸⁷ *Chartes de Cluny*, III, no. 2307. See also in 1009 the gift of one-half of a castle to Bishop Humbert by King Rudolf (*Cart. de Vienne*, no. 38).

In Provence, where this half and half system of holding castles was no doubt encouraged by the example of the *medium plantum*, we can find other examples of this practice. Thus a charter of 984 shows us Pons, bishop of Marseille giving one-half of the castle of Almis to the abbey of Saint-Victor and reserving one-half for himself *"ad allodem,"*[88] and a charter of four years later shows another landowner doing the same in giving one-half of the castle of Gap to Cluny.[89] Another nobleman, called Richard, did the same in the year 1000 in giving property to this same abbey.[90] Sometimes our records seem to show that an allodial owner of a castle, having already granted one-half of it as a fief contented himself with giving one-half of his reserved allodial rights. This seems to explain how in 990 Count William could give to Saint-Victor one-quarter of the castles of Arlerc and Avignon,[91] and why in 1023 Cluny received a gift of one-half of one castle and one-quarter of four others from two brothers, Leodegar and Pons.[92] As late as 1040 this method was still not uncommon, as we learn from documents which tell us of how Rambaud, archbishop of Arles, gave one-half of the castle of Ornon to Saint-Victor of Marseille,[93] and how Viscount William of this city gave one-half of the castle of Mato to this same abbey.[94]

When we turn to Languedoc we find what appears to be the same system in a charter telling of how Viscount William of Béziers and his wife gave back to the church of Béziers in 990 one-half of the castle of Nibian and one-half of that of Morecino.[95] In 1030 we also find a reference to a certain Esco, who gave to Rotmund of Folgerius one-half of the *honorem*, which he says he has *"in meo dominio"* over the *castrum* of Lignano.[96] In 1028 we learn of the one-half of their allod in the castle of Auriac given by a certain Odalric and his brother to Viscount Aton II of Albi,[97] and a little later of how Count Pons of Toulouse gave one-half of the castle of Porta Spina to his wife Marjore.[98] Nor was Aquitaine unacquainted with this method of holding castles. Ademar of Chabannes, for example, tells

[88] *Cart. de Saint-Victor*, no. 70.
[89] *Chartes de Cluny*, III, no. 1784.
[90] *Ibid.*, IV, no. 2529.
[91] *Cart. de Lérins*, nos. 3, 72.
[92] *Chartes de Cluny*, IV, no. 2779.
[93] *Cart. de Saint-Victor*, no. 58.
[94] *Ibid.*, no. 552.
[95] *Cart. de Béziers*, no. 46.
[96] *Ibid.*, no. 62.
[97] *Hist. Gén. de Lang.*, V, no. 190.
[98] *Ibid.*, no. 206.

The New Militarism

us how about 1028 Count Aldouin of Angoulême gave to his brother Geoffrey three-quarters of the castle of Blavia *"in beneficio"* and kept the remaining quarter as an allod.[99] A little later about 1035, according to our sources, the bishop of Limoges gave to Saint-Martial the *fevum* of a new castle which he had received from the duke of Aquitaine, who still possessed the *dominio* or allod of this fortress.[100] About 1050 another document tells us of the *burg* of Manslé, of which one-half had been given *"in feudo"* by the canons of the church of Angoulême.[101]

It is Catalonia, however, which seems to furnish us with the most complete information concerning the workings of this system. As early as 987, for instance, a charter tells us of how Count Borell II of Barcelona gave one-half of the castle of Miralès and its surrounding territory to the bishop of Ausona,[102] and in 999 we hear of how Lady Irvanna sold to a certain Hugh one-half of the castle of Montegut.[103] In 1012 we learn from a charter of the gift of one-half the castle of Cleriana and the devastated land pertaining to it to a marcher lord named Gundallo, a castle which seems to belong to Guitard, abbot of San-Cugat.[104] The same abbey is revealed in a charter of 1013 to have similarly divided the castle of Saint-Martin with a Lady Adelaise.[105]

Even more specific information comes from a document dating from 1037. This tells us how Abbot Guitard of San-Cugat gave the castle of Saint-Vincent of Calders to a certain Bernard and his sons. Bernard and his heirs are to hold one-half of this fortress as an allod for two generations and the other half *"per nostrum fevum."* If they did not rebuild the castle in ten years they were to pay a fine of ten ounces of gold to the abbey.[106] A charter of 1038 shows us Count Raymond Berengar I of Barcelona giving a similar castle, that of Flores, which needed to be rebuilt, to another such marcher lord;[107] and another document of 1040, which mentions a grant of land of San-Cugat to another such lord, illustrates this system again. This latter grant concerns an agreement to rebuild the castle of Arampuña and repopulate its lands over a period of some seven

---

[99] *Ademar de Chabannes*, III, 67, p. 193.
[100] *Cart. de Saint-Etienne de Limoges*, no. 28.
[101] *Cart. d'Angoulême*, no. 100.
[102] *El Archivo Condal de Barcelona*, no. 204.
[103] *El "Libre Blanch" de Santas Creus* [Barcelona], no. 4.
[104] *Cart. de San Cugat*, no. 442.
[105] *Ibid.*, no. 452.
[106] *Ibid.*, no. 544.
[107] *Liber Feudorum*, no. 57.

years. The recipient of this castle and its surrounding territory and his heirs were to have one-half of this castle as an allod and one-half *"pro fevum."* The abbey of San-Cugat reserved for itself, on the other hand, pasturage rights, one-quarter of all castle dues and tithes, and one-third of all captives and booty taken by the castellan and *milites* of this fortress.[108] In 1045 still another charter tells us of a grant of land to a certain Argila by a certain Raymond Isembert in which one-half of the land was to be held by Argila and one-half reserved for Raymond.[109] Finally a charter of about this same date contains an agreement between the abbey of San-Cugat and a certain Gerald, castellan of Cleriana, in which the latter agreed to pay the abbey one-half of the court fines, one-half of the tithes, and one-half of the *censives* for the *castellaris* of which San-Cugat is the allodial owner.[110]

These many and varied examples of how in the Midi and Catalonia castles were given out as fiefs, however, does not exhaust the ways in which castles were controlled. In addition to the fief or *fevum* of a castle we find in this period still another system used, the *guarda* or *baillem*. The castle of Solignac in the Limousin, which Aton held as castellan from the bishop of Limoges some time between 1024 and 1050, seems to have been such a *guarda*.[111] So were a number of castles and border districts mentioned in charters from Catalonia which date from 991, 992, and 1017.[112] Even a bishop like Frotaire of Cahors could hold the *guarda* of a castle, in this case one which in 985 belonged to Viscount Isarn of Lautrec.[113] During this period then, *guardas*, more limited in scope than fiefs, are also found in our regions and used as a method of entrusting such fortresses to someone who does not possess the allod or *dominio* of them.

What seems clear then is the fact that castles and the districts pertaining to them were, in this period as earlier, owned and granted out in a bewildering series of ways. There was no single system for owning or holding castles, but a variety of them which existed side by side with one another. They could be owned by a church or an individual outright. They could be subject to joint family ownership. Some could be granted out as benefices or fiefs under the 50–50 system, or they could be entrusted to a castellan as *guardas*. Always we find that the revenues of the castle

---

[108] *Cart. de San Cugat*, no. 553.
[109] *Ibid.*, no. 583.
[110] *Ibid.*, no. 586.
[111] *Cart. de Saint-Etienne de Limoges*, no. 96.
[112] *Cart. de San Cugat*, nos. 272, 284, 466.
[113] *Hist. Gén. de Lang.*, V, no. 139.

The New Militarism 307

were divided too between occupier and owners when such a division of control took place. All of which makes it clear that such castles and the rights pertaining to them were considered as *property* in the Midi and Catalonia. Like other property they followed natural laws of division and inheritance, even in the conditional grants of rights. They seem in this sense indistinguishable from other allodial, *aprisio,* or feudal property found in these regions.

Yet when we insist on this view of castles as property, we must still recognize that for this age in the Midi and Catalonia such castles were an unusually *important* type of property. The nobles and ruling families and churchmen of the Midi and Catalonia recognized this fact too. They knew that castles were the key to effective political and economic control over local districts. This explains why in the wills of the leading nobles of this period, castles and their control are always mentioned so specifically. The conditions under which they are left to an heir are always made extremely clear. This is not only true of earlier tenth century wills left by members of the house of Toulouse-Rouergue. It is true also of the later ones of Count Roger the Old of Carcassonne,[114] Viscount William of Béziers,[115] and a number of the more important magnates of the Spanish March.[116]

Nor is it only these wills which make clear how important ownership and control of castles was to the society of the Midi and Catalonia. We have another proof of their importance—a number of examples of oaths and agreements made between the leading nobles and landowners of this period concerning castles. These oaths or agreements, which are generally reproduced in our charters, not in Latin, but in the vulgar tongue, are sometimes spoken of as examples of feudal homage. This is not entirely accurate in many cases as a description of them, for some concern agreements between members of the same family, such as that of Carcassonne, in which no feudal relationship in the ordinary sense of the word existed.[117] What they seem to be, then, are agreements which con-

---

[114] *Ibid.,* no. 162.
[115] *Cart. de Béziers,* no. 49.
[116] *Cart. de San Cugat,* nos. 431–432, 437–439.
[117] See for instance the agreement, dating from 1036, between Counts William and Peter of Carcassonne (*Hist. Gén. de Lang.,* V, no. 209); and the oath or agreement made by Count Roger of Carcassonne with his uncle Bishop Peter (Cros-Meyrévielle, *Documents,* nos. 38, 39). It is also worth noting that the agreement between Bernard and the bishop of Limoges which concerned the castle of Solignac in the Limousin about 1035 is called a *pactum* (*Cart. de Saint-Etienne de Limoges,* no. 96). That dating from 1040 in Dauphiny, though a castle is mentioned, seems to mention no service due at all (*Cart. de Grenoble,* no. 46).

cern castles made between those who actually are in *physical possession* of such fortresses and those who have rights of *dominio* over them. Possession of a castle might be the result of the grant of a fief, or the creation of a *guarda*. It might be the result of part-allodial ownership. But in any case, he who had a share in this castle in the form of allodial ownership or lordship needed to make clear his rights and to protect them from the one who occupied it. Hence these agreements were necessary.

This leads us to a consideration of the agreements themselves. In addition to one similar to the others, about which we have a rather vague and unsatisfactory statement in a charter from the Grenoble region dating from 1040,[118] we possess some thirty such agreements or oaths. They come from a number of regions, from the Limousin, from the Toulousain, from the Albigeois, from Melgueil, from Béziers, from Carcassonne-Razès,[119] and from the Spanish March[120]—a fairly wide distribution over our regions. The largest number come from Catalonia; and all those from regions north of the Pyrenees and most of those from the south of it concern castles. All seem quite similar in form and, generally speaking, in content too. The earliest of them, mentioned in an earlier chapter, dates from 954.[121] The last one we will be considering is dated just after 1050.

In almost all agreements an individual who holds a particular castle swears *fidelitas* to him who has *dominio* or allodial rights over this fortress. This oath almost never, in our examples, is one of general support, but rather a promise not to aid the latter's enemies, not to deliver the castle over to such enemies, sometimes specified by name, and generally to surrender this castle or castles to him upon demand.[122] Exceptions are often

[118] *Cart. de Grenoble*, no. 46 (*circa* 1040).
[119] *Cart. de Saint-Etienne de Limoges*, no. 96 (*c.* 1035) (the Limousin); *Hist. Gén. de Lang.*, V, nos. 139 (985) and 190 (1028) (the Toulousain); 209 (Béziers); 217 (1040), and 412–414 (1035) (the Albigeois); 179 (1020), 185 (1025), 210 (1036), and Cros-Meyrévielle, *Documents*, nos. 38, 39 (1035) (Carcassonne-Razès); *Liber Instrumentorum Memorialium* [Montpellier], nos. 480–484 (1059) (Melgueil).
[120] For agreements, records of agreements, and oaths of fealty in Catalonia during this period see *El "Libre Blanch" de Santas Creus* [Barcelona], no. 2 (978); *Cart. de San Cugat*, nos. 544 (1037), 571 (1044), 599 (1010–1053); *Liber Feudorum*, nos. 109 (1050), 146 (1039–1049), 147 (1050), 150 (1039–1065), 157 (1018–1023), 202 (1039–1050), 203 (1050), 205 (1039–1059), 272 (1018–1023), 284 (1039–1049), 417–418 (1039–1049), 432–433 (1048); *Cart. roussillonnais*, no. 42 (1050).
[121] *Hist. Gén. de Lang.*, II, no. 209.
[122] For an example of such limited provisions for the Toulousain see the agreement between Bishop Frotaire and Viscount Isarn of Lautrec in 985 (*Hist. Gén.*

The New Militarism

specifically mentioned.[123] In return he who has rights of *dominio* over the castle swears to respect the rights of the castellan who occupies this fortress and to protect him in case of need against his enemies, though even here sometimes exceptions are specified.[124] In some cases both parties to these agreements produce *fidejussores* who guarantee these oaths and promise large payments of money in case either part defaults in the performance of their promises.[125]

Now an analysis of these oaths leads one to some interesting conclusions. Their emphasis seems essentially *negative*. He who holds the castle and he who has *dominio* over it emphasize not a positive *fidelitas* to each other, but a negative one—what they will *not* do. The scope of these agreements also seems in general very limited.[126] They seem to concern not *fidelitas* in the Carolingian or Northern French sense of the word, but *fidelitas* as regards a particular piece of property. One is not swearing

---

de Lang., V, no. 139). For the Narbonnaise see the agreement between William Ebroin and Viscount Berenger of Narbonne in 1020 (*ibid.*, no. 372). For Eastern Languedoc see the agreement between Guillem of Pouget and Lord Guillem of Montpellier in 1059 (*Liber Instrumentorum Memorialium* [Montpellier], nos. 480–481). Or for Catalonia see, among others, the agreement of 1050 between Abbot Berengar and Count Raymond Berenger I of Barcelona in *Liber Feudorum*, no. 437, and that of Count Ermengol of Urgell and Count Raymond Berenger I in 1039–1065 (*ibid.*, no. 1050). See also agreements dating from 1039–1049 found in *ibid.*, nos. 241, 284, 417–418, 431–433.

[123] For examples of such special conditions see the agreement of Bernard and Bishop Jordain about 1035 in *Cart. de Saint-Etienne de Limoges*, no. 96. Or that of Count William and Viscount Berenger of Narbonne in which William promised to aid the latter against all enemies *except* Count Hugh of Rouergue, Count William of Toulouse, Count Bernard of Melgueil, and his own sons Peter, Roger, and Pons (*Hist. Gén. de Lang.*, V, no. 210). For Catalonia one of the best such examples is the pact, called a *conventia*, between Count Ermengol of Urgell and the count of Barcelona which dates from 1039–1049 (*Liber Feudorum*, no. 146). Or see the exception made of the viscount of Cardona in the general oath of fealty which the lord of the castle of Tarati made to Count Raymond of Barcelona, *circa* 1039–1050 (*ibid.*, no. 205). For other such exceptions see *ibid.*, no. 202, and *Cart. roussillonnais*, no. 42.

[124] See note above.

[125] For examples of such guarantors or *fidejussores* see *Cart. de Saint-Etienne de Limoges*, no. 96, and *Liber Feudorum*, no. 157.

[126] It is precisely the limited or *specific* nature of these agreements, pacts, conventions, or oaths which seems to distinguish them from those we normally think of as feudal. This seems even truer of them than the general *fidelitas* of Carolingian times, as specified in the *Manual of Dhuoda*, limited and negative though that *fidelitas* was.

homage *to a man;* one is swearing a limited *fidelitas* for a castle or castles. One gets the impression that castles were important property, and that owners and those who occupied them needed to specify the exact way in which they were to be controlled, but that in so doing they did not, as in Northern French feudalism, set up any general personal tie of loyalty. And this was to continue to be true in the Midi and the Spanish March long after this period.[127] The basis of power was still the *allod*, considered property, above all, in the Roman sense of the word, and even castles and their control reflected this point of view.

So far in this chapter we have concerned ourselves only with the increase in the number of castles to be found and the methods by which they were owned, granted out as fiefs or *guardas*, and safeguarded for owner and possessor alike. But there still remains another important question which needs to be examined—the effect of such castles upon Southern France and Catalonia during this period. Here we must emphasize what we began to find was true during the preceding period, that a castle had become more than a mere fortress. It had become the center of a territory or district which in varying degrees was subject to the authority of its castellan and its *milites*. In almost every region south of Poitou and Burgundy, it had become what contemporary sources call a *mandamenta*.

In Dauphiny and Provence where, from 950 on, the castle had tended to be an instrument of government for organizing regions which had no law and order, we would expect to find a good deal of evidence of such *mandamenta* centering about castles during this period. And we do. In 1015, for instance, a charter which mentions a *"castellum novum"* in Dauphiny speaks of its *"apendiciis et mandemences."*[128] In Provence we find even more abundant references to the territories which pertained to castles in charters which date from 988, 990, 1000, 1009, 1010, 1012, 1022, 1023, 1025, 1027, 1030, 1031, 1033, 1038, and 1040.[129] Nor need we be surprised that in the Spanish March, where from the time of Count

---

[127] In this respect there seems to be no essential difference between the types of oaths and agreements found in the Midi and Catalonia *during this period* and those of the late eleventh, twelfth, and early thirteenth century which Richardot calls *"francs fiefs."* See H. Richardot, "Francs fiefs: essai sur l'exemption totale ou partielle des services de fief," in *Revue historique de droit français et étranger*, XXVII (1949). This pattern, then, seems to be a continuing one reflecting fundamental Southern French and Catalan patterns of political action and thought.

[128] *Cart. de Vienne*, no. 43.

[129] *Chartes de Cluny*, III, no. 1784; IV, nos. 2771, 2779; *Cart. de Lérins*, nos. 3, 240; and *Cart. de Saint-Victor*, nos. 58, 64, 135, 250, 253, 330, 475, 488, 490, 625, 684, 772.

Guifred, frontier land was organized around the castle, this still remained true throughout this period. This accounts for references to territory belonging to castles found in charters dating from 976, 977, 981, 983, 986, 988, 990, 991, 992, 993, 994, 999, 1001, 1005, 1006, 1010, 1012, 1018, 1020, 1030, 1031, 1036, 1037, 1038, and 1045.[130]

What seems to be a more significant development though, is the spread of this system into other parts of the Midi where, prior to 975, it was rarer than in Provence and the Spanish March. Thus, in the Massif Central region of Auvergne, Rouergue, and Velay we can see the beginnings of such *mandamenta* in references to *"in territorio* Castelluc" in 983, the *mandamenta* of the castle of Ussarie in 986, the *mandamenta* of the castle of Cairovolo between 996 and 1031, the *"vicaria de* Castro Capitoliensi" in 1030, or the *podium* of Mons Barcolomio *"cum boschaticum"* in 1050.[131] In Western Aquitaine we find a reference late in the tenth century to the *caslania* of the *castrum* of Tulle, the *"vicaria de* Castro Traliburcense" in 1016, and Castro Fronciaco *"cum omnibus in circuitui terris et castellis"* in 1028.[132]

In Languedoc a document of 978 mentions the *circuitu* of the castle of Saint-Martin; the castle of Sexago *"cum ipsa caslania et ipsa virgarias"* is referred to in one of 1002 and so is that of Minerbe and the land pertaining to it in the same year.[133] In 1010 we hear of the *castrum* of Melgueil and its *mandamenta,* and in 1034 of the castle of Cula *"cum ipsa terra."*[134] To these direct references to land surrounding castles which were subject to their authority, we should add references to the special dues their castellans and *milites* levied on regions nearby which give us indirect

---

[130] *Cart. de San Cugat,* nos. 112 (976), 122 (977), 151 (981), 184 (983), 246 (986), 272 (988), 286 (990), 292 (991), 341 (992), 361 (993), 400 (994), 402 (999), 599 (1001), 499 (1005), 470 (1006), 478 (1010), 512 (1012), 544 (1018), and 583 (1020). See also *El Archivo Condal de Barcelona,* no. 188 (1030); *Hist. Gén. de Lang.,* V, nos. 144 (1031) and 175 (1036); *Archivo Catedral de Barcelona,* no. 26 (1037); and *Liber Feudorum,* nos. 57 (1038) and 58 (1045).

[131] *Cart. de Sauxillanges,* no. 376 (Castelluc); *Cart. de Saint-Egidius,* nos. 97 (Ussarie), 189 (Cairovolo), 227 (Mons Barcolomio); *Cart. de Saint-Chaffre,* no. 228 (Capitoliensi). See also *"in territorio de illa Roca"* in *Cart. de Brioude,* no. 299, and *"parrochia castri Saint-Desiderius"* in a charter of 1031–1060 (*Cart. de Saint-Egidius,* no. 96).

[132] *Cart. de Tulle,* no. 290; *Cart. de Saint-Jean d'Angély,* no. 78; *Ademar de Chabannes,* III, 68, p. 194.

[133] *Hist. Gén. de Lang.,* V, nos. 130, 162; and Cros-Meyrévielle, *Documents,* no. 35.

[134] *Cart. de Maguelonne,* I, no. 4; Cros-Meyrévielle, *Documents,* no. 37.

evidence of the development of such *mandamenta*. These dues were particularly heavy, when levied on land belonging to churchmen, and aroused the hostility of monastic establishments in particular. Thus charters of such establishments call them *"malos consuetudines"* or *"malos toltos"* in Auvergne.[135] They refer to them as *"usos"* or *"usura"* in Rouergue,[136] and "unjust rights," "unjust customs" or *"malos consuetudines"* in the Limousin.[137] In Velay we find them again called *"malos consuetudines"* or *"pravos usos,"*[138] in Gascony *"mala exactione et rapina,"*[139] in Languedoc *"malos albergos,"*[140] in Dauphiny *"servicium et hospitalia,"*[141] In both Provence and the Spanish March the general term *tasca* seems to include not only the *cens* but such additional levies too.[142]

What were these exactions levied upon surrounding territory by castellans and *milites* in the castles of this period—exactions which called forth the terms of approbrium mentioned above? Perhaps the most important one was what was frequently known as the *albergum* or *receptum*, or even *hospitalia*. Originally it seems to have been a special additional levy of the Carolingian period or one used to a limited extent in the domains of the great abbeys.[143] By this time it had become a tax in kind used to provide food for the *milites* of a castle, since it is often referred to as an *albergum* or *receptum* for so many *milites* or *caballarios*.[144] Levied on the land, it in effect came to be an additional payment similar to a *cens*. Similar to this levy were special dues which we find laid upon the peas-

---

[135] See *Cart. de Sauxillanges*, nos. 378, 403, 419, 635, 781; and *Cart. de Brioude*, no. 107.

[136] *Cart. de Conques*, nos. 27, 94, 346.

[137] *Cart. de Vigeois*, no. 11; and *Cart. de Tulle*, no. 469.

[138] *Cart. de Saint-Barnard de Romans*, no. 67; and *Cart. de Saint-Chaffre*, nos. 284, 311.

[139] *Cartulaire de l'abbaye de Sainte-Croix de Bordeaux*, ed. Ducaunnes Duval, in *Archives Historiques de la Gironde*, XXVII (1892), (hereafter cited as *Cart. de Sainte-Croix*), no. 2.

[140] *Cart. de Gellone*, no. 37. See a charter of 1030 in which they are called *"taschas, tortas et usaticos"* (*Cart. de Béziers*, no. 62). Or one of 1036 in which there is a mention of *"ipsas ministerialias, ipsas questas et ipsos donos,"* in *ibid.*, no. 63.

[141] *Cart. de Saint-Barnard de Romans*, no. 56; and *Chartes de Maurienne*, no. 4.

[142] For the Spanish March see *Cart. de San Cugat*, nos. 419, 445, 449, 476, 495; and *Hist. Gén. de Lang.*, V, no. 212. For Provence see *Chartes de Cluny*, III, no. 1866; *Cart. de Saint-Victor*, nos. 135, 437; and *Cart. de Lérins*, nos. 46, 307.

[143] For instance note the *receptum* at Beaulieu in 971 (*Cart. de Beaulieu*, no. 50).

[144] See *Cart. d'Aniane*, no. 236; *Cart. de Conques*, nos. 23, 254, 273, 285; *Cart. de Saint-Victor*, no. 101; and *Cart. de Gellone*, nos. 93, 98.

The New Militarism

antry's livestock—their pigs, sheep, goats, horses, cows, and even chickens—particularly important in mountainous pastoral regions like the Massif Central, the Alps, or the Pyrenees.[145] Then there was the *banalités* or dues which came from seigneurial monopoly of mill and oven,[146] the *portaticum*,[147] and a host of others. To these levies should be added dues or services of various sorts of a menial variety, which are mentioned several times in contemporary documents—even military service or *"hostem, pediaticum et cavalcadem"* which seems to have been largely confined to the Spanish March where it was a survival of Carolingian customs.[148]

Were rights of justice also included as part of the rights of such *mandamenta*? This seems probable as far as the Spanish March is concerned, and even in other parts of the Midi where *vicaria* were a part of the *caslania* or territory pertaining to a castle.[149] It seems less certain elsewhere, especially in portions of Aquitaine, Provence, and the Valley of the Rhone where justice was still essentially a seigneurial right exercised by a landowner, who controlled a large allodial estate and controlled the justice for his tenants and peasant *coloni*. But even in such regions there seems to have been a tendency to combine rights of justice with the other rights or dues levied by the castellan and *milites* over the surrounding countryside. Gradually and inexorably, it would seem, such castellans were not only creating territories or districts about their fortresses, but usurping rights to *cens* and tithes, and levying new onerous dues and services upon their neighbors. They were also becoming dispensers of justice and replacing older minor officials like the vicars and *judices* in their role of judges over the humbler members of the society of the Midi and Catalonia. Slowly, but surely, many parts of the Midi seem to have been approaching the situation found around a castle in Pallars in 1010 where *"bannum et placitos, parados et albergos et servicios"* and *"hostem et cavalcadem"* were levied upon the nearby population.[150]

The results of the spread of castles and their increase in number, then, went far beyond the creation of a new class of *milites* imbued with a new

---

[145] See *Cart. de Gellone*, no. 93; *Cart. de Saint-Barnard de Romans*, no. 56; *El "Libre Blanch" de Santas Creus* [Barcelona], no. 2.

[146] Only in Provence do we find such dues of *fornum* specified in the documents of this period, though they may have also existed elsewhere.

[147] *Cart. de Saint-Barnard de Romans*, no. 56.

[148] *El "Libre Blanch" de Santas Creus* [Barcelona], no. 2.

[149] See reference to *placitos* in a document of 1046 in *Cart. de San Cugat*, no. 589.

[150] *Marca hispanica*, ap. 153.

and different military spirit. Whether castles were created as the result of definite policies, as in Dauphiny, Provence, and the Spanish March, or whether they grew more haphazardly as in the rest of the Midi, the result was the same. New, almost cellular units, appeared in the countryside, which we call *mandamenta*. The castles, which formed the center of such territories, required new dues and services from neighbors, as well as usurping older *cens* and tithes; and a new justice began to be dispensed. This sort of government—for, legal or illegal, government it was—was much resented by allodial landholders, peasants, and churchmen alike, who saw in it a threat to their freedom, their livelihood, and the exercise of their legal rights. Led by the Church, they attempted to combat this trend in movements known as the Peace and Truce of God which we will examine in the next chapter. By 1050, then, the new militarism had become powerful enough not only to create castles and *milites* everywhere, but also to create a new system of *mandamenta* which threatened the allodial landholding system and Church of the Midi and which was to lead directly to a new era in lands south of Poitou and Burgundy.

CHAPTER XVI

The Church (975–1050)

IN THE YEAR 975 the Church was the most important single institution in Southern France and Catalonia. Its new and older monastic foundations had steadily grown in power and influence, as abbeys spread into regions like Gascony and Alpine areas east of the Rhone where for decades they had been unknown. Its princes, the great bishop-abbots of the period, were the actual rulers of many regions of Southern France and Catalonia. Its administration, which was adjusted to the prevailing family system of powerful landowners, provided patronage and favor which linked these nobles to its organization. Its protection in an age which provided little, had attracted to it smaller proprietors as well as larger ones who turned over to its abbeys and churches their property in return for a relatively mild yoke of tithe, *cens,* and *tasca.* In many ways this continued to be so during the years from 975 to 1050 also. One cannot examine evidence of an increase in the domains of abbeys like Sauxillanges, Brioude, Saint-Chaffre, Savigny, Saint-André-le-Bas, Saint-Victor of Marseille, Lérins, Aniane, Gellone, Conques, Cuxa, or San-Cugat,[1] for instance, without be-

---

[1] About 170 charters dating from this period show the growth of Sauxillanges (see the *Cart. de Sauxillanges*). Though Brioude's domain does not seem to have increased as much as Sauxillanges', during these years some 40 charters in the *Cart. de Brioude,* show the abbey's continued growth. Some 60 charters in the *Cart. de Saint-Chaffre,* show a growth of the abbey's lands in Velay, Vivarais, Forez, the Lyonnais, Savoy, Dauphiny, Auvergne, Provence, and even in Northern Italy. According to the charters of the *Cart. de Savigny* this was a period of rapid growth, but mainly in the local region of the Lyonnais and Forez. Saint-André-le-Bas, like Savigny, experienced a growth and expansion of its holdings, but mainly close to Vienne. See some four score charters of the *Cart. de Saint-André-le-bas* for this growth. Saint-Victor de Marseille according to its catulary really began to expand until its land spread all over Provence and the Alpine regions nearby ac-

ing impressed by their power and importance. Nor can one help but be struck by the authority of the great church officials of the period, like Abbot Guitard of San-Cugat,[2] Bishop Oliba of Cuxa and Ripoll,[3] Archbishop Burchard of Lyon[4] or Bishop Etienne III of Auvergne.[5] This was

---

cording to more than 200 charters of this period (*Cart. de Saint-Victor*). It even accumulated land in distant Catalonia. Lérins also expanded its domains, but mainly in a region centering about the Riviera, according to its cartulary. But it did have land given it in Auvergne also (See *Cart. de Lérins*, no. 219). Judging from its cartulary, Aniane grew steadily but modestly during these years. Some 30 charters show the expansion of its holdings mainly near the abbey itself in Eastern Languedoc (*Cart. d'Aniane*). Judging from charters Gellone's domains grew steadily in the Melgueil-Béziers region. But the abbey also acquired some extensive holdings to the north in the Albigeois and Rouergue (*Cart. de Gellone*). The *Cart. de Conques* shows this period was one of great growth for the abbey's landed endowment. Over 180 charters exist which show gifts to Conques. Most are from Rouergue and the Albigeois. Some however are from Quercy, the Limousin, Auvergne, Vivarais, and even Provence. On Cuxa's growth during these years see P. Ponsch, "Le domaine foncier de Saint-Michel de Cuxa au IXe, X^e, et XIe siècles," in *Études Roussillonnaises*, II (1952). More than 200 charters illustrate how San Cugat's lands grew in extent during this period. Most impressive of all is the list of castles which it owned along the entire border of Catalonia. See the charters given the abbey by Pope Sylvester II in 1002 and by Pope John in 1007 which trace the extent of San Cugat's domains (*Cart. de San Cugat*, nos. 382, 412).

[2] Charters dating from 1011 and 1012 show the power which Abbot Guitard was able to exercise (*Cart. de San Cugat*, nos. 437–439, 442, 447, 449). All concern San-Cugat's ownership of important castles. See also his influence shown in a dispute with an important marcher lord in 1020 (*ibid.*, no. 479).

[3] For some examples of Oliba's power note how he presided over the Synod of Taluges in 1027 where the Peace of God was proclaimed (*Recueil des Historiens des Gaules et de la France*, ed. D. Bouquet *et alii*, XI, 514). Or see how he intervened in this same year to protect the rights of two villages in Roussillon (*Cart. roussillonnais*, no. 32). On his career see R. de Abadal i de Vinyals, *L'Abat Oliva, bisbe de Vic, i la seva època*.

[4] Note the privileges which Archbishop Burchard helped give Cluny in 994 (*Chartes de Cluny*, III, no. 2255), and his action in excommunicating those who were disturbing the abbey of Saint-Pierre de Lyon about the year 1000 (*Cart. Lyonnais*, no. 8). See also the important councils held at Vienne in 1023 (*Cart. de Saint-André-le-bas*, no. 32); and a little later also *Cartulaire de Saint-Maurice de Vienne*, ed. U. Chevalier, in *Cartulaire de Saint-André-le-bas de Vienne*, appendix L, p. 59. On the vain attempts of his nephew to succeed to his position and power see Raoul Glaber, *Historiarum libri V*, V, 4, 21–22, pp. 130–132.

[5] A number of charters reveal the power exercised by this bishop (*Cart. de Sauxillanges*, nos. 701, 476; *Cart. de Brioude*, no. 105; *Chartes de Cluny*, IV, no. 2682).

an age in which St. Odilon of Cluny could act as the arbiter of Auvergne[6] and in which Papal intervention was effective in the power politics of the Limousin.[7]

Yet, as the years progressed from 975 to 1050, it became steadily more apparent that all was not well with this powerful Church. More and more its close relationship with the great noble landholding families began to change from one of close collaboration and mutual respect to one in which secular domination had become the rule. The Church in the Midi and Spanish March began to become so secularized that, despite its power, it was threatened with complete absorption into the family system of these regions. In an immediate sense, an even more dangerous situation threatened it, that which proceeded from the new militarism emanating from the new rising castles and their *milites*. This new militarism found land which belonged to abbeys and cathedral churches very tempting indeed, and so the new military class began to build castles, legal and illegal, on or near Church land and to extort heavy new exactions from proprietors and peasants who were under Church protection. They usurped Church revenues. By force or intimidation, they took over important Church offices. Faced by this threat the Church struck back by enlisting Pope, enlightened nobles, and Cluny on its side, and important churchmen began to put public pressure on their dangerous neighbors, the castellans and *milites*. This pressure finally took organized form as the Peace of God and the Truce of God which rapidly spread throughout Southern France and Catalonia. As a result, by 1050 the Church had begun to make some headway against this new militarism and was holding it at bay in many regions south of Poitou and Burgundy.

But such a program, even though it produced some victories, was not enough. It still did not touch the heart of the problem—the prevailing secularism of a Church which was completely involved in the power politics of the period on a local level. As long as an archbishopric of Narbonne could be bought for 100,000 *solidi*,[8] and abbeys could be passed from one hand to another by secular nobles as if they were private property,[9] the danger to the Church remained a real one. By 1050 only a few

---

[6] See a number of charters on Abbot Odilon's activities in Auvergne (*Cart. de Saint-Flour*, nos. 4, 6; *Cart. de Sauxillanges*, no. 635).

[7] *Ademar de Chabannes*, III, 36, pp. 159–160.

[8] *Hist. Gén. de Lang.*, V, no. 251, and P. Ponsch, "Le Confluent et ses comtes du IXe au XIIe siècle," in *Études Roussillonnais*, I (1951), 295.

[9] For examples of such lay control of abbeys see the will of Viscountess Adelaise

voices were raised against this threat to the Church in Southern France and Catalonia, but at least some protests were finally being heard. They were to swell in volume until they led directly to the Gregorian Reform movement of the last years of the eleventh century and to a new and more spiritual Church.

With this general pattern of development in mind, let us examine evidence of the continuing spread and growth of monasteries during these years. One of the more interesting aspects of this movement concerns the building of new priories and abbeys in parts of the Midi where up to this time few existed. One of these regions was Western Gascony. Here, in the last years of the tenth century, at last we begin to find an active monastic movement. It was at about this period, for instance, that the priory of La Réolle was founded,[10] and that we begin to hear of two new abbeys, Blasement, and Lucq, the latter located not far from Bayonne in Southwestern Gascony.[11] By the first years of the eleventh century these three houses had been joined by other new or restored foundations, Sainte-Croix and Sainte-Marie near Bordeaux and Sorde further in the interior.[12] Soon after 1050 Centulle IV, viscount of Béarn, gave the newly built Sainte-Foi of Morlaas to Cluny.[13] Gascony, like the rest of the Midi, began to be a land covered with abbeys.

In Alpine and other regions near the Rhone Valley these years saw a similar movement. In 1016 Humbert, bishop of Grenoble, and his brother

---

of Narbonne about 990, or of Count Roger of Carcassonne about the year 1000 in *Hist. Gén. de Lang.*, V, nos. 152, 162. Other examples are to be found in the power exercised by Count Pons of Toulouse according to *ibid.*, no. 206, and *Cart. de Tulle*, no. 1306.

[10] The first mention of this abbey seems to date from 978 (*Cart. de la Réolle*, no. 132), though there is an account of the founding of the abbey in *ibid.*, no. 94. See also a charter of Pope Benedict which mentions this monastery in 981 (*ibid.*, no. 138).

[11] On the abbey of Blasement see *ibid.*, no. 14. Our first proof of the existence of the abbey of Lucq seems to come from a charter dating from 988 (*Cart. de Lucq*, no. 3). We also have a mention of still another Gascon monastery in a charter dating from 980 (*Hist. Gén. de Lang.*, V, no. 133).

[12] A charter of 1027 tells of how this abbey was founded at Bordeaux (*Cart. de Saint-Croix*, no. 1). A series of charters give us our first references to the abbey of Sorde during these years (*Cart. de Saint-Jean de Sorde*, nos. 2, 3, 15). A countess of Bordeaux in 1043 founded this establishment according to *Cart. de Sainte-Croix*, no. 80.

[13] *Cartulaire de Sainte-Foi de Morlaas*, ed. L. Cadier, in *Bulletin de la société des sciences, lettres et arts de Pau*, 2nd Ser. XIII (1886), no. 1.

The Church (975–1050)

Count Guigo founded a new abbey in Dauphiny.[14] A few years later a second was established at Suse.[15] Our sources also tell us of others which appear to be new or restored foundations, one in Savoy, about 1031[16] and two others near Grenoble mentioned in 1040 and 1042,[17] respectively. Further to the south near Valence we hear of two other new ones which were placed under the supervision of the abbey of Saint-Chaffre in the years 1010 and 1011.[18]

Provence too felt this impetus toward monastic growth as it began to enter a more orderly era resulting from its organization by Count William into a principality. About the year 1000, for instance, we learn that Count Josfred had restored the abbey of Sparro near Aix, which had been destroyed by the Moslems, according to our source;[19] and at about the same time a charter tells us of a new foundation at Valentiolo, which is coming under the control of Cluny.[20] Near Nice we hear of the new abbeys of Vence and Saint-Pons.[21] A document, dating from 1034, tells us of a priory near Fréjus, called a *cella,* belonging to the abbey of Saint-Victor of Marseille.[22] Ten years later we learn from our sources of a gathering of important nobles and churchmen, headed by Count Bertrand of Provence, which founded the abbey of Saint-Promasius near the castle of Forcalquier,[23] and of another near Gap, which restored the abbey of Bremetense which had been destroyed by the pagans.[24] In much of Provence the monastic movement was revived after a period in which for many decades abbeys had ceased to exist.

We could continue such a list of new foundations in the rest of the Midi too, like Saint-Flour in Auvergne, Gallargues near Nîmes, or Dorat and the almonry of Saint-Martial in the Limousin, or Saint-Etienne de Baigne and Notre Dame de Saintes in Saintonge.[25] But this is not neces-

---

[14] *Cart. de Grenoble,* no. 33.
[15] Raoul Glaber, *Historiarum libri V,* IV, 3, 6–7, pp. 96–97.
[16] *Cart. de Saint Sulpice en Bugey,* no. 2.
[17] *Cart. de Grenoble,* nos. 19, 20, 34.
[18] *Cart. de Saint-Chaffre,* nos. 314, 375.
[19] *Cart. de Saint-Victor,* no. 269. See also the Papal privileges given to the restored abbey of Saint-André of Avignon in 999 (*Hist. Gén. de Lang.,* V, no. 157).
[20] *Chartes de Cluny,* III, nos. 1866, 1990, 1991.
[21] See reference to this monastery of Vence in *Cart. de Saint-Victor,* no. 272. There is a mention of the election of the abbot of Saint-Pons of Nice in a charter of 1004 *Cart. de Saint-Pons de Nice,* no. 2.
[22] *Cart. de Saint-Victor,* no. 558.
[23] *Ibid.,* no. 659.
[24] *Ibid.,* no. 691.
[25] See *Cart. de Saint-Flour,* no. 6 on the early history of Saint-Flour, and *Hist.*

sary. It seems clear that down to 1050 new abbeys were founded in every part of Southern France, especially in regions like Gascony, Savoy, Dauphiny, and Provence, where they had been few in number and where their foundation represented a definite monastic revival. Only in the Spanish March, as a matter of fact, is there evidence of some slowing down during this period in the rate of founding of new religious houses, and here this was to prove only temporary. When the frontiers of Christian Spain began to move south in the Reconquista which began about 1050, new abbeys followed the frontier as it moved forward at the expense of the Moslems who had long dominated the fertile Ebro Valley.

Even more striking is evidence of the expansion of the domains and power of certain important abbeys throughout the Midi and Spanish March. Cluny, which was already important in these regions before 975, is a good example of this. After 975 it continued to spread its influence as new monastic foundations became a part of its congregation of abbeys, not only in Auvergne and the Rhone Valley, where it had long exerted considerable authority, but elsewhere as well. Particularly significant in this regard was Cluny's growth in the southwestern part of the Midi, where, shortly before 1050, Moissac and Lézat[26] came under Cluniac control and where shortly thereafter, Sainte-Foi of Morlaas followed their example.[27] From this region Cluny's influence began to spill across the Pyrenees into Northwestern Spain where it was to play a major role in the Reconquista.[28]

It needs to be emphasized, however, that the example of Cluny was by no means unique. The abbey of Saint-Chaffre in Velay played a similar role, as its domains and affiliated houses spread along the Rhone Valley as far north as the Lyonnais[29] and as far south as Provence[30] and even into

---

Gén. de Lang., V, no. 188 on Gallargues. See a reference to the foundation of Dorat by Count Boson of La Marche in a charter of 987 (*Recueil de textes et d'analyses concernant le chapitre de Saint-Pierre de Dorat*, ed. J. Font-Réaulx, in *Bulletin de la société archéologique et historique du Limousin*, LXXII (1927), no. 2. Charters of 1020 and 1025 mention Saint-Martial in *Cart. de l'aumônerie de Saint-Martial de Limoges*, nos. 14, 29. For the beginnings of Saint-Etienne about the year 1000 see *Cartulaire de l'abbaye de Saint-Etienne de Baigne en Saintogne*, ed. R. Chalet, nos. 263, 270, 271. The *Cart. de Notre Dame de Saintes*, nos. 1 and 78 contain the first references to Notre Dame de Saintes.

[26] *Cart. de Tulle*, no. 1306. *Chartes de Cluny*, III, no. 1950.

[27] *Cart. de Sainte-Foi de Morlaas*, no. 1.

[28] On the expansion of Cluny's influence into Northwestern Spain see M. Defourneaux, *Les Francais en Espagne aux XIe et XIIe siècles*.

[29] *Cart. de Saint-Chaffre*, no. 387.

[30] *Ibid.*, nos. 321, 390, 391, 393.

northern Italy.³¹ The abbey of Conques which had long been important became even more so in this period and came to acquire land as far south as the Spanish March.³² So too did Saint-Victor of Marseille.³³ In Aquitaine, Fleury's affiliated priories spread into Gascony.³⁴ In Catalonia domains belonging to San Cugat spread all along the frontiers of the Spanish March,³⁵ while we have evidence of the authority of Lagrasse in Pallars and Ribagorça.³⁶ Even more than in the period prior to 975, the great abbeys of the Midi and Catalonia were bursting their regional bonds and exercising authority over more extended areas. Nor was this merely a spread of domains and affiliated religious houses. It often included, rather significantly, a military-political authority of some consequence. The castles which the abbey of San Cugat possessed along the frontiers of Barcelona and Manressa made it a military power to be reckoned with in this part of Spain,³⁷ just as the castle which Savigny built about 1000 gave it an all but independent authority in the Lyonnais.³⁸ Similar fortresses owned by abbeys like Saint-Victor of Marseille, Saint-Pons of Thomières, and Conques³⁹ gave to them also a certain power in their local regions which the secular society of *principes* and *milites* had to take into consideration.

All of this helps to explain why ruling families in the Midi and Catalonia found control of archbishoprics, bishoprics, and abbeys in their regions such an important basis for their authority after 975, as had been the case earlier. They continued to make every effort to dominate these religious establishments by seeing that members of their families were selected as church officials or as the *prepositi, defensores,* and *custodes* who handled their landed endowment. Everywhere the system was the same. In Eastern Gascony, we find the newly re-established archbishopric of Auch had, by this period, come under the control of nearby local ruling families, with Archbishop Raymond, uncle of the count of Fézensac, hold-

---

³¹ *Ibid.*, no. 367. On lands belonging to Saint-Chaffre in Alpine regions of Savoy and Dauphiny see *ibid.*, nos. 357, 433, 434, 435.
³² *Cart. de Conques,* no. 73. See also reference to land in the Narbonnaise in *ibid.*, no. 411.
³³ *Cart. de Saint-Victor,* nos. 1044, 1046–1052.
³⁴ *Cart. de la Réolle,* no. 99.
³⁵ For example see *Cart. de San Cugat,* no. 387.
³⁶ *Hist. Gén. de Lang.,* V, no. 167.
³⁷ *Cart. de San Cugat,* nos. 387, 412.
³⁸ *Cart. de Savigny,* no. 430.
³⁹ For examples of such castles see *Cart. de Saint-Victor,* nos. 58, 135, 243, 255; *Hist. Gén. de Lang.,* V, no. 226; *Cart. de Conques,* nos. 34, 142, 167, 355.

ing this important office during the first years of the eleventh century.[40] His successor, St. Austinde, had equally important family ties which linked him to the noble families of this region.[41] Down to 1029 the archbishop of Bordeaux was Séguin, from a family which had been important in this part of Gascony since the ninth century, and his successor, chosen, according to Ademar of Chabannes, from a family of Frankish origin, marks the beginning of Poitevin authority over the Bordelais.[42] Bernard, son of Count Raymond Dat, was bishop of Oriolo in 980,[43] just as Gumbald, the brother of Duke William Sánchez of Gascony, was bishop of Baza in 1046.[44] In Gascony family control of church offices was the order of the day.

Nearby, in Catalonia, the same state of affairs prevailed. In the late tenth century members of the viscontal family began to occupy the office of bishop of Barcelona as well as the *abbatia* of San-Cugat, which was the most important monastic foundation of the region,[45] while Peter, of the House of Carcassonne, a brother of Countess Ermissende, was made bishop of Gerona.[46] It would appear that the abbeys of Ripoll and Cuxa chose as abbots members of the House of Cerdanya-Besalu of which Bishop Oliba was certainly the most distinguished representative.[47] Then about 1016 they extended their family influence by purchasing the archbishopric of Narbonne,[48] and, a little later the bishopric of Urgell.[49] During most of this period this family also controlled the nunnery of Saint Joan de les Abadesses.[50]

To the north in Languedoc the right to fill the archbishopric of Narbonne seems to have been a prerogative of the viscontal family of the city,[51] until its purchase for Guifred of Cerdanya-Besalu, and so was the naming

[40] *Cart. d'Auch*, no. 11.
[41] On his kinship with important noble families of this region see A. Brueils, *St. Austinde et la Gascogne au XIe siècle*.
[42] *Ademar de Chabannes*, III, 34, pp. 163–164.
[43] *Hist. Gén. de Lang.*, V, no. 133.
[44] *Cart. de la Réolle*, no. 90.
[45] *El Archivo Condal de Barcelona*, no. 26.
[46] *Cart. de Carcassonne*, I, 244–245, and *Hist. Gén. de Lang.*, V, nos. 189, 209.
[47] On Oliba's relationship with the House of Cerdanya-Besalu see Abadal, *L'abat Oliva*, pp. 18–39.
[48] *Hist. Gén. de Lang.*, V, no. 251.
[49] Ponsch, "Le Confluent et ses comtes," p. 295.
[50] *Ibid*.
[51] See the will of Aimery, archbishop of Narbonne, which dates from 977 (*Hist. Gén. de Lang.*, V, no. 127); and that a little later of Viscountess Adelaise (*ibid.*, no. 151).

The Church (975–1050)

of abbots of Caunes, one of whom in 993 was Udalguerius, a brother of Viscount Raymond and Archbishop Ermengaud.[52] According to the will of Count Roger the Old in 1002, the Carcassonne house could dispose of a number of abbeys like Saint-Hilaire and Montolieu as if they were their own private property;[53] just as Viscount William could will the bishopric of Béziers to his daughter like any other family allod.[54] Not only did the family of Marquis Bernard of Anduze and his wife, Countess Garsinde, control the bishoprics of Nîmes and LePuy for a period;[55] in 1035 they also had rights over the abbeys of Aniane and Gellone.[56] About 1030 we find a similar situation in Melgueil, where Bishop Peter of Maguelonne was a son of Countess Senegunde and a cousin of Count Bernard.[57]

When we turn to Provence we find that the viscounts of Marseille controlled this city's bishopric[58] and the abbey of Saint-Victor. Their control of this latter was amply attested by a charter which gives us details concerning an election of the monastery's abbot in 1005.[59] Their power also extended over the archbishopric of Aix.[60] In 1018 records indicate that the bishopric of Nice was in the hands of the local counts of this region,[61] just as similar families in Antibes and Grasse controlled their bishoprics in 1038 and 1032[62] respectively. During this same period our sources reveal that the archbishopric of Arles was controlled in the same way by the local lords of this city.[63] When we turn our attention to regions which lay further to the north in the Valley of the Rhone, we find the counts of Valence choosing the bishop of this region from members of their

---

[52] *Cart. de Carcassonne*, IV, 3.
[53] *Hist. Gén. de Lang.*, V, no. 162.
[54] *Cart. de Béziers*, no. 46.
[55] The *Cronique de la Monastère de Saint-Pierre-de-Le-Puy*, in *Hist. Gén. de Lang.*, V, col. 18–20 mentions control of LePuy by the Anduze family. See also a charter of 1020 which mentions Bernard, lord of Anduze, and his sons Frédol, bishop of LePuy, and Gerald, bishop of Nîmes (*Cart. de Nîmes*, no. 120). On the election of Frédol as bishop of LePuy see also *Cart. de Saint-Petrus Aniacensis* [LePuy], ed. A. Molinier, in *Hist. Gén. de Lang.*, V, no. 416.
[56] *Hist. Gén. de Lang.*, V, no. 206.
[57] *Cart. de Gellone*, no. 8.
[58] *Cart. de Saint-Victor de Marseille*, nos. 69, 169.
[59] *Ibid.*, nos. 1053, 1054.
[60] *Ibid.*, no. 15.
[61] *Cartulaire de l'ancienne Cathédral de Nice, Sainte-Réparte*, ed. E. Cais de Pierlas, no. 11.
[62] *Cart. de Lérins*, nos. 131, 140.
[63] *Cart. de Saint-Victor*, nos. 58, 116.

family[64] and for a brief period controlling the see of LePuy as well.[65] They seem to have shared this right with the counts of Gevaudun, who also for a period exercised control over the abbey of Saint-Chaffre du Monastier in Velay.[66] In Dauphiny the counts of Gravaisdun, who were related to the House of Valence, regularly provided bishops of Grenoble from members of their family.[67] The nearby important archbishopric of Lyon was, for a period, controlled by the royal family of Burgundy-Provence, since Burchard, its archbishop, was a brother of King Rudolf and in 1031 his nephew made an attempt to succeed him in this office.[68] In 1024, by placing a certain Léger on the archbishopric of Vienne, the family of Sylvius got control of this important office as well as the abbey of Saint-Barnard de Romans.[69] This same family also had some pretensions to control over Saint-Chaffre du Monastier in Velay.[70] Even St. Odilon of Cluny was not above seeing that a nephew should succeed to the bishopric of LePuy.[71] In Auvergne a similar nepotism seems to have prevailed, where Bishop Etienne III of Auvergne was a brother of Count Robert of Clermont and a member of the family which had long supplied this see with bishops.[72] By 1035 the Trencavels not only were in possession of the bishopric of Nîmes,[73] they also had enough authority over that of Albi to sell it outright for some 5,000 *solidi*.[74] However, in 1045 a charter reveals they were still in control of the bishopric.[75] To the west in Languedoc the House of Toulouse not only served as *custodes* of important abbeys like Moissac[76] and Lézat;[77] they also seem to have had the right of selecting the bishops of Toulouse, a right they may have

---

[64] For references to Bishops Lambert and Pons of Valence who were members of this family see *Cart. de Saint-Chaffre*, nos. 314, 315, and *Chartes de Cluny*, IV, no. 2921.

[65] For the election of Bishop Ademar of this family of Valence see *Cart. de Saint-Petrus Aniacensis* [LePuy], no. 416.

[66] *Cronique de Saint-Pierre de LePuy*, cols. 14–23, and *Cart. de Saint-Chaffre*, no. 140.

[67] *Cart. de Grenoble*, no. 33.   [68] *Cart. de Vienne*, no. 38.

[69] *Cart. de Saint-Barnard de Romans*, nos. 74, 78, 80.

[70] On Sylvius and his encroachment upon lands belonging to Saint-Chaffre see *Cart. de Saint-Chaffre*, no. 311.

[71] *Cronique de Saint-Pierre de LePuy*, col. 21–23.

[72] We find this in a charter dating from 994–1046 (*Cart. de Sauxillanges*, no. 476).

[73] *Hist. Gén. de Lang.*, V, nos. 203, 205.

[74] *Ibid.*, no. 214.   [75] *Ibid.*, no. 225.

[76] *Cart. de Tulle*, XXII, 154–155.

[77] *Hist. Gén. de Lang.*, V, no. 173.

The Church (975-1050)

shared with certain viscontal families of this region.[78] In the Limousin lay abbots seem to have regularly been chosen from members of the leading local viscontal families,[79] just as the bishopric of Limoges appears to have been regularly filled by bishops chosen from the family of the viscounts of Limoges.[80] In the same way in Angoulême, during the first years of the eleventh century, the bishop was a brother of Count Geoffrey of Angoulême who controlled this part of Aquitaine.[81]

There seems to be no need to continue this examination of family control of church offices by looking into the family affiliations of the *prepositi* and other laymen who held such offices during these years. Suffice it to say that they continued to be chosen, as had been the case earlier, from the ranks of less important local landholding families or *milites*. Thus they seem to reflect the same kind of family influence over the Church which we find dictated the choosing of archbishops, bishops, and abbots. Even more than had been the case in earlier periods, these decades saw a Church which was the repository of family interests and family power and which had become almost a part of the family system that controlled authority in Southern France and Catalonia. As the wealth, the power, and the influence of a family grew, so did its control over the Church establishments which were located nearby. As it declined, so did its influence in the choice of important church officials and lay vicars and *prepositi* who administered church domains.

So natural, as a matter of fact, did this system seem to the society of the Midi and the Spanish March in the late tenth century and the first half of the eleventh, that it was not often seriously questioned, though it was certainly anything but canonical. What did cause growing concern was something else: namely the more direct, more brutal control of Church lands and Church offices than the older system of family influence sanctioned. This, of course, was the result of the new militarism and the exactions which castellans of fortresses and their *milites* began to impose upon nearby Church establishments. It was against such practices that protests began to arise in our region.

---

[78] Hugh who was bishop of Toulouse in the late tenth century was a member of the Toulouse-Rouergue family. See his will in *Cart. de Saint-Sernin*, no. 280. His successor, Frotaire, was probably of the Lautrec family (*Hist. Gén. de Lang.*, V, no. 139). The next bishop, Raymond, was probably of the Toulousain house (*ibid.*, no. 165).

[79] See *Cart. d'Uzerche*, nos. 31, 58, 1039; and *Cart. de Tulle*, no. 290.

[80] One finds a mention of bishops of this family in *Cart. d'Uzerche*, nos. 31, 426, 1020.

[81] *Cart. de Savigny*, no. 633.

The first efforts to limit the excesses of the new militarism in various parts of the Midi began late in the tenth century. One of the first of such efforts seems to have occurred in Velay, according to a contemporary chronicle. This tells how Guy, who was bishop of LePuy and later abbot of Saint-Chaffre, and who had been chosen for this office, no doubt, because of family connections (his nephews were counts of Gevaudun), ordered all *milites* in his region to keep the peace and forced his nephews to give back the *"rura et castella"* which they had seized.[82] At about the same time, about 985, a charter tells us how the nearby Count Lambert of Valence gave to a newly reformed abbey the right to protect itself by means of fortifications from the rapacity of evil men (*"pravorum hominum"*).[83]

These two examples of a resistance to the new militarism of the period were more than matched by certain actions of Archbishop Burchard of Lyon, who, like Bishop Guy of LePuy, seems to be a good example of family influence over the local church, since he was the king of Burgundy's brother. Nevertheless, we find him fighting the same battle, excommunicating those who were encroaching on the domains of the abbey of Saint-Pierre of Lyon,[84] and complaining in 984 of the sad state of Church property in his province due to such usurpations.[85] In 994 this same primate is shown in our sources holding an important church council, which was attended by Archbishop Teubald of Vienne and a number of other churchmen of the Rhone Valley, as well as some prominent laymen. At this council the matter of Cluny's lands in this region was considered, and it was decreed that no *judex*, count, or person controlling armed men could build a castle *on* or *near* lands which belonged to Cluny, or levy any special dues or exactions upon such property.[86] It seems probable that this Church council stiffened local resistance to the activities of the new military class in this region. At any rate, six years later in 1000 we learn of a similar assembly of churchmen and nobles, local in nature, held by the abbot of Saint-André-le-Bas which condemned sacrileges to the Church.[87] In the same year Artald, a local noble in the Lyonnais, gave up exactions

---

[82] *Cronique de Saint-Pierre de LePuy*, col. 14–15.

[83] *Chartes de Cluny*, II, no. 1716.

[84] *Cart. Lyonnais*, no. 8. See the excommunication pronounced by the bishop of Grenoble for a similar offense in his part of Dauphiny in 976–978 in *Cart. de Grenoble*, no. 25.

[85] *Cart. Lyonnais*, no. 9.

[86] *Chartes de Cluny*, III, no. 2255.

[87] *Cart. de Saint-André-le-bas*, no. 210. See also Artald's return of land in 992 which his father had usurped from Savigny (*Cart. de Savigny*, no. 533).

he was levying on the domains of this same abbey;[88] and a neighboring house, Savigny, built a castle to protect its domains from the same kind of encroachment.[89]

Despite such councils and assemblies sponsored by churchmen and their pronouncements, however, the pressure and encroachment upon Church domains continued. In 1012, for instance, the abbey of Saint-Chaffre had to summon a nobleman, Sylvius, to its court before he agreed to give up the exactions he was levying upon its domains as *"defensor."*[90] And the election of Sylvius' grandson Léger as archbishop of Vienne in 1025 was certainly no triumph for the antimilitary party of the Church in the Valley of the Rhone, followed as it was by this primate's ruthless appropriation of the patrimony of Saint-André-le-Bas[91] and his similar actions regarding that belonging to Saint-Barnard de Romans, where he also served as abbot.[92] But the struggle continued nevertheless. In 1024 for instance, Savigny seems to have successfully persuaded a certain Vurchard to give up dues he was exacting from property belonging to this abbey in return for a payment to him of some 500 *solidi*.[93] Then three years later in 1027 Cluny received from King Robert of France, who now controlled Burgundy, an important charter which had repercussions on neighboring regions in the Midi and which, like that of 994, forbade anyone to build fortresses near land which belonged to Cluny or its associated Church establishments.[94]

By the year 1030 the result of all this was a more general movement on the part of the Church to limit the effects of the new militarism upon its lands and its authority, as Raoul Glaber's *Chronicle* makes clear.[95] In the Middle Rhone region and elsewhere this resulted in new Church councils, which were held in 1031 and 1037,[96] and which were attended by both leading churchmen and members of the lay nobility. These councils ordered the laity to return churches which they had seized from Savigny and other abbeys. They did more than this. Out of such mixed

---

[88] *Cart. de Saint-André-le-bas*, no. 182.
[89] *Cart. de Savigny*, no. 430.
[90] *Cart. de Saint-Chaffre*, no. 311.
[91] *Cart. de Saint-André-le-bas*, no. 209.
[92] *Cart. de Saint-Barnard de Romans*, nos. 74, 80.
[93] *Cart. de Savigny*, nos. 679, 680.
[94] *Chartes de Cluny*, IV, no. 2800.
[95] Raoul Glaber, *Historiarum libri V*, IV, 5, 14–16, p. 103.
[96] Mansi, *Sacrorum conciliorum nova et amplissima collectio*, XIX, col. 507. *Cart. de Saint-Barnard de Romans*, no. 79.

assemblies we begin to find rules being elaborated which were to become what we now know as the Peace of God. One such assembly was held in 1037, and was attended by the bishops, abbots, counts, and *principes* of Valence and Vienne. This gave to the abbey of Saint-Barnard de Romans the right to refuge, one of the first acts of its kind setting up such a sanctuary in a Church establishment in the Midi.[97] Yet as late as 1050, Pope Leo IX was attempting to protect this abbey from encroachment and usurpations of its lands and felt it necessary to reaffirm its privileges in a special Papal bull.[98] The battle of the Church against the new militarism was still not won by 1050 in the Middle Rhone region, though some progress had been made in the struggle.

This pattern of Church resistance to the militarism of this age, with its exactions and usurpation of Church lands, was not, however, confined to the Rhone Valley and regions immediately contiguous to it. We find it proceeding in Auvergne, in Rouergue, and in Gevaudun, where the new militarism, which resulted from rising castles and their covetous *milites*, presented problems to the Church of these regions too. It is in an Auvergnat cartulary, as a matter of fact, that we read about an early eleventh-century council, held by Bishop Guy of LePuy, which was attended by bishops from Toulouse, Rodez, Elne, Lodève, Glandève, Auvergne, Vivarais, and Valence, as well as by important nobles and *principes* of the laity. This council prohibited the building of castles or the levying of special exactions except on one's own allod, benefice, or *commande*.[99] This of course represents the same prohibitions found in the charter which Archbishop Burchard procured from his council for Cluny in 994, except that now these provisions were given a *general* application and were assented to by a body of bishops who represented a majority of the regions to be found in the Midi. It may have had some *immediate* local effect, for it is at about this time that we find Duke William of Aquitaine, who was the overlord of much of Auvergne, giving up exactions he and his predecessors were accustomed to levy upon the church of LePuy and other religious establishments of the region.[100]

Encroachment upon Church property, however, did not cease as a result

[97] *Cart. de Saint-Barnard de Romans*, no. 79.
[98] *Ibid.*, no. 93. See in the same year the record of similar encroachments of another landowner upon the domains of the abbey of Saint-Sulpice (*Cart. de Saint-Sulpice*, no. 3).
[99] *Cart. de Sauxillanges*, no. 15.
[100] *Chartes de Cluny*, III, no. 2277.

The Church (975-1050)

of this council, despite the active intervention of St. Odilon of Cluny,[101] and the support which the counts of Clermont gave to those who were opposed to the new militarism and disorders which it produced. True, a few *milites* like Maurice and Artmann, who gave up exactions they were levying on land belonging to Sauxillanges, appear to have been impressed by St. Odilon.[102] Others, like those *milites* whom Renco, bishop of Auvergne, had to threaten with excommunication about 1040, proved more refractory and had to be bought off by the monks.[103] Almost as difficult to deal with were those important military figures of Southern Auvergne, Etienne and his brother Austorg, who refused to give up the dues *"per vacas"* which they were levying on domains belonging to the abbey of Conques until they were paid 140 *solidi*.[104] Auvergne, like nearby Gevaudun, remained an area in the Midi so disorderly that the Peace of God still needed to be enforced there all through the eleventh century.[105]

The same pressures on the Church and its property are to be found in Western Aquitaine west of Auvergne and Rouergue. We have already noted how an abbey in the Limousin as early as 971 felt it necessary to forbid its own men or officials, in this case its *judices servum*, to become *milites*.[106] A little later an initial Church council seems to have been held at Charroux which attempted, like those in Velay and the Rhone Valley, to halt abuse which resulted from the new militarism.[107] It seems doubtful, however, if such efforts were crowned by much success, since abuses continued. About the year 1000, for instance, in giving some land to the abbey of Tulle, Viscount Rainald of Aubusson felt it necessary to promise that he would not thereafter interfere with this property as a *"defensor."* This gives a rather sinister but realistic idea of what the term *defensor* now really meant.[108] A little later, about 1020, a charter tells us of some property that belonged to the church of Limoges which

---

[101] *Cart. de Saint-Flour*, no. 4.
[102] *Cart. de Sauxillanges*, nos. 417, 419, 620, 635.
[103] *Ibid.*, no. 378.
[104] *Cart. de Conques*, no. 285, 441. On Ictor's sale of his unjustly exercised rights to Conques in 1019 see *ibid.*, no. 394. On similar action by his son Robert to Sauxillanges at about this time see *Cart. de Sauxillanges*, no. 406.
[105] C. Brunel, "Les juges de la paix en Gévaudun au milieu du XIe siècle," in *Bibliothèque de l'Ecole des Chartes*, CIX (1951).
[106] *Cart. de Beaulieu*, no. 50.
[107] See how Count Boson de La Marche returned land to Uzerche as a result of this council (*Cart. d'Uzerche*, no. 46).
[108] *Cart. de Tulle*, no. 350.

a certain Etienne had usurped and held illegally for two years.[109] Still later, we find the bishop and canons of this same church complaining that their own *prepositus* had taken over some of their church property and given it "furtively" to his brother, who proceeded to use it to reward three of his *milites*.[110] It is at about this time too that the viscounts of Comborn and Carlat seem to have joined together to take over almost the entire domain of the abbey of Aurillac;[111] just as the former had done with that of Tulle,[112] and the lords of Castelnau with Beaulieu's patrimony.[113] The lands belonging to the abbeys of the Limousin were threatened with appropriation by the lords of the region. We even learn from a charter of 1027 that Bishop Jordain of Limoges and his mother acted in similar fashion by usurping property which belonged to the abbey of Saint-Martial of Limoges.[114]

All of this explains why Church councils, held at Bourges and in the Limousin in 1031, were of such importance to the Church in this part of Aquitaine. These councils seem to have been attended by the leading *principes* and churchmen of the region, and to have had the full backing of the dukes of Aquitaine. They provided a forum where monks like those of Beaulieu could go to enlist aid in their attempt to halt abuses and protest the conditions forced upon them by the militarized nobility of their particular regions.[115] Calling for an excommunication of offenders, these councils ordered such deplorable conditions corrected and threatened to lay an interdict upon the lands of those who continued to usurp Church property. Perhaps the fulminations of such councils had some effect, for soon afterwards we begin to hear of reforms and of certain local nobles giving up exactions they were levying upon neighboring abbeys. Such seems to have been the case with the domains of the abbey of Uzerche.[116] We also learn of a local Church council of barons and churchmen, presided over by Bishop Hildegare of Limoges in 1039, which forbade both interference in the election of abbots and the usurpation of Church property in the Limousin.[117] Soon after this council met, a charter, dating from

[109] *Cart. de Saint-Etienne de Limoges*, no. 46.
[110] *Ibid.*, no. 156.
[111] *Ibid.*
[112] *Cart. de Tulle*, no. 290.
[113] P. Labbé, *Sacrosancta Concilia*, IX, col. 898.
[114] *Cart. de l'aumônerie de Saint-Martial de Limoges*, no. 36.
[115] Labbé, *Sacrosancta Concilia*, IX, col. 898, and XIX, col. 507.
[116] *Cart. d'Uzerche*, nos. 179, 441, 452.
[117] *Ibid.*, no. 1039.

The Church (975–1050)

1044, tells us of the return of a number of *villas* to the abbey of Uzerche by Viscount Guy of Limoges,[118] an action which may have forced a local *miles* to act similarly a year later.[119] Even in Southern Limousin and Quercy we find evidence that Viscount Bernard of Tulle was giving up similar levies on the domains of the abbey of Tulle at about this period.[120] By 1050 the situation had improved sufficiently, so that the duke of Aquitaine could give to the bishopric of Limoges a charter which guaranteed that the election of its bishop could take place without outside interference.[121] In the Limousin and Quercy, where the new militarism had borne most heavily upon the Church and its rights and property, reforms had begun, at last, to change the situation, though much still remained to be done.

Nor were such reforms confined to the Limousin and Quercy. We find evidence of them elsewhere in Aquitaine, where again the power and prestige of the dukes of Aquitaine was marshalled to assist Church reform. In 1026 a charter tells us of a wood, belonging to the abbey of Saint-Jean d'Angély which was restored to it by Viscount Kaledon of Aunay who had usurped it.[122] Five years later a *miles*, called Rainald, with the consent of Duke William of Aquitaine, returned to this same abbey a *mansus* he was occupying;[123] and in 1039 under the same conditions William, lord of Parthenay, gave up dues he was levying on land which also belonged to this monastery.[124] It was about this time too that we find Bishop Rohan of Angoulême threatening to excommunicate *anyone* who gave church property as fiefs.[125] We begin to find a successful effort to curb the new militarism and stop the usurpation of church lands and the illegal exactions between Poitou and the Garonne, just as we find a similar movement in the same period in Auvergne and the Valley of the Rhone.

Naturally enough this movement to curb the abuses of the new militarism also spread into more southerly portions of the Midi: into Languedoc, Gascony, Provence, and Catalonia. As early as 993 a charter of Pope John the XVI had placed the abbeys of Saint-Hilaire, Cuxa, and Lézat under the protection of Cluny,[126] and in 997 an important local lord of this region, Amelius, had returned land belonging to Lézat, which he

---

[118] *Ibid.*, no. 1092. [119] *Ibid.*, no. 109.
[120] *Cart. de Tulle*, no. 469.
[121] *Cart. de Saint-Etienne de Limoges*, nos. 175–176.
[122] *Cart. de Saint-Jean d'Angély*, no. 48.
[123] *Ibid.*, no. 197. [124] *Ibid.*, no. 186.
[125] *Cart. d'Angoulême*, no. 30.
[126] *Chartes de Cluny*, III, no. 1950.

had usurped.[127] A little later, about 1015 and 1025, charters show us Count William of Toulouse acting in similar fashion and giving back to this same abbey property he had taken from it.[128] At about the same period in nearby Gascony, we learn from our sources that Viscount William Forto restored land to the abbey of Mas Grenier, because he had violated the monastery's right of sanctuary by seizing a certain Bernard who was taking refuge there.[129] At about the same period another document tells us of the restoration of land belonging to Saint-Sernin of Toulouse by certain local landholding nobles.[130] Nevertheless, usurpation of church lands continued to be a serious problem. So much so, that we find Pope John XIX sending a letter to Count William of Toulouse threatening excommunication if a certain Viscount Arnold Eudes, called a *miles* by the Pope, did not stop taking over lands which belonged to the abbey of Moissac.[131] By 1047 Count William's son, Count Pons of Toulouse, took the obvious step and gave Moissac to Cluny,[132] and a little later accepted a similar Cluniac connection for the abbey of Lézat, which was also under his protection as its *custodis* or *defensor*.[133] In this part of the Midi too, a combination of Papal pressure and comital influence, aided by Cluny, began to halt usurpation of Church property by the new military class and to check the more flagrant exactions which *milites* were levying on Church domains.

To the south in the Narbonnaise we again find a similar resistance on the part of the Church to usurpation of its property by the lay nobles of the region. A charter of 998, for instance, tells us of the return of land which they had usurped from the abbey of Montolieu by two local magnates of the regions,[134] and in 1002 after a court case, Viscount Arnold of Carcassonne was forced to restore property he had taken from the abbey of Saint-Hilaire.[135] It was this kind of lay pressure upon the Church of this region which no doubt caused an important Church council to meet at Taluges in 1027, presided over by Bishop Oliba and attended by many important nobles and churchmen of this part of the Midi and Catalonia.[136]

[127] *Hist. Gén. de Lang.*, V, no. 155.
[128] *Ibid.*, nos. 173, 184.
[129] *Ibid.*, no. 174.
[130] *Cart. de Saint-Sernin*, nos. 47, 99, 147, 232.
[131] *Hist. Gén. de Lang.*, V, no. 195.
[132] *Cart. de Tulle*, XXII, 154–155.
[133] *Chartes de Cluny*, III, no. 1950.
[134] *Cart. de Carcassonne*, I, 196.
[135] Cros-Meyrévielle, *Documents*, no. 34.
[136] *Recueil des Historiens des Gaules et de la France*, XI, 514.

The Church (975–1050) 333

At this council the same kind of rules were promulgated which we find in similar councils which met in Aquitaine, Velay, and the Valley of the Rhone. The Peace of God was proclaimed with regulations designed to curb the abuses of the new militarism as they affected both the Church and the society of Southern France and Catalonia.

The great Church council of Taluges seems to have had some effect upon the society of this region. At any rate in 1036 a charter tells us that Count Roger the Young of Carcassonne returned important domains belonging to the abbey of Saint-Polycarpe in Razès.[137] Twelve years later the abbeys of Saint-Just of Narbonne and Lézat recovered lands which had been usurped as well.[138] Even more important is evidence of a wholesale return of property which had been taken from abbeys like Aniane and Gellone and the cathedral church of Béziers. Documents dating from this period, most of them from the years 1030 to 1050, show us some thirteen *guirpitios*, giving back land and rights to Gellone,[139] four to six which did the same for Aniane,[140] and several for the church of Béziers and the nearby abbey of Saint-Nazaire.[141] All these restorations of Church land and rights seem to have taken place before informal courts presided over by important churchmen and attended by leading landowners and *milites* of this part of Languedoc. A similar return of church lands at Nîmes is mentioned in a document of 1007,[142] and three more in charters dating from the years 1043–1060.[143] In nearby Provence we find less evidence of this sort of activity, but even here, in 1032, we learn of a gift of land to the abbey of Saint-Victor of Marseille by the archbishop of Aix.[144] At about the same time another series of charters tell us of the restoration of Church property in the Arles area of Provence to this same abbey.[145] Only in Catalonia does such return of Church property seem a rare occurrence, probably because the usurpation of Church land was still less of a problem there than in the rest of the Midi.

All of this leads us to some conclusions concerning the Church in the

---

[137] *Hist. Gén. de Lang.*, V, no. 208.
[138] *Ibid.*, no. 227.
[139] *Cart. de Gellone*, nos. 11, 16, 33, 34, 54, 86, 107, 133, 146, 221, 248, 305, and *Hist. Gén. de Lang.*, no. 206.
[140] *Cart. d'Aniane*, nos. 142, 146, 230, 244, 277, 332.
[141] *Hist. Gén. de Lang.*, V, no. 149, and *Cart. de Béziers*, no. 66.
[142] *Cart. de Nîmes*, no. 104.
[143] *Ibid.*, nos. 137, 140, 141.
[144] *Cart. de Saint-Victor*, no. 237. See also the *guirpitio* of the *villa* of Valentiola to Cluny at about this time (*Chartes de Cluny*, III, nos. 2066, 2268).
[145] *Cart. de Saint-Victor*, nos. 167, 186, 293.

Midi and Catalonia during this period. Our sources make it clear to us that the coming of castles and *milites* to lands south of Poitou and Burgundy caused serious problems for the Church in these regions. Aided by the system of family control of Church establishments, which had long existed in the Midi and Catalonia, the castellans and *milites* who occupied these fortresses encroached upon the domains of nearby Church establishments, levying dues of a new and onerous sort and in many cases usurping Church lands, which were then distributed as fiefs to members of the new military class. As early as the last years of the tenth century the Church reacted against such practices, particularly in regions like the Limousin and the Valley of the Rhone. It did so by enlisting the support of both Cluny and the Papacy, and by holding Church councils on a local and regional level. These councils included among those who attended, not only the leading churchmen but also important nobles of the regions concerned. They condemned the building of castles and the levying of the new onerous types of exactions which were a feature of the new militarism.

At first such councils were relatively unsuccessful. But when in 1027, 1031, and 1037 more important councils were held, followed up by local assemblies of the same character in various parts of the Midi, we begin to see some results. In part, no doubt, this was due to decisive support for the movement on the part of important lay nobles. In Aquitaine, for instance, it was the backing of the dukes of Aquitaine which helped most.[146] In Auvergne that of the counts of Clermont.[147] In the Toulousain that of the counts of Toulouse.[148] In Eastern Languedoc that of the principal noble families. All of these saw the dangers to them of the new militarism, and cooperated with the Church of their regions in checking its abuses. Perhaps even more important these councils elaborated a definite program, the Peace of God, which was more specific and workable than earlier fulminations and decrees against the building of castles and usurpation of Church property. As a result by 1050 we can see evidence from all over the Midi and Catalonia that the abuses of the new militarism had been checked, and that land was being restored to its Church owners and in many cases exactions given up. A beginning had at least been made

---

[146] See Labbé, *Sacrosancta Concilia*, IX, col. 898, on action taken by the duke of Aquitaine to free the Church of his region from lay control.

[147] See for example the action taken by the count of Clermont in 1011 according to *Chartes de Cluny*, IV, 2682, and in 1047 according to *Chartes de Charroux*, no. 4.

[148] See action taken by Count Pons as regards the abbeys of Lézat and Moissac and other church establishments in notes 128–133.

of bringing the new militarism under some form of control, though much still needed to be done.

But all of this still failed to touch the real problem which the Church in the Midi needed to face—its domination by local families in the regions where Church establishments were located. A Bishop Guy of LePuy, an Archbishop Burchard of Lyon, a Bishop Hildegare of Limoges, or a Bishop Oliba, or even an Archbishop Pons of Aix, sincere though they might be as opponents of the new militarism, were still the product of a family-run Church, who owed their positions to the operation of this system in the Midi and Catalonia. In some ways the same thing can even be said of St. Odilon of Cluny. They were still far removed in spirit from the Gregorian Reform movement of the late eleventh century, which was to demand a Church, not only free of military domination and control, but a spiritual Church whose officials were free of any form of lay investiture and simony. Already in the provisions of councils that asked for free election of abbots in the Limousin[149] and in the charter which the duke of Aquitaine gave the bishopric of Limoges that provided for his free election, we can see this new spirit emerging.[150] But by 1050 it was only beginning to affect the rest of the Midi and Catalonia, and was not to triumph until well into the twelfth century. By the mid eleventh century then, the Church of Southern France and the Spanish March was beginning to emerge successfully from its struggle with the new militarism of these regions, but its purification from the more subtle forms of family control and influence still remained a problem for the future.

Yet even when we emphasize the limitations which attended this aspect of the Cluny Reform movement and the Peace of God, which Cluny and others in the Church did so much to bring about, we must note a very important fact: the evidence of the great authority throughout our region which the Papacy and Cluny, due to this movement, were able to exert. We have already commented on how Cluny's influence, as seen in her affiliated houses, by 1050 had spread until every region, from the Pyrenees to the Loire and from Provence and Dauphiny to the Atlantic, was affected by it, and how it was even crossing the mountains into Northwestern Spain.

What needs more emphasis still, though, is evidence of the authority and influence over Southern France and Catalonia which the pre-Gregorian Papacy was beginning to wield. We not only find popes actively in-

[149] *Cart. d'Uzerche*, no. 1039.
[150] *Cart. de Saint-Etienne de Limoges*, nos. 175–176.

tervening in Catalonia,[151] as Kehr has emphasized; we find their authority reflected in the charters they granted to monastic establishments in Dauphiny, in Velay, in the Limousin, in Gascony, and in Provence.[152] We find them setting up abbeys as sanctuaries in the Alps,[153] admonishing *milites* in Gascony,[154] and getting a bishop released from captivity in Limoges.[155] Already by 1050 the Popes had moved in to fill the vacuum left by the decline of royal Northern French influence in the Midi and Catalonia, and the inability of the kings of Provence-Burgundy to build an effective kingdom in the Valley of the Rhone. A basis had been laid for the work of Gregory VII, Urban II, Alexander III, and Innocent III in lands south of Poitou and Burgundy.

Thus we see an increase in Papal and Cluniac influence over the Church of the Midi and Catalonia; and a Church which still was vigorous and vital enough to rally society and check certain abuses of the new prevailing militarism of the period, and to make a beginning toward the creation of a new, more spiritual, Church. Abuses still remained, it is true, but they were beginning to feel a breath of reform which was to produce the age of the crusades and Gregory VII.

[151] See Papal charters given to the abbey of San Cugat in 1002 and 1007 (*Cart. de San Cugat*, nos. 387, 412).

[152] *Cart. de Saint-Barnard de Romans*, nos. 92, 93 (Dauphiny); *Cart. de Saint-Chaffre*, no. 375 (Velay); *Chartes de Charroux*, nos. 72–75 (the Limousin); *Cart. de la Réolle*, no. 99 (Gascony), *Hist. Gén. de Lang.*, V, no. 157 (Provence).

[153] *Cart. de Saint-Barnard de Romans*, no. 93.

[154] *Hist. Gén. de Lang.*, V, no. 195.

[155] *Ademar de Chabannes*, III, 36, p. 160.

CHAPTER XVII

The Continued Failure of Principalities

DURING THE period from 975 to 1050 when militarism was growing in the Midi and the Spanish March and a powerful Church was waging a valiant and not unsuccessful attempt to curb its excesses, little progress was made in government. In many ways, as a matter of fact, the failure of the family system which controlled Southern France and the Spanish March was even more noticeable after 975 than it had been before. For to the failure of families like the dukes of Gascony and the kings of Provence-Burgundy to evolve an effective governing system, we must add similar failures of those noble houses who controlled regions like Carcassonne-Razès, Cerdanya-Besalu, and Provence. By the year 1050 actual control of most of the Midi and Catalonia was in the hands of a large number of less important families, whose authority was local in character and who seem to have borne the general title of *principes*. They tended to control the castles and churches in their own local areas without much interference from outside authority. Vestiges of greater influence over a wider region still remained for many families like that of Toulouse-Rouergue, but the time had not yet come when such influence could be transformed into effective power. By the end of this period, of all the noble houses of these regions, only the counts of Barcelona and the duke of Aquitaine had begun the process of building toward a more centralized and effective political system, and they were only able to do this in the last decades before 1050. And even for them the real period of political centralization was to come later in the century.

In this Midi and Catalonia of independent nobles and *principes* it was Cluny and the Papacy, as we have emphasized, who wielded whatever effective outside political influence existed—not the French monarchs from the North. For instance such rulers gave only a handful of charters to the abbeys of Catalonia in contrast to their earlier activities along this line. All of them seem to have been issued by Lothaire, the last of the Carolingians—two dating from 981 for Roussillon,[1] one for the abbey of Ripoll in 982,[2] and the last two granted to the abbeys of San-Cugat and Saint-Peter of Rhodes in 986.[3] When the French crown passed to the Capetian house in 987, however, and when it became apparent that no effective assistance against the Moslems could be expected from the rulers of this house, the nobles of the Spanish March dropped any pretence of formal ties to the French crown. Instead they looked for leadership to Rome and the Papacy, or made arrangements and marriage alliances with other local noble houses of the Midi to the north of them. Only a purely theoretical connection remained with the French monarchy. It was one provided by the use of Capetian reigns to date their charters.

If this seems true in Catalonia, it was even truer for the rest of the Midi. When Hugh Capet became king, few lords of Southern France, except the dukes of Aquitaine, supported him, and indeed we have a record of only one abbey, that of Paunat, which solicited his protection.[4] When he and his son Robert, in alliance with the Poitevin dukes, attempted to intervene in the Limousin, the result was a failure. They could not capture castles which belonged to the count of La Marche.[5] Worse still, according to a contemporary chronicle, they had to endure an open insult from this upstart marcher lord, who, when he was taunted as to how he became a count, a title to which he certainly had little right, contemptuously answered, "Who made you kings?"[6]

A few years later Robert, Hugh Capet's successor, was able to do a little better in Auvergne. There he was at least recognized as king. But even here it is difficult to be sure that he was so recognized in his own right.[7] It seems more probable that his influence over this region was more the result of the fact that the countess of Clermont was a sister of his wife Queen Constance. Robert and his successor Henry were able to achieve considerable control over Burgundy,[8] but to the south their role remained

[1] *Catalunya Carolingia*, II, 211–213.

[2] *Ibid.*, pp. 170–174.

[3] *Ibid.*, pp. 197–200, 241–244.

[4] *Cart. de Paunat*, no. 12.

[5] *Ademar de Chabannes*, III, 34, 45, pp. 157, 167. Note that King Robert also failed in attempting to chastize Eudes, *princeps* of Deols, in 1014 (*ibid.*, III, 51, p. 174).

[6] "Aquitaniae Historiae Fragmentum," in *ibid.*, p. 205.

[7] On the activities of these early Capetians in this part of France see P. Lauer, *Robert I et Raoul de Bourgogne, rois de France*.

[8] See J. Richard, *Les ducs de Bourgogne et la formation du duché du XIe au*

The Continued Failure of Principalities 339

a negligible one. Only as their powerful vassals, the dukes of Aquitaine, expanded their authority south were the Capetians able to exert any influence over the Midi, and then only indirectly. By 1050 the Capetian monarchy had become a Northern French institution, for all practical purposes without much meaning for those who lived south of Poitou and Burgundy. And so it was to remain for another century.

Remembering this lack of influence of the Capetian house, let us examine the political system of the Midi and Catalonia. Perhaps the most striking thing of all is the lack of political cohesion which an examination of these regions discloses. The Auvergne region, for instance, during this period seems to have been divided among the counts of Clermont,[9] the counts of Gevaudun,[10] the dukes of Aquitaine,[11] and a series of independent viscontal and seigneurial families like the viscounts of Carlat, the viscounts of LePuy, the lords of Bourbon, the *comtors* of Nonette, and a number of others.[12] Under the uninspired rule of King Conrad the Peaceful, King Rudolf, and their German imperial successors, the Middle Rhone Valley region, politically speaking, presents an equally chaotic picture. Here a series of new families like the counts of Savoy,[13] the counts of Gravaisdun,[14] and the counts of Lyonnais-Forez[15] were competing for

---

*XIV*e *siècle*, pp. 30–137. See also a charter of 1022 which attests to his authority in Velay (*Cart. de Saint-Egidius*, no. 98).

[9] For information concerning the power of the counts of Clermont in Auvergne see M. Boudet, Introduction to the *Cart. de Saint-Flour*, p. cxxii. See references to their authority over the abbey of Sauxillanges in *Cart. de Sauxillanges*, nos. 279, 401, 402, 476, 572, 635. See also *Cart. de Lérins*, no. 214.

[10] Charters of 986, 999, and 1011 attest to the influence of the counts of Gevaudun in Auvergne and especially at Brioude *Cart. de Brioude*, nos. 91, 321, and *Grand Cart. de Brioude*, no. LIV.

[11] See references to Duke William of Aquitaine in *Chartes de Cluny*, III, nos. 2277, 2682; *Cart. de Brioude*, nos. 92, 323; and *Chartes de Charroux*, no. 4.

[12] See Introduction to *Cart. de Saint-Flour*, pp. cvii–clxvi.

[13] See G. de Manteyer, "Les origines de la maison de Savoie en Bourgogne (910–1060)," in *Mélanges d'archéologie et d'histoire de l'École française à Rome*, XIX (1899), and "Les origines de la maison de Savoie en Bourgogne, Notes additionnelles," in *Le Moyen Age*, V (1901). See a charter of 1015 which mentions their authority in this region (*Cart. de Grenoble*, no. 18). For a somewhat later period see *Cart. de Saint-Sulpice*, no. 2; *Cart. de Saint-Chaffre*, nos. 434, 435; *Cart. de Grenoble*, nos. 19, 20; and *Cart. de Saint-André-le-bas*, nos. 211–213.

[14] On the counts of Gravaisdun and their authority in Dauphiny which included control of the bishopric of Grenoble see *Chartes de Cluny*, IV, no. 2307; *Cart. de Saint-Chaffre*, nos. 355, 356; and *Cart. de Grenoble*, nos. 15, 16, 34. About 1050 this family seems to have lost control over parts of this Alpine region to the more aggressive counts of Savoy.

[15] On Count Artald, who founded a new line of counts in the Lyonnais at the

authority with older houses like that of Valence[16] or the viscounts of Lyon and Vienne.[17] In the Limousin viscounts continued to multiply and to compete with each other also without any effective interference from outside overlords.[18] In many ways a similar situation existed in Rouergue, Quercy, and the Albigeois. To the southwest in Gascony the ruling families who controlled Commignes, Bigorre, Astarac, Fézensac, Béarn, and Tartas, to name only a few of the more important ones, quarrelled with one another and made any attempt on the part of its dukes to create a strong duchy an impossibility.[19] The same is true of Pallars and Ribagorça which not only appear to have lost all political cohesion during this period due to internal subdivision of authority, but to have become subject to outside influences that were exerted by the rulers of Aragón and the counts of Urgell and Barcelona.[20]

Amidst this prevailing pattern of political chaos, however, in several parts of the Midi and Catalonia we do find, during this period, attempts to create something approaching territorial states. None of them ultimately succeeded, but by examining them in some detail we can, per-

---

end of the tenth century see E. Fournial, "Recherches sur les comtes de Lyon du IX⁰ et X⁰ siècles" in *Le Moyen Age*, LVIII (1952), 231–249. See a charter of 992 which probably refers to Count Artald in *Cart. de Savigny*, no. 53. For a reference to Count Gerald, who probably succeeded him, note a charter of 1017 in *ibid.*, no. 602.

[16] We find references to this noble house which controlled Valence in *Chartes de Cluny*, III, nos. 1715, 1716; IV, no. 2832; *Cart. de Saint-Petrus Aniacensis* [LePuy], no. 425; and *Cart. de Saint-Chaffre*, nos. 314, 315.

[17] These viscounts are mentioned in *Cart. de Vienne*, no. 33, and *Cart. de Saint-André-le-bas*, no. 140.

[18] The pages of Ademar de Chabannes reveal the quarrels of the lords of the Limousin, such as the struggle between Viscount Guido of Limoges and Boson II, count of La Marche in 999 over a castle (*Ademar de Chabannes*, III, 35, p. 159); or the quarrel between Viscount Guido and the bishop of Angoulême about 1000 (*ibid.*, III, 36, pp. 159–160). Note also the mention of how this same Viscount Guido's castle was besieged by five counts in 990 ("Aquitaniae Historiae Fragmenta," in *ibid.*, p. 205).

[19] On the situation which existed in Gascony during this period see C. Samarin, "Les institutions en Gascogne" in F. Lot and R. Fawtier, *Histoire des Institutions de la France*, I, 186–192.

[20] On the relations maintained between the counts of Urgell and those of Pallars see *Liber Feudorum*, nos. 120, 121. On those between the latter and Aragón see *ibid.*, nos. 58, 59. See also *ibid.*, nos. 36, 57, 107, 109, and *Hist. Gén. de Lang.*, V, no. 212. On Ribagorça see *Hist. Gén. de Lang.*, nos. 115 and 117.

The Continued Failure of Principalities

haps, learn something of the nature of these regions' governmental problems and the reasons why they were able to make so little political progress. We will concentrate on seven of these attempts to create principalities. They are Carcassonne-Razés, Anduze, Provence, La Marche, Angoulême, Cerdanya-Besalu, and last of all Toulouse-Rouergue. Since almost every section of the Midi and Spanish March is represented by these examples they should give us an insight into Southern France and Catalonia, as a whole, from the standpoint of government in this period.

The first such potential principality, that of Carcassonne-Razès, was made possible by the earlier failures and weaknesses of the House of Toulouse-Rouergue, which we have examined at some length in a previous chapter. When Count Raymond Pons died about 950 and a little later his wife Countess Garsinde dissipated his holdings in gifts to her friends, her relatives, and a series of abbeys, neither her cousins the counts of Rouergue, nor the Toulousain heir, Count William Taillefer, were able to build up a powerful state in Languedoc or even to maintain the position which Raymond Pons had held.[21] This gave to the House of Carcassonne-Razès, in the person of Count Roger the Old and his wife Countess Adelaise, its opportunity. Controlling important abbeys like Montolieu, Saint-Hilaire, and Caunes,[22] they were able to expand their authority to the west until they not only controlled Razès, but also that area which was to become the county of Foix.[23] They even had an interest in the newly created county of Commignes.[24] Through the Narbonne relatives of Adelaise, countess of Carcassonne, they gained considerable influence over Narbonne and its archbishopric.[25] By marrying their daughter Ermissende to the heir to the county of Barcelona they

---

[21] See Chapter II, Section IV, on the earlier failure of the House of Toulouse-Rouergue to build a principality in this part of the Midi.

[22] The will of Count Roger the Old of 1002 mentions certain *abadias* which he has *already* given to his son Bishop Peter of Gerona (*Hist. Gén. de Lang.*, V, no. 162). For Roger's earlier control of these abbeys see Cros-Meyrévielle, *Documents*, nos. 30, 31, 34, and *Cart. de Carcassonne*, IV, 3. Charters which refer to this family's later control of these church establishments are found in Cros-Meyrévielle, *Documents*, nos. 38, 39; *Cart. de Carcassonne*, II, 75; and *Hist. Gén. de Lang.*, V, no. 189.

[23] Count Roger's will of 1002 mentions the county of Razès (*Hist. Gén. de Lang.*, no. 162).

[24] Roger, son of Count Roger the Old was count of Foix in 1034 (Cros-Meyrévielle, *Documents*, no. 37).

[25] *Hist. Gén. de Lang.*, V, no. 130.

were able to exert some influence over Catalonia, which explains why one of their sons, Peter, became the bishop of Gerona.[26] No wonder in a charter of 984, Roger could refer to himself as count and marquis.[27]

It seems probable that this new eminence of the House of Carcassonne in the Midi and Catalonia aroused feelings of jealousy and alarm among neighboring ruling families: particularly the House of Cerdanya-Besalu, which coveted territory in Capçir that Count Roger regarded as his own, and which was disturbed by the close ties he had developed with the House of Barcelona. As a result we learn of a conflict between Count Roger and Count Oliba Cabreta of Besalu. Our information concerning these hostilities is scant indeed, being largely confined to information contained in a charter in which Roger, in a gift to the abbey of Saint-Hilaire, mentions his victory.[28] This would imply that he held his own. On the other hand it is equally clear that Count Oliba Cabreta also made gains at Carcassonne's expense in the Pyrenean area to the south.[29] So it seems probable that when Oliba died in Rome about 990, Roger could breathe a sigh of relief. His will, dating from 1002, shows that he still possessed authority over a considerable portion of the Midi.[30]

Yet this potentially powerful principality soon disintegrated, despite Roger's attempts to hold it together as shown in his will. When he left his authority and domains to his heirs he seems to have stipulated that these heirs should only dispose of their holdings to each other and thus keep them in the family.[31] Like most wills this soon became a dead letter. Each of his heirs—his brother, who was in control of Foix; his son Peter, bishop of Gerona; and his other two sons, Raymond and Bernard—soon went their separate ways. By 1016 the rival House of Cerdanya-Besalu was able to purchase the archbishopric of Narbonne for Guifred, a member of their family.[32] Carcassonne's domains were divided among a series of heirs until they lost whatever unity they had had earlier.[33] Soon after

[26] *Ibid.*, no. 162, and Cros-Meyrévielle, *Documents*, no. 37.

[27] *Hist. Gén. de Lang.*, V, no. 137. In 1002 he is also called *princeps Carcassonne* (*ibid.*, no. 161).

[28] Cros-Meyrévielle, *Documents*, no. 31.

[29] See P. Ponsch, "Le Confluent et ses comtes du IXe au XIIe siècle" in *Études Roussillonnaises*, II (1952), 285–295.

[30] *Hist. Gén. de Lang.*, V, no. 162.

[31] *Ibid.*   [32] *Ibid.*, no. 251.

[33] See charter of 1025 (*ibid.*, no. 185); or charters of 1034 (Cros-Meyrévielle, *Documents*, nos. 37, 38, 39); or charter of 1036 (*Hist. Gén. de Lang.*, V, nos. 208, 209, 210); or that of 1050 (*ibid.*, no. 229). All reveal the progressive fragmentation of the domains of Count Roger the Old.

1050 even the nuclear county of Carcassonne was to be the subject of contention between the counts of Barcelona, the counts of Toulouse, and the Trencavel house of Béziers. The work of Count Roger the Old had ended in failure.

When we turn to eastern Languedoc we find another interesting case, that which concerns the House of Anduze. The beginnings of this family seem more modest than those of Carcassonne, since this house was descended from a castellan who held Anduze in the last years of the ninth century.[34] After 975 its power and prestige began to increase rapidly. Perhaps the most important cause of this rise was the marriage of Bernard of Anduze to Garsinde, heiress to a major portion of the viscounties of Béziers and Agde.[35] As a result, early in the eleventh century, a potentially powerful principality had been created which stretched from Nîmes to Béziers and north toward Velay. Two sons of Bernard and Garsinde became bishops of Nîmes and LePuy,[36] respectively, and the family appears to have maintained control over the abbeys of Aniane, Gellone, and other religious establishments near Béziers and Agde.[37] In this period Bernard, like Roger of Carcassonne, refers to himself as *princeps* and marquis and his wife Garsinde bears the title of countess.[38]

Yet it is clear that no permanent principality in eastern Languedoc emerged from all this. Like Carcassonne, the House of Anduze fell upon evil days when its founders, Marquis Bernard and Countess Garsinde, died. The bishoprics of LePuy and Nîmes came under the control of rival houses.[39] The abbeys of Aniane and Gellone regained a large measure of

[34] Frédélon, of the castle of Anduze, the progenitor of this clan, is first mentioned in an earlier ninth century charter (*Cart. de Nîmes*, no. 32).

[35] See the will of Viscount William of Béziers dating from 990 (*Cart. de Béziers*, no. 49). Garsinde is mentioned again in charters of 1006, 1013, 1024, and 1029 (*ibid.*, no. 54; *Cart. de Conques*, no. 18; *Hist. Gén. de Lang.*, V, no. 182; and *Cart. de Gellone*, no. 6). The charters of 1013 and 1024 also mention her husband Bernard.

[36] Frédélon (or Frédol) of the castle of Anduze is mentioned as being made bishop of LePuy in *Chronique de la Monastère de Saint-Pierre de LePuy*, in *Hist. Gén. de Lang.*, V, cols. 18–20. He also is referred to in *Cart. d'Aniane*, nos. 146–148. Both he, his brother, the bishop of Nîmes, and other members of the family are mentioned in a charter of 1020 (*Cart. de Nîmes*, no. 120).

[37] A charter of 1037 mentions that the *abbatias* of Aniane and Gellone are under the control of Bermund and his brother, Count Peter (*Hist. Gén. de Lang.*, V, no. 206).

[38] Bernard is called *marquis* in 1013 (*ibid.*, no. 171), and *princeps* in 1024 (*ibid.*, no. 182). Garsinde is called countess in both charters.

[39] See *Cronique de Saint-Pierre de LePuy*, cols. 21–24, on how a new family got

independence.[40] Family lands and rights were divided between Count Perre, who held Béziers, and Bermund, who succeeded to Anduze.[41] By 1050 only traces of Anduze's authority still remained, and much of this soon passed into the hands of the House of Trencavel which succeeded to their authority in Nîmes and Béziers.

Lest this be considered an unusual case, the story of the county of Provence during this period reveals much the same situation. About the year 950 King Conrad of Burgundy-Provence gave this part of his domains to a certain Count Boson of Arles.[42] Boson seems to have had two sons, an older one, Roubaud, and a younger one, William, both of whom bore the title of count.[43] William proved to be a man possessing unusual gifts as a warrior and administrator. With the assistance of the counts of the High Alps and the viscounts of Marseille and Fos, he drove the Moslems from Fraxinetum and reorganized disorderly regions east of the Rhone to create, almost single-handedly, a large, well-organized duchy, marquisate, or county of Provence.[44] He well deserved the title of duke which he bore from this time on, as well as that of *Pater Patriae* given him in a contemporary charter.[45] He controlled the royal *fisc* within his domains,[46] and held courts whose competence seems to have been unquestioned, and was in fact in every way independent of his nominal suzerain at Vienne.[47] During his lifetime only he bore the title of marquis while his brother had to content himself with that of count.[48]

When William died, about 994, his brother Count Roubaud seems to have succeeded him as head of the family, and to have assumed William's

---

control of the bishopric of LePuy. On the change in the bishopric of Nîmes which went to the Trencavel family see *Hist. Gén. de Lang.*, V, no. 217.

[40] *Hist. Gén. de Lang.*, V, no. 206.
[41] *Ibid.* On Count Perre's holdings later on see *ibid.*, no. 209.
[42] *Chartes de Cluny*, II, no. 1052.
[43] *Cart. de Saint-Victor*, nos. 29, 598.
[44] Raoul Glaber, *Historiarum libri V*, I, 4, 9, p. 12. See also a later charter of 993 which tells how Count William organized Provence after the expulsion of the Moslems (*Cart. de Saint-Victor*, no. 77).
[45] Charters from 979 and 992 call him *marquis* (*Cart. de Saint-Victor*, no. 1042; and *Hist. Gén. de Lang.*, V, no. 153). This later charter calls him *princeps* also.
[46] The charter of 992 says the land William took from the pagans was his as a gift of the king [of Burgundy] (*Cart. de Saint-Victor*, no. 1042). Other later charters dating from 1018–1032, 1030, and 1040, refer to regalian and comital rights over *villas* belonging to the *fisc* (*ibid.*, nos. 1061, 155, 172).
[47] *Ibid.*, nos. 29, 654.
[48] See note 45.

The Continued Failure of Principalities 345

title of marquis,[49] which he in turn passed on to his own son William II, who bore it as late as 1032.[50] Roubaud's daughter Emma married Count William of Toulouse.[51] Yet the heirs of William I also kept some authority. It seems probable that it was Williams' daughter who was the Constance who married King Robert of France, while her sister became countess of Clermont.[52] Soon after 1018 two other heirs of Marquis William, Bertrand and Josfred, ruled in Provence as co-counts also.[53]

Perhaps it was this diffusion of authority which explains the failure of the family of Provence to maintain the highly organized principality of its founder, Marquis William. However that may be, it seems apparent that by 1030, if not earlier, the power of the counts of Provence had begun to disappear. General courts ceased to be held and the counts of remote regions like Sisteron, Vintmille, Antibes, Nice, and Fréjus began to act in an independent manner.[54] So did the viscounts of Marseille, to whom William's heirs were forced to grant land belonging to the comital *fisc* as outright allods.[55] By 1050 what had, for the period, been an unusually well-organized principality had become one in which the major noble families were all but independent. It was also one which soon was to see even the marquisate disputed between the counts of Toulouse, the counts of Forcalquier, and eventually the counts of Barcelona. After an excellent beginning Provence followed the same path leading to dissolution and disintegration which, we have already noted, was followed by Carcassonne and Anduze.

Leaving this southern area of the Midi let us next turn to two other examples of the same sort in a region quite remote from the Mediterranean. I refer to the House of La Marche and that of Angoulême which developed in a part of Western Aquitaine that lay between Poitou and the Garonne and from Limousin to the Atlantic. In choosing these two examples we find a particular interest in the fact that they represent two ruling families which were following diametrically opposed political policies and yet ended up with the same general results. The first ex-

[49] *Chartes de Cluny*, III, no. 1987.
[50] *Cart. de Saint-Victor*, nos. 652, 656; and *Hist. Gén. de Lang.*, V, no. 172.
[51] *Cart. de Lérins*, no. 149.
[52] Raoul Glaber, *Historiarum libri V*, III, 9, 40, p. 89.
[53] A charter of 1030 calls Josfred and Bertrand counts of Provence (*Cart. de Saint-Victor*, no. 155). In one of 1031 Bertrand calls himself *"comes vel gubernator Provintiae regionis"* (*ibid.*, no. 455). In 1034 another calls them *principes* of all Provence (*ibid.*, no. 333).
[54] See *Cart. de Lérins*, nos. 40, 113, 144, 167 for examples of this independence.
[55] For an example of this comital bounty see *Cart. de Saint-Victor*, no. 34.

ample, La Marche, represents a family which led the resistance of the nobles of this region to the advance of the Poitevin dukes of Aquitaine. The second, that of Angoulême, presents a picture of a ruling house which was, perhaps, the leading ally of these dukes during their period of expansion.

Let us first consider the House of La Marche. The origins of the first counts of La Marche are obscure. All we really know is that sometime about 950 a certain Marquis Boson, seems to have been in control of some territory in the northern part of the Limousin.[56] The location of his small principality—which barred the route that the counts of Poitou had to follow south into the Limousin—and indeed its very name of La Marche make one suspect that he was given this land by Count Raymond I of Rouergue or other Limousin nobles opposed to Poitevin ambitions. This, however, is only conjecture. It is clear, however, that once established in this region Count or Marquis Boson proved a doughty adversary to the dukes of Aquitaine. So did his successors. As a result of their prestige as warriors and their victories over their Poitevin adversaries they were able to add the county of Périgord to their holdings, by marrying its heiress,[57] and about the year 1000 also made an ally of the viscount of Limoges, whose sister wed one of their house.[58] At the turn of the millenium, under the leadership of Count Boson II, they appear to have headed a powerful coalition of anti-Poitevin nobles in the Limousin.[59] At the same time, their control of Périgord brought them into close alliance with the House of Toulouse who had long maintained friendly relations with the counts of this region. As late as 1040 this alliance was still in existence which helps to explain the marriage between Almodis of La Marche and Count Pons of Toulouse.[60]

Nevertheless the family of La Marche were not destined to create a strong principality in this part of Western Aquitaine. When Count Boson II died his heirs followed the prevailing practice and divided up his domain. Bernard got La Marche and Adelbert, Périgord.[61] So divided Boson's successors could not resist the dukes of Aquitaine, nor

[56] On the possible origins of this house see R. Mertier, *La Senechausée de la Basse-Marche*, pp. 21–26. It is in 958 that Boson I is first called *marchio*. (L. Albanes-Chevalier, *Gallia Christiana Novissima*, II, *Inst.*, col. 169).

[57] *Ademar de Chabannes*, III, 34, p. 156.

[58] *Ibid.*, III, 25, p. 148.

[59] *Ibid.*, III, 34, pp. 156–157.

[60] See reference made to Almodis and her husband Count Pons of Toulouse in a charter of 1047 which gave Moissac to Cluny (*Cart. de Tulle*, XXII, 154–155).

[61] *Ademar de Chabannes*, III, 20, p. 138.

were they able to rally the jealous bickering lords of the Limousin to any unity under their leadership. Soon La Marche had to surrender to Duke William the Great of Aquitaine[62] and by 1027 Limoges followed suit.[63] A principality which might have become strong disintegrated. By the end of the century a new Poitevin family held La Marche, the original basis of the power and authority of Count Boson the Old.

Equally instructive is an examination of how the counts of Angoulême failed. These counts were descended from Count Turpio, who established himself in this part of Aquitaine in the late ninth century. In 975 they and their cousins controlled not only Angoulême and Périgord, but also the county of Agen which they received from the counts of Toulouse.[64] They probably also had some authority over Saintonge.[65] When the county of Périgord came into the possession of the counts of La Marche, William Taillefer II, the count of Angoulême, appears to have been unhappy about it. At any rate he countered by allying himself to Count Fulk III of Anjou, whose sister he married.[66] Since Fulk was a close ally of the counts of Poitou this had the effect of making Angoulême the leading ally of the dukes of Aquitaine in this region. This alliance seems to have resulted in some solid advantages for Count William II. Though he did not gain Périgord, which remained in the hands of the family of La Marche, he was able, with Duke William's assistance, to expand his power into the Bordelais,[67] and about 1020 to become a power in Saintonge as well.[68] At the time of his death, about 1028, he was probably the leading magnate in this part of Aquitaine, allied to Poitou and Anjou and having a son who was married to the daughter of the reigning duke of Gascony.

This eminence, however, proved temporary and illusory. Upon the death of Count William in 1028 his sons, Aldouin and Geoffrey, began

---

[62] "Aquitaniae Historiae Fragmenta," in *ibid.*, p. 208.

[63] See reference to the presence of Duke William of Aquitaine in 1027 (*Cart. de Saint-Etienne de Limoges*, no. 69).

[64] *Ademar de Chabannes*, III, 20, p. 138.

[65] See references to their land and their authority in Saintonge in 1021 (*Cart. de Saint-Jean d'Angély*, no. 251).

[66] *Ademar de Chabannes*, III, 41, p. 163. Ademar says that Fulk held castles in Poitou and Saintonge *"pro benefico,"* that is to say as fiefs from them.

[67] Ademar tells of the help which Count William Taillefer of Angoulême gave to Duke William of Aquitaine in his struggle with Boson II of La Marche (*ibid.*, III, 42, p. 165). He also mentions his expansion into the Bordelais and his authority there (*ibid.*, III, 68, p. 194).

[68] On control over Saintonge exercised by Count William in 1024 see *ibid.*, III, 66, p. 186.

quarrelling over their inheritance in the Bordelais.[69] Revolts broke out in Saintonge.[70] The duke of Aquitaine and the count of Anjou took advantage of the situation to intervene. As a result Saintonge was lost to the House of Angoulême.[71] Even more important a few years later another heiress to Gascony, the daughter of Duke William Sánchez, married into the House of Poitou.[72] From this union came claims that the dukes of Aquitaine had to Gascony, which in 1053 they were able to vindicate by force of arms. As a result, in this period what had promised to be a strong principality in Angoulême and neighboring regions had disintegrated into weakness. The counts of Angoulême became minor nobles dependent upon the dukes of Aquitaine, who had gained not only all of Aquitaine but Gascony as well.

Our sixth example of a failure to create a strong principality involves Catalonia and the House of Cerdanya-Besalu. By 975 this family, which was descended from Count Miró, the brother of Count Guifred, and who were cousins of the House of Barcelona, had begun to consolidate their authority over their part of Catalonia. In the course of this consolidation they began to adopt policies generally hostile to Count Borell II of Barcelona, who represented the older traditions of Guifred's marquisite over all the counties of Catalonia. By the time Count Oliba Cabreta had personally united his family's possessions in Besalu, Cerdanya, and Berga, a strong principality seemed a reality, not only one which controlled these central Pyrenean counties, but one which exercised an influence far beyond them, through family control of the great abbeys of Ripoll, Cuxa, Saint-Joan de les Abadesses, and even Lagrasse.[73] Yet such authority did not content Count Oliba. He therefore extended his domains to the north at the expense of the House of Carcassonne, and to the west at the expense of the House of Ampurias-Roussillon.[74] He took the title of marquis and

[69] *Ibid.*, III, 67, p. 193.

[70] *Ibid.*, III, 66, p. 186.

[71] *Ibid.* See also proof of ducal power in this region in *Cart. de Saint-Jean d'Angély*, nos. 148, 197, 244, 252. See Count Aldouin of Angoulême mentioned as present at a conclave in 1030. He may have still kept some authority there at this period (*ibid.*, no. 158). By 1037, apparently this is no longer true (*ibid.*, no. 42). See also *Cart. de Notre Dame de Saintes*, no. 1 (which dates from 1947).

[72] On this ducal connection with Gascony which preceded its conquest soon after 1050 see *Ademar de Chabannes*, III, 39, pp. 161–162.

[73] See R. de Abadal i de Vinyals, *L'abat Oliva, bisbe de Vic, i la seva època*, pp. 15–49, and Ponsch, "Le Confluent et ses comtes," pp. 270–290 on the power of the House of Cerdanya-Besalu in this period.

[74] Ponsch, "Le Confluent et ses comtes," pp. 290–295.

The Continued Failure of Principalities

began to assume a leadership over Catalonia which the weakness and general incompetence of Count Borell II of Barcelona made it easy for him to do.[75]

When Count Oliba died in 990, by his will he divided his domains among his sons and his widow. One of the sons, Bernard, received Besalu with the promise of Vallespir too when his mother died. Guifred, the other, got Cerdanya, Confluent, and Berga. Perhaps this family's chief weakness had been its failure to control any bishoprics. This was soon remedied. After an effort to get Pope Benedict VIII to set up a new bishopric in Besalu failed,[76] Berengar, one of the family, was made bishop of Elne in 993.[77] A little later in 1008 Oliba, a brother of Counts Bernard and Guifred was made bishop of Ausona,[78] and in 1016 the archbishopric of Narbonne was purchased for a son of Count Guifred, who bore the same name.[79] Still a little later the bishopric of Urgell was purchased for still another scion of this house.[80] By the end of the second decade of the eleventh century the House of Besalu-Cerdanya had come to control bishoprics to the north, the south, the east, and the west of their domains.

Yet such power was not to last. When Count Guifred of Cerdanya-Confluent-Berga died, his will, as was the custom, divided his domains among his seven children.[81] Nor was his brother Count Bernard Taillefer more successful in keeping his lands intact after his death.[82] As this disintegration took place due to inheritance, leadership over Catalonia gradually slipped from the grasp of this family into that of the House of Barcelona, which was now taking charge of the advance south into Moslem territory which we know as the Reconquista. By the time Raymond, count of Cerdanya, was willing to allow the powerful Count Raymond Berengar I of Barcelona to purchase his allegiance in 1058, the future belonged to the House of Barcelona and a powerful principality of Besalu-Cerdanya was no longer a possibility.

There still remains one final family which we need to consider to round out our picture, that of Toulouse-Rouergue. In an earlier chapter we noted

---

[75] *Ibid.*, pp. 289–290.
[76] C. Brousse, "La vicomté de Castellnou," in *Études Roussillonnaises*, III (1953), 115–120.
[77] *Marca hispanica*, I, appendix 176–178.
[78] *Hist. Gén. de Lang.*, V, no. 158.
[79] *Ibid.*, no. 251.
[80] Ponsch, "Le Confluent et ses comtes," p. 295.
[81] Dom Luc D'Achery, *Spicelegium*, III, 392.
[82] Ponsch, "Le Confluent et ses comtes," pp. 302–305.

how by 975 this family had failed to create an effective principality in the Midi, despite the considerable authority which it possessed.[83] This remained the situation after this period too. Yet throughout these years we can see that they still possessed sufficient authority so that the possibility that they might do so still existed. For example Raymond II of Rouergue was able to pass down to his son, Count Hugh, a certain suzerainty over Rouergue and neighboring regions,[84] and enough power over Narbonne to allow him to receive one-half of the 100,000 *solidi* purchase price of its archbishopric in 1016.[85]

Even more impressive is evidence of the influence wielded by Count William Taillefer of Toulouse, the cousin of Count Hugh, particularly in Western Languedoc. A charter dating from 1006 refers to William as count of Toulouse, Albi, and Quercy,[86] and another from Lézat, dating from 1015, calls him *marchio*.[87] Another bearing a date of 1025 from this same abbey refers to him as *"marchio prefatus in pago Tholosano."*[88] His position was of enough importance so that it was he to whom Pope John XIX appealed to restrain one of his *milites* who was usurping churches belonging to the abbey of Moissac;[89] and a little later his authority over Toulouse proper is shown in a charter in which he gave up dues which he was levying on the market of this city.[90]

Nor does his influence and authority seem to have been confined to this region alone. The will of the archbishop of Narbonne, Ermengaud, of 1005, mentions him in leaving him some falcons as a legacy,[91] and in the year 1020 he was among the notables present at a ceremony in which Countess Garsinde of Anduze and her sons gave some property to the abbey of Gellone.[92] We also find him present frequently in Provence where his wife Countess Emma had inherited considerable property from her father, Marquis Roubaud. Charters which mention both him and his wife in this region date from 992, 1005, 1006, 1015, and 1024.[93]

After Count William's death his son, Count Pons, seems to have in-

[83] See Chapter II, Section IV.
[84] *Cart. de Conques,* no. 8.
[85] *Hist. Gén. de Lang.,* V, no. 251. Count Hugh is also mentioned in the Narbonnais in 1032 and 1035 (*ibid.,* nos. 198, 207).
[86] *Ibid.,* no. 165.   [87] *Ibid.,* no. 173.
[88] *Ibid.,* no. 184.   [89] *Ibid.,* no. 195.
[90] *Cart. de Saint-Sernin,* nos. 134–137.
[91] *Hist. Gén. de Lang.,* V, no. 164.
[92] *Cart. de Gellone,* no. 6.
[93] *Hist. Gén. de Lang.,* V, no. 153 (992), 172 (1015), 182 (1024); *Cart. de Saint-Victor,* nos. 15 (1005), 653 (1006).

The Continued Failure of Principalities

herited from him and his mother Countess Emma considerable power and a good deal of property. Thus we find him, according to a charter of 1030, possessing considerable rights over certain castles in Albigeois[94] and in 1037 giving to his new wife Majore a number of castles, churches, and other rights in this region and in the Nimois and Provence.[95] In 1040, according to a charter, he gave to Cluny considerable property in Diens,[96] and in 1038 he divided with the Trencavels the purchase price of the bishopric of Albi.[97] In 1047 in still another charter in which he is called count palatine of Toulouse we find him giving to Cluny the abbey of Moissac.[98]

None of this means that either the family of Rouergue or their relatives of the family of Toulouse were able by 1050 to create any principality in this part of the Midi. But it does make clear that they were able to maintain considerable influence and considerable property in the form of rights over castles and Church establishments. Soon after 1050, Raymond of Saint-Gilles, the younger son of Count Pons and Almodis, was to build upon this prestige and such possessions to create a true principality in Languedoc, one that could match in power those which had already been formed by the counts of Barcelona and the dukes of Aquitaine.[99]

This leads us to an important question. What does a careful analysis of the failure of these seven families to create principalities during this period reveal to us concerning the political life of the Midi and Catalonia? Why did the efforts of the Houses of Carcassonne, Anduze, Provence, La Marche, Angoulême, Cerdanya-Besalu, and Toulouse-Rouergue all end in failure, just as had those in the preceding period in the Midi and in Catalonia? What went wrong?

We might begin by emphasizing that it is difficult to find an answer to this question in external enemies, with the possible exception of the House of La Marche. In every other example we have examined it is clear that while all these houses had outside enemies, it was not such enemies which kept principalities of a permanent nature from arising. We must look elsewhere. When we do we at once become aware that each of the

---

[94] *Cart. de Conques,* no. 34. See also the reference to him and to his control over a castle in the Albigeois in 1040 in *Hist. Gén. de Lang.,* V, no. 217.
[95] *Ibid.,* no. 206.
[96] *Chartes de Cluny,* IV, nos. 2948, 2949.
[97] *Hist. Gén. de Lang.,* V, no. 214.
[98] *Cart. de Tulle,* XXII, 154–155.
[99] See an excellent account of the early career of Raymond of Saint-Gilles, the younger son of Count Pons, in J. Hill and L. Hill, *Raymond IV de St. Gilles.*

families who attempted to form principalities had one thing in common: the way in which they inherited their land and their authority. And in each of the cases which we have examined, disintegration followed hard upon the division of the principality or domains in question among a number of heirs, a process which was sometimes repeated a number of times. In Carcassonne, for instance, the lands and the authority of Count Roger the Old in a very short time found their way into the hands of a number of members of his family:[100] his brother, his nephews, and his sons. The same kind of a *divisio* followed the death of Marquis Bernard of Anduze and his wife, Countess Garsinde.[101] In Provence in the course of two generations the patrimony of Marquis William I in like manner was divided among his heirs and his relatives, who were descended from Marquis Roubaud, his brother, and the counts of Toulouse.[102] Nor were the ruling families which we have been examining in Aquitaine immune from similar developments. The division of La Marche and Périgord among the heirs of Count Boson II,[103] like the quarrels between Aldouin II and Geoffrey II of Angoulême[104] over their inheritance in the Bordelais, show the same process at work.

Even more striking is the way in which Cerdanya-Besalu disintegrated after first Count Oliba Cabreta and then his heirs divided up their property and authority among their descendants.[105] The division of authority between the House of Rouergue and that of Toulouse seems equally revealing as a cause of failure to develop a principality here.[106] Therefore it seems fair to say that ruling families were unable to create principalities in the Midi and in Catalonia chiefly because of the way they insisted on dividing their domains and their rights among various heirs: widows, brothers, sons, and daughters. Under such a system no principality could last for more than two generations at the most; and all political power and cohesion were lost in the resulting fragmentation which took place.

There seems to be some indication, though, that some of the rulers of this period were aware of this fact and strove to deal with it within the

[100] See *Hist. Gén. de Lang.*, V, nos. 185, 208, 209, 229, and Cros-Meyrévielle, *Documents*, nos. 37–39.

[101] *Hist. Gén. de Lang.*, V, nos. 206, 208.

[102] See notes 50 and 51 on how members of this family divided their land and authority.

[103] *Ademar de Chabannes*, III, 45, pp. 167–168.

[104] *Ibid.*, III, 66, p. 193.

[105] D'Achery, *Spicilegium*, III, 392.

[106] See notes 84–92 on the way this house found its possessions and its authority divided.

The Continued Failure of Principalities 353

limits which the family system imposed upon them. When Count Roger of Carcassonne provided in his will that none of his property or his rights which he left to his heirs could be disposed of except to another member of the family,[107] he was trying to keep disintegration at a minimum. It also seems possible that the system whereby the oldest member of the family bore the title of marquis after William I's death was used by the House of Provence to keep a certain family unity alive.[108] Perhaps we can see the same kind of family headship in the case of the House of Toulouse-Rouergue with such a position passing from Raymond Pons to Raymond I and II of Rouergue and then back to William Taillefer and Pons of the Toulousain branch of the family.[109] Even in Cerdanya-Besalu we seem to see a pattern whereby brothers rather than sons succeed to certain portions of the family inheritance.[110] In Aquitaine Aldouin II, the older brother, clearly had a position superior to the younger, Geoffrey II.[111]

Examination of certain other ruling families of the Midi seems to show similar efforts to maintain a family solidarity, efforts which were often relatively successful. Such seems to have been the case with the viscounts of Marseille whose family always seems to sign charters *en masse*,[112] or the counts of Gevaudun where Count Pons and his brother Bertrand seem to act in concert.[113] Such attempts, however, to make a family an effective political instrument seem to have been doomed to failure. No family sys-

---

[107] *Hist. Gén. de Lang.*, V, no. 162.

[108] See notes 48–51 on attempts to maintain a head of the House of Provence.

[109] Chapter II, Section IV, describes how the headship of the family passed from the Toulousain house to the Rouergue branch before 975. Then, following the death of Count Raymond II of Rouergue the title of *marchio* passed to Count William of Toulouse (see charter of 1015 in *Hist. Gén. de Lang.*, V, no. 173). William kept this title and passed it on to his son Count Pons after his death.

[110] See Abadal, *L'abat Oliva* and *Els Primers Comtes Catalans* on this Catalan pattern of inheritance which was repeated a number of times.

[111] *Ademar de Chabannes*, III, 67, p. 193.

[112] For examples see a series of charters dating between the years 1000 and 1030 which reveal action by the entire viscontal family of Marseille (*Cart. de Saint-Victor*, nos. 18, 69, 110, 111, 155, 169, 185, 249, 585). See also a charter of 1029 in which seventeen descendants and heirs of a certain Martin, called Blanchi, join in giving some property to *Saint-Victor de Marseille* (*Ibid.*, no. 656).

[113] Pons and Bertrand of the House of Gevaudun are called *"clarissimi consules Aquitaniae"* in *Cronique de Saint-Pierre de LePuy*, col. 14–16. They are also shown acting jointly in two charters which date from 995 and 999 (*Chartes de Cluny*, III, no. 2305; and *Grand Cart. de Brioude*, no. LIV). For the distant Riviera region of Provence see a charter of 1041 which shows that Otto and Conrad, as co-counts of Vintmille were acting similarly in concert (*Cart. de Lérins*, no. 167).

tem could provide the necessary clear political authority which even the government of Southern France in the late tenth century demanded. Family control, however limited and circumscribed it might be, could only end in divided and discordant policies which made government impossible. The prevailing system of family inheritance and control, then, was the principal reason why principalities failed to develop in the period after 975, as they had before that date.

In addition to family control and the system of inheritance it prescribed, however, we find still another tendency which made territorial states of any size all but impossible in the Midi and Catalonia. I refer to the tendencies, even the pressures, which we find to transfer or change to allodial ownership all lands or rights given out by ruling families to those who were their subordinates. This was no new tendency in these regions. It had existed since late Carolingian times, as we have noted. What is important to note is that it continued as a very powerful and pervasive one.

Provence, which had been organized with great care by Marquis William I in the last quarter of the tenth century as an effective principality, gives us a good example of this tendency at work. As far as we can tell Marquis William originally granted to his lords domains over which in most cases he kept some authority, especially over the castles which they built upon them. He also kept in his own hands, judging from charters, a large amount of property which belonged to the *fisc* of the counts. Soon after his death, however, this situation began to change. Provence's nobles began to transform their rights over such lands and castles into full allodial ownership, and in addition to take over land belonging to the comital *fisc*. In some cases this appears to have been done with the consent of William's successors. In other cases it was the result of usurpation. When they sought to justify such a change in the status of land we find the usurpers quoting Roman law in the charters of the period, saying that this law gives a man the right to do as he wishes with his property. This seems to have been the case in two charters dating from 1018 and 1028[114] from the region of Nice. Even more specific as an example of this point is a charter of Lérins which dates from 1035 in which an assembly of nobles, including a bishop from this region, agree that any man, *miles* or *rusticus*, can freely give land *"ex suo honore"* to the abbey of Lérins.[115] No clearer evidence of the transformation of feudal to allodial land could be found.

Such statements in charters of the period, however, were merely a justi-

---

[114] *Cart. de Nice*, no. 11 (1018); *Cart. de Saint-Pons de Nice*, no. 4 (1028).
[115] *Cart. de Lérins*, no. 74.

The Continued Failure of Principalities 355

fication of what was already a common practice in this part of Provence. In 1002, 1003, and 1032[116] our documents tell us of land given as allods to Church establishments which the owners clearly state were originally grants given them by the counts of Provence. Nor was this practice confined to the area of the Riviera, that is to say Nice, Antibes, Fréjus. In 1010 we find a certain priest called Walbert giving to a church without comital permission land which he states he received from the count *"ad medium vestem."*[117] And a charter of 1032 tells us of another landowner who is giving property to the abbey of Saint-Victor of Marseille which he states his *lord*, Count Geoffrey of Provence gave to him *"ad proprium allodem."*[118]

It is when we examine the relationship which existed between the counts of Provence and their powerful subordinates, the viscounts of Marseille, however, that we can see this change from comital fief and *fisc* to allodial ownership most clearly illustrated. Some time between 1018 and 1032, for instance, we learn from a charter that King Rudolf of Burgundy, for a payment of four ounces of gold, renounced any rights he might have over a *villa* which was part of the *fisc* which belonged to the counts of Provence. What happened to this *villa*? It was given to Viscountess Odila of Marseille as an allod.[119] A little later, about 1030, we find references in another charter to Count Josfred and Count Bertrand giving up their rights to lands, again belonging to their *fisc*, which the viscounts of Marseille gave to the abbey of Saint-Victor.[120] By 1044 this practice seems to have become so general that a document dating from this year shows us Count Josfred agreeing *in advance* to give up his rights over *any* land which Viscount Fulco of Marseille wishes to give this same monastery.[121] When we add to this evidence from a charter of 1038 in which Count Josfred relinquished his rights over a number of castles and property which were in the possession of the same Viscount Fulco,[122] we can see how slowly but surely the allodial principle triumphed in Provence over the rights which the counts possessed there as overlords.

There is a good deal of evidence that this same tendency to transform

---

[116] *Cart. de Nice*, no. 18 (1002), 19 (1003); *Cart. de Saint-Victor*, no. 504 (1032).

[117] *Cart. de Saint-Victor*, no. 133. For two other charters mentioning allodial land which was once given out by lords see *ibid.*, nos. 227, 548.

[118] *Ibid.*, no. 504.
[119] *Ibid.*, no. 1061.
[120] *Ibid.*, no. 155.
[121] *Ibid.*, no. 34.
[122] *Ibid.*, nos. 447, 448.

fiefs into allods was found in other parts of the Midi as well as in Provence. In Dauphiny a later charter tells how the fortresses of Dauphiny, which belonged allodially to the bishops of Grenoble, were usurped by those who possessed them and transformed into allods during this period.[123] In Aquitaine the specific example of the castle of Blavia is another case in point. Our sources tell us that initially, following its conquest, this fortress was given to the count of Angoulême as a fief by the duke of Aquitaine.[124] Yet a little later it had become the allodial possession of this family, and in 1028 was given out by Count Aldouin as a fief.[125] Just so a new castle at Limoges, belonging to the duke of Aquitaine, soon after 1032 was transformed into an allod belonging to the bishop of Limoges. The wording of the charter which reveals to us this change seems to be a masterpiece of calculated ambiguity. It says *"ipse Willelmus comes totum illum fevum dedit mihi in allodem extra episcopum."*[126] It should not surprise us to find a charter of this same region dating from 1040 which contains the old phrase that a man has the right to do as he wishes with his property according to Roman law, that usual defense of allodial rights in regions where a resistance to fiefs is to be found.[127]

In Languedoc we notice the same tendency at work. That well-known gift of property made to Guy or Guillem, the founder of the House of Montpellier, by Count Bernard of Melgueil in 985 states that this land is being given to him *"pro suo servicio vel benevolentia,"* but it is clear that the property in question was an allod and not a fief.[128] In 989 a charter, which tells us of the exchange of property between Viscount William of Béziers and Bishop Matfred cites that familiar phrase that a man has a right to dispose of his property as he wishes.[129] In 1006 another somewhat later document shows us a certain Austinde citing Roman law in the same way in exchanging with Abbot Deusdet land which he says he got as an *"allodem vel beneficium"* from the viscount of Narbonne.[130] Again in 1030 Bishop Peter of Gerona, in violating the will of his father which forbade giving family property outside of the family, cites the authority of Roman law and gives a church and some other property to the abbey

[123] *Cart. de Grenoble,* no. 16.
[124] *Ademar de Chabannes,* III, 42, pp. 165–166.
[125] *Ibid.,* III, 67, p. 193.
[126] *Cart. de Saint-Etienne de Limoges,* no. 28.
[127] *Cart. de Beaulieu,* no. 104.
[128] *Liber Instrumentorum Memorialium* [Montpellier], no. 70.
[129] *Hist. Gén. de Lang.,* V, no. 155.
[130] *Ibid.,* no. 166.

The Continued Failure of Principalities

of Montolieu.[131] Even such an important lord as Count Pons of Toulouse does the same in citing the authority of Roman, Salic, and Gothic law in a charter giving to his wife Majore a bridal gift in 1037 of a number of castles and churches in Albi, Nîmes, and Provence.[132] Perhaps he did so because his title to such property was doubtful. The land in Albi was probably some over which his Rouergue cousins had certain rights. That in Provence property which he possessed jointly with other members of the family of the counts of Provence.

It does not seem necessary to cite similar examples of property given as allods by the counts of Barcelona to important nobles of Catalonia during the period of the late tenth or early eleventh century. Such grants, suffice it to say, were as numerous as those found elsewhere in the Midi.[133] All of which seems to indicate that the failure of principalities in the Midi and Catalonia during this period was as much the result of the loss of control over land which was given out to supporters as it was to the distribution of land among numerous heirs. By 1050 principalities had failed to develop, in no small measure, because the tendency of property to become allodial still was so strong that it kept rulers from using conditional grants of land as a method of building up their power over a wider region. What helped destroy the *fisc* of the Carolingians in the Midi and Catalonia continued to deplete those of their successors who were attempting to build up authority in the same regions.

But we need also to recognize two other things which worked against principalities and their formation during this period. The first was the growth of castles, which we mentioned in an earlier chapter. In a society in which the allodial principle was strong, and the government weak and limited in its effectiveness, castles built upon domains belonging to them could often be a positive danger to rulers. Such castles were either from the start allodially owned by those who built them or tended to become

[131] *Ibid.*, no. 189.
[132] *Ibid.*, no. 206.
[133] See for example a charter of 977 in which Count Borell II sold land and castles to Lord Unifredo (*Cart. de San Cugat*, no. 126); or a sale of land in Urgell by the same count in 979 to a certain Rescindo (*Hist. Gén. de Lang.*, V, no. 132); or a gift of land and castles as allods in 980 by Count Borell to a son of Viscount Guitard (*El Archivo Condal de Barcelona*, no. 186); or the sale of land by this same count to Vivas in 989 (*ibid.*, nos. 211, 214, 215); and to Lord Hennego in the same year (*Cart. de San Cugat*, no. 239). See other examples in charters dating from 989, 990, 992, and 995 in *Cart. de San Cugat*, nos. 240, 295; and *El Archivo Condal de Barcelona*, nos. 225, 232. Obviously in this period the count of Barcelona was disposing of his comital *fisc* as allods to his nobles and *fideles*.

so. In either case they gave to their possessors a practical independence which made it difficult for a ruler or potential ruler to deal with them. This, of course, is the reason for those agreements which we have noted between castellans and overlords of such fortresses, agreements which are to be found in our region at such an early date.[134] But if the possessor of such a castle disregarded the agreement which he had made, what then? How could he be brought back to his sworn allegiance or punished by the overlord with whom he had made such an agreement, a man who had limited military power at his disposal and no real means at hand for reducing such a castle by siege. The pages of Ademar of Chabannes, with his accounts of unsuccessful sieges of the fortresses of Aquitaine during this period, show how difficult action in such matters could be for a ruler.[135] Thus wherever they were numerous, castles, in practice, generally tended to reduce the authority of a ruler of a potential principality and enhance the power of those who actually held such fortresses. Castles, then, helped further weaken principalities south of Poitou and Burgundy.

Finally, the attempt on the part of the Church to curb the abuses of the new militarism, as they affected Church property and authority, also helped to make it difficult for ruling families to maintain or even build up principalities. As long as the Church directed its attention to militarism *per se* this was not so. But when the Church went beyond the Peace of God, with its emphasis upon ending exactions upon Church land, and began to attack secular control of the Church *per se* this was another matter.[136] Now the Church was striking at the very basis of family rule in the Midi and Catalonia, its control over the land. In so doing, therefore, it helped make principalities more difficult to maintain, for to question family control in the election of Church officials was not a matter which the rulers of the Midi could view lightly. Whether it was an Aniane or a Gellone escaping from the control of the House of Anduze,[137] or a bishopric of Limoges lost to the viscounts of Limoges,[138] or an archbishopric of Bordeaux ceasing to be a local Gascon affair and becoming more Aqui-

[134] See Chapter I, Section V, on the conditions by which castles were held during this period in the Midi and Catalonia.

[135] On these struggles over control of castles in the Limousin and the rest of Aquitaine see *Ademar de Chabannes*, III, 34, pp. 156–157; 35, p. 159; 42, p. 166; 45, p. 167; 51, p. 174; 66, p. 186; 67, p. 193.

[136] See for example the charter of 1039 from the Limousin which forbade lay control of the election of abbots or lay intervention in the affairs of the abbeys of Uzerche and Saint-Martial (*Cart. d'Uzerche,* no. 1039).

[137] *Hist. Gén. de Lang.,* V, no. 206.

[138] *Cart. de Saint-Etienne de Limoges,* nos. 175–177.

The Continued Failure of Principalities

tanian,[139] the effect was the same: to diminish the ability of a local family to control its local area and thus also to reduce this family's chances of building and maintaining a principality of some strength and permanence.

By 1050, then, with the exception of the counts of Barcelona and the dukes of Aquitaine, whom we will examine in detail later on, none of the ruling families of the Midi and Catalonia had been able to create strong, permanent principalities. All efforts to do so foundered as a result of the system of inheritance which was used, and the tendency toward allodial possession of land. To these two older tendencies one should add the difficulty of controlling the castles which had appeared and the *milites* who garrisoned them. Even the Church, the real bulwark of the authority of the ruling families of the Midi and Catalonia also proved to be an uncertain basis of authority as its reaction against the new militarism threatened to take the form of an opposition to all secular control of its establishments.

As a result all government that existed during this period more and more came to rest in the hands of a large class or aristocracy of nobles, churchmen, castellans, and important landowners whom contemporary documents call *principes*. Whatever order was kept, they kept. Whatever government existed, existed only by their consent. The *princeps* having failed, the *principes* took over, and to them we must look to see how the Midi and Catalonia were really governed.

[139] *Ademar de Chabannes*, III, 69, p. 194.

CHAPTER XVIII

The *Principes* and Public Order

IN OUR LAST three chapters we have seen how a new militarism grew in the Midi and Catalonia, how a powerful Church began, with some success, to curb its most extreme manifestations, and how efforts to create principalities of real permanence and with real authority ended in failure almost everywhere. As a result of all this, except in portions of the Spanish March and Aquitaine, by 1050 there existed no governmental structures, either feudal or nonfeudal in nature, which could assure peace and order for this society. Local nobles were supreme in their local regions. Sometimes such nobles bear titles of count or viscount. Sometimes they are called barons. Sometimes, as in parts of Auvergne and Catalonia, they are called *comtor* or *conditor*.¹ The actual title seems unimportant. Whatever title they bear they seem alike; they are independent magnates controlling their domains, large or small, by virtue of their own strength and authority, and little bound to others except by ties so fragile that they could easily be broken. In short, between 975 and 1050 Southern France and much of Catalonia was in the hands of an aristocracy of nobles whom we might well refer to as *principes*, just as their own age tended to do.²

Within their own private domains such *principes* did maintain a system of *dominio* or a private administration which might be called government. They made use of subordinate officials called *viguiers* or vicars to administer justice and *judices* whose functions are less certain.³ They

---

¹ Amblard, *comptor* of Nonette, is mentioned in *Cart. de Saint-Flour*, nos. 5, 6. In Catalonia *comtores* or *conditores* are mentioned in a charter of 994. (*Cart. de San Cugat*, no. 298), and one of 1050 (*Liber Feudorum*, no. 147).

² See the excellent description of the situation in the Limousin during this period in G. Tenant de la Tour, *L'homme et la terre de Charlemagne à Saint Louis*, pp. 200–295.

³ In Catalonia charters dating from 990 and 999 contain references to such of-

levied upon these domains the *cens* and even certain other dues and exactions of a more onerous sort, some legal and some illegal in character. On Church lands which tended to be organized as *commandes* or *guardas* entrusted to these same nobles, the same system tended to be used.[4] Everywhere in the Midi and Catalonia, then, there existed, during this period, a kind of local government which we would do well to think of as seigneurial, almost in the classic sense of the word, either an older milder system preferred by the great allodial landholders and the Church, or the new harsher type which was exercised over nearby regions by the castellans and *milites* of the new fortresses. It is when one proceeds beyond such jurisdictions and local control that one finds oneself in another world— one in which no real governmental system existed at all. No power existed which could supervise the *principes* as they exercised their authority or which could restrain them as they restrained and controlled their own subordinate officials. Here the failure to create principalities in the Midi and Catalonia with any real authority over more than a local district becomes apparent as a failure with serious consequences for the society of the period.

In our last chapter an attempt was made to explain why this situation existed, even in such a region as Provence, which initially had a workable system imposed upon it by Marquis William I but which by 1030 had disintegrated into the same kind of area—controlled by nobles, *principes*, and castellans—which we find elsewhere in Southern France. Since no *princeps* could create a strong permanent principality in the face of the family system of the time, the tendency of land to become allodial, and the power of a new militarism and a reforming Church, the *principes* took over the ruins of such efforts and ruled supreme.

Having noted this vital and important fact, however, we must go on to emphasize that this did not result in either anarchy or complete and total disorder. Faced by the political realities of the period, the society of the Midi and Catalonia found a way to keep peace and order which allowed

---

ficials (*Cart. de San Cugat*, nos. 247, 343). See also the right which a landowner possessed over a *villa* in Pallars according to a charter of 1010 (*Marca hispanica*, I, ap. 163). See the same situation reflected during the years 1004–1020 in Auvergne (*Cart. de Saint-Flour*, no. 5; and *Cart. de Sauxillanges*, no. 804); or in Rouergue according to a charter of 1019 (*Cart. de Conques*, no. 304).

[4] See references to such *commandes* in Auvergne in 1025 (*Cart. de Sauxillanges*, no. 781); or in Rouergue about 1030 (*Cart. de Conques*, nos. 23, 366); or about 1050 (*ibid.*, nos. 94, 452); or in Dauphiny about 1050 (*Cart. de Saint-Barnard de Romans*, no. 91).

Map 5. SOUTHERN FRANCE AND CATALONIA (*circa* 1050).

key to symbols

Noble Families Dominating the Regions (all boundaries are approximate)

Aq—Aquitaine
Ar—Aragón
As—Astarac
AG—Auvergne-Gevaudun
 (disorganized)
AR—Ampurias-Roussillon
Ba—Barcelona
Bu—Kingdom of Burgundy
 (disorganized)
Ca—Carcassonne
Co—Commignes

CB—Cerdanya-Besalu
 (disorganized)
Fo—Foix
Ga—Gascony
 (disorganized)
La—Languedoc
 (disorganized)
Na—Navarre
PR—Pallars-Ribagorça
 (disorganized)
TR—Toulouse-Rouergue
Ur—Urgell

a maximum of independence to allodial landowner, churchman, castellan, and noble in whom real authority was vested. This society evolved a way of maintaining some of the necessary benefits of government in an age in which no over-all institutions could be provided for this purpose.

The system which evolved for this purpose was not a feudal one, though feudal elements existed in it. Nor was it new. It actually was an outgrowth of those informal tribunals which more and more, about the middle of the tenth century, replaced the Carolingian court system and handled the *guirpitios* of this period.[5] By 975 it was in full flower everywhere north of the Spanish March and continued to expand throughout the years we are discussing. We can describe it in simple fashion, as a system whereby assemblies, councils, or groups of important lay and clerical magnates were gathered together on an informal basis whenever a matter arose which affected their interests in a collective way. In other words when a matter came up which could not be handled within the framework of private seigneurial jurisdiction or the family system, others were called in to advise and to give their assent to a particular act or action. We might say, then, that the substitute for institutions of government by 975 was the collective judgment of a group of the *principes* who had an interest in, or knowledge of, a particular problem or procedure.

Any important magnate could hold such a meeting, assembly, or court in Southern France during this period. It might be an abbot of an important monastery, a bishop, or an archbishop. It might be an important lay noble, a *princeps*, or even a less important one. It might even be an important personage from outside the region, like a St. Odilon of Cluny, visiting the Midi to use his influence to restrain the excesses of the new militarism in a region like Auvergne. All that was necessary was that the person calling together such an assembly be able to get a gathering of important personages who could then consider a certain matter which was important to him and to those who came in response to his appeal.

The occasion for such an assembly of notables or magnates could vary in many ways. It might be called to consider the election of an important Church official, or to guarantee privileges to a Church establishment or even to found a new monastery or nunnery. It could be used to announce important gifts of property to such a church or abbey. It could be assembled to witness a *guirpitio*, that formal relinquishing of land or rights usurped from a particular Church establishment. It could meet to

---
[5] See Chapter II, Section IV, on the beginnings of this system of informal courts or assemblies before which *guirpitios* took place.

help settle property disputes between landowners. It could be called together to arrange for the building of a bridge or to reduce dues which were restraining trade. On a more formal regional scale it could be called together to proclaim the Peace of God in areas of the Midi and Catalonia. It could even be used to witness the imposition of a penance upon an important noble personage.

Who tended to make up such assemblies? They varied in their character generally speaking in regions where the family system was a powerful factor. They always included the important members of a family whose business was being considered by such a body, and almost always the principal representatives of important neighboring noble families or important churchmen. Our documents of the period describe them in various ways. Sometimes they are simply called by name or by title. Sometimes they are referred to as *principes*, sometimes as barons, sometimes as *seniores*, sometimes as *nobiles*, and most often as *boni homines*. We even find them called *friends* and *neighbors*. Some of them seem to have been bound by ties of *fidelitas* to the individual who summoned such an assembly in which case they are referred to as *fideles* in the charters of the period.

How were they expected to act or to function? In many cases our information makes it clear that they were simply witnesses, present to add the weight and prestige of their persons to the action being taken by him who called them together. In other cases there seems to have been formed a deliberative body which attempted to arbitrate a dispute or to reach a solution agreeable to the parties concerned. They seem to have acted in this way when such a dispute, if allowed to continue, menaced the public by threatening to lead to violence. In other words they reflect for us the presence of a relatively effective *public opinion* in the broad sense of the word, which was the only possible substitute for political institutions available to a society which had little or no government.

From the several hundred examples of such assemblies found in the sources of the period let us examine the actions of a few councils, meetings, or courts, whatever they may be called in our charters. Let us begin with the Toulousain. Here we find three such assemblies which concerned themselves with the exactions that certain individuals were levying on the market of the city of Toulouse. The first, mentioned in a charter which dates from between 1004 and 1010, was a council of noblemen which made a certain Donat give up the dues he was levying on the market. Donat states that he does so *"cum consilio"* of Count William and Bishop

Raymond of Toulouse and other *"principium terre."*[6] This apparently did not settle the matter, for a little later we find a mention of another court or council which felt it necessary to deal with this matter. This council or court was composed of Count William again and the archbishop of Narbonne and a number of other bishops, including those of Toulouse, Carcassonne, Béziers, and Maguelonne, which threatened excommunication of any who continued such exactions.[7] In the year 1050, however, the matter seems to have come up again, and this time we find it is Count William himself who agrees to give up such exactions before a group or assembly of *"boni homines."*[8] Each of these assemblies was quite different from the others. Yet each of them could deal with such a specific question as the market of Toulouse and the dues levied upon it. For another example of such an assembly, the charter in which Count Pons of Toulouse gives to Cluny the abbey of Moissac is revealing too. Pons says he is making this gift *"cum consilio"* of his wife Countess Almodis and a number of noblemen whom he calls *"principium mihi."*[9] But even a simple individual layman or churchman could also hold such a court. Thus we learn from a document of 1036 that a monk of Montolieu, having sought out a certain Bernard Odalric, who unjustly held a church belonging to this abbey, gathered together a group of noblemen who witnessed the *guirpitio* of this church by Bernard in return for a payment of some twenty *solidi*.[10]

When we turn to Gascony we find references to still other kinds of assemblies. One, dating from 985, seems to be an assembly gathered to witness the penance which Archbishop García I laid upon Count William of Astronove for marrying a wife within the prohibited degree.[11] The assembly, we are told, consisted of certain *principes*, such as the duke of Gascony, Count William's brothers—Bernard, Raymond, and García—the bishop of Toulouse, and a number of other important personages. A

[6] *Cart. de Saint-Sernin*, no. 134.
[7] *Ibid.*, nos. 135–137.
[8] *Ibid.*, no. 138.
[9] *Cart. de Tulle*, no. 1306.
[10] *Hist. Gén. de Lang.*, V, no. 207. There are a number of other such gatherings we know of in this region which took place during these years. None were held by a nobleman who had a right to hold such a court, per se, and all were held with *boni homines*, nobles, or *principes* present. See *Hist. Gén. de Lang.*, IV, 772–773; V, no. 163; "Cart. de Lézat" [unprinted], X, 69; and *Cart. de Saint-Sernin*, no. 232.
[11] *Cart. d'Auch*, nos. 51, 52.

little later another assembly, referred to as a court, met in 1027 to found the abbey of Sainte-Croix. This court, says the charter, provided land for this establishment and was composed of *"omnes principes Burdegalensium."*[12]

North of Gascony in Western Aquitaine the same kind of assembly seems to have been common. One such was called together in 1027 to judge a lady accused of poisoning Count William II of Angoulême.[13] Ademar of Chabannes says that it was attended by the *"principes et nobiles"* of Angoulême, Périgord, and Saintonge. Or we read in a charter how Duke William of Aquitaine gave a church to the abbey of Saint-Jean d'Angély in 1038 in the presence of a gathering which is composed of men called by the Duke in his charter *"primatibus meis et principibus."*[14] Again another charter of 1040 informs us of certain *principes* present in 1040 when Abbot Ademar of Saint-Etienne de Baigne made a new division of family property with his brother Itier.[15]

In the nearby Limousin soon after 992 a charter tells us how Viscount Archimbaud gave a church to the abbey of Uzerche *"cum consilio et voluntate fidelium nostrorum,"* and how Bishop Hildegare of Limoges added certain rights "with the consent of the barons who live near this abbey."[16] In 1025 our sources mention another gift of a church, this time by Viscount Ademar, to Saint-Martial of Limoges, done *"cum voluntate fidelium nostrorum Widoni et Gauzfredi ceterorumque propinquium atque amicorum nostrorum."*[17] A little later, in 1039, when Bishop Hildegare forbids interference in the election of the abbots of Uzerche and Saint-Martial he does so, says the charter, *"cum consilio canonicum ac baronem circa monasterium consistentiam."*[18] In 1045 the charter given Bishop Jordain by Duke William of Aquitaine which regulated the election of the bishops of Limoges mentions that this is done *"in praesenti nobilium, clericorum vel laicorum."*[19] Three years later, when land is given to found a nunnery, we learn that among those present on this oc-

[12] *Cart. de Sainte-Croix*, no. 1. For other examples of such assemblies which our sources often report were attended by *principes* see *Cart. de la Réolle*, no. 153 (c. 980), and *Cart. de Lucq*, no. 4 (c. 1040–1050).
[13] *Ademar de Chabannes*, III, 66, pp. 191–192.
[14] *Cart. de Saint-Jean d'Angély*, no. 181.
[15] *Cart. de Saint-Etienne de Baigne*, no. 120.
[16] *Cart. d'Uzerche*, no. 46.
[17] *Cart. de l'aumônerie de Saint-Martial de Limoges*, no. 29.
[18] *Cart. d'Uzerche*, no. 1039.
[19] *Cart. de Saint-Etienne de Limoges*, nos. 175–177.

casion were the bishops of Angoulême, Périgord, and Limoges, three viscounts of the region, and a number of noblemen.[20]

In Auvergne when a certain noble landowner called Robert gave the abbey of Sauxillanges, about 1030, a large gift of property, the charter says he does so *"cum consilio amicorum meorum."*[21] Still another document of the same period shows another important Auvergnat noble called Artmann giving up exactions he had been levying on Church property *"cum consilio fidelium meorum,"* in this case identified as the *milites* of his castle of Nonette.[22] Still a third noble, a certain Robert, son of Ictor, gives the same abbey a *mansus* in the presence of an assembly which he calls *"ejusdem regionibus seniores."*[23] It is in this same part of France that we hear of *"principes et nobiles"* who attend the council at which the bishops of the region proclaim the Peace of God;[24] and here St. Odilon of Cluny, in addition to holding a series of assemblies which persuaded nobles to return land they had usurped from Sauxillanges, ordered the *"principes illis terrae"* to come before him to explain their exactions over land belonging to the priory of Saint-Flour.[25]

In Rouergue about 1020 we find a certain magnate, called Gerald Richard, giving back to the abbey of Conques a large tract of land, including a forest, before an assembly which included in its membership Bishop Frotaire and a number of other important landowners.[26] And a priest, Hugh, and his brother at about this time before a court of Conques, presided over by Abbot Odalric and consisting of a number of monks and laymen, gave their property to this establishment too.[27] About 1035 at Albi a somewhat similar assembly met and decided to build a new bridge across the river Tarn. Among those present there were the bishops of

---

[20] *Cart. d'Uzerche*, no. 842. For other examples of such assemblies found in Western Aquitaine and the Limousin see *Cart. de Dorat*, no. 2 (987); *Cart. de Vigeois*, no. 24 (1001–1031); *Cart. d'Uzerche*, no. 47 (1025); *Cart. de Saint-Etienne de Limoges*, nos. 24 (1047–1050), 69 (1027); *Cart. de Savigny*, no. 633 (c. 1028); *Cart. de Saint-Jean d'Angély*, no. 158 (1030), 193 (1040); *Cart. d'Angoulême*, no. 6 (1040); and *Cart. de Paunat*, no. 6.

[21] *Cart. de Sauxillanges*, no. 539.

[22] *Ibid.*, no. 18.

[23] *Ibid.*, no. 406.

[24] *Ibid.*, no. 15.

[25] *Cart. de Saint-Flour*, nos. 5, 6. For other examples of such assemblies see the charters of the period from Auvergne such as *Cart. de Sauxillanges*, nos. 279, 290, 378, 419, 476, 635 (996–1049), and *Cart. de Brioude*, no. 331 (1011).

[26] *Cart. de Gellone*, no. 82.

[27] *Cart. de Conques*, no. 31.

Albi, Nîmes, Rodez, and Cahors, the abbot of Saint-Sernin of Albi, and Viscount Aton of the same city.[28]

In Velay and nearby Valence similar assemblies seem to be common too. In 996, for instance, a charter tells us of a certain Hunald who gave property to the abbey of Saint-Chaffre *"cum authoritate virorum qui chartam signaverunt,"*[29] and four years later in giving to Saint-Chaffre a monastery Viscount Etienne of Gevaudun says he does so with the consent of the bishops of LePuy and Viviers, of Pons, count of Gevaudun, and his brother Bertrand, and all *"amicis et fidelibus nostris."*[30] A charter of 1012 from the Lyonnais mentions that a certain Aigro and his brother gave a church and other property to the abbey of Savigny *"cum consilio amicorum meorum,"*[31] a phrase repeated by Lord Guerin eight years later in making a similar gift to this same monastery *"cum consilio amicorum et parentum meorum."*[32] In charters of 984 and 1007,[33] which mention the archbishop's confirmation of the elections of Hugh and Durand as abbots of Savigny, the archbishop says he is acting with the consent of the lords of the region. Just so, in 1033, a long, acrimonius dispute between Savigny and Abbess Astrudis over the church of Saint-Sernin was finally settled by a council which included in its membership not only the archbishops of Lyon and Vienne but also others who are called *"aliorum principium"* among whom some *milites* are mentioned.[34] And when in 1044 a certain *miles* agreed to give up dues that he was levying upon the church of Saint-Etienne of Lyon, he did so only after he had been summoned to appear before an assembly presided over by Archbishop Oldaric and composed of *"quam plurimos nobilium clericorum et laicorum."*[35]

To the south of Lyon we have evidence of other such assemblies or councils meeting during this period. There was one which was composed of bishops, counts, and noblemen whom Bishop Hugh called "his friends" and who witnessed his gift of a church and other property at Geneva to

---

[28] *Hist. Gén. de Lang.*, V, no. 205. This charter calls these men the *principes* of Albi. For other examples of such assemblies in this region see *ibid.*, no. 142 (987); *Cart. de Conques*, nos. 23 (1010–1053), 83 (1031–1065), 175 (997–1004).

[29] *Cart. de Saint-Chaffre*, no. 141.

[30] *Ibid.*, no. 375.

[31] *Cart. de Savigny*, no. 583.

[32] *Ibid.*, no. 652.

[33] *Ibid.*, no. 427 (984), 581 (1007).

[34] *Ibid.*, no. 648.

[35] *Chartes de Cluny*, IV, no. 2960. For a record of other such assemblies in this region see *Cart. de Savigny*, nos. 256 (976), 553 (992), 602 (1017); *Cart. de Saint-Chaffre*, no. 56 (1034); and *Chartes de Cluny*, IV, no. 2921 (circa 1050).

Cluny in 993;[36] or the so-called public council which forced Lord Sylvius in 995 to return land he had usurped to the abbey of Saint-Barnard de Romans;[37] or that composed of brothers, *fideles*, and friends which witnessed a gift made to Saint-Chaffre by Aquinas of Dauphiny in 1024.[38] No wonder we find that it was a similar assembly of bishops, abbots, and *principes* of Vienne and Valence which met to confirm Saint-Barnard's right of sanctuary,[39] and that it was before a *"coram principibus"* of nobles and bishops that a certain Aimon in 1050 made a *guirpitio* of land in Savoy which he had usurped from the abbey of Saint-Sulpice.[40]

Turning to Provence we find in our records even more examples of such assemblies of mixed noblemen and churchmen which seem to have been held for all sorts of purposes in every part of this region. This seems particularly true when the over-all structure of justice dispensed by general courts began to weaken soon after the death of Marquis William I in 994.[41] Thus, it is in this same year that we find Almeradus, bishop of Riez, attending a court presided over by Lord Garnier, *prepositus* of Cluny, and giving up exactions he was levying on the *villa* of Valentiolo.[42] Ten years later, in 1004, a charter mentions a group of important noblemen, including Marquis Roubaud and his wife, William of Antibes, and other magnates who met to elect an abbot of Saint-Pons of Nice.[43] A year later our sources tell us how a great assembly of magnates and churchmen met to give privileges to the abbey of Saint-Victor of Marseille. It included Count Roubaud of Provence, Bishop Pons of Marseille, Count William of Toulouse, and a number of abbots and other churchmen.[44] Still another document of a year later mentions these same noblemen and certain others who met to choose a new abbot for this same monastery. The nobles mentioned are called *"fideles laici."*[45]

[36] *Chartes de Cluny*, III, no. 1984.
[37] *Cart. de Saint-Barnard de Romans*, no. 56.
[38] *Cart. de Saint-Chaffre*, no. 357.
[39] *Cart. de Saint-Barnard de Romans*, no. 79.
[40] *Cart. de Saint-Sulpice*, no. 3. For other examples of such assemblies see *Cart. de Saint-André-le-bas*, nos. 32 (1023), 179 (1003), 212 (1046), 241 (1036–1050); *Cart. de Saint-Barnard de Romans*, nos. 74 (1025), 96 (1050); *Cart. de Saint-Maurice de Vienne*, no. 50 (1028).
[41] The last record of such a general court or *placitum generale* held in Provence dates from 984 (*Cart. de Saint-Victor*, no. 654).
[42] *Chartes de Cluny*, III, no. 2268.
[43] *Cart. de Saint-Pons de Nice*, no. 2.
[44] *Cart. de Saint-Victor*, no. 15.
[45] *Ibid.*, no. 1054.

The Principes and Public Order

After the year 1026 such assemblies seem even more common in Provence. Thus in this year we learn that Viscount William of Marseille gave an allod to Saint-Victor in Sisteron in the presence of members of his family and *"ceteri circumadstantes milites,"* who signed the charter as witnesses to his gift.[46] A similar large group of witnesses were present when Bishop Josselin and his kinsmen and other landowners gave the abbey of Saint-Martin near Fréjust to Saint-Victor of Marseille in 1030;[47] and when Lambert and his wife, in the presence of the bishops of Sisteron, Antibes, and Nice in 1033, gave a number of churches to the abbey of Lérins.[48] Our records also show us another large gathering of notables in 1040, when Archbishop Rambaud of Arles gave the castle of Auriol to Saint-Victor,[49] and when Count Otto and Conrad of Vintmille, a year later, gave the abbey of Saint-Michael to Lérins *"in presantia multones homines ipsius loci."*[50] A charter of 1045 tells us that it was a council *"episcoporum ac provincialum nobiliorum"* which used ordeals to decide a dispute between Viscount Pierre of Gap and the abbey of Saint-Victor;[51] and a similar council, or assembly of *"milites et boni homines,"* meeting in 1050, gave permission to Abbot Pons of Saint-Sernin of Vence to give his monastery to the church of this *civitas*.[52] Thus it was a court presided over by Lord Acbert of Digne and consisting of members of his family and *"multis militibus adstantibus et aliorum multum"* which settled a dispute in 1055 between Saint-Victor and certain allodial landholders of the region.[53] Wherever we look in Provence we find assemblies meeting and acting as they do in the rest of the Midi.

Turning to Languedoc west of Toulouse again we find evidence of many such assemblies. In 985 a charter tells us of how a group of the "men of Montpellier" and Bishop Pierre of Melgueil and Viscount Aimery of Narbonne met and reached an agreement concerning tolls levied on commerce of Montpellier with Narbonne, both that arriving by sea and that by land.[54] Later, in 998, before a court consisting of a number of *boni homines* and presided over by Abbot Etienne, two brothers gave up land

[46] *Ibid.*, no. 655.
[47] *Ibid.*, no. 599.
[48] *Cart. de Lérins*, no. 144.
[49] *Cart. de Saint-Victor*, no. 58.
[50] *Cart. de Lérins*, no. 167. See also the record of a council or assembly which met nearby in 1044 (*Cart. de Saint-Victor*, no. 659).
[51] *Cart. de Saint-Victor*, no. 691.
[52] *Cart. de Lérins*, no. 97.
[53] *Cart. de Saint-Victor*, no. 739.
[54] *Liber Instrumentorum Memorialium* [Montpellier], no. 149.

belonging to the abbey of Montolieu, which they were occupying unjustly.[55] In 1013, when Countess Garsinde of Anduze and her sister Viscountess Senegunde of Millau were disputing ownership of a *villa* at Palaiz, the matter was settled by a court held at Béziers whose members included a number of abbots, noblemen, and *"aliorum bonorum hominum."* The charter which tells us of this court calls its members *"seniores et boni homines."*[56] At least a score of *guirpitios* of land belonging to the abbeys of Aniane and Gellone during this period took place before similar assemblies or courts of noblemen who lived near these establishments.[57] Even more interesting is a record of an agreement reached between these two rival abbeys, sometime between 1031 and 1048, which was negotiated before a group of notables or *"laicorum hominum."* This agreement concerned the building of a bridge near these two abbeys.[58] Still another important assembly of notables met in 1029 to witness the gift of lands to these two abbeys by Marquis Bernard of Anduze and his wife Countess Garsinde.[59] This included among its members the count of Toulouse, the viscount of Albi, and a number of important bishops and churchmen. A similar group of noblemen formed a court or council which met at Narbonne in 1023 to arbitrate a dispute between a landowner named Rainard and the abbey of Saint-Paul of Narbonne,[60] just as we find another assembly which met two years earlier to elect an abbot of Caunes, an assembly which included Count Pierre of Carcassonne, his nephew, Viscount Aton of Nîmes, and a number of other magnates whom the charter calls *"principes et clienti nostri."*[61]

We do have a record of one case involving such court or assembly or council which gives us perhaps the best possible idea of how they functioned in the Midi during this period. This case seems to have concerned a dispute in 1053 between two noblemen of Béziers and the canons of Saint-Nazaire over a certain church which both parties claimed. To settle this matter an assembly or court of the *seniores* or nobility of the region

[55] *Cart. de Carcassonne,* I, 196. See also a charter of 998 describing an assembly of churchmen, nobles, and *fideles* present when Viscount Stephen of Gevaudun founded the abbey of Langogne (*Hist. Gén. de Lang.,* V, no. 156).

[56] *Cart. de Conques,* no. 18.

[57] See for instance *Cart. de Gellone,* nos. 11, 16, 24, 33, 34, 54, 86, 107, 133, 146, 248, 305; *Cart. d'Aniane,* nos. 142, 146, 230, 244, 277, 332; *Hist. Gén. de Lang.,* V, no. 206.

[58] *Cart. de Gellone,* nos. 18, 20.

[59] *Ibid.,* no. 6.

[60] *Hist. Gén. de Lang.,* V, no. 180.

[61] *Cart. de Carcassonne,* IV, 75.

met and called both parties before them. When no agreement could be reached, despite the efforts of these assembled nobles, they recommended that the matter be settled by judicial combat, *"cum scuto et bacalo,"* says the charter. Neither side regarded this as a proper solution, apparently, and so another court or *placitum* met to settle the matter, this time one presided over jointly by the bishop and viscount of the city, and including a number of nobles and *"boni homines"* who were not present at the first court. After a good deal of argument the lay landowners agreed to give up their claims to this property upon payment of some 300 *solidi* by the canons of Saint-Nazaire. This agreement settled the dispute at last.[62]

Now an examination of this case shows us how assemblies and courts of this type functioned in the Midi. In the first place we can see that these assemblies were informal gatherings rather than formal ones. They seem to have no clear jurisdiction over the parties concerned who may refuse to accept their verdict, as happened in the case of the initial court with its verdict of a judicial combat. Third, they strive to reach an agreement satisfactory to both parties rather than to lay down the law as such, hence the payment of 300 *solidi* in return for giving up a claim to the disputed land by the two landowners in question. They seem like bodies which arbitrate disputes rather than give a formal verdict. And finally if one court cannot solve a problem, this case proves that another one can be called together to meet and finally settle it.

There still remains one final region which needs to be examined. That region is Catalonia. Here we find a situation somewhat different from elsewhere in the Midi, because the essential structure of the Carolingian court system and of Visigothic law had not disappeared. Like Provence at the time of Marquis William I, the Spanish March preserved a more organized government than was the case north of the Pyrenees. Thus we find in our documents evidence from the years 978, 985, 989, 1011, 1013, 1017, 1018, 1025, 1033, 1036, and 1037[63] that Carolingian-type courts continued to be held in the Barcelona region; as well as evidence dating from the years 987, 1010, 1020, 1027, 1030, and 1031,[64] that they are still found in Cerdanya-Besalu and Roussillon. Our sources make it clear

---

[62] *Cart. de Béziers*, no. 66.

[63] *Liber Feudorum*, no. 320 (978); *Catalunya Carolingia*, II, 72–73 (985); *El Archivo Condal de Barcelona*, no. 2 (989); *Cart. de San Cugat*, nos. 437–439 (1011), 452 (1013), 464 (1017), 470 (1018), 496 (1025), 529 (1033), 542 (1036), 545 (1037).

[64] *El Archivo Condal de Barcelona*, no. D (987); *Hist. Gén. de Lang.*, V, nos.

that the procedure in use is still in accordance with Visigothic law, and that the usual *judices* and *boni homines* attended these tribunals to assist the counts or their representatives in arriving at a judgment in accordance with the law.

Along with this formal legal system and equally important, however, we begin to find another of a more private sort which also developed during these years. One of the first proofs of such a system is to be found in charters which inform us of certain wills by which important landowners of Catalonia bequeathed their property and their rights to their heirs. Thus in 981 documents tell us of how two important magnates, Viscount Guitard of Barcelona and Lord Galindo, left their property to heirs in wills sworn as valid before a *judex* and a panel of *boni homines*.[65] In 985 this procedure, which seems to have been new and rather unusual in Catalonia, was used again in the case of a will left by Ramio, who died as a captive in Cordova, and one by Viscount Ernimiro of Cardona. Lord Ramio's will was probated before a *judex* and a group of *boni homines*;[66] Viscount Ernimiro's before an assembly, which consisted of his *co-milites* Ennego, Borrucio, Jotfred, Senior, and other lords of the Catalan border marches.[67] By 992 such procedures had become regularized, and we find a series of these wills in charters dating from 992, 993, 994, 1002, 1010, 1024, 1027, 1032, 1045, and 1046.[68] Some, like that of Adalberto of the viscontal family of Barcelona in 1010, which disposed of castles like Mogio and Albaniya, which he owned, were to result in law suits later on in the courts of the counts of Barcelona.[69] All seem to reflect a more private jurisdiction than the legal procedures used before this period allowed.

Along with this new method of probating wills of important personages before assemblies or courts of their peers gathered together informally for this purpose, we find other uses of assemblies which met outside the formal legal system of the region and which resemble in many ways those

---

168 (1010), 193 (1020); *Cart. roussillonnais*, nos. 32 (1027), 33 (1030), 34 (1031).

[65] *Cart. de San Cugat*, nos. 136, 139.

[66] *Ibid.*, no. 171.

[67] *Hist. Gén. de Lang.*, V, no. 141.

[68] *Archivo Catedral de Barcelona*, no. 26 (994); *Cart. de San Cugat*, nos. 280, 281 (992), 294 (993), 372–374 (1002), 431, 432 (1010), 491 (1024), 505 (1027), 526 (1032), 581 (1045), 587 (1046).

[69] See final settlement of the dispute raised by this will in *Cart. de San Cugat*, nos. 437–439.

which we have just been describing in the Midi. One of the earliest of these which we find is a court in 988, which was presided over by Bishop Godemar of Gerona and Abbot Oddo of San-Cugat, and which included a number of *boni homines*.[70] This court or assembly managed to persuade a certain landowner, called Sentimiro, to reach an agreement with the abbey of San-Cugat, an agreement called a *pacto* or *conventio*, concerning some land which his brother had left to this monastery, land which he had been unwilling to relinquish. Though the wording is a little different, obviously here we see in Catalonia the same kind of *guirpitio* which was so common during this period in the Midi. In 996 we have a record of a similar *guirpitio* in which the family of a certain Sunifred relinquished to this same monastery certain water rights which it claimed, and did so before a body of men called *"procures et boni homines."*[71] Soon more important noblemen were following this kind of procedure. Witness a court of similar nature which, in the year 1000, was presided over by Bishop Berengar of Elne and Viscount Sunifred of Cerdanya and which included a number of laity and churchmen;[72] or that mixed body of lay and ecclesiastical *boni homines* before which Sunyer, count of Pallars and his family, appeared in 1007 to give up property they were occupying which belonged to the abbey of San-Vincent of Oveix.[73] Cases involving similar disputes in the Barcelona region are also found in documents dating from 1028, 1036, and 1045,[74] in Besalu in 1018,[75] in Roussillon in 1036 and 1037,[76] and in Pallars in 1037.[77]

Thus we can see that in Catalonia too, as in the rest of the Midi, the informal agreement or the private will, made legal and binding by being arranged or probated before groups of *principes, nobiles, milites,* or *boni homines,* began to replace action taken before more formal courts, though the formal Carolingian courts and legal system never completely disappeared.[78] In fact, it seems probable that if the counts of Barcelona had not begun, about 1060, a system of legal reforms which produced that

[70] *Ibid.*, no. 218.   [71] *Ibid.*, no. 317.
[72] *Hist. Gén. de Lang.*, V, no. 158.
[73] *Ibid.*, no. 167.
[74] *Cart. de San Cugat*, nos. 508 (1028), 542 (1036), 577 (1045).
[75] *Hist. Gén. de Lang.*, V, no. 175.
[76] *Ibid.*, no. 207 (1036); *Cart. de San Cugat*, no. 545 (1037).
[77] *Hist. Gén. de Lang.*, V, no. 212.
[78] Valls-Taberner comments on the use of two different sorts of judicial procedures in Catalonia. One he calls "arbitration" and the other formal use of courts as provided in the *Lex Visigothorum.* See F. Valls-Taberner, "La Cour Comtale Barcelonaise" in *Revue historique de droit français et étranger*, XIV, (1935).

body or code of law we call the *Usatches*,⁷⁹ the Spanish March might have followed the same path as the rest of the Midi. It would have had a system in which law and order were maintained only as a result of informal assemblies of important laymen and churchmen, who met and settled disputes where no governmental machinery existed for this purpose.

How can we sum up, then, the way in which lords south of Poitou and Burgundy managed to keep order and minimize disputes in an age without an adequately functioning government? The answer seems clear. In Southern France, and to a certain extent in Catalonia, the substitute for governmental machinery was a practice of periodically gathering together important magnates and churchmen in informal courts, councils, or assemblies. By means of such gatherings the society of the period was able to transcend the narrow limits of Church and private seigneurial jurisdiction. This made possible the building of bridges, the election of abbots, the ordering of privileges of various sorts, and most important of all the settling of disputes. While in theory such assemblies often had no true jurisdiction over the matters with which they concerned themselves, in practice they tended to represent public opinion to such an extent that they were generally able to get results, and particularly to arbitrate disputes which were brought before them. They could even lay down courses of action or programs, like the Peace of God, which could then be implemented on a more local level by assemblies less important than the regional councils which first proclaimed them.⁸⁰ The existence of such a system explains why in the Midi and Catalonia peace generally prevailed in this period, despite the growth of militarism and the failure of principalities. And from them were to be derived local courts and, more important, later assemblies which were to be used to deal with conflicts like those that took place between the counts of Toulouse, the kings of Aragón, and other major powers in the Midi.⁸¹

We are now able to consider a final question. To what extent were these courts, assemblies, and gatherings feudal? The answer seems clear. In some of them we do find a feudal element. Some of those who attended them did so as the *fideles* of those who called them together.⁸² But such *fideles* seem in general to have been in the minority. Judging from the

[79] *Ibid.*, pp. 672–682.
[80] See the general statements of Raoul Glaber, *Historiarum libri V*, V, 17, p. 103.
[81] We need some detailed studies on such informal assemblies in the Midi in later periods. They were both numerous and important.
[82] For example see *Cart. d'Uzerche*, no. 46; *Cart. de l'aumônerie de Saint-Martial*

The Principes *and Public Order*

examples of such assemblies or courts down to 1050 attendance always seems to have been based more on the region in which they were located or an interest in the matter they were called to deal with than any individual ties of loyalty which demanded court service. In spirit, throughout this period, such gatherings seem more Carolingian in this sense than feudal. And they were to remain so until Southern France in the twelfth and thirteenth century began to come under the control of Northern French monarchs.

It would be a mistake, however, to conclude this discussion of the political system found in the Midi and Catalonia from 975 to 1050 on such a note. For by this time we are able, at last, to discern the beginnings of two principalities in lands lying south of Poitou and Burgundy. The first of these was a new duchy of Aquitaine. The second was a new county of Barcelona. Each of these in its own way illustrates a new and growing trend toward political consolidation which at *last* we see gathering strength in these regions.

Let us first consider the duchy of Aquitaine, which was an outgrowth of the county of Poitou. Though the counts of Poitou had long had claims to Auvergne, the Limousin, and the rest of Western Aquitaine, as well as taking the title of duke of Aquitaine, they had had little real control over these regions. After 975, as the power of their principal rivals, the House of Toulouse-Rouergue declined, they began to renew their efforts to expand. At first, despite assistance given them by the kings of France, they made little progress. Any allegiance received from the Limousin was of a temporary nature,[83] and Angoulême under its able counts went its own way.[84] As for Auvergne, their control over portions of it was generally only nominal.[85]

Gradually, however, they began to do better, for they had certain ad-

---

de Limoges, no. 29; *Cart. de Sauxillanges*, no. 18; *Cart. de Saint-Chaffre*, no. 375; and *Cart. de Carcassonne*, IV, 75.

[83] Ademar de Chabannes mentions one of these intermittent periods of Poitevin influence in the Limousin about 990 (*Ademar de Chabannes*, III, 42, pp. 165–166). This is confirmed by a charter of 987 from Dorat (*Cart. de Dorat*, no. 2). See efforts of the duke of Aquitaine in 1006 directed against the counts of La Marche (*Ademar de Chabannes*, III, 45, p. 167).

[84] At least down to 1028. On the alliance between the dukes and Count William Taillefer of Angoulême see *Ademar de Chabannes*, III, 42, pp. 165–166. On their alliance with the Angevin House about 1010 (*ibid.*, III, 41, pp. 163–164). On Angoulême expansion into Gascony see *ibid.*, III, 68, p. 194.

[85] See Introduction to the *Cart. de Saint-Flour*, pp. cvii–clxii, on the situation in Auvergne where the Poitevin House was able to exercise very little influence.

vantages. In the first place they were able to maintain in their nuclear county of Poitou a centralized Carolingian administration, and the dukes were able, about the year 1000, to graft upon this structure a centralized feudalism much like that developing in nearby Anjou and Normandy.[86] They had, therefore, a well organized base from which they could move south and east at the expense of their rivals. Secondly, they perceived the advantages of supporting Church reform or at least the Church's opposition to the abuses of the new militarism, which gave them allies of importance in the rest of Aquitaine.[87] By 1027 their well organized armies of vassals, assisted by the count of Anjou, had conquered much of the Limousin[88] and within a year or so had control of Saintonge.[89] Soon all Western Aquitaine was under their control and they were supreme north of the Garonne.[90] Then in 1053 Gascony fell to them also.[91] By the end of our period a great duchy of Aquitaine had appeared between the Loire and the Pyrenees.

It needs to be emphasized, however, that this large new duchy of Aquitaine was still in many ways not a true principality. In the Limousin, in Auvergne, and in Gascony the authority of the dukes was still very nominal. The society of these regions clung to its nonfeudal family struc-

[86] See the excellent articles by Garaud on the control they exercised over their nuclear county of Poitou. M. Garaud, "Les circonscriptions administratives du comté de Poitiers et les auxiliares du comté au Xe siècle," in *Le Moyen Age*, LIX (1953), and "Les Vicomtes de Poitou," in *Revue historique de droit français et étranger*, XVI (1938). Garaud doubts that the dukes had complete authority over all Poitevin viscounts until the eleventh century.

[87] P. Labbé, *Sacrosancta Concilia*, IX, col. 898; and *Cart. de Saint-Etienne de Limoges*, nos. 175–177.

[88] See references to their authority at Limoges in 1027 in *Cart. de Saint-Etienne de Limoges*, no. 69; and "Aquitaniae Historiae Fragmenta," in *Ademar de Chabannes*, p. 208.

[89] See the account of Duke William's successful intervention in Saintonge by the 1020's in *Ademar de Chabannes*, III, 66, p. 186. For charters showing William's authority here see *Cart. de Saint-Jean d'Angély*, nos. 42, 74, 184, 186, 197, 252.

[90] See references to the marriage of Sancia, sister of the duke of Gascony, to a member of the Poitevin family during this period, a marriage which helped establish their first influence in this region, and to their successful intervention in the affairs of the Church of Gascony (*Ademar de Chabannes*, III, 39, 69, pp. 161–162, 194). By this time (c. 1030) the duke's authority was recognized throughout most of Aquitaine.

[91] For an excellent account of the conquest of Gascony in 1053 see P. Chaplais, "Le traité de Paris de 1259 et l'inféodation de la Gascogne allodiale," in *Le Moyen Age*, LXI (1955).

ture, its distrust of centralized authority, and its reliance on allodial rights. As Henry II and Richard the Lionhearted were to discover, it was difficult to change the Limousin and the rest of Western Aquitaine into a region whose lords behaved like English barons, while Gascony was to remain distinctive and opposed to centralized feudal institutions even longer. But at least by 1053 a beginning had been made of creating something approaching a principality in a part of the Midi where nothing like it had existed down to the year 1000.

The county of Barcelona, the other principality which needs to be examined, presents a somewhat different story. Here, as in Poitou, there were rulers who had had, since Count Guifred's time, some real pretense of authority over more than their nuclear counties of Barcelona, Gerona, and Ausona. Here too we find the same story of late tenth century failures, as Count Borell II gradually lost out to his cousins of Cerdanya-Besalu and began to find it difficult to control his own marcher lords.[92] His policy of dependence on Cordova proved equally disastrous, as the sack of Barcelona in 985[93] and the later Moslem attack of 1002–1003 clearly showed.[94] By the time of Count Borell's death, it seemed that the days of a strong marquis of Catalonia of the House of Barcelona were over.

Then things began to change. Borell's successor Count Raymond Borell and his wife, the able Countess Ermissende, began a new era for the House of Barcelona. Raymond Borell and his kinsman Count Ermengol began to lead Catalan armies south into Moslem territory,[95] one expedition reaching Cordova itself. They revitalized the judicial system by making their court one in which justice was available.[96] They began to recover a

[92] For records of the sale of castles and lands to marcher lords by Count Borell II and his son between 977 and 995 see *Cart. de San Cugat*, nos. 126, 211, 214, 215, 239, 240, 295; *El Archivo Condal de Barcelona*, nos. 186, 225, 232; and *Hist. Gén. de Lang.*, V, no. 132.

[93] R. de Abadal i de Vinyals, *Els Primers Comtes Catalans*, pp. 327–347.

[94] For instance see reference to Moslem destruction of the border castle of La Granada about 1002–1003, *El Archivo Catedral de Barcelona*, no. 27.

[95] On Count Ermengol of Urgell's successful attack on the Moslems in 1008 see *Ademar de Chabannes*, III, 38, p. 161.

[96] The first such evidence of a revitalized comital control through use of the court system is revealed in charters dating from 1011 which tell how Count Raymond Borell intervened in a dispute between the abbey of San-Cugat and the viscontal family of Barcelona (*Cart. de San Cugat*, nos. 437–439). A second such intervention took place in 1013 in a dispute between this same abbey and the family of another marcher lord (*ibid.*, no. 452). This case was not finally settled until 1017 (*ibid.*, no. 464).

measure of control over castles belonging to marcher lords who had for some decades ignored the rights of the counts over such fortresses.[97] They brought a new prestige again to their house. When Count Raymond Borell died, Countess Ermissende continued to act with vigor,[98] at the very moment when Cerdanya-Besalu was in the process of disintegrating.

Finally, in 1039, Raymond Berengar the Old, the real architect of Barcelona's greatness, became count. He reorganized and strengthened the judicial institutions of his counties still further, a process which led to the codification of Barcelona's laws in the famous *Usatches,* the work of the great jurist Bonefill March, which Raymond Berengar and his council of magnates promulgated in 1060.[99] Even more than his predecessors he understood the importance of control of castles, and forced the marcher lords who possessed them to do him homage for them and to recognize the rights which he had over them as count.[100] Nor did he neglect Church reform, supporting it until by 1061 he and his magnates could proclaim a Peace of God by comital princely authority.[101] Finally, he made the important discovery that the most effective method that could be used to control the new feudalism of the time was the use of money. He began to purchase support from his barons, and in the 1040's through the payment of some 20,000 *solidi* secured the loyalty of Count Ermengol of Urgell and his *milites* and castellans. He followed it up with other payments to the *conditores* and castellans of Urgell about 1050.[102] Soon he

[97] Note also the count's intervention in 1012 in a dispute concerning control of the castle of Santa-Oliva owned by San-Cugat and controlled by a marcher lord called Isembert (*ibid.,* no. 449).

[98] Countess Ermissende and her son Count Raymond Berengar presided over a series of courts in 1018, 1020, 1025, and 1033 (*Cart. de San Cugat,* nos. 470, 476, 496, 529). See the homage of Count Guifred to Countess Ermissende for a number of castles in Gerona and Ausona between 1018 and 1023 (*Liber Feudorum,* no. 272), as well as the homage which Count Ermengol of Urgell did to Count Raymond Berengar for castles in Urgell (*ibid.,* no. 157). For another example of the count's power in 1037 over castles see *Cart. de San Cugat,* no. 545.

[99] On the *Usatches* which were written down first in 1058 or 1060, see F. Valls-Taberner, "Els 'usalia de curialibus usibus Barchinonae," and "Carta constitucional de Raymond Berenger I de Barcelona," in *Obras Selectas Estudios Histórico-Júdicos,* II, 55–75. See also his "El Problema de la formacio dels usatges de Barcelona," in *ibid.,* pp. 45–49.

[100] For a partial list of such homages see *Liber Feudorum,* nos. 109, 150, 202, 205, 241, 284, 417–418, 437.

[101] On the Peace of God proclaimed by the count see Valls-Taberner, "La Cour Comtale Barcelonaise," pp. 664–666.

[102] *Liber Feudorum,* no. 46. For other examples of this use of money to buy allegiance see *ibid.,* nos. 36, 117, 212.

was to buy the loyalty of his cousins in Cerdanya-Besalu and assume power over all of Catalonia.

Thus at last a new county of Barcelona began to arise as a strong principality. Prestige and booty gained in battle against the Moors, judicial centralization, Church reform, and control over military lords through feudal ties and gold, laid the foundation of a new strong Catalan state, which was to compete with the duchy of Aquitaine and a revived county of Toulouse—established by Raymond of Saint-Gilles—for leadership in Southern France. In Catalonia and Aquitaine by 1050, if not elsewhere, we can see the beginnings of a new political centralization which was to transform the political life of the regions south of Poitou and Burgundy.

CHAPTER XIX

Southern French and Catalan Society (975–1050)

By THE middle of the eleventh century Southern France and Catalonia were on the threshold of a new and important era. Within some fifty years its nobles and *milites* were to be storming the walls of Antioch and Jerusalem and carrying their pennons deep into Moslem Spain. With political weakness a thing of the past they were creating powerful principalities in Aquitaine, in Languedoc, and in Catalonia, whose rulers were strong enough to deal with the kings of France and England, the monarchs of Aragón and Castile, or the emperors of Germany, on terms of equality. Their newly expanding cities of Bordeaux, Toulouse, Lyon, Marseille, Narbonne, and Barcelona were becoming important centers in a world of revived commerce and industry. And in Aquitaine poets were busy creating a new and important literary form—the troubadour lyric—whose effect upon the entire western world was to be incalculable. By 1100 lands which lay south of Poitou and Burgundy were ready to play an important role in Western European civilization.

What was the nature of this protean society which evolved during the years 975 to 1050? How did it differ from that which preceded it, as it coped with its new militarism and saw most of its efforts to create strong principalities end in failure? Above all to what extent by 1050 was the society of Southern France and Catalonia feudal, and what was the exact nature of its feudalization?

Here it might be well to emphasize what an examination of the military system, the government, and the Church during this period has already made quite clear: which is that the feudalization of most of these aspects of life was by no means complete. There was a new military system, but this militarization did not always mean feudalization. It was quite compatible with allodial ownership in many cases. The Church too was threatened by militarization during this period and made a rather successful attempt to curb its effects upon its land and its organization, but it did so without abandoning the older system of family control of its establishments which it had inherited from an earlier period. All efforts to form principalities failed except in parts of Aquitaine and Catalonia, but this did not mean that feudal government took its place. Rather we find the substitute for government in the Midi and Catalonia tended to be those informal periodic meetings of magnates in assemblies or courts which, if they did contain feudal elements, were still essentially nonfeudal in nature. Though there were elements which we might call feudalistic in the military system, the Church, and the organization of such government as is to be found, by 1050 it would be difficult to characterize the lands which lay south of Poitou as feudal in any classic sense of the word.

This leads us directly to still another aspect of the society of the Midi and Catalonia—landholding, which, when examined in detail, should furnish us with another indication of the extent and nature of such feudalization as is to be found by the mid-eleventh century. Again in this period, as in earlier ones, our source of information regarding this are the numerous charters, dating from this period, which show us the kind of land people gave to Church establishments or to other individuals. Taking some 1,800 charters as the basis of our analysis we note the following: of these 1,783 charters, to be exact, some 120 deal with land that seems to be in some respect feudally held, while the rest concern allods. Based on these figures, then, feudally held land formed only 7 per cent of the total in the hands of private individuals in Southern France and Catalonia during the years 975 to 1050. While this is almost double the percentage of property held in this fashion in the preceding period, it is very little more when one considers the over-all picture. Judging from this pattern of landholding one must regard the feudalization of the Midi and Catalonia as still relatively limited in 1050.

A more detailed analysis of these figures, though, should prove revealing for various areas of the Midi and the Spanish March. For Western Aquitaine, that is to say Saintonge, Angoulême, Périgord, and the Limousin, we have some 184 charters which refer to gifts or transfers of property.[1] Only 11 of this total refer to land which seems to be feudally held.

[1] These charters are from the *Cart. de Vigeois*, *Cart. de Saint-Etienne de Limoges*, *Cart. d'Uzerche*, *Cart. de Tulle*, *Cart. de Beaulieu*, *Cart. de Dorat*, *Cart. de Paunat*, *Cart. de Conques*, *Cart. de l'aumônerie de Saint-Martial de Limoges*, *Chartes de Cluny*, *Cart. de Saint-Jean d'Angély*, *Cart. d'Angoulême*, *Cart. de Notre Dame de Saintes*, *Cart. de Saint-Etienne de Baigne*, *Chartes de Charroux*, and *Cart. de Savigny*.

Of the rest, which seem clearly to be allodial, some 50 are small holdings, 55 medium-sized holdings, and 68 large tracts or estates. For Eastern Aquitaine—that is to say the Massif Central region of Auvergne, Rouergue, and the Albigeois—some 395 charters show only 32 which deal with feudally held land.[2] Here, among those which concern allods, we find 71 which deal with large estates, 79 medium-sized property, and 213 small holdings. The over-all percentage of feudally-held land runs about 6 per cent for Western Aquitaine and 8 per cent for the area of the Massif Central.

Turning east to the Middle Rhone region of Velay, the Lyonnais, Savoy, Dauphiny, Valence, and Vivarais, we find some 432 charters which date from this period.[3] Down to 1050 only 19 of them represent land feudally held, and the rest, or approximately 5 per cent, is allodial property—a little less than the percentage found in Aquitaine. In this region, judging from our charters, small holdings seem to be more numerous than property of large size, since 242 of these charters deal with small holdings, 85 with property of medium size, and 95 with large holdings or roughly the same proportion as in the Massif Central.

Turning to the south of these regions, let us shift our attention to Provence, Languedoc, and Gascony which form the rest of the Midi north of the Pyrenees. For Provence we possess much more abundant materials dating from these years than was true earlier. In examining some 202 charters we find that 20 of them, or 10 per cent, deal with land which is feudal in character, the rest concern allods.[4] Here again the size of allodial holdings is of some interest to us, for 81 of these charters concern large estates, 61 of them medium-sized property, and 61 land which is small in size. This represents not only a slightly larger proportion of feudally held land than seems to be found in Aquitaine and the Middle Rhone region, but a larger proportion of large-size holdings too. When we consider Languedoc, which here is taken to mean Septimania and the

[2] From the *Cart. de Conques, Hist. Gén. de Lang., Cart d'Aniane, Cart. de Vabres, Cart. de Saint-Flour, Cart. de Brioude, Grand Cart. de Brioude, Cart. de Sauxillanges, Cart. de Saint-Egidius, Chartes de Cluny, Chartes de Charroux,* and *Cart. de Lérins.*

[3] From the *Cart. de Savigny, Cart. d'Ainay, Cart. Lyonnais, Chartes de Cluny, Cart. de Saint-Chaffre, Cart. de Saint-Egidius, Cart. de Saint-Barnard de Romans, Hist. Gén. de Lang., Cart. de Conques, Cart. de Grenoble, Chartes de Maurienne, Cart. de Saint-André-le-bas, Cart. de Vienne,* and *Cart. de Saint-Sulpice.*

[4] From the *Cart. de Saint-Victor, Hist. Gén. de Lang., Chartes de Cluny, Cart. de Lérins, Cart. de Saint-Pons de Nice, Cart. de Nice, Cart. de Saint-Chaffre,* and *Cart. de Conques.*

Toulousain, we have some 266 charters upon which we can draw for information.[5] These reveal some 42, or 16 per cent, which are concerned with feudally held property, a higher proportion than we have found anywhere else in the Midi. As for size of holdings, 98 of our charters concern large-sized property, 65 medium sized, and 61 small-sized pieces of land, or somewhere between Provence and Western Aquitaine on the one hand and the Middle Rhone region and the Massif Central on the other, as far as the proportion of large to small holdings is concerned. For Gascony we have less information, but some 31 charters give us a scattering of property holdings which present us with a partial picture at least.[6] Of these, 30 charters deal with allodial property and only 1 with feudally held land, with the size of holdings being 4 small in size, 7 medium sized, and 20 of a *villa* or more. Judging from this evidence then, Gascony seems to have the smallest percentage of feudally held land and the largest percentage of large estates of any region north of the Pyrenees.

Finally we have the Spanish March. Here some 535 charters give us some interesting information.[7] Only 37, or 6 per cent, of these charters seem to be concerned with land which is feudally held. The other 498 concern allods. Of the charters which concern allods, 198 seem to refer to small holdings, 183 to medium-sized property, and 117 to larger holdings, which seems about the median for the rest of our regions north of the Pyrenees.

From an analysis of these charters, then we can perhaps hazard a few observations on how individuals held their land in Southern France and Catalonia during this period. They seem to show that Gascony was the region which was the least feudalized, with the Spanish March, the Middle Rhone region, and Western Aquitaine following in that order.

---

[5] From the *Cart. de Nîmes*; *Cart. d'Aniane*; *Hist. Gén. de Lang.*; "Cart. de Psalmodi" [unprinted]; "Cartulaire des Trencavels" [unprinted]; *Cart. de Gellone*; *Cart. de Béziers*; *Cart. d'Agde*; "Cart. de l'Évêché d'Agde" [unprinted]; *Liber Instrumentorum Memorialium* [Montpellier]; *Cart. de Maguelonne*; *Cart. de Conques*; *Cart. de Carcassonne*; Cros-Meyrévielle, *Documents*; *Cart. de Fontjoncouse*; *Cart de Saint-Sernin*; "Cart. de Lézat" [unprinted]; and *Chartes de Cluny*.

[6] From the *Cart. de la Réolle, Cart. d'Auch, Hist. Gén. de Lang.*, "Cart de Lézat" [unprinted], *Cart. de Lucq, Cart. de Saint-Jean de Sorde, Cart. de Sainte-Croix*, and the *Cart. de Sainte-Foi de Morlaas*.

[7] From the *Cart. de San Cugat*; *Hist. Gén. de Lang.*; *El Archivo Condal de Barcelona*; *Catalunya Carolingia*, II; *Marca hispanica*; *Cart. roussillonnais*; *Cart. de Conques*; *El "Libre Blanche" de Santas Creus* [Barcelona]; *Archivo Catedral de Barcelona*; *Liber Feudorum*; and *Cart. de Saint-Victor*.

They also indicate that Languedoc was the most feudalized, with Provence and the Massif Central close behind in the percentage of land feudally held. Except for Gascony and Languedoc, however, each of which represents an extreme case, judging from our evidence, none of these regions differed very much one from the other in the degree of their feudalization, and in only one area, Languedoc, did the amount of land feudally held exceed 10 per cent of the total.

We should not leave this question of the amount of land which was feudally held, however, without approaching it in still another way, through an examination of the amount of Church land which charters show us was given out to members of the laity as *commandes, guardas, precaria,* or fiefs. This too is an indication of the degree of feudalization of the land of various parts of Southern France and Catalonia. Judging from our documents certain areas were more feudalized than others in this respect. Those that seem to have the highest percentage of feudalized Church lands during this period are Languedoc,[8] as a whole, probably first, then the Limousin,[9] then Rouergue,[10] and then the Middle Rhone Valley.[11] Then finally we have Catalonia, Gascony, Provence, the rest of Western Aquitaine and Auvergne[12] following in that order. Adding together evidence of the feudalization of Church land and the amount of feudally held property belonging to private individuals, which is revealed to us in our charters, we find that Gascony is still the region which is the least affected by feudalism, Languedoc the area most affected by it. The other regions lie somewhere in between without too much differentiation among them being possible in this respect.

One final point also needs to be made concerning our evidence of the feudalization of land. That is that our charters showing transfers of such property during this period reveal that most of those which concern feudal land, perhaps 75 per cent of them, date from the years 1025 to

[8] Charters from Languedoc list some twenty-nine grants of *precaria* or *commandes* or *guardas* which date from this period. Seven are from the Nîmes area, thirteen from the rest of Eastern Languedoc, three from the Narbonne region, and six from near Toulouse.

[9] Charters from the Limousin give us a record of some sixteen such grants. Most seem to refer to large tracts of land.

[10] From Rouergue and the Albigeois, according to our sources, we have record of twenty such grants. Again many seem to represent large tracts of land.

[11] Our sources show us some thirty such grants coming from this region.

[12] Our Catalan documents list some twenty *precaria* of various sorts. The figure for Gascony is two and for Provence only three. Western Aquitanian charters of the period give us information on only two such *precaria* and for Auvergne the figure is only five.

1050. Thus we seem to find the tendency or pressures toward feudalization were stronger toward the end of this period than they were earlier. This, as a matter of fact, is what we would expect to be the case, since we know that it was during this same period, starting about the 1020's and 1030's that the Church began to react most strongly to militarization, and that the better organized feudalism of the dukes of Aquitaine and the counts of Barcelona became a factor of some importance in Aquitaine and the Spanish March. By 1050, then, it seems probable that the movement toward a more feudal society in Southern France and Catalonia was still growing in importance and in scope, and was to continue to do so throughout the remainder of the eleventh century.

This examination of feudalization, as seen in the landholding system used by the society of Southern France and Catalonia, then, seems to emphasize the following—down to 1050 feudalism, while still growing, remained a factor of little importance in the way land was owned or held. The allod still reigned supreme. Despite this fact, however, in certain parts of the Midi we find evidence that feudalism had some importance, and was to become even more important in the years ahead. Like other aspects of the society of the Midi and the Spanish March, upon which we have commented during this period, the system of landholding shows us a society which contained feudalistic elements but which, in essence, was not feudal at all.

Nevertheless, we have evidence that even this degree of feudalization, such as it was, met considerable resistance. This was true not only of the Church, which organized opposition to certain manifestations of it in a military sense, but also of allodial landowners. In whatever region feudalism began to gain strength, such landowners opposed its manifestations as they had done in earlier periods. In Eastern Languedoc, which was becoming one of the most feudalized regions of the Midi, they did so, in part, by adding to charters referring to property which they were giving to the Church a phrase forbidding that this land be given out as a fief or benefice. More common, however, was their continued citing of the authority of Roman and Visigothic law as giving a man the right to do as he wished with his own property. We find statements to this effect in charters from the Limousin dating from 988 and 1050,[13] from Rouergue and the Albigeois in 984 and 1037,[14] from Velay about 1030,[15] from

[13] *Cart. de Saint-Etienne de Limoges,* no. 114; and *Cart. de Beaulieu,* no. 104.
[14] *Hist. Gén. de Lang.,* V, nos. 137, 206. See also a charter of 1003 from Auvergne (*Cart. de Conques,* no. 326).
[15] *Cart. de Saint-Chaffre,* no. 433.

Provence in 1018 and 1028,[16] from the Narbonnaise in 989, 1027, and 1030[17] and from the Toulousain in 1000 and 1015.[18] All evidence seems to point to the fact that the actual provisions of Roman and Visigothic law as they affected private property were hazy indeed for the society of the Midi north of Roussillon during this period,[19] but the remembrance of these legal systems as the protectors of allodial right still remained a reality, which society in Southern France could invoke in opposing the feudalization of its land and in protecting the right of a landowner to dispose of his property as he wished.

The charters of this period, however, do more than help illuminate and clarify the degree of feudalization of private property in Southern France and Catalonia. They help explain still other aspects of the social system. By comparing information found in these documents with that which can be found in those of the period from 900 to 975, we are able to say with some degree of confidence that by 1050 the *villa* system was tending to disappear in many areas. This does not mean that we do not still find a mention of such estates in our charters, for we do, particularly in Gascony[20] and in the Limousin[21] where they still seem not uncommon. They are also found, according to our documents in the Upper Rhone Valley[22] and in that part of Provence near the older settled regions of Arles, Avignon, and Marseille.[23] But they seem rare elsewhere south of

[16] *Cart. de Nice*, no. 11; and *Cart. de Saint-Pons de Nice*, no. 4.

[17] *Hist. Gén. de Lang.*, V, nos. 159, 189, and Cros-Meyrévielle, *Documents*, no. 36.

[18] *Cart. de Saint-Sernin*, no. 47; and *Hist. Gén. de Lang.*, V, no. 174.

[19] On the lack of any real understanding of Roman law during this period see an excellent article by A. Gouron, "Les étapes de la pénétration du droit romain au XIIe siècle dans l'ancienne Septimanie," in *Annales du Midi*, LXIX (1957).

[20] See references to *villas* in Gascony in *Cart de la Réolle*, no. 152 (980); *Cart. de Lucq*, nos. 1 (985), 2 (1000), 3 (988), 4 (1040–1050); *Cart. de Sorde*, nos. 2 (1010–1032), 9 (1010–1032); *Cart. de Sainte-Croix*, no. 1 (1027).

[21] For references to *villas* in the Limousin see *Cart. d'Uzerche*, nos. 31 (977), 47 (1025), 52 (1044), 174 (1001), 248 (1003–1040), 347 (998–1003); *Cart. de Vigeois*, no. 35 (996–1020); *Cart. de Tulle*, nos. 350 (1000), 469 (1050); *Cart. de Saint-Etienne de Limoges*, no. 12 (1017–1023); *Cart. de l'aumônerie de Saint-Martial de Limoges*, no. 32 (1029); *Cart. de Conques*, no. 27 (1031–1060).

[22] For mention of *villas* see *Cart. de Saint-Barnard de Romans*, no. 52 (995); *Cart. de Saint-Chaffre*, nos. 375 (1000), 154 (1001), 56 (1034); *Cart. de Vienne*, nos. 38 (1009), 41 (1011), 44 (1016); *Cart. de St. Egidius*, no. 98 (1022); *Cart. de Saint-André-le-bas*, nos. 32 (1023), 209 (1025), 206 (1040).

[23] For references to *villas* see *Hist. Gén. de Lang.*, V, no. 133 (979); *Chartes de Cluny*, III, nos. 1784 (988), 1837 (990); IV, nos. 2916, 2917 (1037); *Cart. de Saint-Victor*, nos. 1061 (1018–1032), 155 (1030).

Poitou and Burgundy, especially in Languedoc, Catalonia, Rouergue, Auvergne, and most of Western Aquitaine.

Why is this so? Why did *villas*, which had been the more normal method of exploiting the soil in the Midi and Catalonia, tend to disappear by the middle of the eleventh century? No final answer can be given to this question until a great deal more research has been done upon certain aspects of the landholding system of these regions. But at least there are some possibilities which might be advanced. The first possible cause of their disappearance lies in the way in which the inheritance system of the period functioned. The division of property among *all* the heirs of an individual worked to destroy the unity of the *villa*. We can see that clearly in the type of estates left by some landowners during this period. These estates tend to consist of scattered *mansi* located in a number of *villas* instead of a compact *villa* with all its contiguous and pertaining *mansi*.[24] Fragmentation was inevitable under such rules of inheritance.

In the second place in a number of regions, particularly in Catalonia and parts of Provence, the castle began to replace the *villa* as the unit of rural exploitation. Where this happened the basis of older agricultural life changed inevitably. The castellan and his *milites* had a different point of view toward the area which they dominated than did the old allodial *villa* owner. They tended to dominate a larger region, or a *mandamenta*, which might consist of a number of *villas* or villages.[25] Their purpose was, in most cases, military rather than economic. Hence, where castles were most numerous, we naturally find the older *villa* system disappearing too. And interestingly enough the castle itself, like the *villa*, by 1050 had begun to be subject to the fragmentation process inevitable under the Midi's rules for inheritance. As we find a *villa* divided into a number of *mansi* owned by various different proprietors, so we find castles divided and subdivided in the same way, especially in Provence, where our records are particularly complete for this period.[26]

[24] See two excellent articles which describe this situation in Rouergue and Auvergne. C. Higounet, "Observations sur la seigneurie rurale et l'habitat en Rouergue du IXe au XIVe siècle," in *Annales du Midi*, LXII (1950); and G. Fournier, "La Seigneurie en Basse-Auvergne aux XIe et XIIe siècles," in *Mélanges Louis Halphen*. An article on Provence of importance, though it underestimates the number of *villas* which survived, is R. Latouche, "Quelques aperçus sur le manse en Provence au Xe et XIe siècles," in *Recueil de Travaux Offerts à M. C. Brunel*, II.

[25] See, for instance, that charter of 1015 issued by King Rudolf, in which lands attached to a *"Castellum Novum"* are mentioned (*Cart. de Vienne*, no. 43).

[26] For some examples of such divided castles and their territories in Provence

As the *villa* began to disappear, or better perhaps began to be absorbed into the *mandamenta* system of the Midi and Catalonia, we also find something else happening. We find the old traditional system of serfdom disappearing with it. It is interesting to note that, in contrast to earlier periods, charters from these years seldom mention serfs. One charter from Navarre speaks of them,[27] as does a document from Gascony dating from the year 1000.[28] Still others from Western Aquitaine contain references to this class: one from Saintonge dating from 989,[29] one from Angoulême dating from 1040,[30] and four from the Limousin in 1000, 1020, 1035, and 1040.[31] In addition, we do have a mention of serfs in an Auvergnat charter of 1040,[32] and in two from Dauphiny which date from 1009 and 1011.[33] This is all. What we seem to be seeing is a gradual disappearance of this class everywhere in the Midi except the Limousin, that old center of the Roman *villa* system, where some still remained, though, judging from our documents, even here they were much less numerous than earlier.

It is tempting, of course, to relate the disappearance of the older serfdom to that of the *villa*, and it is true that where *villas* disappeared serfs tended to do so also. But we should also, in this period, as in earlier ones, mention the fact that this disappearance as a class was probably also the result of free land; the clearing of new soil which gave them a chance to improve their lot by cultivating such land on an *aprisio* or *medium plantum* basis and so rise to at least tenant status. Even more important, however, in explaining the end of the older servile class was the growth of *mandamenta*. Such castle jurisdiction over nearby areas forced all cultivators, serf and *censive* alike, to accept burdens of an onerous nature which made the older distinction between *mancipius* or *colonus* and free tenant paying a *cens* meaningless.[34] Where castles were numerous, then,

---

see *Cart. de Saint-Victor*, nos. 58 (1040), 70 (984), 135 (1010), 255 (1034); *Cart. de Lérins*, nos. 3, 72 (990); *Chartes de Cluny*, IV, no. 2779 (1023).

[27] *Cart. de Conques*, no. 73 (996–1031).

[28] *Cart. de Lucq*, no. 2.

[29] *Cart. de Saint-Jean d'Angély*, no. 5.

[30] *Cart. d'Angoulême*, no. 31, mentions land owing services which seem to be of a servile nature.

[31] *Cart. de Saint-Etienne de Limoges*, no. 161. This charter mentions the freeing of the serfs concerned. See also *Cart. de l'aumônerie de Saint-Martial de Limoges*, no. 14; *Cart. de Saint-Etienne de Limoges*, no. 147; and *Cart. de Vigeois*, no. 15.

[32] *Chartes de Cluny*, III, no. 2100.

[33] *Cart. de Vienne*, nos. 38, 93.

[34] See Chapter I, Section V, on these dues. For an excellent example of this new

a new serfdom arose and the old serfdom simply tended to be forgotten. This, in many parts of the Midi and Catalonia, is what appears to have happened, until the new movement which helped the peasants achieve greater freedom in the *bastides* of the twelfth and thirteenth century became a reality in the Midi and the Spanish March.

Last of all, before we leave the question of landholding, we should add a word concerning the role of women in the society of the Midi during this period, a role which remained an extremely important one. One might expect that the growth of a more militarized society during these years would tend to make them less important than had been the case earlier. Such, however, was not the case. Our charters make it abundantly clear that they could still freely inherit and dispose of property and act as free agents controlling their own estates. Their position in the governing system of the period continued to be an important one. A Queen Irmengaude of Burgundy could control a number of castles and even whole counties in her own right.[35] So could a Countess Emma of Toulouse, as heiress to a portion of Provence.[36] Our documents seem to show, for instance, that Countess Garsinde of Anduze was a more important personage than her husband, Marquis Bernard,[37] while Viscountess Adelaise of Narbonne could act as if in no small measure Eastern Languedoc was in her control.[38] Similar ladies of great authority existed in the Limousin and Auvergne during these years,[39] while Count Pons of Toulouse as a bridal gift to his wife Majore felt it fitting to bestow upon her a number of important fortresses in Languedoc and Provence.[40] No wonder Raoul Glaber regarded Queen Constance—the new wife of King Robert of France—who was a product of a region where women were so powerful, with suspicion and hostility.[41]

Catalonia, however, is where we see women of particular power during this period. Countess Ermissende of Barcelona seems to be the equal

---

serfdom see a charter of 1025 from Rouergue which mentions that the *cens* owed by two *mansi* includes the labor service of one man out of seven who must furnish his own bread (*Cart. de Conques*, no. 196).

[35] *Cart. de Vienne*, no. 93.

[36] *Hist. Gén. de Lang.*, V, nos. 172, 181.

[37] See the vast inheritance she received in 990 from her father, Viscount William of Béziers (*Cart. de Béziers*, no. 49).

[38] *Hist. Gén. de Lang.*, V, nos. 130, 152.

[39] For instance see reference to land belonging to Beatrice, countess of Chamboulières in the mid-eleventh century (*Cart. de Tulle*, no. 340).

[40] *Hist. Gén. de Lang.*, V, no. 206.

[41] Raoul Glaber, *Historiarum libri V*, III, 9, 40, p. 89.

of her husband, Count Raymond Borell, and after his death seems to have owned castles in her own right and to have received the homage of their castellans.[42] So did Viscountess Jerosolima[43] and Countess Almodis,[44] who after two earlier marriages, one of them to Count Pons of Toulouse, finally wound up as the consort of Count Raymond Berengar I of Barcelona and shared power with him. Wherever one turns, one finds a series of remarkable and powerful ladies who, acting on their own, could control the destinies of whole regions in the Midi and Catalonia and set the stage for their successors whom the troubadours were to praise with such fervency later. By 1050 women in these regions had developed such authority and influence that their later prestige had become all but inevitable.

Such seems to be the information concerning the society of these regions which an examination of the landholding system provides for us. We see a society in which feudalism was a growing force, but a force not powerful enough, as yet, to triumph over allodial ownership. We see an older *villa* system with its attendant serfdom tending to disappear, due to the system of inheritance which was used, or to be absorbed into the new military system of castles and *mandamenta*. We find ladies of great importance and power occupying positions of prestige and authority. But what of the economic factors at work in these regions? How did they change and affect the life and society of the period?

Let us first examine evidence of continuing agrarian progress in clearing the soil and putting new land into cultivation. In the period before 975, as has been pointed out, a good deal was accomplished in this respect. Such progress in many regions of the Midi continued also after 975. Some five charters from Auvergne mention *medium plantum*. Two of them date from 985 and 1030 and the remainder from the general period 994–1050.[45] Our information is somewhat less specific for nearby Rouergue, but we do have some general references to the clearing of new land for cultivation in 976, between 996 and 1004, about 1000, and in 1012,[46] as well as a specific mention of a *medium plantum* in a charter which dates from about 1030.[47] Three references to such clearings come

[42] See *Liber Feudorum*, no. 272; and *Cart. de San Cugat*, nos. 479, 545, 571.
[43] *Liber Feudorum*, no. 202.
[44] On Almodis' authority in Catalonia see F. Valls-Taberner, "La Cour Comtale Barcelonaise" in *Revue historique de droit français et étranger*, XIV (1935), 675–682.
[45] *Cart. de Sauxillanges*, nos. 96, 509, 521, 596.
[46] *Cart. de Conques*, nos. 274, 337, 397, 174, 298.
[47] *Ibid.*, no. 138.

from documents which concern Velay—one, which probably was a *medium plantum*, is mentioned in a charter of 1030,[48] and two others in charters of a later date refer to *assarts* in wooded mountainous regions.[49]

We do not, however, find as much evidence of progress in clearing the land in the Massif Central region of the Midi as we do in the Lyonnais, Dauphiny, and Savoy to the east. Here such activity seems to have been particularly important, judging from our documents. Charters from the Lyonnais refer to cultivation of new land in 1007, 1010, and between 1022 and 1032,[50] while some eighteen of them, dating from the period 976 to 1050, mention such activities in Dauphiny and Savoy.[51] Some of the charters which mention new land being brought into cultivation seem particularly interesting because they mention the use of a *medium plantum* system in which seven instead of five years are allowed to elapse, once the land is alloted to a cultivator, before it is divided between the original proprietor and those who were putting it into cultivation.[52]

Nor was such activity confined to the Middle Rhone region. In Provence charters which date from 977, 984, 993, 1001, and 1010[53] seem to refer to a similar system of putting unused land into cultivation, sometimes land which was granted out in very large tracts by its proprietors. Nearby, in Eastern Languedoc, we find the same kind of system in use too—witness charters from Nîmes dating from 978 and 994[54] and two from the Maguelonne region, which date from 1010 and from between 996 and 1031.[55] In one of the grants of such land from the Nîmes area the land, once put into cultivation, seems to have been divided between allodial owner and cultivator on a 25–75 basis instead of on a 50–50 basis as was more normal elsewhere with a *medium plantum*.[56] Even in the Narbonnaise, in addition to one reference to an *aprisio* in 979,[57] we

---

[48] *Chartes de Cluny*, III, no. 2330.
[49] *Cart. de Saint-Egidius*, nos. 107, 108.
[50] *Cart. d'Ainay*, in *Cart. de Savigny*, nos. 25, 148; and *Cart. de Savigny*, no. 627.
[51] *Cart. de Grenoble*, nos. 8, 9, 16, 18; *Chartes de Maurienne*, no. 3; *Cart. de Saint-Barnard de Romans*, nos. 73, 96; *Cart. de Vienne*, nos. 52, 119; *Cart. de Saint-André-le-bas*, nos. 26, 27, 62, 80, 158, 161, 169, 186, 188.
[52] *Ibid.*, nos. 62, 80.
[53] *Cart. de Saint-Victor*, nos. 72 (977), 70 (984), 77 (993), 133 (1010), 174 (1001).
[54] *Cart. de Nîmes*, nos. 73 (978), 90 (994); also in 1021, *ibid.*, no. 121.
[55] *Cart. de Maguelonne*, I, no. 4 (1010); *Cart. d'Aniane*, no. 180 (996–1031). See also a charter of about 1050 which mentions a *bastida* (*ibid.*, no. 146).
[56] *Cart. de Nîmes*, no. 90.
[57] *Cart. de Carcassonne*, IV, 74.

find *medium plantum* referred to in documents dating from 990 and 1031.[58]

Curiously enough, however, when we examine charters originating in Gascony and Western Aquitaine we find little evidence of such activity in contrast to the situation in the areas of the Massif Central, Languedoc, Provence, and the Valley of the Rhone, and even in contrast to the previous period in the Limousin itself. We find only two references to such land being cleared, one dating from 980 which mentions a gift of coastal marsh land to Saint-Jean d'Angély by the duke of Aquitaine,[59] and one in a charter of 1035 from Foix which tells us of an *aprisio*.[60] Why this part of the Midi should have lagged behind the rest of Southern France in this respect it is difficult to imagine. Perhaps one answer lies in the continuing pattern of *villa* proprietorship in Gascony and this part of Aquitaine, for such a system of landownership may well have been opposed to the use of *aprisiones* and *medium plantum*. Whatever the cause of this, it was to remain true of this part of the Midi for several centuries, until here, too, at last in the late thirteenth and early fourteenth century new *bastides* began to increase the amount of land in cultivation and fill up waste places with a new peasant population.

It is when we turn to the Spanish March, however, that we find the most evidence of a continuing movement in the countryside devoted to clearing the soil and putting into cultivation vacant land. Some of this seems to date from the last years of the tenth century—either land near the Moslem frontiers which was taken over by cultivators on an *aprisio* basis, as revealed in charters dating from 976, 977, and 982,[61] or that further in the interior which charters dating from 981, 984, 986, 991, 994, 998, and 999 show us was put into cultivation under what seems to be a *medium plantum* system.[62] Soon after the year 1000 both systems seem to have been in common use, but here, as in Provence, the tracts of land were often large ones, organized around castles which were being built along the frontiers. Perhaps it all began with the great expedition against Cordova in 1009. But, whatever the cause, after this date we can find

[58] *Hist. Gén. de Lang.*, V, nos. 151, 197.
[59] *Cart. de Saint-Jean d'Angély*, no. 331.
[60] *Hist. Gén. de Lang.*, V, no. 207. A charter dating from 983–1036 also mentions what it calls new land in this part of Gascony planted in vines (*Cart. de la Réolle*, no. 6).
[61] *Cart. de San Cugat*, nos. 115, 144; and *Liber Feudorum*, no. 320.
[62] *Cart. de San Cugat*, nos. 139, 160, 192, 266, 295, 302, 335, 344; and *El Archivo Condal de Barcelona*, no. 203.

ample evidence of an advance south at the expense of the Moslems, of the building of new castles on land wrested from the Moors, and of the colonization of such land by peasant cultivators. By 1050 in Catalonia, as elsewhere in Spain, the Reconquista had begun, and with it the settlement of frontier areas on a vast scale. What had begun slowly in Carolingian times in Southern France and Catalonia, had now become an agrarian movement of great importance, using *aprisio* and *medium plantum* to bring new land into cultivation and to provide more foodstuffs and a better status for the peasant population and for society in general.

While we should not minimize the importance of agrarian progress in most of Southern France and the Spanish March during this period, which resulted in the production of an agricultural abundance unknown earlier, it is important to note that this agrarian progress, vital as it was, was probably less important, economically speaking, than another development of the period. I refer to the renewal of trade and commerce which also took place during these years. This revival reversed the tendency toward economic localism, which for more than a century had characterized the life of the Midi and Catalonia. It seems to have begun in the last years of the tenth century, when a revived commerce in Northern France and along the Atlantic coasts of Aquitaine and Gascony met a similar revived trade coming from Italy and the Mediterranean. These two streams of commerce met in the Midi and began to end this region's isolation, economically speaking, from the main currents of commerce of the Mediterranean and the Northern Seas of Europe.[63]

We find many indications of this revival. A Maguelonne, on the Mediterranean shores near Melgueil, which had long been abandoned by its canons, was refortified and reoccupied.[64] A merchant class in the town of Montpellier, which had newly appeared in response to revived commerce, by 985 had become important enough to concern itself with dues which were being levied upon its goods going to Narbonne.[65] By 1040 there was sufficient traffic reaching the interior of this part of Languedoc so that a bridge across the Hérault had become a necessity, and the monks of the abbeys of Aniane and Gellone agreed to build it, incidentally, with the proviso that no tolls be levied on those who used it.[66] At Toulouse, starting about the year 1000 we find a charter which shows a concern re-

[63] See A. Lewis, *The Northern Seas A.D. 300–1100*, pp. 445–446.
[64] *Hist. Gén. de Lang.*, V, nos. 55–56.
[65] *Liber Instrumentorum Memorialium* [Montpellier], no. 149.
[66] *Cart. de Gellone*, no. 20.

garding the market of the town and exactions levied on merchants coming there to trade.[67] This concern is reflected in two later charters of 1010 and 1050 dealing with the market and exactions which affected its prosperity.[68] One of these charters shows churchmen from all over Languedoc cooperating by reducing abuses which hindered trade. Another mentions *Goti* coming there to trade, which probably refers to Spanish merchants from Catalonia.[69] In Angoulême the bishop of the region found water mills located on the river Boehme important enough to merit his protection,[70] and in the Albigeois a whole group of churchmen and *principes* of the region agreed to build a new bridge across the river Tarn at Albi.[71]

As trade became more important we find it resulting in the growth and expansion of a number of the old *civitates,* who began to outgrow their older fortifications. In 1019 we hear of new walls and fortifications at Vienne,[72] which probably explains why a charter mentions a stone mason or *murator* who is living in the city.[73] At about this same period in 1015 we hear of similar fortifications being built at Nîmes.[74] A little later about 1050 the suburbs of the town of Béziers had become important enough to be sold as a fief to an important nobleman by its bishop,[75] while even earlier, about 990, a suburb of Narbonne, called Villanova is mentioned in the will of its Viscountess Adelaise.[76] By 1033 Barcelona had outgrown its older fortifications and had to build new walls,[77] and Limoges at the same period had to be refortified also.[78]

One of the results of this economic growth in Southern France and Catalonia was a certain revival of moribund mints and the opening of new ones, for the first time in more than a century. A charter of 988 which mentions the money of Melgueil now indicates a new mint in operation near Montpellier.[79] A decade or so later our documents reveal that

---

[67] *Cart. de Saint-Sernin,* no. 135.
[68] *Ibid.,* nos. 137, 138.
[69] *Ibid.,* no. 136.
[70] *Cart. d'Angoulême,* nos. 30, 36.
[71] *Hist. Gén. de Lang.,* V, no. 205.
[72] *Cart. de Vienne,* no. 46.
[73] *Cart. de Saint-André-le-bas,* no. 79.
[74] *Cart. de Nîmes,* no. 92.
[75] *Cart. de Béziers,* no. 65.
[76] *Hist. Gén. de Lang.,* V, no. 151.
[77] *El Archivo Condal de Barcelona,* no. 40.
[78] *Cart. de Saint-Etienne de Limoges,* nos. 175–177.
[79] *Cart. de Nîmes,* no. 84.

Southern French and Catalan Society (975-1050)

similar mints had reopened at Albi[80] and Rodez[81] too. During this period Count Gausfred II began to coin money too,[82] and the *solidi* of Vich began to circulate in parts of Catalonia.[83] We find the money of Arles, called *ottochini*, known by name as far west as Rouergue[84] and as far to the east as Fréjus, where a charter of 1032 mentions it as being in use.[85]

In the western portion of Southern France we find the same thing happening. About 1040 Agen again began to mint coins,[86] thereby joining Angoulême and Bordeaux, both of which had started to do so a little earlier in the century,[87] while in 1047 Count Geoffrey of Anjou reopened the mint of Saintes by importing moneyers from nearby Angoulême.[88] At about the same period coins, for the first time in centuries, began to be minted at Béarn in Western Gascony.[89] In every region of the Midi and Catalonia we find ourselves in the presence of economic forces which make the opening of new mints advisable to meet the needs of a revived commerce.

As this happened coins began to circulate more widely too. An early eleventh century coin hoard recently discovered at Corrèze in the southern part of the Limousin illustrates this fact. This hoard contains over 2,500 coins in all: of these 1,960 are *barbarins* of Saint-Martial of Limoges, 483 are from LePuy, 44 from Limoges, 14 from Angoulême, 4 from Turenne, and 1 from Clermont. Though the majority of these coins show a strong local basis for their circulation, as a whole the coins in this hoard reveal an area of some size in which they tended to circulate from Angoulême to LePuy, and from Clermont to Turenne.[90] This kind of circulation of money explains why we find in charters from Provence a mention of the money of both LePuy and Vienne,[91] and why in Rouergue there

---

[80] *Hist. Gén. de Lang.*, V, no. 206.
[81] See reference to *solidi* of Rodez in *Cart. de Conques*, nos. 316, 333, 336, 339, among others.
[82] See J. Botet y Siso, *Les monedes catalanes*, I, 17-70.
[83] *Ibid.*, pp. 167-185.   [84] *Cart. de Conques*, no. 328.
[85] *Cart. de Lérins*, no. 31.
[86] A. Blanchet and A. Dieudonné, *Manuel de Numismatique*, IV, 220-221.
[87] *Ibid.*, pp. 215-216.
[88] *Cart. de Notre Dame de Saintes*, no. 75.
[89] Blanchet and Dieudonné, *Manuel de Numismatique*, IV, 87-92.
[90] L. de Nussac, "Trouvaille de monnaies médiévales à Argentat," in *Bulletin de la société historique et archéologique de la Corrèze*, LXVI (1944).
[91] *Cart. de Nîmes*, no. 92; *Cart. de Lérins*, no. 31; and *Cart. de Saint-Victor*, no. 172.

are constant references to the *solidi* of Limoges and LePuy also.⁹² Like commerce itself money had, by 1050, ceased to be merely a local affair.

As such mints opened and the money they coined began to circulate more widely, we begin to find evidence that it was used in larger quantities too by the society of the period. In 1027 the bishop of Limoges could sell some property to the abbey of Saint-Martial and receive 2,500 *solidi* for it,⁹³ just as a certain landowner, Tesalage, could do the same with some land for which he got 3,000 *solidi* from the canons of Saint-Etienne of Limoges.⁹⁴ In 1047 Count Geoffrey had 1,000 *solidi* at his disposal to buy out the *miles* who had a monopoly of the right to coin money at Saintes,⁹⁵ and at Albi there was sufficient cash available so that Bishop Frotaire and his brother could sell its bishopric for some 5,000 *solidi*.⁹⁶ At about the same period in 1035 Count Hugh of Rouergue could get 1,000 *solidi* by selling an allod to Viscount Berengar.⁹⁷

All this evidence of wealth in the hands of the magnates and churchmen of the Midi, however, pales before the evidence of that available during this period to important nobles of the Spanish March. The 100,000 *solidi* which Count Guifred of Cerdanya found available to purchase the archbishopric of Narbonne for his son in 1016,⁹⁸ is almost matched by the huge money subsidies which Count Raymond Berengar I of Catalonia poured out to assure the loyalty and support of Count Ermengol of Urgell.⁹⁹ Nor do we find only silver here in such large quantities. After the year 1000 we find much gold too, which is mentioned over and over again in charters dating from this period.¹⁰⁰ Perhaps some of this gold arrived in Catalonia as a result of trade with Moslem Spain. It seems more probable, however, that it was the result of booty won from the Moors or subsidies paid out by Moslem rulers to their Christian adversaries in a vain effort to secure their faltering fortunes and thrones as the Reconquista began. Whatever its origin, it not only gave Catalonia new

⁹² *Cart. de Conques,* nos. 95, 97–99, 104–108, 122, 125, 127.
⁹³ *Cart. de l'aumônerie de Saint-Martial de Limoges,* no. 36.
⁹⁴ *Cart. de Saint-Etienne de Limoges,* no. 69.
⁹⁵ *Cart. de Notre Dame de Saintes,* no. 75.
⁹⁶ *Hist. Gén. de Lang.,* V, no. 214.
⁹⁷ *Ibid.,* no. 207.
⁹⁸ *Ibid.,* no. 251.
⁹⁹ *Liber Feudorum,* nos, 46, 47.
¹⁰⁰ See, among many other references to gold, *Cart. de San Cugat,* nos. 337 (998), 343 (999), 397 (1005); and *Liber Feudorum,* no. 212 (1049). Most Catalan charters mention gold *by weight,* but in some cases they speak of *mancusi* or coins.

wealth, it also began to reach the Midi as well. It helps explain how in 1034 the abbot of Caunes had two ounces of gold which he could loan to Viscountess Ermissende[101] and how that magnate of Béziers, Rainald, could afford twelve ounces of the same metal to buy feudal rights over part of the city from Bishop Berengar in 1050.[102] It may even help explain how sometime between 1018 and 1032 the viscontal family of Marseille had available the four ounces of gold which they used to purchase from King Rudolf of Burgundy the rights he still had over a *villa* which they wanted, which had once belonged to his royal *fisc*.[103]

Revived trade and commerce and booty from Moslem Spain began to change the society of the Midi and Catalonia after 975. It helped to stimulate the growth of new towns, like Montpellier, and older *civitates*. In these new and older towns gradually there began to appear a new class of people in response to this economic revival, a class of merchants, traders, and artisans whom we can now call the bourgeois. Already as early as the year 1000 this new class was beginning to make their presence felt in protests over dues which were being levied upon their commerce.[104] Soon they were to amass sufficient wealth and power so that, as a class, they could join the *milites* and allodial landowners as *boni homines* and begin to play a role in local and regional government and in the life of Southern France and Catalonia.

The new and more abundant supply of money which began to become available to the society of the period, however, did more than create a new class, the bourgeois. It began to make possible a more orderly government in many regions. Where the allodial tradition of landholding, the family system of inheritance and control, and the new castles had helped strengthen a resistance to centralized government by rulers who, thanks to them, had no effective means of enforcing their rights, money gave them a new chance to succeed in their endeavors. A count of Barcelona buying allegiance, or a count of Saintes buying out a feudal moneyer were a foretaste of the future. Soon counts of Barcelona were to expand their authority in the Midi and the Spanish March, and a Count Raymond of Saint-Gilles was to control the county of Toulouse, in no small measure

---

[101] *Hist. Gén. de Lang.*, V, no. 200.
[102] *Cart. de Béziers*, no. 65.
[103] *Cart. de Saint-Victor*, no. 1061. See also references, in a charter of the Limousin from this period, to three ounces of gold (*Cart. de Tulle*, no. 654) and in an Auvergnat charter to two ounces of gold (*Cart. de Sauxillanges*, no. 406).
[104] See *Liber Instrumentorum Memorialium* [Montpellier], no. 149; and *Cart. de Saint-Sernin*, nos. 135–138.

because they controlled abundant supplies of hard cash with which they could buy support which the society of the period was unwilling to give on any other basis. A new governmental system, based on the use of money by rulers, was already in the making which was to transform the political, as well as the economic, life of regions which lay south of Poitou and Burgundy.

Between 975 and 1050, then, the society of Southern France and Catalonia changed in a number of ways. With a few exceptions it tended to remain essentially one based on allodial ownership of land, with political institutions of a weak, voluntary sort. Despite its growing militarization, it did not become essentially feudal. At the same time its older serfdom and *villa* system tended to disappear, and in part to be replaced by a new bondage exercised from its many castles, with the *mandamenta* they controlled determining in part the nature of local government. This, however, did not unduly interfere with progress in clearing the soil and expanding in most regions the area which was under cultivation. The Church met the challenge of the new militarism successfully enough to preserve its independence and take steps which were to lead later on to a more spiritual Church life, free from secular control. Perhaps most important of all, the society of this period began to be affected vitally by the revival of trade and commerce and a golden flow of booty from Moslem Spain. As this happened a new element—money—entered the picture. This created a new class in Southern France and Catalonia—the bourgeois, which soon took its place as equal in power to the *milites,* the churchmen, and the older allodial magnates who controlled landed wealth. Most important of all it gave to rulers who were wise enough to use it, a new weapon. With money at their disposal such rulers slowly but surely began to create *at last* a governmental system which worked for regions which had known little effective government since the time of Charlemagne and Louis the Pious. The age of the *principes* was over. An era of true principalities was at hand.

Conclusion

THE SOCIETY which had emerged in Southern France and Catalonia by 1050 differed in many ways from that found in these same regions in 718 on the eve of Moslem and Carolingian intervention in the affairs of the Midi. Yet in one respect it was similar. In 718 the social pattern which existed south of the Loire and north of the Pyrenees was generally similar in every region, except in tribal Gascony and in Catalonia, which had been overrun by the Moors. Life in the Limousin or the Valley of the Rhone was remarkably similar, judging from our scanty sources, to that found in Septimania, the Toulousain, or Provence near the mouths of the Rhone. By 1050 this was even truer. Regional differences existed in the mid-eleventh century as they had existed even in 950. Gascony, which had never known Roman or Visigothic law or where it had disappeared leaving no trace, kept certain unusual legal procedures. Visigothic law gave a different cast to the legal system which was used in Catalonia. The *aprisio* continued in 1050 important in the Spanish March long after it had disappeared north of the Pyrenees. Gascony and Western Aquitaine kept a prevailing *villa* system intact to a greater degree than the rest of the Midi, but lagged in clearing their vacant land for cultivation.

Nevertheless one should not overestimate such regional differences. By 1050, and even earlier, we can clearly view this whole region as an area enjoying a civilization generally similar in character in every portion of it, and different from that found in Northern France. All of the Midi and Catalonia by the eleventh century had the same kind of social classes, the same kind of Church, the same kind of military system, the same method of landholding, the same weak feudalism, the same lack of government, the same type of voluntary courts or assemblies which kept the peace. We can say, by this time, that we are dealing with what, for want of a better term, we might call a special civilization. All this explains why a Raymond of Saint-Gilles could rally the nobles of these regions to follow him as Provençals on the First Crusade; why troubadour lyrics could spread so rapidly from the Limousin to Gascony, Catalonia, Languedoc, and the Valley of the Rhone; and how a count of Barcelona could effectively operate in Languedoc, and his successors, as kings of Aragón, could become counts of Provence. By 1050 a new and unusual society had emerged in lands which lay south of Poitou and Burgundy.

How did this society of 1050 differ from the earlier one of 718? In the first place, by the mid-eleventh century the society of these regions was a much more vital one. Two new classes had appeared, the *milites* and the bourgeois. One was the product and result of the new castles which had arisen in the course of the tenth century; the other had emerged as a result of the revival of trade and commerce and the new growth of towns. In the countryside a new, freer, and more independent peasantry was to be found on the *aprisiones* and *medium plantum* which were created out of vacant and uncultivated land, as the *villa* system disappeared and the older serfdom with it. Only near castles was a new and different serfdom appearing. The Church, vigorous and growing, was busy checking the abuses of the new militarism and beginning to demand a more spiritual life, free of secular control. In Aquitaine and Catalonia new principalities, making use of money in a new way, were appearing. The society of the Midi and Catalonia, then, in 1050 was richer, more militarized, and more productive in its agricultural and commercial life than it had been in 718. At the same time it had a more vigorous Church and in certain areas the beginnings of more effective regional government. It was a society ready to play an important role in the medieval civilization of Western Europe.

How did all this come about? What caused the emergence of this vital and unusual civilization in Southern France and Catalonia? First of all we need to assess the role of the Carolingians in this process—a role frequently overestimated or even misunderstood. Perhaps their most important contribution was the conquest of Septimania and the Spanish March and their partial pacification of Gascony. As a result of this, both Septimania and Catalonia became integrated with the rest of the Midi, an integration that survived the decay of Carolingian authority, while enough ties were established between the Gascons and their Southern French neighbors so that in the tenth century Gascony too could become a part of Southern French civilization in a real sense, despite its backward, primitive society.

On the other hand, little of the political system which the Carolingians imposed upon the Midi and Spanish March survived the end of the ninth century, except perhaps in Catalonia. Though the names of the officials

Conclusion 403

which they introduced—counts, viscounts, and vicars—survived, their functions did not. Nor did the territorial boundaries which they established always survive either in later counties, viscounties, or *vicaria*. The feudalism which they introduced either disappeared into the allodial and family system which prevailed, or was modified into a system of *precaria* and benefices closer to that found in these regions in pre-Carolingian times. Their military organization disappeared also, except perhaps in Catalonia, until a new and different one, based upon castles and *milites*, appeared in the late tenth century. Except in Catalonia, so did their judicial system, which became a system of informal regional assemblies and courts keeping order by invoking public opinion to obtain agreements on a voluntary basis. By the tenth century little of the Carolingian political system had survived which could form the basis of later government, either feudal or nonfeudal.

Where the Carolingians made the most important contribution to the Midi and Spanish March, as a matter of fact, was in what they did for the Church. The revival which they encouraged in the Church of Aquitaine, Septimania, and the Spanish March never completely stopped, though they were less successful in this respect in Gascony and Provence. From this revival stemmed a renewed Church and monastic growth which spread from the Massif Central and Languedoc and Catalonia, until by the end of the tenth century a vigorous Church was one of the realities in every part of these lands which lay south of Poitou and Burgundy. Similarly the *aprisio* system, which they sponsored in Septimania and Catalonia, and the *medium plantum,* which seems to have begun during their rule, were important as means of clearing new land for cultivation, and from the tenth century on, changed the face of Southern France and the Spanish March and helped free the peasantry from its ancient bondage to serfdom and the *villa* system.

Though we must agree that a debt is due the Carolingians on the part of Southern France and Catalonia, we still must emphasize that the particular type of society which emerged by 1050 was more the result of certain indigenous instincts than it was of Carolingian influence. What were these instincts or traditions? The first was the insistence upon land being allodial. From the time of Louis the Pious the society of Southern France and Catalonia fought for allodial rights. As a result Carolingian benefices and *aprisiones* disappeared by 900, and every later attempt to create a true principality failed also, as those to whom land was given on feudal terms transformed it into allods. If Charles the Bald failed in this respect, so did Louis of Provence, William the Pious of Auvergne, Count Ebles

Manzur of Poitou, Count Raymond Pons of Toulouse, Marquis William I of Provence, and many others.

The second important instinct or tradition of these regions was its emphasis on family control of property, political power, and the Church. This, like the emphasis on the allod, doomed Carolingian feudalism and government, and helped make all later attempts to create principalities impossible. This family system also helps to explain why women became powerful in the Midi and Catalonia at an early period and remained so, and why the Church in this region was so different from that found elsewhere. At a time when all other political institutions had disappeared, it was the family system which survived as the basis of public order and control of private property.

The third instinct was one which insisted on viewing feudal ties less as a matter of personal loyalty in the Carolingian or Northern French sense than as individual agreements over property as such. Even before Charlemagne this seems to have been the case in regard to early *precaria* and benefices given out by private individuals and the Church. It remained so later. As a result the feudalism that we find by the eleventh century in our regions concentrates on the fief and conditions under which it is held, generally demanding at least a *cens* in payment for it, instead of upon the loyalty of *fidelitas* which should exist between lord and vassal of which the fief was a payment or tangible token. Such a feudalism at best could be only a fragile affair of little value in the establishment of an effective governmental system.

Finally to make this system work the society of Southern France and Catalonia added, in the tenth century, its own contribution of a unique sort: the informal court or assembly which represented independent families, churchmen, *milites,* and other magnates, and which met on a local or regional basis to keep peace, settle disputes, and handle other matters of importance. Until counts of Barcelona and dukes of Aquitaine began to use money and power in a new way, this was the closest thing to government which we find in Southern France. Out of it were to come those representative assemblies and local town councils which were to be so important for the future in these regions.

The society of the Midi, then, was different from that of Northern France by 1050, because its original elements, the contributions that the Carolingians made to it, and the basic instincts were different from those north of the Loire. And it was to remain different until the armed might of Northern French monarchs and nobles forcibly integrated it into a new France which was being built in the twelfth and thirteenth centuries.

BIBLIOGRAPHY

I. Primary Materials 407
   A. Unprinted Sources, 407
   B. Printed Sources, 407
      1. General Collections, 407
      2. Royal Sources, 407
         a. General Records, 407
         b. Royal Charters (In Historical Order), 408
      3. Narrative Sources, 409
      4. Printed Cartularies, Volumes Containing Charters (Except for Royal Charters), and Other Collected Records, 411
         a. General Works, 411
         b. Works Dealing with Particular Locations, 412

II. Secondary Materials 415

Primary Materials

UNPRINTED SOURCES

"Cartulaire de l' Évêché d'Agde," in Archives de l'Herault, Montpellier.
"Cartulaire de Lézat," in Archives de Toulouse (printed edition recently available).
"Cartulaire de Psalmodi," in Archives de Nîmes.
"Cartulaire des Trencavels" in Société archéologique et historique de Montpellier.

PRINTED SOURCES

General Collections

Bibliotheca Rerum Germanicarum, ed. P. Jaffé, 6 vols. Berlin: 1864–1873.
España sagrada, ed. E. Flórez, Vols. VI, X, XVII, XXIX. Madrid: 1751–1795.
Mansi, *Sacrorum conciliorum nova et amplissima collecto*, New ed., 31 vols. Florence and Venice: 1757–1798.
Migne, *Patrologia cursus completus series latina*, 221 vols. Paris: 1844–1859.
Recueil des Historiens des Gaules et de la France, ed. D. Bouquet *et alii*, 24 vols. Paris: 1738–1904.
Villanueva, J., *Viaje literario a las iglesias de España*, Vols. VI–XI, XIII–XIV. Madrid and Valencia: 1821–1850.

Royal Sources

GENERAL RECORDS

Böhmer, J., and E. Mühlbacher, *Regesta Imperii: Die Regester des Kaiserreichs unter der Karolingern (751–908)*, 2nd ed. Innsbruck: 1908.
Boretius, A., and V. Krause, *Capitularia regum Francorum*, 2 vols., in *Mon. Ger. Hist. Capitularia*.
Haenel, G., *Lex Romana Visigothorum*. Zagreb: 1877.
Krause, V. *See* Boretius, A.
Lauer, P., and C. Samarin, *Les diplômes originaux des Mérovingiens*. Paris: 1908.
Maasen, F., *Concilia aevi Merowingici*, in *Mon. Ger. Hist. Leges*, Vol. III.
Mansi, *Sacrorum conciliorum nova et amplissima collectio*, Vols. XIV–XX. Florence and Venice: 1757–1798.
Werminghoff, A., *Concilia aevi karolini*, in *Mon. Ger. Hist. Leges*, Vol. III.
Zeumer, K., *Formulae Merovingici et karoli aevi*, in *Mon. Ger. Hist. Leges*, Vol. V.

ROYAL CHARTERS (IN HISTORICAL ORDER)

Mühlbacher, E., *Die Urkunden der Karolinger*, I: *Die Urkunden Pippins, Karlomanns und Karls des Grossen*, in *Mon. Ger. Hist. Diplomata Karolinorum.*
Kehr, P., *Die Urkunden Karls III*. Berlin: 1937.
Lot, F., P. Lauer, and G. Tessier, *Diplomata Karolinorum*. Paris: 1936–1945.
Ludovici Pii imperatoris diplomata, in *Recueil des Historiens des Gaules et de la France*, Vol. VI. Paris: 1749.
Karli Calvi diplomata, in *Recueil des Historiens des Gaules et de la France*, Vol. VIII. Paris: 1752.
Ludovici Balbi diplomata, in *Recueil des Historiens des Gaules et de la France*, Vol. IX. Paris: 1756.
Carlomani regis diplomata, in *Recueil des Historiens des Gaules et de la France*, Vol. IX. Paris: 1756.
Karoli Grassi imperatoris diplomata, in *Recueil des Historiens des Gaules et de la France*, Vol. IX. Paris: 1756.
Odonis regis diplomata, in *Recueil des Historiens des Gaules et de la France*, Vol. IX. Paris: 1756.
Roberti Francorum regis diplomata, in *Recueil des Historiens des Gaules et de la France*, Vol. IX. Paris: 1756.
Rodulfi regis diplomata, in *Recueil des Historiens des Gaules et de la France*, Vol. IX. Paris: 1756.
Regis Hugonis Capeti diplomata, in *Recueil des Historiens des Gaules et de la France*, Vol. X. Paris: 1760.
Roberti regis diplomata, in *Recueil des Historiens des Gaules et de la France*, Vol. X. Paris: 1760.
Henrici I Francorum regis diplomata, in *Recueil des Historiens des Gaules et de la France*, Vol. XI. Paris: 1767.
Lot, F., G. Tessier, *et alii*, *Recueil des actes de Charles II le Chauve*, 3 vols. Paris: 1943–1955.
Lauer, P., *Recueil des actes de Charles III le Simple*, 2 vols. Paris: 1940–1949.
Lauer, P., *Recueil des actes de Louis IV*. Paris: 1914.
Halphen, L. and F. Lot, *Recueil des actes de Lothaire et Louis V*. Paris: 1908.
Levillain, L., *Recueil des actes de Pépin I et Pépin II, rois d'Aquitaine*. Paris: 1926.
Poupardin, R., *Recueil des actes des rois de Provence (855–928)*. Paris: 1920.
Abadal i de Vinyals, R. de, *Catalunya Carolingia*, II: *Els Diplomes Carolingis a Catalunya*. Barcelona: 1926–1952.
—, *Catalunya Carolingia*, III: *Els Comtats de Pallars i Ribagorça*. Barcelona: 1955.
—, "Els precepts comtals carolingis per al Pallars," in *Boletín de la Real Academia de Buenas Letras de Barcelona*, Vol. XXVI (1954–1958).

Bibliography

Narrative Sources

Ademar de Chabannes, *Chronique*, ed. A. Chavanon. Paris: 1897.
Agobardi Lugdunensis archepiscopi Epistolae, ed. E. Dummler, in *Mon. Ger. Hist. Epistolae*, Vol. V.
Aimonus, *Liber inventionis sive translationis beati Vincentii ex Hispania in Castiense monasterium*, in Migne, *Patrologia Latina*, Vol. CXV, col. 939-960.
Annales Anianenses (Annals of Aniane) in *Hist. Gén. de Lang.*, Vol. II.
Annales Barcinonenses, ed. G. Pertz, in *Mon. Ger. Hist. Scriptores*, Vol. XXIII.
Annales Bertiniani, ed. E. Waitz. Hanover: 1883.
Annales Engolensis, ed. G. Pertz, in *Mon. Ger. Hist. Scriptores*, Vol. XVI.
Annales Floriacenses, ed. G. Pertz, in *Mon. Ger. Hist. Scriptores*, Vol. II.
Annales Laurissenses, ed. G. Pertz, in *Mon. Ger. Hist. Scriptores*, Vol. I.
Annales Luricanes, ed. E. Waitz, in *Mon. Ger. Hist. Scriptores*, Vol. I.
Annales Mettenses priores, ed. B. de Simson, Hanover: 1909.
Annales Regni Francorum, ed. G. Kurze. Hanover: 1895.
Annales remanies, ed. G. Pertz, in *Mon. Ger. Hist. Scriptores*, Vol. I.
Annales Xantenenses and Annales Vedastini, ed. B. de Simson. Hanover: 1909.
"Aquitaniae Historiae Fragmenta," in Ademar de Chabannes *Chronique*, ed. A Chavanon. Paris: 1897.
Astronomus, *Vita Hludovici imperatoris*, ed. G. Pertz, in *Mon. Ger. Hist. Scriptores*, Vol. II.
Bondurand, E., *L'education Carolingienne: Le Manuel de Dhuoda*. Paris: 1887.
Chronici Fontanellensis fragmentum, ed. G. Pertz, in *Mon. Ger. Hist. Scriptores*, Vol. II.
Chronicon ecclessiae Sancti Pauli Narbonnensis, in *Hist. Gén. de Languedoc*, Vol. V.
Chronicon Moisacense (Chronicle of Moissac), ed. G. Pertz, in *Mon. Ger. Hist. Scriptores*, Vol. I.
Chronicon Nemausense, in *Mon. Ger. Hist. Scriptores*, Vol. III; and in *Hist. Gén. de Languedoc*, Vol. V.
Chronicon Sancti Saturni Tolesae, in *Hist. Gén. de Languedoc*, Vol. V.
Chronicon Ucenense (Chronicle of Uzès), in *Hist. Gén. de Languedoc*, Vol. II.
Chronicon Vetus Magalonense, in *Hist. Gén. de Languedoc*, Vol. V., and in *Catulaire de Maguelonne*, Vol. I, ed. J. Rouguette. Montpellier: 1912.
Chronicum Aquitanicum, ed. G. Pertz, in *Mon. Ger. Hist. Scriptores*, Vol. II.
Chroniques de Saint-Martial de Limoges, ed. H. Duplès-Agier. Paris: 1874.
Chronique de la Monastère de Saint-Pierre de LePuy, in *Hist. Gén. de Languedoc*, Vol. V.
Chronique de Nantes, ed. R. Merlot. Nantes: 1896.

Chronilogia et series regum Gothorum, in *Hist. Gén. de Languedoc*, Vol. II.
Divisis terminorum episcopatum provinciae Narbonensis, in *Hist. Gén. de Languedoc*, Vol. II.
Einhard, *Vie de Charlemagne*, ed. L. Halphen, in *Mon. Ger. Hist. Epistolae*, Vol. V.
Ermold Niger, *Carmina in homorem Hludovici I*, ed. E. Dummler, in *Mon. Ger. Hist. Scriptores*, Vol. I.
Flodoard, *Annales*, ed. P. Lauer. Paris: 1906.
Flodoardus, *Historia Remensis ecclesiae*, ed. P. Heller and E. Waitz, in *Mon. Ger. Hist. Scriptores*, Vol. XIII.
Fredegarius, *Chronicon quod dicitur Fredegarii continuatio*, ed. R. Krusch, in *Mon. Ger. Hist. Scriptores rerum Merov.*, Vol. II.
Gesta Comitum Barcinonensium, ed. L. Barrau-Dihigo and R. Masso-Torrents. Barcelona: 1925.
Gesta Dagoberti, ed. R. Krusch, in *Mon. Ger. Hist. Scriptores rerum Merov.*, Vol. II.
Havet, J. *Lettres de Gerbert*. Paris: 1889.
Hincmar, *Opera*, in Migne, *Patrologia latina*, Vols. CXXVI–CXXVII.
Inventione et translation des reliques de S. Basile, martyr, à Nîmes, in *Hist. Gén. de Languedoc*, Vol. II.
Isidore of Seville, *Historia Gothorum*, in Migne, *Patrologia latina*, Vol. XC.
Johannis VIII, *Papae Epistolae*, in Migne, *Patrologia latina*, Vol. CXXVI.
Julian of Toledo, *Historia Excellentissimi Wambae Regis*, in *España sagrada*, Vol. VI.
Khodâdbeh, Ibn, *Book of Routes*, ed. R. de Geoje, in *Biblioteca Geographiae Arabiae*, Vol. IX. London: 1899.
Liudprand of Cremona, *Works*, ed. F. Wright. London: 1930.
Loup de Ferrières, *Correspondence*, ed. L. Levillain, 2 vols. Paris: 1927–1933. Also in *Mon. Ger. Hist. Epistolae*, Vol. I.
Millás-Vallicrosa, J., *Els textos d'historiadors musalmans referents a la Catalunya carolingia*, in *Cuaderns d'Estudi*, Vol. XIV. Barcelona: 1922.
—, *Historiadors aràbics referents a la reconquista catalana*. Barcelona: 1936.
Miracles de Sainte Foy, ed. D. Bouquet, in *Recueil des Historiens des Gaules et de la France*, Vol. VII.
Miracula Sancti Martialis Lemovicensis, ed. D. Bouquet, in *Recueil des Historiens des Gaules et de la France*, Vol. III.
Nithard, *Histoire des fils de Louis le Pieux*, ed. P. Lauer. Paris: 1926.
Odo, *Vita Sancti Geraldi Aureliacensis*, in Migne, *Patrologia latina*, Vol. CXXXIII.
Raoul Glaber, *Historiarum libri V*, ed. R. Prou. Paris: 1886.
Richer, *Histoire de France*, ed. R. Latouche, 2 vols. Paris: 1930–1937.
Theganus, *Vita Hludovici imperatoris*, ed. G. Pertz, in *Mon. Ger. Hist. Scriptores*, Vol. II.

Bibliography

Theodulfus, bishop of Orleans, *Pavrensis ad Judices*, ed. E. Dummler, in *Mon. Ger. Hist. Poet. Lat. Aevi*, Vol. I.
Translatio S. Faustae Martyris, in *Acta Sanctorum*, Jan. I, cols. 1091–1092.
Translatio Sanctae Faustae e Vasconia, ed. D. Bouquet, in *Recueil des Historiens des Gaules et de la France*, Vol. VII.
Vie de Saint Didier, ed. R. Poupardin, Vol. VIII. Paris: 1900.
Vita Benedicti Anianensis, ed. E. Waitz, in *Mon. Ger. Hist. Scriptores*, Vol. XV, and in Migne, *Patrologia latina*, Vol. CV.
Vita Sancti Guilelmi ducis ac monarchi, in *Acta Sanctorum*, May VI, cols. 811–820.
Vita Sancti Hilarii Arelatensis, in Migne, *Patrologia latina*, Vol. I.

Printed Cartularies, Volumes Containing Charters (Except for Royal Charters), and Other Collected Records

GENERAL WORKS

Alart, B., *Un jugement inédit de l'an 865 concernant la ville de Pradès*. Perpignan: 1873.
Albanes-Chevalier, L., *Gallia Christiana Novissima*. Marseille: 1901.
Baluze, E., *Histoire Généalogique de la Maison d'Auvergne*. Paris: 1708.
—, *Historiae Tutelensis libri tres*. Paris: 1707.
Brunel, C., *Les plus anciennes chartes en langue provençale*. Paris: 1926.
D'Achery, Dom Luc, *Spicelegium*, 3 vols. Paris: 1862–1867.
DeVic, C., and J. Vaissette, *Histoire Générale de Languedoc*, ed. Privat, Vols. II and V. Toulouse: 1879–1892.
Gallia Christiana in provincias ecclesiasticas distributas, Vol. V. Paris: 1718.
Jacotin, A., *Preuves de la maison de Polignac*, 5 vols. Paris: 1895–1906.
Labbé, P., *Sacrosancta Concilia*, Vols. IX, XIX. Venice: 1729, 1732.
Lacarra, J. (ed.), *Documentos para el estudio de la repoblación del valle de Ebro*, in *Estudios de Edad Media de la Corona de Aragón*, Vols. II–V. Zaragoza: 1946–1954.
Lasteyrie, R. de, *Étude sur les comtes et vicomtes de Limoges antérieurs à l'an 1000* (pièces justificatives). Paris: 1874.
Manteyer, G., *La Provence du Ier au XIIe siècle* (pièces justificatives). Paris: 1908.
Marca, P. de, *Histoire de Béarn*, 2 vols. (pièces justificatives). Pau: 1894–1912.
—, *Marca hispanica sive limes hispanicus*, 2 vols. (pièces justificatives). Paris: 1688.
Miguel Rossell, F. (ed.), *Liber Feudorum Maior*, 2 vols. Barcelona: 1945–1947.
Pouhardin, R. (ed.), *Une charte inédite de Bernard Plantevelue*, in *Annales du Midi*, Vol. XIV (1902).

WORKS DEALING WITH PARTICULAR LOCATIONS

AGDE. *Cartulaire du chapitre de l'église d'Agde*, ed. J. Rouquette. Montpellier: 1925.
AINAY. *See* SAVIGNY.
ANGOULÊME. *Cartulaire de l'église d'Angoulême*, ed. I. Nanglard, Vol. I. Angoulême: 1900.
ANIANE. *Cartulaire d'Aniane*, ed. A. Cassan and E. Meynial. Montpellier: 1910.
AUCH. *Cartulaires du chapitre de l'église métropolitaine Sainte Marie d'Auch*, ed. C. Lacaye La Playne-Barris, in *Archives Historiques de la Gascogne*, fasc. III. Auch: 1899.
AVIGNON. *Les Chartes du pays d'Avignon (439–1040)*, ed. G. Manteyer, in *Mémoires de l'Académie de Vaucluse*, Vol. II. Mâcon: 1914.
BAIGNE. *Cartulaire de l'abbaye de Saint-Etienne de Baigne en Saintonge*, ed. R. Chalet. Niort: 1868.
BARCELONA. *El Archivo Condal de Barcelona en los Siglos IX–X*, ed. F. Udina-Martorell. Barcelona: 1951.
—. *El Archivo Catedral de Barcelona*, ed. S. Puig y Puig. Barcelona: 1906.
—. *El "Libre Blanch" de Santas Creus* [Barcelona], ed. F. Udina-Martorell. Barcelona: 1947.
BEAULIEU. *Cartulaire de l'abbaye de Beaulieu*, ed. M. Deloche. Paris: 1859.
BÉZIERS. *Livre Noir ou Cartulaire du chapitre cathédral de Béziers*, ed. J. Rouquette. Montpellier: 1918.
BORDEAUX. *Cartulaire de l'abbaye de Sainte-Croix de Bordeaux*, ed. P. Ducaunnes-Duval, in *Archives Historiques de la Gironde*, Vol. XXVII (1892).
—. *Diplômes Carolingiens de l'église cathédrale Saint-André de Bordeaux* in *Le Moyen Age*, Vol. XIX (1915–1916).
BRIOUDE. *Cartulaire de Brioude*, ed. H. Doniol. Clermont-Ferrand: 1869.
—. *Le Grand Cartulaire de Saint-Julien de Brioude, essai de reconstruction*, ed. Anne Marie and Marcel Boudet. St. Etienne: 1935.
CARCASSONNE. J. Cros-Meyrévielle, *Histoire du comté et de la vicomté de Carcassonne*, (pièces justificatives). Carcassonne: 1912.
—. *Cartulaire et archives des communes de l'ancien diocèse et de l'arrondissement de Carcassonne*, ed. M. Mahul, 6 vols. Paris: 1857–1872.
CARLAT. *Documents historiques relatifs à la vicomté de Carlat*, ed. G. Saigne and the count of Dienne, 2 vols. Monaco: 1900.
CHAFFRE. *Cartulaire de l'abbaye de Saint-Chaffre du Monastier*, ed. U. Chevalier. Paris: 1884.
CHAMALIÈRES. *Cartulaire de Chamalières-sur-Loire en Velay*, ed. A. Chassaing. Paris: 1895.

Bibliography 413

CHARROUX. *Chartes et documents pour servir à l'histoire de l'abbaye de Charroux*, ed. P. Monsabert, in *Archives Historiques du Poitou*, Vol. XXXIX. Poitiers: 1910.
CLUNY. *Recueil des chartes de l'abbaye de Cluny*, ed. A. Bernard and A. Bruell, 4 vols. Paris: 1876–1903.
CONQUES. *Cartulaire de l'abbaye de Conques en Rouergue*, ed. A. Desjardins. Paris: 1879.
DIE. *Cartulaire de l'église de Die*, ed. U. Chevalier. Grenoble: 1868.
DORAT. *Recueil de textes et d'analyses concernant le chapitre de Saint-Pierre de Dorat*, ed. J. de Font-Réaulx, in *Bulletin de la société archéologique et historique du Limousin*, Vol. LXXII (1927).
FONTJONCOUSE. *Cartulaire de la seigneurie de Fontjoncouse*, ed. G. Mouynes, in *Bulletin de la commission archéologique et littéraire de Narbonne*, Vol. I. (1877).
GELLONE. *Cartulaire de Gellone*, ed. A. Cassan and E. Meynial. Montpellier: 1900.
GIRONDE. *Cartulaire du prieuré conventual de Saint-Pierre de la Réolle*, ed. C. Grellet-Balguerie, in *Archives Historiques de la Gironde*, Vol. V (1864).
GRENOBLE. *Cartulaire de l'église Cathédrale de Grenoble*, ed. J. Marion. Paris: 1869.
LEPUY. *Cartularium conventus St. Egidii Camaleriarum*, ed. H. Fraisse. LePuy: 1871.
—. *Cartulaire de Saint Petrus Aniacenses*, ed. A. Molinier, in *Hist. Gén. de Lang.*, Vol. V.
LÉRINS. *Cartulaire de l'abbaye de Lérins*, ed. H. Moris and E. Blanc, 2 vols. Paris: 1883–1902.
LIMOGES. *Cartulaire de l'église de Saint-Etienne de Limoges*, ed. J. de Font-Réaulx, in *Bulletin de la société archéologique et historique du Limousin*, Vol. LXIX (1922).
—. *Cartulaire de l'aumônerie de Saint-Martial de Limoges*, ed. A. Leroux, in *Documents historiques de la Marche et du Limousin*, Vol. II. Limoges: 1885.
LIMOUSIN. *Chartes du Limousin antérieures au XIIIe siècle*, ed. A. Leroux. Tulle: 1900.
LUCQ. *Cartulaire de Saint-Vincent de Lucq*, ed. L. Barrau-Dihigo, in *Revue de Béarn et des Pays Basques*, Vol. I (1904).
LYON. *Cartulaire Lyonnais*, ed. M. Guigue, Vol. I. Lyon: 1885.
—. *Documents inédits des IXe, X^e et XIe siècles relatifs à l'église de Lyon*, ed. U. Chevalier. Lyon: 1867.
MAGUELONNE. *Cartulaire de Maguelonne*, ed. J. Rouquette and A. Villemagne, Vol. I. Montpellier: 1912.

MARSEILLE. *Cartulaire de l'abbaye de Saint-Victor de Marseille*, ed. B. Guéraud. Marseille: 1857.
MAZ D'AZIL. *L'Abbaye du Maz d'Azil: Monographie et Cartulaire (817–1774)*, ed. D. Cau-Durban. Foix: 1897.
MAURIENNE. *Chartes du diocèse de Maurienne*, ed. A. Billiot and F. Abrieux, in *Académie Impériale de Savoie: Documents*, II. Champéry: 1861.
MONTÉLIMAR. *Cartulaire Municipal de la ville de Montélimar*, ed. U. Chevalier. Montélimar: 1871.
MONTPELLIER. *Liber Instrumentorum Memorialium: Catulaire des Guillems*, ed. A. Germain. Montpellier: 1884.
MORLAAS. *Cartulaire de Sainte-Foi de Morlaas*, ed. L. Cadier, in *Bulletin de la société des sciences, lettres et arts de Pau*, 2nd Ser., Vol. XIII (1886).
NICE. *Cartulaire de l'ancienne Cathédrale de Nice, Sainte-Réparte*, ed. E. Cais de Pierlas. Turin: 1888.
—. *Cartulaire de l'abbaye de Saint-Pons-hors-les-murs de Nice*, ed. E. Cais de Pierlas and G. Saige. Monaco: 1903.
NÎMES. *Cartulaire de l'église cathédrale de Notre Dame de Nîmes*, ed. E. Germer-Durand. Nîmes: 1874.
PAUNAT. *Fragments du cartulaire du Monastère de Paunat*, ed. R. Poupardin and A. Thomas. Toulouse: 1906.
POITOU. *Chartes et documents pour servir à l'histoire de l'abbaye de Saint-Maixent*, ed. A. Richard, in *Archives historiques du Poitou*, Vols. XVI, XVIII (1886).
—. *Chartes poitivines (833–1160) de l'abbaye de Saint Florent de Samaur*, ed. P. Marchegay, in *Archives historiques du Poitou*, Vol. II (1873).
—. *Cartulaire de l'abbaye de Saint-Cyprien de Poitiers*, ed. Redet, in *Archives historiques du Poitou*, Vol. III (1874).
ROMANS. *Cartulaire de Saint-Barnard de Romans*, ed. U. Chevalier. Romans: 1898.
ROUSSILLON. *Cartulaire roussillonnais*, ed. B. Alart. Perpignan: 1880.
SAINTES. *Cartulaire de l'abbaye royale de Notre Dame de Saintes*, ed. T. Graslier, in *Cartulaires inédits de la Saintonge*, Vol. II. Niort: 1871.
SAINT-FLOUR. *Cartulaire du Prieuré de Saint-Flour*, ed. M. Boudet. Monaco: 1902.
SAINT-JEAN D'ANGÉLY. *Cartulaire de Saint-Jean d'Angély*, ed. G. Musset. Paris: 1901.
SAINT-JEAN DE SORDE. *Cartulaire de Saint-Jean de Sorde*, ed. P. Raymond. Pau: 1873.
SAINT-SULPICE EN BUGEY. *Cartulaire de Saint-Sulpice en Bugey*, ed. M. Guigue. Lyon: 1884.

Bibliography

SAN CUGAT DES VALLES. *Cartulario de San Cugat des Valles*, ed. J. Ruis Serra. 3 vols. Barcelona: 1947–1949.
SAN SALVADOR DE OÑA. *Collección diplomática de San Salvador de Oña*, ed. J. del Alamo, Vol. I. Madrid: 1950.
SARLAT. *Chartier du monastère de Sarlat*, ed. G. Marnier, in *Bulletin de la société archéologique du Périgord*, Vol. XI (1884).
SAUXILLANGES. *Cartulaire de Sauxillanges*, ed. H. Doniol. Clermont: 1864.
SAVIGNY. *Cartulaire de l'abbaye de Savigny, suivi du petit cartulaire de l'abbaye d'Ainay*, ed. A. Bernard. Paris: 1853.
TOULOUSE. *Cartulaire de l'abbaye de Saint-Sernin de Toulouse*, ed. C. Douais. Toulouse: 1887.
TULLE. *Cartulaires des abbayes de Tulle et de Roc-Amador*, ed. J. Champéval, in *Bulletin de la société scientifique, historique et archéologique de la Corrèze*, Vols. IV–XVIII (1887–1902).
UZERCHE. *Cartulaire de l'abbaye d'Uzerche*, ed. J. Champéval. Tulle: 1900.
VABRES. *Cartulaire de Vabres* (sections), ed. A. Molinier, in *Hist. Gén. de Lang.*, Vol. II.
VALPUESTA. *Chartes de l'église de Valpuesta du IXe au XIe siècle*, ed. L. Barrau-Dihigo, in *Revue Hispanique*, Vol. VII (1900).
VIENNE. *Cartulaire de l'abbaye de Saint-André-le-bas-de Vienne*, ed. U. Chevalier. Vienne: 1869.
—. *Cartulaire de Vienne*, ed. U. Chevalier, in *Cartulaire de l'abbaye de Saint-André-le-bas de Vienne*. Vienne: 1869.
—. *Cartulaire de St. Maurice de Vienne*, ed. U. Chevalier, in *Cartulaire de Saint-André-le-bas de Vienne*. Vienne: 1869.
VIGEOIS. *Cartulaire de l'abbaye de Vigeois*, ed. M. de Montegut. Limoges: 1907.

Secondary Materials

Abadal i de Vinyals, R. de, *L'abat Oliva, bisbe de Vic, i la seva època*. Barcelona: 1948.
—, "La batalla del adopcionisme en la desintegración de la Iglesia visigoda," in *Real Academia de Buenas Letras de Barcelona*. Barcelona: 1949.
—, "La Catalogne sous l'empire de Louis le Pieux," in *Études Roussillonnaises*, Vols. IV–VI (1955–1957).
—, "Com neix i com creix un gran monestir pirinenc abans de l'any mil," in *Analecta Monserratensia*, Vol. VIII (1954–1955).
—, "El comte Bernat de Ribagorça i la llegenda de Bernardo de Carpio," in *Estudios dedicados a Menéndez-Pidal*, Vol. III. Madrid: 1951.
—, "Un diplôme inconnu de Louis le Pieux pour le comte Oliba de Carcassonne," in *Annales du Midi*, Vol. LXI (1949).

—, "La expedición de Carlomagno a Zaragoza, el hecho histórico," in *Coloquios de Roncesvalles. Augusto 1955*. Zaragoza: 1956.

—, "Origen y proceso de consolidación de la sedes ribagorzana de Rodo," in *Estudios de Edad Media de la Corona de Aragón*, Vol. III. Zaragoza: 1952.

—, "El paso de Septimania del dominio godo al franco a través de la invasión sarracena," in *Cuadernos de Historia de España*, Vol. XIII. Buenos Aires: 1953.

—, *La Plana de Vich*. Vich: 1954.

—, *Els Primers Comtes Catalans*. Barcelona: 1958.

Adelson, H., "Early Medieval Trade Routes," in *American Historical Review*, Vol. LXV (1960).

Anchel, R. *Les Juifs de France*. Paris: 1946.

Aubenas, R., "Les châteaux forts des Xe et XIe siècles," in *Revue historique de droit français et étranger*, Vol. XV (1937).

—, *Etude sur le notariat provençal au Moyen-âge*. Aix: 1931.

—, "La famille dans l'ancienne Provence," in *Annales d'histoire économique et sociale*, Vol. VIII (1936).

Auzias, L., *L'Aquitaine Carolingienne (778–987)*. Toulouse: 1937.

—, "Recherches d'histoire carolingienne, I: Les fluctuations politiques de quelques grands d'Aquitaine (846–74)," in *Annales du Midi*, Vol. XLIV (1932).

—, "Recherches d'histoire carolingienne, II: Le personnel comtal et l'autorité comtale en Septimanie méridionale (872–78)," in *Annales du Midi*, Vol. XLV (1933).

—, "Les relations de Bernard Plantevelue avec les princes carolingiens de 880 à 885," in *Le Moyen Age*, Vol. XXXI (1935).

Barlangue, G., *L'abbaye Saint-Pierre de Moissac, des origines au début du XIVe siècle*, in *Bibliotèque de l'Ecole des Chartes*, Vol. CX (1952).

Barrau-Dihigo, L. "Notes sur le codex de Meya," in *Revue des Bibliothèques*, Vols. XXX–XXXI (1921).

—, "Les origines du royaume de Navarre," in *Revue Hispanique*, Vol. VII (1900).

—, "Recherches sur l'histoire politique du royaume asturien," in *Revue Historique*, Vol. CLII (1921).

Bautier, R., "Notes historiques sur la Marche d'Espagne: Le Confluent et ses comtes au IXe siècle," in *Mélanges Felix Grat*. Paris: 1946.

Bernard, F., *Les origines féodales en Savoie et en Dauphiné*. Grenoble: 1950.

Binúe, E. *El langage técnic del feudalismo en el siglo X en Catalunya*. Barcelona: 1957.

Blanchet, A., and A. Dieudonné, *Manuel de Numismatique*, 4 vols. Paris: 1912–1937.

Bloch, M., *Les charactères originaux de l'histoire rurale française*, 2 vols. Paris: 1955–1956.

—, "Economie-Nature ou économie-argent: un pseudo-dilemme," in *Annales d'histoire sociale,* Vol. I (1939).
—, "Les formes de la rupture de l'hommage dans l'ancien droit féodal," in *Nouvelle revue historique de droit français et étranger,* Vol. XXXVI (1912).
—, "Le problème de l'or au Moyen age," in *Annales d'histoire économique et sociale,* Vol. V (1933).
—, *La Société Féodale,* 2 vols. Paris: 1939-1940.
Blumenkranz, B., *Juifs et chrétiens dans le monde occidental, 430-1096.* Paris: 1960.
Bofarull y Mascaro, P. de, *Los condes de Barcelona vindicados,* 2 vols. Barcelona: 1836.
Bongert, Y., *Recherches sur les cours laïques de X^e au XIIIe siècle.* Paris: 1949.
Botet y Siso, J., *Condado de Gerona: Los condes beneficiarios.* Gerona: 1890.
—, *Les monedes catalanes,* 2 vols. Barcelona: 1908.
Bouches du Rhône: Encyclopédie départementale, Vol. II. Marseille: 1924.
Boudon, L. A., *Histoire du Velay.* Thouars: 1930.
Bousquet, L., "Un épisode des invasions normandes en Rouergue d'après la charte de donation de l'église de Cannec," in *Revue Rouergue,* Vol. XV (1950).
Boussard, J., "Serfs et 'colliberti' (XIe et XIIe siècles)," in *Bibliothèque de l'Ecole des Chartes,* Vol. CVII (1949).
Boutruche, R., "Les courants de peuplement dans l'Entre-Deux-Mers," in *Annales d'histoire économique et sociale,* Vol. VII (1935).
—, *Seigneurie et féodalité.* Paris: 1959.
—, *Une société provinciale en lutte contre le régime féodal: L'alleu en Bordelais et en Bazadais de XIe au XIIIe siècle.* Rodez: 1947.
Bressalles, Mgr., *Saint Agobard, évêque de Lyon.* Paris: 1949.
Breuils, A., *St. Austinde et la Gascogne au XIe siècle.* Auch: 1895.
Brouens, M., "Le peuplement germanique de la Gaule entre Méditerranée et l'ocean," in *Annales du Midi,* Vol. XLVIII (1956).
Brousse, C., "La vicomté de Castellnou," in *Etudes Rouissillonnaises,* Vol. III (1953).
Brunel, C., "Les juges de la paix en Gévaudun au milleu du XIe siècle," in *Bibliothèque de l'Ecole des Chartes,* Vol. CIX (1951).
Brutails, A. *Etude sur la population rurale dans le Roussillon au Moyen Age.* Paris: 1878.
Busquet, R., "Rois de Bourgogne et comtes de Provence," in *Provence Historique,* Vol. III (1950-1951).
Calmette, J., "A propos de la famille de Joffre le Poilu," in *Annales du Midi,* Vol. XXXVII (1925).
—, "A propos d'un duché de Roussillon au Xe siècle," in *Etudes Médiévales.* Toulouse: 1946.

—, "Bourgogne et Midi à l'epoque Carolingienne," in *Annales de Bourgogne*, Vol. XIII (1941).
—, "Les comtes Bernard sous Charles le Chauve," in *Mélanges Louis Halphen*. Paris: 1951.
—, "Les comtes d'Auvergne et les comtes de Velay sous Charles le Chauve," in *Annales du Midi*, Vol. XVI (1904).
—, "Comtes de Toulouse inconnus," in *Mélanges Antoine Thomas*. Paris: 1927.
—, "Les comtés et les comtes de Toulouse et de Rodez sous Charles le Chauve," in *Annales du Midi*, Vol. XVII (1905).
—, *De Bernardo, Sancti Wilelmi filio*. Toulouse: 1902.
—, "Un diplôme original du Comte Frédélon," in *Annales du Midi*, Vol. XLII (1930).
—, "La Famille de Saint Guillem," in *Annales du Midi*, Vol. XVIII (1906).
—, "La Famille de Saint Guillem et l'ascedance de Robert le Fort," in *Annales du Midi*, Vol. XL (1928).
—, "Gaucelme, Marquis de Gothie sous Louis le Pieux," in *Annales du Midi*, Vol. XVIII (1906).
—, "Un jugement original de Wifred le Velu pour l'abbaye d'Amer (17 Avril 898)," in *Bibliothèque de l'Ecole des Chartes*, Vol. LXVII (1906).
—, "Le Marquis de Gothie," in *Annales du Midi*, Vol. XIV (1902).
—, "Les Marquis de Gothie sous Charles le Chauve," in *Annales du Midi*, Vol. XIV (1902).
—, "Note sur les premiers comtes Carolingiens d'Urgell," in *Mélanges d'archéologie et d'histoire de l'école française à Rome*, Vol. XXII (1902).
—, "Notes sur Wifred le Velu," in *Revista de Archivos, Bibliotecas y Museos*, Vol. V (1901).
—, "Onfroy, Marquis de Gothie," in *Etudes Médiévales*, Toulouse: 1946.
—, "Les origines de la première maison comtale de Barcelone," in *Mélanges d'archéologie et d'histoire de l'école française à Rome*, Vol. XX (1900).
—, *La Question des Pyrénees et la Marche d'Espagne au Moyen Age*. Paris: 1947.
—, "Rampon, Comte de Gerona et Marquis de Gothie," in *Le Moyen Age*, Vol. V (1901).
—, "Le sentiment national dans la Marche d'Espagne au IXe siècle," in *Mélanges Ferdinand Lot*. Paris: 1927.
—, "Le siège de Toulouse par les Normands," in *Annales du Midi*, Vol. XXIX (1917).
—, *La société féodale*, 4th ed. Paris: 1938.
Cantor, N., "The Crisis of Western Monasticism," in *American Historical Review*, Vol. LXCI (1961).
Carabie, R., *La propriété foncière dans le très ancien droit Normand: I. La propriété domaniale*. Caen: 1943.

Carreras y Candi, F., "Lo Montjuich de Barcelona," in *Memorias de la Real Academia de Buenas Letras de Barcelona*, Vol. VIII (1901).
—, "Relaciones de los vizcondes de Barcelona con los árabes," in *Homenaje de D. Francisco Codera*. Zaragoza: 1904.
Castaigng-Sicard, M., "Donations Toulousaines du Xe au XIIIe siècles," in *Annales du Midi*, Vol. LXX (1958).
Catel, G. *Histoire des comtes de Toulouse*. Toulouse: 1623.
—, *Mémoires de L'histoire de Languedoc*. Toulouse: 1633.
Cavet, E. *Etude historique sur l'établissement des Espagnols dans la Septimanie*. Montpellier: 1898.
Chaplais, F., "Le traité de Paris de 1259 et l'inféodation de la Gascogne allodiale," in *Le Moyen Age*, Vol. LXI (1955).
Chaume, M., "Bérenger, Comte de Toulouse," in *Annales du Midi*, Vol. LII (1940).
—, "Les comtes d'Autun des VIIIe et IXe siècles," in *Mémoires de la société éduenne*, Vol. XLVIII (1937).
—, "Onfroi, Marquis de Gothie, ses origines et ses attaches familiales," in *Annales du Midi*, Vol. LII (1940).
—, "L'Origine Carolingienne des ducs féodaux d'Aquitaine," in *Annales du Midi*, Vol. LIX (1947).
—, *Les origines du duché de Bourgogne*, 4 vols. Dijon: 1927–1935.
—, "Les premières Croisades bourguignones au delà des Pyrénées," in *Annales de Bourgogne*, Vol. XVIII (1946).
—, "Le problème des origines de la Maison de Savoie," in *Annales de Bourgogne*, Vol. III (1931).
—, "Sur une esquisse d'histoire agraire et rurale au haut moyen âge," in *Annales de Bourgogne*, Vol. XIV (1942).
Chénon, E., *Histoire de la propriété des alleux en France*. Paris: 1888.
—, *Histoire générale du droit français public et privé des origines à 1815*, 2 vols. Paris: 1926–1929.
—, "Le rôle juridique de l'osculum dans l'ancien droit français," in *Mémoires de la société des Antiquaires de France*, 8th ser, Vol. VI (1924).
Chevrier, G., "Conjectures sur l'originalité du droit féodal dans les deux Bourgognes," in *Annales de Bourgogne*, Vol. XXIII (1951).
—, "Contribution à l'étude de l'acte à cause de mort au moyen âge," in *Mémoires de la société historique de droit et des institutions des anciens pays bourguignons, comtois et romans*, No. 12 (1948–1949).
—, *Déclin et renaissance du testament en droit bourguignon*. Dijon: 1952.
—, "L'évolution de l'acte à cause de mort en Dauphiné du VIIe à la fin du Xe siècle," in *Recueil de la société historique de droit et des institutions des pays du droit écrit*, Vol. I (1948).
—, "Sur les origines des cours de justice féodales," in *Annales de Bourgogne*, Vol. XXI (1949).

Codera y Zaidín, F., "Embajadas de príncipes cristianos en Córdova en los últimos años de Alhaquem II," in *Colección de Estudios Árabes*, Vol. IX. Madrid: 1917.

—, "Expedición a Pamplona de los condes francos Elbo y Aznar," in *Colección de Estudios Árabes*, Vol. VII. Zaragoza: 1903.

—, "Límites probables de la dominación árabe en la cordillera pirenaica," in *Colección de Estudios Árabes*, Vol. VIII. Madrid: 1915.

—, "Mohamed Atavil, rey Moro de Huesca," in *Colección de Estudios Árabes*, Vol. VII. Zaragoza: 1903.

Coll i Alenthorn, M., "La historiographia de Catalunya en el período primitivo," in *Estudis Romanços*, Vol. III (1951–1952).

Columbi, G., *Episcopi Valentiniani*, Vol. VII. Valence: 1754.

Coulbourn, R. (ed.), *Feudalism in History*. Princeton: 1956.

Courteault, P., *Histoire de Gascogne et de Béarn*. Paris: 1938.

David, M., *Le serment de sacre du IXe au Xe siècle*. Strasbourg: 1951.

Declareuil, J., *Histoire générale du droit français des origines à 1789*. Paris: 1925.

Défourneaux, M., *Les Français en Espagne aux XIe et XIIe siècles*. Paris: 1949.

—, "Charlemagne et la monarchie Asturienne," in *Mélanges Louis Halphen*. Paris: 1951.

Degret, A., "Le pouvoir royal en Gascogne sous les derniers Carolingiens et les premiers Capétiens," in *Revue des Questions Historiques*, Vol. XXVIII (1902).

Delage, F., and G. Brussel, "Un domaine carolingien au Limousin, Cavalicus," in *Bulletin de la société archéologique et historique du Limousin*, Vol. LXXXIV (1952–1954).

Delcambre, E., "Géographie historique du Velay, du pagus, au comté et au baillage," in *Bibliothèque de l'Ecole des Chartes*, Vol. XCVIII (1937).

Déléage, A., "Les forteresses de la Bourgogne franque," in *Annales de Bourgogne*, Vol. III (1931).

—, *La vie économique et sociale en Bourgogne dans le haut moyen âge*, 3 vols. Mâcon: 1941.

Depoin, J., "Les comtes héréditaires d'Angoulême de Vougrin Ier à Audoin II," in *Bulletin de la société archéologique et historique de la Charente*, Vol. XXX (1904).

De Vic, C., and J. Vaissette, *Histoire Générale de Languedoc*, ed. Privat, Vols. II–IX. Toulouse: 1872–1894.

Dhondt, J., *Etude sur la naissance des principalités territoriales en France*. Bruges: 1948.

Duby, G., "Recherches sur l'évolution des institutions judiciaires pendent le Xe et le XIe siècles dans le sud de la Bourgogne," in *Le Moyen Age*, Vols. LII–LIII (1946–1947).

—, *La société aux XIe et XIIe siècles dans la région mâconnaise*. Paris: 1953.

Bibliography

—, "Les villes du sud-est de la Gaule du VIIIe au XIe siècle," in *La Città dell'alto medioevo*, Vol. VI (Spoleto: 1959).
Dumas, A., "Encore la question: Fidèles or vassaux?" in *Nouvelle revue historique de droit français et étranger*, Vol. XLIV (1920).
—, "Quelques observations sur la grande et la petite propriété à l'époque carolingienne," in *Revue historique de droit français et étranger*, Vol. IV (1926).
Dupont, A., *Les cités de la Narbonnaise première depuis les invasions germaniques*. Nîmes: 1943.
—, "Considérations sur la colonisation et la vie rurale dans le Roussillon et la Marche d'Espagne," in *Annales du Midi*, Vol. LXVII (1955).
—, "L'exploitation du sel sur les etangs de Languedoc (IXe–XIIIe siècle)," in *Annales du Midi*, Vol. LXX (1958).
—, *Les relations commerciales entre les cités maritimes du Languedoc et les cités méditerranéennes d'Espagne et d'Italie*. Nîmes: 1942.
Duprat, E., *Essai sur l'histoire politique d'Avignon pendant le haut Moyen Age*, in *Mémoires de l'Académie de Vaucluse*, Vol. I. Mâcon: 1908.
—. See also *Bouches du Rhône*.
Eichel, A., *Charles le Simple*. Paris: 1899.
Esmein, A., *Cours élémentaire d'histoire du droit français*, 15th ed. Paris: 1925.
Estey, F., "The Fideles in the County of Mâcon," in *Speculum*, Vol. XXX (1955).
Fage, R., "La propriété en Bas Limousin pendant le Moyen Age," in *Bulletin de la société archéologique et historique du Limousin*, Vol. LXXVI (1947).
Favre, E., *Eudes, comte de Paris et roi de France (882–898)*. Paris: 1892.
Favre, F., "Étude sur la condition des personnes et des terres en Bas Languedoc du Xe au XIIIe siècle," in *Le Moyen Age*, Vol. XXIX (1933).
Fawtier, R., and F. Lot. *Histoire des institutions françaises au Moyen Age*, Vol. I. Paris: 1957.
Fazy, M., *Les origines du Bourbonnais*, 2 vols. Moulins: 1924.
Février, P., "La donation faite à Lérins par le comte Leibulfe," in *Provence Historique*, Vol. VI (1956).
Fichtenau, H., *Der karolingische Imperium*. Zurich: 1949.
Flach, J., "La Marche d'Espagne," in *Estudis Universitaris Catalans*, Vol. XVI. Barcelona: 1931.
—, *Les origines de l'ancienne France: X^e et XIe siècles*, 4 vols. Paris: 1886–1917.
Fliche, A., and V. Martin, *L'Église au pouvoir des Laïcs*, in *Histoire de l'Église*, Vol. VI. Paris: 1948.
Fontana, M., "La Réforme Grégorienne en Provence orientale," in *Annales de la Faculté de Lettres d'Aix en Provence, Travaux et Mémoires*, Vol. VIII (1926).

Font y Ríus, J., *Instituciones medievales españolas*, 2 vols. Madrid: 1949.
—, "Els origens del co-senyoriu Andorra," in *Pireneos*, Vol. XI (1955).
Fournial, E., "Notes sur la chronologie de quelques chartes du Cartulaire de Vabres," in *Revue Rouergue*, Vol. XX (1957).
—, "Recherches sur les comtes de Lyon au IXe et Xe siècles," in *Le Moyen Age*, Vol. LVIII (1952).
Fournier, G., "La Seigneurie en Basse-Auvergne aux XIe et XIIe siècles," in *Mélanges Louis Halphen*. Paris: 1951.
—, *Le peuplement rural en Basse-Auvergne durant le haut moyen âge*. Paris: 1962.
Fustel de Coulanges, G., *Histoire des institutions politiques de l'ancienne France*, Vol. VI. Paris: 1892.
Gallet, L., *Les traités de pariage dans la France féodale*. Paris: 1935.
Ganshof, F., "Benefice and Vassalage in the Age of Charlemagne," in *The Cambridge Historical Journal*, Vol. VI (1939).
—, "Charlemagne et le serment," in *Mélanges Louis Halphen*. Paris: 1951.
—, "Contribution à l'étude des cours féodales en France," in *Revue historique de droit français et étranger*, Vol. VI (1928).
—, "Une Crise dans le règne de Charlemagne, les années 778 et 779," in *Mélanges Charles Gaillard*. Lausanne: 1944.
—, "Depuis quand a-t-on pu en France être vassal de plusieurs seigneurs," in *Mélanges Paul Fournier*. Paris: 1929.
—, "La Juridiction de Seigneur sur son vassal à l'époque Carolingienne," in *Revue de l'Université de Bruxelles*, Vol. XXVII (1922).
—, "Note critique sur la biographie de Nithard," in *Mélanges Paul Thomas*. Bruges: 1930.
—, "Note sur la date de deux documents administratives émanant de Louis le Pieux," in *Receuil des travaux offerts à M. C. Brunel*, Vol. I. Paris: 1955.
—, "Note sur les origines de l'union du bénéfice avec la vassalité," in *Etudes d'histoire dédiées à la mémoire de Henri Pirenne*. Bruxelles: 1937.
—, "Notes sur les ports de Provence du VIIIe au Xe siècle," in *Revue Historique*, Vol. CLXXXIII (1938).
—, "Observations sur l'Ordinatio Imperii de 817," in *Festschrift Guido Kisch*. Stuttgart: 1955.
—, "L'origine des rapports féodo-vassiliques," in *I problemi della Civiltà Carolingia*. Spoleto: 1954.
—, *Qu'est-ce que la féodalité?* 3rd ed. Bruxelles: 1957. Trans. by P. Grierson as *Feudalism*, 2nd ed. New York: 1961.
—, *Recherches sur les capitulaires*. Paris: 1958.
Garaud, M., "Les circonscriptions administratives du comté de Poitiers et les auxiliaires du comté au Xe siècle," in *Le Moyen Age*, Vol. LIX (1953).
—, "La construction des châteaux et les déstinées de la *vicaria* et du *vicarius*

Carolingiens en Poitou," in *Revue historique de droit français et étranger,* Vol. XXXI (1953).

—, "Les origines des Pagi poitevins au moyen âge," in *Revue historique de doit français et étranger,* Vol. XXVI (1948).

—, "Les Vicomtes de Poitou," in *Revue historique de droit français et étranger,* Vol. XVI (1938).

Gariel, E., *Les monnaies royales de France sous la race carolingienne.* Strasbourg: 1883.

Génestal, R., *Le Parage Normand.* Caen: 1911.

Gouron, A., "Les étapes de la pénétration du droit romain au XIIe siècle dans l'ancienne Septimanie," in *Annales du Midi,* Vol. LXIX (1957).

Gouron, M., *Les étapes successives de Nîmes.* Nîmes: 1947.

Grierson, P., "Le sou d'or d'Uzès," in *Le Moyen Age,* Vol. LX (1954).

—, "The 'Patrinonium Petri in Illis Partibus' and the Pseudo-Imperial Coinage In Frankish Gaul," in *Revue Belge de Numismatique,* Vol. CV (1959).

Guilhiermoz, P., *Essai sur les origines de la noblesse en France au moyen âge.* Paris: 1902.

Halphen, L., "À propos du capitulaire de Quierzy," in *Revue Historique,* Vol. LXXXVI (1906).

—, *Charlemagne et l'empire Carolingien.* Paris: 1949.

—, *Le comté d'Anjou au XIe siècle.* Paris: 1906.

—, *Études critiques sur l'histoire de Charlemagne.* Paris: 1921.

—, "L'idée d'état sous les Carolingiens," in *Revue Historique,* Vol. CLXXXIV (1939).

—, "La place de la royauté dans le système féodal," in *Anuario de historia del derecho español,* Vol. IX (1933).

Herlihy, D., "Agrarian Revolution in France and Italy, 801–1150," in *Speculum,* Vol. XXXIII (1958).

—, "Church Property on the European Continent, 701–1200," in *Speculum,* Vol. XXXVI (1961).

Higounet, C., "Les Aznars, un tentatif de groupement des comtés gascons et pyrénéens au IXe siècle," in *Annales du Midi,* Vol. LXI (1949).

—, "Les chemins de Saint-Jacques et les sauvetés de Gascogne," in *Annales du Midi,* Vol. LXIII (1951).

—, "Chronique du Midi Carolingien," in *Annales du Midi,* Vol. LXVIII (1956).

—, *Le comté de Commignes de ses origines à son annexation à la Couronne,* Vol. I. Toulouse: 1949.

—, "Esquisse d'une géographie des châteaux des Pyrénées françaises au moyen âge," in *Primero Congreso de Pirineistas.* Zaragoza: 1950.

—, "Mouvements de population dans le Midi du XIe au XVe siècle," in *Annales économiques et sociales,* Vol. I (1955).

—, "Observations sur la seigneurie rurale et l'habitat en Rouergue du IXe au XIVe siècle," in *Annales du Midi*, Vol. LXII (1950).
—, "L'occupation du sol du pays entre Tarn et Garonne au moyen âge," in *Annales du Midi*, Vol. LXIV (1952).
Hilaire, J., "Les régimes matrimoniaux aux XIe et XIIe siècles dans la région de Montpellier," in *Recueils de la société historique de droit et des institutions des pays du droit écrit*, Vol. III (1955).
Hill, J., and L. Hill, *Raymond IV de St. Gilles*. Toulouse: 1959.
Hollyman, K., *Le développement du vocabulaire féodal pendant le haut Moyen Age*. Geneva: 1957.
Hoyt, R., *Feudal Institutions*. New York: 1951.
Ibarra, Rodríguez E., "La reconquista de los Estados pirenaicos hasta la muerte de Sancho el Mayor," in *Hispania, Revista española de historia*, Vol. VI. Madrid: 1942.
Imbart de la Tour, P., "Les colonies agricoles et l'occupation des terres désertes à l'époque carolingienne," in *Mélanges Paul Fabre*. Paris: 1902.
—, *Les élections épiscopales dans l'Eglise de la France du IXe au XIIe siècle*. Paris: 1890.
—, *Les origines religieuses de la France: les paroisses rurales du IVe au XIe siècle*. Paris: 1910.
Jaurguin, J., *La Vasconie*, 2 vols. Paris: 1902.
Justo, Fr. P., *Sancho el Mayor de Navarra*. Navarra: Institución del Príncipe de Viana, 1950.
Katz, S., *The Jews in the Visigothic and Frankish Kingdoms of Spain and Gaul*. Cambridge, Massachusetts: 1937.
Keeney, B., *Judgment of Peers*. Cambridge, Massachusetts: 1949.
Kehr, P., *Papsturkunden in Spanien: Vorarbeiten zur Hispania Pontifica I. Katalanien II. Navarra und Aragon* in *Abhandlungen der Gessellshaft der Wissenshaften*, Vols. XVIII (1926) and XXVI (1928).
Kendrick, T., *A History of the Vikings*. London: 1930.
Kleinclausz, A., *L'Empire Carolingien*. Paris: 1902.
Krause, V., *Geschichte des Institutes der Missi Dominici* in *Deutsches Archiv für Geschichte des Mittelalters*, 2 Jahrung (1938).
Kurth, G., *Etudes Franques*, 2 vols. Paris: 1919.
Lacarra, J., "A propos de la colonisation franca en Navarre et in Aragon," in *Annales du Midi*, Vol. LXV (1953).
—, *Un arancel de aduanas del siglo*, Vol. XI. Zaragoza: 1950.
—, *El desarollo urbano de las ciudades de Navarra y Aragón en la Edad Media*, Zaragoza: 1950.
—, *Orígines del condado de Aragón*. Zaragoza: 1945.
—, "Panorama de la Historia urbana en la Península Ibérica desde el siglo V al X," in *La Città dell'alto medioeva*. Spoleto: 1956.

—, "Textos navarros del Códice de Roda," in *Estudios de Edad Media de la Corona de Aragón*, Vol. I. Zaragoza: 1945.
—, *Vasconia medieval: Historia y Filología*. San Sebastián: 1957.
—, and L. Vásquez de Porgo. *Peregrinaciones a Santiago de Compostela*, 3 vols. Madrid: 1948–1949.
Lambert, H., "Le Livre de St. Jacques et les routes du pèlerinage de Compostelle," in *Revue Géographique des Pyrénées et du Sud-Ouest*, Vol. XIX (1943).
Latouche, R., *Histoire de Nice*. Nice: 1951.
—, *Histoire du Comté de Nice*. Paris: 1932.
—, *Les origines de l'économie occidentale*. Paris: 1956.
—, "Quelques aperçus sur le manse en Provence au Xe et au XIe siècles," in *Recueils des travaux offerts à M. C. Brunel*, Vol. II (Paris: 1953).
—, "Sainte-Foy-de-Conques et le problème d'or aux temps Carolingiens," in *Annales du Midi*, Vol. XLVII (1956).
Lauer, P., "Les Actes carolingiens suspects de l'abbaye de Lagrasse," in *Bulletin de la commission des travaux historiques*. Paris: 1926–1927.
—, *Louis IV d'Outremer*. Paris: 1900.
—, *Robert I et Raoul de Bourgogne, rois de France*. Paris: 1912.
Le Gentilhomme, P., *Mélanges de Numismatique Merovingienne*. Paris: 1940.
—, "Le Monnayage et la circulation monétaire dans les royaumes barbares en occident (V^e–VIIIe siècles)," in *Revue Numismatique*, Vol. VII–VIII (1943–1945).
Leicht, P., "Il Feudo in Italia nell'età Carolingia," in *I problemi della Civiltà Carolingia*. Spoleto: 1954.
—, "Gasindi e Vassali," in *Rendiconti della Reale Academia Nazionale dei Lincei: Classe di Scienze Morali, storiche e filologiche*, Vol. III (1927).
—, "L'Introduzione de feudo nell'Italia franca e normanna," in *Revista di storia del diritto italiano*, Vol. XII (1939).
Lemarignier, J., "Les Fidèles du roi de France," in *Recueils de travaux offerts à M. C. Brunel*, Vol. II (Paris: 1955).
—, *Recherches sur l'hommage en Marche et les frontières féodales*. Lille: 1945.
Letonnelier, G., "Essai sur l'origine des châtelains et des mandaments en Dauphiné," in *Annales de l'Université de Grenoble*, Vol. I (1889).
Lesne, E., "Les diverses acceptions du terme 'beneficium' du VIIIe au XIe siècle," in *Revue historique de droit français et étranger*, Vol. II (1924).
—, *Histoire de la propriété ecclésiastique en France*, 6 vols. Lille: 1910–1943.
Levillain, L., "Ademar de Chabannes, généalogiste," in *Bulletin de la société des antiquaires de l'ouest*, Vol. XXIX (1934).
—, "De quelques personages nommés Bernard dans les Annales de Hincmar," in *Mélanges Felix Grat*. Paris: 1946.
—, *Examen des chartes de Corbie*. Paris: 1901.
—, "Giraut, Comte de Vienne," in *Le Moyen Age*, Vol. LV (1949).

—, "Les Nibelungen historiques et leurs alliances de famille," in *Annales du Midi*, Vol. XLIX–L (1937–1938).

—, "Les personages du nom de Bernard (Bernard Veau, Bernard de Gothie, Bernard Plantevelue) dans la seconde moitié du IXe siècle," in *Le Moyen Age*, Vol. LIV (1948).

Lévi-Provençale, E., *L'Espagne Musulmane au Xe siècle*. Paris: 1932.

—, *Histoire de l'Espagne Musulmane*. Cairo: 1944.

Lewis, A., "Le commerce maritime et la navigation sur les côtes de la Gaule atlantique du Ve au VIIIe siècle," in *Le Moyen Age*, Vol. LIX (1953).

—, "The Development of Town Government in Twelfth Century Montpellier," in *Speculum*, Vol. XXII (1947).

—, *Naval Power and Trade in the Mediterranean A.D. 500–1100*. Princeton: 1951.

—, *The Northern Seas A.D. 300–1100*. Princeton: 1958.

—, "Seigneurial Administration in Twelfth Century Montpellier," in *Speculum*, Vol. XXII (1947).

Lot, F., "Une année du règne de Charles le Chauve," in *Le Moyen Age*, Vol. VI (1902).

—, "Amaugin, Comte de Bordeaux," in *Annales du Midi*, Vol. XVI (1904).

—, *Les Derniers Carolingiens: Lothaire, Louis V, Charles de Lorraine*. Paris: 1892.

—, "Etudes Carolingiennes: Les Comtes d'Auvergne entre 846 et 877; Les Comtes d'Autun entre 864 et 878," in *Bibliothèque de l'Ecole des Chartes*, Vol. CII (1941).

—, *Etudes sur le règne de Hughes Capet*. Paris: 1903.

—, *Fidèles ou vassaux?* Paris: 1904.

—, *La fin du Monde Antique*, 2nd ed. Paris: 1951.

—, "Garsia-Sanche, duc de Gascogne," in *Annales du Midi*, Vol. XVI (1904).

—, "La grande invasion normande de 856–62," in *Le Moyen Age*, Vol. XII (1908).

—, *L'impôt foncier et la capitation personnelle sous le Bas Empire et à l'époque franque*. Paris: 1928.

—, "Les judgements d'Aix et de Quierzy," in *Bibliothèque de l'Ecole des Chartes*, Vol. LXXXII (1921).

—, "La Loire, l'Aquitaine et la Seine de 862 à 866 et Robert le Fort," in *Bibliothèque de l'Ecole des Chartes*, Vol. LXXVI (1915).

—, "Origine et nature du bénéfice," in *Anuario de historia del derecho español*, Vol. X (1934).

—, "Le serment de fidélité à l'époque franque," in *Revue Belge*, Vol. XII (1933).

—, "La vicaria et le vicarius," in *Revue historique de droit français et étranger*, Vol. X (1893).

—, and L. Halphen, *Le règne de Charles le Chauve (842–877)*. Paris: 1902.

Bibliography

—. See also Fawtier, R.
Luchaire, A., *Manuel des institutions françaises: Période des Capétiens directs.* Paris: 1902.
Lutti, B., *I Saraceni in Provenza, in Liguria e nelle Alpi Orientali.* Bordighera: 1952.
Lyon, B., *From Fief to Indenture.* Cambridge, Massachusetts: 1957.
Malafosse, J. de, "Contribution à l'étude de crédit dans le Midi aux Xe et XIe siècles," in *Annales du Midi,* Vol. LXIII (1951).
Manteyer, G. de, "Les origines de la maison de Savoie en Bourgogne (910–1060)," in *Mélanges d'archéologie et d'histoire de l'école française à Rome,* Vol. XIX (1899).
—, "Les origines de la maison de Savoie en Bourgogne. Notes additionnelles," in *Le Moyen Age,* Vol. V (1901).
—, *La Provence du Ier au XIIe siècle.* Paris: 1908.
Marovall, J., *El concepto de España en la Edad Media.* Madrid: 1954.
Mas, J., *Notes historiques del Bisbat de Barcelona,* Vols. VIII–XII. Barcelona: 1908–1915.
Masdeu, J., *Saint Joan de les abadesses.* Vich: 1926.
Mateu y Llopis, F., "De la Hispania tarraconense visigoda a la Marca hispánica Carolina," in *Analecta Sacra Tarraconensis,* Vol. XIX. Barcelona: 1947.
Melchior, G., *Les Establissements des Espagnols dans les Pyrénées Méditerranéennes du VIIIe et IXe siècles.* Montpellier: 1919.
Menédez-Pidal, R., "Los Godos y el origen de la epopeya española," in *I Goti in Occidenti Problemi.* Spoleto: 1956.
Merlet, R., "La famille de Bérenger," in *Mélanges Ferdinand Lot.* Paris: 1925.
Mertier, R., *La Senauchausée de la Basse-Marche.* Paris: 1912.
Mitteis, H., *Lehnrecht und Staatsgewalt.* Weimar: 1933.
Molinier, A., "Étude sur l'administration féodale en Languedoc," in *Hist. Gén. de Lang.,* Vol. VII.
—, "Sur les invasions Arabes dans le Languedoc," in *Hist. Gén. de Lang.,* Vol. II.
Moliné, A., *L'organisation judiciaire, militaire et financière des associations de la Paix.* Toulouse: 1902.
Mollat, G., "Restitutions des églises privées du IXe au XIe siècle," in *Revue historique de droit français et étranger,* Vol. XXVII (1949).
Monod, G., "Du rôle de l'opposition des races et des nationalités dans la dissolution de l'empire carolingien," in *Annuaire de l'Ecole des Hautes Etudes,* Vol. XXII (1896).
Morel-Fatio, A., *Catalogue raisonné de la collection des deniers merovingiens des VIIe et VIIIe siècles de la trouvaille de cimiez.* Paris: 1890.
Mundy, J., *Liberty and Political Power in Toulouse (1050–1300).* New York: 1954.

Navel, H., "Recherches sur les institutions féodales en Normandie," in *Bulletin de la société des Antiquaires de Normandie,* Vol. LI (1948–1951).
Newman, W., *Le domaine royal sous les premiers Capétiens (987–1160).* Paris: 1937.
Nicolau d'Oliver, L., "La Catalogne à l'époque romane: Le cadre historique et social," in *Bibliothèque de la Fondation Catalane à l'Université de Paris,* Vol. II (1932).
—, "L'escola poètica de Ripoll en els sigles X–XII," in *Annuari de l'Institut d'Estudis Catalans,* Vol. VI. Barcelona: 1923.
—, "Gerbert y la cultura catalana del siglo X," in *Estudis Universitaris Catalans,* Vol. IV (1910).
Nussac, L. de, "Trouvaille de monnaies médiévales à Argentat," in *Bulletin de la société historique et archéologique de la Corrèze,* Vol. LXVI (1944).
Odegaard, C., "Carolingian oaths of fidelity," in *Speculum,* Vol. XVI (1941).
—, "The Concept of Royal Power in Carolingian Oaths of Fidelity," in *Speculum,* Vol. XX (1945).
—, *Vassi and Fideles in the Carolingian Empire.* Cambridge, Massachusetts: 1945.
Olivier-Martin, F., *Histoire du droit français des origines à la Revolution.* Paris: 1948.
Ourliac, P., "L'origine des comtes de Commignes," in *Recueil de travaux offerts à M. C. Brunel,* Vol. II (Paris: 1955).
Painter, S., "Castellans in the Plain of Poitou in the Eleventh and Twelfth Century," in *Speculum,* Vol. XXXI (1956).
Parisot, R., *Le royaume de Lorraine sous les Carolingiens (843–923).* Paris: 1894.
Pérez de Urbel, J., "Lo viejo y lo nuevo sobre el origin del Reino de Pamplona," in *Al-Andalus,* Vol. XIX (1954).
Perroy, E., *La féodalité en France du Xe au XIIe siècle.* Paris: 1958.
—, *Les institutions publiques et privées de l'ancienne France.* Paris: 1935.
Petot, P., "L'hommage servile: essai sur la nature juridique de l'hommage," in *Revue historique de droit français et étranger,* Vol. VI (1928).
Pfister, C., *Études sur le règne de Robert le Pieux.* Paris: 1947.
Ponsch, P., "A propos de la date du décès de Wilfred le Velu," in *Études Roussillonnaises,* Vol. II (1952).
—, "Le Confluent et ses comtes du IXe au XIIe siècle," in *Études Roussillonnaises,* Vol. I (1951).
—, "Le domaine foncier de Saint-Michel de Cuxa au IXe, X[e], et XIe siècles," in *Études Roussillonnaises,* Vol. II (1952).
—, "Le légitimisme Carolingien en Roussillon (987)," in *Études Roussillonnaises,* Vol. II (1952).
—, "Les origines de l'abbaye d'Arles," in *Études Roussillonnaises,* Vol. IV (1954–1955).

—, "Les origines de Saint-Michel de Cuxa," in *Études Roussillonnaises*, Vol. II (1952).
—, "Le role de Saint-Michel de Cuxa dans la formation de l'historiographie de Catalogne et l'historiographie de la legénde de Wilfred le Velu," in *Études Roussillonnaises*, Vol. IV (1954).
Portal, C., *Histoire de la région Albigeoise*. Albi: 1911.
Portejoie, P., "Le régime des fiefs d'après la coutume de Poitou," in *Mémoires de la société des Antiquaires de l'ouest*, Vol. III (1959).
Poupardin, R., "Les grandes familles comtales à l'époque Carolingienne," in *Revue Historique*, Vol. LXXII (1900).
—, *Le Royaume de Bourgogne (888–1038)*. Paris: 1907.
—, *Le Royaume de Provence sous les Carolingiens*. Paris: 1901.
Prou, M., *Catalogue des Monnaies Carolingiennes*. Paris: 1896.
Rabanis, M., *Les Mérovingiens d'Aquitaine: Essai historique et critique sur la charte d'Aláon*. Paris: 1856.
Rambault, L., "La Numismatique Provençale," in *Bouches du Rhône: Encyclopédie départementale*, Vol. II. Marseille: 1924.
Rapports du IXᵉ Congrès International des Sciences Historiques, Vol. I. Paris: 1950.
Regné, J., *Étude sur la condition des Juifs de Narbonne du Vᵉ au XIVᵉ siècle*. Narbonne: 1913.
Rey, R., *Les vielles églises fortifiées du Midi de la France*. Paris: 1925.
Richard, A., *Histoire des Comtes de Poitou (778–1126)*, 2 vols. Paris: 1903–1904.
Richard, J., *Les ducs de Bourgogne et la formation du duché du XIᵉ au XIVᵉ siècle*. Dijon: 1954.
Richardot, H., "A propos des personnes et des terres féodales. Conversions, dissociations, interférences," in *Études d'histoire du droit privé offerts à Pierre Petot*. Paris: 1959.
—, "Le fief routurier à Toulouse," in *Revue historique de droit français et étranger*, Vol. XIII (1935).
—, "Francs fiefs: essai sur l'exemption totale ou partielle des services de fief," in *Revue historique de droit français et étranger*, Vol. XXVII (1949).
—, "L'hommage: Sa nature et ses applications dans l'ancien droit français," in *Études de droit contemporain: Contributions françaises aux IIIᵉ et IVᵉ Congrès internationaux de droit comparé*. Paris: 1959.
—, "Notes sur les routuriers possesseurs de fiefs nobles," in *Annales de la Faculté de Droit d'Aix*, Vol. XLIII (1950).
—, "Quelques textes sur la reprise de censive en fief," in *Revue historique de droit français et étranger*, Vol. XXVIII (1950).
Rubio, J., " 'Donationes post obitum' y 'donationes reservato usufructu' en la alta Edad Media de León y Castilla," in *Anuario de historia del derecho español*, Vol. IX (1933).

Salin, E., *La Civilisation Merovingienne*, 3 vols. Paris: 1950–1956.
Samarin, C., "Les institutions en Gascogne," in R. Fawtier and F. Lot, *Histoire des institutions françaises au Moyen Age*, Vol. I. Paris: 1957.
—, "Le plus ancien cartulaire de Sant-Mond (Gers)," in *Bibliothèque de l'Ecole des Chartes*, Vol. CX (1952).
Sánchez-Albórnoz, C., "Alphonso III y el particularismo Castellano," in *Cuadernos de Historia de España*, Vol. XIII. Buenos Aires: 1953.
—, "La auténtica batalla de Clajevo," in *Cuadernos de Historia de España*, Vol. IX. Buenos Aires: 1948.
—, *La España Musulmana*. Buenos Aires: 1946.
—, "España y el feudalismo Carolingia," in *I problemi della Civiltà Carolingia*. Spoleto: 1954.
—, "La potestad real y los señorios en Léon y Castillo en los siglos VIII a XIII," in *Revista de Archivos, Bibliotecas y Museos*, 3rd ser., Vol. XXXI (1914).
—, *El "stipendium" hispano-godo y los orígines del beneficio pre-feudal*. Buenos Aires: 1947.
—, *En torno a los orígines del feudalismo*, 3 vols. Mendoza: 1942.
Serra Vilàro, J., *Baronies de Pinos i Metaplana*, 3 vols. Barcelona: 1930–1954.
—, "Senyoriu de la viscomtal familia Miró," in *Boletín del Centro Excursionista de Catalunya*. Barcelona: 1909.
Serrano y Sans, J., *Noticias y documentos históricos del Condado de Ribagorça*. Madrid: 1912.
Shetelig, H., *An Introduction to the Viking History of Western Europe*. Oslo: 1940.
Sobqueros, S., *Els barons de Catalunya*. Barcelona: 1957.
Société Jean Bodin, Recueils I. *Les liens de la vassalité et les immunites* (Bruxelles: 1936; 2nd ed. Bruxelles: 1958). III. *La Tenure* (Bruxelles: 1938). IV. *Le Domaine* (Weteren: 1949).
Sola Molas, J., *El condado de Ausona en medio-evo*, Vol. II. Vich: 1933.
Soldevila, F., *Historia de Catalunya*, Vols. I–II. Barcelona: 1934–1936.
Stephenson, C., *Medieval Feudalism*. Ithaca: 1942.
—, "The Origins and Significance of Feudalism," in *American Historical Review*, Vol. XLVI (1946).
Tenant de la Tour, G., *L'homme et la terre de Charlemagne à Saint Louis*. Paris: 1943.
Tessier, G., "A propos de quelques actes toulousains du IX⁰ siècle," in *Recueil de travaux offerts à M. C. Brunel*, Vol. II. Paris: 1955.
Thomas, G., *Les comtes de la Marche de la maison de Charroux (X⁰ siècle–1177)*. Paris: 1928.
Thomas, P., *Le droit de propriété des laïcs sur les églises*. Paris: 1906.
Thompson, J., *The Dissolution of the Carolingian Fisc in the Ninth Century*. Berkeley: 1935.

Tisset, P., *L'Abbaye de Gellone au diocèse de Lodève*. Paris: 1933.
—, "Placentin et son enseignement à Montpellier," in *Recueils de la société historique de droit et des institutions des pays du droit écrit,* Vol. II (1951).
Tulippe, O., *Le manse à l'époque Carolingienne.* Liège: 1936.
Valls-Taberner, F., "La Cour Comtale Barcelonaise," in *Revue historique de droit français et étranger,* Vol. XIV (1936).
—, "Un diplôme de Charles le Chauve pour Sunaire, Comte d'Ampurias-Roussillon," in *Le Moyen Age,* Vol. XV (1919).
—, "Estudi sobre els documents del Comte Guifré de Barcelona," in *Estudis Universitaris Catalans,* Vol. XXI. Barcelona: 1936.
—, "Figures de l'època comtal Catalana," in *Annuari Heraldic.* Barcelona: 1917.
—, "Les genealogies de Roda o de Meya," in *Descursos de la Real Academia de Bonas Lletras.* Barcelona: 1920.
—, *Obras Selectas in Estudios Histórico-Júdicos,* Vol. II. Barcelona: 1954.
—, *Els origines dels comtats de Pallars i Ribagorça.* Barcelona: 1918.
Vasiliev, A., *The Russian Attack on Constantinople in 860.* Cambridge, Massachusetts: 1945.
Verlinden, C., *L'esclavage dans l'Europe Médiévale,* Vol. I. Bruges: 1955.
Vicens-Vives, J., *Aproximacíon a la historia de España.* Barcelona: 1952.
Zotenburg, H., "Sur les invasions Arabes dans le Languedoc," in *Hist. Gen. de Lang.,* Vol. II.

INDEX

abbeys: ravaged by Pepin, 27; cultivation of lands by, 84-85, 85 n.; royal protection of, 136; expansion of, 138-145, 172, 243-245, 318-321; lay control of, 144-145, 151-153, 317 and n., 321; tribunals held in, 216; levies against, 312; destruction of, by Moslems, 319; papal intervention in, 336. SEE ALSO Church, Roman Catholic; monastic system; individual abbeys

Abbo (of Rhone Valley): will of, 8 n., 10 and n., 14 n., 15, 16; mention of, 12, 14 and n., 15, 16 and n., 17

Abbo (viscount): 215, 275

abbots: SEE churchmen

Abd-ar-Rahman I: 22, 26, 28

Abd-ar-Rahman III: 191, 221-222

Abraham of Commignes: 39

Acbert (of Digne): 371

Acfred (count of Auvergne): 181, 212, 230

Acfred I (of Carcassonne-Razès): 109, 122

Acfred II (of Carcassonne-Razès): 122, 184 and n., 201 and n., 202

Acut (castle): 294

Adalbert (count in Marseille): 146

Adalberto of Barcelona: 374

Adelaise (abbess of Saint-Joan de les Abadesses): 250, 251 n.

Adelaise (countess of Carcassonne): 231, 275 and n., 341

Adelaise (viscountess of Narbonne): 233, 391, 396

Adelard (bishop of LePuy): 186

Adelbert (count of Périgord): 346

Adellano (castle): 295

Ademar (abbot of Saint-Etienne de Baigne): 367

Ademar (bishop): 324 n.

Ademar (count of Poitou): 106, 112 and n., 122, 181, 185

Ademar (count of Scalas): 218, 230

Ademar (viscount): 367

Adfaix, Turre of (castle): 295

Adoptionism: 41

Agde: as bishopric, 6; fortifications of, 9; destruction in, 24 and n.; control of, 251, 343, 344. SEE ALSO Saint-Andrew of Agde

Agen: mint at, 86, 173, 397; control of, 206, 347

Agepitus II (pope): 191-192, 248

Agilbert (bishop of Béziers): 159

Agobard (archbishop of Lyon): 66

Agoldi (castle): 294

Agremundo (castle): 229

agricultural development: under Carolingians, 69-84, 403; and monastic revival, 84-86, 85 n.; of 9th century, 169-173 *passim;* and expansion of cultivation, 278-283, 392-395; of 11th century, 390-395, *passim*, 400-402 *passim*. SEE ALSO colonization

Aguarnius (bishop of Cahors): 67, 84

Agudo (castle): 298

Aiga (countess of Turenne): 170 and n.

Aigobert: 78, 79

Aimery: 265

Aimery (archbishop of Narbonne): 322 n.

Aimery (lay abbot): 258

Aimery (viscount of Narbonne): 371

Ainay (abbey): 244

Aix-en-Provence: archbishopric of, 6, 323; moslem raids near, 222; archbishop of, 333

Aix-la-Chapelle: as seat of Carolingian authority, 41, 43, 51, 53, 64; conference of border counts at, 45, 47 n.; *hispani* take grievance to, 70 and n., 71

—, Council of: 39, 47 n., 83

Aizo: 46, 93, 172

Aláo (abbey): 48, 82

Albaniya. SEE Saint-Peter of Albaniya

Albaniya (castle): 374

Albi: viscontal control of, 116, 196, 206,

207, 350, 372; bishopric of, 250, 265–266, 324, 351, 368, 398; assembly at, 368; mint at, 397; mention of, 7, 231, 357. SEE ALSO Albigeois; Saint-Sernin of Albi; Saint-Velesius of Albi
Albi (castle): 293
Albigeois: Frankish landowners in, 13; Moslems in, 18, 21; serfs in, 169; control of, 206, 351; fortifications in, 238, 292–293, 299; landholding in, 265, 384, 386 n., 387; agricultural development of, 278; political development of, 278; political development of, 340; mention of, 10, 26 and n. SEE ALSO Albi; Rouergue-Albigeois
—, church in: restoration of, 15; usurpation of property of, 147; property of, 156, 247, 248, 387
Albinaño (castle): 298, 299, 303
Aldouin (count of Angoulême): rule of, 106, 122, 132, 226, 296; properties of, 302, 305, 356
Aldouin II: 347, 348 n., 352, 353
Aléran (count): 104
Ales (castle): 298
Alet (abbey): 82 n.
Alexander (archbishop of Vienne): 244
Alexander III: 336
Alguaire (castle): 221
Allidaf (viscount): 150
allods: transfer of property into, 212–214, 253, 354–355, 403, 404; castles as, 230–235, 301–310 *passim*; Church ownership of, 238, 255 n., 256, 371; prevalence of, 273, 383–385; limitations on, 328; and political power, 354–357. SEE ALSO land; landholders; landholding
Almansor (Moslem): 191, 288
Almeradus (bishop of Reiz): 370
Almis (castle): 294, 304
Almodis of La Marche: as wife of Count Pons of Toulouse, 275, 346, 351, 366; power of, 392 and n.; as wife of Raymond Berengar I, 392 and n.
Alpheus: 15 n.
Al-Tamil (lord of Huesca): 221

Altonum (castle): 294
Alzonne (castle): 131, 134, 205 n., 228, 238
Amblard (archbishop of Lyon): 278 n.
Amer (abbey): 244
Ampurias: under Louis the Pious, 44; mint at, 86, 173, 276; fortification of, 131
Ampurias-Roussillon: house of, 109, 112 and n., 197, 348; political stability of, 208. SEE ALSO Ampurias, Roussillon
Anastasius (abbot of Conques): 67
Andorra. SEE Urgell
Anduze: house of, 323 and n., 343–344, 351–352, 358; mention of, 295, 341, 345.
Anduze (castle): 62, 130, 133, 227, 302, 343 and n.
Angély. SEE Saint-Jean d'Angély
Angély (castle): 296
Angevin House. SEE Anjou, house of
Angoulême: fortifications of, 9, 132, 226, 296–297; sacking of, 27, 101; mint at, 86, 397; political development of, 115, 118, 122, 181, 196, 341, 347–348, 377 and n.; secular court in, 125 and n.; Church in, 147, 243, 246, 325; serfdom in, 169, 274, 390; agricultural development in, 279; dukes of Aquitaine in, 288, 347; nature of landholding in, 383–384; house of, 345–348, 351–352, 356; mention of, 367, 368. SEE ALSO Saint-Cybord of Angoulême
Angoulême-Périgord: nature of landholding in, 156, 157, 210, 262; house of, 184, 197, 206, 250. SEE ALSO Angoulême; Périgord
Aniane: castle in, 130
Aniane (abbey): 62, 66, 81, 126, 134, 140 and n., 146, 168, 246, 255, 275, 315, 316 n., 323, 333, 343 and n., 358, 395
Anjou, house of: 288, 377 n., 378
Ansemundus [Misemundus] (Gothic count): 7 n., 8 n., 24, 25, and n., 30, 31

Index 437

Antibes: bishropric of, 323; bishop of, 371, mention of, 345
Appolonius (count): 105 and n., 116, 134, 161, 162
aprisio: nature of, 68, 70–74, 70 n., 79–80, 272–274, 282, 390–395; as method of acquiring allod, 158–160, 163, 164; as method of colonization, 282; regional differences of, 401; begun by Carolingians, 403. SEE ALSO benefices; land; landholding
aprisiones: 64, 65, 71, 128. SEE ALSO landholders
Apt: 193
Aqualonga (castle): 298
Aquinas of Dauphiny: 370
Aquitaine: political development of, 3, 7–8 and n., 43–49, 51–53, 51 n., 58, 64, 289, 377–382 *passim*; castles in, 9–10, 62, 230, 240, 302, 304–305; Carolingians in, 10, 18, 20, 22–23, 26–28, 32, 92, 97; mints in, 13, 86, 173; commerce in, 13, 86, 173–175, 395; Gallo-Romans in, 14; Franks in, 14, 20, 21, 59–60; Moslems in, 20, 21; revolts in, 24, 97, 98 and n., 99; landholding in, 70 and n., 356, 384, 394; Viking raids on, 100–101, 127, 129, 220–221, 221 n., 288; noble families in, 10, 107–108, 179–191 *passim*; vicars in, 119–120; tribunal system of, 214–215; militarism in, 329, 330, 334; feudalism of, 387; mention of, 305, 185, 382
—, church of: bishoprics, 6–7; property of, 11, 82, 156; usurpation of property of, 26, 147; revival of, 84, 137–138, 321, 403; secular control of, 196, 250, 358–359
—, dukes of: power of, 197, 337, 339, 346–348, 377–379, 404; aggression by, 288–289, 289 n., 378 and n.; support of Church by, 331, 378, 394; support of monarchy by, 338, 339; feudalism of, 387; mention of, 305, 351, 356
—, Western: ruling families in, 105–106; monastic decline in, 138; visit of monarchs to, 179–180, 180 n.; control of, 188, 377, 378; trade ships out of, 277; castles in, 311; political development of, 345–348; nature of assembly in, 367; Church in, 367; landholding in, 383–385, 386, and n.; serfs in, 390
Aquitanians: 28, 41, 65
Aquitaro (castle): 298
Aragón: Basques in, 4; Frankish control of, 42; revolt of, 43, 93; Carolingian control of, 64; Moslem attacks on, 221; mention of, 340, 376, 382
Arampuña (castle): 209, 229, 239, 305
archbishoprics: royal protection of, 56 and n., 136, 148 n.; political authority of, 196; family control of, 321. SEE ALSO Church, Roman Catholic; churchmen
Archimbaud (viscount of Limousin): 367
Archinose (castle): 294
Ardaval (castle): 298
Ardebert (priest): 80
Aredus: 11
Arena of Nîmes (castle): 130, 133 and n.
Areng (castle): 298
Argaton (castle): 297
Arlerc (castle): 294, 304
Arles: as ecclesiastic center, 6, 125; fortifications of, 9, 102, 130; Moslems in, 23 and n., 101; capture of, by Franks, 23 and n.; mint at, 86, 173, 175; archbishop of, 129, 175; Italian trading ships in, 277; archbishopric of, 323; mention of, 63, 333, 388
Arles (Auch) (abbey): 140, 142, 143, 146
Arles-sur-Teche (abbey): 81, 142, 143, 152
Arnald (of Commignes): 213, 265
Arnaud (count of Fézensac): 106
Arnold (viscount of Carcassonne): 332
Arnold Eudes (viscount): 332
Arnulf (archbishop of Narbonne): 148–149, 163, 186
Arnulf (bishop of Gerona): 255, 282

Arsinde (countess of Carcassonne): 275, 278
Arsinde (viscountess): 124
Artald (count of Lyon): 225, 326 and n., 339 n.
Artiga (castle): 294
Asnar Galindo (count of Aragón and Urgell-Cerdanya): rule by, 44, 96, 117; attack on Moslems by, 65; *aprisios* of, 71, 73, 75, 160, 164; as usurper of Pallars-Ribagorça, 110; revolt by, 117; mention of, 43, 45, 63, 64
assemblies, regional: nature of, 364–366, 373–377 *passim*, 383, 401–404 *passim*. SEE ALSO *guirpitios*; judicial system; law; tribunals
Astarac (county): 208, 340
Astronomus: 31–32
Astronove: 132, 161
Astrudis (abbess): 369
Asturias: 4, 41, 220, 277
Aton (viscount of Albi): 213, 238, 369
Aton (viscount of Nîmes): 372
Aton II (viscount of Albi): 304
Auch (archbishropric of): 139, 243, 321. SEE ALSO Arles (Auch)
Auch (church): 243
Audelino (castle): 298
Aureolus (count of Aragón): 42, 43, 64
Auriac (castle): 294, 296, 304
Auribello (castle): 294
Aurilbert (bishop of Valence): 233
Aurillac (abbey): castrum at, 132; mention of, 141 and n., 151, 258, 330
Auriol (castle): 294, 371
Aurose (castle): 292
Ausona: castles in, 41, 131, 133, 229, 238, 239, 305; Carolingian aggression in, 93, 129, 131; serfs in, 170; women as landholders in, 170; colonization in, 172; Church in, 173, 248; levies in, 238–239, 239 n.; mention of, 41, 46, 73, 208–209, 379. SEE ALSO Barcelona-Gerona-Ausona
Austrasia: 3
Autun: 18, 21, 201
Auvergne: political control of, 7, 107, 181, 184, 186–187, 196, 201–202, 206,

240, 289, 339; castles in, 10, 225–226, 233, 240, 292, 301, 311, 312; Carolingian invasion of, 24, 26, 27; judicial courts in, 125, 126, 216, 219, 368; house of, 145, 253; landholding in, 166–170 *passim*; 223–224, 262, 266–269 *passim*, 268 n., 384, 386 and n.; serfs in, 169, 274, 390; importance of women in, 170, 391; agricultural development in, 172, 278–280, 392; visit of French monarchs to, 179–180; Toulousain intervention in, 281, 184, 200–201, 204, 266; by William Caput Stupe in, 189 and n.; Poitevin control of, 201, 377 and n.; militarism in, 237, 299 and n., 328, 329, 331, 334; mint in, 276; Robert as king of, 338; system of inheritance in, 389 n.; mention of, 196

—, church in: property of, 127–128, 128 n., 156, 157, 245, 247, 253, 368; power of, 145, 148, 251, 324; and Cluny, 193–194, 248, 320; monastic movement in, 243, 319; and Peace of God, 329

Ava (lady of Auvergne): 275
Avignon: Moslems in, 8 n.; fortifications of, 9, 61, 130; Childebrand in, 9 n.; Franks in, 23 and n.; mint at, 86, 173; coin hoard in, 174; *Villa* system in, 388
Avignon (castle): 294, 304
Avitus (landowner): 13
Ay (castle): 293
Azillan: 216
Aznar (count of Gascony): 44, 45, 65, 93, 96
Aznar family: 104, 211

Balciago (castle): 292
Balcoreigne (castle): 298
Balearics: 42 and n.
Banu Kasi: 6, 42
Banvure (castle): 298
Banyols. SEE Saint-Stephen of Banyols
Bar (castle): 294
Barcelona: and Carolingian aggression, 38, 41, 46, 65, 129; Frankish counts

Index 439

in, 58; fortification of, 61 and n., 131, 229, 299, 396; mint in, 86, 173, 276 and n.; political control of, 99, 377, 379–381, 379 n.; Moslems in, 100, 191, 288, 379 and n.; colonization in, 172; levies in, 239; judicial system in, 373–375, 379–380, 379 n.; expansion of, 382, 396, 399; feudalism of, 387. SEE ALSO Gerona-Besalu-Barcelona
—, bishop of: 209, 245, 322
—, church of: development of, 47–49; property of, 144, 188, 248; usurpation by, 146; monastic revival in, 245; family control of, 250, 322; power of, 321
—, counts of: as vassals of Moslems, 191, 222; founding of nunnery by, 245; power of, 337, 340, 357 and n., 404; conflict of, with neighbors, 343, 345; legal reforms by, 375–376; mention of, 188, 351, 374
—, house of, churchmen in, 250; ownership of castles by, 303, 374; alliances of, 342, 348; power of, 349, 379; new era of, 379–380, 379 n.
Barcelona-Gerona-Ausona: 208–209. SEE ALSO Ausona; Barcelona; Gerona
Barcelona-Urgell, house of: 292 and n. SEE ALSO Barcelona; Urgell
Barholmes (castle): 293
Bartone: 16 n.
Basques: nature of, 4–6; Eudes' policy toward, 22 n.; defense of, against Charlemagne, 28, 38; religion of, 39 and n., 47; as counts of Gascony, 64, 288
Baugisière: hoard at, 13 n.
Béarn (county): 208, 340, 397
Beatti Cassiani (castle): 293
Beaulieu (abbey): mention of, 108 n., 117 n., 141 and n., 142, 143, 144, 145 and n., 147, 148, 149, 151, 157, 162, 167, 219, 226, 231, 238 and n., 245, 255, 257, 259, 330.
—, abbot of: 236
Becces, Turres: 298
Begon (count of Toulouse): 42, 43, 258
Belea (castle): 296

Bellacum (castle): 297, 302
Bello [Bellum] (castle): 292
Bellommen (castle): 293
Bellomonte (castle): 293
Bellon (count of Carcassonne): 45 and n., 63, 108–110 *passim*, 109 n.
Bellum (castle): 226, 292
Belvezet: coin hoard at, 86
Bencio (count of Carcassonne): 122
Benedict VIII (pope): 349
benefices: nature of, 71, 74–80, 75 n., 166, 267–269, 271; payment for, 71, 76, 171, 404; granting of, by Church, 77–78, 153, 166; hereditary, 111 n.; become allods, 163, 171; prohibitions on, 166–168, 328; castles as, 134–135, 233 and n., 234, 235, 303–306; disappearance of, 403. SEE ALSO *aprisio*; *honores*; *precaria*
Bera (count): rule of, 41, 44, 46, 65; and Louis the Pious, 44, 58 and n., 63, 74 n.
Berano (castle): 298
Berbers: in Spain, 3. SEE ALSO Moslems
Berencs (castle): 292
Berengar (bishop of Elne): 349, 375, 399
Berengar (count of Toulouse): reorganization of Gascony by, 43–44; Carolingian frontier under, 46, 54, 92, 93, 132; castle built by, 62; death of, 96
Berengar (viscount): 398
Berengar de Araquel: 234
Berga: military action in, 41, 129, 131; control of, 46, 348, 349; colonization in, 172
Berga (castle): 298, 299
Berga-Cerdanya-Besalu: 41, 229. SEE ALSO Berga; Besalu; Cerdanya
Berga-Urgell: 292. SEE ALSO Berga; Urgell
Berilon (viscount): 163, 212
Bernard: 303
Bernard (bishop): as abbot of Aniane, 254–255
Bernard (bishop of Oriolo): 322
Bernard (count of Auvergne): 107,

115, 145 n. SEE ALSO Bernards of Auvergne
Bernard (count of Carcassonne): 342
Bernard (count of La Marche): 346
Bernard (count of Melgueil): 110, 356
Bernard (count of Périgord): 194, 210, 223, 243, 244
Bernard (count of Septimania): and Louis the Pious, 45, 46, 52 and n., 54 and n., 92, 93, 95–96, 98; death of, 98, 128; usurpation by, 146; mention of, 97, 107
Bernard (count of Toulouse): murder of, 111, 117, 127; mention of, 108 and n., 148 n.
Bernard (count of Turenne): 258 and n.
Bernard (marquis of Anduze): 323 and n., 343, 352, 372, 391
Bernard (marquis of Gothia): 105, 108, 111, 116, 118
Bernard (viscount of Albi): 230, 232, 250
Bernard (viscount of Nîmes): 265
Bernard (viscount of Tulle): 331
Bernard (viscount of Turenne): 257
Bernard Calvinus: 267
Bernard Plantevelue (count of Auvergne): a rule of, 107–108, 108 n., 111, 122, 140 and n.; and murder of Bernard of Toulouse, 127; claims by heirs of, 181, 201. SEE ALSO Bernards of Auvergne
Bernards of Auvergne, house of: 112 and n., 151, 184, 197, 224
Bernard Taillefer: 349
Berry: 7, 10, 26, 27 and n.
Berteiz (countess of Toulouse): 123, 171
Bertha (countess of Rouergue): 206, 275
Bertin (castle): 229
Bertrand (count of Gevaudun): 353 and n., 369
Bertrand (count of Provence): as co-count, 345, 355; mention of, 289, 319
Besalu: control of, 40, 348, 349; Church holdings in, 48, 248; fortification of, 131, 229; royal land gifts in, 163, 187; court system in, 375. SEE ALSO Berga-Cerdanya-Besalu; Cerdayna-Besalu; Gerona-Besalu-Barcelona; Urgell-Cerdanya-Besalu; Vallespir-Besalu-Roussillon
Besalu (castle): 298
Besaura (castle): 131, 229
Bestila: 81
Betses, Turres: 229
Béziers: fortifications of, 9, 24 and n., 62, 295; Visigoths in, 14 n.; control of, 25, 211 and n., 343–344; mint at, 86, 173, 175; viscounts in, 116, 119, 196, 249; secular courts in, 124, 372–373; women as landowners in, 170; house of Toulouse-Rouergue in, 205; money in, 399
—, church of: bishopric, 6, 366; usurpation of property of, 146, 333; property of, 156, 246; family control of, 249, 258, 323; acts against levies, 366. SEE ALSO Saint-Nazaire of Béziers
Bigorre (county): 208, 340
Bisatico (castle): 293
bishops: as members of ruling families, 249–252; power of, 254–255. SEE ALSO churchmen
bishops, lord. SEE churchmen
bishoprics: in Narbonnaise, 6; in Visigothic kingdoms, 6 n.; in Aquitaine, 7 n.; in Spanish March, 48; under Louis the Pious, 49; royal protection of, 56 n., 136; control of, by family system, 151–154, 321; political authority of, 196. SEE ALSO churchmen
Bjorn (Viking): 101, 102
Bladino of Clermont (count of Auvergne): 8 n, 11 n, 27
Blasement (abbey): 296, 318
Blavia (castle): 296, 305, 356
Bligardis: 232
Bobila of Quercy: 15
Bonefill March (jurist): 380
boni homines: in judicial system, 55, 217–219
Bonnevaux: coin hoard of, 174
Bordeaux: as ecclesiastical center, 6–7;

Index   441

fortification of, 9, 60, 61 n.; coin hoards of, 12; trade of, 13, 220, 277; mint at, 86, 173, 397; growth of, 382; archbishopric of, 138,139, 322, 358–359. SEE ALSO Bordelais
Bordelais: 14, 27, 347 and n., 348, 352
Borell (count of Barcelona-Gerona-Ausona-Cerdanya-Urgell): rebuilding of castles by, 41, 61; as a Goth, 63, 109; properties of, 161; political authority of, 191, 209 and n.; founding of abbey by, 245
Borell II (count of Barcelona): 305, 348, 349, 379 and n.
Boric (castle): 294
Bornaz (castle): 292
Borrucio (marcher lord): 374
Boson (count of Arles): 202, 210, 211, 344
Boson (count and duke of Provence): as ruler of Rhone Valley, 92, 103 and n., 110, 112 and n., 194, 214; as king of Provence, 103, 127, 129, 144; death of, 103 and n.; defeat of Moslems by, 203
Boson (viscount of Béziers): will of, 249
Boson, Castrum of (castle): 294
Boson II (count in the Limosin): rule of, 346, 347 n., 352
Boson the Old (count of La Marche): rule of, 200, 223, 235, 346
Botvilla (castle): 297
Bourbon in Auvergne (fortress): 27
Bourbon in Berry (castle): 10
bourgeois: beginnings of, 395, 399; power of, 399, 400, 402
Bourges: 6, 9, 27, 330
Boxetum (castle): 294
Boxia (castle): 228
Bré (castle): 297
Bremetense (abbey): 319
Bresantium [Brésac] (castle): 226, 259
Brézac [Bresantium] (castle): 226, 259
Brezons (castle): 293
Brioude. SEE Saint-Julien de Brioude
—, abbot of: 78
Brioux: coin hoard of, 174

Britain: trade with, 277
Britanny: expedition into, 93
Brosadolz (castle): 293
Brossac (castle): 297
Brosse (castle): 223
Bruso (castle): 294
Buchodenes (castle): 294
Budrono (castle): 292
Buerre, battle of: 23, 30
Buis: hoard at, 13 n.
Burchard (archbishop of Lyon): power of, 225, 316 and n.; attacks on, 289; family ties of, 324, 326, 335
Burg of Villanova (castle): 296
Burghals (nunnery): 245
Burgund (count of Fézenac): 38
Burgundy: as northern boundary of Midi, 3, 180–194 *passim*; military forces of, 14 and n., 23 and n., 41; conquest of, by Charles Martel, 22, 23, 58; retaliation on, by border counts, 27; as kingdom, 263; king of, 326. SEE ALSO Provence-Burgandy

Cabrera (castle): 297
Cagnes (castle): 294
Cagueli (castle): 294
Cahors: rebuilding of, 9; bishop of, 140 n., 369; convent at, 152; viscontal control of, 206, 207; mention of, 11, 231
Cairovolo (castle): 331
Caladio: villas of, 15 n.
Calaf (castle): 298
Calars (castle): 294
Camargue: 102, 130
Camberliaco (castle): 293
Camprodon. SEE Saint-Peter of Camprodon
Canneto (castle): 294
Capçir: 342
Capdeneco (castle): 293
Capetian family: rise of, 91, 92; rivalry of, with Carolingians, 180–181, 190; alliance of, with dukes of Aquitaine, 288; influence of, 338–339; ineffectiveness of, in Midi, 338; mention of, 103, 142

Capitoliensi (castle): 293, 311
Capulso (castle): 293
Carcassonne: political development of, 4, 121–123, 184, 196, 342–343, 345, 352; fortification of, 9, 296; Frankish landowners in, 13; Visigoths in, 14 n.; Moors in, 21, 40; mint at, 86, 173, 276; Gothic counts of, 98, 185–186; royal land grants in, 161–162; land cultivation in, 279. SEE Narbonnaise
—, church of: bishopric, 6; property of, 248; family control of, 322, 323; acts against levies, 366
—, house of: influence of, 152, 342, 351–352; conflict of, with Toulouse, 184; properties of, 234, 307, 348; control of Church by, 322, 323
Carcassonne-Razès: political development of, 44, 204, 207, 211, 212, 341; fortifications of, 231–232; monastic revival in, 243. SEE ALSO Carcassonne; Razès
—, house of: power of, 197, 341–342; conflict of, with neighbors, 292 and n., 342; ineffectiveness of, 337
Cardona (castle): 41, 61, 131
Carlat (castle): 293
Carlat, family of: 206, 289, 339
Carloman (king of France): with Charlemagne in Aquitaine, 28; retirement of, to monastery, 28; viscounts under, 116, 119; land gifts of, 141 n., 144, 147, 162–163; mints under, 174–175; mention of, 103, 128, 180
Carmague: Viking raids from, 102
Carolingians: power of, 3, 24, 47 and n., 50–51, 112–113; expansion under, 10, 18–19, 20, 40–49 *passim*; difficulties of, 29–32, 49, 91–113 *passim*; ecclesiastical policy under, 32 and n., 47–49, 136–137, 137 n.; economic policies of, 33; influence of, in Spain, 40–41; navy under, 42; renaissance of, 68 n., 185; and local nobility, 104–113, 119; military organization of, 129, 133–135; landholding by, 158–159; rivalry of, with Capetians, 180–181, 190; political system of, 402–403; contribution of, to Midi, 402–404. SEE ALSO individual rulers
Casserès (castle): 41, 61, 131, 229
Cassius: 6
Castelaro (castle): 292
Castelars (castle): 289
Castelfels. SEE Santa-Maria de Castelfels
Castelito (castle): 229
Castellacus: castle at, 132
Castellano (castle): 229
castellans: authority of, 359, 361, 364, 389.
Castellanus (abbot of Arles): 48, 66
Castellar (castle): 293
Castellaris (castle): 131, 229
Castellet (castle): 298, 299
Castellione: castle in, 132
Castellnou (castle): 298, 299
Castellnova of Nice (castle): 294
Castelloi (castle): 298
Castello Mousqué (castle): 296
Castello Novo of Limoges (castle): 297
Castellopendente (castle): 296
Castellovum (castle): 294
Castelluc (castle): 10, 24, 225, 311
Castellum, Novum (castle): 293, 301
Castellum Novum (castle): 389 n.
Castelluz (castle): 292
Castelnau [Castro Novo] (castle): 296, 330
Castelnou (castle): 292
Casterole (castle): 225
Castile: Christian king of, 222
castles: as fortification, 60–66, 130–133; power of, 130, 239–241, 283, 307, 310–314, 357–358, 361, 389 and n., 390; sacked by Vikings, 132; ownership and control of, 133–135, 230–235, 301–307, 357–359, 380 and n., 391, 392; exchange of, 210; building of, 222–241 *passim*, 261, 281, 283, 292–299, 305, 399; as basis of militarism, 230, 236–241, 259; occupancy of, 232–241; as benefices, 233 and n., 234; levies of, 237–241, 311–313; payment for, 270 and n., 271; and *guarda* system, 306; agreements and

oaths regarding, 307–310; as *mandamenta*, 310–312; Church ownership of, 321, 371; attitude of Church toward, 328, 334; inheritance of, 389 and n. SEE ALSO castellans; fortification; individual castles
Castres. SEE Saint-Vincent of Castres
Castres (castle): 226
Castro Comitale (castle): 298
Castro de Petro Castellanus (castle): 294
Castro Fronciaco (castle): 311
Castromuris (castle): 294
Castro Novo [Castelnau] (castle): 296, 330
Castro Novo de Moet (castle): 293
Castro Rochareuil (castle): 301
Castro Vetulo (castle): 293
Castrum of Boson (castle): 294
Catalonia: political development of, 6, 44–49, 92, 208–210, 348–349, 379–381, 402; agricultural development of, 18–19, 73–74, 172, 173, 281–283; nationalism in, 44, 45 and n.; *hispani* refugees in, 64; Carolingian expedition to, 65; landholding systems in, 70 and n., 73, 163, 264, 267, 272, 357 and n.; invasion of, by William, 98 and n., 99; power of women in, 123–124, 391–392; judicial system in, 124, 126, 215, 219, 373–376, 375 n.; Moslems in, 127, 129 n., 191, 221, 288; military in, 129 and n., 331; fortifications of, 131, 231, 238, 305; mints in, 173, 277; levies in, 239; Reconquista in, 395
—, church of: monastic expansion of, 47, 66, 82, and n., 84, 137, 245–246, 321; influence of, 191–194, 336; family control of, 250–252, 322
—, governmental authority in: Gothic counts, 98, 185–186; co-counts, 121–123; Moslems, 127, 129 n., 191, 221, 288; viscounts, 196; family system, 196, 211 and n., 249
Caudo Longo (castle): 294
Caunes (abbey): mention of, 77, 79, 81, 125, 142, 143, 146, 323, 341, 372, 398

Causago (castle): 292
Cayles (castle): 293
Cedemilla (castle): 298
Cenceno (castle): 232
cens: nature of, 255–257, 255 n., 270 and n., 271, 313, 314, 391 n. SEE ALSO levies
Centulle IV (viscount of Béarn): 318
Cerdanya: control of, 21–22, 234, 237, 348, 349; Moslem attack on, 99; political development of, 341, 381. SEE ALSO Berga-Cerdanya-Besalu; Urgell-Cerdanya; Urgell-Cerdanya-Besalu; Urgell-Cerdanya-Confluent
Cerdanya-Besalu: disintegration of, 352, 380; tribunals in, 373. SEE ALSO Cerdanya; Besalu
—, house of: power of, 251, 348–349, 379; control of Church by, 322; failure of, 337, 349, 351–352; conflict of, with neighbors, 342
Cerrucium (castle): 132, 134, 161
Cervallo (castle): 229
Cervilione (castle): 229
Cévennes: 29
Chalencon (castle): 293
Chamalières (abbey): 243
Chanoux (castle): 293
Chanteuges (abbey): 188, 202 n., 243
Charenguges (castle): 294
Charlemagne (king and emperor of France): invasion of Spain by, 28; governmental system under, 30–32, 50–68 *passim*, 108, 100; expansion problems of, 37–42 *passim*; and the Church, 39, 81–83, 136–137; death of, 43; system of fortresses under, 60–66; landholding under, 69–87, 159, 172; and rise of local rule, 112; trade and commerce under, 173; agricultural system under, 283. SEE ALSO Carolingians
Charles (prince): 102
Charles Martel (king of Franks): military activities of, 9 and n., 10, 21–24 *passim*, 24 n., 30, 129; confiscation of Church lands by, 10, 26; as Frankish

ruler, 20; government of, 58; mention of, 3. SEE ALSO Carolingians
Charles the Bald (king and emperor): land grants of, 62, 73, 134, 157, 161–163 *passim*; and *aprisiones*, 71; and civil wars, 98 and n., 99, 127; ambitions of, 102–103; as emperor, 103; death of, 103; and rise of local rule, 106–107, 110, 111, 112, 115–116, 119; military under, 128; Church reform under, 137–138; gifts to Church by, 140 n., 141 n., 142–143, 147 and n.; and *vassi*, 165; mints under, 174, 175; political failure of, 403; mention of, 66, 107, 134, 180. SEE ALSO Carolingians
Charles the Fat (king): 92, 103, 111, 175. SEE ALSO Carolingians
Charles the Simple (king): inheritance of, 52, 93; land gifts of, 131, 144, 163, 244, 248; protection of Church by, 148 n., 149; mints under, 174; made king, 181; policies of, 185–186. SEE ALSO Carolingians
Charos (castle): 295
Charroux (abbey): 62, 66, 75, 83
charters, royal: to Church, 140–144; to supporters, 158–164 *passim*; significance of, 180; by Charles the Simple, 185–186; rule, 112; trade and commerce under, 173; agricultural system under, 283
Château Larchier: 132
Châtel (castle): 130, 133 and n., 134
Cherssac (castle): 293
Childebrand: in Rhone Valley, 9 and n., 23 and n., 24. SEE ALSO Carolingians
Choriano (castle): 296
Chorson (duke of Toulouse): 38, 74 n.
Church, Roman Catholic: Moslem raids on, 10, 139; pre-Carolingian, 11; as substitute for secular government, 12, 136, 249, 260; and Carolingians, 32, 39, 136–137, 137–142; in Spain, 39–40, 47; non-Frankish character of, 66–67; loyalty to, 84; power of, 136, 191–194, 249, 252–254, 315, 361; and papacy, 192, 248; protection by, 192, 225, 315; in 10th century, 240–260; and Cluny, 248; sharing of revenues by, 260; nepotism in, 321–325; and feudalism, 386–387, 386 n.; unity of, in Midi, 401. SEE ALSO abbeys; churchmen; Cluny; ecclesiastical rule; monastic system; papacy; pope
—, property of: received as gifts, 12, 14–17, 76, 144, 153–154, 156–158, 163, 167–168, 205–206, 253, 255, 262, 355, 365–371, 383, 387–388; restrictions on, 17 n., 78; castles as, 65–66, 134–135, 231–234, 301–305, 371; protection of, 65–66, 148–150, 266; nature of, 73, 257, 283, 315 and n.; given away, 76–78, 166, 260, 269–271, 386; allodial, 156–157, 355; expansion of, 243–249; usurpation of, 22, 26, 145–149, 147 n., 164, 317, 326–334 *passim*, 350, 356, 368
—, protection of: by rulers, 56 and n., 82, 136–138; by papacy, 248; by Cluny, 248
—, secular control of: nature of, 32, 137–142, 151–154, 179, 249–260 *passim*, 317, 320–325, 334, 335, 351, 404; opposition to, 335, 358–359, 400, 402
— and militarism: Church-owned castles, 65–66, 134–135, 231–234, 301–305, 371; levies against Church, 317, 334, 358, 361, 366, 368, 369; Church military power, 321; Church reaction, 312, 314, 317, 325–334 *passim*, 358, 359, 366, 382–383, 402
— reform: under Carolingians, 81–85, 335–336; economic results of, 84–86; under ruling families, 151, 173, 378, 380; and Cluny, 242, 245, 335; mention of, 69, 336, 403
churchmen: in Carolingian government, 55–58, 63–68; loyalty of, to monarch, 136–137; influence of, 148–150, 153, 207, 216, 315–316, 316 n., 359, 364; political independence of, 190, 196, 209; and colonization, 203; as members of ruling families, 152–153, 249–252, 260, 321–325; election of, 335,

Index 445

358 and n., 367; holding of assembly by, 364, 366; and commercial problems, 396. SEE ALSO archbishoprics; bishops; bishoprics
Cleriana (castle): 229, 305, 306
Clermont: fortification of, 9, 27; mint at, 86, 173, 174, 276; viscounts of, 201, 202; churchmen from, 250 and n.; counts of, 329, 334, 339 and n.; countess of, 338, 345; coins from, 397
Clothair II: 14 n.
Clovis: 3
Cluny: protection by, 193–194, 311; gifts to, 193–194, 318, 332, 351, 369–370; abbot of, captured by Moslems, 222; influence of, 244, 248, 249, 258–260, 327, 335, 337; landholding by, 247; intervention of, against militarism, 317, 326, 334; role of, in Reconquista, 320; expansion of, 320; mention of, 194, 319, 324, 329
Cluny Reform movement: 242, 245, 335
Cohec (castle): 297
coins: use of, in Midi, 12–13, 173–175, 276–278, 396–400, 404. SEE ALSO hoards, coin; mints; monetary system
Colliensi (castle): 296
Collio (castle): 296
Colongellos (castle): 294
colonization: nature of, 172–173, 274, 282–283; in Middle Rhone, 203, 281, 283; of Spanish frontier, 272, 395; in Catalonia, 282; in Gascony, 394. SEE ALSO agricultural development
commerce: revivals of, 69, 86, 382, 395–400, 402; in 9th century, 173–174; localism of, 175, 276–277; levies on, 395, 399. SEE ALSO economic system
Commignes: comital control of, 207, 340, 341
Concay (castle): 297
Condorcet (castle): 294
Confluent: secular courts in, 124; serfs in, 170; repopulation of, 172; Church holdings in, 247; control of, 349. SEE ALSO Urgell-Cerdanya-Confluent
Confolencs (castle): 296
Conques (abbey): mention of, 62, 66, 76, 80 n., 83, 85 n., 139, 140 and n., 142, 167, 223, 245, 247, 254, 258, 265, 277, 279, 292, 315, 316 n., 321, 329 and n., 368
Conrad (king of Burgundy-Provence): and Church, 193, 259; as king, 198, 203; dispersal of properties by, 213, 344 and n.; ineffectiveness of, 222, 275, 339; fortifications of, 231
Conrad of Vintmille: 371
Consolente (castle): 297
Constance (queen of France): 338, 345, 391
Corbi (castle): 131
Cordova: peace with, 42, 93; expeditions against, 288, 379, 394; mention of, 28, 40, 99, 222, 379; caliphate of, 191, 379. SEE ALSO Moslems
Corrèze: coin hoard of, 397
Coruis (castle): 294
Cosilacum (castle): 132
counts: military duty of, 71, 128; judicial authority of, 71, 124, 215; disputes among, 93, 96–97, 100, 127; disloyalty of, 97; nationalities of, 112 and n.; independence of, 121–124, 164, 209–210; control of castles by, 133–135; curb usurpation of Church property, 332. SEE ALSO nobility, local ruling; individual counts
court: SEE assemblies; *guirpitios*; judicial system; law; tribunals
Courts, ecclesiastical: 125–126
Couserans: 7, 14
Crusade, First: 260
Cubelles (castle): 298
Cula (castle): 296
Curul (castle): 298
Cussac (castle): 293
Cuxa. SEE Saint-Michael of Cuxa

Dagobert: 4
Dalmace (abbot of Saint-Chaffre): 250
Dalmatius (viscount of LePuy): 237
Daniel: 165, 167, 209, 298
Dauphiny: landholding in, 14 n., 15, 16, 170, 264, 384; women as landholders in, 170; disorders in, 223–224, 225;

Church in, 223, 247, 324; castles in, 257, 293, 303, 310, 312, 314, 355; *precaria* in, 269; serfs in, 274, 390; agriculture in 279–280, 393; resettlement of, 281, 283; monastic movement in, 319, 320; papal intervention in, 336. SEE ALSO Vienne-Dauphiny
Dax: mint at, 86, 173
Dela (count): 109, 122
Deusdet (abbot): 356
Deusdet (lord): 165, 167
Dhuoda of Uzès: 63
Didier: SEE St. Didier
Dido: 162
Digne: 193
Divisio of 806 A.D.: 52 n.
Diylo (castle): 294
Dodila: 65, 80, 84
Dorat (abbey): 319
Dourgne (castle): 296
Dovera (abbey): 142, 143
Drôme (castle): 294
Dua Castella (castle): 298
Duas Virginias (castle): 295
Ducelea (castle): 294
duke: as title, defined, 54 and n., 55
Dunes (castle): 296
Dunine (castle): 292
Durand (abbott of Savigny): 369
Durbin (castle): 296
Durimane (castle): 227, 296

Eastern Languedoe. SEE Languedoe, Eastern
Ebaino (castle): 292
Ebles (bishop of Limoges, abbot of Saint-Hilaire): family connections of, 188, 189, 250; fortifications built by, 226, 231; power of, 254; mention of, 200
Ebles (Frankish count): 45, 65, 93
Ebles Manzure: rule of, 106, 200; conflict of, with House of Toulouse, 181 and n., 224; as ally of Raoul, 187; death of, 189; titles of, 198 and n.; defeat of Vikings by, 220; decline of power of, 403–404
Ebolatus: 76

Ebrard, Turre of (castle): 293
Ebroin: 79
Ebro Valley: 41, 221
ecclesiastical courts: nature of, 125–126
ecclesiastical rule: under Carolingian system, 55–68; power of ruling families in, 249–255; and beginnings of ecclesiastical principality, 255–257. SEE ALSO abbeys; church, Roman Catholic; churchmen; Cluny; monastic system
Echelles [Scalas] (castle): 226
economic system: pre-Carolingian, 12–13, 19; during Carolingian conquest, 33; development of, 84–86, 171–175, 395–400, 402; localism of, 174–175, 261, 276–277. SEE ALSO coins; commerce; hoards, coin; landholding; mints, monetary system
Eixalada (abbey): 138, 141, 146
Eleanor of Aquitaine: 276
Elne: bishopric of, 6, 48, 82; Moslems in, 47; church holdings in, 85 n., 142, 246; usurpation of church land in, 146; bishop of, 160, 328; land grants by church of, 168
Elnone (castle): 292
Embrun: 6
Emma (abbess of Saint-Joan de les Abadesses): 152 and n., 171, 216, 250 and n.
Emma (countess of Toulouse): 345, 350, 351, 391
Enneco (ruler of Navarre): 42
Ennego (marcher lord): 374
Ermenard: 135
Ermengardis (abbess of Burghals): 250–251
Ermengaud (archbishop of Narbonne): 323, 350
Ermengaud (count of Toulouse-Rouergue): as co-comital ruler, 108, 122; homage by, 187; titles of, 198; family of, 204–205; mention of, 210
Ermengaude (queen of Burgundy): 302
Ermengol (count of Urgell): power of, 209, 234, 292 n., 302; attack on Mos-

lems by, 379 and n.; selling of allegiance by, 380 and n., 398
Ermenicus: 162, 165
Ermenon (count of Périgord and Pitou): 97, 100, 105–106, 127, 184
Ermissende (countess of Barcelona): power of, 123, 275, 379–380 n., 391–392; family ties of, 322, 341
Ermissende (viscountess): 399
Ernimiro (viscount of Cardona): 374
Ervilla (castle): 298
Ervillo (castle): 302
Eschelles. SEE Scalas
Escoules, Les (abbey): 48
Espolede (castle): 293
Etienne (abbot): 371
Etienne II (bishop of Auvergne): authority of, 201, 250, 254, 258 and n., 278–279; tribunal of, 216–217, 268
Etienne III (bishop of Auvergne): 316, 324
Etienne (viscount of Gevaudun): 369
Eudes (count of Toulouse): co-comital rule of, 108, 122, 204; role of viscount under, 116
Eudes (duke of Aquitaine): power of, 3; Gascons as allies of, 10 n.; and Charles Martel, 20 and n., 21, 30; in conflicts with Moslems, 14, 21 and n., 22; alliance of, with Cerdanya, 21–22, 22 n.; death of, 22
Eudes (king of France): ineffectiveness of, 92, 111 and n., 185, 190 and n.; made king, 103, 180 and n.; land grants of, 144, 163; and usurpation suits, 149–150; mints under, 174

Falconis (castle): 229
Fallat (castle): 298
family system. SEE nobility, local ruling
Far (castle): 298
Favat (castle): 294
Ferreolus (abbot of Brioude): 67
feudalism: introduction of, 267; nature of, in Midi, 378–380, 382–392 *passim*, 401; disappearance of, 403, 404. SEE ALSO fief
Fézensac (county in Gascony): organization of, 38, 58, 104, 207, 208, 340; count of, 39, 321
fideles: as landholder, 160–165 *passim*
fidelitas: nature of, 57, and n., 74–76, 136, 180, 257
fief: origin of, 77 and n.; opposition to, 265, 266, 356; nature of, 267–268; Church property as, 331, 386; transfer of, to allod, 355. SEE ALSO benefice; feudalism; landholding; *precaria*
Figeac (abbey): 231
fisc, royal: distribution of, 76, 158–163, 212; exhaustion of, 163, 166
Flaisoe (castle): 294
Fleury (abbey): 321
Florensiaco (castle): 295
Flores (castle): 305
Foix (castle): 296
Foix (county): 341 and n., 342
Folet (castle): 298
Fons Cooperta (*villa*): 71
Fontaneto (castle): 298
Fonte Rubio (castle): 298
Fontjoncouse: 70. SEE ALSO John of Fontjoncouse
Forcalquier: counts of, 345
Forcalquier (castle): 294, 319
Fores (castle): 298, 299
Forez: 193, 263, 274, 293. SEE ALSO Lyonnais-Forez
Fornells (castle): 298
fortifications: pre-Carolingian, 9–10; nature of, 60–65, 130–135; as factor in land grants, 160; expansion of, 235–236, 396. SEE ALSO castles
Fos (castle): 13, 61 n., 222, 294
Fouilloux (castle): 226
Fracta Bute (castle): 297
Franausius (deacon): 80
Franks: as landowners, 13 and n., 14; military forces of, 14, 21–26, 30, 41, 65; colonization of Midi by, 14 n., 31–32, 32 n., 59–68 *passim*; vassalage of, 17 n.; and Charlemagne, 28; and Pepin, 31 and n.; as Carolingian counts, 45 and n., 64; as local officials, 58. SEE ALSO Salic law

Fraxinetum: as Moslem pirate base, 102, 203, 222, 223, 240, 344
Frédol (archbishop of Narbonne): 125
Frédol (bishop of LePuy): 323 n.
Frédélon [Frédol] (castellan of Anduze): as progenitor of house of Anduze, 343 and n.
Frédélon (count of Toulouse): family of, 58, 107–108, 249; surrender of Toulouse by, 98; and viscontal system, 115; ownership of castle by, 230
Frédélon (viscount of Toulouse): tribunal held by, 215
Fréjus: 345
Frisians: 20 and n.
Fronciac (castle): 296
Fronciaco, Castro (castle): 311
Fronsac (castle): 28, 61, 302
Frontiniaco (castle): 295
Frotaire (archbishop of Bordeaux and Bourges): power of, 101, 108 n., 138, 152, 167, 254; protection of Church properties by, 148–149
Frotaire (bishop): 368
Frotaire (bishop of Albi): 250, 398
Frotaire (bishop of Cahors): 306
Frotaire (bishop of Toulouse): 227, 233, 325 n.
Fruesendi (*rocca*): 131, 134
Fulco (viscount of Marseille): 355
Fulcrad (duke): 101
Fulk III (count of Anjou): 347 and n.

Gaillac. SEE Saint-Michael of Gaillac
Galindo (lord of Barcelona): 374
Gallargues (abbey): 319
Gallo-Romans: descendants of, 13, 14, 66–67
Gap (castle): 294, 304
Gap (county): 240, 247
García I (archbishop): 366
García Malo (count): 43
García Mucí: 43
Garcí of Aragón: 190
Gariago (castle): 298
Garnier (lord of Cluny): 370
Garnomo (castle): 9
Garnulf (abbot of Beaulieu): 167

Garonne region: 28, 100
Garonne River: 3, 4, 13, 15
Garsinde (countess of Anduze and Béziers): power of, 323, 391 and n.; and Church, 323, 350; marriage of, 343; death of, 352; dispute with sister by, 372
Garsinde (countess of Toulouse): power of, 124, 204, 275; will of, 207, 227, 263, 274 n.; possession of fortresses by, 230, 231, 232; levies under, 238; gifts of, to Church, 253 and n., 277; dissipation of properties by, 211, 341
Garza (castle): 240
Gascons: nature of, 4–6, 14; in Carolingian army, 10 and n., 27, 28, 41, 65; as allies of Waiffre, 26 and n., 27; as Hunald's allies, 28; *aprisio* rights of, 73
Gascony: revolt in, 43; attacks on, by Moslems, 100; Vikings in, 100–101, 127, 138, 220; hereditary dukes of, 112 and n., 184, 207–208, 337; mints in, 173; division of, into counties, 211 and n.; nature of landholding in, 264, 384–390 *passim,* 386 n.; Basques of, 288; castles in, 296, 312; *milites* in, 300; levies in, 312; militarism in, 311; alliances of, 347, 348; assemblies in, 366; *villa* system in, 388–390 *passim,* 394; land cultivation in, 394 and n.; in, 395; primitiveness of, 401, 402
—, church of: and ecclesiastical rule, 6–7, 39; problems of, 47 and n.; and religious revival, 82, 243, 245, 318, 320, 321; monastic movement in, 138–139, 139 n., 318; and papal intervention, 193, 336; family control of, 321–322, 358; holdings of, 332, 366–367
—, political development of: pre-Carolingian, 4–7, 7 n.; and Carolingian expansion, 18–49 *passim*; non-Gascons as rulers in, 58; and Carolingian authority, 64, 402; control of local families in, 104, 179–191 *passim,* 196, 207–208, 340, 378–379, 378 n.; House

Index

of Toulouse in, 204; and agression of dukes of Aquitaine, 288, 378 and n.; and integration into Midi, 402
—, Western: dukes of Aquitaine in, 289; monastic movement in, 318; mints in, 397
Gaucelm (count of Ampurias-Roussillon): rule of, 44, 46, 49, 54, 84, 92, 107; and family rivalry, 45
Gausfred (count in Limousin): 122
Gausfred II (count): mint under, 397
Gavan (castle): 298
Geccago (castle): 292
Gédéon: 16, 17
Geilin (count of Middle Rhone): 203
Geilin (count of Valence-Velay): 198
Gellito (castle): 229, 303
Gellone (abbey): 42 and n., 140 and n., 231, 238, 246, 255, 315, 316 n., 323, 333, 343 and n., 350, 358, 395
Geminas (castle): 294
Geneva: assembly at, 369
Geneva (castle): 293
Geoffrey (count of Ampurias-Roussillon): 188, 198
Geoffrey (count of Angoulême): 296, 302, 305, 325
Geoffrey (count of Anjou): 397, 398
Geoffrey (count of Provence): 355
Geoffrey II of Aquitaine: 353
Geoffrey II of Angoulême: 347, 352
Gerald (archbishop of Aix): 244, 258
Gerald (bishop of Nîmes): 323 n.
Gerald (count of Auvergne): 106
Gerald (count of Vienne): defeat of, by Charles the Bald, 102–103; system of viscounts under, 115, 118; in military campaigns, 129; usurpation of Church properties by, 146; mention of, 105, 120
Gerbert of Aurillac: 258
Gergora (castle): 292
Germany: Pepin's aspirations in, 24; emperor of, 382
Gerona: Frankish control of, 40; Moslems in, 40, 99; Carolingian control of, 46, 99; Church holdings in, 47–49, 82, 143, 144, 163, 248; fortifications of, 61 and n., 131, 134; bishop of, 134; mint of, 173, 276 and n., mention of, 379. SEE ALSO Barcelona-Gerona-Ausona
Gerona-Besalu-Barcelona: reorganization of, 9th century, 44. SEE ALSO Barcelona; Besalu; Gerona
Gerrí (abbey): 49, 82 n.
Gevaudun: William II in, 187; Bernard Plantevelue and heirs in, 201–202; counts of, 324, 326, 328, 339 and n., 353 and n.; Peace of God in, 329
Gibernus: 233
Gisclafred of Carcassonne: 109
Gislebert (bishop): 149
Gislebert (viscount): 118 n.
Glandève: bishop of, 328
Godemar (bishop of Gerona): 375
Godeschalc (bishop of LePuy): 243, 254
gold: as means of exchange, 277 and n., 380 and n., 381; mention of, 398 and n., 399 n. SEE ALSO coins; hoards, coin; monetary system
Gombard (bishop of Angoulême): 152, 250
Gontard (castle): 294
Gordiano (castle): 294
Gordo (castle): 233
Gordon (castle): 294
Gothic law: 63, 214, 266, 357
Goths: as Carolingian allies, 25 and n., 30, 31, 41, 65; as Carolingian counts, 40, 45 and n., 63, 184, 185–186; *aprisio* rights of, 73
Gotmar (bishop of Ausona): 159, 171
Gotmar (bishop of Barcelona): 188
Gouraud (landowner): 78
government, pre-Carolingian: in the Midi, 7–8, 19
—, Carolingian: in Midi and Spanish March, 50–68, 68 n., 114–128; weaknesses of, 91–92, 97, 376, 401; women in, 121, 123–124, 391–392; viscounts in, 114–119; vicars in, 119–120; influence of noble families in, 179–191 *passim*; and caliphate of Cordova, 191; influence of papacy in, 191–193;

influence of Cluny on, 193-194; local nature of, 361, 400 ; money as factor in, 399-400; regional development of, 402
Granada, La (castle): 298, 379 n.
Granario (castle): 297
Grasse: bishopric of, 323
Grasse (castle): 294
Gratos (castle): 229
Gravaisdun: counts of, 250, 324, 339 and n.
Greeks: as pirates in Marseille, 101
Gregorian Reform movement: 318, 335
Gregory VII (pope): 336
Grenoble: monastic revival in, 244, 319
—, bishopric of: power of, 196, 254, 303, 326 n., 356; building of fortifications by, 232; family control of, 250 and n., 339 n.
Grenoble (castle): 293
Gualter (castle): 221
Guanin (castle): 294
guarda: nature of, 234 and n., 306. SEE ALSO castles; landholding
Guardec (castle): 294
Guerin (lord in Lyonnais): 369
Guido (viscount of Limoges): 340 n.
Guifred (archbishop of Narbonne): 322, 342, 349, 398
Guifred (count of Cerdanya-Confluent-Berga): 349, 380 n., 398
Guifred the Hairy (count of Barcelona-Gerona-Urgell-Cerdanya-Confluent): colonization under, 73, 118, 120, 128, 133, 172-173, 238; royal grants to, 109, 163, 186; growth of territory of, 109-110, 129, 131, 163, 186, 221; viscounts under, 116, 118; vicars under, 120; as co-comital authority, 122; military expansion by, 129, 131, 221; death of, 129, 221; castles built by, 133, 238; control of Church by, 145, 152, 171; titles of, 198; mention of, 197, 208, 210, 348, 379
Guigo (count of Grenoble): 319
Guillaume (viscount of Marseille): 249
Guillaumette (countess of Melgueil): 110, 124, 152, 171

Guillem [Guy] (of Montpellier): 356
Guillem, St. SEE William [St. Guillem]
Guinelda (countess of Barcelona-Cerdanya): 123
guirpitios: nature of, 217-219, 217 n., 333, 364 and n., 375. SEE ALSO assemblies; judicial system; tribunals
Guitard (abbot of San Cugat): 305, 316 and n.
Guitard (viscount of Barcelona): 374
Gumbald (bishop of Baza): 322
Guy (bishop of LePuy, abbot of Saint-Chaffre): 326, 328, 335
Guy (count of Clermont): 197
Guy (viscount of Limoges): 331
Guy [or Guillem] (of Montpellier): 356

Hastings (Viking): 101, 102
Hennego (marcher lord): 209, 210, 231, 239, 298, 302
Henry I (king of France): 338
Henry II (king of England): 379
Heristal. SEE Pepin of Heristal
Hildebert (viscount of Limoges): 162
Hildegare (bishop of Limoges): 330, 335, 367
Hilduco: 161
Hincmar of Rheims: 137
hispani [*spani*]: Spanish refugees called, 39-40, 47, 64; in *aprisio* system, 70, 73
homage: buying of, 380 and n. SEE ALSO *fidelitas*
hoards, coin: types of coins found in, 12-13, 86, 103; as sign of economic localism, 13, 174-175, 276-277, 397; expanding commerce shown by, 86, 103 n., 397. SEE ALSO coins; economic system; gold; mints; monetary system
Honoratius (bishop of Marseille): 249 and n., 254
honores: nature of, 54-57 *passim*, 74-75, 74 n., 79, 111 and n.; comital control of, 117-118, 121-123, 164; women as holders of, 123-124; of Church, 154; decline of system of, 166. SEE ALSO *aprisio;* benefice; fief; *precaria*

Index

Hostalde, Turre (castle): 229
Hucbert (bishop of Nîmes): 216
Huesca: 41, 222
Hugh (abbot of Savigny): 369
Hugh (bishop of Toulouse): properties of, 234, 263; family ties of, 204, 205 n., 249, 235 n.; mention of, 207, 227
Hugh (count of Arles, king of Italy): in ruling family of Provence, 111, 115, 118, 197, 214; viscounts under, 115, 118; titles of, 198; control of Rhone Valley by, 202, 210; royal gifts to, 212; as king, 212; as viceroy, 222; mention of, 214, 277
Hugh (count of Rouergue): 350, 398
Hugh (count of Toulouse): 213, 265
Hugh Capet (king of France): 181, 338
Humber (count of Berry): 31
Humbert (bishop of Grenoble): 281 n., 303 and n., 318–319
Humbert (count of Bourges): 11 n., 27, 64
Humbert (count of Savoy): 289
Humfrid (marquis): 99, 100, 105, 118, 131, 162
Hunald (duke of Aquitaine): as successor to Eudes, 3, 22, 30; conflicts of, with Carolingians, 23, and n., 24, 28, 30, 37
Hungarian raid: 222 and n.

Igiga (lord): 298–302
Inchas (castle): 130, 133 and n.
Incia: 130
Ingelbert: family of, 252
Innocent III (pope): 336
Inter Castello (castle): 294
Investure controversy: 242, 260
Ionis (castle): 293
Ireland: trade with, 277
Irmengaude (queen of Burgundy): 391
Irmena (abbess of Cahors): 152, 170 and n.
Isarn (bishop of Grenoble): colonization under, 203 and n., 281; defense of, against Moslems, 222; building of

451

fortifications by, 228, 232, 257; family connections of, 250
Isarn (count of Pallars): as co-count, 122; as Moslem prisoner, 221; founding of nunnery by, 245; family of, 250 n., 251
Isarn (viscount of Lautrec): 306
Isembert: 162
Isembert (marcher lord): 380 n.
Islam. SEE Moslems
inheritance, system of: 352–354, 389, 399
Italy: as Carolingian kingdom, 51, 52 and n.; Louis II as emperor of, 102–103
Itier: 367

Jerosolima (viscountess): 392
Jews: in Midi, 174, 277, 278
John (hero of Pont): 70
John XI (pope): 192
John XVII (pope): 331
John XIX (pope): 332, 350
John of Fontjoncouse: *aprisiones* of, 74, 159, 164; heirs of break *fidelitas*, 76 and n.; mention of, 58 n., 65, 114
Jordain (bishop of Limoges): 330, 367
Josfred (co-count of Provence): 319, 345, 355
Josselin (bishop): 371
Jotfred (marcher lord): 374
judicial system: pre-Carolingian, 8; in Midi, 55 and n., 124–126, 364, 373, 403; role of viscounts in, 114–116; power of Church in, 136; informality of, 214–219; failure of, 370; in Barcelona, 379–380, 379 n.; regional differences of, 402. SEE ALSO assemblies; *guirpitios;* law; tribunals
Judith (queen of France): 52
Juncariot (castle): 295

Kaledon (viscount of Aunay): 331
Karissima of Auvergne: 80
Karissima (abbess of Saint-Sernin): 147, 170
Kastellionem (castle): 131, 229
knights. SEE military system; *milites*

LaFara (castle): 293
La Granada (castle): 298, 379 n.
Lagrasse (abbey): mention of, 77, 81, 84, 85 n., 134, 140 and n., 142, 143, 146, 152, 153, 168, 186, 192, 231, 243, 246, 248, 251, 321, 348
Laiers (castle): 239
La Marche: division of, 211 and n., 352; defense of, 288; political development of, 341; and Périgord, 346, 347; disintegration of, 347; mention of, 200, 338
—, house of: political development of, 345–347; failure of, 351–352
Lambert: 371
Lambert (bishop of Valence): 324 n.
Lambert (count of Valence): 326
Lamber (viscount of Marillac): 223
Lambisco (castle): 240
land: cultivation of, 17–19, 18 n., 40, 169, 278; Wamba's law about, 17 n.; as Church endowments, 136, 138, 142–144, 156, 245, 383; granting of, 166; charters about, 223–224; acquired through conquest, 223–224; as basic form of wealth and power, 261; payment for, 166–168, 171, 279–280; transfer of, 166, 262–265, 383, 386, 389. SEE ALSO agricultural development; allods; colonization; landholders; landholding
landholders: usurpation by, 146–150; benefices of Church to, 153; women as, 170–171, 275; independence of, 209; in judicial system, 150, 216, 313, 368; Church control over, 257; allodial grants by, 279–280, 282; antagonism of, against castles, 307, 312–314 *passim;* power of, 313, 359; property rights of, 265–266, 387–388. SEE ALSO *apriciones*
—, allodial: 19, 80, 279–280, 364, 387, 389
landholding: systems of, 13–19, 155–169, 262–283 *passim,* 354–357; in pre-Carolingian Midi, 14–19, 69–70; under Carolingian rule, 57, 69–87; as cause of internal disorder, 223–224;

size of, 273, 383–385; in 11th century, 383–395, 403; inheritance of, 389; in Midi, 401. SEE ALSO agricultural development; allods; *aprisio;* benefices; castles; colonization; guarda; landholder
—, allodial system of: development of, 155–166, 272; nature of, 80, 171, 261–267, 282–283, 382–392, 399, 400, 403
Landry (count of Saintes): 97, 105, 106, 127
Langogne (abbey): 372 n.
Languedoc: fortifications in, 230, 302, 304, 311, 312; militarism in, 300 and n., 331, 334; family control of Church in, 322–324; Church properties in, 333; landholding in, 356, 384–386 and n., 387; assemblies in, 371–372; agriculture in, 393; commerce in, 395–396
—, political development of: co-comital rule in, 122; authority of minor officials in, 196; House of Toulouse-Rouergue in, 205, 207, 213; viscontal control in, 207; family control in, 196, 210, 341, 343; and creation of principality, 351; mention of, 382
—, Eastern: 295, 391
—, Western: 81, 296, 350
Larchier, Château: 132
Lardariola (castle): 293
La Réolle (priory): 318 and n.
Laurico (castle): 293
Lauro (castle): 298
Lautrec (viscounts of): 207
Lautrec (castle): 292
law. SEE ecclesiastical law; Gothic law; Roman law; Salic law; Theodosian Code
Lay Investiture: 287
Ledrad (bishop): 83
Léger (archbishop of Vienne): 327
Leibulf (count of Provence): 44, 46, 54, 63, 65, 93
Lemignano (castle): 230
Lempteus: allods of, 80
Leo IX (pope): 328

Index

Leocono (castle): 293
Léon (king): 222
Leone (castle): 298
Leopardo (viscount): 209, 231
Leorte (castle): 228
LePuy: fortifications of, 9, 132, 228; viscontal control of, 117, 118, 201, 202, 250, 339; mint of, 173, 276 and n.; visiting monarchs in, 179–180, 180 n.; privileges of Church in, 189; burg of, 232; coins from, 397–398
—, bishop of: political authority of, 196; and militarism, 326; mention of, 369
—, bishopric of: family control of, 323 and n., 324, 343
—, see of: 324
Lérida: 41, 129, 222, 229
Lérins (abbey): 11, 62, 83 and n., 139 and n., 315, 316 n., 354, 371
Les Escoules (abbey): 48
levies: of Charles Martel, 9; by Waiffre, 10; for support of military, 237–239; by castellons, 311–313, 317; Church protest against, 325–334 passim, 358; by landowners, 361. SEE ALSO cens
Lézat (abbey): 192, 244, 320, 324, 331, 332, 333, 350
Lézat (castle): 296
Lignano (castle): 295, 304
Limoges: fortifications of, 9, 10 n., 60, 61 n., 226, 231, 396; capture of, by Pepin, 27; mint in, 86, 173, 174, 276; viscounts in, 116, 119, 325; political control of, 196, 200, 346, 358; division of, into viscounties, 211 and n.; Church holdings in, 246; usurpation from church in, 329–330; surrender of, 347; growth of, 396; coins from, 397–398; mention of, 367, 368. SEE ALSO Saint-Etienne of Limoges; Saint-Martial of Limoges
—, bishopric of: properties of, 167, 305, 306, 307 n., 356, 398; family control of, 250 and n., 325, 358; reform in elections of, 331, 335, 367
—, Castello Novo of (castle): 297

Limousin: fortifications in, 10, 132, 226–238 *passim*, 296–297, 302, 306; Frankish elements in, 13–14, 13 n., 60; political development of, 122, 200–201, 207, 346, 377 and n., 378; judicial courts in, 125, 126, 215, 219, 367–368, 368 n.; civil disorders in, 127; usurpation in, 147, 330; royal land grants in, 161–162; serfdom in, 169, 274, 390; importance of women in, 170, 391; viscounties in, 211 and n.; nature of landholding in, 213, 223–224, 267, 271, 383–390 *passim*, 386 n.; *milites* in, 236; mint in, 276; agriculture in, 279, 280; levies in, 312, 331; royal intervention in, 338; Poitevin advances in, 346
—, Church in: gifts to, 11, 156, 157, 367–368, 387; benefices given by, 166, 167; and monastic revival, 243; property of, 194, 246, 247; family control of, 250, 251, 325; and papal intervention, 317, 336; acts against militarism, 329–331, 334; elections of officials in, 335
—, rulers of: Pepin, 27; French monarchs, 179; Toulousain overlords, 181, 206; viscounts, 196, 206, 207; dukes of Aquitaine, 288 and n.
Limousin-Quercy: landholding in, 262, 266. SEE ALSO Limousin; Quercy
Liutard (count of Fézensac): 38, 62, 66, 80 n., 84
Livorte (castle): 297
Llaiers (castle): 229
Llop (count): as co-count, 122
Llop ibn Mohammed: 221
Lodet (castle): 296
Lodève: 4, 6, 130, 168, 328
Loire region: 27, 63, 100
Lomargue: 208
Lombards: 24 and n., 30
lord abbot. SEE churchmen
Lordanis (castle): 298
lords, marcher. SEE marcher lords
Lorraine: ruler of, 102–103
Lothaire I (king and emperor of middle kingdom): expedition under, 46; as

sub-king, 52; as emperor, 92, 93, 102, 142, 338; influence of, 180, 189–190; mention of, 98, 159. SEE ALSO Carolingians
Lothaire II (king of Lorraine): 102–103, 146, 166
Louis (king of Provence): rule of, 103, 111, 113, 167, 185, 214; dispersal of lands by, 144, 163, 212; political failure of, 403
Louis I (the Pious): campaigns of, 38–41; political organization of, 42, 44–49, 50–68 *passim*, 400; in Aix-la-Chapelle, 43, 45, 47 n.; and Church, 48–49, 81–85, 82 n., 136–137, 137 n., 140 n., 142; as king of Aquitaine, 51 and n.; as emperor, 51–52, 52 n.; system of fortresses under, 60–66; landholding under, 69–87, 159, 168, 172; edict to *aprisiones* by, 70–71; premature division of empire by, 92–93, 92 n.; sons' revolt against, 92–94; counts appointed by, 106; and rise of local rule, 112; land grants by, 161; trade and commerce under, 173; mention of, 105, 107, 223, 224, 403. SEE ALSO Carolingians
Louis II (son of Louis the Pious): as sub-king, 52; feud of, with Lothaire, 98. SEE ALSO Carolingians
Louis II (emperor of Italy): 102–103
Louis III (king of northern France): 103
Louis IV: 179–180, 180 n., 181, 188–189, 243
Louis the Blind: 198, 202, 222, 225
Louis the Stammerer: 111 n., 144
Loup. SEE Lupo
Lucano (castle): 229
Lucca (castle): 298
Lucq (abbey): 296, 318
Lunel (castle): 295
Lunet (castle): 227
Lunis (castle): 294
Lupo [Loup] (duke): 6, 7 n., 26, 28, 37–38, 41, 65
Lupo Centulle: 43 and n., 44
Lurs (castle): 294

Lyon: as ecclesiastic center, 6; Church properties in, 83; fortification of, 130, 228; viscounts of, 340 and n.; expansion of, 382. SEE ALSO Lyonnais, Saint-Etienne of Lyon; Saint-Pierre of Lyon
—, archbishopric of: political authority of, 196, 369; family control of, 324
Lyonnais: usurpation in, 128; Hungarian raid on, 222 n.; landholding in, 224, 225, 263, 279, 280, 384; fortifications in, 228, 293, 301, 327; *milites* in, 237; serfs in, 274; assemblies in, 369; agriculture in, 393. SEE ALSO Lyon
—, Church in: property of, 156, 247, 369; benefices given by, 166; and influence of Cluny, 193; and monastic movement, 244, 320; power of, 321
—, rulers of: Charles Martel, 23 and n.; Lothair, 92; William II, 187; Bernard Plantevelue, 201–202.
Lyonnais-Forez: 269 and n., 271, 339. SEE ALSO Lyon; Lyonnais; Forez
lyric, troubadour: 382, 392, 401

Magna, Turre (castle): 295
Maguelonne [Melgueil] bishopric of, 6, 152; count of, 7 n., 63; bishop of, 75, 366; cathedral at, 82; Moslem pirate base at, 102; ruling family of, 110, 112 and n.; women as landholders in, 170; mint in, 173; Church holdings in 169, 246; family control of Church in, 323; land cultivation in, 393; restoration of, 395; monetary system in, 396; mention of, 9
Maguelonne [Melgueil] (castle): 130–131, 295, 296, 311
Majore (countess of Toulouse): 351, 357
Malaracua (castle): 294
Malerdula (castle): 298
Mallato (castle): 298
Mallesti (castle): 131
mandamenta: nature of, 239–241, 310–314, 389–390
Mandillac (castle): 293

Index 455

Manressa: castle at, 131, 229
Manslé (castle): 297, 305
mansus: defined, 156
Manual of Dhuoda: 57
marcher lords: 299, 305, 379, and n., 380
Marcillac (abbey): 231
Maressa (castle): 229
Marestay (castle): 297
Marfines (castle): 297
Marfinus (landowner): 77, 79
Marigno (castle): 240
Marillac (castle): 118 n., 132, 297
Marro (castle): 229
Marsan (county): 208
Marseille: on trade route, 13; *villa* system in, 15, 388; Franks in (23 n.; fortifications of, 60 and n.; attacks on, 60, 101, 222; mint at, 86, 173; secular courts at, 124; family control of Church in, 249, 258, 323; viscounts of, 289, 345, 353 and n., 399; landholding in, 302, 345, 355; growth of, 382. SEE ALSO Saint-Victor of Marseille
Marsens (castle): 294
Martignac (castle): 297
Mas Grenier (abbey): 332
Masquefa (castle): 210, 229, 231, 303
Massai (castle): 297
Massif Central: control of, by Waiffre, 26; agricultural development of, 173, 282, 393; landholding in, 384–386
Matas (castle): 118 n., 132
Matfred (bishop of Béziers): 356
Matfred (count of Urgell): 49, 84
Matfred (viscount of Narbonne): 228
Matilda (queen of Provence-Burgundy): 235, 259, 275
Mato (castle): 304
Mauguio: fortification of, 9, 24 and n., 32, 60 and n.; count of, 63
Maurienne: fortification of, 62, 130, 134; bishop of, 134, 144; monastic revival in, 244
Maurontius (bishop of Marseille): 7 n., 32 n., 66
Maurontius (patrician of Provence): 8 n., 10 and n., 23 and n., 24 and n., 30
Mayeuil. SEE St. Mayeuil
Maz d'Azil (abbey): 76, 83
Mediam (castle): 298
medium plantum, system of: 273; 279–282, 392–394
Medolio (castle): 298
Melgueil. SEE Maguelonne
Melgueil (castle). SEE Maguelonne
Mellando (castle): 295
Melle: mint at, 86, 173, 174, 276
Melle (castle): 227
Mercariolo (castle): 295
merchant class. SEE bourgeois
Mercurio (castle): 9, 293
Merlen (castle): 298
Mermens (castle): 293
Merovingians: 3, 4, 14 n., 20, 24, 32
Mesoa (castle): 62, 75 n., 131, 134, 160, 295
Metrannus: 16
Mezengo (castle): 228
Middle Rhone Valley. SEE Rhone Valley, Middle
Midi: political geography of, 3–6; in early 8th century, 3–6, 12–19, 18 n.; government of, 7, 9–10; military organization of, 9–10, 61–63, 239–240; economy of, 12–19; land use in, 13–19, 18 n.; conquest of, 20–30, 32–33; Carolingians in, 20–30; social changes in, 32–33; frontier of, 41–52; castle system in, 61–63, 239–240; women in government of, 123; family system of rule in, 249; power of, 402
militarism: as threat to Church, 259, 317, 382–383; necessity for, 287–292; opposition to, 287, 330–335, 358, 359, 378, 381, 383, 387; development of, 287–301, 313–314, 376, 382, 400, 402; power of, 314, 325–327, 361; usurpation by, 331, 332; curbing of, 331, 332, 333
military service: landholders in, 71, 76; land as payment for, 171; aristocracy in, 258; as payment for land grants,

267-268, 270, 271, 273; as payment for castle protection, 313
military system: pre-Carolingian, 9-10, 19; Franks in, 21, 59-65; Carolingian policy of, 57, 65; non-Franks in, 65; nature of, 127-135; ineffectiveness of, 129; necessity for, 220-235; castles in, 225-235, 260, 261, 277; development of, 235-241, 401, 403; new society in, 283; power of Church in, 321. SEE ALSO castles
milites, system of: nature of, 71, 235-241, 236 n., 237 n., 287; as new class, 259, 313; Church opposition to, 259, 326, 329, 331, 332, 334; power of, 284, 359, 399, 400, 402; growth of, 292; in castles, 299-301; levies by, 312-313, 332; as assembly participants, 374. SEE ALSO castles; militarism
Millia (castle): 9
Milon (count): 75
Minerbe (castle): 131, 296, 311
mints: in Midi, 7, 13, 86, 173, 186, 276; disappearance of, 33; comital control of, 54; increase in, 396-397. SEE ALSO coins; monetary system
Mirabels [Miravels] (castle): 268, 296
Miralès (castle): 209, 229, 234, 237, 305
Miralles (castle): 298
Miravels. SEE Mirabels
Miró (count of Barcelona): 209 n., 245
Miró the Old (count of Cerdanya-Besalu): Catalonia under, 109-110, 122, 197; as co-comital ruler, 122; colonization under, 128, 172; military success of, 129; property of, 161; 210 and n.; and heirs, 208, 209, 348; mention of, 239
Misemundus. SEE Ansemundus
missi: nature of, 56-57, 57 n., 114-116 *passim*
Moet, Castro Novo de (castle): 293
Mogio (castle): 298, 303, 374
Moissac (abbey): mention of, 12, 15 n., 18 n., 83, 84, 134, 140 and n., 161, 231, 233, 320, 324, 332, 346 and n., 350, 351
monarchs, French: power of, 145, 179, 185, 190, 248-249, 249 n, 337; in Midi, 179-180, 180 n.; and local rulers, 382
monasteries. SEE abbeys; monastic system; individual abbeys
monastic system: pre-Carolingian, 11; development of, 47-49, 140-145, 318-321, 403; revival in, 66, 69, 81-84, 137-138, 283; economic effects of, 84-87; and local ruling families, 151; and Church vitality, 243-245; reform in, 258. SEE ALSO abbeys; individual abbeys
Moncieux (castle): 226, 233 n., 270 n.
monetary system: coin hoards as indication of, 12-13; in Midi and Catalonia, 173-175, 277, 404. SEE ALSO coins; economic system; gold; hoards, coins; mints; silver
moneylending: 277 n., 278 and n.
Mons Barcolomio (castle): 311
Monserrat (abbey): 189
Mons Meruli (castle): 293
Mons Pantiaro (castle): 292
Montbui (castle): 298
Mont Burton (castle): 259, 275
Montchâtfer (castle): 297
Monte Asenario (castle): 226
Monte Aspero (castle): 131, 134
Montecalmense (castle): 62, 66, 134
Montecarlo (castle): 298
Montegut (castle): 292, 298, 302, 305
Monte Juliaco (castle): 298
Montgrony (castle): 131, 229
Montmell (castle): 229, 239
Montolieu (abbey): mention of, 81, 84, 131, 134, 140, 142, 144, 146, 149, 168, 186, 192, 205 and n., 232, 238, 246, 265, 323, 332, 341, 357, 372
Montpellier: house of, 356; mention of, 371, 395, 396, 399
Mont Rochefort (castle): 293
Montserrat (abbey): 245
Moors. SEE Moslems
Moralès (castle): 209, 298

Index 457

Morecino (castle): 304
Morera (castle): 294
Moriocipium (castle): 295
Morlaas, Sainte-Foy of (abbey): 139, 318, 320
Moslems: conquest of Spain by, 3, 6, 21 n., 22; in Catalonia, 6, 191; in Provence, 8 n., 10 and n., 129, 139, 203, 222–223; attack on Toulouse by, 9; campaigns of, in Midi, 10, 18–21, 40, 61, 91, 99–102, 127, 220–221, 278, 401; defeat of, by Franks, 14, 22–23, 29–30; control of Pyreness by, 22; at Arles, 23 and n., 129; in Rhone Valley, 23, 139; at Narbonne, 25 and n.; revolt of, against Abd-ar-Rahman I, 28; Navarre regained by, 42–43; Church weakened by, 47; invasion of Cerdanya by, 99; peace negotiated with, 100; attack of, on Barcelona, 191, 379 and n.; capture of Abbot Mayeuil by, 194; as marcher lords, 221–222; at Fraxinetum, 240, 344; fleet of, 288; in Spanish March, 288, 320; in Ebro Valley, 299; at Aix, 319; booty of, 398–400 *passim*; colonized territory of, 395; as source of gold, 398; payment of subsidies by, 398. SEE ALSO Berbers; Cordova
Mota (castle): 294
Mousqué, Castello (castle): 296
Mozérat (castle): 132
Mugins (castle): 294
Mulier (castle): 229
Muret (castle): 293
Musa: Arab and Berber forces of, 3

Nantes (castle): 62, 66, 294
Narbonne: mint at, 7, 13, 86, 173, 276; Visigoths in, 8 n., 14 n.; fortification of, 9, 131, 134, 230, 296; on trade route, 13; Moslems in, 21 and n., 23, 25, 40; political development of, 23 n., 25 and n., 63, 184, 341, 350; goths in, 31; *hispani* in, 40; landholding in, 70 and n.; viscounts in, 115 and n., 118, 119, 196, 207, 322; judicial system in, 124, 126, 372; royal land grants in, 143, 144, 161–163 *passim*; Jews in, 277 and n.; and Montpellier, 371, 395; expansion of, 382
—, archbishop of: and benefice dispute, 75; properties of, 186, 228, 232; political authority of, 196; against levies, 366; mention of, 115, 134
—, archbishopric of: usurpation of properties of, 146; royal protection for, 148 n.; family control of, 249, 317, 322, 341, 342, 349, 350, 398
—, bishopric of: 6
—, church of: immunities granted to, 82 and n.; revival of, 84, 243; property of, 246, 248; family control of, 258. SEE ALSO Saint-Just of Narbonne; Saint-Paul of Narbornne
Narbonne-Carcassonne. SEE Carcassonne; Narbonne
Narbonnaise: pre-Carolingian government in, 3–8 *passim;* Visigoths in, 8 and n., 14, 21; military class in, 10; Moslems in, 18, 21; Carolingians in, 20, 24 and n., 25; Franks in, 23, 25 and n., 31; monastic revival in, 81; landholding in, 81, 156, 263, 265, 393; viscontal system in, 116; women as landowners in, 170; *tribunals* in, 215, 219; Toulousain intervention in, 181, 205, 265; restitution of Church property in, 332. SEE ALSO Carcassonne; Narbonne; Septimania
Navarre: Spanish Basques in, 4; under Carolingian authority, 41, 42, 64; Moslems in, 43, 100, 221; attacks on, by Carolingians, 45, 65, 93; mention of, 222, 390
Nebule (castle): 229
Neustria: 3
Nibelungen, The: 58
Nibian (castle): 304
Nice: *rocca* at, 294; family control of bishopric of, 323; accounts of, 345; bishop of, 371. SEE ALSO Saint-Pons of Nice
—, Castellnova of (castle): 294
Nîmes: fortification of, 9, 130, 227, 295,

396; Arena of, 24 n.; Franks in, 25 and n., 31, 53, 58; Pepin in, 25 and n.; revolt of, 25, 30; tribunal held at, 116, 124, 126, 214; viscounts in, 116, 196, 206, 207; mint at, 173, 175; house of Toulouse-Rouergue in, 205–206; landholding in, 213, 393; castle in 240; Countess Majore's properties in, 357; bishop of, 368–369. SEE ALSO Arena of Nîmes; Notre-Dame of Nîmes
—, bishopric of: usurpation of properties of, 146, 149; family control of, 323, 324, 343; mention of, 6
—, church of: immunities granted to, 82; property of 156, 246; secular control of, 252; and monastic movement, 319; restitution of property to, 333. SEE ALSO Saint-Basil of Nîmes; Saint-Marie of Nîmes
Nimfridius of Narbonne: 66
Niolo (castle): 297
Nizezius: 12, 15 and n.
Nobiliaco (castle): 297
nobility, local ruling: rise of, 91–113 *passim;* control of Church by, 144–145, 151–154, 260, 317, 321–325; 358–359, 383; usurpation by, 145–150, 330; as landholders, 161–163, 166, 403, 404; power of, 166, 179–191, 283, 337, 355–359, 360–364 *passim,* 404; independence of, 185, 189 and n.; 190; political development of, 196–214, 404; cooperation among, 210–211, 211 n.; giving of lands by, 212, 355–357, 357 n.; ownership of castles by, 231, 232–233; as churchmen, 249–252; gifts of, to Church, 271; in military, 287; and militarism, 317, 334; restitution of Church properties by, 332; quarreling among, 340 and n.; subordinates of, 354–357
Noirmoutier (island): 100
Nonette (castle): 289, 292, 368
Normandy: 378
Notre-Dame of Nîmes (church): 206
Notre Dame de Saintes (abbey): 319
Novalese (abbey): 12

Novum (castle): 292
Novum, Castellum (castle): 389 n.
Novum Castellum(castle) : 293, 301
Novumvillaco (castle): 62
Nure (castle): 298
Nuret (castle): 229

Odalric: 38
Odalric (abbot of Conques): 368
Odalric (viscount): 219, 223
Oddo (abbot of San Cugat): 375
Odene (castle): 298
Odila (viscountess of Marseille): 355
Odilon. SEE St. Odilon
Oldaric (archbishop of Lyon): 369
Oleras (castle): 294
Olerdula (castle): 209, 229
Oliba (bishop): power of, 251, 255 and n., 316 and n., 332; family ties of, 322, 335, 349
Oliba I (count of Carcassonne): mention of, 77, 79, 84, 96, 109 and n., 142
Oliba II (count of Carcassonne): 109, 116, 121, 146, 149, 162, 184
Oliba Cabreta: power of, 209, 348; aggression of, 292 and n., 342, 348; division of properties of, 349, 352
Oliola (castle): 221
Olivella (castle): 298
Olone (castle): 229
Omelas (castle): 295
Oppida Noneda (castle): 301
Orbaciaco (*villa*): 147
ordeals: use of, in court decision, 371
Oriat (castle): 298
Orion (castle): 294
Oris (castle): 298
Ornon (castle): 304
Orpino (castle): 298
Ostend (castle): 226
Otto (bishop): 251 n.
Otto (count): 371
Oveix. SEE San-Vincent of Oveix

Pailhares (castle): 293
Palacionem (castle): 294
Paladl (castle): 298
Palejano (castle): 296

Index 459

Pallars: Spanish Basques in, 4; comital control of, 40, 122, 340; monastic movement in, 47–49 *passim*, 66, 245, 321; fortification of, 132, 229; Moslem aggression in, 221–222; levels in, 239; landholding in, 272; assembly in, 375

Pallars-Ribagorça: political development of, 44, 180, 208; ruling families in, 110–111, 197; viscontal rule in, 115, 118; political changes in, 208; landholding in, 264. SEE ALSO Pallars; Ribagorça

Pallerios (castle): 292, 301

Palumbi (castle): 229

Pampeluna: 22, 28, 42

papacy: influence of, in Midi, 191–192, 249, 260, 336, 337–338; intervention in abbey affairs by, 192–193; and militarism, 317, 328, 332–335 *passim*; mention of 24 n., 37. SEE ALSO Church, Roman Catholic; Pope

Pareds (castle): 297

Parisio (castle): 234

patricians of Provence: 3, 7 n., 8, 12

Paulianus (castle): 295

Paunat (abbey): 338

Pavelleno (castle): 295

Pax (castle): 298

Peace of God [Truce of God]: as movement against new militarism, 287, 317, 333, 334; development of, 328; in Auvergne, 329; in Gevaudun, 329; limitations of, 335; proclamation of, 365, 368, 376, 380; mention of, 259, 314, 358

Pedinates (castle): 295

Pepin (son of Charlemagne): as ruler of Italy, 51 and n., 52 n. SEE ALSO Carolingians

Pepin (son of Charles Martel): in Narbonnaise, 8 n., 24–25; campaign of, in Aquitaine, 9, 10, 18, 30; wars of, with Waiffre, 15 n., 23 n., 24–28, 26 n.; campaigns of, outside Midi, 24; death of, 28; government policy of, 58, 63–64; gifts to Church by, 82; military under 129. SEE ALSO Carolingians

Pepin I (king of Aquitaine, son of Louis the Pious): rule of, 43, 52 and n., 53, 92, 93; expedition of, to Catalonia, 46; gifts to Church by, 84, 140 n., 142; death of, 97. SEE ALSO Carolingians

Pepin II (king of Aquitaine, son of Pepin I): named king by nobles, 97; and civil wars, 97–99, 127; death of, 99; as ally of Vikings, 99; military under, 128; gifts to Church by, 140 n., 143; land grants of, 161 and n.; mention of, 100 n., 105. SEE ALSO Carolingians

Pepin of Heristal: 3

Perelada: 229

Périgord: fortifications of, 9, 10, 60, 61 n., 296–297; Pepin in, 27; sacking of, by Vikings, 101; co-comital rule in, 122; nature of landholding in, 168, 383–384; serfdom in, 169; domination of, by House of Toulouse, 181; comital control of, 207, 367, 368; informal tribunals in, 219; control of, by House of La Marche, 346, 347; disintegration of, 352. SEE ALSO Angoulême-Périgord

Perpignan: 14 n.

Perrucé (castle): 10

Persc (castle): 292

Peter (bishop of Gerona): 322, 341 n., 342, 356

Peter (bishop of Maguelonne): 323

Petro Castellano (castle): 240

Petro Castellanus, Castro de (castle): 294

Petro Foco (castle): 294

Pictanis (castle): 294

Pierrapertusa (castle): 296

Pierre (bishop of Melgueil): 371

Pierre (count of Carcassonne): 372

Pierre (viscount of Gap): 371

Pilep (castle): 62

Pinaud: 77, 79

Pinna Nigra (castle): 298

Plaissac: 13

Plana de Courts (castle): 297
Podietum de Malanate (castle): 294
Podium Odolinum (castle): 294
Poitiers: fortification of, 9; Moslems in, 18, 22; Frankish–Carolingian wars in, 22, 27, 29; mint at, 86; sacking of, by Vikings, 101. SEE ALSO Poitou; Saint-Cybard of Poitiers; Saint-Hilaire of Poitiers
Poitou (county): political development of, 7, 106, 117, 377–378, 378 n; fortification of, 10, 132, 296–297; surrender of, to Pepin, 27; as northern boundary of Midi, 180; house of Toulouse in, 204; landholding in, 262; mint in, 276; aggression of, dukes of, 346. SEE ALSO Poitiers
—, house of: claim to Auvergne by, 181; alliances of, 184, 338, 347, 348, 278 n; in favor with Louis IV, 188–189; power of, 187, 197–200 *passim*, 322, 347
Polignac, viscount of: 116
Pons (abbot of Saint-Sernin: 371
Pons (archbishop of Aix): 335
Pons (bishop of Marseille): 304, 370
Pons (bishop of Valence): 324 n.
Pons (count of Gevaudun): 353 and n., 369
Pons (count of Toulouse): properties of, 302, 304, 350–351; curbing of usurpation by, 332; Almodis as wife of, 346, 392; Majore as wife of, 351, 357; gift to Cluny by, 366; holding of assembly by, 366; as son of William Taillefer, 353 and n.
Pons (viscount of Marseille): 249
Pontilans (castle): 298
Ponus (castle): 131
Pope: and Charles the Bald, 103 and n.; mention of, 137. SEE ALSO Church, Roman Catholic; papacy
Por (castle): 131, 231
Porales (castle): 294
Porcano (castle): 295
Porta Spina (castle): 296, 304
Portiars (castle): 295
Pouget (castle): 295

precaria: nature of, 16–19 *passim,* 77–80 *passim;* church property as, 252, 253 and n., 256–257, 260, 269–273; *cens* in payment for, 270 and n., 271. SEE ALSO *aprisio;* benefices; landholding
Primaliano (castle): 298
principality: beginnings of, in Midi, 337–352, 377–382, 400; failure of, 352–358 *passim,* 361, 376, 383, 403, 404. SEE ALSO individual counties and kingdoms
principes: in Gascony, 6, 7 and n.; as military leaders, 10; nature of, 55, 337, 359, 360–361
Procea (castle): 297
Protadio: 16 n.
Provençals: 41, 65, 401
Provence: political geography of, 3–4, 7 and n.; in 8th century, 3–4, 7 and n.; *villa* system in, 15 and n., 388–390, 389 n.; landholding in, 70 and n., 264, 269, 354, 355, 384–386, 386 n.; *hispani* refugees in, 64; commerce in, 86; noble families in, 196; division of properties in, 212, 352; castle as governing unit in, 240, 300 and n.; serfs in, 274; land cultivation in, 279–280, 281, 283, 393; resettlement in, 281, 283; levies in, 312; political development of, 319, 341, 344–345, 361; disintegration of, 345, 352; assemblies in, 370–371; Countess Emma in, 391
—, church of: early, 6, 11; revival of, 84; monastic movement in, 138–139, 244, 319, 320; usurpation of property of, 145–146, 333; property of, 145–146, 156, 193, 247, 333, 370–371, 388; and Cluny, 193; family control of, 249, 323; and papal intervention, 336
—, conflict in: fortification for, 9, 10 n., 62, 130, 223, 228, 230, 232, 294, 302, 304, 310, 314, 389 n.; civil wars, 102–103, 127; and importance of military, 127; Hungarian attack, 222; and

Index

castles, 240; and militarism, 300 and n., 331
—, peoples in: Moslems, 10 n., 20, 101, 102, 127, 129, 220, 222–223; Gallo-Romans, 14; Franks, 20, 24 and n., 30, 59–60; Lombards, 24 and n.
—, rulers of: Carolingians, 20, 24 and n.; Lothaire, 92; Boson and sons, 103; ruling family, 110–111, 197, 211, 344–345, 351–353 *passim*
Provence-Burgundy: control of, 202–203; royal family of, 324; ineffectiveness of kings of, 336, 337. SEE ALSO Burgundy; Provence
Provincia, Roman: 3
Psalmodi (abbey): monks of, 102 and n., 139; usurpation of, 146; mention of, 65, 143, 186
Puigreig (castle): 298
Pupet (castle): 293, 301

Queralt (castle): 209, 229, 234, 237, 268
Quercy: Church holdings in, 11, 14, 156; fortifications in, 10, 132, 226–227, 230, 231; internal disorder in, 10, 223–224; coin hoards of, 12; serfdom in, 169; Raoul in, 179; properties of Cluny in, 194; political development of, 200, 206, 240, 340, 350; *milites* in, 236; castle as governing unit in, 240; landholding in, 269; militarism in, 331; mention of, 27. SEE ALSO Limousin-Quercy
Queribus (castle): 296
Quiersy, Assembly of: 111 and n.

Radulf (count of Uzès and Nîmes): 25, 58, 110, 122
Rainald: 162
Rainald (lord of Béziers): 399
Rainald (viscount): 146, 329
Rambaud (archbishop of Arles): 304, 371
Ramio: 374
Ramnulf (viscount in Angoulême): 117, 118 n.

Ramón (count of Pallars-Ribagorça): 110, 112 and n., 122, 208, 221
Rampon (count of Barcelona-Gerona): 44, 45, 46, 49, 65, 84
Rancogne (castle): 132
Ranlo (abbess of Saint-Joan): 251, 275
Rannoux I (count of Poitou): 58, 97, 106, 112 and n., 129
Rannoux II (count of Poitou): 106, 118 and n.
Raoul (king of France): interest of, in Midi, 179; named king, 181; gifts by, 186–187, 226, 243; campaign against Vikings by, 187, 220; death of, 188; and *milites*, 236–237
Ravinas (castle): 229, 231
Raymond: 265
Raymond (archbishop of Auch): 321
Raymond (bishop of Toulouse): 325 n., 366
Raymond (count of Carcassonne): 342
Raymond (count of Cerdanya): 292 n., 349
Raymond (count of Saint-Gilles): revival of Toulouse under, 207, 381; power of, 351 and n., 399; as leader of First Crusade, 401
Raymond (count of Toulouse, son of Eudes): as co-comital ruler, 108, 122, 150, 204 and n.; court of, 116; and Charles the Simple, 186; mention of, 163, 205 n., 213
Raymond (count of Toulouse, brother of Frédélon): 108 and n., 117, 145, 172
Raymond (viscount of Narbonne): 323
Raymond I (count of Rouergue): court of, 189 n., 215; will of, 207, 213, 227, 233, 253 and n., 263; properties of, 230, 231, 233, 234, 263; mention of, 246, 253
Raymond II (count of Rouergue): 204, 227, 350, 353 and n.
Raymond Berengar I (count of Barcelona): and system of castle ownership, 303; power of, 349, 380–381, 380 n.; Countess Almodis as consort

of, 392; buying of allegiance by, 398; mention of, 292 n.
Raymond Borell (count of Barcelona): 302, 303, 379–380, 379 n., 392
Raymond Dat (count of Gascony): 322
Raymond Pons (count of Toulouse): power of, 187–188, 210, 341; as ally of Louis IV, 188; titles of, 198 and n., 202 n.; family of, 204–206, 204 n., 253; rights of, over Montolieu, 205 and n.; founding of abbey by, 205 n., 243; dispersal of properties by, 213; levies by, 238; death of, 341; political failure of, 404; mention of, 265
Razès: landholding in, 74 and n.; viscounts in, 118; fortification of, 131, 296; Toulousain overlordship in, 184; castle as governing unit in, 240; Church holdings in, 248. SEE ALSO Carcassonne-Razès; Saint-Polycarpe of Razès
Reconquista: role of Cluny in, 320; leadership of, 349; beginning of, 395; mention of, 288, 398
Reginald (bishop of Béziers), 249
Regulla, Saint-Clement of (abbey): 138, 143
Renco (bishop of Auvergne): 329
Revella (castle): 294
Rheims: 99
Rhoda: 47, 221
Rhodencs (castle): 294
Rhone Valley: as part of Midi, 3; use of money in, 13 and n., 86, 173–175; landholding in, 16, 212, 263–264, 267, 269, 388–390 *passim*; Carolingian conquest of, 18, 23, 24, 30, 58, 103; counts in, 63; noble families in, 110, 111, 179–191 *passim*, 196; viscounts in, 118; civil wars in, 127, 224–225; fortifications of, 130, 228, 230, 232; royal land grants in, 163; political independence of, 180; judicial system in, 214, 219; serfs in, 274; ineffectuality of kings in, 336
—, church in: gifts to, 156; and Cluny, 193–194, 248, 320; and monastic movement, 244, 245, 318–319; control of, 323–324; and militarism, 327–328, 331, 334
—, Middle: political control of, 203, 339; landholding in, 384–386, 386 n.
—, people in: Franks, 14, 24; Burgundians, 14; Moslems, 18, 23 and n.; Charles Martel, 23, 24, 30, 58; Charles the Bald, 103; Louis of Provence, 202; Hugh of Arles, 210
Ribagorça: Spanish Basques in, 4; political development of, 40, 122, 239–240; monastic movement in, 47–49 *passim*, 66, 321; fortification of, 132, 229; Moslem invasion of, 221–222; levies in, 239; landholding in, 272–273. SEE ALSO Pallars-Ribagorça
Richard the Lionhearted: 379
Richelde (countess of Carcassonne): 168
Richelde (countess in Lagrasse): 153
Richelme (viscount in Rousillon): 115, 165
Ripoll (abbey): 141 and n., 145, 173, 246, 251, 255, 316, 322, 348
Robert (count of Clermont): 324
Robert (count of Melgueil): 75, 110
Robert (king of France): 327, 345, 338 and n.
Robert of Auvergne: 368
Roca Savona: 292
Roccamare (castle): 296
Roccamolten (castle): 297, 302
Rochabuna (castle): 294, 295
Rochafullo (castle): 295
Rochamauro (castle): 298
Rochaneuil (castle): 295
Rochareuil, Castro (castle): 301
Rochechouart (castle): 297
Rocheta (castle): 294, 298
Rochos (castle): 293, 301
Rodancs (castle): 294
Rodez: viscontal family of, 206, 207; bishops of, 328, 369; and militarism, 328; mint at, 397
Rodulf (archbishop of Bourges): 127, 151, 167
Rodulf (bishop of Limoges): 161
Roffrac (castle): 297

Index

Roger the Old (count of Carcassonne): ownership of castles by, 302; will of, 307, 323, 341 n., 342, 353; power of, 341–342; division of properties of, 343, 352, 353; titles of, 343; mention of, 265
Roger (count of Limoges): 62, 66, 75 and n.
Roger (count of Turenne): 80 and n., 84
Roger the Young (count of Carcassonne and Foix): 333, 341 n.
Rohan (bishop of Angoulême): 331
Roman law: in the Midi, 19, 55, 59, 67; property rights under, 80 and n., 122, 157–158, 354, 356, 357, 387–388; mention of, 126, 214, 265, 266, 401
Rome: Charles the Bald in, 103 and n. SEE ALSO Church, Roman Catholic; papacy; Pope
Roncesvalles: legend of, 38
Roquador (castle): 227
Rosidors (castle): 229
Rostagnus: 146
Rotrudis (countess of Turenne): 170
Roubaud (count of Provence): 344–345, 350, 352, 370
Rouergue: landholding in, 15 n., 74, 384–387 *passim*, 386 n., Moslems in, 18, 21; fortifications of, 62, 225–227 *passim*, 292–293, 311; political development in, 122, 206, 227, 340–341, 350, 352; judicial system in, 125, 219, 368; civil disorders in, 127, 223–224; serfdom in, 169, 274; agrarian progress in, 278–279, 392; militarism in, 299 and n., 328; castle levies in, 312; inheritance in, 389 n. SEE ALSO Toulouse-Rouergue
—, Church in: property of, 156, 245, 248, 368, 387; *benefices* given by, 166, 167; and militarism, 328
—, house of: 204–205, 352. SEE ALSO Toulouse, house of; Toulouse-Rouergue, house of
Rouergue-Albigeois: landholding in, 262, 265, 269. SEE ALSO Albigeois; Rouergue

Roussillon: as boundary of Midi, 4; conquest of, 25 and n.; Spanish Christians in, 40; under Louis the Pious, 44; counts in, 40; Vikings in, 102; viscounts in, 115–116, 118; judicial system in, 124, 126, 373, 375; Church holdings in, 156, 168, 248, 338; royal land grants in, 161–163 *passim*, 338; serfs in, 170, 274; women as landowners in, 170; repopulation of, 172; fortifications in, 131, 228; *milites* in, 237. SEE ALSO Ampurias-Roussillon; Vallespir-Besalu-Roussillon
Rudolf (abbot of Conques): 265
Rudolf (king of Burgundy): properties of, 281 n., 301, 355, 399; family of, 324; ineffectiveness of, 339
Rusticiago: 15 n.

Saint-Alban (castle): 293
Saint-André de Sureda (abbey): 48, 84, 143
Saint-André de Trésponts (abbey): 48
Saint-André-le-Bas (abbey): 141 and n., 246, 255, 315 and n., 326, 327
Saint-Andrew of Agde (abbey): 11 n., 38
Saint-Angelus (castle): 297
Saint-Armand (abbey): 194, 244
St. Austinde (bishop of Auch): 322
Saint-Barnard (castle): 293
Saint-Barnard de Romans (abbey): mention of, 141 and n., 168, 192, 212, 244, 254, 277 n., 324, 327, 328, 370
Saint-Basil of Nîmes (abbey): 11 n.
St. Benedict (abbot of Aniane): family of, 7 n., 63; and monastic revival, 39, 81 and n., 151; influence of, 66, 82; support of Carolingians by, 137
Saint-Chaffre du Monastier (abbey): mention of, 60, 138, 140 and n., 142, 143, 152, 192, 243, 246, 254, 278, 279, 315 and n., 319, 320, 324 and n., 326, 327, 369, 370
Saint-Clement of Regulla (abbey): 138, 143
Saint-Clinian (abbey): 82 n., 143

Saint-Cybard of Angoulême (abbey): 82, 101, 138, 157, 243
Saint-Cybard of Poitiers (abbey): 138
Saint-Desiderio (castle): 293
St. Didier (bishop of Quercy): 9–16 *passim*
Sainte-Croix (abbey): 318, 367
Sainte-Eulalia (church): 216
Sainte-Felice (castle): 293
Sainte-Foi of Morlaas (abbey): 139, 318, 320
St. Guillem. SEE William [St. Guillem]
Sainte-Maria of Arles (abbey): 48
Sainte-Marie (abbey): 318
Sainte-Marie (castle): 295
Sainte-Marie de Canon (abbey): 243
Sainte-Marie of Nîmes (church): 267, 278
Saintes: fortification of, 9; capture of, by Pepin, 27; mint at, 86, 173, 397, 398, 399; Vikings in, 101; count of, 399. SEE ALSO Notre-Dame de Saintes
Saint-Etienne de Baigne (abbey): 319, 367
Saint-Etienne of Limoges (abbey): mention of, 82, 143, 147, 157, 266, 275, 398
Saint-Etienne of Lyon (church): 144, 146, 166, 369
Saint-Flour (abbey): 319, 368
Saint-Genesius des Fonts (abbey): 48, 85 n., 213
St. Gerald: 151
Saint-Gerri (abbey): 11
Saint-Gervaise (abbey): 139 n.
Saint-Gilles (abbey): 11 n., 351
Saint-Hilaire (abbey): mention of, 81, 135, 140 and n., 143, 146, 226, 246, 264, 323, 331, 332, 341, 342
Saint-Hilaire (castle): 226, 296
Saint-Hilaire of Poitiers (abbey): 22, 138, 188, 254
Saint-Jacques de Joucan (abbey): 131, 186, 231
Saint-Jean d'Angély (abbey): mention of, 138, 188, 243, 262, 331, 367, 394
Saint-Joan de les Abadesses (nunnery): mention of, 141, 142, 145, 152, 159, 171, 173, 216, 232, 239, 245, 246, 250, 251, 255 and n., 322, 348
Saint-Julian (castle): 293, 298
Saint-Julien de Brioude (abbey): mention of, 62, 66, 108 n., 128 and n., 132, 134, 140 and n., 142, 145 and n., 148, 151, 153, 157, 167, 168, 231, 245 and n., 251 and n., 254, 255, 258, 278, 315 and n.
Saint-Just of Narbonne (abbey): 333
Saint-Juste (castle): 62
Saint-Maixent: mint at, 86
Saint-Marcello (castle): 296
Saint-Martial of Limoges (abbey): mention of, 11, 82, 200, 226, 254, 258, 305, 319, 330, 367, 397, 398
Saint-Martin (abbey): 371
Saint-Martin (castle): mention of, 229, 237, 267–268, 296, 298, 305, 311
Saint-Martin (church): 216
Saint-Martin de Lez (abbey): 244
Saint-Martin des Escoules (abbey): 138
Saint-Maurice of Vienne (church): 167, 257
St. Mayeuil (abbot of Cluny): 194, 222
Saint-Medir in Gerona (abbey): 138
Saint-Michael of Cuxa (abbey): mention of, 141 and n., 145, 189, 190, 232, 246, 247, 251, 255, 258, 315, 316 and n., 322, 331, 348, 371
Saint-Michael de la Cluse (priory): 244
Saint-Michael of Gaillac (abbey): 231, 233
Saint-Nazaire of Béziers (abbey): 205, 333, 372–373
St. Odilon (abbot of Cluny): nepotism of, 324, 335; and militarism, 329, 335, 364; assemblies held by, 364, 368; mention of, 194, 317
Saintonge: fortifications of, 132, 227, 296–297; counts of Poitou in, 200–201; landholding in, 262, 383–384; serfs in, 274, 390; dukes of Aquitaine in, 288; monastic movement in, 319; control of, 347–348, 378; nobles of, at assembly, 367

Index

Saint-Paul de Fontclara (abbey): 134, 141, 142, 144
Saint-Paul of Narbonne (abbey): 372
Saint-Peter de Rhodes (abbey): 189, 244, 338
Saint-Peter of Albaniya (abbey): 48, 143
Saint-Peter of Camprodon (abbey): 189
Saint-Pierre of Lyon (abbey): 326
Saint-Polycarpe of Razès (abbey): 81 and n., 142, 143, 144, 152, 333
Saint-Pons (castle): 226, 296
Saint-Pons of Nice (abbey): 319 and n., 370
Saint-Pons of Thomières (abbey): 188, 205 and n., 213, 231, 232, 238, 243, 321
Saint-Promasius (abbey): 319
Saint-Salvador in Urgell (abbey): 138
Saint Savin (abbey): 244
Saint-Sernin (church): 369
Saint-Sernin de Port (priory): 244
Saint-Sernin de Tabernoles (abbey): 48
Saint Sernin of Albi (abbey): 147, 369
Saint-Sernin of Toulouse (abbey): 140 and n., 266, 332
Saint-Sernin of Vence (abbey): 319, 371
Saint-Sour de Geniac (abbey): 244
Saint-Stephen (castle): 131, 297
Saint-Stephen of Banyols (abbey): 48, 84, 85 n.
Saint-Sulpice (abbey): 328 n., 370
Saint-Tiberio (castle): 295
Saint-Ucruze (castle): 293
Saint-Velesius of Albi (abbey): 143 and n.
Saint-Victor of Marseille (abbey): family control of, 7 n., 12, 323; and Moslems, 11, 139 and n., 222; property of, 15 n., 77, 83, 145–146, 148 n., 149, 232, 315 and n., 319, 321, 333, 355; gifts to, 16, 76, 213, 302, 304; decadence of, 139 and n.; abbot of, 254; power of, 370; mention of, 371
Saint-Vincent (abbey): 244
Saint-Vincent (castle): 294
Saint-Vincent de Calders (castle): 298, 305
Saint-Vincent of Castres (abbey): 231
Salaves (castle): 227
Salern (castle): 292
Salerna (castle): 294
Salic law: and property rights, 59–60, 126, 157, 214, 265, 266, 357
Salmegro (castle): 226
Saloman (count of Urgell-Cerdanya-Confluent): 109 and n., 115, 165
Salvense (castle): 295
Sánchez (duke of Gascony): 96, 98, 100 and n., 106, 187, 213
Sancho the Great of Navarre: 288
sanctuary: right of, 332, 370; abbey as, 328, 336
San-Cugat (abbey): mention of, 47, 145, 188, 209, 231, 232, 246, 255 and n., 269, 303, 305, 306, 315, 316 and n., 322, 338, 375, 379 n., 380 n.
Sandila (castle): 298
San-Felix de Guixolds (abbey): 190, 245
Sanila (Goth): 44, 74 n.
San-Pedro de les Puellas (nunnery): 245
San-Salvador in Urgell (abbey): 142
San-Senterada (abbey): 143
Santa-Cecilia de Elins (abbey): 141, 142, 144
Santa-Crucis (castle): 298
Santa-Grata (abbey): 82 n.
Santa-Julia del Mont (abbey): 73, 138, 143
Santa-Maria de Castelfels (abbey): 229, 245
Santa-Oliva (castle): 298, 380 n.
Santa-Perpetua (castle): 298
San-Vincent of Oveix (abbey): 82 n., 375
Saragossa: Spanish Basques in, 4; Carolingian campaign against, 18, 39, 70; Moslems in, 28; mention of, 41, 222
Sarlat (abbey): 194
Sarraix (castle): 294
Sauxillanges (abbey): mention of, 193, 216, 225, 243, 245 and n., 251, 254,

266, 278, 279, 281, 315 and n., 329 and n., 368
Savartione (castle): 296
Savigny (abbey): mention of, 77, 140 and n., 153, 166, 255, 315 and n., 321, 327, 369
Savigny (castle): 293, 327
Savona, Roca: 292
Savoy: castles in, 239; 293; monastic movement in, 319, 320; counts of, 339 and n.; landholding in, 384; agriculture in, 393
Saxony: 37, 47
Scalas [Eschelles] (castle): 10, 226, 240, 257
Séguí: castle at, 132
Séguin (archbishop of Bordeaux): 322
Séguin (count of Bordeaux): 43, 64, 74 n., 100–101, 129
Séguin family: as dukes of Gascony, 104 and n., 105
Ségur (castle): 133
Selma (castle): 298
Sendredo (lord): 209
Senegunde (countess of Toulouse): 232, 265
Senegunde (countess of Melgueil, viscountess of Millau): 323, 372
Senez (castle): 294
Senterada (abbey): 49, 82 n., 84, 85 n.
Sentiae (castle): 293
Septimania: fortifications in, 9, 130, 227, 230; Carolingians in, 18, 26, 39–40, 43, 95–96, 402; *hispani* in, 39, 64, 70; landholding in, 73, 263, 269, 271, 384–385; commerce of, 86; mints in, 86, 173; imperial rule of, 92, 185; noble families in, 179–191 *passim*, 196; judicial procedure in, 214, 219; integration of, into Midi, 402. SEE ALSO Narbonnaise
—, church of: pre-Carolingian, 6–7; revival of, 39, 81 and n., 84, 137, 403; property of, 156, 246; and papal intervention, 193
—, people in: Gallo-Roman, 14; Visigoths, 14 and n.; Moors, 21 n., 22;

Franks, 23, 24 and n., 26, 32; Gothic counts, 40
Sexago (castle): 227, 233, 234, 239, 240, 296, 311
Sex Forno (castle): 294
Sidonius: 13
Sigebert: 80
Sigefred: 84
silver: as means of exchange, 277 and n. SEE ALSO coins, hoards, coin; mints; monetary system
Sinna (castle): 294
Sisteron: independence of, 345; bishop of, 371
slavery: 174, 277
So (castle): 298
Solario (castle): 294
soldiers. SEE *milites*
Solenegra: castle in, 230
Solignac (abbey): 153, 306
Solignac (castle): 117 n., 186, 297
Sorde (abbey): 318 and n.
Sousa (castle): 298
Southern France. SEE Midi
Spain: Catalonia as part of, 6, 20; Carolingian intervention in, 20, 28, 29, 33, 37, 39; navy of, 42; refugees from, 64; under Abd-ar-Rahman III, 221–222; co-existence of, Catalonia, 221–222; aggression in, 288; and Reconquista, 288, 395; influence of Cluny in, 320, 335; trade of, 398. SEE ALSO Catalonia; Spanish March
spani. SEE *hispani*
Spanish March: political development of, 40, 43–68 *passim*, 208, 338, 373; Carolingian expansion into, 47–49, 402; castle system in, 61–63, 229, 230, 234, 239–240, 297–298, 302–303, 310–311, 314, 395; colonization in, 73, 282–283; landholding in, 73, 74, 239–240, 385, 394; Moslem invasions of, 99–100, 127, 220–221, 288; local families in, 179–191 *passim*, 196; co-existence of, with Spain, 221–222; *milites* in, 300–301; levies in, 312, 313; land cultivation in, 394–395; monetary system in, 398

Index

—, church of: reorganization of, 47–48; and monastic movement, 137, 244, 320, 321, 403; influence of, 191–194
Sparro (abbey): 319
Sparro (castle): 294
Spugnole (castle): 229, 231
Stanquillières: castle at, 226
Stanquillières (church): 218
Stephen (viscount): 114
Stephen (viscount of Gevaudun): 372 n.
Stodile (bishop of Limoges): 125, 147, 151, 165
Subirats (castle): 229
Substantion: mint at, 175
Substantion (castle): 62, 131 and n., 227, 295
Sunifred (abbot of Arles): 152
Sunifred (abbot of Lagrasse): 152
Sunifred (count of Urgell-Cerdanya-Confluent): landholdings of, 71, 72, 161, 168; Urgell-Cerdanya under, 96 and n.; Barcelona and Gerona under, 99; defeats Moslem invaders, 99; death of, 99; family ties of, 109, 159
Sunifred (viscount of Cerdanya): 375
Suniofredo (deacon): 298, 302
Sunyer (count of Barcelona): 221
Sunyer (count of Pallars): 375
Sunyer I (count of Ampurias-Roussillon): 109 and n.
Sunyer II (count of Ampurias-Roussillon): 109, 116, 122, 131
Surgiaco (castle): 297
Suse: abbey built at, 319
Sylvius (of Velay): 255 and n., 324, 327, 370

Taganarit (castle): 298
Tamarrit (castle): 298
Tarabaldi (castle): 131
Tarascon (castle): 294
Tarati (castle): 298
Tarik: 3
Tarn River: 15
Tarragona: 221, 240, 299
Tarrassa (castle): mention of, 41, 61 and n., 70 n., 100, 131, 135, 165, 209

Tartas (county): 208, 340
Taverna (abbey): 82 n.
tax. SEE *cens*; levies
Tehes (castle): 293
Teubald (archbishop of Vienne): 326
Teutbert: 147, 212
Theodosian Code: 158
Thomières. SEE Saint-Pons of Thomières
Thouars: 114, 116, 117, 119 n.
title: defined, 197–199, 353, 360
Todela (castle): 298
Toramenus (castle): 294
Torello (castle): 131 n., 134
Tornense (castle): 297
Tortosa: 41
Toulousain, the: gifts to Church in, 11, 156, 365–366, 388; coin hoards of, 12; landholding in, 15 n., 74 and n., 262–263, 265, 384–385, 386 n.; secular court in, 125; agricultural progress in, 172, 278; fortifications in, 227; militarism in, 237, 334; monastic revival in, 243; serfs in, 274 and n.; assemblies in, 365–366, 366 n.
Toulouse: Moslems in, 9, 14, 21; Franks in, 26 and n.; fortification of, 61 and n., 132; mint at, 86, 173, 174, 276; political control of, 96, 98, 350, 399; Viking attacks on, 101, 132; viscounts in, 116–118, 196; co-comital rule in, 122; bishopric of, 324–325, 328, 366; family control, 324–325; and militarism, 328, 366; levies in, 365–366, 395–369; revival of, 381, 382; commerce in, 395–396. SEE ALSO Saint-Sernin of Toulouse
—, counts of: as Carolingian viceroy, 39; control of Pyrenees by, 40; fight Vikings, 129; usurpation of Church properties by, 147 and n.; authority of, in Gascony, 207; and militarism, 334 and n.; conflicts of, with neighbors, 343, 345, 376; mention of, 372
—, house of: development of, 107–112, 108 n., 112 n.; conflicts of, with other families, 181–184, 190, 204, 224; ambitions of, 181; alliances of, 184–185,

346; enemies of, 186; properties of, 211, 213, 233, 263, 265; and House of Rouergue, 352; mention of, 152, 197, 227
Toulouse-Rouergue: 341. SEE ALSO Rouergue; Toulouse
—, house of: control of Church by, 145 and n., 258, 324–325, 325 n.; influence of, 201, 337, 349–351; heirs of, 204–205; gifts to Church by, 205, 206, 253; decline of, 205–209, 341 and n., 351–352, 377; castles of, 307; titles of, 353 and n.; mention of, 267, 289, 353 and n., 267. SEE ALSO Rouergue, house of; Toulouse, house of
Tournon: castle at, 130
Tous (castle): 298
trade. SEE commerce
Traliburcense (castle): 296, 311
Trencavel, house of: authority of, 324, 344; conflict of, with neighbors, 343; purchase of bishopric by, 351
Treslia (castle): 231, 232
tribunals: during 10th century, 214–219; expansion of, 364. SEE ALSO assemblies; *guirpitios*; judicial system; law
Trigantis (castle): 294
troubador lyric: 382, 392, 401
Truce of God. SEE Peace of God
Tudela: 42
Tulle (abbey): mention of, 141 and n., 153, 187, 188, 218, 219, 226, 231, 233, 236, 243, 245, 257, 258, 329, 330, 331
Tulle (castle): 297, 311
Turenne: counts in, 105 and n.; viscounts in, 117, 211 n., 152; family control of Church in, 145, 151–152; division of, 211 and n.; coins from, 397
Turenne (castle): 10, 62, 132, 133 and n.
Turlande (castle): 293
Turpio (bishop of Limoges): 226
Turpio (count of Angouleme): family of, 91 and n., 105, 347; killed by Vikings, 101, 129
Turre (castle in Limoges): 297

Turre of Adfaix (castle): 295
Turre of Ebrard (castle): 293
Turre Hostalde (castle): 229
Turre Magna (castle): 295
Turres (castle in Béziers): 62, 131, 134, 160
Turres (castle in Agde): 62, 66, 297
Turres Becces: 298
Turres Betses: 229

Udalguerius (abbot of Caunes): 323
Ugo Blavia: 281
Ulmo (castle): 233
Umbert (count of Bourges): 8 n.
Urban II: 336
Urgell: Church in, 6, 11 and n., 47–49, 82, 168, 248; Moslems in, 11; Carolingians in, 42; loss of, by Catalonia, 46; monastic movement in, 48–49; land grants in, 161, 168; *milites* in, 237; levies in, 239; and Raymond Berengar, 380 and n. SEE ALSO Barcelona-Urgell; Berga-Urgell; San-Salvador in Urgell
—, bishopric of: 322, 349
—, counts of: 340
—, viscounts of: 234, 237
Urgell-Cerdanya: under Carolingian rule, 40, 41, 44, 63, 96; landholding in, 73. SEE ALSO Cerdanya; Urgell
Urgell-Cerdanya-Besalu: reorganization of 44; ruling family of, 112. SEE ALSO Besalu; Cerdanya; Urgell
Urgell-Cerdana-Confluent: ruling families of, 109. SEE ALSO Cerdanya; Confluent; Urgell
Usalito (castle): 229
Usatches: 376, 380 and n.
usurpation: lawsuits about, 149–150; of Church property, 145–147, 150, 317, 326–329, 332; curbing of, 332; in Provence, 354.
Ussarie (castle): 293, 311
Uxelladuno (castle): 226, 236
Uzerche (abbey): 329 n., 330, 331, 367
Uzès: bishopric of, 6; fortifications in, 9; Franks in, 25 n., 31, 58; mint at,

Index

86, 173, 175, 277; properties of Cluny in, 193

Vabres (abbey): 124, 141 and n., 142, 145 and n., 151, 167, 249
Vacherias (castle): 298
Valence: usurpation in, 128; gifts to Church in, 156, 369; properties of Cluny in, 193; bishop of, 228; fortification of, 233, 293; landholding in, 264, 384; militarism in, 328; assemblies in, 369
—, house of: control of Church by, 323, 324 and n.; political power of, 340
Valentiolo: 319
Valle Fornes (castle): 298
Vallespir: fortifications in, 229; control of, 349
Vallespir-Besalu-Roussillon region: monastic movement in, 48–49. SEE ALSO Besalu; Roussillon; Vallespir
Varrigo (castle): 295
vassi dominici: nature of, 57–58, 57 n., 72 and n., 75–76, 75 n., 120–121; as landholders, 63, 64, 65; in military service, 128. SEE ALSO *aprisiones; fideles;* landholders; *missi; vassus*
vassus: nature of, 31, 165
Vauro (castle): 292
Velay: fortifications in, 9, 228, 232, 293, 301, 311; Moslems in, 18; women as landowners in, 170; agricultural development in, 172, 279, 393; viscontal rule of, 196; family control of, 201–202; landholding in, 264, 269, 384, 387; mint in, 276; militarism in, 299 and n., 326; levies in, 312; assemblies in, 369
—, church in: property of, 156, 246, 247, 369, 387; benefices given by, 166; and papal intervention, 193, 336; and monastic revival, 243; and militarism, 326
Velesius (abbey): 147
Vellosa (castle): 61, 66, 131, 134
Venasque (castle): 130
Vence. SEE Saint-Sernin of Vence
Vennena (castle): 294
Verdun: 277
Vertasionem (castle): 292
Vetulo, Castro (castle): 293
Vetus Brivate (castle): 293
Veuillen (in Poitou): 86
vicar: duties of, 55 and n., 119–120, 215, 240, 360
viceroy: 54
Vich: 46, 397
Victoriacum (castle): 62
Vidde (castle): 229
Vienne: as ecclesiastical center, 6; fortification of, 61, 130, 228, 294, 396; mint at, 86, 173, 276; viscounts in, 115, 196, 340; tribunal in, 124; usurpation in, 128; archbishops in, 196, 369, 370; Jews in, 277 and n., 278; Church holdings in, 246, 259; family control of Church in, 252; landholding in, 263, 269; bishop of, 370. SEE ALSO Saint-Maurice of Vienne; Viennois
—, archbishropic of: power of, 254; family control of, 324
Vienne-Dauphiny: land grants to Church in, 156. SEE ALSO Dauphiny; Vienne
Viennois: under Lothaire, 92; benefices of Church in, 166; Church holdings in, 193, 246; land acquired by conquest in, 224–225; serfs in, 274; castles in, 293. SEE ALSO Vienne
Vigeois (abbey): 11
Vikings: raids of, 61, 97, 99, 100–101, 102, 127, 129, 132, 220, 278, 288; Séguin killed by, 129; sacking of monasteries by, 138; defeat of, by Raoul, 187
villa: importance of, in landholding, 14–19, 81, 274; destruction of, 27, 33; inheritance of, 389 and n.
villa system: nature of 18–19, 388–390; regional differences in, 401; disappearance of, 402, 403
Villademaier (castle): 298
Villamare (castle): 292
Villanova, Burg of (castle): 296
Villo (castle): 298

470   Southern French and Catalan Society

Vintmille: 345, 353 n.
Vintronem (castle): 292
Viridaria (castle): 298
Visalia (castle): 281 n., 293
viscounts: system of, 55 and n., 114–119, 121; courts held by, 115–116, 115 n.; power of, 196, 206; political independence of, 209–210; and Church, 250. SEE ALSO nobility, local ruling; individual viscounts
Visigoths: in Spain, 4, 16 n.; power of 6; mint of, 7; in Midi, 14 and n., 21, 32
Visilia (castle): 303
Vite Albano (castle): 294
Vitrola (castle): 294
Vitry (castle): 62
Vivarais: land grants to church of, 156; landholding in, 264, 384; land cultivation in, 279; fortifications in, 228, 293; militarism in, 328. SEE ALSO Viviers
Vivario (castle): 298
Vivas (bishop of Barcelona): 239
Viviers: church of, 11, 146, 167; bishop of, 369; landholding in, 384. SEE ALSO Vivarais
Viviers (castle): 9 n.
Voltniger (castle): 298
Vulgrin (count of Angoulême-Périgord): wards off Vikings, 101; family of, 106, 112 and n.; viscount under, 117, 118; castles built by, 132, 133
Vultrairo (castle): 297

Wadald (bishop of Marseille): 78
Waiffre (duke of Aquitaine): rule of, 3, 7, 10, 16, 24; wars of, against Pepin, 11, 23 n., 25 and n., 26 and n., 27 and n., 30; Gascons as allies of, 11 n., 26 and n., 27; death of, 27–28
Wamba (king of Visigothic Spain): 4, 16 n.
Warin (count of Auvergne): 44, 93 n., 102, 107, 145 n.
Western Aquitaine. SEE Aquitaine, Western

Western Gascony, SEE Gascony, Western
Western Languedoc. SEE Languedoc, Western
William (count of Arles): 223
William (count of Astronove): 366
William (count of Périgord): 106, 122
William (count of Septimania): 98, 99, 107
William [St. Guillem] (count and duke of Toulouse): campaigns of, 38, 40, 41, 129; family of, 45, 58, 92, 107; and Church, 151; retirement of, to monastery, 42, 53
William (duke, marquis, count of Provence): rule of, 198, 214, 304, 344 and n., 345, 354; colonization under, 281; political reorganization by, 319, 361; death of, 344, 353, 370; political failure of, 404
William (viscount of Béziers): 302, 304, 307, 323, 356
William (viscount of Marseille): 304, 371
William (viscount of Provence): 302
William II (count of Auvergne): 184, 186–187, 201 and n., 243, 258 and n.
William II (marquis of Provence): 345
William Caput Stupe (count of Poitou): 188–189, 189 n., 198 n., 202
William Fierebras of Poitou (duke of Aquitaine): 190, 200, 223, 235
William Forto (viscount): 332
William García (count of Fézensac): 243
William of Antibes: 370
William of Parthenay: 331
William Sánchez (duke of Gascony): 348
William Taillefer (count of Angoulême): 210, 223, 243
William Taillefer (count of Toulouse): mention of, 204, 211, 332, 341, 345, 350, 353, 365–366, 370
William Taillefer II (count of Angoulême): 347 and n., 367, 377 n.
William the Great (duke of Aquitaine): 328, 331, 347 and n., 367

Index

William the Pious (duke of Aquitaine, count of Toulouse): faimly of, 107 and n.; titles of, 197; rule of, 118, 201 and n.; as lay abbot, 145 n., 148; as founder of Cluny, 193; estates of, 202; political failure of, 403
Wimar [Guimar]: 72 and n.
women: as landholders, 123–124, 170–171, 275; influence of, 211, 283, 391–392, 404; as Church officers, 147, 152, 170–171, 216, 250 and n., 251, 275, 369

Yconensium (castle): 226
Yvonis (castle): 293

www.ingramcontent.com/pod-product-compliance
Lightning Source LLC
Chambersburg PA
CBHW022006300426
44117CB00005B/52